Clashing Views in

United States History
Since 1945

THIRD EDITION

Selected, Edited, and with Introductions by

Larry Madaras
Professor Emeritus, Howard Community College

EL CAMINO COLLEGE
LIBRARY
Mc Graw Hill McGraw-Hill
Higher Education

Boston   Burr Ridge, IL   Dubuque, IA   New York   San Francisco   St. Louis
Bangkok   Bogotá   Caracas   Kuala Lumpur   Lisbon   London   Madrid   Mexico City
Milan   Montreal   New Delhi   Santiago   Seoul   Singapore   Sydney   Taipei   Toronto

McGraw-Hill
Higher Education

TAKING SIDES: CLASHING VIEWS IN UNITED STATES HISTORY SINCE 1945,
THIRD EDITION

Published by McGraw-Hill, a business unit of The McGraw-Hill Companies, Inc., 1221 Avenue of the Americas, New York, NY 10020. Copyright © 2008 by The McGraw-Hill Companies, Inc. All rights reserved. Previous edition(s) 2001–2003. No part of this publication may be reproduced or distributed in any form or by any means, or stored in a database or retrieval system, without the prior written consent of The McGraw-Hill Companies, Inc., including, but not limited to, in any network or other electronic storage or transmission, or broadcast for distance learning.

Some ancillaries, including electronic and print components, may not be available to customers outside the United States.

Taking Sides® is a registered trademark of the McGraw-Hill Companies, Inc.
Taking Sides is published by the **Contemporary Learning Series** group within the McGraw-Hill Higher Education division.

1 2 3 4 5 6 7 8 9 0 DOC/DOC 0 9 8 7

MHID: 0-07-351519-1
ISBN: 978-0-07-351519-9
ISSN: 1530-0765

Managing Editor: *Larry Loeppke*
Production Manager: *Beth Kundert*
Senior Developmental Editor: *Jill Peter*
Editorial Assistant: *Nancy Meissner*
Production Service Assistant: *Rita Hingtgen*
Permissions Coordinator: *Lori Church*
Senior Marketing Manager: *Julie Keck*
Marketing Communications Specialist: *Mary Klein*
Marketing Coordinator: *Alice Link*
Project Manager: *Jane Mohr*
Design Specialist: *Tara McDermott*
Senior Administrative Assistant: *DesAnna Dausener*
Senior Operations Manager: *Pat Koch Krieger*
Cover Graphics: *Maggie Lytle*

Compositor: ICC Macmillan Inc.
Cover Image: Courtesy of National Archives (NLNS-5364-19)

Library of Congress Cataloging-in-Publication Data

Main entry under title:
    Taking sides: clashing views on controversial issues in American history since 1945/selected, edited, and with introductions by Larry Madaras.—3rd ed.

Includes bibliographical references and index.
    1. United States—History—1945—. I. Madaras, Larry, *comp.*
                                973.92

Preface

The success of the first eight editions of *Taking Sides: Clashing Views on Controversial Issues in American History* encouraged me to develop a volume that specializes in controversial issues in American history since 1945. I remain faithful to the series' original objectives, methods, and format. My aim has been to create an effective instrument to enhance classroom learning and to foster critical thinking. Historical facts presented in a vacuum are of little value to the educational process. For students, whose search for historical truth often concentrates on *when* something happened rather than *why* and on specific events rather than on the *significance* of those events, *Taking Sides* is designed to offer an interesting and valuable departure. The understanding that the reader arrives at based on the evidence that emerges from the clash of views encourages the reader to view history as an *interpretive* discipline, not one of rote memorization.

The issues in this book are arranged in chronological order and can be easily incorporated into any American history survey course. Each issue has an issue *introduction*, which sets the stage for the debate that follows in the pro and con selections and provides historical and methodological background to the problem that the issue examines. Each issue concludes with a *postscript*, which ties the readings together, briefly mentions alternative interpretations, and supplies detailed *suggestions for further reading* for the student who wishes to pursue the topics raised in the issue. Also, Internet site addresses (URLs) have been provided on the *Internet References* page that accompanies each unit opener, which should prove useful as starting points for further research. At the back of the book is a listing of all the *contributors to this volume* with a brief biographical sketch of each of the prominent figures whose views are debated here.

Changes to the third edition In this edition, I have continued my efforts to maintain a balance between the traditional political, diplomatic, and cultural issues and the new social history, which depicts a society that benefited from the presence of African Americans, women, and workers of various racial and ethnic backgrounds. With this in mind, I present three entirely new issues: "Was Rock and Roll Responsible for Dismantling America's Traditional Family, Sexual, and Racial Customs in the 1950s and 1960s?" (Issue 5), "Were the 1980s a Decade of Affluence for the Middle Class?" (Issue 14), and "Is George W. Bush the Worst President in American History?" (Issue 15). Nine issues have been reshaped with either new frameworks, new readings, or both: "Was It Necessary to Drop the Atomic Bomb to End World War II?" (Issue 1), "Was President Truman Responsible for the Cold War?" (Issue 2), "Was President Kennedy Responsible for the Cuban Missile Crisis?" (Issue 6), "Did the Great Society Fail?" (Issue 9), "Has the Women's Movement of the 1970s Failed to Liberate American Women?" (Issue 11), "Was Richard Nixon America's Last

Liberal President?" (Issue 12), "Did President Reagan Win the Cold War?" (Issue 13), "Is George W. Bush the Worst President in American History?" (Issue 15), and "Is the Environmental Crisis 'An Inconvenient Truth'?" (Issue 17). Only six issues remain the same for the second edition.

A word to the instructor An *Instructor's Resource Guide with Test Questions* (multiple choice and essay) is available through the publisher for the instructor. *Using Taking Sides in the Classroom,* which discusses methods and techniques for integrating the pro-con approach into any classroom setting, is also available. An online version of *Using Taking Sides in the Classroom* and a correspondence service for *Taking Sides* adopters can be found at http://www.mhcls.com/usingts/.

Taking Sides: Clashing Views in United States History since 1945 is only one title in the Taking Sides series. If you are interested in seeing the table of contents for any of the other titles, please visit the Taking Sides Web site at http://www.mhcls.com/takingsides/.

Acknowledgments Many individuals have contributed to the successful completion of this text. I am particularly indebted to Maggie Cullen, the late Barry A. Crouch, Virginia Kirk, Joseph and Helen Mitchell, Jean Soto, and David Stebenne, who shared their ideas and pointed me toward potentially useful historical works. A special note of gratitude goes to former student, Christopher Higgins. Although we find ourselves on opposite sides of the political spectrum, I gained numerous ideas from our conversations and from his suggested lists of books and articles, which have found their way into this reader. My thanks also are extended to Lynn Wilder, Catalina Ruiz, and Erica Perez, who performed indispensable typing duties connected with this project. Ela Cibrowski, James Johnson, and Sharen Gover in the library at Howard Community College provided essential help in acquiring books and articles on the computer and on interlibrary loan. Finally, I am sincerely grateful for the commitment, encouragement, and patience in correcting errors in recent years by Jill Peter, senior developmental editor for the Taking Sides series, and the entire staff of McGraw-Hill Contemporary Learning Series.

Larry Madaras
Howard Community College

Contents In Brief

Contents

UNIT 1   AMERICAN HIGH: 1945–1962   1

Issue 1.   Was It Necessary to Drop the Atomic Bomb to End World War II?   2

YES: **Robert James Maddox,** from *American Heritage* (May/June 1995)   *4*

NO: **Tsuyoshi Hasegawa,** from *Racing the Enemy: Stalin, Truman, and the Surrender of Japan* (Harvard University Press, 2005)   *13*

Professor of American history Robert James Maddox contends that the atomic bomb became the catalyst that forced the hard-liners in the Japanese army to accept the emperor's plea to surrender, thus avoiding a costly, bloody invasion of the Japanese mainland. Professor of American history Tsuyoshi Hasegawa argues that the Soviet entrance into the war played a greater role in causing Japan to surrender than did the dropping of the atomic bombs.

Issue 2.   Was President Truman Responsible for the Cold War?   26

YES: **Arnold A. Offner,** from "'Another Such Victory': President Truman, American Foreign Policy, and the Cold War," *Diplomatic History* (Spring 1999)   *28*

NO: **John Lewis Gaddis,** from *We Now Know: Rethinking Cold War History* (Oxford University Press, 1997)   *35*

Professor Arnold A. Offner argues that Harry S. Truman was a parochial nationalist whose limited vision of foreign affairs precluded negotiations with the Russians over cold war issues. John Lewis Gaddis argues that after a half century of scholarship, Joseph Stalin was uncompromising and primarily responsible for the cold war.

Issue 3.   Did Communism Threaten America's Internal Security after World War II?   50

YES: **John Earl Haynes and Harvey Klehr,** from *Venona: Decoding Soviet Espionage in America* (Yale University Press, 1999)   *52*

NO: **Richard M. Fried,** from *Nightmare in Red: The McCarthy Era in Perspective* (Oxford University Press, 1990)   *63*

History professors John Earl Haynes and Harvey Klehr argue that army code-breakers during World War II's "Venona Project" uncovered a disturbing number of high-ranking U.S. government officials who seriously damaged American interests by passing sensitive information to the Soviet Union. Professor of history Richard M. Fried argues that the early

1950s were a "nightmare in red" during which American citizens had their First and Fifth Amendment rights suspended when a host of national and state investigating committees searched for Communists in government agencies, Hollywood, labor unions, foundations, universities, public schools, and even public libraries.

Professor of political science John S. Spanier argues that General Douglas MacArthur was fired because he publicly disagreed with the Truman administration's "Europe first" policy and its limited war strategy of containing communism in Korea. Biographer D. Clayton James and assistant editor Anne Sharp Wells argue that General MacArthur was relieved of duty because there was a lack of communication between the Joint Chiefs of Staff and the headstrong general, which led to a misperception over the appropriate strategy in fighting the Korean War.

Professor Glen C. Altschuler maintains that rock and roll's "switchblade beat" opened wide divisions in American society along the fault lines of family, sexuality, and race. Writer J. Ronald Oakley argues that although the lifestyles of youth departed from their parents, their basic ideas and attitudes were still the conservative ones that mirrored the conservativism of the affluent age in which they grew up.

Political analyst Ronald Steel believes that President Kennedy mishandled the Cuban missile crisis when his hastily organized decision-making committee of 14 experts emphasized military ultimatums over diplomatic solutions. Historian Robert Weisbrot argues that the new sources uncovered the past 20 years portray Kennedy as a president who had absorbed the values of his time as an anti-Communist, cold warrior who nevertheless acted as a rational leader who was conciliatory toward his opponent in the Soviet Union in resolving the Cuban missile crisis.

Professor of history Brian VanDeMark argues that President Lyndon Johnson failed to question the viability of increasing U.S. involvement in the Vietnam War because he was the prisoner of America's global containment policy and because he did not want his opponents to accuse him of being soft on communism or endanger support for his Great Society reforms. H. R. McMaster, an active-duty army tanker, maintains that the Vietnam disaster was not inevitable but a uniquely human failure whose responsibility was shared by President Johnson and his principal military and civilian advisors.

Writer and lecturer F. Carolyn Graglia argues that women should stay at home and practice the values of "true motherhood" because contemporary feminists have discredited marriage, devalued traditional homemaking, and encouraged sexual promiscuity. According to Professor Sara M. Evans, despite class, racial, religious, ethnic, and regional differences, women in America experienced major transformations in their private and public lives in the twentieth century.

According to professor of history Joan Hoff-Wilson, the Nixon presidency reorganized the executive branch and portions of the federal bureaucracy and implemented domestic reforms in civil rights, welfare, and economic planning, despite its limited foreign policy successes and the Watergate scandal. According to Professor Bruce J. Schulman, Richard Nixon was the first conservative president of the post-World War II era who undermined the Great Society legislative program of President Lyndon Baines Johnson and built a new Republic majority coalition of white, northern blue-collar workers, and southern and sunbelt conservatives.

Social scientist Tamar Jacoby believes that legal immigration quotas should be increased to over 400,000 per year because the newest immigrants keep America's economy strong because they work harder and take jobs that native-born Americans reject. Syndicated columnist Patrick J. Buchanan argues that America is no longer a nation because immigrants from Mexico and other Third World Latin American and Asian countries have turned America into a series of fragmented multicultural ethnic enclaves that lack a common culture.

NASA scientist Jim Hansen believes that the world will become a more desolate place to live in the foreseeable future unless we reduce or sequester the carbon emissions that are warming the atmosphere. Kevin Shapiro, a research fellow in neuroscience at Harvard University, believes the increase in CO_2 in the atmosphere is significant but not a cause for panic because what we "know" about global warming comes from computer-simulated models that have various biased built-in assumptions.

Introduction

The Study of History

Larry Madaras

In a pluralistic society such as ours, the study of history is bound to be a complex process. How an event is interpreted depends not only on the existing evidence but also on the perspective of the interpreter. Consequently, understanding history presupposes the evaluation of information, a task that often leads to conflicting conclusions. An understanding of history, then, requires the acceptance of the idea of historical relativism. Relativism means that redefinition of our past is always possible and desirable. History shifts, changes, and grows with new and different evidence and interpretations. As with the law and even with medicine, beliefs that were unquestioned 100 or 200 years ago have been discredited or discarded since.

Relativism, then, encourages revisionism. There is a maxim that "the past must remain useful to the present." Historian Carl Becker argued that every generation should examine history for itself, thus ensuring constant scrutiny of our collective experience through new perspectives. History, consequently, does not remain static, in part because historians cannot avoid being influenced by the times in which they live. Almost all historians commit themselves to revising the views of other historians, synthesizing theories into macrointerpretations, or revising the revisionists.

Schools of Thought

Three predominant schools of thought have emerged in American history since the first graduate seminars in history were given at the Johns Hopkins University in Baltimore, Maryland, in the 1870s. The progressive school dominated the professional field in the first half of the twentieth century. Influenced by the reform currents of Populism, progressivism, and the New Deal, these historians explored the social and economic forces that energized America. The progressive scholars tended to view the past in terms of conflicts among groups, and they sympathized with the underdog.

The post–World War II period witnessed the emergence of a new group of historians who viewed the conflict thesis as overly simplistic. Writing against the backdrop of the Cold War, these neoconservative, or consensus, historians argued that Americans possess a shared set of values and that the areas of agreement within the nation's basic democratic and capitalistic framework were more important than the areas of disagreement.

In the 1960s, however, the civil rights movement, women's liberation, and the student rebellion (with its condemnation of the war in Vietnam) fragmented the consensus of values upon which historians and social scientists of the 1950s centered their interpretations. This turmoil set the stage for the emergence of another group of scholars. New Left historians began to reinterpret the past once again. They emphasized the significance of conflict in American history, and they resurrected interest in those groups ignored by the consensus school. In addition, New Left historians critiqued the expansionist policies of the United States and emphasized the difficulties confronted by Native Americans, African Americans, women, and urban workers in gaining full citizenship status.

Consensus and New Left history is still being written. The most recent generation of scholars, however, focuses on social history. Their primary concern is to discover what the lives of "ordinary Americans" were really like. These new social historians employ previously overlooked court and church documents, house deeds and tax records, letters and diaries, photographs, and census data to reconstruct the everyday lives of average Americans. Some employ new methodologies, such as quantification (enhanced by advancing computer applications) and oral history, while others borrow from the disciplines of political science, economics, sociology, anthropology, and psychology for their historical investigations.

Contemporary history divides less easily into discernable schools of thought and is often difficult to interpret because of the short time span—at most 55 years—that has elapsed. Consensus and New Left history is still being written, but a new conservative historiography that is often aligned with the modern conservative political movement has also begun to emerge and is reflected in several issues in this reader.

Writers of the recent past have been less affected by social history—the framework used by most professional historians to interpret America. Most history written about America since 1945 centers on the traditional political, military, and diplomatic perspectives. There are several reasons for this. In the twentieth century—and especially since the passage of the New Deal—the role of the national government as a social service and regulatory institution has become a dominant force in people's individual lives. The traditional roles of the president as commander in chief and chief diplomat were transformed by World War II and the subsequent Cold War. Because of the development of the atomic bomb and subsequent nuclear weapons, which accompany the world's strongest armed forces, the United States has abandoned its traditional policy of political isolationism. The controversies surrounding America's role in world affairs is reflected in several issues in this reader.

Interpretations of recent American history are driven in part by the availability of primary sources. Many traditional sources are missing, while modern technology has created new types of material. Social historians are hampered by the fact that detailed information about individuals from the U.S. census is closed to researchers for 100 years. Furthermore, historians have to compete with psychologists, economists, sociologists, and journalists in evaluating the modern social and cultural atmosphere. A time perspective about significant or insignificant changes or continuities in American life is also missing.

There is, however, an abundance of official records available with which to interpret the recent past. In addition to congressional investigations and documents published in the Foreign Relations of the United States series, the Freedom of Information Act has enabled researchers to access—often with many bureaucratic snags—FBI and other intelligence and cabinet agencies' files. These records have altered historians' interpretations of foreign policy, as reflected in several of the issues in this reader. The traditional historian misses the old-fashioned correspondence, however. The eloquent letters of Presidents Theodore Roosevelt and Woodrow Wilson are absent among our modern presidents. There is not enough material to fill a 46-volume edition of the personal papers of George Bush or Bill Clinton, unlike earlier presidents. New sources, such as oral histories, phone logs, and diaries (an old source), cannot make up for the missing letters. Tape recordings of phone conversations and official meetings—especially during the Kennedy, Johnson, and Nixon administrations—are quite revealing. Unfortunately, because the "Watergate tapes" forced Richard Nixon's resignation, subsequent presidents have been reluctant to tape their daily meetings. Airplane diplomacy with only officially issued communiqués, fax memos, and e-mail have also altered the sources that future historians will use. The long-term effect of "Monicagate" may not be the impeachment of President Clinton, but it may make any public official reluctant to put into writing the (public) affairs of the moment.

The proliferation of historical approaches, which are reflected in the issues debated in this book, has had mixed results. On the one hand, historians have become so specialized in their respective time periods and methodological styles that it is difficult to synthesize the recent scholarship into a comprehensive text for the general reader. On the other hand, historians now know more about the American past than at any other time in our history. They dare to ask new questions or ones that were previously considered to be germane only to scholars in other social sciences. Although there is little agreement about the answers to these questions, the methods employed and issues explored make the "new history" a very exciting field to study.

The topics that follow represent a variety of perspectives and approaches. Each of these controversial issues can be studied for its individual importance to American history. Taken as a group, they interact with one another to illustrate larger historical themes. When grouped thematically, the issues reveal continuing motifs in the development of American history.

War, Diplomacy, and Internal Security

World War II brought the end of Nazi Germany and Imperial Japan. It was the war that was really supposed to end all wars. But it produced two major unintended consequences. The Manhattan Project was a secret enclave of thousands of scientists who lived in the desert in Los Alamos, New Mexico, in order to develop an atomic bomb. The first successful test in the desert of New Mexico occurred two months after the war in Germany had ended. Two atomic bombs—Fat Man and Little Boy—were ready to be used against the Japanese. Were there alternatives to dropping the atomic bombs on Japan to end the war? Were the alternatives rejected for political reasons: (1) keep Russia out of the Asian war: (2) make the Russians "more manageable" in Eastern European peace negotiations? In the first selection in Issue 1, Professor Robert James Maddox rejects these contentions and argues that military considerations were dominant. President Truman, he says, dropped both atomic bombs in order to shorten the war, save American and Japanese lives, and convince the military hard-liners to surrender because there were no acceptable alternatives. Professor Tsuyoshi Hasegawa plays down the role of the A-bombs in bringing about Japan's surrender. After a careful examination of Japanese, Russian, and American archives, he concludes that it was the Russian declaration of war and not the two atomic bombs at Hiroshima and Nagasaki that caused the Japanese to surrender out of fear of having part of northern Japan occupied by the Russians after the war ended.

A second unintended consequence was the reemergence of the rivalry between the United States and the Soviet Union. Who started the Cold War? Was it inevitable, or should one side take more of the blame? In Issue 2, Professor Arnold A. Offner argues that President Harry S. Truman was a parochial nationalist whose limited vision of foreign affairs precluded negotiations with the Russians over Cold War issues. But John Gaddis, the most important American scholar of the Cold War, argues that after a half century of scholarship, Joseph Stalin was uncompromising and primarily responsible for the Cold War.

After World War II, many Americans believed that the Russians not only threatened world peace but could also subvert America's own democratic form of government. How legitimate was the great Red Scare? Did communist subversion threaten America's internal security? In the first reading in Issue 3, John Earl Haynes and Harvey Klehr contend that recently released World War II intelligence intercepts prove that a sizable number of high-level government officials passed sensitive information to Russian intelligence. But Richard M. Fried argues that the 1950s became a "Red nightmare" when state and national government agencies overreacted in their search for communists in government agencies, schools, labor unions, and even Hollywood, violating citizens' rights of free speech and defense against self-incrimination under the First and Fifth Amendments.

The nuclear arms race led to the Cold War's greatest crisis when Premier Nikita Khrushchev attempted to establish offensive nuclear missiles on the island of Cuba, less than 100 miles from Miami, Florida. Should President Kennedy receive an A or an F grade for the way he handled the crisis? Political journalist Ronald Steel argues in Issue 6 that President Kennedy mishandled the crisis when his hastily organized decision-making committee of 14 experts emphasized military ultimatums over diplomatic solutions. But Colby University historian Robert Weisbrot argues that the new sources uncovered the past 20 years portray Kennedy as a president who had absorbed the values of his time as an anti-Communist cold warrior who nevertheless acted in a firm, rational, yet conciliatory, manner toward his opponent in resolving the Cuban missile crisis.

No discussion of American foreign policy is complete without some consideration of the Vietnam War. Was America's escalation of the war inevitable in 1965? In Issue 10, Brian VanDeMark argues that President Lyndon Johnson was a prisoner of America's global "containment" policy and was afraid to pull out of Vietnam because he feared that his opponents would accuse him of being soft on communism and that they would also destroy his Great Society reforms. H. R. McMaster blames Johnson and his civilian and military advisers for failing to develop a coherent policy in Vietnam.

Now that the Cold War is over, historians must assess why it ended so suddenly and unexpectedly. Did President Ronald Reagan's military build-up in the 1980s force the Soviet Union into economic bankruptcy? In Issue 13, John Lewis Gaddis gives Reagan high marks for ending the Cold War. By combining a policy of militancy and operational pragmatism, he argues, Reagan brought about the most significant improvement in Soviet-American relations since the end of World War II. According to Daniel Deudney and G. John Ikenberry, however, the Cold War ended only when the Soviets saw the need for international cooperation to end the arms race, prevent a nuclear holocaust, and liberalize their economy. They contend that Western global ideas, not the hard-line containment policy of the early Reagan administration, caused Soviet president Mikhail Gorbachev to abandon traditional Russian communism.

American Presidents Since World War II

The Korean War provided the first military test case of America's Cold War policy of "containing" the expansion of communism. The conflict explored in Issue 4 also provided a classic case of civilian control over military officials. Should President Truman have fired General Douglas MacArthur? John S. Spanier argues that MacArthur was fired because he publicly disagreed with the Truman administration's Europe-first policy and its limited war strategy of containing communism in Korea. D. Clayton James, writing with Anne Sharp Wells, maintains that General MacArthur was relieved of duty because there was a lack of communication between the Joint Chiefs of Staff and the headstrong general as well as a misperception over the appropriate strategy for fighting the Korean War.

The perspective gained by the passage of time often allows us to reevaluate the achievements and failures of a given individual. Such is the case with Richard Nixon, president of the United States from 1969 to 1974. Because he was forced to resign the presidency to avoid impeachment proceedings resulting from his role in the Watergate scandal, Nixon remains a controversial political figure. How will Nixon, who died in 1994, be remembered? In Issue 12, Joan Hoff-Wilson downplays the significance of the Watergate scandal in assessing Nixon's legacy. She believes that President Nixon should be applauded for reorganizing the executive branch and portions of the federal bureaucracy and for implementing domestic reforms in civil rights, welfare, and economic planning, despite its limited foreign policy successes and the Watergate scandal. But Professor Bruce Schulman argues that Nixon was not the last liberal twentieth-century president, but America's first modern conservative executive. By 1971, Nixon had recognized that the center of the American political spectrum had shifted rightward, and he shifted his policies accordingly in the areas of civil rights, environmentalism, and welfare reform.

In the 30-plus years since Nixon's departure, the American political spectrum has continued to shift to the right. Even Democratic Presidents Carter and Clinton could by no stretch of the imagination be considered liberals. Our present executive, George W. Bush, traces his economic legacy of tax cuts as a fiscal stimulus back to the Reagan presidency. Issue 15 presents two diametrically opposed views of the current president. Princeton historian Sean Wilentz thinks that George Bush will be considered one of the worst presidents in American history because he is oblivious to the major economic and social problems facing the nation, has waged a partisan war in Iraq under false pretenses, and has turned an inherited surplus into the largest deficit ever with his proposed tax cuts for the wealthiest Americans. But publishing mogul Conrad Black disagrees: George Bush, he argues, will rank with Lincoln and FDR among our most important presidents because he is waging a successful war against terrorism, while his nation-building agenda will bring peace, stability, freedom, and democracy to the Arab world.

Social, Cultural, and Economic Changes Since 1945

Carl N. Degler has labeled the years from 1945 to 1963 as the age of "anxiety and affluence." Issue 5 deals with this unique period in U.S. history. The population explosion that took place after World War II led to a youth culture who challenged the value system of their parents. Tensions between parents and children have always existed in America. Do different tastes in dress and music reflect revolutionary or surface changes? Professor Glenn C. Altschuler maintains that rock and roll's "switchblade beat" opened wide division in American society along the fault lines of family, sexuality, and race. But writer J. Ronald Oakley argues that although the lifestyles of youth departed from their parents, their basic ideas and attitudes were still the conservative ones that mirrored the conservatism of the affluent age in which they grew up.

The 1960s was an era of great turmoil. President Johnson hoped to be remembered as the president who extended the New Deal reforms of the 1930s to the bottom third of the population. So controversial were Johnson's domestic reforms that some members of the Bush administration blamed the Los Angeles riots in the spring of 1992 on the Great Society. In Issue 9, Charles Murray argues along this line. Not only did the retraining, anticrime, and welfare programs of the Great Society not work, says Murray, but they also contributed to the worsening plight of U.S. inner cities today. In contrast, Joseph A. Califano, Jr., maintains that the 1960s' reforms brought about positive revolutionary changes in the area of civil rights, education, health care, the environment, and consumer protection.

America's anxiety peaked on November 22, 1963, when President John F. Kennedy was assassinated while riding in a motorcade through downtown Dallas, Texas. The identity of the president's killer or killers has been a matter of great controversy and speculation ever since. In Issue 7, the President's Commission on the Assassination of President John F. Kennedy concludes that

Lee Harvey Oswald was the sole assassin of President Kennedy and that he was not part of any organized conspiracy. Michael L. Kurtz disagrees with the conclusions of the commission, which he maintains ignored evidence of Oswald's connections with organized criminals and pro-Castro and anti-Castro supporters as well as forensic evidence that pointed to multiple assassins.

The American public experienced a shock in the late 1970s due to the normal expectations of constant growth. Rising oil prices, foreign economic competition, and double-digit interest and inflation rates created an economic recession. Issue 14 debates whether the 1980s was a decade of affluence or decline for middle-class Americans. According to Professor J. David Woodard, supply-side economics unleashed a wave of entrepreneurial and technological innovation that transformed the economy and restored America's confidence in the Golden Age from 1983 to 1992. Political journalist Thomas Byrne Edsall argues that the Reagan revolution brought about a policy realignment that reversed the New Deal and redistributed political power and economic wealth to the top 20 percent of Americans.

The final issue in this book (Issue 17) is of great concern to most Americans: Is the earth out of balance? In other words, is there really an environmental crisis? NASA scientist Jim Hansen believes that the world will become a more desolate place to live in the foreseeable future unless we reduce or sequester the carbon emissions that are warming the atmosphere. Kevin Shapiro, a research fellow in neuroscience at Harvard University, believes the increase in CO_2 in the atmosphere is significant but not a cause for panic because what we "know" about global warming comes from computer simulation models that have various biased built-in assumptions.

The Outsiders: African Americans, Women, and Immigrants

Groups outside the mainstream made great strides in the 1960s. This was particularly true of African Americans, who regained civil and political rights denied them since the end of the 1890s. Issue 8 focuses on the second revolution and, in particular, the role of Martin Luther King, Jr. In the first selection, Adam Fairclough demonstrates the importance of King's leadership to the civil rights movement in 1960. In the second selection, Clayborne Carson plays down the mythical image of King and asserts that bestowing praise solely on King for the civil rights movement takes credit away from many of the local leaders who desegregated their communities through the creation of grassroots organizations. Carson argues that King is a product of a movement that would have occurred even if King had never lived.

Two ongoing controversies that have continued into the twenty-first century are analyzed in this reader. Issue 16 debates whether or not the United States should remain a nation of immigrants. Tamar Jacoby, who supports allowing immigration to continue, maintains that the newest immigrants keep America's economy strong because they work harder and take jobs that native-born Americans reject. Patrick J. Buchanan, however, argues that America is no longer a nation because immigrants from Mexico and other Third World Latin

American and Asian countries have turned it into a series of fragmented multi-cultural ethnic enclaves that lack a common culture. Therefore, he contends, immigration should be drastically curbed.

A direct lineage of the civil rights revolution was the women's liberation movement of the 1970s. Did it help or harm women? In Issue 11, writer and lecturer F. Carolyn Garglia argues that women should stay at home and practice the values of "true motherhood" because contemporary feminists have discredited marriage, devalued traditional homemaking, and encouraged sexual promiscuity. But feminist and activist scholar Sara M. Evans takes a much more positive view of the women's movements for suffrage and liberation in the past 100 years. Despite their class, racial, religious, ethnic, and regional differences, Evans argues that women in America experienced major transformations in their private and public lives in the twentieth century.

Conclusion

The process of historical study should rely more on thinking than on memorizing data. Once the basics of who, what, when, and where are determined, historical thinking shifts to a higher gear. Analysis, comparison and contrast, evaluation, and explanation take command. These skills not only increase our knowledge of the past, but they also provide general tools for the comprehension of all the topics about which human beings think.

The diversity of a pluralistic society, however, creates some obstacles to comprehending the past. The spectrum of differing opinions on any particular subject eliminates the possibility of quick and easy answers. In the final analysis, conclusions are often built through a synthesis of several different interpretations, but even then they may be partial and tentative.

The study of history in a pluralistic society allows each citizen the opportunity to reach independent conclusions about the past. Since most, if not all, historical issues affect the present and future, understanding the past becomes necessary if society is to progress. Many of today's problems have a direct connection with the past. Additionally, other contemporary issues may lack obvious direct antecedents, but historical investigation can provide illuminating analogies. At first, it may appear confusing to read and to think about opposing historical views, but the survival of our democratic society depends on such critical thinking by acute and discerning minds.

Internet References . . .

Cold War Policies 1945–1991

This site presents U.S. government policies during the Cold War, listed year by year from 1945 through 1991, as well as links to related sites.

http://ac.acusd.edu/history/20th/coldwar0.html

Oingo: History of the Korean War

This Oingo site provides dozens of links on the Korean War covering the history of the war, specific missions, political and social issues, and General Douglas MacArthur.

http://www.oingo.com/topic/53/53130.html

CNN Interactive: Cold War

Experience CNN's landmark documentary series in this award-winning Web site covering the Cold War years. Navigate interactive maps, see rare archival footage online, and read recently declassified documents, among other activities.

http://www.conn.com/SPECIALS/cold.war/

The Cold War Museum

Click on a decade on this site's timeline for information about important events that took place during those years, including the Korean War, the Cuban Missile Crisis, and the assassination of President John F. Kennedy.

http://www.coldwar.org

John McAdams, "The Kennedy Assassination"

http://mcadams.posc.mu.edu

The Lee Harvey Oswald Page

The purpose of this site, maintained by independent researcher W. Tracy Parnell, is to provide information to researchers and students about Lee Harvey Oswald, accused assassin of President John F. Kennedy, as well as general assassination-related material. (See also Unit 2 opener for more information sites on the Kennedy assassination.)

http://www.madbbs.com/-tracy/lho/

American High: 1945–1962

*T*he post-war years were a period of both affluence and anxiety. America emerged from World War II as one of the strongest nations in the world, both militarily and economically. Both the reconstruction and revitalization of world trade were dependent upon American loans and its industrial production. Presidents Truman, Eisenhower, and Kennedy managed an economy whose major problem was to keep inflation under control for a prosperous blue-collar labor force and an emerging baby boomer, white-collar class. The rich got richer, and the middle class did like-wise. African Americans, working, women, and rural America were not only left behind but invisible.

World War II ended in 1945 with a bang. But the peace that every-one had hoped for never came. Whether the bomb was used for military or political reasons soon became irrelevant. An "iron curtain" was hung over Eastern Europe, and by 1947 a "cold war" between the Western powers and the Russians was in full swing. In 1949 China came under communist control, the Russians developed an atomic bomb, and com-munist subversion of high-level U.S. government officials in the State and Treasury Departments of the U.S. government was uncovered. A year later American soldiers were fighting a hot war of "containment" against communist expansion in Korea.

For the most part, Americans were wealthy beyond their fondest dreams. But they were also scared of losing it all in a third world war. It almost came in October 1962, when the Americans and the Russians faced off in the Cuban Missile Crisis. Both sides backed off, but it appeared to be a victory for the United States when the Russians pulled their missiles out of Cuba. The Kennedy promise came to an abrupt halt 13 months later, when the president was assassinated. The "American high" was over.

- Was It Necessary to Drop the Atomic Bomb to End World War II?

- Was President Truman Responsible for the Cold War?

- Did Communism Threaten America's Internal Security after World War II?

- Should President Truman Have Fired General MacArthur?

- Was Rock and Roll Responsible for Dismantling America's Traditional Family, Sexual, and Racial Customs in the 1950s and 1960s?

- Was President Kennedy Responsible for the Cuban Missile Crisis?

1

ISSUE 1

Was It Necessary to Drop the Atomic Bomb to End World War II?

YES: Robert James Maddox, from *American Heritage* (May/June 1995)

NO: Tsuyoshi Hasegawa, from *Racing the Enemy: Stalin, Truman, and the Surrender of Japan* (Harvard University Press, 2005)

ISSUE SUMMARY

YES: Professor of American history Robert James Maddox contends that the atomic bomb became the catalyst that forced the hard-liners in the Japanese army to accept the emperor's plea to surrender, thus avoiding a costly, bloody invasion of the Japanese mainland.

NO: Professor of American history Tsuyoshi Hasegawa argues that the Soviet entrance into the war played a greater role in causing Japan to surrender than did the dropping of the atomic bombs.

America's development of the atomic bomb began in 1939 when a small group of scientists led by well-known physicist Albert Einstein called President Franklin D. Roosevelt's attention to the enormous potential uses of atomic energy for military purposes. In his letter, Einstein warned Roosevelt that Nazi Germany was already experimenting in this area. The program to develop the bomb, which began very modestly in October 1939, soon expanded into the $2 billion Manhattan Project, which combined the talents and energies of scientists (many of whom were Jewish refugees from Hitler's Nazi Germany) from universities and research laboratories across the country. The Manhattan Project was the beginning of the famed military-industrial-university complex that we take for granted today.

Part of the difficulty in reconstructing the decision to drop the atomic bomb lies in the rapidity with which events moved in the spring of 1945. On May 7, 1945, Germany surrendered. Almost a month earlier the world was stunned by the death of FDR, who was succeeded by Harry Truman, a former U.S. senator who was chosen as a compromise vice presidential candidate in 1944. The man from Missouri had never been a confidant of Roosevelt. Truman did not even learn of the existence of the Manhattan Project until

12 days after he became president, at which time Secretary of War Henry L. Stimson advised him of a "highly secret matter" that would have a "decisive" effect upon America's postwar foreign policy.

Because Truman was unsure of his options for using the bomb, he approved Stimson's suggestion that a special committee of high-level political, military, and scientific policymakers be appointed to consider the major issues. The committee recommended unanimously that "the bomb should be used against Japan as soon as possible . . . against a military target surrounded by other buildings . . . without prior warning of the nature of the weapon."

A number of scientists disagreed with this report. They recommended that the weapon be tested on a desert island before representatives of the United Nations and that an ultimatum be sent to Japan warning of the destructive power of the bomb. These young scientists suggested that the bomb be used if the Japanese rejected the warning, and only "if sanction of the United Nations (and of public opinion at home) were obtained."

A second scientific committee created by Stimson rejected both the test demonstration and warning alternatives. This panel felt that if the bomb failed to work during the demonstration, there would be political repercussions both at home and abroad. If a specific warning was given, the American military leaders were afraid that POWs would be stationed in the target area.

Thus, by the middle of June 1945, the civilian leaders were unanimous that the atomic bomb should be used. During the Potsdam Conference in July, Truman learned that the bomb had been successfully tested in New Mexico. The big three—Truman, Atlee, and Stalin—issued a warning to Japan to surrender or suffer prompt and utter destruction. When the Japanese equivocated in their response, the Americans replied by dropping an atomic bomb on Hiroshima on August 6, which killed 100,000 people, and a second bomb on August 9, which leveled the city of Nagasaki. During this time the emperor pleaded with the Japanese military to end the war. On August 14 the Japanese accepted the terms of surrender with the condition that the emperor not be treated as a war criminal.

Was it necessary to drop the atomic bombs on Japan in order to end the war? In the following selections, two viewpoints are advanced. Robert James Maddox, a long-time critic of cold war revisionist history, argues that Truman believed that the use of the atomic bomb would shorten the war and save lives, particularly American ones. Maddox also asserts that the bombs at Hiroshima and Nagasaki allowed the emperor to successfully plead with army hard-liners to end the war. Professor Tsuyoshi Hasegawa casts the use of the atomic bomb in a wider setting. "Truman issued the Potsdam Proclamation," he says, "not as a warning to Japan, but to justify the use of the atomic bomb." He also challenges "the commonly held view that the atomic bomb provided the immediate and decisive knockout blow to Japan's will to fight. Instead, the Soviet entry into the war played a greater role than the atomic bombs in inducing Japan to surrender."

YES

Robert James Maddox

The Biggest Decision: Why We Had to Drop the Atomic Bomb

On the morning of August 6, 1945, the American B-29 Enola Gay dropped an atomic bomb on the Japanese city of Hiroshima. Three days later another B-29, *Bock's Car*, released one over Nagasaki. Both caused enormous casualties and physical destruction. These two cataclysmic events have preyed upon the American conscience ever since. The furor over the Smithsonian Institution's *Enola Gay* exhibit and over the mushroom-cloud postage stamp last autumn are merely the most obvious examples. Harry S. Truman and other officials claimed that the bombs caused Japan to surrender, thereby avoiding a bloody invasion. Critics have accused them of at best failing to explore alternatives, at worst of using the bombs primarily to make the Soviet Union "more manageable" rather than to defeat a Japan they knew already was on the verge of capitulation.

⋅❀⋅

By any rational calculation Japan was a beaten nation by the summer of 1945. Conventional bombing had reduced many of its cities to rubble, blockade had strangled its importation of vitally needed materials, and its navy had sustained such heavy losses as to be powerless to interfere with the invasion everyone knew was coming. By late June advancing American forces had completed the conquest of Okinawa, which lay only 350 miles from the southernmost Japanese home island of Kyushu. They now stood poised for the final onslaught.

Rational calculations did not determine Japan's position. Although a peace faction within the government wished to end the war—provided certain conditions were met—militants were prepared to fight on regardless of consequences. They claimed to welcome an invasion of the home islands, promising to inflict such hideous casualties that the United States would retreat from its announced policy of unconditional surrender. The militarists held effective power over the government and were capable of defying the emperor, as they had in the past, on the ground that his civilian advisers were misleading him.

From *American Heritage*, May/June 1995, pp. 70–74, 76–77 © 1995 by Forbes, Inc. Reprinted by permission of *American Heritage* magazine, a division of Forbes, Inc.

Okinawa provided a preview of what invasion of the home islands would entail. Since April 1 the Japanese had fought with a ferocity that mocked any notion that their will to resist was eroding. They had inflicted nearly 50,000 casualties on the invaders, many resulting from the first large-scale use of kamikazes. They also had dispatched the superbattleship *Yamato* on a suicide mission to Okinawa, where, after attacking American ships offshore, it was to plunge ashore to become a huge, doomed steel fortress. *Yamato* was sunk shortly after leaving port, but its mission symbolized Japan's willingness to sacrifice everything in an apparently hopeless cause.

The Japanese could be expected to defend their sacred homeland with even greater fervor, and kamikazes flying at short range promised to be even more devastating than at Okinawa. The Japanese had more than 2,000,000 troops in the home islands, were training millions of irregulars, and for some time had been conserving aircraft that might have been used to protect Japanese cities against American bombers.

Reports from Tokyo indicated that Japan meant to fight the war to a finish. On June 8 an imperial conference adopted "The Fundamental Policy to Be Followed Henceforth in the Conduct of the War," which pledged to "prosecute the war to the bitter end in order to uphold the national polity, protect the imperial land, and accomplish the objectives for which we went to war." Truman had no reason to believe that the proclamation meant anything other than what it said.

Against this background, while fighting on Okinawa still continued, the President had his naval chief of staff, Adm. William D. Leahy, notify the Joint Chiefs of Staff (JCS) and the Secretaries of War and Navy that a meeting would be held at the White House on June 18. The night before the conference Truman wrote in his diary that "I have to decide Japanese strategy—shall we invade Japan proper or shall we bomb and blockade? That is my hardest decision to date. But I'll make it when I have all the facts."

⋅◈⋅

Truman met with the chiefs at three-thirty in the afternoon. Present were Army Chief of Staff Gen. George C. Marshall, Army Air Force's Gen. Ira C. Eaker (sitting in for the Army Air Force's chief of staff, Henry H. Arnold, who was on an inspection tour of installations in the Pacific), Navy Chief of Staff Adm. Ernest J. King, Leahy (also a member of the JCS), Secretary of the Navy James Forrestal, Secretary of War Henry L. Stimson, and Assistant Secretary of War John J. McCloy. Truman opened the meeting, then asked Marshall for his views. Marshall was the dominant figure on the JCS. He was Truman's most trusted military adviser, as he had been President Franklin D. Roosevelt's.

Marshall reported that the chiefs, supported by the Pacific commanders Gen. Douglas MacArthur and Adm. Chester W. Nimitz, agreed that an invasion of Kyushu "appears to be the least costly worthwhile operation following Okinawa." Lodgment in Kyushu, he said, was necessary to make blockade and bombardment more effective and to serve as a staging area for the invasion of Japan's main island of Honshu. The chiefs recommended a target date of

November 1 for the first phase, code-named Olympic, because delay would give the Japanese more time to prepare and because bad weather might postpone the invasion "and hence the end of the war" for up to six months. Marshall said that in his opinion, Olympic was "the only course to pursue." The chiefs also proposed that Operation Cornet be launched against Honshu on March 1, 1946.

❧❦❧

Leahy's memorandum calling the meeting had asked for casualty projections which that invasion might be expected to produce. Marshall stated that campaigns in the Pacific had been so diverse "it is considered wrong" to make total estimates. All he would say was that casualties during the first thirty days on Kyushu should not exceed those sustained in taking Luzon in the Philippines—31,000 men killed, wounded, or missing in action. "It is a grim fact," Marshall said, "that there is not an easy, bloodless way to victory in war." Leahy estimated a higher casualty rate similar to Okinawa, and King guessed somewhere in between.

King and Eaker, speaking for the Navy and the Army Air Forces respectively, endorsed Marshall's proposals. King said that he had become convinced that Kyushu was "the key to the success of any siege operations." He recommended that "we should do Kyushu now" and begin preparations for invading Honshu. Eaker "agreed completely" with Marshall. He said he had just received a message from Arnold also expressing "complete agreement." Air Force plans called for the use of forty groups of heavy bombers, which "could not be deployed without the use of airfields on Kyushu." Stimson and Forrestal concurred.

Truman summed up. He considered "the Kyushu plan all right from the military standpoint" and directed the chiefs to "go ahead with it." He said he "had hoped that there was a possibility of preventing an Okinawa from one end of Japan to the other," but "he was clear on the situation now" and was "quite sure" the chiefs should proceed with the plan. Just before the meeting adjourned, McCloy raised the possibility of avoiding an invasion by warning the Japanese that the United States would employ atomic weapons if there were no surrender. The ensuing discussion was inconclusive because the first test was a month away and no one could be sure the weapons would work.

In his memoirs Truman claimed that using atomic bombs prevented an invasion that would have cost 500,000 American lives. Other officials mentioned the same or even higher figures. Critics have assailed such statements as gross exaggerations designed to forestall scrutiny of Truman's real motives. They have given wide publicity to a report prepared by the Joint War Plans Committee (JWPC) for the chiefs' meeting with Truman. The committee estimated that the invasion of Kyushu, followed by that of Honshu, as the chiefs proposed, would cost approximately 40,000 dead, 150,000 wounded, and 3,500 missing in action for a total of 193,500 casualties.

That those responsible for a decision should exaggerate the consequences of alternatives is commonplace. Some who cite the JWPC report profess to see more sinister motives, insisting that such "low" casualty projections call into question the very idea that atomic bombs were used to avoid heavy losses. By discrediting that justification as a cover-up, they seek to bolster their contention that the bombs really were used to permit the employment of "atomic diplomacy" against the Soviet Union.

The notion that 193,500 anticipated casualties were too insignificant to have caused Truman to resort to atomic bombs might seem bizarre to anyone other than an academic, but let it pass. Those who have cited the JWPC report in countless op-ed pieces in newspapers and in magazine articles have created a myth by omitting key considerations: First, the report itself is studded with qualifications that casualties "are not subject to accurate estimate" and that the projection "is admittedly only an educated guess." Second, the figures never were conveyed to Truman. They were excised at high military echelons, which is why Marshall cited only estimates for the first thirty days on Kyushu. And indeed, subsequent Japanese troop buildups on Kyushu rendered the JWPC estimates totally irrelevant by the time the first atomic bomb was dropped.

⁓◈⁓

Another myth that has attained wide attention is that at least several of Truman's top military advisers later informed him that using atomic bombs against Japan would be militarily unnecessary or immoral, or both. There is no persuasive evidence that any of them did so. None of the Joint Chiefs ever made such a claim, although one inventive author has tried to make it appear that Leahy did by braiding together several unrelated passages from the admiral's memoirs. Actually, two days after Hiroshima, Truman told aides that Leahy had "said up to the last that it wouldn't go off."

Neither MacArthur nor Nimitz ever communicated to Truman any change of mind about the need for invasion or expressed reservations about using the bombs. When first informed about their imminent use only days before Hiroshima, MacArthur responded with a lecture on the future of atomic warfare and even after Hiroshima strongly recommended that the invasion go forward. Nimitz, from whose jurisdiction the atomic strikes would be launched, was notified in early 1945. "This sounds fine," he told the courier, "but this is only February. Can't we get one sooner?" Nimitz later would join Air Force generals Carl D. Spaatz, Nathan Twining, and Curtis LeMay in recommending that a third bomb be dropped on Tokyo.

Only Dwight D. Eisenhower later claimed to have remonstrated against the use of the bomb. In his *Crusade in Europe*, published in 1948, he wrote that when Secretary Stimson informed him during the Potsdam Conference of plans to use the bomb, he replied that he hoped "we would never have to use such a thing against any enemy," because he did not want the United States to be the first to use such a weapon. He added, "My views were merely personal and immediate reactions; they were not based on any analysis of the subject."

Eisenhower's recollections grew more colorful as the years went on. A later account of his meeting with Stimson had it taking place at Ike's headquarters in Frankfurt on the very day news arrived of the successful atomic test in New Mexico. "We'd had a nice evening at headquarters in Germany," he remembered. Then, after dinner, "Stimson got this cable saying that the bomb had been perfected and was ready to be dropped. The cable was in code . . . 'the lamb is born' or some damn thing like that." In this version Eisenhower claimed to have protested vehemently that "the Japanese were ready to surrender and it wasn't necessary to hit them with that awful thing." "Well," Eisenhower concluded, "the old gentleman got furious."

⁓◉⁓

The best that can be said about Eisenhower's memory is that it had become flawed by the passage of time. Stimson was in Potsdam and Eisenhower in Frankfurt on July 16, when word came of the successful test. Aside from a brief conversation at a flag-raising ceremony in Berlin on July 20, the only other time they met was at Ike's headquarters on July 27. By then orders already had been sent to the Pacific to use the bombs if Japan had not yet surrendered. Notes made by one of Stimson's aides indicate that there was a discussion of atomic bombs, but there is no mention of any protest on Eisenhower's part. Even if there had been, two factors must be kept in mind. Eisenhower had commanded Allied forces in Europe, and his opinion on how close Japan was to surrender would have carried no special weight. More important, Stimson left for home immediately after the meeting and could not have personally conveyed Ike's sentiments to the President, who did not return to Washington until after Hiroshima.

On July 8 the Combined Intelligence Committee submitted to the American and British Combined Chiefs of Staff a report entitled "Estimate of the Enemy Situation." The committee predicted that as Japan's position continued to deteriorate, it might "make a serious effort to use the USSR [then a neutral] as a mediator in ending the war." Tokyo also would put out "intermittent peace feelers" to "weaken the determination of the United Nations to fight to the bitter end, or to create inter-allied dissension." While the Japanese people would be willing to make large concessions to end the war, "For a surrender to be acceptable to the Japanese army, it would be necessary for the military leaders to believe that it would not entail discrediting warrior tradition and that it would permit the ultimate resurgence of a military Japan."

Small wonder that American officials remained unimpressed when Japan proceeded to do exactly what the committee predicted. On July 12 Japanese Foreign Minister Shigenori Togo instructed Ambassador Naotaki Sato in Moscow to inform the Soviets that the emperor wished to send a personal envoy, Prince Fuminaro Konoye, in an attempt "to restore peace with all possible speed." Although he realized Konoye could not reach Moscow before the Soviet leader Joseph Stalin and Foreign Minister V. M. Molotov left to attend a Big Three meeting scheduled to begin in Potsdam on the fifteenth, Togo sought to have negotiations begin as soon as they returned.

American officials had long since been able to read Japanese diplomatic traffic through a process known as the MAGIC intercepts. Army intelligence (G-2) prepared for General Marshall its interpretation of Togo's message the next day. The report listed several possible constructions, the most probable being that the Japanese "governing clique" was making a coordinated effort to "stave off defeat" through Soviet intervention and an "appeal to war weariness in the United States." The report added that Undersecretary of State Joseph C. Grew, who had spent ten years in Japan as ambassador, "agrees with these conclusions."

Some have claimed that Togo's overture to the Soviet Union, together with attempts by some minor Japanese officials in Switzerland and other neutral countries to get peace talks started through the Office of Strategic Services (OSS), constituted clear evidence that the Japanese were near surrender. Their sole prerequisite was retention of their sacred emperor, whose unique cultural/religious status within the Japanese polity they would not compromise. If only the United States had extended assurances about the emperor, according to this view, much bloodshed and the atomic bombs would have been unnecessary.

A careful reading of the MAGIC intercepts of subsequent exchanges between Togo and Sato provides no evidence that retention of the emperor was the sole obstacle to peace. What they show instead is that the Japanese Foreign Office was trying to cut a deal through the Soviet Union that would have permitted Japan to retain its political system and its prewar empire intact. Even the most lenient American official could not have countenanced such a settlement.

⋯◉⋯

Togo on July 17 informed Sato that "we are not asking the Russians' mediation in *anything like unconditional surrender* [emphasis added]." During the following weeks Sato pleaded with his superiors to abandon hope of Soviet intercession and to approach the United States directly to find out what peace terms would be offered. "There is . . . no alternative but immediate unconditional surrender," he cabled on July 31, and he bluntly informed Togo that "your way of looking at things and the actual situation in the Eastern Area may be seen to be absolutely contradictory." The Foreign Ministry ignored his pleas and continued to seek Soviet help even after Hiroshima.

"Peace feelers" by Japanese officials abroad seemed no more promising from the American point of view. Although several of the consular personnel and military attachés engaged in these activities claimed important connections at home, none produced verification. Had the Japanese government sought only an assurance about the emperor, all it had to do was grant one of these men authority to begin talks through the OSS. Its failure to do so led American officials to assume that those involved were either well-meaning individuals acting alone or that they were being orchestrated by Tokyo. Grew characterized such "peace feelers" as "familiar weapons of psychological warfare" designed to "divide the Allies."

Some American officials, such as Stimson and Grew, nonetheless wanted to signal the Japanese that they might retain the emperorship in the form of a constitutional monarchy. Such an assurance might remove the last stumbling block to surrender, if not when it was issued, then later. Only an imperial rescript would bring about an orderly surrender, they argued, without which

Japanese forces would fight to the last man regardless of what the government in Tokyo did. Besides, the emperor could serve as a stabilizing factor during the transition to peacetime.

There were many arguments against an American initiative. Some opposed retaining such an undemocratic institution on principle and because they feared it might later serve as a rallying point for future militarism. Should that happen, as one assistant Secretary of State put it, "those lives already spent will have been sacrificed in vain, and lives will be lost again in the future." Japanese hard-liners were certain to exploit an overture as evidence that losses sustained at Okinawa had weakened American resolve and to argue that continued resistance would bring further concessions. Stalin, who earlier had told an American envoy that he favored abolishing the emperorship because the ineffectual Hirohito might be succeeded by "an energetic and vigorous figure who could cause trouble," was just as certain to interpret it as a treacherous effort to end the war before the Soviets could share in the spoils.

There were domestic considerations as well. Roosevelt had announced the unconditional surrender policy in early 1943, and it since had become a slogan of the war. He also had advocated that peoples everywhere should have the right to choose their own form of government, and Truman had publicly pledged to carry out his predecessor's legacies. For him to have formally *guaranteed* continuance of the emperorship, as opposed to merely accepting it on American terms pending free elections, as he later did, would have constituted a blatant repudiation of his own promises.

Nor was that all. Regardless of the emperor's actual role in Japanese aggression, which is still debated, much wartime propaganda had encouraged Americans to regard Hirohito as no less a war criminal than Adolf Hitler or Benito Mussolini. Although Truman said on several occasions that he had no objection to retaining the emperor, he understandably refused to make the first move. The ultimatum he issued from Potsdam on July 26 did not refer specifically to the emperorship. All it said was that occupation forces would be removed after "a peaceful and responsible" government had been established according to the "freely expressed will of the Japanese people." When the Japanese rejected the ultimatum rather than at last inquire whether they might retain the emperor, Truman permitted the plans for using the bombs to go forward.

Reliance on MAGIC intercepts and the "peace feelers" to gauge how near Japan was to surrender is misleading in any case. The army, not the Foreign Office, controlled the situation. Intercepts of Japanese military communications, designated ULTRA, provided no reason to believe the army was even considering surrender. Japanese Imperial Headquarters had correctly guessed that the next operation after Okinawa would be Kyushu and was making every effort to bolster its defenses there.

General Marshall reported on July 24 that there were "approximately 500,000 troops in Kyushu" and that more were on the way. ULTRA identified new units arriving almost daily. MacArthur's G-2 reported on July 29 that "this threatening development, if not checked, may grow to a point where we attack on a ratio of one (1) to one (1) which is not the recipe for victory." By the time the first atomic bomb fell, ULTRA indicated that there were 560,000 troops in southern Kyushu (the actual figure was closer to 900,000), and projections for November 1 placed the number at 680,000. A report, for medical purposes, of July 31 estimated that total battle and non-battle casualties might run as high as 394,859 *for the Kyushu operation alone*. This figure did not include those men expected to be killed outright, for obviously they would require no medical attention. Marshall regarded Japanese defenses as so formidable that even after Hiroshima he asked MacArthur to consider alternate landing sites and began contemplating the use of atomic bombs as tactical weapons to support the invasion.

The thirty-day casualty projection of 31,000 Marshall had given Truman at the June 18 strategy meeting had become meaningless. It had been based on the assumption that the Japanese had about 350,000 defenders in Kyushu and that naval and air interdiction would preclude significant reinforcement. But the Japanese buildup since that time meant that the defenders would have nearly twice the number of troops available by "X-day" than earlier assumed. The assertion that apprehensions about casualties are insufficient to explain Truman's use of the bombs, therefore, cannot be taken seriously. On the contrary, as Winston Churchill wrote after a conversation with him at Potsdam, Truman was tormented by "the terrible responsibilities that rested upon him in regard to the unlimited effusions of American blood."

❧

Some historians have argued that while the first bomb *might* have been required to achieve Japanese surrender, dropping the second constituted a needless barbarism. The record shows otherwise. American officials believed more than one bomb would be necessary because they assumed Japanese hard-liners would minimize the first explosion or attempt to explain it away as some sort of natural catastrophe, precisely what they did. The Japanese minister of war, for instance, at first refused even to admit that the Hiroshima bomb was atomic. A few hours after Nagasaki he told the cabinet that "the Americans appeared to have one hundred atomic bombs . . . they could drop three per day. The next target might well be Tokyo."

Even after both bombs had fallen and Russia entered the war, Japanese militants insisted on such lenient peace terms that moderates knew there was no sense even transmitting them to the United States. Hirohito had to intervene personally on two occasions during the next few days to induce hard-liners to abandon their conditions and to accept the American stipulation that the emperor's authority "shall be subject to the Supreme Commander of the Allied Powers." That the militarists would have accepted such a settlement before the bombs is farfetched, to say the least.

Some writers have argued that the cumulative effects of battlefield defeats, conventional bombing, and naval blockade already had defeated Japan. Even without extending assurances about the emperor, all the United States had to do was wait. The most frequently cited basis for this contention is the *United States Strategic Bombing Survey*, published in 1946, which stated that Japan would have surrendered by November 1 "even if the atomic bombs had not been dropped, even if Russia had not entered the war, and even if no invasion had been planned or contemplated." Recent scholarship by the historian Robert P. Newman and others has demonstrated that the survey was "cooked" by those who prepared it to arrive at such a conclusion. No matter. This or any other document based on information available only after the war ended is irrelevant with regard to what Truman could have known at the time.

What often goes unremarked is that when the bombs were dropped, fighting was still going on in the Philippines, China, and elsewhere. Every day that the war continued thousands of prisoners of war had to live and die in abysmal conditions, and there were rumors that the Japanese intended to slaughter them if the homeland was invaded. Truman was Commander in Chief of the American armed forces, and he had a duty to the men under his command not shared by those sitting in moral judgment decades later. Available evidence points to the conclusion that he acted for the reason he said he did: to end a bloody war that would have become far bloodier had invasion proved necessary. One can only imagine what would have happened if tens of thousands of American boys had died or been wounded on Japanese soil and then it had become known that Truman had chosen not to use weapons that might have ended the war months sooner.

Tsuyoshi Hasegawa  **NO**

Racing the Enemy: Stalin, Truman, and the Surrender of Japan

Assessing the Roads Not Taken

The end of the Pacific War was marked by the intense drama of two races: the first between Stalin and Truman to see who could force Japan to surrender and on what terms; and the second between the peace party and the war party in Japan on the question of whether to end the war and on what conditions. To the very end, the two races were inextricably linked. But what if things had been different? Would the outcome have changed if the key players had taken alternative paths? Below I explore some counterfactual suppositions to shed light on major issues that determined the outcome of the war.

What if Truman had accepted a provision in the Potsdam ultimatum allowing the Japanese to retain a constitutional monarchy? This alternative was supported by Stimson, Grew, Forrestal, Leahy, McCloy, and possibly Marshall. Churchill also favored this provision, and it was part of Stimson's original draft of the Potsdam Proclamation. Undoubtedly, a promise to retain the monarchy would have strengthened the peace party's receptivity of the Potsdam ultimatum. It would have led to intense discussion much earlier among Japanese policymakers on whether or not to accept the Potsdam terms, and it would have considerably diminished Japan's reliance on Moscow's mediation.

   Nevertheless, the inclusion of this provision would not have immediately led to Japan's surrender, since those who adhered to the mythical notion of the *kokutai* would have strenuously opposed the acceptance of the Potsdam terms, even if it meant the preservation of the monarchy. Certainly, the three war hawks in the Big Six would have objected on the grounds that the Potsdam Proclamation would spell the end of the armed forces. But peace advocates could have accused the war party of endangering the future of the imperial house by insisting on additional conditions. Thus, the inclusion of this provision would have hastened Japan's surrender, though it is doubtful that Japan would have capitulated before the atomic bomb was dropped on Hiroshima and the Soviet Union entered the war. The possibility of accepting the Potsdam terms might have been raised immediately after the atomic bombing on Hiroshima. This provision might have tipped the balance in favor of the peace party after the Soviet invasion, thus speeding up the termination of the war.

Why, then, didn't Truman accept this provision? One explanation was that he was concerned with how the public would react to a policy of appeasement. Domestic public opinion polls indicated an overwhelmingly negative sentiment against the emperor, and inevitably Archibald McLeish, Dean Acheson, and others would have raised strident voices of protest. Byrnes had warned that a compromise with the emperor would lead to the crucifixion of the president.

But would it have? Although public opinion polls were overwhelmingly against the emperor, newspaper commentaries were evenly split between those who advocated the abolition of the emperor system and those who argued that the preservation of the monarchical system could be compatible with eradication of Japanese militarism. Truman could have justified his decision on two powerful grounds. First, he could have argued that ending the war earlier would save the lives of American soldiers. Second, he could have explained that this decision was necessary to prevent Soviet expansion in Asia, though he would have had to present this argument carefully so as not to provoke a strong reaction from the Soviet Union.

Truman's refusal to include this provision was motivated not only by his concern with domestic repercussions but also by his own deep conviction that America should avenge the humiliation of Pearl Harbor. Anything short of unconditional surrender was not acceptable to Truman. The buck indeed stopped at the president. Thus, as long as Truman firmly held to his conviction, this counterfactual supposition was not a real alternative.

But the story does not end here. Another important, hidden reason motivated Truman's decision not to include this provision. Truman knew that the unconditional surrender demand without any promise to preserve a constitutional monarchy would be rejected by the Japanese. He needed Japan's refusal to justify the use of the atomic bomb. Thus so long as he was committed to using the atomic bomb, he could not include the provision promising a constitutional monarchy.

What if Truman had asked Stalin to sign the Potsdam Proclamation without a promise of constitutional monarchy?   In this case, Japanese policymakers would have realized that their last hope to terminate the war through Moscow's mediation was dashed. They would have been forced to confront squarely the issue of whether to accept the Potsdam surrender terms. The ambiguity of the emperor's position, however, still remained, and therefore the division among policymakers was inevitable, making it likely that neither the cabinet nor the Big Six would have been able to resolve the differences.

Japan's delay in giving the Allies a definite reply would surely have led to the dropping of the atomic bombs and Soviet participation in the war. Would Japan have surrendered after the first atomic bomb? The absence of a promise to preserve the monarchical system in the Potsdam terms would have prevented the peace party, including Hirohito and Kido, from acting decisively to accept surrender. Ultimately, the Soviet invasion of Manchuria would still have provided the coup de grace.

What if Truman had invited Stalin to sign the Potsdam Proclamation and included the promise to allow the Japanese to maintain a constitutional monarchy? This would have forced Japanese policymakers to confront the issue of whether to accept the Potsdam terms. Undoubtedly, the army would have insisted, if not on the continuation of the war, at least on attaching three additional conditions to the Potsdam Proclamation in order to ensure its own survival. But the promise of preserving the monarchical system might have prompted members of the peace party to intercede to end the war before the first atomic bomb, although there is no guarantee that their argument would have silenced the war party. The most crucial issue here is how the emperor would have reacted to the Potsdam terms had they contained the promise of a constitutional monarchy and been signed by Stalin in addition to Truman, Churchill, and Chiang Kai-shek. Undoubtedly, he would have been more disposed to the Potsdam terms, but the promise of a constitutional monarchy alone might not have induced the emperor to hasten to accept the ultimatum. A shock was needed. It is difficult to say if the Hiroshima bomb alone was sufficient, or whether the combination of the Hiroshima bomb and Soviet entry into the war was needed to convince the emperor to accept surrender. Either way, surrender would have come earlier than it did, thus shortening the war by several days.

Nevertheless, these counterfactual suppositions were not in the realm of possibility, since Truman and Byrnes would never have accepted them, for the reasons stated in the first counterfactual. The atomic bomb provided them with the solution to previously unsolvable dilemmas. Once the solution was found to square the circle, Truman and Byrnes never deviated from their objectives. An alternative was available, but they chose not to take it.

This counterfactual was dubious for another reason. If Stalin had been asked to join the ultimatum, he would never have agreed to promise a constitutional monarchy. Stalin's most important objective in the Pacific War was to join the conflict. The promise of a constitutional monarchy might have hastened Japan's surrender before the Soviet tanks crossed the Manchurian border—a disaster he would have avoided at all costs. This was why Stalin's own version of the joint ultimatum included the unconditional surrender demand. Had Stalin been invited to join the ultimatum that included the provision allowing Japan to retain a constitutional monarchy, he would have fought tooth and nail to scratch that provision. Ironically, both Stalin and Truman had vested interests in keeping unconditional surrender for different reasons.

What if Hiranuma had not made an amendment at the imperial conference on August 10, and the Japanese government had proposed accepting the Potsdam Proclamation "with the understanding that it did not include any demand for a change in the status of the emperor under the national law"? Hiranuma's amendment was an egregious mistake. Although the three war hawks in the Big Six attached three additional conditions to acceptance, they lacked the intellectual acumen to connect their misgivings to the fundamental core of the *kokutai* debate. Without Hiranuma's amendment the emperor would have supported the one-conditional acceptance of the Potsdam terms as formulated at the first imperial conference;

this condition was compatible, albeit narrowly, with a constitutional monarchy that Stimson, Leahy, Forrestal, and Grew would have accepted. If we believe Ballantine, Byrnes and Truman might have accepted the provision. But Hiranuma's amendment made it impossible for the American policymakers to accept this condition without compromising the fundamental objectives of the war.

On the other hand, given Truman's deep feelings against the emperor, even the original one condition—retention of the emperor's status in the national laws—or even the Foreign Ministry's original formula (the preservation of the imperial house) might have been rejected by Truman and Byrnes. Nevertheless, either formula might have been accepted by Grew, Dooman, and Ballantine, and would have strengthened the position advocated by Stimson, Leahy, Forrestal, and McCloy that Japan's first reply should be accepted.

What if the Byrnes Note had contained a clear indication that the United States would allow the Japanese to retain a constitutional monarchy with the current dynasty? The rejection of Japan's conditional acceptance of the Potsdam terms as amended by Hiranuma was not incompatible with the promise of a constitutional monarchy. The lack of this promise triggered the war party's backlash and endangered the peace parry's chances of ending the war early. Had the Byrnes Note included the guarantee of a constitutional monarchy under the current dynasty, Suzuki would not have temporarily defected to the war party, and Yonai would not have remained silent on August 12. War advocates would have opposed the Byrnes Note as incompatible with the *kokutai*. Nevertheless, a promise to preserve the monarchy would have taken the wind out of their sails, especially, given that the emperor would have more actively intervened for the acceptance of the Byrnes Note. Stalin would have opposed the Byrnes Note if it included the provision for a constitutional monarchy, but Truman was prepared to attain Japan's surrender without the Soviet Union anyway. This scenario thus might have resulted in Japan's surrender on August 12 or 13 instead of August 14.

Without the atomic bombs and without the Soviet entry into the war, would Japan have surrendered before November 1, the day Operation Olympic was scheduled to begin? The *United States Strategic Bombing Survey,* published in 1946, concluded that Japan would have surrendered before November 1 without the atomic bombs and without Soviet entry into the war. This conclusion has become the foundation on which revisionist historians have constructed their argument that the atomic bombs were not necessary for Japan's surrender. Since Barton Bernstein has persuasively demonstrated in his critique of the *Survey* that its conclusion is not supported by its own evidence, I need not dwell on this supposition. The main objective of the study's principal author, Paul Nitze, was to prove that conventional bombings, coupled with the naval blockade, would have induced Japan to surrender before November 1. But Nitze's conclusion was repeatedly contradicted by the evidence provided in the *Survey* itself. For instance, to the question, "How much longer do you think the war might have continued had the atomic bomb not been dropped?" Prince Konoe answered: "Probably it would have lasted all this year." Bernstein introduced numerous other testimonies by Toyoda, Kido, Suzuki, Hiranuma, Sakomizu, and others to contradict the *Survey*'s conclusion. As Bernstein asserts, the *Survey* is "an unreliable guide."

The Japanese leaders knew that Japan was losing the war. But defeat and surrender are not synonymous. Surrender is a political act. Without the twin shocks of the atomic bombs and Soviet entry into the war, the Japanese would never have accepted surrender in August.

Would Japan have surrendered before November 1 on the basis of Soviet entry alone, without the atomic bomb? Japanese historian Asada Sadao contends that without the atomic bombs but with Soviet entry into the war, "there was a possibility that Japan would not have surrendered before November 1." To Asada the shock value was crucial. Whereas the Japanese anticipated Soviet entry into the war, Asada argues, the atomic bombs came as a complete shock. By contrast, Bernstein states: "In view of the great impact of Soviet entry . . . in a situation of heavy conventional bombing and a strangling blockade, it does seem quite probable—indeed, far more likely than not—that Japan would have surrendered before November without the use of the A-bomb but after Soviet intervention in the war. In that sense . . . there may have been a serious 'missed opportunity' in 1945 to avoid the costly invasion of Kyushu without dropping the atomic bomb by awaiting Soviet entry."

The importance to Japan of Soviet neutrality is crucial in this context. Japan relied on Soviet neutrality both militarily and diplomatically. Diplomatically, Japan pinned its last hope on Moscow's mediation for the termination of the war. Once the Soviets entered the war, Japan was forced to make a decision on the Potsdam terms. Militarily as well, Japan's Ketsu-go strategy was predicated on Soviet neutrality; indeed, it was for this reason that the Military Affairs Bureau of the Army Ministry constantly overruled the intelligence section's warning that a Soviet invasion might be imminent. Manchuria was not written off, as Asada claims; rather, the military was confident that Japan could keep the Soviets neutral, at least for a while. When the Soviets invaded Manchuria, the military was taken by complete surprise. Despite the bravado that the war must continue, the Soviet invasion undermined the confidence of the army, punching a fatal hole in its strategic plan. The military's insistence on the continuation of war lost its rationale.

More important, however, were the political implications of the Soviet expansion in the Far East. Without Japan's surrender, it is reasonable to assume that the Soviets would have completed the occupation of Manchuria, southern Sakhalin, the entire Kurils, and possibly half of Korea by the beginning of September. Inevitably, the Soviet invasion of Hokkaido would have been raised as a pressing issue to be settled between the United States and the Soviet Union. The United States might have resisted the Soviet operation against Hokkaido, but given the Soviets' military strength, and given the enormous casualty figures the American high command had estimated for Olympic, the United States might have conceded the division of Hokkaido as Stalin had envisaged. Even if the United States succeeded in resisting Stalin's pressure, Soviet military conquests in the rest of the Far East might have led Truman to concede some degree of Soviet participation in Japan's postwar occupation. Whatever the United States might or might not have done regarding the Soviet operation in Hokkaido or the postwar occupation of Japan, Japanese leaders were well aware of the danger of allowing Soviet expansion to continue beyond Manchuria, Korea, Sakhalin, and the Kurils. It was for this reason that the Japanese policymakers came together at the last moment to surrender under the Potsdam terms, that the military's insistence on continuing the war collapsed, and that the military accepted surrender relatively easily. Japan's decision to surrender was above all a political decision, not a military one. Therefore, even without the atomic bombs, the war most likely would have ended shortly after Soviet entry into the war—before November 1.

Would Japan have surrendered before November 1 on the basis of the atomic bomb alone, without the Soviet entry into the war? The two bombs alone would most likely not have prompted the Japanese to surrender, so long as they still had hope that Moscow would mediate peace. The Hiroshima bombing did not significantly change Japan's policy, though it did inject a sense of urgency into the peace party's initiative to end the war. Without the Soviet entry into the war, it is not likely that the Nagasaki bomb would have changed the situation. Anami's warning that the United States might have 100 atomic bombs and that the next target might be Tokyo had no discernible impact on the debate. Even after the Nagasaki bomb, Japan would most likely have still waited for Moscow's answer to the Konoe mission.

The most likely scenario would have been that while waiting for the answer from Moscow, Japan would have been shocked by the Soviet invasion in Manchuria sometime in the middle of August, and would have sued for peace on the Potsdam terms. In this case, then, we would have debated endlessly whether the two atomic bombs preceding the Soviet invasion or the Soviet entry would have had a more decisive impact on Japan's decision to surrender, although in this case, too, clearly Soviet entry would have had a more decisive impact.

Richard Frank, who argues that the atomic bombings had a greater impact on Japan's decision to surrender than Soviet involvement in the war, relies exclusively on contemporary sources and discounts postwar testimonies. He emphasizes especially the importance of Hirohito's statement at the first imperial conference, the Imperial Rescript on August 15, and Suzuki's statements made during cabinet meetings. This methodology, though admirable, does not support Frank's conclusion. Hirohito's reference to the atomic bomb at the imperial conference comes from Takeshita's diary, which must be based on hearsay. None of the participants who actually attended the imperial conference remembers the emperor's referring to the atomic bomb. The Imperial Rescript on August 15 does refer to the use of the "cruel new bomb" as one of the reasons for the termination of the war, with no mention of Soviet entry into the war. But during his meeting with the three marshals on August 14, the emperor referred to both the atomic bomb and Soviet entry into the war as the decisive reasons for ending the war. Moreover, the Imperial Rescript to the Soldiers and Officers issued on August 17 refers to Soviet entry as the major reason for ending the war and makes no reference to the atomic bomb. In contemporary records from August 6 to August 15 two sources (the Imperial Rescript on August 15 and Suzuki's statement at the August 13 cabinet meeting) refer only to the impact of the atomic bomb, three sources only to Soviet entry (Konoe on August 9, Suzuki's statement to his doctor on August 13, and the Imperial Rescript to Soldiers and Officers on August 17), and seven sources both to the atomic bomb and Soviet involvement. Contemporary evidence does not support Frank's contention.

Without Soviet participation in the war in the middle of August, the United States would have faced the question of whether to use the third bomb sometime after August 19, and then the fourth bomb in the beginning of September, most likely on Kokura and Niigata. It is hard to say how many atomic bombs it would have taken to convince Japanese policymakers to abandon their approach to Moscow. It is possible to argue, though impossible to prove, that the Japanese military would still have argued for the continuation of the war after a third or even a fourth bomb.

Could Japan have withstood the attacks of seven atomic bombs before November 1? Would Truman and Stimson have had the resolve to use seven atomic bombs in succession? What would have been the impact of these bombs on Japanese public opinion? Would the continued use of the bombs have solidified or eroded the resolve of the Japanese to fight on? Would it have hopelessly alienated the Japanese from the United States to the point that it would be difficult to impose the American occupation on Japan? Would it have encouraged the Japanese to welcome the Soviet occupation instead? These are the questions we cannot answer with certainty.

On the basis of available evidence, however, it is clear that the two atomic bombs on Hiroshima and Nagasaki alone were not decisive in inducing Japan to surrender. Despite their destructive power, the atomic bombs were not sufficient to change the direction of Japanese diplomacy. The Soviet invasion was. Without the Soviet entry into the war, the Japanese would have continued to fight until numerous atomic bombs, a successful allied invasion of the home islands, or continued aerial bombardments, combined with a naval blockade, rendered them incapable of doing so.

Legacies

The Bomb in American Memory

After the war was over, each nation began constructing its own story about how the war ended. Americans still cling to the myth that the atomic bombs dropped on Hiroshima and Nagasaki provided the knockout punch to the Japanese government. The decision to use the bomb saved not only American soldiers but also the Japanese, according to this narrative. The myth serves to justify Truman's decision and ease the collective American conscience. To this extent, it is important to American national identity. But as this book demonstrates, this myth cannot be supported by historical facts. Evidence makes clear that there were alternatives to the use of the bomb, alternatives that the Truman administration for reasons of its own declined to pursue. And it is here, in the evidence of roads not taken, that the question of moral responsibility comes to the fore. Until his death, Truman continually came back to this question and repeatedly justified his decision, inventing a fiction that he himself later came to believe. That he spoke so often to justify his actions shows how much his decision to use the bomb haunted him.

On August 10 the Japanese government sent a letter of protest through the Swiss legation to the United States government. This letter declared the American use of the atomic bombs to be a violation of Articles 22 and 23 of the Hague Convention Respecting the Laws and Customs of War on Land, which prohibited the use of cruel weapons. It declared "in the name of the Japanese Imperial Government as well as in the name of humanity and civilization" that "the use of the atomic bombs, which surpass the indiscriminate cruelty of any other existing weapons and projectiles," was a crime against humanity, and demanded that "the further use of such inhumane weapons be immediately ceased." Needless to say, Truman did not respond to this letter. After Japan accepted the American occupation and became an important ally of the United States, the Japanese government has never raised any protest about the American use of the atomic bombs. The August 10 letter remains the only, and now forgotten, protest lodged by the Japanese government against the use of the atomic bomb.

To be sure, the Japanese government was guilty of its own atrocities in violation of the laws governing the conduct of war. The Nanking Massacre of 1937, biological experiments conducted by the infamous Unit 731, the Bataan March, and the numerous instances of cruel treatment of POWs represent only a few examples of Japanese atrocities. Nevertheless, the moral lapses of the Japanese do not excuse those of the United States and the Allies. After all, morality by definition is an absolute rather than a relative standard. The forgotten letter that the Japanese government sent to the United States government on August 10 deserves serious consideration. Justifying Hiroshima and Nagasaki by making a historically unsustainable argument that the atomic bombs ended the war is no longer tenable. Our self-image as Americans is tested by how we can come to terms with the decision to drop the bomb. Although much of what revisionist historians argue is faulty and based on tendentious use of sources, they nonetheless deserve credit for raising an important moral issue that challenges the standard American narrative of Hiroshima and Nagasaki.

The Stalinist Past

Soviet historians, and patriotic Russian historians after the collapse of the Soviet Union, justify the Soviet violation of the Neutrality Pact by arguing that it brought the Pacific War to a close, thus ending the suffering of the oppressed people of Asia and the useless sacrifices of the Japanese themselves. But this book shows that Stalin's policy was motivated by expansionist geopolitical designs. The Soviet leader pursued his imperialistic policy with Machiavellian ruthlessness, deviousness, and cunning. In the end he managed to enter the war and occupy those territories to which he felt entitled. Although he briefly flirted with the idea of invading Hokkaido, and did violate the provision of the Yalta Agreement to secure a treaty with the Chinese as the prerequisite for entry into the war, Stalin by and large respected the Yalta limit. But by occupying the southern Kurils, which had never belonged to Russia until the last days of August and the beginning of September 1945, he created an intractable territorial dispute known as "the Northern Territories question" that has prevented rapprochement between Russia and Japan to this day. The Russian government and the majority of Russians even now continue to cling to the myth that the occupation of the southern Kurils was Russia's justifiable act of repossessing its lost territory.

Stalin's decisions in the Pacific War are but one of many entries in the ledger of his brutal regime. Although his imperialism was not the worst of his crimes compared with the Great Purge and collectivization, it represented part and parcel of the Stalin regime. Certainly, his conniving against the Japanese and the blatant land-grabbing that he engaged in during the closing weeks of the war are nothing to praise. Although the crimes committed by Stalin have been exposed and the new Russia is making valiant strides by shedding itself of the remnants of the Stalinist past, the Russians, with the exception of a few courageous historians, have not squarely faced the historical fact that Stalin's policy toward Japan in the waning months of the Pacific War was an example of the leader's expansionistic foreign policy. Unless the Russians come to this realization, the process of cleansing themselves of the Stalinist past will never be completed.

The Mythology of Victimization and the Role of Hirohito

It took the Japanese a little while to realize that what happened to the Kurils during the confused period between August 15 and September 5 amounted to annexation of Japan's inherent territory, an act that violated the Atlantic Charter and the Cairo Declaration. But the humiliation the Japanese suffered in the four-week Soviet-Japanese War was not entirely a result of the Soviet occupation of the Kurils. The Soviet occupation of the Kurils represented the last of many wrongs that the Soviets perpetrated on the Japanese, beginning with the violation of the Neutrality Pact, the invasion of Manchuria, Korea, southern Sakhalin, and the deportation and imprisonment of more than 640,000 prisoners of war. The "Northern Territories question" that the Japanese have demanded be resolved in the postwar period before any rapprochement with the Soviet Union (and Russia after 1991) is a mere symbol of their deep-seated resentment of and hostility toward the Russians who betrayed Japan when it desperately needed their help in ending the war.

Together with the Soviet war against Japan, Hiroshima and Nagasaki have instilled in the Japanese a sense of victimization. What Gilbert Rozman calls the Hiroshima syndrome and the Northern Territories syndrome are an inverted form of nationalism. As such they have prevented the Japanese from coming to terms with their own culpability in causing the war in Asia. Before August 14, 1945, the Japanese leaders had ample opportunities to surrender, for instance, at the German capitulation, the fall of Okinawa, the issuance of the Potsdam Proclamation, the atomic bomb on Hiroshima, and Soviet entry into the war. Few in Japan have condemned the policymakers who delayed Japan's surrender. Had the Japanese government accepted the Potsdam Proclamation unconditionally immediately after it was issued, as Sato and Matsumoto argued, the atomic bombs would not have been used, and the war would have ended before the Soviets entered the conflict. Japanese policymakers who were in the position to make decisions—not only the militant advocates of war but also those who belonged to the peace party, including Suzuki, Togo, Kido, and Hirohito himself—must bear the responsibility for the war's destructive end more than the American president and the Soviet dictator.

In postwar Japan, Hirohito has been portrayed as the savior of the Japanese people and the nation for his "sacred decisions" to end the war. Indeed, without the emperor's personal intervention, Japan would not have surrendered. The cabinet and the Big Six were hopelessly divided, unable to make a decision. Only the emperor broke the stalemate. His determination and leadership at the two imperial conferences and his steadfast support for the termination of the war after the decisive meeting with Kido on August 9 were crucial factors leading to Japan's surrender.

This does not mean, however, that the emperor was, in Asada's words, "Japan's foremost peace advocate, increasingly articulate and urgent in expressing his wish for peace." He was, as all other Japanese leaders at that time, still pinning his hope on Moscow's mediation, rejecting the unconditional surrender demanded by the Potsdam Proclamation until the Soviet entry into the war. After the Soviets joined the fight, he finally changed his mind to accept the Potsdam terms. In Japan it has been taboo to question the motivation that led Hirohito to accept surrender. But the findings of this book call for a reexamination of his role in the ending of the Pacific War. His delay in accepting the Allied terms ensured the use of the bomb and Soviet entry into the war.

Although Hirohito's initiative after August 9 should be noted, his motivation for ending the war was not as noble as the "sacred decision" myth would have us believe. His primary concern was above all the preservation of the imperial house. He even flirted with the idea of clinging to his political role. Despite the myth that he said he did not care what happened to him personally, it is likely that he was also in fact deeply concerned about the safety of his family and his own security. At the crucial imperial conference of August 10, Hiranuma did not mince words in asking Hirohito to take responsibility for the tragedy that had befallen Japan. As Konoe, some of the emperor's own relatives, and Grew, the most ardent supporter of the Japanese monarchy, argued, Hirohito should have abdicated at the end of the war to make a clean break with the Showa period that marked anything but what "Showa" meant: enlightened peace. His continuing reign made Japan's culpability in the war ambiguous and contributed to the nation's inability to come to terms with the past.

Thus this is a story with no heroes but no real villains, either—just men. The ending of the Pacific War was in the last analysis a human drama whose dynamics were determined by the very human characteristics of those involved: ambition, fear, vanity, anger, and prejudice. With each successive decision, the number of remaining alternatives steadily diminished, constraining ever further the possibilities, until the dropping of the bomb and the destruction of the Japanese state became all but inevitable. The Pacific War could very well have ended differently had the men involved made different choices. But they did not.

So they left it for us to live with the legacies of the war. The question is, Do we have the courage to overcome them?

POSTSCRIPT

Was It Necessary to Drop the Atomic Bomb to End World War II?

The "official" history defends the use of the atomic bombs against Japan. After some early doubts by some publicists and church leaders, the hardening cold war with Russia after 1947 caused the decision makers to defend their policy. The atomic bombs were dropped for military reasons. It forced the Japanese to end the war quickly and saved both Japanese and American lives. In a much quoted article, "The Decision to Use the Atomic Bomb," *Harper's Magazine* 194 (February, 1947), former Secretary of Defense Henry L. Stimson asserted that the two invasions of Kyushu and Honshu might be expected to cost over a million casualties to American forces. While the real military estimates for the invasions were nowhere near a million, Truman's ghost writers in his *Memoirs I, Year of Decisions* (Doubleday, 1955) estimated casualties at 500,000.

The official interpretation was basically unchallenged until the 1960s when a revisionist school emerged, which blamed the Americans rather than the Russians for the cold war. In a series of articles and a published doctoral dissertation, *Atomic Diplomacy: Hiroshima and Potsdam* (Simon and Schuster, 1965, rev. ed. 1985), Gar Alperovitz argued that President Truman reversed Roosevelt's policy of cooperation with our Russian allies, rejected alternatives such as a test demonstration, blockade, or a specific warning, and dropped the bombs to make the Russians more manageable in Eastern Europe. Not all historians, even revisionists, accepted Alperovitz's use of the bomb as a trump card. Critics argued that Alperovitz had too narrow a perspective and did not see the continuity in policy between the Roosevelt and Truman administrations. Alperovitz also was selective in his use of sources and quoted from participants whose memory was faulty or self-serving. He especially relied on the diary of Secretary of War Henry L. Stimson, a 77-year-old career diplomat whom Truman respected but whose advice he rejected. Finally, Alperovitz made Truman appear to be more decisive in making decisions than he really was and that the Japanese government was united and willing to surrender if the Americans allowed the imperial dynasty to survive.

Most revisionists did not go as far as Alperovitz in arguing that the bombs were dropped primarily for political reasons. Moderate revisionists such as Barton J. Bernstein who has written at least two dozen articles on the subject accept the premise that while military objectives were important, there was a diplomatic "bonus" whereby sole possession of the bomb gave us military superiority over the Russians. This edge lasted until the fall of 1949 when the Russians successfully tested their own A-bomb.

The new orthodoxy among historians was a moderate revisionist interpretation of both military and political objectives. Such an interpretation was unheard of by the general public. When the Smithsonian tried to host a full-scale fiftieth anniversary exhibit of the events surrounding the A-bomb, a huge controversy developed. Under pressure from the Air Force Associated, the American Legion, and Congress, the original exhibit was cancelled. Only the Enola Gay, the plane that dropped the first bomb on Hiroshima, was displayed with minimal comment. For a full-scale analysis of the controversy and the development of A-bomb historiography, see Barton J. Bernstein, "Afterward: The Struggle Over History: Defining the Hiroshima Narrative," in Philip Nobile, ed., *Judgment at the Smithsonian* (Marlowe, 1995), and Michael J. Hogan, ed., *Hiroshima as History and Memory* (Cambridge University Press, 1996). See also Barton J. Bernstein, "The Atomic Bombings Reconsidered," *Foreign Affairs* (January/February 1995) where he argues that the distinction between civilian and military casualties became blurred with the saturation bombing of enemy targets in World War II.

In the plethora of books and articles published in 1995 on the fiftieth anniversary of the dropping of the atomic bomb, Professor Robert James Maddox's *Weapons for Victory: The Hiroshima Decision Fifty Years Later* (University of Missouri Press, 1995) stands out in its defense of the military reasons why Truman dropped the bomb. A long review essay by Donald Kagan on "Why America Dropped the Bomb," *Commentary* (September 1995) and "Letters from Readers" in the December 1995 issue thank Maddox and make similar points.

Maddox makes a compelling case for the military circumstances surrounding the decision to drop the atomic bomb on Japan. The Americans had suffered 50,000 casualties in the capture of the island of Okinawa in the spring of 1945. This was considered a preview of the impending invasion of Japan. Maddox points out that estimates of casualties were mere guesswork at a given time and that Army Chief of Staff George C. Marshall himself increased these numbers considerably when he realized that the Japanese were stationing hundreds of thousands of troops on their main islands.

Tsuyoshi Hasegawa has written the most recent scholarly account of why the Japanese surrendered. In *Racing the Enemy: Stalin, Truman and the Surrender of Japan,* Hasegawa has done extensive research in Russian and Japanese archives as well as American archives. He bypasses the usual debate between traditionalists and revisionists, which argues whether the bomb was dropped for military or political reasons. By engaging in multi-archival research, Hasegawa examines the varied and often conflicting political, military, and territorial objectives in ending the war of Truman, Stalin, the emperor, and the Japanese military. Hence, with the title *Racing with the Enemy*, Hasegawa lets no one off the hook. Truman never seriously considered other options to dropping the bomb because he wanted to avenge the sneak attack at Pearl Harbor. As he wrote a group of church leaders a few days after the bombings of Hiroshima and Nagasaki: "I was greatly disturbed over the unwarranted attack by the Japanese on Pearl Harbor and their murder of our prisoners of war. The only language they seem to understand is the one we have been using to bomb them. When you have to deal with a beast, you have to treat him as a beast."

Unlike most revisionists, however, Hasegawa is just as critical of the policies of the Russians and the Japanese. Stalin had his own expansionist aims. He was determined to recover the territories promised him at the Yalta Conference of February 1945 for his entrance into the Asian war once Germany was defeated. Stalin demanded and was given back all the possessions and territorial spheres of influence in Asia that Russia lost to Japan after the 1904–1905 Russo-Japanese war. After the first bomb was dropped, Stalin rushed his entry into the Asian war by a week and proceeded to take even the Northern Sakalin Islands, which was not part of the Yalta agreements. Hasegawa is also one of the few historians to seriously explore the Japanese decision-making process. He moves beyond the seminal research of *Japan's Decision to Surrender* (Stanford University Press, 1954) written over 50 years ago by his former teacher, Robert J. C. Butow, who discussed conflicts between the extreme militarists and the Japanese moderates who wanted to pursue a surrender with the condition of keeping the emperor as the nominal leader of the country. While Butow and most Japanese view the emperor as a hero who broke the deadlock between hard-liners and moderates in ending the war, Hasegawa views the emperor's intervention in the deadlock not as a "noble" decision to end the war, but as an attempt that was ultimately successful "to preserve the imperial house." Hasegawa's most controversial contention is that "the bomb provided a solution to the previously unsolvable dilemma that faced Truman: to achieve Japan's unconditional surrender before Soviet entry into the war. Truman issued the Potsdam Proclamation, not as a warning to Japan, but to justify the use of the atomic bomb. This challenges the commonly held view that the atomic bomb provided the immediate and decisive knockout blow to Japan's will to fight. Indeed, the Soviet entry into the war played a greater role than the atomic bombs in inducing Japan to surrender (p. 5). This interpretation conflicts with Richard B. Frank's *Downfall: The End of the Imperial Japanese Empires* (Random House, 1999), which argues that when the emperor announced his decision in the early morning hours to surrender, he gave three reasons: (1) the fear of a domestic upheaval; (2) inadequate defense preparations to resist the invasion; (3) the vast destructiveness of the atomic bomb and the air attacks. The emperor, says Frank, did not refer to Soviet intervention (p. 345). *Downfall* basically substantiates the arguments of Professor Maddox.

In addition to the Bernstein essay and Hogan collection, J. Samuel Walker has provided two useful essays on "The Decision to Use the Bomb: A Historiographical Update," *Diplomatic History* 14 (Winter 1990) and "Recent Literature on Truman's Atomic Bomb Decision: The Search for Middle Ground," *Diplomatic History* 29/2 (April 2005). A useful collection of primary sources is Robert H. Ferrell, ed., *Truman and the Bomb: A Documentary History* (High Plains Publishing, 1996), and Michael B. Stoff, Jonathan F. Fanton, and R. Hal Williams, eds., *The Manhattan Project: A Documentary Introduction to the Atomic Age* (Temple University Press, 1991), which contains facsimiles of original documents.

ISSUE 2

Was President Truman Responsible for the Cold War?

YES: Arnold A. Offner, from "Another Such Victory": President Truman, American Foreign Policy, and the Cold War, *Diplomatic History* (Spring 1999)

NO: John Lewis Gaddis, from *We Now Know: Rethinking Cold War History* (Oxford University Press, 1997)

ISSUE SUMMARY

YES: Arnold A. Offner argues that President Harry S. Truman was a parochial nationalist whose limited vision of foreign affairs precluded negotiations with the Russians over cold war issues.

NO: John Lewis Gaddis argues that after a half century of scholarship, Joseph Stalin was uncompromising and primarily responsible for the cold war.

Less than a month before the war ended in Europe the most powerful man in the world, President Franklin Delano Roosevelt, died suddenly from a brain embolism. A nervous impetuous and an inexperienced Vice President Harry S. Truman became the president. Historians disagree whether Truman reversed Roosevelt's relationship with Stalin or whether the similarities in policy were negated by Truman's blunt negotiating style compared with FDR's suave, calm approach. But disagreements emerged over issues such as control over the atomic bomb (see Issue 1), Germany, Poland, and the economic reconstruction of Europe.

The question of Germany was paramount. During the war it was agreed that Germany would be temporarily divided into zones of occupation with the United States, Great Britain, and the newly liberated France controlling the Western half of Germany while the Russians were in charge of the Eastern half. Berlin, which was 90 miles inside of the Russian zone, would also be divided into zones of occupation. Arguments developed over boundaries, reparations and transfers of industrial equipment and agricultural foodstuffs between zones. In May, 1946, the Americans began treating the western zones as a separate economic unit because the Russians were transferring the food from their zone back to the Soviet Union. In September, 1946, Secretary of State James Byrnes announced that the Americans would continue to occupy their half of Germany indefinitely with military troops. By 1948, a separate democratic West German government was established. The Russians protested by blocking ground access to the western zones of Berlin. But the Americans continued to supply the West Berliners with supplies through an airlift. After 10 months, because of the bad publicity, the Russians abandoned the Berlin blockade and created a separate communist East German government.

Roosevelt and Churchill had conceded Russian control over Eastern Europe during the World War II Conferences. The question was how much control. Stalin was not going to allow anti-Communist governments to be established in these countries. He had no understanding of how free elections were held. Consequently, when the cold war intensified in 1947 and 1948, Russian-dominated Communist governments were established in Hungary, Poland and Czechoslovakia.

In February 1946, Stalin delivered a major speech declaring the incompatibility of the two systems of Communism and Capitalism. The next month, Winston Churchill, now a retired politician, delivered his famous speech at a commencement in Fulton, Missouri, with the Truman administration's consent in which he complained about the "iron curtain" that Russia was imposing on Eastern Europe. At the same time, George Kennan, a bright multi-linguist American diplomat who spent years in Germany and Russia and would become the head of Truman's policy planning staff, wrote a series of telegrams and articles which set the tone for the specific policies the Truman administration would undertake. Kennan had coined the phrase "containment," a word that would be used to describe America's foreign policy from Truman to the first President Bush. Containment would assume various meanings and would be extended to other areas of the globe besides Europe in ways Kennan claims were a misuse of what his original intentions were. Nevertheless the Truman administration took steps to stop further Russian expansionism.

In 1947, a series of steps were undertaken both to "contain" Russian expansionism and to rebuild the economies of Europe. On March 12, in an address before a Republican-controlled Congress, Truman argued in somewhat inflated rhetoric that "it must be the policy of the United States to support free peoples who are resisting attempted subjugation by armed minorities or by outside pressures." In the same speech in what became known as the "Truman Doctrine," the President requested and received $400 million economic and military assistance to Greece and Turkey. Almost as an afterthought, American military personnel were sent to oversee the reconstruction effort, a precedent that would later be used to send advisers to Vietnam.

In June 1947, Secretary of State George C. Marshall announced a plan to provide economic assistance to all European nations. This included the Soviet Union, who rejected the program and formed its own economic recovery group. In April 1948, Congress approved the creation of the Economic Cooperation Administration, the agency that would administer the program. The Marshall Plan would be remembered as America's most successful foreign aid program. Seventeen billion dollars were channeled to the western European nations. By 1950, industrial production had increased 64 percent since the end of the war while the communist parties declined in membership and influence.

When did the cold war begin? Was it inevitable? Or should one side take most of the blame?

YES

Arnold A. Offner

"Another Such Victory": President Truman, American Foreign Policy, and the Cold War

As the twenty-first century nears, President Harry S. Truman's reputation stands high. This is especially true regarding his stewardship of foreign policy although, ironically, he entered the Oval Office in 1945 untutored in world affairs, and during his last year in the White House Republicans accused his administration of having surrendered fifteen countries and five hundred million people to communism and sending twenty thousand Americans to their "burial ground" in Korea. Near the end of his term, Truman's public "favorable" rating had plummeted to 23 percent.

Within a decade, however, historians rated Truman a "near great" president, crediting his administration with reconstructing Western Europe and Japan, resisting Soviet or Communist aggression from Greece to Korea, and forging collective security through NATO. In the 1970s the "plain speaking" Truman became a popular culture hero. Recently, biographers have depicted him as the allegory of American life, an ordinary man whose extraordinary character led him to triumph over adversity from childhood through the presidency, and even posited a symbiotic relationship between "His Odyssey" from Independence to the White House and America's rise to triumphant superpower status. Melvyn P. Leffler, in his *A Preponderance of Power,* has judged Truman to have been neither a naif nor an idealist but a realist who understood the uses of power and whose administration, despite serious, costly errors, prudently preserved America's national security against real or perceived Soviet threats.

Collapse of the Soviet Union and Europe's other Communist states, whose archives have confirmed Truman's belief in 1945 that their regimes governed largely by "clubs, pistols and concentration camps," has further raised the former president's standing. This has encouraged John Lewis Gaddis and others to shift their focus to Stalin's murderous domestic rule as the key determinant of Soviet foreign policy and the Cold War. As Gaddis has contended, Stalin was heir to Ivan the Terrible and Peter the Great, responsible for more state-sanctioned murders than Adolf Hitler, and treated world politics as an extension of domestic politics: a zero sum game in which his gaining security

From *Diplomatic History*, vol. 32, no. 2, Spring 1999, pp. 127–143, 153–155. Copyright © 1999 by Blackwell Publishing, Ltd. Reprinted by permission.

meant depriving all others of it. For Gaddis and others, that is largely the answer to the question of whether Stalin sought or caused the Cold War.

But as Walter LaFeber has said, to dismiss Stalin's policies as the work of a paranoid is greatly to oversimplify the Cold War. Indeed, historians of Stalin's era seem to be of the preponderant view that he pursued a cautious but brutal realpolitik. He aimed to restore Russia's 1941 boundaries, establish a sphere of influence in border states, provide security against a recovered Germany or Japan or hostile capitalist states, and gain compensation, notably reparations, for the ravages of war. Stalin calculated forces, recognized America's superior industrial and military power, put Soviet state interests ahead of Marxist-Leninist ideology, and pursued pragmatic or opportunistic policies in critical areas such as Germany, China, and Korea.

Thus, the time seems ripe, given our increased knowledge of Soviet policies, to reconsider President Truman's role in the Cold War. As Thomas G. Paterson has written, the president stands at the pinnacle of the diplomatic-military establishment, has great capacity to set the foreign policy agenda and to mold public opinion, and his importance, especially in Truman's case, cannot be denied. But contrary to prevailing views, I believe that his policymaking was shaped by his parochial and nationalistic heritage. This was reflected in his uncritical belief in the superiority of American values and political-economic interests and his conviction that the Soviet Union and communism were the root cause of international strife. Truman's parochialism also caused him to disregard contrary views, to engage in simplistic analogizing, and to show little ability to comprehend the basis for other nations' policies. Consequently, his foreign policy leadership intensified Soviet-American conflict, hastened the division of Europe, and brought tragic intervention in Asian civil wars.

In short, Truman lacked the qualities of the creative or great leader who, as James MacGregor Burns has written, must broaden the environment in which he and his citizenry operate and widen the channels in which choices are made and events flow. Truman, to the contrary, narrowed Americans' perception of their world political environment and the channels for policy choices and created a rigid framework in which the United States waged long-term, extremely costly global cold war. Indeed, before we celebrate America's victory in this contest we might recall that after King Pyrrhus's Greek forces defeated the Romans at the battle of Asculum in 280 B.C., he reflected that "another such victory, and we are undone."

II

Truman's parochialism and nationalism, and significant insecurity, were rooted in his background, despite his claim to have had a bucolic childhood of happy family, farm life, and Baptist religiosity. In fact, young Harry's poor eyesight, extended illness, and "sissy" piano playing alienated him from both his peers and his feisty father and fostered ambivalence in him toward powerful men. On the one hand, Truman deferred to "Boss" Thomas Pendergast, his dishonest political benefactor, and to Secretaries of State George Marshall and Dean

Acheson, whose manner and firm viewpoints he found reassuring. On the other hand, he denounced those whose style or ways of thinking were unfamiliar. This included the State Department's "striped pants boys," the military's "brass hats" and "prima donnas," political "fakirs" [sic] such as Teddy and Franklin Roosevelt, and "professional liberals." For Truman, Charles de Gaulle, Josef Stalin, Ernest Bevin, and Douglas MacArthur were each, at one time or another, a "son of a bitch."

Truman's need to demonstrate his authority underlay his upbraiding of both Soviet Foreign Minister Vyacheslav Molotov in April 1945 for Russia's alleged failure to keep its agreements and his secretary of state, James Byrnes, for allegedly exceeding his authority at the Moscow Conference of Foreign Ministers (CFM) that December. Truman naively likened Stalin to Pendergast, who, like Harry's father, always kept his word, but then took great umbrage at the thought that the Soviet leader had broken his word over Poland, Iran, or Germany. Truman also blamed MacArthur for misleading him at their Wake Island meeting in 1950 about Chinese intentions in the Korean War, but this was equally Truman self-deception.

Truman's self-tutelage in history derived largely from didactic biographies of "great men" and empires. This enhanced his vision of the globe but provided little sense of complexity or ambiguity and instilled exaggerated belief that current events had exact historical analogues that provided the key to contemporary policy. The new president was "amazed" that the Yalta accords were so "hazy" and fraught with "new meanings" at every reading, which probably contributed to his "lackluster" adherence to them. Shortly, Truman uncritically applied analogues about 1930s appeasement of Nazi Germany to diplomacy with the Soviet Union and crises in Iran, Greece, Turkey, and Korea.

Further, young Harry's Bible reading and church going did not inspire an abiding religiosity or system of morals so much as a conviction that the world was filled with "liars and hypocrites," terms he readily applied to his presidential critics, and a stern belief, as he wrote in 1945, that "punishment always followed transgression," a maxim that he applied to North Korea and the People's Republic of China (PRC).

Truman's early writings disdained non-Americans and minorities ("Chink doctor," "dago," "nigger," "Jew clerk," and "bohunks and Rooshans"), and in 1940 he proposed to deport "disloyal inhabitants." As president in 1945 he questioned the loyalty of "hyphenate" Americans, and in 1947 he signed Executive Order 9835, creating an unprecedented "loyalty" program that jettisoned basic legal procedural safeguards and virtually included a presumption of guilt.

Truman's command of men and bravery under fire in World War I were exemplary but not broadening. He deplored Europe's politics, mores, and food and sought only to return to "God's country." He intended never to revisit Europe: "I've nearly promised old Miss Liberty that she'll have to turn around to see me again," he wrote in 1918, and in 1945 he went reluctantly to Potsdam to his first and only European summit.

Nonetheless, Truman identified with Wilsonian internationalism, especially the League of Nations, and as a senator he supported President Franklin

Roosevelt on the World Court, neutrality revision, rearmament, and Lend Lease for Britain and Russia. He rightfully said "I am no appeaser." But his internationalism reflected unquestioned faith in American moral superiority, and his foreign policy proposals largely comprised military preparedness. He was indifferent to the plight of Republican Spain and too quickly blamed international conflict on "outlaws," "savages," and "totalitarians." After Germany invaded the Soviet Union in 1941, he hastily remarked that they should be left to destroy one another—although he opposed Germany's winning—and he likened Russian leaders to "Hitler and Al Capone" and soon inveighed against the "twin blights—atheism and communism." Hence, while Truman supported the fledgling United Nations and the liberalization of world trade, the man who became president in April 1945 was less an incipient internationalist than a parochial nationalist given to excessive fear that appeasement, lack of preparedness, and enemies at home and abroad would thwart America's mission (the "Lord's will") to "win the peace" on its terms.

President Truman inherited an expedient wartime alliance that stood on shaky ground at Yalta in February 1945 and grew more strained over Soviet control in Romania and Poland and U.S. surrender talks with German officials at Bern that aroused Stalin's fears of a separate peace. Truman lamented that "they didn't tell me anything about what was going on." He also had to depend on advisers whose views ranged from Ambassador Averell Harriman's belief that it was time to halt the Russians' "barbarian invasion" of Europe to counsel from FDR emissaries Joseph Davies and Harry Hopkins to try to preserve long-term accord. Truman's desire to appear decisive by making quick decisions and his instinct to be "tough" spurred his belief that he could get "85 percent" from the Russians on important matters and that they could go along or "go to hell."

Initially, the president's abrupt style and conflicting advice produced inconsistent policy. His mid-April call for a "new" government in Poland and his "one-two to the jaw" interview with Molotov brought only a sharp reply from Stalin, after which the United States recognized a predominantly Communist Polish government. In May, Truman approved "getting tough" with the Russians by suddenly curtailing Lend Lease shipments, but Anglo-Soviet protests caused him to countermand the cutoffs. He then refused Prime Minister Winston Churchill's proposal to keep Anglo-American troops advanced beyond their agreed occupation zones to bargain in Germany and soon wrote that he was "anxious to keep all my engagements with the Russians because they are touchy and suspicious of us."

Still, Truman determined to have his way with the Russians, especially in Germany. Tutored in part by Secretary of War Henry L. Stimson, he embraced the emergent War-State Department position that Germany was key to the balance of power in Europe and required some reconstruction because a "poor house" standard of living there meant the same for Europe, and might cause a repeat of the tragic Treaty of Versailles history. Truman replaced Roosevelt's reparations negotiator, Isador Lubin, with conservative oil entrepreneur Edwin Pauley, who brushed off both Soviet claims to Yalta's $20 billion in reparations and State Department estimates that Germany could pay

$12–14 billion. Truman also said that when he met with Churchill and Stalin he wanted "all the bargaining power—all the cards in my hands, and the plan on Germany is one of them."

The other card was the atomic bomb, which inspired Truman and Byrnes to think that they could win their way in Europe and Asia. Byrnes told the president in April that the bomb might allow them to "dictate our terms" at the war's end and in May indicated his belief that it would make the Russians more "manageable." Stimson counseled Truman that America's industrial strength and unique weapon comprised a "royal straight flush and we mustn't be a fool about how we play it," that it would be "dominant" in any dispute with Russia over Manchuria, and a "weapon" or "master card" in America's hand in its "big stakes" diplomacy with the Russians.

The president readily analogized diplomacy with his poker playing and, as Martin J. Sherwin has shown, believed that use of his atomic "ace-in-the-hole" would allow him to wrest concessions from Stalin. Truman had incentive to delay a summit meeting until the bomb was ready and to take no steps to obviate its use. In late spring he passed over proposals to modify unconditional surrender that sought to induce Japan's quick capitulation, and he would not give the Japanese or Russians notice of the atomic bomb.

Truman set sail for Potsdam highly disposed to atomic diplomacy, albeit not "blackmail." His nationalist perspective shaped his thinking. He aimed to advance American interests only: "win, lose, or draw—and we must win." En route, he approved Pauley's policy to give "first charge" priority to German occupation and maintenance costs over reparations. "Santa Claus is dead," Truman wrote, and the United States would never again "pay reparations, feed the world, and get nothing for it but a nose thumbing." Further, after Stimson brought word on 16 July of the successful atomic test in New Mexico and urged an early warning and offer to retain the Emperor as means to induce Japan's rapid surrender, Truman and Byrnes refused. That ended the last, brief chance at atomic restraint.

After meeting Stalin on 17 July Truman wrote that he was unfazed by the Russian's "dynamite" agenda because "I have some dynamite too which I'm not exploding now." The following day he asserted that the "Japs will fold up" before Russia entered the Pacific war, specifically "when Manhattan appears over their homeland." Truman agreed with Byrnes that use of the bomb would permit them to "out maneuver Stalin on China," that is, negate the Yalta concessions in Manchuria and guarantee that Russia would "not get in so much on the kill" of Japan or its occupation. Assured by 24 July that the bomb would be ready before Russia's entry, the president had to be persuaded even to hint to Stalin that he had a new weapon and afterward exulted in the mistaken belief that the Russian leader had not caught on to the bomb. Truman then hastened to issue the Potsdam Declaration without Soviet signature on 26 July and signed his "release when ready" order on the bombs on the 31st.

News of the bomb's power also greatly reinforced Truman's confidence to allow Byrnes to press European negotiations to impasse by refusing the Russians access to the Ruhr, rejecting even their low bid for $4 billion in industrial reparations, and withdrawing the Yalta accords. Convinced that the

New Mexico atomic test would allow the United States to "control" events, Byrnes pushed his famous 30 July tripartite ultimatum on German zonal reparations, Poland's de facto control over its new western border (including Silesia) with Germany, and Italy's membership in the UN. "Mr. Stalin is stallin'," Truman wrote hours before the American-set deadline on 31 July, but that was useless because "I have an ace in the hole and another one showing," aces that he knew would soon fall upon Japan.

Truman won his hand, as Stalin acceded to zonal reparations. But Truman's victory was fraught with more long-term consequences than he envisioned. He had not only equated his desire to prevent use of taxpayer dollars to help sustain occupied Germany with the Russians' vital need for reparations but also given them reason to think, as Norman Naimark has written, that the Americans were deaf to their quest for a "paltry" $10 billion or less to compensate for Germany's having ravaged their nation. Further, America's insistence on zonal reparations would impede development of common economic policy for all of Germany and increase likelihood of its East-West division.

In addition, use of two atomic bombs on Hiroshima and Nagasaki—the second was not militarily necessary—showed that for Truman and Byrnes, the prospect of political gain in Europe and Asia precluded serious thought not to use the bombs. And this may have led the Russians to conclude that the bombs were directed against them, or their ability to achieve their strategic interests. But Stalin would not be pressured; he was determined to pursue a Russian atomic bomb.

Shortly, Truman backed Byrnes's "bomb in his pocket" diplomacy at the London CFM, which deadlocked over Russian control in Eastern Europe and American control in Japan. Truman told Byrnes to "stick to his guns" and tell the Russians "to go to hell." The president then agreed with "ultranationalist" advisers who opposed international atomic accord by drawing misleading analogies about interwar disarmament and "appeasement" and by insisting that America's technological-industrial genius assured permanent atomic supremacy. Truman held that America was the world's atomic "trustee"; that it had to preserve the bomb's "secret"; and that no nation would give up the "locks and bolts" necessary to protect its "house" from "outlaws." The atomic arms race was on, he said in the fall of 1945, and other nations had to "catch up on their own hook."

In the spring of 1946, Truman undercut the Dean Acheson-David Lilienthal plan for international control and development of atomic resources by appointing as chief negotiator Bernard Baruch, whose emphasis on close inspections, sanctions, no veto, and indefinite American atomic monopoly virtually assured Russian refusal. Despite Acheson's protests, Truman analogized that "if Harry Stimson had been backed up in Manchuria [in 1931] there would have been no war." And as deadlock neared in July 1946, the president told Baruch to "stand pat."

Ultimately the UN commission weighing the Baruch Plan approved it on 31 December 1946. But the prospect of a Soviet veto in the Security Council precluded its adoption. Admittedly, Stalin's belief that he could not deal with the United States on an equal basis until he had the bomb and Soviet insistence on retention of their veto power and national control of resources and facilities may have precluded atomic accord in 1946. Still, Baruch insisted that the United States could get its way because it had an atomic monopoly, and American military officials sought to preserve a nuclear monopoly as long as possible and to develop a strategy based on air power and atomic weapons. As David Holloway has written, neither Truman nor Stalin "saw the bomb as a common danger to the human race."

Meanwhile, Byrnes's diplomacy in Moscow in December 1945 had produced Yalta-style accords on a European peace treaty process, Russian predominance in Bulgaria and Romania and American primacy in China and Japan, and compromise over Korea, with Soviet disputes with Iran and Turkey set aside. But conservative critics cried "appeasement," and in his famous but disputed letter of 5 January 1946, an anxious president charged that Byrnes had kept him "completely in the dark"; denounced Russian "outrage[s]" in the Baltic, Germany, Poland, and Iran and intent to invade Turkey; and said that the Russians understood only an "iron fist" and "divisions" and that he was tired of "babying" them. In fact, Truman knew of most of Byrnes's positions; they had hardly "babied" Russia since Potsdam; and no Russian attack was imminent. The letter reflected Truman's new "get tough" policy, or personal cold war declaration, which, it must be emphasized, came six weeks before George Kennan's Long Telegram and Churchill's Iron Curtain speech.

Strong American protests in 1946 caused the Russians to withdraw their troops from Iran and their claims to joint defense of the Turkish Straits. In the latter case, Truman said he was ready to follow his policy of military response "to the end" to determine if Russia intended "world conquest." Once again he had taken an exaggerated, nationalist stance. No one expected a Russian military advance; America's action rested on its plans to integrate Turkey into its strategic planning and to use it as a base of operations against Russia in event of war. And in September Truman approved announcement of a Mediterranean command that led to the United States becoming the dominant naval power there by year's end.

Meanwhile, Truman ignored Secretary of Commerce Henry Wallace's lengthy memoranda during March–September 1946 that sought to promote economic ties with Russia and questioned America's atomic policies and global military expansiveness. The president then fired Wallace after he publicly challenged Byrnes's speech on 6 September in Stuttgart propounding West German reconstruction and continued American military presence there. The firing was reasonable, but not the rage at Wallace as "a real Commy" and at "parlor pinks and soprano-voiced men" as a "national danger" and "sabotage front" for Stalin.

Equally without reason was Truman's face value acceptance of White House special counsel Clark Clifford's "Russian Report" of September 1946 and accompanying "Last Will of Peter the Great." Clifford's report rested on a hasty compilation of apocalyptic projections of Soviet aim to conquer the world by military force and subversion, and he argued that the United States had to prepare for total war. He wrote in the "black and white" terms that he knew Truman would like and aimed to justify a vast global military upgrade and silence political critics on the left and right. Tsar Peter's will was an old forgery purporting to show that he had a similar design to conquer Eurasia. Truman may have found the report so "hot" that he confined it to his White House safe, but he believed the report and the will and soon was persisting that the governments of the czars, Stalin, and Hitler were all the same. Later he told a mild critic of American policy to read Tsar Peter's will to learn where Russian leaders got their "fixed ideas."

It was a short step, Clifford recalled, from the Russian Report to Truman's epochal request in March 1947 for military aid to Greece and Turkey to help "free peoples" fight totalitarianism. Truman vastly overstated the global-ideological aspects of Soviet-American conflict. Perhaps he sought to fire "the opening gun" to rouse the public and a fiscally conservative Republican Congress to national security expenditures. But he also said that this was "only the beginning" of the "U.S. going into European politics," that the Russians had broken every agreement since Potsdam and would now get only "one language" from him. He added in the fall of 1947 that "if Russia gets Greece and Turkey," it would get Italy and France, the iron curtain would extend to western Ireland, and the United States would have to "come home and prepare for war."

Truman's fears were excessive. Stalin never challenged the Truman Doctrine or Western primacy in Turkey, now under U.S. military tutelage, and Greece. He provided almost no aid to the Greek rebels and told Yugoslavia's leaders in early 1948 to halt their aid because the United States would never allow the Greek Communists to win and break Anglo-American control in the Mediterranean. When Marshal Josip Broz Tito balked, Stalin withdrew his advisers from Yugoslavia and expelled that nation from the Cominform. Tito finally closed his borders to the Greek rebels in July 1949.

Perhaps U.S. officials feared that Britain's retreat from Greece might allow Russia to penetrate the Mediterranean, or that if Greek Communists overthrew the reactionary Greek regime (Turkey was not threatened) they might align Athens with Moscow. Still, the Truman administration's costly policy never addressed the causes of Greece's civil war; instead, it substituted military "annihilation of the enemy for the reform of the social and economic conditions" that had brought civil war. Equally important, Truman's rhetorical division of the world into "free" versus "totalitarian" states, as Gaddis once said, created an "ideological straitjacket" for American foreign policy and an unfortunate model for later interventions, such as in Korea—"the Greece of the Far East," as Truman would say—and in French Indochina.

The Truman Doctrine led to the Marshall Plan in June 1947, but they were not "two halves of the same walnut," as Truman claimed. State Department officials who drew up the European Recovery Plan (ERP) differentiated it from what they viewed as his doctrine's implications for "economic and ultimately military warfare." The Soviets likened the Truman Doctrine to retail purchase of separate nations and the Marshall Plan to wholesale purchase of Europe.

The Soviet view was narrow, although initially they had interest in participating and perhaps even harbored dreams that the United States would proffer a generous Lend Lease-style arrangement. But as the British quickly saw, Soviet participation was precluded by American-imposed financial and economic controls and, as Michael J. Hogan has written, by the integrated, continental approach to aid rather than a nation-by-nation basis that would have benefited war-devastated Russia. Indeed, in direct talks in Paris, U.S. officials refused concessions, focused on resources to come from Russia and East Europe, and insisted on German contributions to the ERP ahead of reparations payments or a peace treaty—and then expressed widespread relief when the Soviets rejected the ERP for themselves and East Europe.

The Marshall Plan proved to be a very successful geostrategic venture. It helped to spur American-European trade and Western European recovery, bring France into camp with Germany and satisfy French economic and security claims, and revive western Germany industrially without unleashing the 1930s-style "German colossus" that Truman's aides feared. The Marshall Plan was also intended to contain the Soviets economically, forestall German-Soviet bilateral deals, and provide America with access to its allies' domestic and colonial resources. Finally, as the British said, the Truman administration sought an integrated Europe resembling the United States, "God's own country."

The Marshall Plan's excellent return on investment, however, may have cost far more than the $13 billion expended. "The world is definitely split in two," Undersecretary of State Robert Lovett said in August 1947, while Kennan forewarned that for defensive reasons the Soviets would "clamp down completely on Czechoslovakia" to strengthen their hold on Eastern Europe. Indeed, the most recent evidence indicates that Stalin viewed the Marshall Plan as a "watershed" event, signaling an American effort to predominate over all of Europe. This spurred the Soviets into a comprehensive strategy shift. They now rigged the elections in Hungary, proffered Andrei Zhdanov's "two camps" approach to world policy, created the Cominform, and blessed the Communist coup in Czechoslovakia in February 1948. Truman, in turn, concluded that the Western world confronted the same situation it had a decade earlier with Nazi Germany, and his bristling St. Patrick's Day speeches in March 1948 placed sole onus for the Cold War on the Soviet Union. Subsequently, Anglo-American talks at the Pentagon would culminate in NATO in April 1949.

Meanwhile, the U.S. decision to make western Germany the cornerstone of the ERP virtually precluded negotiations to reunify the country. In fact, when Secretary of State Marshall proposed during a CFM meeting in the spring of 1947 to offer current production reparations to the Russians to induce agreement to unify Germany, the president sternly refused. Marshall complained of lack of "elbow room" to negotiate. But Truman would not yield, and by the time of the next CFM in late 1947 the secretary showed no interest in Russian reparations or Ruhr access. Despite America's public position, Ambassador to Moscow Walter Bedell Smith wrote, "we really do not want nor intend to accept German unification on any terms that the Russians might agree to, even though they seemed to meet most of our requirements."

The Americans were by then onto their London Conference program to create a West German state and, as Stalin said in February 1948, "The West will make Western Germany their own, and we shall turn Eastern Germany into our own state." In June the Soviet dictator initiated the Berlin blockade to try to forestall the West's program, but Truman determined to "stay period." He believed that to withdraw from Berlin would seriously undermine U.S. influence in Europe and the ERP and destroy his presidential standing, and he remained determined to avert military confrontation.

But Truman saw no connection between the London program and the blockade, as Carolyn Eisenberg has written. Further, his belief that "there is nothing to negotiate" and accord with General Lucius Clay's view that to withdraw from Berlin meant "we have lost everything we are fighting for" exaggerated the intent of Stalin's maneuver and diminished even slim chances for compromise on Germany, including Kennan's "Plan A" for a unified, neutralized state with American and Soviet forces withdrawn to its periphery. As Marshall said in August 1948, there would be "no abandonment of our position" on West Germany.

Eventually, Truman and the airlift prevailed over Stalin, who gave in to a face-saving CFM in May 1949 that ended the blockade, with nothing else agreed. The new secretary of state, Acheson, said that the United States intended to create a West German government "come hell or high water" and that Germany could be unified only by consolidating the East into the West on the basis of its incipient Bonn Constitution. Likewise Truman said in June 1949 that he would not sacrifice West Germany's basic freedoms to gain "nominal political unity."

Long convinced that the United States was locked in "a struggle with the USSR for Germany," the president showed no interest when Stalin made his most comprehensive offer on 10 March 1952, proposing a Big Four meeting to draft a peace treaty for a united, neutral, defensively rearmed Germany free of foreign troops. Whether Stalin was seeking a settlement to reduce great power conflict over a divided Germany has been debated. His note came only after the United States and its allies were near contractual accord on West German sovereignty and Acheson had just negotiated his "grand slam" providing for German forces to enter a proposed European Defense Community (EDC) linked to NATO. Acheson held that Stalin had thrown a "golden apple" of discord over the iron curtain to forestall a sovereign, industrially strong, and rearmed West Germany joining an American-led alliance system.

Truman gave full sway to Acheson, who hesitated to reject Stalin's offer out of hand. But he insisted that the allies "drive ahead" with the German contractuals and EDC. He also got support from West German Chancellor Konrad Adenauer to shape uniform allied replies, with conditions, such as UN-supervised elections in all of Germany prior to negotiations and unified Germany's right to join any "defensive European community," that he knew Stalin would reject. Further, although Truman and Acheson had just coaxed Kennan to become ambassador to Moscow, they never asked his advice or gave him a policy clue despite meeting with him three times in April. This confirmed Kennan's view that "we had no interest in discussing the German problem with the Soviet Government in any manner whatsoever."

Stalin, meanwhile, told East German leaders in April 1952 that the West would never accept any proposal they made and that it was time to "organize your own state" and protect its border. The United States won the so-called battle of the notes, although exchanges continued. But the allies concluded the German contractuals and the EDC in late May. And when the French then reverted to proposing a four power meeting on Germany, Acheson said that four power control was long past. He then shaped the note so that it "puts onus on Sovs sufficiently to make it unlikely that Sovs will agree to mtg on terms proposed." He was right, and in September the note writing drew to its anticlimactic closure.

Prospect for accord based on Stalin's note was remote, but not just because Stalin wanted, as Vojtech Mastny has written, either a unified "pro-Soviet though not necessarily communist" Germany or a full-fledged East German satellite. Truman had no interest in a unified, neutral, or demilitarized Germany and now believed that a rearmed FRG was as vital to NATO as West Germany was to ERP. German unity was possible only on the basis of West over East. Thus, Ambassador Kennan said after talking to U.S. officials linked to NATO in the fall of 1952 that they saw no reason to withdraw U.S. forces from Germany "at any time within the foreseeable future under any conceivable agreement with Russia." This meant that the "split of Germany and Europe" would continue. And it did, for the next forty years. . . .

⌐◉⌐

No one leader or nation caused the Cold War. The Second World War generated inevitable Soviet-American conflict as two nations with entirely different political-economic systems confronted each other on two war-torn continents. The Truman administration would seek to fashion a world order friendly to American political and economic interests, to achieve maximum national security by preventing any nation from severing U.S. ties to its traditional allies and vital areas of trade and resources, and to avoid 1930s-style "appeasement." Truman creditably favored creation of the UN, fostered foreign aid and reconstruction, and wished to avert war, and, after he recognized his "overreach" in Korea, he sought to return to the status quo ante.

Nonetheless, from the Potsdam Conference through the Korean War, the president contributed significantly to the growing Cold War and militarization of American foreign policy. He assumed that America's economic-military-moral superiority assured that he could order the world on its terms, and he ascribed only dark motives to nations or leaders who resisted America's will. Monopoly control of the atomic bomb heightened this sense of righteous power and impelled his use of atomic bombs partly to outmaneuver the Russians in China and over Japan. Truman also drew confidence from the bombs that he could deny the Soviets any fixed sum of German reparations despite their feasibility, the Yalta accords, and the apparent disregard of Russia's claim to compensation for its wartime suffering. American-imposed zonal reparations policy only increased the East-West divide and diminished prospects to reunite Germany, although Stalin evidently remained open to the idea of a united and neutralized Germany until 1949 and conceivably as late as 1952. But Truman, as Marshall learned in the spring of 1947, had little interest in negotiating such an arrangement, and his administration's decision that year to make western Germany the cornerstone of the Marshall Plan and Western Europe's reconstruction virtually precluded

German unification except by melding East into West. Formation of NATO and insistence that a unified Germany be free to join a Western military alliance reinforced division of Germany and Europe.

It is clear that Truman's insecurity with regard to diplomacy and world politics led him to seek to give the appearance of acting decisively and reinforced his penchant to view conflict in black and white terms and to divide nations into free or totalitarian societies. He shied from weighing the complexities of historic national conflicts and local or regional politics. Instead, he attributed nearly every diplomatic crisis or civil war—in Germany, Iran, Turkey, Greece, and Czechoslovakia—to Soviet machination and insisted that the Russians had broken every agreement and were bent on "world conquest." To determine his response he was quick to reach for an analogy, usually the failure of the Western powers to resist Germany and Japan in the 1930s, and to conclude that henceforth he would speak to the Russians in the only language that he thought they understood: "divisions." This style of leadership and diplomacy closed off both advocates and prospects for more patiently negotiated and more nuanced or creative courses of action.

Truman also viscerally loathed the Chinese Communists, could not comprehend Asian nationalism, demonized Asian opponents, and caused the United States to align itself with corrupt regimes. He was unable to view China's civil war apart from Soviet-American conflict. He brushed off criticism of America's intervention in behalf of the frightful GMD, refused to open channels of communication with the emergent PRC, and permitted the American-armed, Taiwan-based GMD to wage counterrevolutionary war against China's new government, whose sovereignty or legitimacy he never accepted. The Korean War then overtook his administration. The president decided to preserve South Korea's independence but set an unfortunate if not tragic precedent by refusing to seek formal congressional sanction for war. His decision to punish North Korea and implement "rollback," and his disdain for the PRC and its concerns before and after it entered the war, brought unnecessary, untold destruction and suffering to Asians and Americans and proved fatal to his presidency. Still, in his undelivered farewell address Truman insisted that "Russia was at the root" of every problem from Europe to Asia, and that "Trumanism" had saved countless countries from Soviet invasion and "knocked the socks off the communists" in Korea.

In conclusion, it seems clear that despite Truman's pride in his knowledge of the past, he lacked insight into the history unfolding around him. He often could not see beyond his immediate decision or visualize alternatives, and he seemed oblivious to the implications of his words or actions. More often than not he narrowed rather than broadened the options that he presented to the American citizenry, the environment of American politics, and the channels through which Cold War politics flowed. Throughout his presidency, Truman remained a parochial nationalist who lacked the leadership to move America away from conflict and toward détente. Instead, he promoted an ideology and politics of Cold War confrontation that became the modus operandi of successor administrations and the United States for the next two generations.

John Lewis Gaddis  **NO**

We Now Know:
Rethinking Cold War History

[Joseph] Stalin appears to have relished his role, along with [Franklin D.] Roosevelt and [Winston] Churchill, as one of the wartime Big Three. Such evidence as has surfaced from Soviet archives suggests that he received reassuring reports about Washington's intentions: "Roosevelt is more friendly to us than any other prominent American," Ambassador Litvinov commented in June 1943, "and it is quite obvious that he wishes to cooperate with us." Whoever was in the White House, Litvinov's successor Andrei Gromyko predicted a year later, the Soviet Union and the United States would "manage to find common issues for the solution of . . . problems emerging in the future and of interest to both countries." Even if Stalin's long-range thinking about security did clash with that of his Anglo-American allies, common military purposes provided the strongest possible inducements to smooth over such differences. It is worth asking why this *practice* of wartime cooperation did not become a *habit* that would extend into the postwar era.

The principal reason, it now appears, was Stalin's insistence on equating security with territory. Western diplomats had been surprised, upon arriving in Moscow soon after the German attack in the summer of 1941, to find the Soviet leader already demanding a postwar settlement that would retain what his pact with Hitler had yielded: the Baltic states, together with portions of Finland, Poland, and Romania. Stalin showed no sense of shame or even embarrassment about this, no awareness that the *methods* by which he had obtained these concessions could conceivably render them illegitimate in the eyes of anyone else. When it came to territorial aspirations, he made no distinction between adversaries and allies: what one had provided the other was expected to endorse. . . .

On the surface, this strategy succeeded. After strong initial objections, Roosevelt and Churchill did eventually acknowledge the Soviet Union's right to the expanded borders it claimed; they also made it clear that they would not oppose the installation of "friendly" governments in adjoining states. This meant accepting a Soviet sphere of influence from the Baltic to the Adriatic, a concession not easily reconciled with the Atlantic Charter. But the authors of that document saw no feasible way to avoid that outcome: military necessity required continued Soviet cooperation against the Germans. Nor were they themselves prepared to relinquish spheres of influence in Western Europe and the Mediterranean, the Middle East, Latin America, and East Asia. Self-determination was a sufficiently malleable concept that each of the Big Three could have endorsed, without sleepless nights, what the Soviet government had said about the Atlantic Charter: "practical application of these principles will necessarily adapt itself to the circumstances, needs, and historic peculiarities of particular countries."

That, though, was precisely the problem. For unlike Stalin, Roosevelt and Churchill would have to defend their decisions before domestic constituencies. The *manner* in which Soviet influence expanded was therefore, for them, of no small significance. Stalin showed little understanding of this. Having no experience himself with democratic procedures, he dismissed requests that he respect democratic proprieties. "[S]ome propaganda work should be done," he advised Roosevelt at the Tehran conference after the president had hinted that the American public would welcome a plebiscite in the Baltic States. "It is all nonsense!" Stalin complained to [Soviet Foreign Minister V. M.] Molotov. "[Roosevelt] is their military leader and commander in chief. Who would dare object to him?" When at Yalta F.D.R. stressed the need for the first Polish election to be as pure as "Caesar's wife," Stalin responded with a joke: "They said that about her, but in fact she had her sins." Molotov warned his boss, on that occasion, that the Americans' insistence on free elections elsewhere in Eastern Europe was "going too far." "Don't worry," he recalls Stalin as replying, "work it out. We can deal with it in our own way later. The point is the correlation of forces."

The Soviet leader was, in one sense, right. Military strength would determine what happened in that part of the world, not the enunciation of lofty principles. But unilateral methods carried long-term costs Stalin did not foresee: the most significant of these was to ruin whatever prospects existed for a Soviet sphere of influence the East Europeans themselves might have accepted. This possibility was not as far-fetched as it would later seem. . . . [Stalin] would, after all, approve such a compromise as the basis for a permanent settlement with Finland. He would initially allow free elections in Hungary, Czechoslovakia, and the Soviet occupation zone in Germany. He may even have *anticipated an enthusiastic response* as he took over Eastern Europe. "He was, I think, surprised and hurt," [W. Averell] Harriman [one of Roosevelt's closest advisors] recalled, "when the Red Army was not welcomed in all the neighboring countries as an army of liberation." "We still had our hopes," [Nikita] Khrushchev remembered, that "after the catastrophe of World War II, Europe too might become Soviet. Everyone would take the path from capitalism to socialism." It could be that there was another form of romanticism at work here, quite apart from Stalin's affinity for fellow authoritarians: that he was unrealistic enough to expect ideological solidarity and gratitude for liberation to override old fears of Russian expansionism as well as remaining manifestations of nationalism among the Soviet Union's neighbors, perhaps as easily as he himself had overridden the latter—or so it then appeared—within the multinational empire that was the Soviet Union itself.

If the Red Army could have been welcomed in Poland and the rest of the countries it liberated with the same enthusiasm American, British, and Free French forces encountered when they landed in Italy and France in 1943 and 1944, then some kind of Czech–Finnish compromise might have been feasible. Whatever Stalin's expectations, though, this did not happen. That non-event, in turn, removed any possibility of a division of Europe all members of the Grand Alliance could have endorsed. It ensured that an American sphere of influence would arise there largely by consent, but that its Soviet counterpart could sustain itself only by coercion. The resulting asymmetry would account, more than anything else, for the origins, escalation, and ultimate outcome of the Cold War.

❧

. . . It has long been clear that, in addition to having had an authoritarian vision, Stalin also had an imperial one, which he proceeded to implement in at least as single-minded a way [as the American]. No comparably influential builder of empire came close to wielding power for so long, or with such striking results, on the Western side.

It was, of course, a matter of some awkwardness that Stalin came out of a revolutionary movement that had vowed to smash, not just tsarist imperialism, but all forms of imperialism throughout the world. The Soviet leader constructed his own logic, though, and throughout his career he devoted a surprising amount of attention to showing how a revolution and an empire might coexist. . . .

Stalin's fusion of Marxist internationalism with tsarist imperialism could only reinforce his tendency, in place well before World War II, to equate the advance of world revolution with the expanding influence of the Soviet state. He applied that linkage quite impartially: a major benefit of the 1939 pact with Hitler had been that it regained territories lost as a result of the Bolshevik Revolution and the World War I settlement. But Stalin's conflation of imperialism with ideology also explains the importance he attached, following the German attack in 1941, to having his new Anglo-American allies confirm these arrangements. He had similar goals in East Asia when he insisted on bringing the Soviet Union back to the position Russia had occupied in Manchuria prior to the Russo-Japanese War: this he finally achieved at the 1945 Yalta Conference in return for promising to enter the war against Japan. "My task as minister of foreign affairs was to expand the borders of our Fatherland," Molotov recalled proudly many years later. "And it seems that Stalin and I coped with this task quite well." . . .

❧

From the West's standpoint, the critical question was how far Moscow's influence would extend *beyond* whatever Soviet frontiers turned out to be at the end of the war. Stalin had suggested to Milovan Djilas that the Soviet Union would impose its own social system as far as its armies could reach, but he was also very cautious. Keenly aware of the military power the United States and its allies had accumulated, Stalin was determined to do nothing that might involve the USSR in another devastating war until it had recovered sufficiently to be certain of winning it. "I do not wish to begin the Third World War over the Trieste question," he explained to disappointed Yugoslavs, whom he ordered to evacuate that territory in June 1945. Five years later, he would justify his decision not to intervene in the Korean War on the grounds that "the Second World War ended not long ago, and we are not ready for the Third World War." Just how far the expansion of Soviet influence would proceed depended, therefore, upon a careful balancing of opportunities against risks. . . .

Who or what was it, though, that set the limits? Did Stalin have a fixed list of countries he thought it necessary to dominate? Was he prepared to stop in the face of resistance within those countries to "squeezing out the capitalist order"? Or would expansion cease only when confronted with opposition from the remaining capitalist states, so that further advances risked war at a time when the Soviet Union was ill-prepared for it?

Stalin had been very precise about where he wanted Soviet boundaries changed; he was much less so on how far Moscow's sphere of influence was to extend. He insisted on having "friendly" countries around the periphery of the USSR, but he failed to specify how many would have to meet this standard. He called during the war for dismembering Germany, but by the end of it was denying that he had ever done so: that country would be temporarily divided, he told leading German communists in June 1945, and they themselves would eventually bring about its reunification. He never gave up on the idea of an eventual world revolution, but he expected this to result—as his comments to the Germans suggested—from an expansion of influence emanating from the Soviet Union itself. "[F]or the Kremlin," a well-placed spymaster recalled, "the mission of communism was primarily to consolidate the might of the Soviet state. Only military strength and domination of the countries on our borders could ensure us a superpower role."

But Stalin provided no indication—surely because he himself did not know—of how rapidly, or under what circumstances, this process would take place. He was certainly prepared to stop in the face of resistance from the West: at no point was he willing to challenge the Americans or even the British where they made their interests clear. . . . He quickly backed down when confronted with Anglo-American objections to his ambitions in Iran in the spring of 1946, as he did later that year after demanding Soviet bases in the Turkish Straits. This pattern of advance followed by retreat had shown up in the purges of the 1930s, which Stalin halted when the external threat from Germany became too great to ignore, and it would reappear with the Berlin Blockade and the Korean War, both situations in which the Soviet Union would show great caution after provoking an unexpectedly strong American response.

What all of this suggests, though, is not that Stalin had limited ambitions, only that he had no timetable for achieving them. Molotov retrospectively confirmed this: "Our ideology stands for offensive operations when possible, and if not, we wait." Given this combination of appetite with aversion to risk, one cannot help but wonder what would have happened had the

West tried containment earlier. To the extent that it bears partial responsibility for the coming of the Cold War, the historian Vojtech Mastny has argued, that responsibility lies in its failure to do just that. . . .

Stalin's policy, then, was one of imperial expansion and consolidation differing from that of earlier empires only in the determination with which he pursued it, in the instruments of coercion with which he maintained it, and in the ostensibly anti-imperial justifications he put forward in support of it. It is a testimony to his skill, if not to his morality, that he was able to achieve so many of his imperial ambitions at a time when the tides of history were running against the idea of imperial domination—as colonial offices in London, Paris, Lisbon, and The Hague were finding out—and when his own country was recovering from one of the most brutal invasions in recorded history. The fact that Stalin was able to *expand* his empire when others were contracting and while the Soviet Union was as weak as it was requires explanation. Why did opposition to this process, within and outside Europe, take so long to develop?

One reason was that the colossal sacrifices the Soviet Union had made during the war against the Axis had, in effect, "purified" its reputation: the USSR and its leader had "earned" the right to throw their weight around, or so it seemed. Western governments found it difficult to switch quickly from viewing the Soviet Union as a glorious wartime ally to portraying it as a new and dangerous adversary. President Harry S. Truman and his future Secretary of State Dean Acheson—neither of them sympathetic in the slightest to communism—nontheless tended to give the Soviet Union the benefit of the doubt well into the early postwar era. . . .

Resistance to Stalin's imperialism also developed slowly because Marxism-Leninism at the time had such widespread appeal. It is difficult now to recapture the admiration revolutionaries outside the Soviet Union felt for that country before they came to know it well. . . . Because the Bolsheviks themselves had overcome one empire and had made a career of condemning others, it would take decades for people who were struggling to overthrow British, French, Dutch, or Portuguese colonialism to see that there could also be such a thing as Soviet imperialism. European communists—notably the Yugoslavs—saw this much earlier, but even to most of them it had not been apparent at the end of the war.

Still another explanation for the initial lack of resistance to Soviet expansionism was the fact that its repressive character did not become immediately apparent to all who were subjected to it. . . .

One has the impression that Stalin and the Eastern Europeans got to know one another only gradually. The Kremlin leader was slow to recognize that Soviet authority would not be welcomed everywhere beyond Soviet borders; but as he did come to see this he became all the more determined to impose it everywhere. The Eastern Europeans were slow to recognize how confining incorporation within a Soviet sphere was going to be; but as they did come to see this they became all the more determined to resist it, even if only by withholding, in a passive but sullen manner, the consent any regime needs to establish itself by means other than coercion. Stalin's efforts to consolidate his empire therefore made it at once more repressive and less secure. Meanwhile, an alternative vision of postwar Europe was emerging from the other great empire that established itself in the wake of World War II, that of the United States, and this too gave Stalin grounds for concern. . . .

***

What is there new to say about the old question of responsibility for the Cold War? Who actually started it? Could it have been averted? Here I think the "new" history is bringing us back to an old answer: that *as long as Stalin was running the Soviet Union a cold war was unavoidable.*

History is always the product of determined *and* contingent events: it is up to historians to find the proper balance between them. The Cold War could hardly have happened if there had not been a United States and a Soviet Union, if both had not emerged victorious from World War II, if they had not had conflicting visions of how to organize the postwar world. But these long-term trends did not in themselves *ensure* such a contest, because there is always room for the unexpected to undo what might appear to be inevitable. *Nothing* is ever completely predetermined, as real triceratops and other dinosaurs discovered 65 million years ago when the most recent large asteroid or comet or whatever it was hit the earth and wiped them out.

Individuals, not asteroids, more often personify contingency in history. Who can specify in advance—or unravel afterwards—the particular intersection of genetics, environment, and culture that makes each person unique? Who can foresee what weird conjunctions of design and circumstance may cause a very few individuals to rise so high as to shape great events, and so come to the attention of historians? Such people may set their sights on getting to the top, but an assassin, or a bacillus, or even a carelessly driven taxicab can always be lurking along the way. How entire countries fall into the hands of malevolent geniuses like Hitler and Stalin remains as unfathomable in the "new" Cold War history as in the "old."

Once leaders like these do gain power, however, certain things become highly probable. It is only to be expected that in an authoritarian state the chief authoritarian's personality will weigh much more heavily than those of democratic leaders, who have to share power. And whether because of social alienation, technological innovation, or economic desperation, the first half of the twentieth century was particularly susceptible to great authoritarians and all that resulted from their ascendancy. It is hardly possible to imagine Nazi Germany or the world war it caused without Hitler. I find it increasingly difficult, given what we know now, to imagine the Soviet Union or the Cold War without Stalin.

For the more we learn, the less sense it makes to distinguish Stalin's foreign policies from his domestic practices or even his personal behavior. Scientists have shown the natural world to be filled with examples of what they call "self-similarity across scale": patterns that persist whether one views them microscopically, macroscopically, or anywhere in between. Stalin was like that: he functioned in much the same manner whether operating within the international system, within his alliances, within his country, within his party, within his personal entourage, or even within his family. The Soviet leader waged cold wars on all of these fronts. The Cold War *we* came to know was only one of many from *his* point of view.

Nor did Stalin's influence diminish as quickly as that of most dictators after their deaths. He built a *system* sufficiently durable to survive not only his own demise but his successors' fitful and half-hearted efforts at "de-Stalinization." They were themselves its creatures, and they continued to work within it because they knew no other method of governing. Not until [Mikhail] Gorbachev was a Soviet leader fully prepared to dismantle Stalin's structural legacy. It tells us a lot that as it disappeared, so too did the Cold War and ultimately the Soviet Union itself.

This argument by no means absolves the United States and its allies of a considerable responsibility for how the Cold War was fought—hardly a surprising conclusion since they in fact won it. Nor is it to deny the feckless stupidity with which the Americans fell into peripheral conflicts like Vietnam, or their exorbitant expenditures on unusable weaponry: these certainly caused the Cold War to cost much more in money and lives than it otherwise might have. Nor is it to claim moral superiority for western statesmen. None was as bad as Stalin—or Mao—but the Cold War left no leader uncorrupted: the wielding of great power, even in the best of times, rarely does.

It is the case, though, that if one applies the always useful test of counterfactual history—drop a key variable and speculate as to what difference this might have made—Stalin's centrality to the origins of the Cold War becomes quite clear. For all of their importance, one could have removed Roosevelt, Churchill, Truman, Bevin, Marshall, or Acheson, and a cold war would still have probably followed the world war. If one could have eliminated Stalin, alternative paths become quite conceivable. For with the possible exception of Mao, no twentieth-century leader imprinted himself upon his country as thoroughly and with such lasting effect as Stalin did. And given his personal propensity for cold wars—a tendency firmly rooted long before he had even heard of Harry Truman—once Stalin wound up at the top in Moscow and once it was clear his state would survive the war, then it looks equally clear that there was going to be a Cold War whatever the west did. Who then was responsible? The answer, I think, is authoritarianism in general, and Stalin in particular.

POSTSCRIPT

Was President Truman Responsible for the Cold War?

Offner takes issue with President Truman's recent biographers, Robert H. Ferrell, *Harry S. Truman: A Life* (University of Missouri Press, 1994), Alonzo L. Hamby, *Man of the People: A Life* of Harry S. Truman (Oxford, 1995) and especially David McCullough's bestseller, *Truman* (Simon & Schuster, 1992), all of whom rank Truman among the near-great presidents. All of the most recent polls of presidents place Truman among the ten greatest. Offner calls Truman a "parochial nationalist." His outlook on foreign policy was ethnocentric in spite of his command in combat in a Missouri national guard unit in World War One. He deplored Europe's politics, customs and food. In his early writings, he expressed disdain for "chinks," "dagos," "niggers," "Jew clerks," "bohunks" on "Rooshans."

Brash and impulsive in temperament, Offner accuses Truman of making rash and quick decisions to cover over his insecurities. Truman, he says, often relied on strong personalities such as Boss Tom Pendergast, who pushed Truman up the ladder of Missouri politics and General George Marshall and career diplomat Dean Acheson among others who helped formulate "the containment policy" in 1946 to prevent the Russians from imposing an iron curtain around all of Europe.

Offner also charges the Truman administration of practicing "Atomic diplomacy" at the end of the war, when we were the sole possessor of the A-bomb, to make the Russians more manageable in Europe. He also argues that the Truman doctrine, the Marshall plan, refusing to compromise on the German questions and the formation of the North Atlantic Treaty Organization (NATO) run roughshod over a country who suffered many more military losses and severe damage to its economy and physical infrastructure.

In his attempt to place most of the blame for the cold war on Truman, Offner overstates his case. He calls Truman a parochial nationalist, yet the former President, though not formerly educated, read widely biographies of great leaders and military history. He also, as Offner admits, performed heroically as an officer in a Missouri national guard unit in combat and as a United States Senator supported FDR's foreign policy "on the World Court, neutrality revision, rearmament and Lend Lease for Britain and Russian before America's Entrance into World War Two."

Offner also downplays the uncertainties facing American foreign policy at the end of the war. For example, FDR had hoped that a revised international organization such as the United Nations might succeed in preventing future world wars because it would be stronger and supported by the major powers than the failed League of Nations.

Offner plays up Truman's insecurities which was true, but then accuses him of making both rash decisions and relying on strong foreign policy advisers such as George Kennan, George Marshall, and Dean Acheson. But why wouldn't Truman be insecure? He was chosen as Vice-President in 10944 to replace the controversial Henry Wallace because he came from Missouri, a border state which made him acceptable to southern conservative democrats, yet with a voting record that supported FDR's New Deal liberal domestic programs.

When he became president after Roosevelt's sudden death on April 12, 1945, Truman knew very little of the intricacies of Roosevelt's agreements with Churchill and Stalin. In fact, both Henry Stinson, the Secretary of Defense and Senator James Byrnes both claim to have informed Truman about the "Manhattan Project's" development of atomic bombs which would be ready for use in the summer of 1945.

Professor John Gaddis accepts the fact that Truman was insecure. He also believes that for all of 1945 up to early 1946, the Truman administration was responding to the political and economic uncertainties of the post-World War Two environment. While the United States took the lead in creating the World Bank and the International Monetary Fund to supply money for rebuilding Europe's destroyed infrastructure, these institutions were woefully inadequate to the task. It was also unclear whether the United States was going to re-enter its own recession as had occurred at the end of the First World War which turned into the great depression of the 1930s.

Gaddis believes that the united States created its Western European empire by invitation through the implementation of the Truman Doctrine, the Marshall Plan, the rebuilding of West Germany and the formation of NATO. On the other hand, Russia created its empire by force. Starting in Romania in 1945 and in Poland and Hungary in 1947 and ending with the murder or suicide of Masuryk government in Czechoslovakia in 1948, the Russians imposed totalitarian governments on its citizens.

Gaddis places most of the blame for the cold war on Stalin, an authoritarian imperialist who "equated world revolution with the expanding influence of the Soviet state." Truman was constrained by the democratic electoral system of checks and balances and a Republican-controlled Congress from 1946 to 1948. But Stalin had no such constraints. He purged all his real and potential revolutionary opponents in the 1930s and also the late 1940s and pursued foreign policy objectives as a romantic revolutionary. What limits did Stalin have? Gaddis said Stalin was premise where he wanted Soviet boundaries changed but was imprecise about how far Moscow's sphere of influence would extend without confronting Western resistance.

In summary, if Gorbachev was the Soviet leader in 1945, there may have been alternate paths to the cold war. But with Stalin in charge, says Gaddis, "there was going to be a cold war whatever the West did."

Gaddis' interpretation goes too far in blaming most of the cold war on Stalin. He argues that new sources from the former USSR and the Eastern European countries demonstrate the control that Stalin exerted. But as Tony Judt points out, these sources are quite limited and they do not tell us about the operations of the Politburo and the twelve men who along with Stalin made decisions. See Tony Judt, "Why the Cold War Worked," *The New York Review of Books* (October 9, 1997) and "A Story Still to be Told," *The New York Review of Books* (March 23, 2006) for critical reviews of Gaddis' *We Now Know: Rethinking Cold War History* (Oxford University Press, 1997) and *The Cold War: A New History* (Penguin Press, 2005). The best critiques of Gaddis are three of his earlier books, *The United States and the Origins of the Cold War, 1941–1947* (Columbia University Press, 1972), *Russia, the Soviet Union and the United States: An Interpretative History,* 2nd ed. (McGraw Hill, 1990) and *Strategies of Containment: A Critical Appraisal of America's Postwar Foreign Policy* (Oxford, 1978).

The literature on the cold war is enormous. Students who wish to study the cold war in greater detail should consult *Containment: Documents on American Policy and Strategy, 1945–1950* edited by Thomas H. Etzold and John Lewis Gaddis (Columbia University Press, 1978). Another comprehensive work is Melvyn P. Leffler, *A Preponderance of Power: National Security, the Truman Administration, and the Cold War* (Stanford University Press, 1992). The two best readers to excerpt the various viewpoints on the cold war are Thomas G. Paterson and Robert J. McMahon, eds., *The Origins of the Cold War,* 3rd ed. (D. C. Heath, 1991) and Melvyn P. Leffler and David S. Painter, eds., *Origins of the Cold War: An International History* (Routledge, 1994). Finally David Reynolds has edited a series of essays in *The Origins of the Cold War: International Perspectives* (Yale University Press, 1994).

Bibliographies are contained in all the previous books. The most up-to-date is Melvin P. Leffler, "Cold War and Global Hegemony, 1945–1991," *OAH Magazine of History* (March 2005). Gaddis' argument with the revisionists is nicely summarized in Karen J. Winkler, "Scholars Refight the Cold War," *The Chronicle of Higher Education* (March 2, 1994), pp. 8–10.

ISSUE 3

Did Communism Threaten America's Internal Security after World War II?

YES: John Earl Haynes and Harvey Klehr, from *Venona: Decoding Soviet Espionage in America* (Yale University Press, 1999)

NO: Richard M. Fried, from *Nightmare in Red: The McCarthy Era in Perspective* (Oxford University Press, 1990)

ISSUE SUMMARY

YES: History professors John Earl Haynes and Harvey Klehr argue that army code-breakers during World War II's "Venona Project" uncovered a disturbing number of high-ranking U.S. government officials who seriously damaged American interests by passing sensitive information to the Soviet Union.

NO: Professor of history Richard M. Fried argues that the early 1950s were a "nightmare in red" during which American citizens had their First and Fifth Amendment rights suspended when a host of national and state investigating committees searched for Communists in government agencies, Hollywood, labor unions, foundations, universities, public schools, and even public libraries.

The 1917 triumph of the Bolshevik revolution in Russia and the ensuing spread of revolution to other parts of Eastern Europe and Germany inspired American radicals that the revolution was near. It also led to a wave of anti-Bolshevik hysteria. In the fall of 1919 two groups of radicals—one native-born, the other foreign-born—formed the Communist and Communist Labor Parties. Ultimately they would merge, yet between them they contained only 25,000 to 40,000 members.

The popular "front" policy, which lasted from 1935 to 1939, was the most successful venture undertaken by American Communists. The chief aim of the American Communists became not to increase party membership but to infiltrate progressive organizations. They achieved their greatest successes in the labor movement, which badly needed union organizers. As a consequence Communists controlled several major unions, such as the West Coast long-shoremen and the electrical workers, and attained key offices in the powerful

United Autoworkers. Many American novelists, screenwriters, and actors also joined communist front organizations, such as the League of American Writers, and the Theatre Collective produced "proletarian" plays.

In the 1930s and 1940s the American Communist Party's major success was its ability to establish a conspiratorial underground in Washington. The release of the Venona intercepts of American intelligence during World War II indicates that some 349 American citizens and residents had a covert relationship with Soviet intelligence agencies.

During the war the Federal Bureau of Investigation (FBI) and Office of Strategic Services (OSS) conducted security clearances that permitted Communist supporters to work at high-level jobs if they met the qualifications. This changed in February 1947. In order to impress the Republicans that he wished to attack communism at home, President Harry S. Truman issued an executive order that inaugurated a comprehensive investigation of the loyalty of all government employees by the FBI and the Civil Service Commission.

Truman's loyalty program temporarily protected him from charges that he was "soft" on communism. His ability to ward off attacks on his soft containment policy against communism ran out in his second term. Alger Hiss, a high-level state department official, was convicted in 1949 of lying about his membership in the Ware Communist cell group. In September Truman announced to the American public that the Russians had successfully tested an atomic bomb. Shortly thereafter the Chinese Communists secured control over all of China when their nationalist opponents retreated to the island of Taiwan. Then on June 24, 1950, North Korea crossed the "containment" line at the 38th parallel and attacked South Korea.

The Republican response to these events was swift, critical, and partisan. Before his conviction, Hiss had been thoroughly investigated by the House UnAmerican Activities Committee. Had he led President Franklin D. Roosevelt and others to a sell-out of the Eastern European countries at the Yalta Conference in February 1945? Who lost China? Did liberal and leftist state department officials stationed in China give a pro-Communist slant to U.S. foreign policies in Asia?

Within this atmosphere Truman's attempt to forge a bipartisan policy to counter internal subversion of government agencies by Communists received a mortal blow when Senator Joseph A. McCarthy of Wisconsin publicly identified 205 cases of individuals who appeared to be either card-carrying members or loyal to the Communist Party.

How legitimate was the second great red scare? Did communism threaten America's internal security in the cold war era? In the following selections, John Earl Haynes and Harvey Klehr contend that a sizeable number of high-level government officials had passed sensitive information to Russian intelligence, while Richard M. Fried argues that the 1950s became a "red nightmare" when state and national government agencies overreacted in their search for Communists, violating citizens' rights of free speech and a defense against self-incrimination under the First and Fifth Amendments.

YES

John Earl Haynes and
Harvey Klehr

Venona and the Cold War

The Venona Project began because Carter Clarke did not trust Joseph Stalin. Colonel Clarke was chief of the U.S. Army's Special Branch, part of the War Department's Military Intelligence Division, and in 1943 its officers heard vague rumors of secret German-Soviet peace negotiations. With the vivid example of the August 1939 Nazi-Soviet Pact in mind, Clarke feared that a separate peace between Moscow and Berlin would allow Nazi Germany to concentrate its formidable war machine against the United States and Great Britain. Clarke thought he had a way to find out whether such negotiations were under way.

Clarke's Special Branch supervised the Signal Intelligence Service, the Army's elite group of code-breakers and the predecessor of the National Security Agency. In February 1943 Clarke ordered the service to establish a small program to examine ciphered Soviet diplomatic cablegrams. Since the beginning of World War II in 1939, the federal government had collected copies of international cables leaving and entering the United States. If the cipher used in the Soviet cables could be broken, Clarke believed, the private exchanges between Soviet diplomats in the United States and their superiors in Moscow would show whether Stalin was seriously pursuing a separate peace.

The coded Soviet cables, however, proved to be far more difficult to read than Clarke had expected. American code-breakers discovered that the Soviet Union was using a complex two-part ciphering system involving a "one-time pad" code that in theory was unbreakable. The Venona code-breakers, however, combined acute intellectual analysis with painstaking examination of thousands of coded telegraphic cables to spot a Soviet procedural error that opened the cipher to attack. But by the time they had rendered the first messages into readable text in 1946, the war was over and Clarke's initial goal was moot. Nor did the messages show evidence of a Soviet quest for a separate peace.What they did demonstrate, however, stunned American officials. Messages thought to be between Soviet diplomats at the Soviet consulate in New York and the People's Commissariat of Foreign Affairs in Moscow turned out to be cables between professional intelligence field officers and Gen. Pavel Fitin, head of the foreign intelligence directorate of the KGB in Moscow. Espionage, not diplomacy, was the subject of these cables. One of the first cables rendered into coherent text was a 1944 message from KGB officers in

From John Earl Haynes and Harvey Klehr, *Venona: Decoding Soviet Espionage in America* (Yale University Press, 1999). Copyright © 1999 by Yale University. Reprinted by permission of Yale University Press. Notes omitted.

New York showing that the Soviet Union had infiltrated America's most secret enterprise, the atomic bomb project.

By 1948 the accumulating evidence from other decoded Venona cables showed that the Soviets had recruited spies in virtually every major American government agency of military or diplomatic importance. American authorities learned that since 1942 the United States had been the target of a Soviet espionage onslaught involving dozens of professional Soviet intelligence officers and hundreds of Americans, many of whom were members of the American Communist party (CPUSA). The deciphered cables of the Venona Project identify 349 citizens, immigrants, and permanent residents of the United States who had had a covert relationship with Soviet intelligence agencies. Further, American cryptanalysts in the Venona Project deciphered only a fraction of the Soviet intelligence traffic, so it was only logical to conclude that many additional agents were discussed in the thousands of unread messages. Some were identified from other sources, such as defectors' testimony and the confessions of Soviet spies.

The deciphered Venona messages also showed that a disturbing number of high-ranking U.S. government officials consciously maintained a clandestine relationship with Soviet intelligence agencies and had passed extraordinarily sensitive information to the Soviet Union that had seriously damaged American interests. Harry White—the second most powerful official in the U.S. Treasury Department, one of the most influential officials in the government, and part of the American delegation at the founding of the United Nations—had advised the KGB about how American diplomatic strategy could be frustrated. A trusted personal assistant to President Franklin Roosevelt, Lauchlin Currie, warned the KGB that the FBI had started an investigation of one of the Soviets' key American agents, Gregory Silvermaster. This warning allowed Silvermaster, who headed a highly productive espionage ring, to escape detection and continue spying. Maurice Halperin, the head of a research section of the Office of Strategic Services (OSS), then America's chief intelligence arm, turned over hundreds of pages of secret American diplomatic cables to the KGB. William Perl, a brilliant young government aeronautical scientist, provided the Soviets with the results of the highly secret tests and design experiments for American jet engines and jet aircraft. His betrayal assisted the Soviet Union in quickly overcoming the American technological lead in the development of jets. In the Korean War, U.S. military leaders expected the Air Force to dominate the skies, on the assumption that the Soviet aircraft used by North Korea and Communist China would be no match for American aircraft. They were shocked when Soviet MiG-15 jet fighters not only flew rings around U.S. propeller-driven aircraft but were conspicuously superior to the first generation of American jets as well. Only the hurried deployment of America's newest jet fighter, the F-86 Saber, allowed the United States to match the technological capabilities of the MiG-15. The Air Force prevailed, owing more to the skill of American pilots than to the design of American aircraft.

And then there were the atomic spies. From within the Manhattan Project two physicists, Klaus Fuchs and Theodore Hall, and one technician,

David Greenglass, transmitted the complex formula for extracting bomb-grade uranium from ordinary uranium, the technical plans for production facilities, and the engineering principles for the "implosion" technique. The latter process made possible an atomic bomb using plutonium, a substance much easier to manufacture than bomb-grade uranium.

The betrayal of American atomic secrets to the Soviets allowed the Soviet Union to develop atomic weapons several years sooner and at a substantially lower cost than it otherwise would have. Joseph Stalin's knowledge that espionage assured the Soviet Union of quickly breaking the American atomic monopoly emboldened his diplomatic strategy in his early Cold War clashes with the United States. It is doubtful that Stalin, rarely a risk-taker, would have supplied the military wherewithal and authorized North Korea to invade South Korea in 1950 had the Soviet Union not exploded an atomic bomb in 1949. Otherwise Stalin might have feared that President Harry Truman would stanch any North Korean invasion by threatening to use atomic weapons. After all, as soon as the atomic bomb had been developed, Truman had not hesitated to use it twice to end the war with Japan. But in 1950, with Stalin in possession of the atomic bomb, Truman was deterred from using atomic weapons in Korea, even in the late summer when initially unprepared American forces were driven back into the tip of Korea and in danger of being pushed into the sea, and then again in the winter when Communist Chinese forces entered the war in massive numbers. The killing and maiming of hundreds of thousands of soldiers and civilians on both sides of the war in Korea might have been averted had the Soviets not been able to parry the American atomic threat.

Early Soviet possession of the atomic bomb had an important psychological consequence. When the Soviet Union exploded a nuclear device in 1949, ordinary Americans as well as the nation's leaders realized that a cruel despot, Joseph Stalin, had just gained the power to destroy cities at will. This perception colored the early Cold War with the hues of apocalypse. Though the Cold War never lost the potential of becoming a civilization-destroying conflict, Stalin's death in March 1953 noticeably relaxed Soviet-American tensions. With less successful espionage, the Soviet Union might not have developed the bomb until after Stalin's death, and the early Cold War might have proceeded on a far less frightening path.

Venona decryptions identified most of the Soviet spies uncovered by American counterintelligence between 1948 and the mid-1950s. The skill and perseverance of the Venona code-breakers led the U.S. Federal Bureau of Investigation (FBI) and British counterintelligence (MI5) to the atomic spy Klaus Fuchs. Venona documents unmistakably identified Julius Rosenberg as the head of a Soviet spy ring and David Greenglass, his brother-in-law, as a Soviet source at the secret atomic bomb facility at Los Alamos, New Mexico. Leads from decrypted telegrams exposed the senior British diplomat Donald Maclean as a major spy in the British embassy in Washington and precipitated his flight to the Soviet Union, along with his fellow diplomat and spy Guy Burgess. The arrest and prosecution of such spies as Judith Coplon, Robert Soblen, and Jack Soble was possible because American intelligence was able to read Soviet reports about their activities. The charges by the former Soviet spy Elizabeth Bentley that several dozen mid-level government officials, mostly secret Communists, had assisted Soviet intelligence were corroborated in Venona documents and assured American authorities of her veracity.

With the advent of the Cold War, however, the spies clearly identified in the Venona decryptions were the least of the problem. Coplon, Rosenberg, Greenglass, Fuchs, Soble, and Soblen were prosecuted, and the rest were eased out of the government or otherwise neutralized as threats to national security. But that still left a security nightmare. Of the 349 Americans the deciphered Venona cables revealed as having covert ties to Soviet intelligence agencies, less than half could be identified by their real names and nearly two hundred remained hidden behind cover names. American officials assumed that some of the latter surely were still working in sensitive positions. Had they been promoted and moved into policy-making jobs? Had Muse, the unidentified female agent in the OSS, succeeded in transferring to the State Department or the Central Intelligence Agency (CIA), the successor to the OSS? What of Source No. 19, who had been senior enough to meet privately with Churchill and Roosevelt at the Trident Conference? Was the unidentified KGB source Bibi working for one of America's foreign assistance agencies? Was Donald, the unidentified Navy captain who was a GRU (Soviet military intelligence) source, still in uniform, perhaps by this time holding the rank of admiral? And what of the two unidentified atomic spies Quantum and Pers? They had given Stalin the secrets of the uranium and plutonium bomb: were they now passing on the secrets of the even more destructive hydrogen bomb? And how about Dodger, Godmother, and Fakir? Deciphered Venona messages showed that all three had provided the KGB with information on American diplomats who specialized in Soviet matters. Fakir was himself being considered for an assignment representing the United States in Moscow. Which of the American foreign service officers who were also Soviet specialists were traitors? How could Americans successfully negotiate with the Soviet Union when the American negotiating team included someone working for the other side? Western Europe, clearly, would be the chief battleground of the Cold War. To lose there was to lose all: the task of rebuilding stable democracies in postwar Europe and forging the NATO military alliance was America's chief diplomatic challenge. Yet Venona showed that the KGB had Mole, the appropriate cover name of a Soviet source inside the Washington establishment who had passed on to Moscow high-level American diplomatic policy guidance on Europe. When American officials met to discuss sensitive matters dealing with France, Britain, Italy, or Germany, was Mole present and working to frustrate American goals? Stalin's espionage offensive had not only uncovered American secrets, it had also undermined the mutual trust that American officials had for each other.

The Truman administration had expected the end of World War II to allow the dismantling of the massive military machine created to defeat Nazi Germany and Imperial Japan. The government slashed military budgets, turned weapons factories over to civilian production, ended conscription, and returned millions of soldiers to civilian life. So, too, the wartime intelligence and security apparatus was demobilized. Anticipating only limited need for foreign intelligence and stating that he wanted no American Gestapo, President Truman abolished America's chief intelligence agency, the Office of Strategic Services. With the coming of peace, emergency wartime rules for security vetting of many government employees lapsed or were ignored.

In late 1945 and in 1946, the White House had reacted with a mixture of indifference and skepticism to FBI reports indicating significant Soviet espionage activity in the United States. Truman administration officials even whitewashed evidence pointing to the theft of American classified documents in the 1945 *Amerasia* case because they did not wish to put at risk the continuation of the wartime Soviet-American alliance and wanted to avoid the political embarrassment of a security scandal. By early 1947, however, this indifference ended. The accumulation of information from defectors such as Elizabeth Bentley and Igor Gouzenko, along with the Venona decryptions, made senior Truman administration officials realize that reports of Soviet spying constituted more than FBI paranoia. No government could operate successfully if it ignored the challenge to its integrity that Stalin's espionage offensive represented. In addition, the White House sensed that there was sufficient substance to the emerging picture of a massive Soviet espionage campaign, one assisted by American Communists, that the Truman administration was vulnerable to Republican charges of having ignored a serious threat to American security. President Truman reversed course and in March 1947 issued a sweeping executive order establishing a comprehensive security vetting program for U.S. government employees. He also created the Central Intelligence Agency, a stronger and larger version of the OSS, which he had abolished just two years earlier. In 1948 the Truman administration followed up these acts by indicting the leaders of the CPUSA under the sedition sections of the 1940 Smith Act. While the Venona Project and the decrypted messages themselves remained secret, the substance of the messages with the names of scores of Americans who had assisted Soviet espionage circulated among American military and civilian security officials. From the security officials the information went to senior executive-branch political appointees and members of Congress. They, in turn, passed it on to journalists and commentators, who conveyed the alarming news to the general public.

Americans' Understanding of Soviet and Communist Espionage

During the early Cold War, in the late 1940s and early 1950s, every few months newspaper headlines trumpeted the exposure of yet another network of Communists who had infiltrated an American laboratory, labor union, or government agency. Americans worried that a Communist fifth column, more loyal to the Soviet Union than to the United States, had moved into their institutions. By the mid-1950s, following the trials and convictions for espionage-related crimes of Alger Hiss, a senior diplomat, and Julius and Ethel Rosenberg for atomic spying, there was a widespread public consensus on three points: that Soviet espionage was serious, that American Communists assisted the Soviets, and that several senior government officials had betrayed the United States. The deciphered Venona messages provide a solid factual basis for this consensus. But the government did not release the Venona decryptions to the public, and it successfully disguised the source of its information about Soviet espionage. This decision denied the public the incontestable evidence afforded by the messages of the Soviet Union's own spies. Since the information about Soviet espionage and American Communist participation derived largely from the testimony of defectors and a mass of circumstantial evidence, the public's belief in those reports rested on faith in the integrity of government security officials. These sources are inherently more ambiguous than the hard evidence of the Venona messages, and this ambiguity had unfortunate consequences for American politics and Americans' understanding of their own history.

The decision to keep Venona secret from the public, and to restrict knowledge of it even within the government, was made essentially by senior Army officers in consultation with the FBI and the CIA. Aside from the Venona codebreakers, only a limited number of military intelligence officers, FBI agents, and CIA officials knew of the project. The CIA in fact was not made an active partner in Venona until 1952 and did not receive copies of the deciphered messages until 1953. The evidence is not entirely clear, but it appears that Army Chief of Staff Omar Bradley, mindful of the White House's tendency to leak politically sensitive information, decided to deny President Truman direct knowledge of the Venona Project. The president was informed about the substance of the Venona messages as it came to him through FBI and Justice Department memorandums on espionage investigations and CIA reports on intelligence matters. He was not told that much of this information derived from reading Soviet cable traffic. This omission is important because Truman was mistrustful of J. Edgar Hoover, the head of the FBI, and suspected that the reports of Soviet espionage were exaggerated for political purposes. Had he been aware of Venona, and known that Soviet cables confirmed the testimony of Elizabeth Bentley and Whittaker Chambers, it is unlikely that his aides would have considered undertaking a campaign to discredit Bentley and indict Chambers for perjury, or would have allowed themselves to be taken in by the disinformation being spread by the American Communist party and Alger Hiss's partisans that Chambers had at one time been committed to an insane asylum.

There were sensible reasons . . . for the decision to keep Venona a highly compartmentalized secret within the government. In retrospect, however, the negative consequences of this policy are glaring. Had Venona been made public, it is unlikely there would have been a forty-year campaign to prove that the Rosenbergs were innocent. The Venona messages clearly display Julius Rosenberg's role as the leader of a productive ring of Soviet spies. Nor would there have been any basis for doubting his involvement in atomic espionage, because the deciphered messages document his recruitment of his brother-in-law, David Greenglass, as a spy. It is also unlikely, had the messages been made public or even circulated more widely within the government than they did, that Ethel Rosenberg would have been executed. The Venona messages do not throw her guilt in doubt; indeed, they confirm that she was a participant in her husband's espionage and in the recruitment of her brother for atomic espionage. But they suggest that she was essentially an accessory to her husband's activity, having knowledge of it and assisting him but not acting as a principal. Had they been introduced at the Rosenberg trial, the Venona messages would have confirmed Ethel's guilt but also reduced the importance of her role.

Further, the Venona messages, if made public, would have made Julius Rosenberg's execution less likely. When Julius Rosenberg faced trial, only two Soviet atomic spies were known: David Greenglass, whom Rosenberg had recruited and run as a source, and Klaus Fuchs. Fuchs, however, was in England, so Greenglass was the only Soviet atomic spy in the media spotlight in the United States. Greenglass's confession left Julius Rosenberg as the target of public outrage at atomic espionage. That prosecutors would ask for and get the death penalty under those circumstances is not surprising.

In addition to Fuchs and Greenglass, however, the Venona messages identify three other Soviet sources within the Manhattan Project. The messages show that Theodore Hall, a young physicist at Los Alamos, was a far more valuable source than Greenglass, a machinist. Hall withstood FBI interrogation, and the government had no direct evidence of his crimes except the Venona messages, which because of their secrecy could not be used in court; he therefore escaped prosecution. The real identities of the sources Fogel and Quantum are not known, but the information they turned over to the Soviets suggests that Quantum was a scientist of some standing and that Fogel was either a scientist or an engineer. Both were probably more valuable sources than David Greenglass. Had Venona been made public, Greenglass would have shared the stage with three other atomic spies and not just with Fuchs, and all three would have appeared to have done more damage to American security than he. With Greenglass's role diminished, that of his recruiter, Julius Rosenberg, would have been reduced as well. Rosenberg would assuredly have been convicted, but his penalty might well have been life in prison rather than execution.

There were broader consequences, as well, of the decision to keep Venona secret. The overlapping issues of Communists in government, Soviet espionage, and the loyalty of American Communists quickly became a partisan battleground. Led by Republican senator Joseph McCarthy of Wisconsin, some conservatives and partisan Republicans launched a comprehensive attack on the loyalties of the Roosevelt and Truman administrations. Some painted the entire New Deal as a disguised Communist plot and depicted Dean Acheson, Truman's secretary of state, and George C. Marshall, the Army chief of staff under Roosevelt and secretary of state and secretary of defense under Truman, as participants, in Senator McCarthy's words, in "a conspiracy on a scale so immense as to dwarf any previous such venture in the history of man. A conspiracy of infamy so black that, when it is finally exposed, its principals shall be forever deserving of the maledictions of all honest men." There is no basis in Venona for implicating Acheson or Marshall in a Communist conspiracy, but because the deciphered Venona messages were classified and unknown to the public, demagogues such as

McCarthy had the opportunity to mix together accurate information about betrayal by men such as Harry White and Alger Hiss with falsehoods about Acheson and Marshall that served partisan political goals.

A number of liberals and radicals pointed to the excesses of McCarthy's charges as justification for rejecting the allegations altogether. Anticommunism further lost credibility in the late 1960s when critics of U.S. involvement in the Vietnam War blamed it for America's ill-fated participation. By the 1980s many commentators, and perhaps most academic historians, had concluded that Soviet espionage had been minor, that few American Communists had assisted the Soviets, and that no high officials had betrayed the United States. Many history texts depicted America in the late 1940s and 1950s as a "nightmare in red" during which Americans were "sweat-drenched in fear" of a figment of their own paranoid imaginations. As for American Communists, they were widely portrayed as having no connection with espionage. One influential book asserted emphatically, "There is no documentation in the public record of a direct connection between the American Communist Party and espionage during the entire postwar period."

Consequently, Communists were depicted as innocent victims of an irrational and oppressive American government. In this sinister but widely accepted portrait of America in the 1940s and 1950s, an idealistic New Dealer (Alger Hiss) was thrown into prison on the perjured testimony of a mentally sick anti-Communist fanatic (Whittaker Chambers), innocent progressives (the Rosenbergs) were sent to the electric chair on trumped-up charges of espionage laced with anti-Semitism, and dozens of blameless civil servants had their careers ruined by the smears of a professional anti-Communist (Elizabeth Bentley). According to this version of events, one government official (Harry White) was killed by a heart attack brought on by Bentley's lies, and another (Laurence Duggan, a senior diplomat) was driven to suicide by more of Chambers's malignant falsehoods. Similarly, in many textbooks President Truman's executive order denying government employment to those who posed security risks, and other laws aimed at espionage and Communist subversion, were and still are described not as having been motivated by a real concern for American security (since the existence of any serious espionage or subversion was denied) but instead as consciously antidemocratic attacks on basic freedoms. As one commentator wrote, "The statute books groaned under several seasons of legislation designed to outlaw dissent."

Despite its central role in the history of American counterintelligence, the Venona Project remained among the most tightly held government secrets. By the time the project shut down, it had decrypted nearly three thousand messages sent between the Soviet Union and its embassies and consulates around the world. Remarkably, although rumors and a few snippets of information about the project had become public in the 1980s, the actual texts and the enormous import of the messages remained secret until 1995. The U.S. government often has been successful in keeping secrets in the short term, but over a longer period secrets, particularly newsworthy ones, have proven to be very difficult for the government to keep. It is all the more amazing, then, how little got out about the Venona Project in the fifty-three years before it was made public.

Unfortunately, the success of government secrecy in this case has seriously distorted our understanding of post-World War II history. Hundreds of books and thousands of essays on McCarthyism, the federal loyalty security program, Soviet espionage, American communism, and the early Cold War have perpetuated many myths that have given Americans a warped view of the nation's history in the 1930s, 1940s, and 1950s. The information that these messages reveal substantially revises the basis for understanding the early history of the Cold War and of America's concern with Soviet espionage and Communist subversion.

In the late 1970s the FBI began releasing material from its hitherto secret files as a consequence of the passage of the Freedom of Information Act (FOIA). Although this act opened some files to public scrutiny, it has not as yet provided access to the full range of FBI investigative records. The enormous backlog of FOIA requests has led to lengthy delays in releasing documents; it is not uncommon to wait more than five years to receive material. Capricious and zealous enforcement of regulations exempting some material from release frequently has elicited useless documents consisting of occasional phrases interspersed with long sections of redacted (blacked-out) text. And, of course, even the unexpurgated FBI files show only what the FBI learned about Soviet espionage and are only part of the story. Even given these hindrances, however, each year more files are opened, and the growing body of FBI documentation has significantly enhanced the opportunity for a reconstruction of what actually happened.

The collapse of the Union of Soviet Socialist Republics in 1991 led to the opening of Soviet archives that had never been examined by independent scholars. The historically rich documentation first made available in Moscow's archives in 1992 has resulted in an outpouring of new historical writing, as these records allow a far more complete and accurate understanding of central events of the twentieth century. But many archives in Russia are open only in part, and some are still closed. In particular, the archives of the foreign intelligence operations of Soviet military intelligence and those of the foreign intelligence arm of the KGB are not open to researchers. Given the institutional continuity between the former Soviet intelligence agencies and their current Russian successors, the opening of these archives is not anticipated anytime soon. However, Soviet intelligence agencies had cooperated with other Soviet institutions, whose newly opened archives therefore hold some intelligence-related material and provide a back door into the still-closed intelligence archives.

But the most significant source of fresh insight into Soviet espionage in the United States comes from the decoded messages produced by the Venona Project. These documents, after all, constitute a portion of the materials that are still locked up in Russian intelligence archives. Not only do the Venona files supply information in their own right, but because of their inherent reliability they also provide a touchstone for judging the credibility of other sources, such as defectors' testimony and FBI investigative files.

Stalin's Espionage Assault on the United States

Through most of the twentieth century, governments of powerful nations have conducted intelligence operations of some sort during both peace and war. None, however, used espionage as an instrument of state policy as extensively as did the Soviet Union under Joseph Stalin. In the late 1920s and 1930s, Stalin directed most of the resources of Soviet intelligence at nearby targets in Europe and Asia. America was still distant from Stalin's immediate concerns, the threat to Soviet goals posed by Nazi Germany and Imperial Japan. This perception changed, however, after the United States entered the world war in December 1941. Stalin realized that once Germany and Japan were defeated, the world would be left with only three powers able to project their influence across the globe: the Soviet Union, Great Britain, and the United States. And of these, the strongest would be the United States. With that in mind, Stalin's intelligence agencies shifted their focus toward America.

The Soviet Union, Great Britain, and the United States formed a military alliance in early 1942 to defeat Nazi Germany and its allies. The Soviet Union quickly became a major recipient of American military (Lend-Lease) aid, second only to Great Britain; it eventually received more than nine billion dollars. As part of the aid arrangements, the United States invited the Soviets to greatly expand their diplomatic staffs and to establish special offices to facilitate aid arrangements. Thousands of Soviet military officers, engineers, and technicians entered the United States to review what aid was available and choose which machinery, weapons, vehicles (nearly 400,000 American trucks went to the Soviet Union), aircraft, and other matériel would most assist the Soviet war effort. Soviet personnel had to be trained to maintain the American equipment, manuals had to be translated into Russian, shipments to the Soviet Union had to be inspected to ensure that what was ordered had been delivered, properly loaded, and dispatched on the right ships. Entire Soviet naval crews arrived for training to take over American combat and cargo ships to be handed over to the Soviet Union.

Scores of Soviet intelligence officers of the KGB (the chief Soviet foreign intelligence and security agency), the GRU (the Soviet military intelligence agency), and the Naval GRU (the Soviet naval intelligence agency) were among the Soviet personnel arriving in America. These intelligence officers pursued two missions. One, security, was only indirectly connected with the United States. The internal security arm of the KGB employed several hundred thousand full-time personnel, assisted by several million part-time informants, to ensure the political loyalty of Soviet citizens. When the Soviets sent thousands of their citizens to the United States to assist with the Lend-Lease arrangement, they sent this internal security apparatus as well. A significant portion of the Venona messages deciphered by American code-breakers reported on this task. The messages show that every Soviet cargo ship that arrived at an American port to pick up Lend-Lease supplies had in its crew at least one, often two, and sometimes three informants who reported either to the KGB or to the Naval GRU. Their task was not to spy on Americans but to watch the Soviet merchant seamen for signs of political dissidence and potential defection.

Some of the messages show Soviet security officers tracking down merchant seamen who had jumped ship, kidnapping them, and spiriting them back aboard Soviet ships in disregard of American law. Similarly, other messages discuss informants, recruited or planted by the KGB in every Soviet office in the United States, whose task was to report signs of ideological deviation or potential defection among Soviet personnel.

A second mission of these Soviet intelligence officers, however, was espionage against the United States. . . . The deciphered Venona cables do more than reveal the remarkable success that the Soviet Union had in recruiting spies and gaining access to many important U.S. government agencies and laboratories dealing with secret information. They expose beyond cavil the American Communist party as an auxiliary of the intelligence agencies of the Soviet Union. While not every Soviet spy was a Communist, most were. And while not every American Communist was a spy, hundreds were. The CPUSA itself worked closely with Soviet intelligence agencies to facilitate their espionage. Party leaders were not only aware of the liaison; they actively worked to assist the relationship.

Information from the Venona decryptions underlay the policies of U.S. government officials in their approach to the issue of domestic communism. The investigations and prosecutions of American Communists undertaken by the federal government in the late 1940s and early 1950s were premised on an assumption that the CPUSA had assisted Soviet espionage. This view contributed to the Truman administration's executive order in 1947, reinforced in the early 1950s under the Eisenhower administration, that U.S. government employees be subjected to loyalty and security investigations. The understanding also lay behind the 1948 decision by Truman's attorney general to prosecute the leaders of the CPUSA under the sedition sections of the Smith Act. It was an explicit assumption behind congressional investigations of domestic communism in the late 1940s and 1950s, and it permeated public attitudes toward domestic communism.

The Soviet Union's unrestrained espionage against the United States from 1942 to 1945 was of the type that a nation directs at an enemy state. By the late 1940s the evidence provided by Venona of the massive size and intense hostility of Soviet intelligence operations caused both American counterintelligence professionals and high-level policy-makers to conclude that Stalin had already launched a covert attack on the United States. In their minds, the Soviet espionage offensive indicated that the Cold War had begun not after World War II but many years earlier.

Richard M. Fried

"Bitter Days": The Heyday of Anti-Communism

Even independent of [Joseph] McCarthy, the years 1950–1954 marked the climax of anti-communism in American life. The Korean stalemate generated both a bruising debate over containment and a sourness in national politics. Korea's sapping effect and a series of minor scandals heightened the Democratic Party's anemia. In addition, the 1950 congressional campaign, revealing McCarthyism's apparent sway over the voters and encouraging the GOP's right wing, signaled that anti-communism occupied the core of American political culture. "These," said liberal commentator Elmer Davis in January 1951, "are bitter days—full of envy, hatred, malice, and all uncharitableness."

Critics of these trends in American politics had scant power or spirit. Outside government, foes of anti-Communist excesses moved cautiously lest they be redbaited and rarely took effective countermeasures. Liberals seldom strayed from the safety of the anti-Communist consensus. Radicals met the hostility of the dominant political forces in Cold War America and fared poorly. In government, anti-communism ruled. Senate resistance to McCarthy was scattered and weak. In the House, HUAC [House Un-American Activities Committee] did much as it pleased. [President Harry S.] Truman upheld civil liberties with occasional eloquence, but he remained on the defensive, and his Justice Department often seemed locked in near-alliance with the Right in Congress. [Dwight D.] Eisenhower, when not appeasing the McCarthyites, appeared at times no more able to curb them than had Truman.

Even at his peak, McCarthy was not the sole anti-Communist paladin, though he cultivated that impression. As McCarthyism in its broader sense outlived the personal defeat of McCarthy himself, so, in its prime, it exceeded his reach. Its strength owed much to the wide acceptance, even by McCarthy's critics, of the era's anti-Communist premises. Along with McCarthy, they made the first half of the 1950s the acme of noisy anti-communism and of the ills to which it gave birth.

Soon after the 1950 campaign, skirmishing over the Communist issue renewed in earnest. In December Senator Pat McCarran joined the hunt for subversives by creating the Senate Internal Security Subcommittee (SISS). As chairman of that panel (and the parent Judiciary Committee), the crusty Nevada Democrat packed it with such like-minded colleagues as Democrats

James Eastland and Willis Smith and Republicans Homer Ferguson and William Jenner. While McCarthy darted about unpredictably, McCarran moved glacially but steadily to his objective, crushing opposition.

McCarran's panel spotlighted themes that McCarthy had raised giving them a more sympathetic hearing than had the Tydings Committee. In February 1951, federal agents swooped down on a barn in Lee, Massachusetts, seized the dead files of the Institute of Pacific Relations (IPR) and trucked them under guard to Washington. After sifting this haul, a SISS subcommittee opened an extended probe of the IPR, which led to a new inquest on "who lost China" and resulted in renewed loyalty and security proceedings, dismissals from the State Department and prosecution—all to McCarthy's greater, reflected glory.

The subcommittee acquired a reputation—more cultivated than deserved—for honoring due process. SISS was punctilious on some points: evidence was formally introduced (when an excerpt was read, the full text was put in the record); hearings were exhaustive (over 5,000 pages); witnesses were heard in executive session before they named names in public; their credentials and the relevance of their testimony were set forth; and some outward courtesies were extended.

The fairness was only skin-deep, however. Witnesses were badgered about obscure events from years back and about nuances of aging reports. Diplomat John Carter Vincent was even asked if he had plans to move to Sarasota, Florida. When he termed it a most "curious" question, counsel could only suggest that perhaps the Florida Chamber of Commerce had taken an interest. The subcommittee strove to ensnare witnesses in perjury. One China Hand called the sessions "generally Dostoyevskian attacks not only on a man's mind but also his memory." To have predicted Jiang's decline or Mao's rise was interpreted as both premeditating and helping to cause that outcome.

A product of the internationalist do-goodery of YMCA leaders in the 1920s, the IPR sought to promote peace and understanding in the Pacific. It had both national branches in countries interested in the Pacific and an international secretariat. Well funded by corporations and foundations in its palmier days, the IPR had more pedigree than power. McCarran's subcommittee insisted that IPR's publications pushed the Communist line on China. Louis Budenz testified that the Kremlin had assigned Owen Lattimore the job of giving the IPR journal, *Pacific Affairs,* a Party-line tilt. Budenz claimed that when he was in the Party, he received "official communications" describing Lattimore (and several China Hands) as Communists.

McCarran's panel spent a year grilling Lattimore, other IPR officials, and various China experts and diplomats as it tried to knit a fabric of conspiracy out of its evidence and presuppositions. McCarran claimed that, but for the machinations of the coterie that ran IPR, "China today would be free and a bulwark against the further advance of the Red hordes into the Far East." He charged that the IPR-USSR connection had led to infiltration of the government by persons aligned with the Soviets, of faculties by Red professors, and of textbooks by proCommunist ideas. He called Lattimore "a conscious and articulate instrument of the Soviet conspiracy."

The hearings revealed naiveté about communism, showed that IPR principals had access to important officials during the war, and turned up levels of maneuvering that sullied IPR's reputation for scholarly detachment. Proven or accused Reds did associate with the IPR and may well have sought leverage through it. There were tendentious claims in IPR publications, as in one author's simplistic dichotomy of Mao's "democratic China" and Jiang's "feudal China." Lattimore was a more partisan editor of *Pacific Affairs* than he conceded. However, in political scientist Earl Latham's measured assessment, the hearings "show something less than subversive conspiracy in the making of foreign policy, and something more than quiet routine." Nor was it proven that IPR had much influence over policy. Perhaps the China Hands had been naive to think that a reoriented policy might prevent China's Communists from falling "by default" under Soviet control and thus might maintain American leverage. Yet those who argued that unblinking support of Jiang could have prevented China's "loss" were more naive still.

Unable to prove, in scholarly terms, its thesis of a successful pro-Communist conspiracy against China, SISS could still carry it politically. The loyalty-security program helped enforce it. New charges, however stale, motivated the State Department Loyalty-Security Board to reexamine old cases of suspected employees, even if they had been previously cleared. Moreover, nudged by the Right, Truman toughened the loyalty standard in April 1951, putting a heavier burden of proof on the accused. Thus under Hiram Bingham, a Republican conservative, the Loyalty Review Board ordered new inquiries in cases decided under the old standard. . . .

The purge of the China Hands had long-term impact. American attitudes toward China remained frozen for two decades. Battered by McCarthyite attacks, the State Department's Far Eastern Division assumed a conservative bunkerlike mentality. Selected by President John F. Kennedy to shake the division up, Assistant Secretary of State Averell Harriman found it "a disaster area filled with human wreckage." Personnel who did not bear wounds from previous battles were chosen to handle Asian problems. Vincent's successor on the China desk was an impeccably conservative diplomat whose experience lay in Europe. JFK named an ambassador to South Vietnam whose prior work had been with NATO. In the 1950s, the field of Asian studies felt the blindfold of conformity as the momentum of U.S. foreign policy carried the country toward the vortex of Vietnam.

‹◦›

The IPR Investigation was but one of many inquiries during the early 1950s that delved into Communist activities. The Eighty-first Congress spawned 24 probes of communism; the Eighty-second, 34; and the Eighty-third, 51. HUAC busily sought new triumphs. In 1953, 185 of the 221 Republican Congressmen asked to serve on it. But HUAC faced the problem all monopolies meet when competitors pour into the market. Besides McCarran and McCarthy, a Senate labor subcommittee probed Red influences in labor unions, two committees combed the U.N. Secretariat for Communists, and others dipped an oar in when the occasion arose.

In part HUAC met the competition with strenuous travel. Hearings often bore titles like "Communist Activities in the Chicago Area"—or Los Angeles, Detroit, or Hawaii. The Detroit hearings got a musician fired, a college student expelled, and UAW Local 600 taken over by the national union. In 1956 two Fisher Body employees were called before a HUAC hearing in St. Louis. When angry fellow workers chalked such slogans as "Russia has no Fifth amendment" on auto bodies and staged a work stoppage, the two men were suspended. The impact of junketing congressional probers was often felt in such local fallout rather than in federal punishments (though many witnesses were cited for contempt of Congress). That indeed was the point. A witness might use the Fifth Amendment to avoid perjury charges, but appearing before a committee of Congress left him open to local sanctions.

Lawmakers fretted over communism in the labor movement. The presence of left-wing unionists in a defense plant offered a frequent pretext for congressional excursions. HUAC addressed the issue often; McCarthy, occasionally; House and Senate labor subcommittees paid close heed. The liberal anti-Communist Hubert Humphrey held an inquiry designed both to meet the problem and to protect clean unions from scattershot redbaiting. Lest unions be handled too softly, in 1952 Pat McCarran, Herman Welker, and John Marshall Butler conceived the formidably labeled "Task Force Investigating Communist Domination of Certain Labor Organizations."

Attacks on radical union leadership from both within and without the labor movement proliferated in the early 1950s. During 1952 hearings in Chicago, HUAC jousted with negotiators for the Communist-led United Electrical Workers just as they mounted a strike against International Harvester. In 1953 McCarthy's subcommittee also bedeviled UE locals in New York and Massachusetts. Such hearings often led to firings and encouraged or counterpointed raids by rival unions. They hastened the decline of the left wing of the labor movement.

The UE was beset on all sides. When the anti-communist International United Electrical Workers Union (IUE), led by James Carey, was founded, Truman Administration officials intoned blessings. The Atomic Energy Commission pressured employers like General Electric to freeze out the UE; IUE literature warned that plants represented by the UE would lose defense contracts. The CIO lavishly funded Carey's war with the UE. Three days before a 1950 election to decide control of a Pittsburgh area local, the vocal anti-Communist Judge Michael Musmanno arrived at a plant gate to campaign for the IUE. Bedecked in naval uniform, he was convoyed by a detachment of National Guardsmen, bayonets fixed and flags unfurled. Many local Catholic clergy urged their flocks to vote for the IUE on the basis of anti-communism. Carey's union won a narrow victory.

These labor wars sometimes produced odd bedfellows. Carey criticized McCarthy, but the latter's 1953 Boston hearings helped the IUE keep control of key GE plants in the area. GE management declared before the hearings that it would fire workers who admitted they were Reds; it would suspend those who declined to testify and, if they did not subsequently answer the charges, would dismiss them. Thus besieged, the UE often settled labor disputes on a take-what-it-could basis.

Where left-wing unions maintained reputations for effective bargaining, anti-communism had limited effect. The UE's tactical surrender of its youthful militancy probably eroded its rank-and-file support more than did any redbaiting. Yet the Longshoremen's Union, despite Smith Act prosecutions against its leaders in Hawaii and the effort to deport Harry Bridges, kept control of West Coast docks. (Indeed, having come to tolerate Bridges by the 1950s, business leaders had lost enthusiasm for persecuting him.) Similarly, the Mine, Mill and Smelter Workers Union held onto some strongholds despite recurrent redbaiting. Weaker leftist unions like the United Public Workers or the Fur and Leather Workers succumbed to raiding and harassment.

In an era when mainline labor was cautious, organizing initiatives often did originate with more radical unions and so fell prey to anti-Communist attack. In 1953 a CIO retail workers' union, some of whose organizers were Communists, struck stores in Port Arthur, Texas. A commission of inquiry named by Governor Allen Shivers (then seeking reelection) found "clear and present danger" of Communist sway over Texas labor. Shivers claimed he had foiled a Communist-led union's "well-laid plans to spread its tentacles all along the Gulf Coast and eventually into *your* community." Other Southern organizing drives succumbed to redbaiting too.

By the 1950s, labor's assertiveness had waned; where it persisted, it met defeat; and new organizing drives were few. Internal dissent—indeed, debate—was virtually stilled. Its momentum sapped and its membership reduced by over a third, the CIO merged with the AFL in a 1955 "shotgun wedding." Having won a place within the American consensus, labor paid a dear price to keep it.

Conservatives feared Communist influence in the nation's schools as well as in its factories. The influence of the "Reducators" and of subversive ideas that ranged, in various investigators' minds, from outright communism to "progressive education" perennially intrigued legislators at the state and national levels.

The Communists' long-running control of the New York Teachers Union alarmed the Senate Internal Security Subcommittee. Previously, the 1940–41 Rapp-Coudert inquiry had led to the dismissal of a number of New York City teachers. In 1949 the Board of Education began a new purge. From 1950 to early 1953, twenty-four teachers were fired and thirty-four resigned under investigation. By one estimate, over three hundred New York City teachers lost their jobs in the 1950s. SISS thus served to reinforce local activities with its 1952–53 hearings in New York City. The refusal by Teachers Union leaders to testify about their affiliations established grounds for their dismissal under Section 903 of the city charter.

Ultimately, the probers failed in their aim to expose Marxist-Leninist propagandizing in Gotham's classrooms. Bella Dodd, a former Communist and Teachers Union leader, claimed that Communist teachers who knew Party dogma "cannot help but slant their teaching in that direction." A Queens College professor said he knew a score of students whom the Communists had "ruined" and turned into "misfits." Yet aside from a few parents' complaints and "one case where I think we could prove it," the city's school superintendent had no evidence of indoctrination. Though Communists had obviously acquired great leverage in the Teachers Union, SISS located its best case of university subversion in a book about *China*.

HUAC quizzed educators too, but its scrutiny of the movie industry earned higher returns when it resumed its inquiry into Hollywood in 1951. By then the Hollywood Ten[*] were in prison, the film industry's opposition to HUAC was shattered, and the blacklist was growing. Fear washed through the movie lots. The economic distress visited on Hollywood by the growth of television further frazzled nerves. Said one witness, the renewed assault was "like taking a pot shot at a wounded animal." When subpoenaed, actress Gale Sondergaard asked the Screen Actors Guild for help, its board rebuffed her, likening her criticism of HUAC to the Communist line. The Screen Directors Guild made its members take a loyalty oath.

Yet few secrets were left to ferret out: the identity of Hollywood's Communists had long ceased to be a mystery. Early in the 1951 hearings, Congressman Francis Walter even asked why it was "material . . . to have the names of people when we already know them?" For HUAC, getting new information had become secondary to conducting ceremonies of exposure and penitence. Would the witness "name names" or not?

Of 110 witnesses subpoenaed in 1951, 58 admitted having had Party involvements. Some cogently explained why they had since disowned communism. Budd Schulberg recalled that while he was writing *What Makes Sammy Run,* the Party told him to submit an outline, confer with its literary authorities, and heed its artistic canons. *The Daily Worker* received his book favorably, but after being updated on Party aesthetics, the reviewer wrote a second piece thrashing the novel. One screenwriter recalled how the Party line on a studio painters' strike shifted perplexingly in 1945: we "could walk through the picket lines in February, and not in June."

Witnesses seeking to steer between punishment and fingering co-workers faced tearing ethical choices. Naming known Reds or those previously named might stave off harm, but this ploy was tinged with moral bankruptcy. Some soured ex-Communists did resist giving names, not wanting, in actor Larry Parks's phrase, to "crawl through the mud to be an informer." Some named each other; some said little, ducking quickly behind the Fifth Amendment. Others told all. The 155 names that writer Martin Berkeley gave set a record. Others gabbed freely. Parrying with humor the oft-asked question—would he defend America against the Soviets?—actor Will Geer, already middle-aged, cheerfully agreed to fight in his way: growing vegetables and entertaining the wounded. The idea of people his vintage shouldering arms amused him; wars "would be negotiated immediately."

---

[*][The Hollywood Ten were members of the film industry who refused to testify before Congress in 1947 about communist infiltration of the industry.—Ed.]

In this as in all inquiries, witnesses trod a path set with snares. The courts disallowed the Hollywood Ten's use of the First Amendment to avoid testifying, so a witness's only protection was the Fifth Amendment guarantee against self-incrimination. Even this route crossed minefields. *Blau v. U.S.* (1950) ruled that one might plead the Fifth legitimately to the question of Party membership. However, the 1950 case of *Rogers v. U.S.* dictated caution: one had to invoke the Fifth at the outset, not in the middle, of a line of questions inching toward incrimination. Having testified that she herself held a Party office, the court ruled, Jane Rogers had waived her Fifth Amendment privilege and could not then refuse to testify about others.

HUAC tried to quick-march Fifth-takers into pitfalls. One gambit was a logical fork: if answering would incriminate him, a witness might use the Fifth; but if innocent, he could not honestly do so. Thus, the committee held, the witness was either guilty or lying—even though the courts did not accept this presumption of guilt. However, a new odious category, the "Fifth-Amendment Communist," was born. Such witnesses, whether teachers, actors, or others, rarely hung onto their jobs.

Legal precedent also demanded care in testifying about associations. One witness pled the Fifth in response to the question of whether he was a member of the American Automobile Association. HUAC members enjoyed asking if witnesses belonged to the Ku Klux Klan, hoping to nettle them into breaking a string of refusals to answer. On their part, witnesses devised novel defenses like the so-called "diminished Fifth." A witness resorting to the "slightly diminished Fifth" would deny present CP membership but refuse to open up his past or that of others; those using the "fully diminished Fifth," on the other hand, testified about their own pasts but no one else's. (The "augmented Fifth" was like the slightly diminished Fifth, but the witness also disclaimed any sympathy for communism.)

The question of whether to testify freely or take the Fifth convulsed the higher precincts of American arts and letters. Writer Lillian Hellman, subpoenaed in 1952, took the bold step of writing HUAC's chairman that she would take the Fifth only if asked to talk about others. She realized that by answering questions about herself, she waived her privilege and was subject to a contempt citation, but better that than to "bring bad trouble" to innocent people. She simply would not cut her conscience "to fit this year's fashions." When she testified, she did invoke the Fifth but scored a coup with her eloquent letter and managed to avoid a contempt citation. In 1956 the playwright Arthur Miller also refused to discuss other people but, unlike Hellman, did not take the Fifth. (His contempt citation was later overturned.)

Art came to mirror politics. Miller had previously written *The Crucible*, whose hero welcomed death rather than implicate others in the seventeenth-century Salem witch trials. Admirers stressed the play's relevance to modern witch-hunts. In contrast, Elia Kazan, who had named names, directed the smash movie *On the Waterfront*, whose hero (Marlon Brando), implored by a fighting priest (Karl Malden) to speak out, agreed to inform against criminals in a longshoremen's union. None of these works dealt with communism, but their pertinence to current political issues was not lost. Among the arbiters of

American culture, these moral choices prompted heated debate, which still reverberated in the 1980s.

The issues were not only philosophical. The sanctions were real. Noncooperative witnesses were blacklisted, their careers in Hollywood shattered. Many drifted into other lines of work. Many became exiles, moving to Europe, Mexico, or New York. Some suffered writer's block. Some families endured steady FBI surveillance and such vexations as sharply increased life insurance premiums (for an assertedly dangerous occupation). Being blacklisted so dispirited several actors that their health was impaired, and premature death resulted. Comedian Philip Loeb, blacklisted and unemployable, his family destroyed, committed suicide in 1955.

Even though several hundred members of the entertainment industry forfeited their livelihoods after HUAC appearances, the studios, networks, producers, and the committee itself did not admit publicly that a blacklist existed. (Privately, some were candid. "Pal, you're dead," a soused producer told writer Millard Lampell. "They told me that I couldn't touch you with a barge pole.") In this shadow world, performers and writers wondered if their talents had indeed eroded. Had one's voice sharpened, one's humor dulled?

For blacklisting to work, HUAC's hammer needed an anvil. It was duly provided by other groups who willingly punished hostile or reluctant witnesses. American Legion publications spread the word about movies whose credits were fouled by subversion; Legionnaires (and other local true believers) could pressure theatre owners, if necessary, by trooping down to the Bijou to picket offending films. The mere threat of such forces soon choked off the supply of objectionable pictures at the source. Indeed, Hollywood, responding to broad hints from HUAC and to its own reading of the political climate, began making anti-Communist potboilers. These low-budget "B" pictures did poorly at the box office. They provided insurance, not profits.

Though entertainment industry moguls justified screening employees' politics by citing the threat from amateur censors, usually professional blacklisters made the system work. Blacklisting opened up business vistas on the Right. In 1950 American Business Consultants, founded by three ex-FBI agents, published *Red Channels,* a compendium listing 151 entertainers and their Communist-front links. *Counterattack,* an ABC publication started in 1947, periodically offered the same type of information. In 1953 an employee left ABC to establish Aware, Inc., which sold a similar service. Companies in show biz subscribed to these countersubversive finding aids and paid to have the names of those they might hire for a show or series checked against "the files." Aware charged five dollars to vet a name for the first time, two dollars for rechecks. It became habit for Hollywood, radio and TV networks, advertisers, and stage producers (though blacklisting had its weakest hold on Broadway) not to employ entertainers whose names cropped up in such files.

A few found ways to evade total proscription. Writers could sometimes submit work under pseudonyms. Studios asked some writers on the blacklist to doctor ailing scripts authored by others. The blacklisted writers received no screen credits and were paid a pittance, but at least they were working. Ostracized actors did not have this option. Said comedian Zero Mostel: "I am a man of a thousand faces, all of them blacklisted." A TV producer once called a talent agent to ask, "Who have you got like John Garfield?" He had Garfield himself, the agent exclaimed; but, of course, the blacklisted Garfield was taboo.

Unlike actors, blacklisted writers could also find work in television, which devoured new scripts ravenously. As in film, some used assumed names. Others worked through "fronts" (whence came the title of Woody Allen's 1976 movie). They wrote, but someone else put his name to the script (and might demand up to half of the income). Mistaken-identity plot twists worthy of a Restoration comedy resulted. One writer using a pseudonym wrote a script that he was asked, under a second pseudonym, to revise. Millard Lampell submitted a script under a phony name; the producers insisted that the script's writer appear for consultation; told that he was away and unavailable, they went for a quick fix: they asked Lampell to rewrite his own (unacknowledged) script.

The obverse of blacklisting was "clearance." Desperate actors or writers could seek absolution from a member of the anti-Communist industry. Often, not surprisingly, the person to see was one who had played a part in creating the blacklist. Roy Brewer, the chief of the International Alliance of Theatrical Stage Employees, had redbaited the leftist craft guilds, but helped rehabilitate blacklistees, as did several conservative newspaper columnists. The American Legion, which issued lists of Hollywood's undesirables, also certified innocence or repentance. A listee might get by with writing a letter to the Legion. Or he might be made to list suspect organizations he had joined and to tell why he joined, when he quit, who invited him in, and whom he had enticed. Thus the written route to clearance might also require naming names.

To regain grace, some sinners had to repent publicly, express robust patriotism in a speech or article, or confess to having been duped into supporting leftist causes. Typically, a blacklistee had to be willing to tell all to the FBI or to HUAC. Even liberal anti-Communists were "graylisted," and some had to write clearance letters. Humphrey Bogart had bought trouble by protesting the 1947 HUAC hearings against the Hollywood Ten. In his article, "I'm No Communist," he admitted he had been a "dope" in politics. Actor John Garfield, whose appearance before HUAC sent his career and life into a tailspin, was at the time of his death about to publish an article titled "I Was a Sucker for a Left Hook."

Like teachers and entertainers, charitable foundations also triggered the suspicion of congressional anti-Communists. These products of capitalism plowed back into society some of the vast wealth of their Robber Baron founders, but conservatives found their philanthropic tastes too radical. In 1952 a special House committee led by Georgia conservative Eugene Cox inquired into the policies of tax-exempt foundations. Did not "these creatures of the capitalist system," asked Cox, seek to "bring the system into disrepute" and to assume "a socialistic leaning"? . . .

❧

How deeply did anti-communism gouge the social and political terrain of the 1950s? With dissent defined as dangerous, the range of political debate

obviously was crimped. The number of times that books were labeled dangerous, thoughts were scourged as harmful, and speakers and performers were
rejected as outside the pale multiplied. Anti-Communist extremism and accompanying pressures toward conformity had impact in such areas as artistic expression, the labor movement, the cause of civil rights, and the status of minorities
in American life.

For some denizens of the Right, threats of Communist influence materialized almost anywhere. For instance, Illinois American Legionnaires warned
that the Girl Scouts were being spoonfed subversive doctrines. Jack Lait and
Lee Mortimer's yellow-journalistic *U.S.A. Confidential* warned parents against
the emerging threat of rock and roll. It bred dope use, interracialism, and sex
orgies. "We know that many platter-spinners are hopheads. Many others are
Reds, left-wingers, or hecklers of social convention." Not every absurdity
owed life to the vigilantes, however. A jittery Hollywood studio cancelled a
movie based on Longfellow's "Hiawatha" for fear it would be viewed as "Communist peace propaganda."

Books and ideas remained vulnerable. It is true that the militant Indiana
woman who abhorred *Robin Hood*'s subversive rob-from-the-rich-and-give-to-
the-poor message failed to get it banned from school libraries.Other locales
were less lucky. A committee of women appointed by the school board of
Sapulpa, Oklahoma, had more success. The board burned those books that it
classified as dealing improperly with socialism or sex. A spokesman claimed
that only five or six "volumes of no consequence" were destroyed. A librarian
in Bartlesville, Oklahoma, was fired for subscribing to the *New Republic,
Nation,* and *Negro Digest.* The use of UNESCO [United Nations Educational,
Scientific, and Cultural Organization] materials in the Los Angeles schools
became a hot issue in 1952. A new school board and superintendent were
elected with a mandate to remove such books from school libraries.

Local sanctions against unpopular artists and speakers often were effective.
In August 1950, a New Hampshire resort hotel banned a talk by Owen Lattimore
after guests, apparently riled by protests of the Daughters of the American Revo-
lution and others, remonstrated. Often local veterans—the American Legion and
Catholic War Veterans—initiated pressures. The commander of an American
Legion Post in Omaha protested a local production of a play whose author,
Garson Kanin, was listed in *Red Channels.* A founder of *Red Channels* warned an
American Legion anti-subversive seminar in Peoria, Illinois, that Arthur Miller's
Death of a Salesman, soon to appear locally, was "a Communist dominated play."
Jaycees and Legionnaires failed to get the theatre to cancel the play, but the
boycott they mounted sharply curbed the size of the audience.

Libraries often became focal points of cultural anxieties. Not every confrontation ended like those in Los Angeles or Sapulpa, but librarians felt they
were under the gun. "I just put a book that is complained about away for a
while," said one public librarian. Occasionally, books were burned. "Did you
ever try to burn a book?" asked another librarian. "It's *very* difficult." One
third of a group of librarians sampled in the late 1950s reported having
removed "controversial" items from their shelves. One-fifth said they habitually
avoided buying such books.

Academics, too, were scared. Many college and university social scientists polled in 1955 confessed to reining in their political views and activities. Twenty-seven percent had "wondered" whether a political opinion they had expressed might affect their job security or promotion; 40 percent had worried that a student might pass on "a warped version of what you have said and lead to false ideas about your political views." Twenty-two percent had at times "refrained from expressing an opinion or participating in some activity in order not to embarrass" their institution. Nine percent had "toned down" recent writing to avoid controversy. One teacher said he never expressed his own opinion in class. "I express the recognized and acknowledged point of view." Some instructors no longer assigned *The Communist Manifesto.*

About a hundred professors actually lost jobs, but an even greater number of frightened faculty trimmed their sails against the storm. Episodes far short of dismissal could also have a chilling effect. An economist at a Southern school addressed a business group, his talk, titled "Know Your Enemy," assessed Soviet resources and strengths. He was denounced to his president as a Communist. Another professor was assailed for advocating a lower tariff on oranges. "If I'd said potatoes, I wouldn't have been accused unless I had said it in Idaho." Some teachers got in mild trouble for such acts as assigning Robert and Helen Lynds' classic sociological study, *Middletown,* in class or listing the Kinsey reports on human sexuality as recommended reading. A professor once sent students to a public library to read works by Marx because his college's library had too few copies. Librarians logged the students' names.

The precise effect of all this professed anxiety was fuzzy. Many liberals claimed that Americans had been cowed into silence, that even honest anti-Communist dissent had been stilled, and that basic freedoms of thought, expression, and association had languished. The worriers trotted out appropriate comparisons: the witch trials in Salem, the Reign of Terror in France, the Alien and Sedition Acts, Know-Nothingism, and the Palmer raids. Justice William O. Douglas warned of "The Black Silence of Fear." Prominent foreigners like Bertrand Russell and Graham Greene decried the pall of fear they observed in America. On July 4, 1951, a *Madison Capital-Times* reporter asked passersby to sign a paper containing the Bill of Rights and parts of the Declaration of Independence. Out of 112, only one would do so. President Truman cited the episode to show McCarthyism's dire effects. McCarthy retorted that Truman owed an apology to the people of Wisconsin in view of that paper's Communist-line policies. Some McCarthy allies upheld the wisdom of refusing to sign any statement promiscuously offered.

McCarthy's defenders ridiculed the more outlandish laments for vanished liberties. A New York rabbi who blamed "McCarthyism" for the current spree of college "panty raids" offered a case in point. Conservative journalist Eugene Lyons was amused by an ACLU spokesman, his tonsils flaring in close-up on television, arguing "that in America no one any longer dares open his mouth." Such talk, said Lyons, led to "hysteria over hysteria." In their apologia for McCarthy, William F. Buckley and L. Brent Bozell snickered at such silliness. They found it odd that, in a time when left-of-center ideas were supposedly being crushed, liberals seemed to monopolize symposia sponsored by the major universities, even in McCarthy's home state, and that Archibald MacLeish and Bernard De Voto, two of those who condemned the enervating climate of fear, had still managed to garner two National Book Awards and a Pulitzer Prize. To Buckley and Bozell, the only conformity present was a proper one—a consensus that communism was evil and must be fought wholeheartedly.

But did such an argument miss the point? The successes enjoyed by prominent, secure liberals were one thing; far more numerous were the cases of those less visible and secure who lost entertainment and lecture bookings, chances to review books, teaching posts, even assembly-line jobs. The fight over the Communist menace had gone far beyond roistering debate or asserting the right of those who disagree with a set of views not to patronize them. People, a great number of whom had committed no crime, were made to suffer.

POSTSCRIPT

Did Communism Threaten America's Internal Security after World War II?

The "Venona Transcripts" represent only one set of sources depicting the Soviet spy apparatus in the United States. The Venona papers were not released to the public until 1995. Haynes and Klehr have also collaborated on two documentary collections based on the archives of the American Communist Party, which had been stored for decades in Moscow and were opened to foreign researchers in 1992. See *The Secret World of American Communism* (Yale University Press, 1995) and *The Soviet World of American Communism* (Yale University Press, 1998), both of which contain useful collections of translated Russian documents, which are virtually impossible to access. Haynes and Klehr's work also substantiates charges made by Allen Weinstein and his translator, former KGB agent Alexander Vassiliev, in *The Haunted Wood: Soviet Espionage in America—The Stalin Era* (Random House, 1999).

According to Fried, 24 teachers from New York City were fired and 34 resigned while under investigation between 1950 and early 1953. According to one estimate, over 300 teachers in the city lost their jobs because of their political beliefs. Similar dismissals also took place in public universities and colleges across the country. Book burnings were rare, but many public libraries discarded pro-Communist books or put them in storage. In Bartlesville, Oklahoma, in 1950, librarian Ruth Brown was fired from her job after 30 years ostensibly for circulating magazines like *The New Republic* and *The Nation,* which were deemed subversive. Actually, many agree that she was fired for supporting civil rights activism, a fact that the American Library Association left out in defending her. See Louise S. Robinson, *The Dismissal of Miss Ruth Brown: Civil Rights, Censorship, and the American Library* (University of Oklahoma Press, 2000). Four books represent a good starting point for students: M. J. Heale, *American Anticommunism: Combating the Enemy Within, 1830–1970* (Johns Hopkins University Press, 1990) extends Americans' fears of subversion back to the Jackson years; Ellen Schrecker, *The Age of McCarthyism: A Brief History With Documents* (Bedford Books, 1994) blames both parties for the excesses of the anti-Communist assault against radicals who were fighting against status quo race relations in the 1930s and 1940s; John Earl Haynes, *Red Scare or Red Menace? American Communism and Anticommunism in the Cold War Era* (Ivan R. Dee, 1996), which argues that anticommunism was a reasonable response to a real threat; and Richard Gid Powers, *Not Without Honor: The History of American Anticommunism* (Free Press, 1995), which portrays anticommunism as a mainstream political movement with many variations.

Powers' interpretation has been challenged by Ellen Schrecker's full scale *Many Are the Crimes: McCarthyism in America* (Princeton University

Press, 1999), which is even more radical in the critique of the "Real Scare" than Fried. Most of the recent writings about the 1950s have been supportive of Cold War liberal attitudes. Allen Weinstein, *Perjury: Hiss Chamber* (Knoff, 1978) and Ronald Radosh and Joyce Milton, *The Rosenberg File: A Search for the Truth* (Holt, Rinehart, and Winston, 1983) find at least Julius Rosenberg guilty of spying. Sam Tannerhous, current editor of *The New York Times Book Review* is sympathetic to *Whitteker Chamber: A Biography* (Random House, 1997). A good summary of the literature is found in John Earl Haynes, "The Cold War Debate Continues: A Traditionalist Look at Historical Writing on Domestic Communication and Anti-communism," *The Journal of Cold War Studies* (Winter 2000).

Biographies of Senator McCarthy are generally critical. Academic standards are Thomas Reeves, *The Life and Times of Joe McCarthy* (Stein and Day, 1982) and David M. Oshinsky, *A Conspiracy So Immense: The World of Joe McCarthy* (Free Press, 1983). More fun to read is former *New Yorker* reporter Richard Rovere's *Senator Joe McCarthy* (Harcourt, Brace, Jovanovich, 1959). More recently, Arthur Herman has praise, with qualifications, in *Joseph McCarthy: Reexamining the Life and Legacy of America's Most Hated Senator* (Free Press, 2000).

Two older collections of essays on McCarthyism are Allen J Matusow, ed., *Joseph McCarthy* (Prentice Hall, 1970) and Earl Lathum, ed., *The Meaning of McCarthyism* (D.C. Heath, 1973). In 2003, Green Haven Press published the most recent collection of essays on the McCarthy Hearings.

ISSUE 4

Should President Truman Have Fired General MacArthur?

YES: John S. Spanier, from "The Politics of the Korean War," in Phil Williams, Donald M. Goldstein, and Henry L. Andrews, Jr., eds., *Security in Korea: War, Stalemate, and Negotiation* (Westview Press, 1994)

NO: D. Clayton James with Anne Sharp Wells, from *Refighting the Last War: Command and Crisis in Korea, 1950–1953* (Free Press, 1993)

ISSUE SUMMARY

YES: Professor of political science John S. Spanier argues that General Douglas MacArthur was fired because he publicly disagreed with the Truman administration's "Europe first" policy and its limited war strategy of containing communism in Korea.

NO: Biographer D. Clayton James and assistant editor Anne Sharp Wells argue that General MacArthur was relieved of duty because there was a lack of communication between the Joint Chiefs of Staff and the headstrong general, which led to a misperception over the appropriate strategy in fighting the Korean War.

$\mathbf{O}$n June 25, 1950, North Korea launched a full-scale attack against South Korea. President Harry S. Truman assumed that the Russians were behind the attack and that they wanted to extend communism into other parts of Asia. The United Nations Security Council unanimously passed a resolution condemning North Korea's well-planned, concerted, and full-scale invasion of South Korea and asked for a halt to the invasion and a withdrawal back to the 38th parallel.

The South Koreans, meanwhile, sent Truman a desperate appeal for help, and the president responded quickly. He bypassed Congress and did not ask for an official declaration of war. Instead he responded to the UN resolutions and ordered General Douglas MacArthur to use American naval and air forces to attack North Korean military targets south of the 38th parallel.

It soon became clear that South Korean ground troops could not withstand North Korea's well-coordinated attack. In response, Truman increased

America's military presence by ordering a naval blockade of North Korea and air attacks north of the 38th parallel. Sixteen nations sent troops, but South Korea and the United States contributed 90 percent of the ground troops, and the United States alone supplied 93 percent of the air forces and 85 percent of the naval forces. By September there were 210,000 American ground forces, and MacArthur was the UN commander.

At first the war went badly for the UN forces. The inexperienced South Korean and American troops were nearly pushed off the peninsula until they established a strong defensive perimeter near the southeastern tip of Korea. Then MacArthur launched an amphibious attack on Inchon, near the western end of the 38th parallel, which caught the North Koreans by surprise. Thousands surrendered and others fled across the 38th parallel chased by UN troops.

The attempt to unify the Korean peninsula under a pro-Western, anti-communist government was short-lived. MacArthur had assured Truman at their only face-to-face meeting in mid-October that the Chinese Communists would not enter the war. The general was mistaken. In late November contingents of "Chinese volunteers" entered North Korea and attacked the overextended UN forces. Instead of going home for Christmas as MacArthur had predicted, UN troops were soon pushed back into South Korea. Seoul, the capital of South Korea, was again captured by the Communists in January 1951. By the spring of 1951, however, UN troops had successfully pushed the Chinese Communists back across the 38th parallel.

As early as December 1950, the Truman administration had decided to shift its policy in Korea back to its original goal: contain communist expansion in Korea and restore the status quo prior to the North Korean attack of June 25. Since UN troops were in control of South Korea by the spring of 1951, Truman decided that the UN command would issue a statement that it was ready to arrange a cease-fire. No concessions were made to the Chinese, but it held out the possibility of negotiating broader issues in Asia.

The announcement proposing a truce was never made. When the Joint Chiefs of Staff informed MacArthur of the State Department's proposal, he undercut Truman by issuing his own directive to the Chinese, threatening to expand the war to the "coastal areas and intern bases" of China unless the enemy's commander-in-chief met with MacArthur to end the war and fulfill "the political objectives" of the UN forces in Korea.

Truman boiled over. He relieved MacArthur of all his duties in the Far East. It would be two years and three months before the new president, Dwight D. Eisenhower, would sign the truce accords ending the Korean War.

Should President Truman have fired General MacArthur? In the following selections, John S. Spanier provides a strong defense of Truman's limited war policy. He maintains that MacArthur should have been fired for his public disagreement with this policy of containing communism in Korea. D. Clayton James and Anne Sharp Wells argue that MacArthur was relieved because there was a lack of communication between the Joint Chiefs of Staff and the headstrong general and a misperception over the appropriate strategy in fighting the Korean War.

YES

John S. Spanier

The Politics of the Korean War

Introduction

Prior to June 25, 1950, Korea was outside the U.S. defense perimeter. On June 25, however, the defense of South Korea rose from low to highest priority as U.S. policy-makers considered the consequences of North Korea's aggression, aggression that they believed could not have occurred without Soviet instigation or support.

There were several reasons for this. First, South Korea, while not a U.S. ally, was an American protégé; Washington had helped the South Korean government with economic and military aid and had a responsibility toward the regime it had created.

Second, had the North Koreans gained control over the entire peninsula, they would, in the metaphor used by the Japanese, have "pointed the Korean dagger straight at Japan's heart." After Nationalist China's collapse in 1949, the United States needed Japan as an ally. It thus had to defend South Korea; otherwise, Japan might have chosen a neutral stance in the Cold War, which, with the attack on South Korea, had spread from Europe to Asia.

A third reason for the U.S. intervention was to preserve the recently established North Atlantic Treaty Organization (NATO). In the absence of a strong response in Korea, the United States commitment to Western Europe would have had no credibility.

Finally, the United States sought to achieve a broader milieu goal. President Truman recalled that, during the 1930s, the democracies, working through the League of Nations, had failed to react to the aggressions of Italy, Japan, and Germany. This failure had encouraged further aggression, destroyed the League, and eventually resulted in World War II. The United States wanted a post-war world free from aggression: the United Nations (UN) was still new and was widely perceived as a symbol of a more peaceful world. A failure to act in South Korea, therefore, would not only whet the appetite of the Soviet Union, but would also undermine the UN.

The resulting defense of South Korea was America's first experience with limited war. The interests at stake were compatible with the restoration of the status quo ante; the total defeat of North Korea, the unconditional surrender

From John S. Spanier, "The Politics of the Korean War," in Phil Williams, Donald M. Goldstein, and Henry L. Andrews, Jr., eds., *Security in Korea: War, Stalemate, and Negotiation* (Westview Press, 1994). Copyright © 1994 by Westview Press, a member of the Perseus Books Group, LLC. Reprinted by permission. Notes omitted.

of its armed forces, and the elimination of its government were not, as in World War II, a prerequisite for the achievement of American objectives. A limited war was the rational response to a less than total challenge. It would have made little sense for the United States to defend South Korea by attacking the Soviet Union because it believed Moscow to be the source of aggression. That would have been irrational; countries do not risk their existence for limited, although very important, interests.

This was particularly so in the nuclear era. It was no longer "a question of *whether* to fight a limited war, but of *how* to avoid fighting any other kind." Limited war would allow the United States to escape the all-or-nothing alternative—inaction or attacking the Soviet Union (later, as the U.S. and Soviet nuclear arsenals grew, referred to as suicide-or-surrender alternatives)— ensuring the walls of containment would not be breached and allowing the United States to pursue containment at an acceptable risk and cost without risking a war with the Soviet Union. . . .

The Drive to the Yalu

By definition, the key problem in a limited war is escalation. Escalation may, of course, be a perfectly acceptable, even desirable, course of action under certain circumstances as, for instance, in cease-fire negotiations. Attacking certain targets previously left as "privileged sanctuaries," for example, could provide the extra incentive needed for the adversary to be more conciliatory and end hostilities. However, it should be the political leaders who weigh the military and political risks and costs of escalation. Escalation should be a deliberate, conscious choice, not a quick response to a battlefield decision taken by the theater commander. To grant the theater commander the freedom to conduct the military campaign as he sees fit is to surrender this critical control.

The war, after the American-led forces crossed the thirty-eighth parallel, was a model of how *not* to fight a limited war. Beginning in late October, there were increasing reports of clashes between Chinese troops and South Korean and then American forces. In early November, MacArthur, in his flamboyant style, denounced the Chinese Communist intervention as one of the most flagrant violations of international law in history. Just as soon as he made this announcement, however, the Chinese Communist forces disengaged, arousing considerable speculation about the purpose of the Chinese intervention in Korea. Was it to protect the hydroelectric dams on the Yalu River? Was it to establish a deeper buffer zone, ranging from the narrow neck above Pyongyang, North Korea's capital, to the Yalu River frontier in order to keep U.S. troops at some distance and ensure they would not cross into China? Was it to drive American forces back to the thirty-eighth parallel, restoring the status quo ante? Or was it the total defeat of the coalition forces, unifying all of Korea in the process, the original North Korean objective?

No one really knew. The most likely aim seemed to be some sort of buffer. The initial intervention, followed by the breakoff, might have been intended to communicate to the American government not to approach the Chinese frontier with non-South Korean troops; or perhaps it was for all UN forces to stay south of a buffer area. In any event, the Chinese disengagement may have been intended to explore political solutions that would either preclude Chinese intervention altogether or limit it to northern-most Korea.

Even if it was only a ruse to gain time and build up Chinese forces for a drive to push the Americans into the sea, it is doubtful Chinese leaders were in full agreement about the desirability of a war with the world's most powerful country at a time when the Chinese hold on the mainland was not yet secure and the new regime faced mounting economic problems. Had diplomacy yielded an acceptable alternative that would have provided the new regime with security, a massive Chinese intervention with all its consequences might have been avoided.

Perhaps Truman's decision to pick his general and then let him determine how best to wage the war would have been workable with a general more in sympathy with administration objectives (like Matthew Ridgway, MacArthur's successor) or a less prestigious and politically powerful general, even if he were not particularly sympathetic to administration goals (like Mark Clark). Unfortunately, it proved impossible with MacArthur, the American viceroy in Tokyo.

Although MacArthur enthusiastically endorsed the President's decision in June and swore total loyalty, it was not long before the surface unity between Washington and Tokyo started to come apart. In late July, instead of sending one of his generals to gather information for the Joint Chiefs of Staff about the defensibility of Formosa, MacArthur decided personally to visit the island. At the end of his visit, MacArthur issued a statement warmly praising Chiang, who returned the compliment in a statement that referred not only to plans for the joint defense of Formosa, but talked of having laid the foundation for "Sino-American military cooperation." This suggestion of broader Nationalist-MacArthur (rather than U.S.) cooperation must have concerned the mainland regime, already upset by the second U.S. intervention in the Chinese civil war. MacArthur dismissed criticisms of his visit when he declared the purpose of his trip, which had been strictly military, had been "maliciously misrepresented to the public by those who invariably in the past have propagandized a policy of defeatism and appeasement in the Pacific."

Then, instead of leaving well enough alone, MacArthur sent a long message to the annual conference of the Veterans of Foreign Wars. He elaborated on the strategic significance of Formosa and declared that United States policy on Formosa came from defeatists and appeasers who did not "understand the Orient . . . (and) Oriental psychology," a specialty he had long claimed for himself. When the administration, the target of these verbal attacks, already irritated by MacArthur's visit to Formosa, learned of MacArthur's message, he was ordered to withdraw it—although by then it was too late to stop its widespread dissemination because it had been sent to press associations, newspapers, and magazines.

These were early indications that MacArthur was an uncontrollable force. His position, however, was strengthened when, on the day the Chinese forces broke off contact, the Republicans in the mid-term election increased their Senate representation by five to forty-seven and House representation by twenty-eight to 199 (with the Democrats holding 235 seats). Even more notable still was the defeat of several senior Democratic senators, like Scott Lucas, the majority leader, Millard Tydings, chairman of the Senate Armed Services Committee, and Francis Myers, the Democratic Whip (the first two were targets of Senator McCarthy). Reelected were Republican conservatives Robert Taft (now the party's leading presidential candidate for 1952), Eugene Milliken, Homer Capehart, and Alexander Wiley. Also elected on the Republican side were such pro-Nationalist and pro-McCarthy figures as Nixon and Dirksen.

The election was clearly overshadowed by McCarthy's tactics, McCarthy's charges and McCarthy's imitators. The upshot was to enhance McCarthy's influence in the Senate and the country and strengthen MacArthur's hand in the conduct of the Korean War as the Republicans stepped up their attacks of appeasement and "softness on Communism" on an administration that, by any objective standards, had repeatedly demonstrated its tough anti-Communist foreign policy. The political price for Truman to take on MacArthur had gone up. MacArthur must have felt virtually untouchable; he certainly acted as if he were.

His orders as he advanced into North Korea were quite specific: he was to destroy the Communist forces, provided that there were no signs of impending or actual Chinese or Soviet intervention; as a matter of policy, he was to use only South Korean troops near the Chinese and Soviet frontiers in order to eliminate any possibility of provocation. Secretary of Defense George Marshall sent him a directive stating he was to feel unhampered tactically and strategically in proceeding north of the parallel, words intended to apply to the crossing of the parallel, but which MacArthur interpreted to mean that he could wage the campaign as he saw fit.

Thus, in late October, MacArthur authorized the use of all ground forces in the drive toward the Yalu, despite the earlier orders against sending any but South Korean forces to the Chinese frontier. The Secretary of Defense and the Joint Chiefs, all junior officers when MacArthur was already a general, handled MacArthur with great solicitousness. The Secretary of State called their approach "timorous."

Perhaps MacArthur had sound reasons for issuing his authorization to proceed north, the JCS said; they "would like information of these reasons since the action contemplated was a matter of concern to them." MacArthur fired back that it was a matter of "military necessity" because of the inadequacies of the South Korean Army. The Army Chief of Staff, General Joseph L. (Lighting Joe) Collins, finding this explanation incredible, considered MacArthur's action a clear violation of his orders and was concerned MacArthur might fail to consult the JCS in a more serious situation.

A second clash between the JCS and MacArthur occurred on the 7th of November, the day after MacArthur had informed the world about the Chinese intervention, when he ordered a bombing attack on the Korean ends of the bridges across the Yalu. When his air component commander Far East Air Force Commander Lieutenant General George E. Stratemeyer checked this order with Washington, the Joint Chiefs were upset. They were concerned that some of the bombs might land on Chinese soil at the very moment when a UN meeting on the Chinese intervention was about to take place and the United States wanted support for a resolution calling on the Chinese to halt their aggression. Bombing along the Yalu would only intensify China's antagonism. While the President was willing to authorize the bombing if there were an immediate and serious threat to U.S. forces, MacArthur had sent no such message. His last message to the JCS on November 4 had been optimistic. He had doubted the Chinese intervention was a full-scale one; the message's tone was one of "don't worry." MacArthur was therefore reminded of previous orders that no bombing closer than five miles to the Chinese frontier was permitted.

MacArthur, furious, shot back a message that men and materiel were "pouring" across all bridges over the Yalu from Manchuria, not just jeopardizing, but threatening "the ultimate destruction" of UN forces. Every hour the bombing was postponed "will be paid for dearly in American and other United Nations blood." Stating he could not accept responsibility for the major calamity that would follow if he were not permitted to bomb the bridges, he demanded the chiefs bring this matter to the President's attention. Truman, seeking to avoid trouble if the issue became public, permitted the bombing to proceed, warning MacArthur again of the danger of escalating the conflict.

Thus, MacArthur, appealing over his military superiors' heads to the Commander in Chief himself, was allowed to do what he had initially intended to do through a fait accompli. He then followed this with a public message that the Chinese had not only grossly violated international law by their intervention, but that more Chinese forces were in reserve in the "privileged sanctuary" of Manchuria. He hinted that this privilege might not last. The chairman of the Joint Chiefs, General Omar Bradley, wrote afterwards that "this night we committed the worst possible error. . . . Right then—that night— the JCS should have taken the firmest control of the Korean War and dealt with MacArthur bluntly." The chiefs were concerned, however, that if they ordered him to a more defensible line across North Korea's "narrow waist," there would be "another burst of outrage, perhaps a tumultuous resignation and angry public charges of appeasement" just as the voters were showing up at the polls.

The climax in this tug of war between Washington and the general came over his decision to launch a "home by Christmas" offensive on November 24 with his forces on the left separated from those on the right (permitting the Chinese to drive through this center). In the weeks leading up to this, disaster might have been averted had MacArthur been ordered to take up defensive positions. The difficulty was that he would have claimed Washington was denying him victory and he might have had to be relieved. Consequently, everyone hesitated and wavered and lost the opportunity to ward off a catastrophe. General Ridgway thought the JCS held MacArthur in "almost superstitious awe" as a "larger than life military figure who had so often been right when everyone else had been wrong." Thus, they were afraid to challenge him and give him a flat order not to advance forward and split his thinly spread armies when Chinese intervention appeared probable and imminent. "Why don't the Joint Chiefs send orders to MacArthur and tell him what to do?"

Ridgway asked one of the JCS members. "He wouldn't obey the orders. What can we do?" he was told in reply.

Recent evidence suggests the Chinese may have intended a full-scale intervention from the beginning. Nevertheless, it is clear that by not exploring alternatives to the advance to the Yalu and, above all, not restraining MacArthur in order to avoid domestic turmoil, the administration ensured an escalation that prolonged the war to 1953 and only postponed the inevitable clash with its head-strong theater commander.

MacArthur's Dismissal

When, on November 24, MacArthur launched his offensive and the Chinese launched theirs, the UN Command faced what the general called a "new war." MacArthur called for new guidelines. His recommendations were: a naval blockade of the Chinese coast; air bombardment of China's industrial complex, communication network, supply depots, and troop assembly points; the reinforcement of UN troops with Chinese Nationalist troops; and diversionary actions with a possible second front on the mainland facing Formosa.

There is also some evidence MacArthur recommended the use of atomic weapons, although he denied it publicly. These measures MacArthur assured the JCS, would not only win in Korea, but "severely cripple and largely neutralize China's capability to wage aggressive war" and thereby "save Asia from the engulfment otherwise facing it." While publicly claiming his prescription was a formula for victory in Korea, MacArthur had a broader objective, namely, to take advantage of Communist China's intervention to wage a preventive war. Ridgway, who took over the retreating army in Korea and was MacArthur's eventual successor, believed that MacArthur's concept of victory "was no less than the global defeat of communism."

MacArthur also made clear that, if his recommendations were rejected his command would have to be evacuated or be subjected to steady attrition. He could not defeat the Chinese forces unless the restraints imposed by Washington—which were "without precedent in history"—were lifted. Either Washington should let him conduct the war as he saw fit—and then he would win—or the United States should withdraw from Korea altogether.

This either-or position was very suspect in Washington. There was an underlying sense that MacArthur was deliberately exaggerating his predicament in order to compel the administration to accept his recommendations. Indeed, to Ridgway, MacArthur's suggestion of throwing in the towel without putting up any fight and his failure to go to Korea and use some of his famous rhetoric to rally his troops were disgraceful. Bradley wondered why an army with superior ground firepower and complete air superiority could not stem the Chinese advance, especially as Chinese logistical lines became longer and more vulnerable to air strikes.

Truman, in addition, felt MacArthur was trying to allay responsibility for the failure of his offensive by saying "he would have won the war except for the fact that we (in Washington) would not let him have his way . . . I should have relieved General MacArthur then and there." The reason Truman did not do this, he said, was he did not wish it to appear that MacArthur was being fired because the offensive had failed. "I have never believed in going back on people when luck is against them. . .."

The administration therefore did two things. It sent MacArthur a directive, addressed to all officials, that foreign and military policy statements were not to be released until cleared by the State or Defense Departments. It also sent General Collins to Korea. In December, while UN forces were still retreating, Collins reported back to the JCS that the situation was not as critical as MacArthur had pictured it and Korea could be held. MacArthur, however, persisted in his demand that the limitations be lifted and his forces be reinforced or evacuated.

When Collins returned to Korea in January 1951, along with the Air Force Chief of Staff, General Hoyt S. Vandenberg, they discovered General Ridgway, who had been there less than a month, had revitalized the army. From that point, Washington:

> Looked beyond MacArthur to Ridgway for reliable military assessments and guidance. Although we continued to address JCS messages and directives to MacArthur, there was a feeling that MacArthur had been 'kicked upstairs' to chairman of the board and was, insofar as military operations were concerned, mainly a prima donna figurehead who had to be tolerated.

The Republicans, however, did not share the administration's assessment. The Republican right, true to its pre-war isolationism with its twin traditions of rejecting entangling alliances with European states and favoring unilateralism in Asia, opposed sending troops to Europe because that might provoke the Soviets whose manpower the United States could not match. It did so while supporting MacArthur's course of action, even though this would deepen the U.S. involvement in a war with Communist China, which also had vastly superior manpower resources.

The shock of Chinese intervention and the headlong U.S. retreat led the Truman Administration to reject MacArthur's military prescriptions. There were several reasons for this. First, the JCS doubted that air and naval power and the imposition of blockade could bring the conflict to an early conclusion. The successful implementation of MacArthur's strategy would require, contrary to the general's assessment, large reinforcements. Indeed, General Omar N. Bradley, the Chairman of the Joint Chiefs of Staff, thought the only way to gain a decisive result would be to fight an all-out war with China, which would be a lengthy affair and require a large commitment of U.S. forces.

A second concern was that MacArthur's recommendations might bring the Soviet Union into the conflict. The Soviet Union could no more afford to see Communist China defeated than China could tolerate the defeat of North Korea. Indeed, the Soviet Union, not Communist China, was America's principal and most powerful enemy. Therefore, the United States had to concentrate its focus and resources on Western Europe, which, as two world wars had amply demonstrated, was America's "first line of defense." The country could not afford to squander its huge, but nonetheless finite resources in what General

Bradley described as "the wrong war, at the wrong place, at the wrong time, and with the wrong enemy." If there was a right war in the right place, it would have been with the Soviet Union, the primary enemy, fought in Europe, the area of primary security interest. However, the United States did not think it was ready for such a conflict in 1950 and 1951. Ever since the Soviet atomic explosion in 1949, Washington believed that, until the United States had built up its nuclear strength, in part to balance Soviet conventional superiority, it was imperative to avoid confrontation with Moscow.

Third, the European allies strongly opposed MacArthur for the same reasons as the administration: his prescription, if followed, would divert U.S. attention and power away from Europe and risk war with the Soviet Union. The allies were also dismayed by Washington's inability to control or discipline MacArthur. The result was a declining confidence in American political leadership and judgment. Moreover, the European members of NATO sought to counter the pressure exercised on the administration from the right. They were reluctant to condemn China and impose sanctions, in part because they felt MacArthur was not blameless in provoking China's intervention and in part because they feared a condemnation of China would strengthen those forces in the United States that wanted a war with China. The administration, caught in the middle, ultimately managed to obtain support in the UN for a resolution condemning Communist China, but at a price: no follow-up military action.

Thus, the unity of the Atlantic alliance was preserved. MacArthur and the Republicans threatened the cohesion of the alliance, one of the key reasons for the administration's defense of South Korea. Indeed, the United States could not simultaneously "go it alone" in Asia, as MacArthur and his supporters wanted, and pursue a policy of collective security in Europe.

After the Chinese intervention, the Administration took seriously the principles of crisis management, such as presidential control of military options, avoiding options likely to motivate the enemy to escalate, pauses in military operations, and coordinating military moves with political-diplomatic action. The administration also reverted to its initial objective of protecting only the security of South Korea. Without ever explicitly admitting it had made a mistake in crossing the thirty-eighth parallel, the administration recognized that the attempt to reunite Korea and eliminate Communist North Korea had led to a dangerous escalation. Ending the war could only be achieved by restoring the status quo ante on the Korean peninsula.

Further clashes with MacArthur were inevitable, as he was unwilling to reconcile himself to a war limited to Korea and the defense of only South Korea. As MacArthur saw the issue, the only way to prevent future Chinese Communist military expansion was by destroying its capability to wage war now. Negotiations to end the war on the basis of the status quo ante would leave China's war potential intact and, therefore, had to be prevented. The administration's assessment was very different. As UN forces approached the thirty-eighth parallel once more, after having imposed very heavy casualties upon the Chinese, the administration, unwilling to attempt forced reunification a second time, sought to explore the possibilities of ending hostilities on the basis of the prewar partition of the country. Washington believed that if made without threat or recrimination, such an offer might be well received in Beijing.

MacArthur was informed on March 20 that the President, after consultation with the allies, would announce his willingness to discuss suitable terms for concluding the war. On March 24, the general issued his own statement. Pointing out China's failure to conquer all of Korea despite its numerical superiority and the restrictions placed upon him, MacArthur suggested that the enemy "must by now be painfully aware that a decision of the United Nations to depart from its tolerant effort to contain the war to the area of Korea, through expansion of our military operations to his coastal areas and interior bases would doom Red China to the risk of imminent military collapse." He then offered to confer with the Chinese military commander about ending the fighting and achieving the UN objectives without being burdened by such "extraneous matters" as Formosa and China's seat in the UN.

By delivering this virtual ultimatum, asking Beijing to admit that it had lost the war or face an expansion of the conflict and total defeat, MacArthur sought to undercut the administration's effort to achieve a cease-fire and start negotiations to end the war. In a letter to the Republican Minority Leader in the House, Representative Joseph W. Martin, Jr., written on the 19th of March, but not released until April 5, the general elaborated that the restrictions imposed upon him were not in accord with "the conventional pattern of meeting force with maximum counter-force," which "we never failed to do in the past." He said Martin's view of allowing Chiang to open a second front on the Chinese mainland was "in conflict with neither logic nor tradition." The war in Asia must be met with "determination and not half-measures," for it was in Asia that the critical battle was being fought; if this battle was lost, Europe's fall would be inevitable.

The President was furious. MacArthur was continuing to challenge the principle of civilian authority. Not surprisingly, therefore, Truman fired MacArthur. It probably should have been done months earlier, but politically it was a risky and unpopular thing to do. MacArthur himself had finally left Truman with no option. Nevertheless, given the political situation in the United States, it took great courage for the President to fire the General. Indeed, the dismissal created a political furor.

Whether the dismissal of MacArthur encouraged the Chinese to begin cease-fire negotiations shortly afterwards is not known, but it had to reassure them that China itself would not be attacked and that U.S. aims no longer included the forceful unification of Korea. This was reaffirmed by the administration in the congressional hearings held after MacArthur returned triumphantly home. To the degree that there were internal differences in the Chinese leadership about the terms on which to settle the war, MacArthur's firing and administration statements may have strengthened those who—as in the U.S. government—were willing to settle on the basis of the pre-war division. The Soviets also appeared ready to explore the ending of hostilities; it was their UN representative who, responding to U.S. feelers, publicly declared (somewhat obliquely) in June that the Soviet people believed peace was possible.

It is also unknown to what extent the situation on the battlefield contributed to the Chinese and Soviet willingness to negotiate. Ridgway had not only rallied his demoralized and retreating army, but honed it into a deadly fighting force. He stopped repeated Chinese offensives in early 1951 by inflicting immense casualties on Chinese troops through the effective use of artillery and air power. Having suffered about a half million casualties in the eight months since the intervention and, with their May offensive broken, the Chinese were demoralized, unable to resist Ridgway's offensive, and placed on the defensive as their long logistical lines were exposed to constant air attacks and the supply situation became desperate.

Had the administration been willing to continue the offensive, the Chinese would have been in danger of being driven back, perhaps to North Korea's narrow neck. This might have encouraged China to conclude the war before their armies were ripped apart. Instead, when the Soviets and Chinese suggested that they were willing to talk about a cease-fire, the administration immediately agreed and halted the offensive. Pressured by public opinion to end the war and unsure that it could count on domestic support for such a tough bargaining strategy, the administration was unwilling to sacrifice more American lives in order to end the war at lines slightly north of where it had begun. The expectation was of a fairly rapid conclusion to the war. Thus, the cost of the Truman Administration's political weakness and inability to coordinate policy and strategy, so characteristic of the American belief that the two were divorced and that diplomacy would follow the use of force, was very high.

In the event, the negotiations dragged on until 1953. In stopping the offensive, the administration had inadvertently ensured the continuation of the war. The Chinese, reinforced, continued to resist, delaying a settlement while seeking to improve the terms for ending the war at little cost to themselves. During that time, 20,000 Americans were killed, more than in the first year of the war; among all UN forces, the figure of those who died in battle was about twice that of the earlier period.

The tragic irony was that the final terms President Eisenhower accepted were little different from those proposed by the UN early in the negotiations; but Eisenhower could accept terms that Truman could not. The Republican President, a moderate who had opposed Senator Taft for the nomination, was immune to charges by his party's right wing of appeasement and "coddling Communism" (not that it did not try, but finally, forced to fight, Eisenhower destroyed McCarthy). However, Harry Truman, a Democrat, despite his staunch record of anti-Communism in Europe and the containment of Soviet power, was vulnerable to such scurrilous charges even though the United States could have done little to prevent Chiang's regime from committing political suicide. Harry Truman, who had succeeded Franklin Roosevelt when he died, could have run for a second term in 1952. Instead, he chose not to run.

D. Clayton James with
Anne Sharp Wells

 **NO**

MacArthur's Dare Is Called

Differences in Strategy

The dismissal of General [Douglas] MacArthur in April 1951 is a watershed in the history of American strategic direction in the Korean conflict. For the ensuing two years and three months of hostilities and truce negotiations no major challenge would be offered to the Truman administration's manner of limiting the war except for a few Allied leaders who urged more compromises with the communists at Panmunjom than the American wished to make for the sake of a quicker end to the fighting. With the removal of MacArthur, moreover, the post-1945 trend of increasing input by the State Department of military policy was accelerated. By the bellicose nature of his criticism of the Truman administration's direction of the war, MacArthur had placed himself in the position of championing a military solution in Korea in the American tradition of preferring strategies of annihilation, instead of attrition. He left the scene as an uncompromising warrior, though, in actuality, his differences with Truman were not as simplistic as they appeared. During World War II, as in the Korean conflict, for instance, he had argued for a balanced global strategy that accorded high priorities to not only Europe but also Asia and the Pacific. In view of the sites where American boys have died in combat since 1945, perhaps that and other arguments of the fiery old general need not have been dismissed so lightly.

Contrary to popular accounts, the strategic aspect of the Truman–MacArthur controversy was not based on the President's advocacy of limited war and the general's alleged crusading for a global war against communism. MacArthur wanted to carry the war to Communist China in air and sea operations of restricted kinds, but he never proposed expanding the ground combat into Manchuria or North China. Both Washington and Tokyo authorities were acutely aware that the Korean struggle could have escalated into World War III if the Soviet Union had gone to war, but at no time did MacArthur wish to provoke the USSR into entering the Korean War. He predicted repeatedly that none of his actions would lead to Soviet belligerency, which, he maintained steadfastly, would be determined by Moscow's own strategic interests and its own timetable.

Yet there were significant strategic differences between Truman and MacArthur. The "first war," against North Korea, did not produce any major

From D. Clayton James with Anne Sharp Wells, *Refighting the Last War: Command and Crisis in Korea, 1950–1953* (Free Press, 1993). Copyright © 1993 by D. Clayton James. Reprinted by permission of The Free Press, an imprint of Simon & Schuster Adult Publishing Group. Notes omitted.

collisions between the general and Washington except on Formosa policy, which did not reach its zenith until the Communist Chinese were engaged in Korea. The strategic plans of MacArthur for a defensive line at the Naktong, for an amphibious stroke through Inchon and Seoul, and for a drive north of the 38th parallel all had the blessings of the President and the Joint Chiefs before they reached their operational stages. Even the Far East commander's plans for separate advances by the Eighth Army and the X Corps into North Korea and for an amphibious landing at Wonsan, though they raised eyebrows in Washington, did not draw remonstrances from his superiors, who viewed such decisions as within the purview of the theater chief. Sharp differences between MacArthur and Washington leaders only emerged after the euphoric days of October 1950 when it seemed the North Korean Army was beaten and the conflict was entering its mopping-up phase. Perhaps because of the widespread optimism that prevailed most of that month, neither Tokyo nor Washington officials were aware of a strategic chasm developing between them. . . .

Perhaps it might not have been too late to avert war with Communist China if the Joint Chiefs [JCS] had focused less on MacArthur's impudence toward them and more on the strategic consequence at stake in the Far East commander's move, namely, the escalation of the war by Communist China rather than by the USSR. While MacArthur had largely discounted the possibility of the Soviet Union's entry into the war, he had not seemed greatly concerned about Communist China's possible belligerency. As he had cockily assured the President at Wake, his air power would decimate the Chinese Communist Forces if they tried to advance south of the Yalu. The aggressive move up to the border with American troops in the lead was imprudent adventurism on MacArthur's part, but, on the other hand, the Joint Chiefs' timidity toward him and their priority on his effrontery to them at such a critical strategic juncture left them fully as liable as he was for the decisive provocation of Peking. . . .

While the Great Debate was heating up on Capitol Hill, the beginning of MacArthur's end occurred when [Army Chief of Staff General Joseph L.] Collins, his Army superior and the executive agent for the JCS in Far East matters, visited Tokyo and the Korean front on January 15–17, accompanied by Vandenberg, the Air Force chief. Their trip had been precipitated by a false dilemma MacArthur had posed to his superiors the previous week: As Truman saw it, the Tokyo commander declared the only alternatives were to "be driven off the peninsula, or at the very least suffer terrible losses." Collins reported that during their meeting at MacArthur's GHQ [general headquarters] in Tokyo, MacArthur again appealed for the four divisions. Upon visiting Ridgway [MacArthur's eventual successor] and his troops in Korea, however, Collins found a renovated force preparing to go on the offensive. He was able to return to Washington with the good news, backed by Vandenberg's findings also, that MacArthur was not only uninformed about the situation at the front but also deceitful in posing the false dilemma of evacuation or annihilation if they did not approve his proposals and troop requests. Ridgway's counsel, rather than MacArthur's, was thereafter increasingly sought by the Joint Chiefs and the President.

MacArthur had been found wanting in both strategy and stratagem. Far more crucial, the U.S. government had reaffirmed its foremost global priority to be the security of its Atlantic coalition. Similar to his plight during the Second World War, MacArthur again was arguing in futility for greater American strategic concern about Asia and the Pacific against a predominantly Europe-first leadership in Washington. Having spent over twenty-five years of his career in the Far East, MacArthur may have been biased in speaking out for a higher priority on American interests in that region. There is little question, however, that communist expansionism was mounting in East and Southeast Asia and that American leaders knew little about the susceptibilities of the peoples of those areas. To MacArthur, his struggle to get Washington's attention focused on the Pacific and Asia must have seemed as frustrating as the efforts by him and Fleet Admiral Ernest King to get more resources allocated to the war against Japan.

Despite the warmongering allegations leveled against him, MacArthur never proposed resorting to nuclear weapons while he was Far East chief. In December 1952, he did suggest in a private talk with Eisenhower and Dulles, the President-elect and the next secretary of state, that a line of radioactive waste materials be air-dropped along the northern border of North Korea, to be followed by conventional amphibious assaults on both coasts as well as atomic bombing of military targets in North Korea to destroy the sealed-off enemy forces. He saw this as "the great bargaining lever to induce the Soviet [Union] to agree upon honorable conditions toward international accord." It must be remembered, however, that he had been out of command for twenty months, and, besides, Eisenhower and Dulles scorned his counsel and never sought it again.

In truth, Presidents Truman and Eisenhower, not MacArthur, both considered the use or threat of nuclear force in the Korean War. On November 30, 1950, Truman remarked at a press conference that use of the atomic bomb was being given "active consideration," but Allied leaders, with British Prime Minister Clement R. Attlee in the forefront, exhibited such high states of anxiety over his comment that the President never openly discussed that option again. In January 1952, however, he confided in his diary that he was considering an ultimatum to Moscow to launch atomic raids against Soviet cities if the USSR did not compel the North Koreans and Red Chinese to permit progress in the Korean truce negotiations. "This means all out war," he wrote angrily but wisely reconsidered the next day. In the spring of 1953, President Eisenhower tried to intimidate the Chinese and North Koreans into signing an armistice on UN terms by threatening to use nuclear weapons, which by then included hydrogen bombs. MacArthur had nothing to do with these nuclear threats. Nevertheless, the canard of MacArthur as a warmonger who was eager to employ nuclear weapons in the Korean conflict has persisted in popular and scholarly writings over the years.

A Threat to Civil-Military Relations?

MacArthur's record of arrogant and near-insubordinate conduct during the previous decade on the world stage was well known to the leaders in Washington in 1950–1951. During World War II, President Roosevelt and General Marshall, the Army chief of staff, had been greatly annoyed when he attempted to get Prime Ministers Churchill and Curtin to press for more American resources to be allocated to the Southwest Pacific theater in 1942. MacArthur appeared to encourage anti-Roosevelt groups in American politics who tried in vain to stir up a draft of him for the Republican presidential nomination in 1944. As for defiance of his military superiors, MacArthur launched a number of amphibious operations prior to obtaining authorization from the Joint Chiefs. Admiral Morison observes that "the J.C.S. simply permitted MacArthur to do as he pleased, up to a point" in the war against Japan.

On several occasions during the early phase of the occupation of Japan, MacArthur defied Truman's instructions for him to come to Washington for consultations, the general pleading his inability to leave "the extraordinarily dangerous and inherently inflammable situation" in Japan. Truman was so irked that he quoted two of the general's declinations in his memoirs written nearly a decade afterward. In 1948, MacArthur again appeared willing to run against his commander in chief, but his right-wing supporters were unable to secure the Republican nomination for him. His dissatisfaction with Washington directives during the later phases of the occupation almost led to his replacement by a civilian high commissioner. His growing alienation from administration policies during the first eight months of the Korean fighting gave rise to speculation that he might head an anti-Truman ticket in the 1952 presidential race.

The administration officials who testified at the Senate hearings on MacArthur's relief clearly indicated that they viewed his attitude and conduct as insubordinate and a threat to the principle of civilian supremacy over the military. Secretary of Defense Marshall, probably the most admired of the witnesses representing the administration, was adamant about MacArthur's unparalleled effrontery toward his superiors:

> It is completely understandable and, in fact, at times commendable that a theater commander should become so wholly wrapped up in his own aims and responsibilities that some of the directives received by him from higher authorities are not those that he would have written for himself. There is nothing new about this sort of thing in our military history. What is new, and what had brought about the necessity for General MacArthur's removal, is the wholly unprecedented situation of a local theater commander publicly expressing his displeasure at and his disagreement with the foreign and military policies of the United States.
>
> It became apparent that General MacArthur had grown so far out of sympathy with the established policies of the United States that there was a grave doubt as to whether he could any longer be permitted to exercise the authority in making decisions that normal command functions would assign to a theater commander. In this situation, there was no other recourse but to relieve him.

The evidence accumulated in the Senate investigation of May and June 1951 demonstrates that virtually all of his transgressions fell under the category of disobedience of the President's "muzzling directives" of December 6, 1950.

The general's responses, in turn, had revealed his deep opposition to administration policies. The press had widely publicized his blasts; indeed, many of his missives had gone to national news magazines and major newspapers by way of interviews with and correspondence to their publishers and senior editors or bureau chiefs. His false dilemma about evacuation or annihilation, which was rankling enough to his superiors since he seemed to pass responsibility to them, was a frequent theme in his flagrantly defiant public statements. McCarthyism had already left the national press in a feeding frenzy, so it was natural for reporters eager to exploit the popular hostility against Truman and [Dean] Acheson to give lavish attention to the antiadministration barbs of one of the nation's greatest heroic figures of World War II.

Most heinous to Commander in Chief Truman were the general's ultimatum to the head of the Chinese Communist Forces [CCF] on March 24 and his denunciation of administration policy read in the U.S. House of Representatives on April 5. The general had been told that Truman would soon announce a new diplomatic initiative to get a Korean truce before Ridgway's army advanced across the 38th parallel again. MacArthur arrogantly and deliberately wrecked this diplomatic overture by issuing his own public statement directed to the CCF leader, which scathingly criticized Red China's "complete inability to accomplish by force of arms the conquest of Korea," threatened "an expansion of our military operations to its coastal areas and interior bases [that] would doom Red China to the risk of imminent military collapse," and offered "at any time to confer in the field with the commander-in-chief of the enemy forces in the earnest effort to find any military means whereby realization of the political objectives of the United Nations in Korea . . . might be accomplished without further bloodshed."

In sixteen or more instances in the previous four months the volatile Far East chief had made statements sharply chastising the administration for its errors or absence of policy in the Far East. MacArthur was bent now upon some dramatic gesture to salvage his waning stature. By late March, the UN commander became so paranoid that he believed that he had ruined a plot created by some in the United Nations, the State Department, and high places in Washington to change the status of Formosa and the Nationalists' seat in the UN.

Upon reading MacArthur's shocking statement of the 24th, the President firmly but secretly decided that day to dismiss him; only the procedure and the date had to be settled. Truman heatedly remarked to an assistant that the general's act was "not just a public disagreement over policy, but deliberate, premeditated sabotage of US and UN policy." Acheson described it as "defiance of the Chiefs of Staff, sabotage of an operation of which he had been informed, and insubordination of the grossest sort to his Commander in Chief." Astoundingly, however, the President, through the JCS, sent him a brief and mildly worded message on March 25 reminding him of the directives of December 6 and telling him to contact the Joint Chiefs for instructions if the Chinese commander asked for a truce.

The message from Washington on March 20 alerting him to the impending peace move also set off MacArthur's second climatic act of self-destruction in his endeavor to redirect American foreign and military policies to a greater focus on Asia's significance to the self-interests of the United States. That same day the general wrote Representative Joseph W. Martin, Jr., the House minority leader and a strong Asia-first and Nationalist China crusader. Martin had asked for comments on a speech by the congressman hitting Truman's weak support of Formosa, his limited-war strategy in Korea, and his plans to strengthen NATO. In his letter, MacArthur endorsed his friend Martin's views with enthusiasm but offered nothing new, even admitting that his positions "have been submitted to Washington in most complete detail" and generally "are well known." What made the general's comments different this time were their coincidence with the sensitive diplomatic maneuvering, Martin's dramatic reading of the letter on the floor of the House, and the front-page headlines MacArthur's words got. . . .

At the Senate hearings, MacArthur claimed the letter to Martin was "merely a routine communication." On the other hand, Truman penned in his diary on April 6: "MacArthur shoots another political bomb through Joe Martin. . . . This looks like the last straw. Rank insubordination. . . . I call in Gen. Marshall, Dean Acheson, Mr. Harriman and Gen. Bradley before Cabinet [meeting] to discuss situation." Acheson exclaimed that the Martin letter was "an open declaration of war on the Administration's policy." When Truman conferred with the above "Big Four," as he called them, he did not reveal that his mind had been made up for some time; instead, he encouraged a candid discussion of options and expressed his desire for a unanimous recommendation from them as well as the three service chiefs, Collins, Sherman, and Vandenberg.

Over the weekend Truman talked to key members of the Cabinet to solicit their opinions, while top State and Defense officials met in various groupings to discuss the issue. At the meeting of the President and the Big Four on Monday, April 9, the relief of General MacArthur was found to be the unanimous verdict of the President, the Big Four, and the service chiefs. . . .

MacArthur was the first to testify at the Senate hearings [in early May], and when he expounded on the harmonious relationship and identity of strategic views between him and his military superiors, he seems to have believed this sincerely, if naively. One by one, Marshall, Bradley, Collins, Sherman, and Vandenberg would later tell the senators that they were not in accord with MacArthur on matters of the direction of the war, relations with civilian officials, the value of the European allies, and the priority of the war in the global picture, among other differences. Not aware of how united and devastating against him his uniformed superiors would be, MacArthur set about describing a dichotomy in the leadership of the war from Washington, with Truman, Acheson, Harriman, and other ranking civilians of the administration, especially the State Department, which tended to have unprecedented input in military affairs by 1950–1951, being responsible for the policy vacuum, indecisiveness, and protracted, costly stalemate. On the other hand, he and the Pentagon leaders, along with most of the other senior American officers of the various services, wanted to fight in less limited fashion and gain a decisive triumph in order to deter future communist aggression.

MacArthur, thinking he spoke for his military colleagues, told the senators that Truman and his "politicians" favored "the concept of a continued and indefinite campaign in Korea . . . that introduces into the military sphere a political control such as I have never known in my life or have ever studied." He argued that "when politics fails, and the military takes over, you must trust the military." Later he added: "There should be no non-professional interference in the handling of troops in a campaign. You have professionals to do that job and they should be permitted to do it." As for his recommendations for coping with the entry of the Red Chinese onto the battlefield, he maintained that "most" of them, "in fact, practically all, as far as I know— were in complete accord with the military recommendations of the Joint Chiefs of Staff, and all other commanders." Referring to a JCS list of sixteen courses of action that were under consideration on January 12, which included three of the four he had recommended on December 30, he claimed with some hyperbole, "The position of the Joint Chiefs of Staff and my own, so far as I know, were practically identical." He pictured his ties with the JCS as idealistic, indeed, unrealistic; "The relationships between the Joint Chiefs of Staff and myself have been admirable. All members are personal friends of mine. I hold them individually and collectively in the greatest esteem." It was a desperate endeavor to demonstrate that the basic friction lay between the civilian and the military leadership, not between him and the Pentagon, but it became a pathetic revelation of how out of touch he was with the Joint Chiefs. For want of conclusive proof as to his motivation, however, leeway must be allowed for MacArthur's wiliness, which had not altogether abandoned him: He may have been trying to exploit tensions between the State and Defense departments, with few uniformed leaders holding Acheson and his lieutenants in high regard.

Fortunately for MacArthur, Marshall and the Joint Chiefs, who had chafed over Acheson's obvious eagerness to see the proud MacArthur fall, felt an affinity with this senior professional in their field who had long commanded with distinction. They could not bring themselves to court-martial him. Further, Truman's terrible ratings in the polls—worse than Nixon's at the ebb of Watergate—and the firestorm that McCarthyism had produced for him and Acheson weakened him so politically that a court-martial of MacArthur would have been foolhardy in the extreme. During the first five days after MacArthur's relief, a White House staff count showed that Truman received almost thirteen thousand letters and telegrams on the issue, of which 67 percent opposed the President's action. By the end of the Senate hearings on the general's relief, much of the public, Congress, and the press had lost interest in the inquiry, though polls indicated that a majority of those who cared enough to give an opinion now were against MacArthur. The notion that he might have touched off World War III was on its way to becoming one of the more unfortunate myths about the general.

Insubordination, or defiance of authority, was the charge most frequently leveled against MacArthur at the time and later by high-ranking officials of the Truman administration, including those in uniform. Of course, there was no doubt of his insubordination in the minds of the two chief architects of his dismissal, Truman and Acheson. On numerous occasions during his days of testimony before the Senate committees, it will be recalled, MacArthur himself said that the nation's commander in chief was empowered to appoint and dismiss his uniformed leaders for whatever reason, which surely included rank insubordination. There was no serious question about Truman's authority to relieve MacArthur, but the President and the Joint Chiefs found such great difficulty in dismissing him because there was no genuine threat to the principle of civilian supremacy over the military in this case. MacArthur was not an "American Caesar" and held very conservative views of the Constitution, the necessity of civilian control, and the traditions and history of the American military. When the President finally decided to gird his loins and dismiss MacArthur, the action was swift and Ridgway replaced him smoothly and effectively in short order. All the President had to do was issue the order to bring about the change in command, and it was clear that his power as commander in chief was secure and unchallenged. The President and his Far East commander had differed over strategic priorities and the direction of the war, but their collision had not posed a serious menace to civilian dominance over the military in America.

Breakdowns in Command and Communication

A significant and often overlooked reason for the termination of MacArthur's command was a breakdown in communications between him and his superiors. During the Second World War, MacArthur and the Joint Chiefs of Staff sometimes differed in ways that indicated misconceptions more than strategic differences, but the two sides and their key lieutenants had personal ties between them that were lacking between the Tokyo and Washington leaders of 1950–1951. During the Korean War, the camps of Truman and MacArthur strongly influenced each man's perception of the other. This is not to say that on their own Truman and MacArthur would have become cordial friends. But their lieutenants undoubtedly were important in molding their judgments. Their only direct contact had been a few hours at Wake Island on October 15, 1950, of which a very small portion had been spent alone. Despite the fact that they had never met before and were never to talk again, they would go to their graves implacable enemies.

If the Truman-MacArthur personal relationship was limited to one brief encounter, the personal links between the Far East leader and the seven men who were the President's principal advisers on the Korean War—the Big Four and the service chiefs—were almost nil. Acheson never met him. Marshall visited him once during World War II while going to Eisenhower's headquarters numerous times. Bradley and Harriman had no personal ties with MacArthur at all prior to June of 1950, although each traveled to Tokyo to confer with him after the Korean hostilities commenced. None of the Big Four was an admirer of MacArthur's flamboyant leadership style, yet Marshall, who had been his military superior in World War II, had treated him with commendable fairness despite the Southwest Pacific commander's sometimes difficult ways. All of the Big Four were strongly committed to the security of West Europe, and all had considerable experience and friends there.

None of the service chiefs had any personal contacts with MacArthur of any importance prior to the outbreak of war in Korea, whereupon they made a number of trips to Tokyo to meet with him and his senior commanders and staff leaders. Collins was on the faculty of the United States Military Academy during MacArthur's last year as superintendent (1921–1922), and Vandenberg was a cadet for the three years (1919–1922) of his tenure. Neither of them, however, really got to know the aloof superintendent, though both knew much about him, especially his hero image from the battlefields of France and his efforts to bring reforms to the school despite faculty and alumni resistance. Collins and Vandenberg achieved their senior commands in the Second World War in the European theater; the former had seen combat first in the Solomons, which was not in MacArthur's theater. When he was on Admiral Chester W. Nimitz's staff during the war in the Pacific, Sherman conferred with MacArthur at three or more intertheater planning sessions. Sherman, who had the most significant pre-1950 personal contact with MacArthur, was his strongest supporter of the seven men on a number of his ideas and plans, notably the Inchon assault. On the other hand, Marshall, the oldest of the seven (like MacArthur, born in 1880), and the officer with seniority in the service, was the last of the group to be persuaded that MacArthur should be relieved of his commands.

Of these key advisers to the President, Acheson stands out for his vituperativeness toward the Tokyo commander. In a bitter exchange of press statements in the autumn of 1945 contradicting each other over estimated troop strength needed in occupied Japan, Acheson and MacArthur seemed to exhibit a deep and natural incompatibility. Acheson blamed MacArthur in part for trouble in getting his approval as under secretary of state passed by the Senate that fall. When he was secretary of state later, he visited Europe often but never Japan, and in 1949 he was behind the move to oust the general as head of the Allied occupation. Certainly as proud and arrogant as MacArthur, Acheson could be invidious. Writing nearly two decades after the dismissal, Acheson still harbored deep wrath: "As one looks back in calmness, it seems impossible to overestimate the damage that General MacArthur's willful insubordination and incredibly bad judgment did to the United States in the world and to the Truman Administration in the United States." Acheson was the abiding voice in Truman's ear from 1945 onward urging him to dump "the Big General," and it was he who primarily continued to stoke the long-cold coals even after most of his cohorts had let the fire die as far as public statements were concerned.

The sorry spectacle of MacArthur testifying at the Senate hearings about his harmonious relations with the Joint Chiefs not only exposed his ignorance of the situation but also pointed up how poorly the JCS had communicated their doubts and anxieties, as well as their anger, to the theater commander. It was an invitation to trouble to place him in the UN command in the first place because of both his prior record of defying authority and his long career of distinction and seniority in comparison to theirs. It should have been understood from the beginning of the Korean War that his past achievements gave him no claim to special privileges in obeying orders and directives, especially in such an unprecedented limited conflict that could quickly become a third world war. Time after time, especially after the Red Chinese intervention, the Joint Chiefs retreated from the policy guidance and new directives they should have given MacArthur and should have demanded his obedience. Instead, his intimidation of the Joint Chiefs led them to appease him.

On the other hand, MacArthur discovered that he could not awe or intimidate Truman. Indeed, at the end, the President dismissed him so abruptly and crudely that the general heard of it first from a commercial radio broadcast. Speaking as a professional, MacArthur later said, "No office boy, no charwoman, no servant of any sort would have been dismissed with such callous disregard for the ordinary decencies." For MacArthur, his erroneous image of Truman as a fox terrier yapping at his heels instead of a tough, decisive commander in chief was a costly failure in communication.

If the Joint Chiefs had been more responsible in keeping MacArthur on a short leash, perhaps the collision course between the President and the general might have been averted. The absurd spectacle of the Senate investigation into the general's relief, which bestowed upon Pyongyang, Peking, and Moscow an abundance of data on American strategy in the midst of war, surely could have been avoided. While MacArthur's career was terminated by the confrontation, Truman's also was cut short, the controversy mightily affecting his chances for reelection. Truman won over MacArthur, but it was a Pyrrhic victory politically.

MacArthur's relief was, in part, a legacy of World War II and the strategic priorities of that conflict. Roosevelt and his Joint Chiefs of Staff had early agreed to the British priority on the defeat of Germany because the Atlantic community of nations was vital to American national security and the threat by Japan was more distant. In the midst of another Asian war, MacArthur was sacrificed by a different President and his Defense and State advisers, who did not consider American strategic interests as menaced in East Asia as in Europe. It remains to be seen whether a century hence the Far East will loom as important to American self-interests as MacArthur predicted.

POSTSCRIPT

Should President Truman Have Fired General MacArthur?

In 1950 MacArthur's disagreements with Truman were twofold. First, he disliked the Truman administration's Europe-oriented policy of "containment" of Russian expansionism; second, he detested the defensive strategy that was implied in fighting a limited war under a containment policy.

MacArthur's sympathies lay with those who blamed the Truman administration for the "loss of China" to the Communists and hoped that the UN forces would push the Communists out of a reunified Korea. On his visit to Formosa on August 2, 1950, he embarrassed the Truman administration with his remarks that plans had been developed for the effective coordination of Chinese and American forces in case of an attack on the island. A few weeks later he was nearly fired after he sent a long message to the national commander of the Veterans of Foreign Wars, which stated, "Nothing could be more fallacious than the threadbare argument by those who advocate appeasement and defeatism in the Pacific that if we defend Formosa we alienate continental Asia."

Spanier contends that MacArthur stretched orders from the Defense Department and Joint Chiefs of Staff well beyond their original intent. Particularly upsetting to Truman was MacArthur's public statement asking Beijing to admit it lost the war or face expansion of the war into parts of China and risk total defeat. This pronouncement, says Spanier, "undercut the administration's effort to achieve a cease-fire and start negotiations to end the war." It also convinced the president that he had to fire the general. The Joint Chiefs of Staff agreed.

James is the author of a three-volume biography of MacArthur. The third volume—*Triumph and Disaster, 1945-1964* (Houghton Mifflin, 1985)—covers in greater detail MacArthur's role in post–World War II Asia. James admits that MacArthur was arrogant and at times difficult to deal with but asserts that the Joint Chiefs of Staff might have prevented MacArthur's firing if they had exerted more control over him.

Spanier agrees with James that the Joint Chiefs of Staff were timorous in dealing with MacArthur. This was likely because many of the Joint Chiefs were much younger than MacArthur, who was then 70 years old, and were afraid to challenge a "living legend." Furthermore, MacArthur had proven to a highly skeptical Joint Chiefs and Defense Department that his tactical abilities were still sharp, given the success of the surprise landing behind the lines of the enemy at Inchon.

Spanier and James agree that a more aggressive military policy might have ended the war two years earlier. Could UN field commander Matthew Ridgeway or MacArthur have forced the Chinese and North Koreans to accept a divided Korea if they had pushed the Chinese to North Korea's narrow neck? Was the Truman administration too politically weak to do this? Was the administration's policy and strategy poorly coordinated? Could MacArthur have been persuaded to accept a compromise-negotiated settlement?

Students who wish to learn more should start with Richard Lowitt, ed., *The Truman-MacArthur Controversy* (Rand McNally, 1984). Walter Karp explores the aftermath of the controversy in "Truman vs. MacArthur," in *American Heritage* (April/May 1984). There are three books that cover the controversy in detail and are supportive of Truman's decision. Many consider the best to be John W. Spanier, *The Truman-MacArthur Controversy and the Korean War* (W. W. Norton, 1959, 1965). See also Trumball Higgins, *Korea and the Fall of MacArthur: A Precis in Limited War* (Oxford University Press, 1960) and Richard H. Rovere and Arthur Schlesinger, Jr., *The MacArthur Controversy and American Foreign Policy* (Transaction Books, 1992), which was originally published at the height of the controversy in 1951. Other defenses include *Memoirs by Harry S. Truman: Years of Trial and Hope, vol. 2* (Signet Paperback, 1956, 1965) and former secretary of state Dean Acheson's caustic *Present at the Creation* (W. W. Norton, 1969). More recent criticism of MacArthur's vision comes from retired brigadier general Roy K. Flint, former head of the history department at West Point, in "The Truman-MacArthur Conflict: Dilemma of Civil-Military Relationships in the Nuclear Age," in Richard H. Kohn, ed., *The United States Military Under the Constitution of the United States, 1789–1989* (New York University Press, 1991).

MacArthur's defense of his policies and anger over his firing can be found in his *Reminiscences* (McGraw-Hill, 1964) and in Charles A. Willoughby and John Chamberlain, *MacArthur: 1941–1951* (McGraw-Hill, 1954). Willoughby was an intelligence officer on MacArthur's staff.

For a good short history of the war, students should see Burton I. Kaufman, *The Korean War: Challenges in Crisis, Credibility and Command,* 2d ed. (McGraw-Hill, 1997). Kaufman has also edited *The Korean Conflict* (Greenwood Press, 1999), an excellent compendium of chronologies, biographical sketches, and bibliography. Two starting points for all the recent research in Soviet archives pertaining to the Korean War are Rosemary Foot, "Making Known the Unknown War: Policy Analysis of the Korean Conflict Since the Early 1980's" and Robert J. McMahon, "The Cold War in Asia: The Elusive Synthesis." Both are essays from *Diplomatic History* that have been reprinted in Michael J. Hogan, ed., *America in the World: The Historiography of American Foreign Relations Since 1941* (Cambridge University Press, 1995).

ISSUE 5

Was Rock and Roll Responsible for Dismantling America's Traditional Family, Sexual, and Racial Customs in the 1950s and 1960s?

YES: Glenn C. Altschuler, from *All Shook Up: How Rock and Roll Changed America* (Oxford University Press, 2003)

NO: J. Ronald Oakley, from *God's Country: America in the Fifties* (Dembner Books, 1986, 1990)

ISSUE SUMMARY

YES: Professor Glenn C. Altschuler maintains that rock and roll's "switchblade" beat opened wide divisions in American society along the fault lines of family, sexuality, and race.

NO: Writer J. Ronald Oakley argues that although the lifestyles of youth departed from their parents, their basic ideas and attitudes were still the conservative ones that mirrored the conservativism of the affluent age in which they grew up.

Most Americans assume that rock and roll has dominated American popular music since the 1950s, but this is not true. The phrase "rhythm and blues" was coined by the first white rock and roll Cleveland disc jockey Alan Freed who, when he went national, was pushed by a lawsuit in 1954 to abandon the name of his show from "The Moondog House" to "Rock 'n Roll Party." A black euphemism for sexual intercourse, "rock 'n roll" had appeared as early as 1922 in a blues song and was constantly used by black singers into the early 1950s. It's not clear whether DJ Freed consciously made the name change to cultivate a broader audience, but that is precisely what happened. The phrase caught on, and Freed and station WINS secured a copyright for it.

Rock and roll was a fashion of rhythm and blues, black gospel, and country-western music. It combined black and white music, which explains why so many of the early rock singers came from the south and recorded their hit songs in New Orleans or Memphis. Between 1953 and 1955, the first true rockers—Fats Domino, Chuck Berry, and Little Richard—were African-American. Fats Domino came from New Orleans, sang from his piano, and sold over

65 million records between 1949 and 1960, including "Ain't That a Shame," "I'm Walking," and "Blueberry Hill." Even more influential because of his electric guitar riffs, body and leg gyrations, and songs full of wit and clever wordplay was Chuck Berry, whose lifestyle (he did two stints in prison) and songs ("Maybellene," "Johnny B. Good," and "Roll Over Beethoven") influenced two generations of rockers, including sixties British rock bands the Beatles and the Rolling Stones. Another rocker, Little Richard, known as "the Georgia Peach," became famous as much for his flamboyant style of dress with his towering hair and multicolored clothes that reflected a teasing sexuality. He created a string of hits—"Tutti Frutti," "Long Tall Sally," and "Good Golly Miss Molly"—which were recorded as cover records by white artists like Pat Boone. Best known today for his Geico commercial, Little Richard scared the hell out of the parents from white middle-class America.

More threatening to middle-class white American parents was Elvis Presley, the king of rock and roll, and the most influential pop icon in the history of America, but Elvis was not the inventor of rock and roll. His voice was average, and his songs (written by others) were often mediocre. But his rugged good looks and his sexy gyrations on the stage threw young girls into spasms. Most importantly, he was white. More than 30 years after his death, Elvis still defines the age of rock and roll. He continues to sell records, which number over a billion.

Presley was the first star to take advantage of the new teenage consumer market. By the middle 1950s there were 16.5 million teenagers, half in high school and the other half in college or the work force, who possessed a lot of disposable income, available via allowances or part-time jobs. Suburban teenagers had their own rooms replete with radios and record players. "By the end of 1957," says Professor Altschuler, "seventy-eight Elvis Presley items had grossed $55 million." Presley helped plug the products, making personal appearances in department stores. Fans could purchase shoes, skirts, blouses, T-shirts, sweaters, charm bracelets, handkerchiefs, purses, etc. inscribed "Sincerely Yours."

There is little argument that a new generation of teenagers had emerged in the fifties. Historians can trace the adolescent generations to the early twentieth century. The gap between parent and child always existed, but the new value system that set apart the two generations might have occurred earlier had the great depression and World War II not intervened. Television shows were geared to the very young and the parents. Radio had lost its nightly sitcoms to television and switched to news and music formats. Teenagers were tired of their parents' sentimental croon and woon ballads that did not address their feelings. New DJs emerged, who played the rock and roll songs for teenagers who sat in their rooms pretending to do their homework.

How radical was rock and roll music? Was it responsible for the revolution in values that took place in the 1960s? In the first selection, Professor Glenn C. Altschuler argues that "rock 'n roll deepened the divide between the generations, helped teenagers differentiate themselves from others, transformed popular culture in the United States, and rattled the reticent by pushing sexuality into the public arena." But writer J. Ronald Oakley disagrees. "Although their lifestyle had departed from the conventions of their elders," Oakley believes "their basic ideas and attitudes were still the conservative ones that mirrored the conservativism of the affluent age in which they grew up."

YES

Glenn C. Altschuler

"All Shook Up": Popular Music and American Culture, 1945–1955

Rock 'n' Roll Fight Hospitalizes Youth, the *New York Times* announced on April 15, 1957. In a fracas between white and black boys and girls following a rock 'n' roll show attended by ten thousand fans, fifteen-year-old Kenneth Myers of Medford, Massachusetts, was stabbed and thrown onto the tracks at a subway station. Myers missed touching a live rail by inches and scrambled back onto the platform seconds before a train sped into the station. "The Negro youths were responsible for it," police lieutenant Francis Gannon told reporters. "The fight was senseless . . . but we expect difficulty every time a rock 'n' roll show comes in."

For two years the *Times* printed dozens of articles linking destructive activities at, outside, or in the aftermath of concerts to "the beat and the booze" or the music alone. Public interest in rock 'n' roll was so great, *Times* editors even viewed the absence of a riot as newsworthy. "Rock 'n' Rollers Collect Calmly," readers learned, following a concert at the Paramount Theater in New York City. The journalist attributed the good order on this occasion and several others that year to the police, who arrived early and in force, as many as three hundred strong, some of them on horseback, to set up wooden barriers along the sidewalk, separate the crowd from passersby on Times Square, and then station themselves in the aisles and at the rear of the theater to keep the audience "under surveillance." During the performances, the fans "cheered, shrieked, applauded, and jumped up and down." A few dancers were escorted back to their seats, and the police ordered several excited fans who stood up to sit down. But no one had to be removed or arrested for "obstreperous" behavior. The implication was clear: teenage rock 'n' rollers should not be left on their own.

Reports of riotous behavior convinced many public officials to ban live rock 'n' roll shows. After frenzied fans in San Jose, California, "routed" seventy-three policemen, neighboring Santa Cruz refused permits for concerts in public buildings. Mayor Bernard Berry and two commissioners in Jersey City, New Jersey, decided not to allow Bill Haley and the Comets to perform in the municipally owned Roosevelt Stadium. Following several fistfights at a dance attended by 2,700 teenagers that were broken up by twelve police officers, the city council of Asbury Park, New Jersey, ruled that "swing and blues harmonies" would no longer be permitted. . . .

In the mass media, however, alarmists drowned out apologists. That pop singers would not like the competition might be expected, but their condemnations of rock 'n' roll were especially venomous. It "smells phony and false," said Frank Sinatra, at whose feet bobby-soxers had swooned and shrieked in the 1940s. "It is sung, played, and written for the most part by cretinous goons, and by means of its almost imbecilic reiteration and sly, lewd, in plain fact dirty, lyrics it manages to be the martial music of every side-burned delinquent on the face of the earth." Therapists weighed in as well. *Time* magazine informed readers that psychologists believed that teenagers embraced rock 'n' roll because of a deep-seated, abnormal need to belong. Allegiances to favorite performers, *Time* warned, "bear passing resemblance to Hitler's mass meetings." The *New York Times* provided a platform to psychiatrist Francis Braceland, who had a similar view. Branding rock 'n' roll "a cannibalistic and tribalistic" form of music that appealed to the insecurity and rebelliousness of youth, he thought it all the more dangerous because it was "a communicable disease."

A few went further, declaring the music of teenagers a tool in a conspiracy to ruin the morals of a generation of Americans. In their best-seller *U.S.A. Confidential*, journalists Jack Lait and Lee Mortimer linked juvenile delinquency "with tom-toms and hot jive and ritualistic orgies of erotic dancing, weed-smoking and mass mania, with African jungle background. Many music shops purvey dope; assignations are made in them. White girls are recruited for colored lovers. . . . We know that many platter-spinners are hopheads. Many others are Reds, left-wingers, or hecklers of social convention. . . . Through disc jockeys, kids get to know colored and other musicians; they frequent places the radio oracles plug, which is done with design . . . to hook juves [juveniles] and guarantee a new generation subservient to the Mafia."

Rock 'n' roll generated sound and fury. What, if anything, did it signify? The rise of rock 'n' roll and the reception of it, in fact, can tell us a lot about the culture and values of the United States in the 1950s. According to historian James Gilbert, there was a struggle throughout the decade "over the uses of popular culture to determine who would speak, to what audience, and for what purpose." At the center of that struggle, rock 'n' roll unsettled a nation that had been "living in an 'age of anxiety'" since 1945.

The Cold War produced numerous foreign crises—the Berlin Airlift and the Korean War among them. A fear of internal subversion by Communists, stoked by the often irresponsible charges of Senator Joseph McCarthy, resulted in loyalty oaths, blacklists, and a more general suppression of dissent. In a national poll conducted in 1954, more than 50 percent of Americans agreed that all known Communists should be jailed; 58 percent favored finding and punishing all Communists, "even if some innocent people should be hurt"; and a whopping 78 percent thought reporting to the FBI neighbors or acquaintances they suspected of being Communists a good idea. Coinciding with the Cold War, of course, was the nuclear age, and the possibility of a war that would obliterate the human race. The construction of fallout shelters, and instructions to schoolchildren about how to survive an atomic attack ("Fall instantly face down, elbows out, forehead on arms, eyes shut . . . duck and cover"), probably alarmed as much as they reassured.

The family seemed as vulnerable as the nation to internal subversion in the 1950s. "Not even the Communist conspiracy," U.S. Senator Robert Hendrickson asserted, "could devise a more effective way to demoralize, confuse, and destroy" the United States than the behavior of apathetic, absent, or permissive parents. Americans worried about working moms, emasculated dads, and especially about a growing army of teenage terrors, poised to seize control of the house, lock, stock, and living room. These fears, Gilbert has shown, crystallized in a decade-long crusade against juvenile delinquency, replete with dozens of congressional hearings and hundreds of pieces of legislation to regulate youth culture.

Finally, a principled and persistent civil rights movement demanded in the 1950s that the commitment to equal rights for African Americans no longer be deferred. With the Supreme Court decision in *Brown v. Board of Education*, the Montgomery, Alabama, Bus Boycott, and the use of federal troops to escort black students into heretofore all-white Little Rock Central High School in Arkansas, a revolution in race relations was well under way. Americans in the North as well as the South were not at all sure where it was headed.

Rock 'n' roll entered indirectly into Cold War controversies, but in helping young Americans construct social identities, it did provide a discourse through which they could examine and contest the meanings adults ascribed to family, sexuality, and race. That discourse was not always verbal. Rock 'n' roll moved audiences as much with the body language of performers and the beat of the music as with its lyrics, perhaps more. When rock 'n' roll tries to criticize something, critic Greil Marcus believes, "it becomes hopelessly self-righteous and stupid." When the music is most exciting, "when the guitar is fighting for space in the clatter while voices yelp and wail as one man finishes another's lines or spins it off in a new direction—the lyrics are blind baggage, and they emerge only in snatches." Without a consistent or coherent critique, and never fully free from an attachment to traditional 1950s values, rock 'n' roll nonetheless provided a fresh perspective, celebrating leisure, romance, and sex, deriding deferred gratification and men in gray flannel suits stationed at their office desks, and delighting in the separate world of the teenager.

According to media commentator Jeff Greenfield, by unleashing a perception that young bodies were "Joy Machines," rock 'n' roll set off "the first tremors along the Generational Fault," paving the way for the 1960s. "Nothing we see in the Counterculture," Greenfield claims, "not the clothes, the hair, the sexuality, the drugs, the rejection of reason, the resort to symbols and magic—none of it is separable from the coming to power in the 1950s of rock and roll music. Brewed in the hidden corners of black American cities, its rhythms infected white Americans, seducing them out of the kind of temperate bobby-sox passions out of which Andy Hardy films are spun. Rock and roll was elemental, savage, dripping with sex; it was just as our parents feared." . . .

The zeitgeist was evident on the new mass medium, television. Installed in nearly two-thirds of American households by 1955, television spread the gospel of prosperity, barely acknowledging the existence of poverty or conflict.

Whether dramas were set in the Old West of Marshal Matt Dillon or the court-room of Perry Mason, viewers had no difficulty distinguishing right from wrong or the good guys from the bad guys. In the end, justice was always done. Situation comedies, the reigning genre of the 1950s, presented a lily-white, sub-urban United States, full of happy housewives like June Cleaver, fathers like Jim Anderson, who knew best, and cute kids like the Beaver, whose biggest dilemma was the size of his allowance. TV commercials suggested that every viewer could easily afford the most modern appliance and the latest model automobile. When African Americans appeared on the small screen, they played chauffeurs, maids, and janitors or sang and danced. The small screen, then, was mainstream. Another America might be glimpsed occasionally on an Edward R. Murrow doc-umentary, or *Playhouse 90*, or the Army-McCarthy hearings, but with the nightly network news limited to fifteen minutes, television rarely left viewers uncertain or scared.

In the early '50s, popular music sent similar messages. Bing Crosby and Perry Como sang soothing, romantic ballads, while the orchestras of Mantovani, Hugo Winterhalter, Percy Faith, and George Cates created mood music for middle-of-the-road mid-lifers, who hummed and sang along in elevators and dental offices. Seeking to create a calm, warm environment for men and women who made love with the lights out, pop singers, according to Arnold Shaw, adhered to the following precepts: "Don't sing out—croon, hum, reflect, day-dream. Wish on a star, wink at the moon, laze in the sun. . . . Accentuate the positive, eliminate the negative. . . . DO stick with Mister In-Between." Popular black singers—Nat King Cole and Johnny Mathis—harmonized with white tastes, in style, sound, and lyrics. As late as 1955, the top five on the pop charts were "Unchained Melody," "The Ballad of Davy Crockett," "Cherry Pink and Apple-Blossom White," "The Yellow Rose of Texas," and "Melody of Love." Those who knew physical activity began after "I give my heart to you . . ." did not want to talk about it.

Another sound, however, was available. Before it was supplanted by rock 'n' roll, rhythm and blues provided a dress rehearsal on a smaller stage for the agitation that reached the *New York Times* in the second half of the decade. After World War II, the industry substituted rhythm and blues for the harsher-sounding "race records" as the term for recordings by black artists that were not gospel or jazz. But R&B also emerged as a distinctive musical genre, draw-ing on the rich musical traditions of African Americans, including the blues' narratives of turbulent emotions, and the jubilation, steady beat, hand clap-ping, and call and response of gospel. Rhythm and blues tended to be "good time music," with an emphatic dance rhythm. Its vocalists shouted, growled, or falsettoed over guitars and pianos, bass drums stressing a 2–4 beat, and a honking tenor saxophone. "Body music rather than head or heart music," according to Arnold Shaw, appealing to the flesh more than the spirit, rhythm and blues "embodied the fervor of gospel music, the throbbing vigor of boogie woogie, the jump beat of swing, and the gutsiness and sexuality of life in the black ghetto."

Three strains of rhythm and blues music appealed to that market. Louis Jordan was the premier exponent of "the jump blues." Born in Brinkley,

Arkansas in 1908, Jordan played alto sax with the bands of Louis Armstrong and Chick Webb before forming his own combo, the Tympany Five, in 1938. A showman in the tradition of Cab Calloway, Jordan cut records that for a decade kept him at or near the top of the "Harlem Hit Parade," *Billboard* magazine's title for its black charts. But Jordan's exuberant hits, unlike those of Calloway, the Mills Brothers, or Nat King Cole, drew on the manners, mores, and hazards of life in the ghetto.

Jordan's earthy themes, vernacular language, and humorous, amorous, and amused tone are evident in the titles of his songs: "The Chicks I Pick Are Slender, Tender, and Tall," "Is You Is or Is You Ain't Ma Baby?," "Reet, Petite, and Gone," "Beans and Cornbread," "Saturday Night Fish Fry," and "What's the Use of Gettin' Sober (When You Gonna Get Drunk Again)?" Urban blacks may have felt they were laughing, from a distance, at their lower-class, hayseed cousins. Or, as Shaw suggests, Jordan may have communicated to his audience that he was self-confident enough to laugh at himself.

More romantic and idealistic were the vocal or street-corner "doo-wop" groups, whose output resembled the standard juvenile fare of white pop music. These balladeers preferred the "preliminaries" and "hearts and kisses" to sweaty sex, in such songs as "Hopefully Yours" (the Larks), "I'm a Sentimental Fool" (the Marylanders), and "Golden Teardrops" (the Flamingoes). On occasion, as R&B historian Brian Ward suggests, the grain of the voices, the tone of the instruments, and the manipulation of harmonies and rhythms subverted the saccharine lyrics, hinting at "barely contained lust and sexual expectancy." The dominant theme of "doo-wop," though, was adolescent longing and loss.

The third and most controversial strain dominated and defined rhythm and blues. It appealed to urban blacks who had fled from deference and demeaning employment in the South but remained powerless to control key aspects of their lives. Perhaps in compensation, R&B "shouters" proclaimed—and sometimes parodied—their independence and sexual potency with a pounding beat and lyrics that could be vulgar, raunchy, and misogynist. "Let me bang your box," shouted the Toppers; "Her machine is full of suds . . . it will cost you 30 cents a pound," proclaimed the Five Royales. One of the most talented of the shouters was Nebraska native Wynonie Harris, a tall, dapper, handsome man who billed himself as the "hard-drinkin', hard-lovin', hard-shoutin' Mr. Blues." Harris's biggest hit, "Good Rockin' Tonight," recorded in 1947, was vintage jump blues, but he made a career bellowing songs about sex. Telling readers of *Tan* magazine that "deep down in their hearts" black women "wanted a hellion, a rascal," Harris sang of "cheatin' women" and men who were better off satisfying their needs with a mechanical "Lovin' Machine" in songs like "I Want My Fanny Brown" and "I Like My Baby's Pudding." Harris's idol and sometime partner in duets, Big Joe Turner, also found love "nothin' but a lot of misery," but in the macho tradition of R&B shouters, he refused to whine: "Turn off the water works," he tells his woman. "That don't move me no mo'."

Shouters made good use of a new instrument, the electric guitar. The first mass-produced, solid-body electric guitar, the Fender Esquire, became available in 1950. By eliminating the diaphragm top of the acoustic guitar, Leo Fender helped musicians amplify each string cleanly, without feedback. Electricity, argues music historian Michael Lydon, provided "that intensity that made non-believers call it noisy when played low, but made believers know it had to be played loud." In the hands of a master, like bluesman Aaron "T-Bone" Walker, the electric guitar could also be a stage prop, held behind the head when he did the splits, and a phallic symbol, pressed against the body or pointed provocatively at the audience.

In the '40s and early '50s, rhythm and blues fought its way onto the radio and records. As the Federal Communications Commission sifted through a backlog of applications for new radio stations at the end of World War II, white entrepreneurs founded independent stations aimed at urban African Americans, who in the aggregate had considerable disposable income—and nearly all of whom owned radios. In late 1948 and early 1949, WDIA in Memphis abandoned white pop to become the first radio station in the United States to program entirely for blacks, putting former schoolteacher Nat D. Williams on the air as its first black announcer. Its ratings began to climb. Within a few years, 70 percent of the African-Americans in Memphis turned to the station at some time during the day. When thousands in the mid-South joined them, national advertisers flocked to WDIA. Stations throughout the country began to expand "Negro appeal programming." In 1949, WWEZ in New Orleans hired a black DJ, Vernon Winslow ("Doctor Daddy-O"), for "Jivin' with Jax"; that same year, WEDR in Birmingham, Alabama, went all black, and WERD in Atlanta became black owned and operated. Farther west, in Flagstaff, Arizona, KGPH began to feature R&B in 1952. By the mid-'50s, twenty-one stations in the country were "all black"; according to a "Buyer's Guide" survey, more than six hundred stations in thirty-nine states, including WWRL in New York City, WWDC in Washington, D.C., and WDAS in Philadelphia, aired "Negro-slanted" shows. In 1953, *Variety* noted that the "strong upsurge in R&B" provided employment for black disc jockeys, with some five hundred of them "spotted on stations in every city where there is a sizable colored population."

The dramatic shift toward television as the entertainment medium of choice for white adults helped convince executives to reorient radio toward young people's music, and particularly R&B. The kids stayed with radio throughout the '50s, as transistors replaced large, heat-generating vacuum tubes, and cheap portable radios and car radios became available. By 1959, 156 million radios were in working order in the United States, three times the number of TV sets.

As R&B found a niche on radio, independent record producers established R&B labels. The major companies—Capitol, Columbia, Decca, Mercury, MGM, and RCA—stuck with pop music, leaving R&B to the "indies." The latter could compete because after 1948 they could acquire high-quality, low-cost recording equipment. Because producers paid composers and performers as little as $10 and a case of whiskey per song (Bo Diddley once referred to R&B as "Ripoffs and Bullshit"), they could break even with sales of only 1,500 units. Between 1948 and 1954, a thousand "indies" went into business. Unlike the majors, whose offices were in New York City, independents spread across the country. Founded by former jukebox operators, nightclub owners, music journalists, and record manufacturers, only some of whom (like Ahmet Ertegun and Jerry Wexler of Atlantic) knew a lot about music and almost all of whom were white, independent producers grossed $15 million in 1952, much of it on R&B. "I looked for an area neglected by the majors," confessed Art Rupe, founder of Specialty Records in Los Angeles, "and in essence took the crumbs off the table in the record industry."

Bottom-line businessmen, independent producers, and radio station operators often exploited R&B artists, but many of them recognized and endorsed the role that the music industry was playing in the struggle for civil rights. Following World War II, which was in no small measure a war against racism, some progress had been made. When he broke the color barrier in baseball in 1947 Jackie Robinson had, in essence, put the nation on notice that the days of segregation were numbered. A year later, by executive order, President Harry Truman ended the practice in the army. But the hard battles had yet to be fought, let alone won. The laws in southern states separating the races in schools, buses, trains, and public swimming pools and bathrooms had been upheld by the U.S. Supreme Court in a decision, *Plessy v. Ferguson* (1896), that was still in force. Many southerners remained implacably racist. "The Negro is different," insisted Ross Barnett, governor of Mississippi, "because God made him different to punish him. His fore-head slants back. His nose is different. His legs are different, and his color is sure different." Such attitudes made it impossible in 1955 to convict the murderers of black teenager Emmett Till, whose crime was daring to converse with (and perhaps whistle at) a young white woman. Race mixing of any kind, according to Barnett, was unnatural and unthinkable: "We will not drink from the cup of genocide."

In the North, racial antipathy was often muted but no less real. Discrimination in employment in the public and private sectors was pervasive, and African Americans often had to take the most menial jobs. While segregation was not legal in any northern state, the races remained largely separate, with many white neighborhoods implacably opposed to black renters or owners of apartments or houses. The migration of blacks to the North made the situation more volatile. In 1951, Harvey Clark, a graduate of Fisk University, moved his family's furniture into an apartment they had leased in Cicero, Illinois. When the Clarks' van arrived, the police intervened and an officer struck him, advising the veteran of World War II to leave the area "or you'll get a bullet through you." When Clark persisted, four thousand whites trashed the apartment building, destroying furniture and plumbing while the police were "out of town." As the NAACP tried to raise funds to replace the Clarks' furniture, a grand jury investigated, only to return an indictment against an NAACP lawyer, the owner of the apartment, her lawyer, and the rental agent, for conspiring to reduce property values by causing "depreciation in the market selling price." Months later a federal grand jury did indict police and city officials for violating the civil rights of the Clarks, but even then three of the seven defendants were acquitted. Occurring in one of the most "southern" of northern cities, the Cicero riot was hardly a typical occurrence in the 1950s, but it served as a graphic reminder that "the Negro problem" was a national problem.

The music business could not solve the problem, of course, but because it depended so heavily on African-American writers and performers, civil rights advocates pressed record producers and radio station owners to promote integration—and practice what they preached. In his monthly column on rhythm and blues in the music industry publication *Cash Box*, Sam Evans pushed for the employment of more African Americans in all phases of the business. When NBC's San Francisco outlet KNBC hired Wallace Ray in May 1952, Evans detected a "fast growing trend." A qualified black, he suggested, is always available to fill the job: "In short course we expect to find a fair and equal representation, racially speaking, in the record manufacturing and distribution biz." Ernie and George Leaner became the agents for OKeh Records, a division of Columbia, in seven midwestern states, Evans informed readers a few months later, not because they "are Negroes, or because they are fat or skinny, or because they are tall or short. But just because the boys are good sound businessmen and know how to run a record distributing company." Evans took an entire column to sum up racial progress in the jukebox, recording, radio, and television businesses. "We have seen supposedly insurmountable barriers broken down," he claimed. In addition to "Negro talent" onstage, "many industry companies, and allied branches, are today employing young Negro people in positions of responsibility and trust. The day when the Negro was automatically delegated to the broom department is a thing of the past. Now we see typists, accountants, bookkeepers, receptionists, road managers, traveling representatives, A&R [artist and repertoire] men, publicity men, publishers, staff radio announcers, staff radio engineers, plus many other jobs, and all drawn from the huge Negro labor market." With praise came a plea that all applicants for employment be judged "only by personal qualifications rather than by skin pigmentation." In the next decade, as high schools and colleges turned out thousands of educated African-American men and women, Evans predicted, the clarion call would be "Give us jobs, and we will win the Freedom."

Even if the music industry did not discriminate in hiring—and Evans's account was far too sanguine—its most important role was not behind the scenes. Mitch Miller, A&R man for Columbia Records and, it would turn out, no friend of rock 'n' roll, suggested that as whites listened to African-American music and cheered performers on the stage, they struck a blow for racial understanding and harmony. Since jazz and the blues reached relatively few whites, R&B probably had the greatest impact. "By their newfound attachment to rhythm and blues," Miller wrote, "young people might also be protesting the Southern tradition of not having anything to do with colored people. There is a steady—and healthy—breaking down of color barriers in the United States; perhaps the rhythm and blues rage—I am only theorizing—is another expression of it."

In the short run, at least, Miller proved to be too sanguine, too. White teenagers were listening, but as they did a furor erupted over R&B. Good enough for blacks, apparently, the music seemed downright dangerous as it crossed the color line.

Actually buying R&B records required some effort. Most music stores in white neighborhoods did not stock them. Until 1954, New Yorkers usually went to 125th Street to buy best-selling R&B platters. Neither the stores on Broadway nor any Madison Avenue shop carried them. On radio, rhythm and blues got airtime primarily on small, independent stations, and even then, Sam Evans reported, "in the very early hours of the morning or late at night."

In pursuit of R&B, however, white teenagers proved to be resolute and resourceful. At the Dolphin Record Store, located in an African-American neighborhood in Los Angeles, about 40 percent of the customers for rhythm and blues in 1952 were white. There, and in other stores in ethnic neighborhoods, in addition to R&B, the stock included the multicultural musical fare produced in the city. In 1948, for example, "Pachuco Boogie," a song blending Mexican speech patterns with African-American scat singing and blues harmonies, sold two million copies.

Whites habituated black nightclubs throughout the country as well. Although some clubs, fearing trouble from the authorities, restricted them to "white spectator tickets," forbidding them to dance or even sit down, "the whites kept on coming," Chuck Berry remembered. . . .

The vast majority of R&B fans remained orderly, obedient, and buttoned down, but rhythm and blues did release inhibitions and reduce respect for authority in enough teenagers to give credibility to charges that the music promoted licentious behavior. "The first time I ever saw a guy put his hand down a girl's pants was at the Paramount," explained a white fan of Chuck Berry. As a teenager in Granite City, Illinois, Bonnie Bramlett went to the Harlem Club in East St. Louis, even though she knew it "was definitely the wrong neighborhood for white girls." She and her friends had a wonderful time, "sneakin' and smokin' and drinkin' and doin' damn near everything."

By 1954, *Cash Box* was reporting that as R&B records received greater airplay, "the complaints are pouring in from parents." Unless record companies stopped producing all "suggestive and risqué" songs, the publication predicted, adults would prohibit their children from purchasing any R&B records, and the goose that had been laying golden eggs would perish.

The call for self-regulation did not go unheeded. After 1954, R&B records were less raspy and raunchy, with more of the "sweet stylings" of vocal groups like Frankie Lymon and the Teenagers ("Why Do Fools Fall in Love?") and Little Anthony and the Imperials ("Tears on My Pillow"). By then, however, the battleground had shifted: rock 'n' roll had gotten its name.

Alan Freed is generally credited with using the phrase to describe rhythm and blues. Born in Windber, Pennsylvania, just south of Johnstown, in 1921, Freed got his first experience with radio broadcasting when he was a student at Ohio State. A successful disc jockey in Akron, he moved to Cleveland in 1950, first to introduce movies on WXEL-TV, and then as the host of "Request Review" on WJW radio. Freed learned about rhythm and blues from Leo Mintz, the owner of Record Rendezvous, located near Cleveland's black ghetto, and began to showcase R&B music on his show. Billing himself as "Alan Freed, King of the Moondoggers," the DJ rang a cowbell, banged a telephone book, and bellowed a Negro-inflected patter into the microphone as he spun the platters. Freed had a "teenager's mind funneled into 50,000 watts," wrote Clark Whelton of the *New York Times*. He "jumped into radio like a stripper into Swan Lake," giving listeners the musical equivalent of a front-row seat for the San Francisco earthquake: "Freed knocked down the buildings you hated and turned the rest into dance floors."

Black and white listeners, in the city and the suburbs, responded enthusiastically to the music and Freed's showmanship and sincerity. "The Moondog House" became the hottest show in town. With a national reputation, Freed in 1953 took on the management of the Moonglows and the Coronets, organized a concert tour, "The Biggest Rhythm and Blues Show," that opened in Revere, Massachusetts, and closed in New Orleans, and reached an agreement with WNJR to rebroadcast "The Moondog House" in Newark, New Jersey. So great was Freed's perceived power that after he became the first white DJ in Cleveland to play "Crying in the Chapel," by the Orioles, he got the credit for the thirty thousand records of the song sold in the city the next day! In 1954 Freed moved to WINS and soon became the dominant nighttime personality on radio in New York City.

In November, he faced a crisis. Thomas Louis Hardin, a blind street musician, composer, and beggar, who set up shop outside Carnegie Hall, decked out in shabby Viking garb, playing triangular drums he called trimbas, claimed that he had used the name "Moondog" for many years. Charging that Freed had "infringed" on his name, Hardin sued. When it turned out that Freed had played Hardin's recording of "Moondog Symphony" on his program, Judge Carroll Walter awarded Hardin $5,700 and forbade Freed from using the name "Moondog."

Initially "very angry and shocked," Freed quickly decided to change the name of his show to "Rock 'n' Roll Party." He had, in fact, occasionally used the phrase in Cleveland to describe his program, though he did not apply it specifically to the music he played. A black euphemism for sexual intercourse, "rock 'n' roll" had appeared in a song title as early as 1922, when blues singer Trixie Smith recorded "My Daddy Rocks Me (With One Steady Roll)." In 1931, Duke Ellington cut "Rockin' Rhythm," and three years later the Boswell Sisters sang "Rock and Roll." After Wynonie Harris's hit "Good Rockin' Tonight," in 1948 so many songs mentioned rock or rockin' that *Billboard* complained Connie Jordan's "I'm Gonna Rock" was the "umpteenth variation" on Harris's title. In 1952, a Rockin' Records Company did a brisk business in Los Angeles.

"Rock 'n' roll," then, was not, as Freed later claimed, an "inspirational flash" that came to him as a "colorful and dynamic" description of the "rolling, surging beat of the music." Nor did he use the phrase to eliminate the racial stigma of "rhythm and blues." Whether or not Freed consciously sought "to cultivate a broader audience" for the music—that is precisely what happened. With a sale of forty thousand records in the late '40s an R&B hit might reach the Top Ten; a rock 'n' roll smash would sell over a million.

As it entered popular discourse, rock 'n' roll was a social construction and not a musical conception. It was, by and large, what DJs and record producers and performers said it was. In any event, the phrase caught on, and Freed and WINS secured a copyright for it. Louis Jordan might complain, with considerable justification, that "rock 'n' roll was just a white imitation, a white adaptation of Negro rhythm and blues." What's in a name? Alan Freed's choice allowed fans to affirm—without having to think about it—that rock 'n' roll was a distinctive, not a derivative, musical form.

A few months before Freed started plugging his radio "Rock 'n' Roll Party," *Billboard* magazine welcomed a "potent new chanter who can sock over a tune for either the country or the R&B markets. . . . A strong new talent." By 1955, he would be hailed as a rock 'n' roll sensation.

Elvis Aron Presley was born in 1935 in Tupelo, Mississippi. His father, Vernon, a drifter, worked sporadically as a farmer or truck driver; Gladys, his mother, kept the family together. She lavished love on her only child (a twin brother, Jessie Garon, was stillborn). In 1948, when Vernon got a job in a paint factory, the Presleys moved to Memphis. As a teenager, Elvis developed the unique and self-contradictory combination of rebelliousness and adherence to conventional values he would exhibit throughout his life—and bequeath to rock 'n' roll. At Humes High School, he joined ROTC, the Biology Club, the English Club, the History Club, and the Spanish Club. With his family, he attended the Pentecostal Assembly of God. He enjoyed the music of Bing Crosby, Perry Como, Eddie Fisher, and Dean Martin. At the same time, Elvis imagined himself the hero of comic books and movies and contrived to let everyone know he was different. He let his sideburns grow long and got kicked off the high school football team for refusing to cut his hair. He bought clothes at Lansky's on Beale Street, a store patronized by blacks, dressed often in his favorite colors, pink and black, and kept his shirt collar up in back and his hair pomaded in a wave. Elvis later remembered that when his classmates saw him walking down the street, they yelled, "Hot dang, let's get him, he's a squirrel, get him, he just come down outta the trees."

A misfit and an outcast, Elvis was, in essence, a southern juvenile delinquent. Journalist Stanley Booth has described the type, "lounging on the hot concrete of a gas station on a Saturday afternoon, stopping for a second on the sidewalk as if they were looking for someone who was looking for a fight. You could even see their sullen faces, with a toughness lanky enough to just miss being delicate, looking back at you out of old photographs of the Confederate Army. . . . All outcasts with their contemporary costumes of duck-ass haircuts, greasy Levi's, motorcycle boots, T-shirts for day and black leather jackets for evening wear. Even their unfashionably long sideburns (Elvis' were furry) expressed contempt for the American Dream they were too poor to be part of." And yet, Booth concludes, Elvis was an especially daring delinquent, unwilling to become a mechanic, housepainter, bus driver, or cop, as so many "hoods" did. With volcanic ambition, he aspired to become a singer, and a star.

Elvis taught himself chord progressions on the guitar his mother gave him, as he listened to WDIA or the phonograph. A regular at Ellis Auditorium's All-Night Gospel Singings, he was mesmerized by the amplitude of some spirituals and the delicacy of others. Although his parents disapproved, Elvis kept listening to blues men Big Bill Broonzy and Arthur Crudup. African-American music, Greil Marcus speculates, gave him more excitement than he could get from the "twangs and laments" of country music. It provided "a beat, sex, celebration, the stunning nuances of the blues and the roar of horns and electric guitars."

After he graduated from Humes, Elvis drove a truck and worked as a machinist and as an usher at the movies. He gave his paycheck to Gladys Presley but kept enough money for his clothes and accessories. In 1953, he appeared with his beat-up guitar in the office of Sun Studios in Memphis. He wanted to make a record to surprise his mother, he said, but "if you know anyone that wants a singer . . ." "Who do you sound like?" the receptionist asked. "I don't sound like nobody." Elvis recorded two Ink Spots songs, "My Happiness" and "That's When Your Heartaches Begin," with Sam Phillips, the owner of Sun, listening from the control room. The receptionist wrote down next to his name "Good ballad singer," and Presley left, with an acetate and an inkling that he was about to be discovered. He reappeared in January and cut another record. But Sam Phillips did not yet recognize that his ship had just come in.

A native of Florence, Alabama, Phillips had dropped out of school to begin working in radio, as an engineer and disc jockey. He came to Memphis in 1945, joining WREC, the CBS affiliate, to set up national hookups of big band music from the Skyway at the Peabody Hotel. Phillips found the pop songs he played dreadfully dull: "It seemed to me that the Negroes were the only ones who had any freshness left in their music; and there was no place in the South they could go to record." He told just about everyone he met that he was looking for "Negroes with field mud on their boots and patches in their overalls . . . battered instruments and unfettered techniques." In 1950 Phillips opened a small office, recording bar mitzvahs and political speeches to defray the expenses of making demos of new artists and sending them to independent producers around the country. Within a short time, he sold recordings of Howlin' Wolf and B. B. King to Chess in Chicago and Modern Records in Los Angeles. He retained his job at WREC, until he could no longer abide snide coworkers asking him "whether he had been hanging around those niggers." By 1953, Sun Studios was promoting and distributing as well as producing, out of a two-person office. Rufus Thomas's "Bear Cat" was the studio's first success; "Feeling Good," by Little Junior Parker, and "Just Walkin' in the Rain," by the Prisonaires, were in the can. Sun's label, an orange, yellow, and black image of a rooster crowing and the sun rising, looked to a new day, and to an open door for African-American artists.

Sam Phillips's commitment to rhythm and blues never wavered; throughout his career he sought out and recorded black singers. He also realized that in the South, and in the North as well, whites were uneasy about listening to black music. In the '50s, as one jukebox operator noted, putting a "black blues record on a honky tonk machine" in a white establishment was a mistake, "because somebody would go over there and play it, just for devilment, and the whole place would explode." So Phillips kept his eyes open for white country boys who could sing the blues. Marion Keisker, Phillips's colleague at Sun, remembers him saying over and over, "If I could find a white man who had the Negro sound and the Negro feel, I could make a billion dollars."

In the summer of 1954, Phillips received a demo of a song called "Without You" from a black performer he did not know. For some reason, he thought the polite young man with the sideburns should record it. At the Sun Studio, Elvis tried and tried but failed to find the ballad's essence. Phillips persevered, asking the youngster to practice with Scotty Moore, a twenty-two-year-old guitarist. After several rehearsals, Presley and Moore returned, with stand-up bass player Bill Black, and played "I Love You Because," a country ballad. This session, too, went badly. Out of anxiety, or perhaps absent-mindedly, Elvis picked up his guitar to strum and sing "That's All Right," a blues song recorded by Arthur Crudup in 1946. Moore and Black joined in, and suddenly Sam Phillips stuck his head out of the control booth and asked them to play it again. He felt "like someone stuck me in the rear end with a brand new super-sharp pitchfork." It sounds pretty good, he said, but "what is it? I mean, who, who you going to give it [i.e., sell it] to?" Elvis did not have the ragged tone, irregular rhythms, and intonation most blues singers used, but he had found something. Instinctively, Greil Marcus argues, he had turned Crudup's lament for a lost love into a "satisfied declaration of independence. . . . His girl may have left him but nothing she can do can dent the pleasure that radiates from his heart. It's the blues, but free of all worry, all sin; a simple joy with no price to pay." When the trio finished the song, Phillips, by now very excited, realized that if he was to get a record out in a hurry he needed something for the flip side. Within a few days, Presley, Moore, and Black recorded the hillbilly classic "Blue Moon of Kentucky." Here, too, Elvis produced a distinctive tone and sound, transforming a country classic into that hybrid of country and R&B that became known as "rockabilly."

Even before he chose "Blue Moon of Kentucky," Sam Phillips played the acetate for his friend Dewey Phillips, by then at WHBQ, but still the "man with the platinum ear." As they listened, Sam wondered "where you going to go with this, it's not black, it's not white, it's not pop, it's not country." He was delighted when Dewey offered to play the songs on his show. As if by magic, most of Memphis seemed to be listening. When Dewey Phillips played "That's All Right," the switchboard lit up with requests that he play it again—and again and again. Dewey complied, then called the Presley home and asked Gladys to get Elvis, who was out at the movies, to the station for an interview. Within minutes the singer arrived, "shaking all over." Dewey told him to cool it and make sure to say "nothing dirty." During the brief chat, Dewey got Elvis to say that he had been a student at (allwhite) Humes High School: "I wanted to get that out, because a lot of people listening had thought he was colored."

On July 19, 1954, Sun released Elvis Presley's first record. An instant hit in Memphis, it had to overcome initial resistance elsewhere in the South, because disc jockeys did not know how to categorize it. Some DJs told Phillips that Elvis was so "country he shouldn't be played after five A.M."; others said flatly he was too black for their tastes. If he played the record, T. Tommy Cutrer, the top country DJ in Shreveport, Louisiana, told Phillips, his white country audience would "run me out of town." In Houston, Paul Berlin, who was still getting mileage spinning the platters of Tennessee Ernie Ford and Patti Page, said, "Sam, your music is just so ragged, I just can't handle it right now. Maybe later on." Even in Tupelo, Elvis's hometown, Ernest Bowen, the sales manager at WELO, told him the record was "a bunch of crap."

When Phillips prevailed, and disc jockeys played the record, listeners couldn't get enough of it. And they liked "Blue Moon of Kentucky" every bit as much as "That's All Right." A scout for RCA asked Sam Morrison, a record dealer in Knoxville, "It's just a normal rhythm and blues record, isn't it?" No, it isn't, Morrison replied, "it's selling to a country audience." Just then, according to Morrison, a man with "more hair growing out of his ears and nose than on his head" entered the store and in an easy Tennessee drawl said, "By granny, I want that record." By mid-August the record was number 3 on *Billboard* magazine's regional country and western best-sellers.

By then, Elvis was a performer as well as a singer. After a shaky debut in front of a "pure redneck" crowd at the Bon Air Club in Memphis, he backed up Slim Whitman at a hillbilly hoedown in an outdoor amphitheater in Overton Park. Elvis approached the mike, with legs quivering and lips contorted into what looked like a sneer. "We were all scared to death," Scotty Moore recalled, "and Elvis, instead of just standing flat-footed and tapping his foot, well, he was kind of jiggling. . . . Plus I think with those old loose britches that we wore—they weren't pegged, they had lots of material and pleated fronts—you shook your leg, and it made it look like all hell was going on under there. During the instrumental parts he would back off from the mike and be playing and shaking, and the crowd would just go wild, but he thought they were actually making fun of him." By the encore, Elvis knew that the image he had projected, whether by accident or not, with his eyes shut and his legs shaking, was arousing the audience: "I did a little more, and the more I did, the wilder they went."

Elvis was something new under the Sun. Although he did not invent "rockabilly," he introduced it to tens of thousands of teenagers. With loose rhythms, no saxophone or chorus, rockabilly was a "personal, confiding, confessing" sound, as Charlie Gillett has defined it, with instrumentalists responding "more violently to inflections in the singer's voice, shifting into double-time for a few bars to blend with a sudden acceleration in the vocalist's tempo." After Elvis's meteoric rise, Sam Phillips signed other rockabilly singers, including Carl Perkins, Roy Orbison, Johnny Cash, and Jerry Lee Lewis.

Beyond his musical style, Elvis embodied some of the characteristics of his "low-down" social class and of many fellow teenagers. Angry at a world that had excluded him, yet eager for recognition and status, Elvis could be arrogant and prideful—and also emotionally vulnerable, insecure, and deferential. No one has captured Elvis's "authentic multiplicity" better than Greil Marcus, who imagines the singer introducing himself as a "house rocker, a boy steeped in mother love, a true son of the church, a matinee idol who's only kidding, a man with too many rough edges for anyone ever to smooth away," a balladeer yearning to settle affairs, a rock 'n' roller apt to "break away at any time."

By instinct more than design, Elvis contributed to the agitation about race relations during the 1950s. In public, and in the South, he acknowledged his indebtedness to the music of African Americans. "The colored folks been singing and playing it [rock 'n' roll] just like I'm doing now, man, for more years than I know," he told the *Charlotte Observer* in 1956. "They played it like that in the shanties and in their juke joints and nobody paid it no mind until I goosed it up. I got it from them. Down in Tupelo, Mississippi, I used to hear Arthur Crudup bang his box the way I do now and I said that if I ever got to the place where I could feel all old Arthur felt, I'd be a music man like nobody ever saw." Sam Phillips believed that Elvis was without prejudice and that "sneaking around through" his music, but clearly discernible to his fans, was an "almost subversive" identification with and empathy for blacks. Phillips's claim that he and Elvis "went out into this no man's land" and "knocked the shit out of the color line" should be dismissed as retrospective fantasy. He was, perhaps, closer to the mark in asserting that, with respect to race, "we hit things a little bit, don't you think?"

As Alan Freed provided a name, and Elvis an icon, Bill Haley gave rock 'n' roll its anthem. In almost all respects, Haley was an improbable '50s teen idol. Born in Highland Park, Michigan, in 1925, he received his first guitar at age seven and began to play hillbilly music, taking as his models country singer Hank Williams and cowboy star Gene Autry. Billed as the "Ramblin' Yodeler," Haley toiled in obscurity for years, performing at fairs, auction barns, and amusement parks in Delaware, Indiana, and Pennsylvania, decked out in cowboy boots and hat. In the late '40s, he formed his own band, first named the Four Aces of Western Swing, then the Saddlemen. Thwarted by the limited appeal of country music in the region, Haley began to experiment with rhythm and blues. In 1951, the Saddlemen recorded "Rocket 88," a stomping R&B song about an Oldsmobile. A year later came "Rock the Joint," a loud and lively jump blues hit, which sold well in Philadelphia and New Jersey. Haley was now ready to exchange his boots and hat for a Scotch plaid jacket or a tuxedo, shave his sideburns, and rename the Saddlemen "Bill Haley and the Comets." Composed of six or seven men, playing stringed instruments, drums, and a saxophone, with Haley as guitarist and lead singer, the Comets played driving and danceable music. Haley's own composition, "Crazy, Man, Crazy," reached the *Billboard* 's Top Twenty. The tune had a pop beat, *The Cash Box* reported; the lyrics "lend themselves to R&B treatment, and the instrumentalization is hillbilly."

Signed by a major national label, Decca, Haley and the Comets recorded "(We're Gonna) Rock Around the Clock" early in 1954. Bursting with energy, the song used a snare drum to produce a heavy backbeat and featured an electric guitar solo. After just one week on *Billboard*'s pop charts, at number 23, it faded. Late that year, however, with "Shake, Rattle, and Roll," a "cover" of Joe Turner's R&B song, with sanitized lyrics, Haley had a huge hit, selling more than a million copies. In his version, Haley copied the basic R&B beat but did not use many other musical effects—the loosely pronounced words, complex and harmonious backing, the slurred "bluesy" notes. He added guitar work and his own thumping, shouting delivery. The success of this song, and the emergence of rock 'n' roll, convinced Hollywood producers to use "Rock Around the Clock" in the film *Blackboard Jungle*.

As the opening credits of *Blackboard Jungle* rolled across the screen, the soundtrack blared "One, two, three o'clock, four o'clock ROCK." An asphalt schoolyard appeared on the screen, visible through a chain-link fence, and students danced, with a few toughs hovering in the background, a saxophone and electric guitar blaring on. For two minutes and ten seconds, "Rock Around the Clock" issued a clarion call to students to break out of jail and have fun. Whereas *Rebel Without a Cause* and *The Wild Ones* belied their themes of youth rebellion with big band sound tracks, *Blackboard Jungle* found music appropriate to its melodramatic ad campaign: "A drama of teenage terror! They turned a school into a jungle." "It was the loudest sound kids ever heard at that time," Frank Zappa remembered. Bill Haley "was playing the Teenage National Anthem and he was LOUD. I was jumping up and down. *Blackboard Jungle*, not even considering that it had the old people winning in the end, represented a strange act of endorsement of the teenage cause."

Despite a conclusion designed to reassure, with an alliance between a young black student, played by Sidney Poitier, and the teacher, played by Glenn Ford, *Blackboard Jungle* (and, by implication, "Rock Around the Clock") suggested that generational conflict was endemic in American culture. In an unforgettable scene, the class fidgeted as a teacher at North Manual High tried to connect with them by playing his favorite jazz records. When the sound track countered with *their* music, the youths erupted, tossing his 78s across the room, then shattering them, as the hapless teacher dissolved in tears. As they watched the movie, observers noted, some teenagers sang along, danced in the aisles, and slashed their seats. *Blackboard Jungle*, music critic Lillian Roxon has written, had a "special, secret defiant meaning for teenagers only." It suggested to them that "they might be a force to be reckoned with, in numbers alone. If there could be one song, there could be others; there could be a whole world of songs, and then, a whole world." The movie reinforced the association between rock 'n' roll and anarchy in the minds of anxious adults. *Blackboard Jungle, Time* magazine opined, undermined the American way of life, giving aid and comfort to Communists. If it were not withdrawn, predicted Clare Booth Luce, U.S. ambassador to Italy, the film would "cause the greatest scandal in motion picture history." "No matter what the outcome of the film," Senator Estes Kefauver's committee on juvenile delinquency concluded, a substantial number of teenagers would identify with Artie West, the sadistic teenager in *Blackboard Jungle*, who assaults Glenn Ford's young and pretty wife. "It was unfortunate," no less an authority than Alan Freed acknowledged, that Haley's song about having a good time had been used "in that hoodlum-infested movie," which "seemed to associate rock 'n' rollers with delinquents."

Blackboard Jungle was denounced by teachers' organizations, the Daughters of the American Revolution, the American Legion, and the Girl Scouts. Banned in Memphis until MGM threatened an injunction, the film played in several cities with the sound track turned off during the opening and closing credits. Despite—and perhaps because of—these denunciations, *Blackboard Jungle* was a sensational hit. And, with a second chance, "Rock Around the Clock" climbed to the top of the charts. By the end of 1955, two million records had been sold, and by the end of the decade the song was gaining on Bing Crosby's "White Christmas" as the best-selling single in history. Bill Haley did not quite know what had hit him. Thirty years old in 1955, chunky, blind in one eye, with chipmunk cheeks and a spit curl plastered on his forehead, Haley found it difficult to compete with younger, sexier performers. Although he went on to make a short feature film, *Rock Around the Clock*, with Freed, in 1956, and had another gold record, "See You Later, Alligator," Haley seemed out of touch with the culture of rock 'n' roll. "He didn't even know what to call it, for the love of Christ," snorts critic Nick Tosches, citing Haley's comment that the Comets used country and western instruments to play rhythm and blues, "and the result is pop music." Haley was no rebel against the dominant values of the 1950s. While the Comets were on the road, he instituted bed checks and prohibited drinking and dating by members of the band. In 1957, the group recorded "Apple Blossom Time"; a year later, "Ida, Sweet as Apple Cider."

Although Bill Haley was unable to take full advantage of it, rock 'n' roll had emerged as a mass culture phenomenon. At the end of 1956, 68 percent of the music played by disc jockeys was rock 'n' roll, an increase of two-thirds over the previous year. By December 1957 virtually every position on *Billboard*'s Top Ten was occupied by a rock 'n' roller. "Whatever emotional and psychological factors there are behind its acceptance," *Cash Box* editors asserted, "whatever spark it may have touched off in a teenager's makeup, the one fact that remains certain is that youngsters today find what they are looking for in the way of music in Rock 'n' Roll. It seems futile to try to deny this fact or pretend that it is a temporary thing."

As Carl Perkins's "Blue Suede Shoes" and Elvis Presley's "Heartbreak Hotel" surged to the top of the pop, rhythm and blues, and country charts, *The Cash Box* exulted that rock 'n' roll was affecting "the lives of everyone in our country." Rock 'n' roll, the editors believed, provided evidence of and served as an impetus for greater cultural harmony and homogenization in the United States. "Greater mobility and more dynamic means of communication," they explained, "have brought the taste and mode of living of people in various areas of our country to the attention and knowledge of those in other areas." In a banner headline, they predicted that "Rock and Roll May Be the Great Unifying Force!"

They were wrong. Although rock 'n' roll was a commodity, produced and distributed by a profit-making industry, and therefore subject to co-optation by the dominant culture, it continued to resist and unsettle "mainstream" values. For African Americans, rock 'n' roll was a mixed blessing. At times a force for integration and racial respect, rock 'n' roll was also an act of theft that in supplanting rhythm and blues deprived blacks of appropriate acknowledgment, rhetorical and financial, of their contributions to American culture. Rock 'n' roll deepened the divide between the generations, helped teenagers differentiate themselves from others, transformed popular culture in the United States, and rattled the reticent by pushing sexuality into the public arena. Anything but a "great unifying force," rock 'n' roll kept many Americans in the 1950s off balance, on guard, and uncertain about their families and the future of their country.

J. Ronald Oakley  **NO**

God's Country: America in the Fifties

Generation in a Spotlight

As the 1950s opened, America's adolescents were basically a conservative, unrebellious lot. Although the word *teenager* had come into widespread circulation in the 1940s to describe this distinct age group mired in the limbo between puberty and adulthood, the teenagers of the early fifties had not yet developed a distinct subculture. They had few rights and little money of their own, wore basically the same kind of clothing their parents wore, watched the same television shows, went to the same movies, used the same slang, and listened to the same romantic music sung by Perry Combo, Frank Sinatra, and other middle-aged or nearly middle-aged artists. Their idols were Joe DiMaggio, General MacArthur, and other prominent members of the older generation. In spite of what they learned from older kids and from the underground pornography that circulated on school playgrounds, they were amazingly naïve about sex, believing well into their high school years that French kissing could cause pregnancy or that the douche, coitus interruptus, and chance could effectively prevent it. Heavy petting was the limit for most couples, and for those who went "all the way" there were often strong guilt feelings and, for the girl at least, the risk of a bad reputation. Rebellion against authority, insofar as it occurred, consisted primarily of harmless pranks against unpopular adult neighbors or teachers, occasional vandalism (especially on Halloween night), smoking cigarettes or drinking beer, and the decades-old practice of mooning. Although most families had the inevitable clashes of opinion between parents and offspring, there were few signs of a "generation gap" or of rebellion against the conventions of the adult world.

But all of this began to change in the early fifties, and by the middle of the decade the appearance of a distinct youth subculture was causing parents and the media to agonize over the scandalous behavior and rebellious nature of the nation's young people. The causes of the emergence of this subculture are not hard to find. One was the demographic revolution of the postwar years that was increasing the influence of the young by producing so many of them in such a short period of time. Another was the affluence of the period, an affluence shared with the young through allowances from their parents or through part-time jobs. As teenagers acquired their own money, they were able to pursue their own life-style, and now American business and advertisers geared up to promote and exploit a gigantic youth consumer market featuring products designed especially for them. Then there were the effects of progressive education and Spockian child-rearing practices, for while neither was quite as permissive or indulgent toward the young as the critics claimed, they did emphasize the treatment of adolescents as unique people who should be given the freedom to develop their own personality and talents. Another factor was television and movies, which had the power to raise up new fads, new heroes, and new values and to spread them to young people from New York to Los Angeles. And finally, there was rock 'n' roll, which grew from several strains in American music and emerged at mid-decade as the theme song of the youth rebellion and as a major molder and reflector of their values.

One of the earliest landmarks in the history of the youth rebellion came in 1951 with the publication of J. D. Salinger's *The Catcher in the Rye.* Infinitely more complex than most of its young readers or older detractors perceived, this novel featured the actions and thoughts of one Holden Caulfield, a sixteen-year-old veteran of several private schools, who roams around New York City in his own private rebellion from home and school. In colloquial language laced with obscenities absent from most novels of the day, Holden tells the reader of his rejection of the phoniness and corruption of the adult world, of how parents, teachers, ministers, actors, nightclub pianists and singers, old grads, and others lie to themselves and to the young about what the world is really like. *The Catcher in the Rye* was popular throughout the fifties with high school and college students, for while young people might not understand all that Salinger was trying to say, they did identify with his cynical rejection of the adult world and adult values. The book was made even more popular by the attempts of school boards, libraries, and state legislatures to ban it. It was one of the first books, if not the first, to perceive the existence of a generation gap in the supposedly happy, family-oriented society of the early 1950s.

Still another sign of the changes occurring in the nation's youth was the rise of juvenile delinquency. Between 1948 and 1953 the number of juveniles brought into court and charged with crimes increased by 45 percent, and it was estimated that for every juvenile criminal brought into court there were at least five who had not been caught. It was especially disturbing that juvenile crimes were committed by organized gangs that roamed—and seemed to control—the streets of many of the larger cities. Street gangs had existed before in American history, but in the fifties they were larger, more violent, and more widespread than ever before. Thanks to modern communications, they tended to dress alike, to use the same jargon, and share the same values all across the country. And they were not just in America—they appeared in England (Teddy Boys), Sweden ("Skinn-Nuttar" or leather jackets), and other industrial countries across the globe. The youth rebellion, including the criminal fringe that made up part of it, was international.

Learning about these gangs in their newspapers and weekly magazines, Americans were horrified by what they read and by how often they read it. It seemed that hardly a week went by without the occurrence of shocking crimes committed by teenagers or even younger children who did not seem to know the difference between good and bad—or worse, deliberately chose the bad over the good. Sporting colorful names like Dragons, Cobras, Rovers, and Jesters, they carried all kinds of weapons—zip guns, pistols, rifles, knives, chains, shotguns, brass knuckles, broken bottles, razors, lead pipes, molotov cocktails, machetes, and lye and other chemicals. They drank alcoholic beverages, smoked reefers, took heroin and other drugs, had their own twisted code of honor, and organized well-planned attacks on other gangs or innocent victims. They also had their own jargon, borrowed from the criminal underworld and spoken by gangs from coast to coast: *dig, duke, gig, jap, jazz, rumble, turf, cool, chick, pusher, reefer,* and hundreds of other slang terms.

To a nation accustomed to believing in the essential goodness of its young people, the behavior of these delinquent gangs was puzzling and frightening. They seemed to pursue violence for the pure joy of violence and to delight in sadistic actions toward other gangs or innocent victims. They engaged in shootings, stabbings, individual and gang rapes, senseless beatings, and unspeakable tortures. They extorted "protection" money from frightened merchants, sprayed crowds in streets or restaurants or subways with rifle fire, doused people with gasoline and set them ablaze, firebombed bars and nightclubs, stole automobiles, vandalized apartments and public buildings, and fought vicious gang wars over girls or invasion of turf or to avenge some real or imagined slight. They often terrorized and vandalized schools and assaulted teachers and students, leading the *New York Daily News* in 1954 to describe "rowdyism, riot, and revolt," as the new three Rs in New York's public schools.

It was particularly disturbing that these young hoodlums often showed no remorse for their actions, recounting with delight to police or social workers the details of a rape, murder, or torture in which they had been involved. One eighteen-year-old who had participated in the torture and murder of an innocent young man in a public park told police that "last night was a supreme adventure for me. Describing his role in the killing of another gang member, one young man told police that "he was laying on the ground looking up at us. I kicked him on the jaw or someplace; then I kicked him in the stomach. That was the least I could do, was kick 'im. In another incident a gang member described his part in a stabbing by saying: "I stabbed him with a bread knife. You know, I was drunk, so I just stabbed him. [Laughs] He was screaming like a dog.

The rise of juvenile delinquency, and especially its organized forms in the street gangs of the major cities, caused agonizing soul-searching among anxious parents, school authorities, psychologists, and other experts on adolescent and criminal behavior. Parents of delinquents anxiously asked, "What did we do wrong?" and many admitted to school, police, and court authorities that they could not control their children. The experts came up with a whole range of explanations of juvenile criminality, blaming it on poverty, slum conditions, permissive parents, lack of religious and moral training, television, movies, comic books, racism, parents who were too busy working or pursuing their own pleasures to rear their children properly, the high divorce rate with the resulting broken homes, anxiety over the draft, and decline of parental discipline and control. Early in the decade most authorities tended to blame it on the problems of poverty and slum living, but as the decade wore on, it became very clear that many of the delinquents were from middle- and upper-class families that provided a good environment for their children. So then it was blamed on society or on simple "thrill seeking" by bored, pampered, and jaded youths. As the problem worsened, many were inclined to agree with Baltimore psychologist Robert Linder, who claimed that the young people of the day were suffering from a form of collective mental illness. "The youth of the world today," he told a Los Angeles audience in 1954, "is touched with madness, literally sick with an aberrant condition of mind formerly confined to a few distressed souls but now epidemic over the earth."

Whatever the causes of juvenile delinquency, and they were certainly multiple and complex, it was obvious that delinquent and criminal acts by individual adolescents and organized gangs were increasing every year and were making the streets of many large cities dangerous for law-abiding citizens. And while many people thought of the problem as one that plagued primarily the slums of the big cities of the Northeast or California, it soon became clear that it was spreading to large cities all across the country, to the new suburbs, to the rural areas which were so accessible now to middle-class teenagers with automobiles, and to the South, which had often prided itself on not having the problems of the big northern cities. In 1954 *New York Times* education editor Benjamin Fine wrote a much-discussed book on the problem, *1,000,000 Delinquents*, which correctly predicted that during the next year 1 million adolescents would get into serious trouble that would bring them into the courtroom. In that same year *Newsweek* published an article entitled "Our Vicious Young Hoodlums: Is There Any Hope?" By now, many people thought that there was none and found themselves in the unusual position of being afraid of their own children.

By the midfifties Americans had become so saturated with stories of juvenile delinquency that there was a tendency among many to stereotype all teenagers as bad, especially if they adopted the clothing, ducktail haircuts, or language of gangs. But the truth was that few teenagers were juvenile delinquents or gang members, very few used drugs (except for alcohol), and very few ever got into trouble with the police. And many teenagers resented the stereotyped image the adult world had of them. As one seventeen-year-old high school girl said in 1955, "I've never set a fire, robbed a gas station, or beaten a defenseless old man. In fact, I don't even know anyone who has. . . . I wish someone would think of the 95% of us who *aren't* delinquents. Because we're here, too." The young woman was correct, of course, for most teenagers were not delinquents. But they were changing in ways that were disturbing even the parents of "good" teens, and one of the major causes of these changes was the rise of a new musical form, rock 'n' roll. . . .

Born in the small town of Fairmount, Indiana, on February 8, 1931, James Dean led a life much like that of the troubled youth he later came to portray in his movies. His mother died when he was nine, and he was reared on the farm of his aunt and uncle with only brief glimpses of his father. A confused adolescent, he went to California after his graduation from high school, attended Santa Monica City College and UCLA, and played some small parts in movies before going back to New York to study acting in 1951. In 1954 he came back to Hollywood as an admirer of Marlon Brando, motorcycles, and fast cars. He quickly earned a reputation as a lazy, undisciplined, ill-mannered star who often stayed out all night long and then showed up on the set too tired to do good work. His first major film, *East of Eden* (1955), brought him instant fame through his portrayal of the sensitive son suffering from the fear that his father does not love him, but his rise as a teenage idol came later in the year through his performance as a misunderstood and rebellious teenager in *Rebel Without a Cause*. Costarring Natalie Wood and Sal Mineo, the film was released to the theaters in the fall of 1955, only two weeks after Dean's tragic death in a high-speed wreck between his Porsche and a Ford on a lonely California highway. By the time the just-completed *Giant* was released, in November of 1956, an astonishing cult had sprung up around the young star and his death, so senseless, at the age of twenty-four.

The legends that grew up around James Dean were the greatest since the death of Rudolph Valentino. Young people saw Dean as the embodiment of their restlessness, confusion, and rejections, as a rebel fighting, like them, against the rules and conformity the adult world was trying to impose upon them. But while Valentino and most other movie legends had appealed as sex symbols. Dean appealed to an age group—to young males and females between fourteen and twenty-four. Young males saw him as a symbol of their own rebellious and troubled nature, while young girls saw him as an attractive, sensual male who needed mothering as much as sexual love. Although Dean was a good actor with great promise, his acting reputation was exaggerated beyond all reality by the myths and legends that shrouded his life and acting career after his premature death.

Within a few weeks after Dean's death, Warner Brothers was swamped with hundreds of letters. Their number rose to 3,000 a month by January of 1956 and to 7,000 a month by July, some with money enclosed for a picture of the dead star. The fan magazines played the Dean legend for all it was worth, publishing thousands of pictures and stories. In these magazines and across the national teenage grapevine, the rumors flew: that he was not really dead, that he had been so disfigured from the wreck that he had gone into hiding or been sent to a sanatorium, that he was just a vegetable in a secret hospital room known only to his close friends, that he had talked to some of his fans from beyond his grave, and that his tomb in Fairmount, Indiana, had been emptied by grave robbers or by Dean's own miraculous resurrection. Several records appeared—"Tribute to James Dean," "The Ballad of James Dean," "His Name Was Dean." "The Story of James Dean," "Jimmy Jimmy," and "We'll Never Forget You." Dozens of biographies and other literary tributes were rushed to the market, along with the inevitable movie, *The James Dean Story.* When the wreckage of his car was put on display in Los Angeles, over 800,000 people paid to view it. The adulation swept teens all across America and even in Europe. In England, a young man legally changed his name to James Dean, copied his clothing and mannerisms, went to America twice to visit the real Dean's family and grave, and claimed to have seen *Rebel Without a Cause* over 400 times. As *Look* magazine observed, the subject of this almost psychopathic adulation was "a 24-year old who did not live long enough to find out what he had done and was in too much of a hurry to find out who he was."

Along with *The Wild One,* a 1954 film starring Marlon Brando as the leader of a motorcycle gang, *The Blackboard Jungle* and the films of James Dean helped to spawn a series of films aimed specifically at young people. In addition to the films of Elvis Presley and other teen idols, the second half of the fifties saw a spate of second-rate rock movies—*Rock Around the Clock, Don't Knock the Rock, Rock Pretty Baby, Rock Around the World,* and *Let's Rock*—and a series of shallow, trashy movies about young people and delinquency, such as *Girls in Prison, Eighteen and Anxious, Reform School Girl, Hot Rod Rumble,* and *High School Confidential.* For better or worse—mostly worse—teenagers were getting their own movies as well as their own music.

In 1955 teenagers had their music, their movies, their idols—dead and alive—but as yet they had no one who combined all three of these and served as a focal point for their growing consciousness as a subculture. But he was waiting in the wings, for in that year a young performer with a regional reputation was making records and gaining a wide following among teenagers, especially young girls, with live performances in southern cities that were often punctuated by desperate attempts by the police to prevent these screaming fans from rushing the stage to tear off his clothes. He was a James Dean fan, who had seen *Rebel Without a Cause* several times, could recite the script by heart, and had been wearing tight pants, leather jackets, and a ducktail haircut with long sideburns for several years. In 1956 he would burst on the national entertainment stage and proceed to become one of the most popular and influential musical performers of all time, rivaling Rudy Vallee, Bing Crosby, Frank Sinatra, and other singers before him. His name was Elvis Presley, and he was destined to claim the title of King of Rock 'n' Roll. . . .

Record sales soared with the coming of rock 'n' roll. Aided by the affluence of the time, the invention of the 45 rpm and $33^1/_3$ rpm records, and the introduction of high fidelity, record sales had steadily climbed from 109 million in 1945 to 189 million in 1950 and to 219 million in 1953, then with the arrival of rock 'n' roll rose to 277 million in 1955 and to 600 million in 1960. In 1956 alone, RCA Victor sold over 13.5 million Elvis Presley singles and 3.75 million Presley albums. By 1957, the new 45s and $33^1/_3$s had driven the 78s out of production. Teenagers bought most of the inexpensive and convenient 45s and most of the long-playing rock 'n' roll albums, whereas adults bought most of the long-playing albums of traditional popular music, jazz, and classical music. While in 1950 the average record buyer was likely to be in his early twenties, by 1958, 70 percent of all the records sold in the United States were purchased by teenagers. Most of the popular singles were purchased by girls between the ages of thirteen and nineteen, the group most receptive, as one critic said, to "little wide-eyed wishes for ideal love and perfect lovers, little songs of frustration at not finding them." Thanks to these revolutions in the musical world, record sales, which had stood at only $7.5 million in 1940, had risen to a healthy $521 million in 1960.

Why was rock 'n' roll so popular? One of the reasons, of course, was that it was written and performed by young people and was centered upon what was important to them: love, going steady, jealousy, high school, sex, dancing, clothing, automobiles, and all the other joys and problems of being young. The lyrics were just as silly, sentimental, and idealistic as the music of the crooners of the first half of the decade, but it was written just for the young and the singing styles, beat, electrical amplification, and volume of the music was much more dynamic than that of the earlier period. Teens were attracted to its celebration of sexuality, expressed in the more explicit lyrics, driving tempo, movements of the rock 'n' roll performers, and in new dances at high school hops and private parties. Perhaps Jeff Greenfield, a member of this first generation of rock 'n' roll fans, expressed it best in his *No Peace, No Place.* "Each night, sprawled on my bed on Manhattan's Upper West Side, I would listen to the world that Alan Freed created. To a twelve- or thirteen-year-old, it was a world of unbearable sexuality and celebration: a world of citizens under sixteen, in a constant state of joy or sweet sorrow. . . . New to sexual sensations, driven by the impulses that every new adolescent generation knows, we were the first to have a music rooted in uncoated sexuality." And very importantly, rock 'n' roll gave young people a sense of cohesion, of unity, all across the nation. It was *their* music, written for them and for them only, about their world, a world that adults could not share and did not understand. As such, it was one of the major harbingers of the generation gap.

It was not long after teenagers acquired their own music and movies that they also acquired their own television show. *American Bandstand* began as a local television show in Philadelphia in 1952, and in August of 1957 it premiered as a network show on ABC over sixty-seven stations across the country, from 3:00 to 4:30 in the afternoon, with twenty-six-year-old Dick Clark as the host. The first network show featured songs by Jerry Lee Lewis, the Coasters, and other top rock 'n' roll artists, and guest star Billy Williams singing "I'm Gonna Sit Right Down and Write Myself a Letter." Some of the early reviews of the show were not complimentary. According to *Billboard,* "The bulk of the ninety minutes was devoted to colorless juveniles trudging through early American dances like the Lindy and the Box Step to recorded tunes of the day. If this is the wholesome answer to the 'detractors' of rock 'n' roll, bring on the rotating pelvises." But by the end of 1958 the show was reaching over 20 million viewers over 105 stations, and had spawned dozens of imitations on local stations. This was a show about teens, and its consistent high rating and longevity proved that they liked it, regardless of what adults said about it.

American Bandstand had a great influence on popular music and on America's teenagers. Clark's good looks, neat clothing, and civilized manner helped reassure American parents that rock 'n' roll was not a barbarian invasion that was turning the young into juvenile delinquents. All the dancers on the show in the fifties were white, adhered to a strict dress code (coats and ties for boys, dresses and skirts and blouses for girls, and no jeans, T-shirts, or tight sweaters), and followed a strict language code that even prohibited the use of the term "going steady." One of Clark's most embarrassing moments on the show came when a young girl told him that the pin she was wearing was a "virgin pin." Stars with unsavory reputations were not allowed on the show, so when the news of Jerry Lee Lewis's marriage to his thirteen-year-old cousin broke, Clark joined other disc jockeys and promotors across the country in canceling all future appearances of the pioneer rock 'n' roll star. The show also featured the biggest stars of the day and helped launch the careers of Connie Francis, Fabian, Frankie Avalon, and several other singers. The new dances performed on the show—such as "the stroll," "the shake," and "the walk"—were soon copied all across the country. Teenagers everywhere also imitated the slang and the dress of this very influential show and brought the records its regulars danced to. The success of this dance show brought popularity and wealth to its host, who freely admitted that "I dance very poorly," yet became a millionaire by the age of thirty.

The rise of rock 'n' roll, teen movies, teen television shows, and teen magazines helped create the teen idol. Many of the idols were singers, like Elvis Presley, Rick Nelson, Frankie Avalon, Bobby Darin, Fabian, Pat Boone, Connie Francis, and Annette Funicello. Others were movie or television actors, like James Dean and Marlon Brando, though of course many of the singers also went on to move careers which might be called, at best, undistinguished. Most of the idols were teenagers themselves or in their twenties, and it is important to note here that while earlier generations had tended to create idols much older than themselves—like Bing Crosby, Perry Como, and Clark Gable—the teenagers of the late fifties made idols of people from their own generation. And although clean-cut starts like Ricky Nelson or Frankie Avalon were chosen as idols, many young people also idolized Brando and Dean, who seemed so much like them in their agonizing over the problems of life. The inclination of the young to idolize those who portrayed problem youth was puzzling and disturbing to parents who wanted their children to grow up to be clean-cut, middle-class kids who went to church, obeyed their parents and other authorities, drank nothing harder than a soft drink, had no sexual experience before marriage, saved and studied for college, hung around soda shops rather than pool rooms, and after college went into a respectable career with a good income and a secure future. In short, they wanted their children to be like Pat Boone.

Born in Jacksonville, Florida, in 1934, Boone rose to fame while still a college student by winning first place on Ted Mack's *Original Amateur Hour* and *Arthur Godfrey's Talent Scouts* in 1954. He became a regular on Godfrey's morning show, and then began a career as a singer, movie star (*Bernadine* and *April Love,* both in 1957), and television star with his own show (*Pat Boone Chevy Showroom*). Many of his recordings were covers of original black songs like "Tutti-Frutti" and "Ain't That a Shame," and traditional romantic tunes such as "Friendly Persuasion," "April Love," and "Love Letters in the Sand." Boone was an all-American boy, a dedicated Christian and family man who had not been spoiled by his success, although at the age of twenty-four he was already popular and wealthy, earning $750,000 annually. He had an attractive wife, four pretty daughters, a baccalaureate degree from Columbia University, a love of milk and ice cream, and a severe distaste for strong drink, tobacco, and anything else immoral. He attracted wide publicity in 1958 when he refused to kiss Shirley Jones in the movie *April Love,* saying that "I've always been taught that when you get married, you forget about kissing other women." However, after talking it over with his wife, he agreed to do the kissing scene, although "she would prefer to keep that part of our lives solely to ourselves." This old-fashioned wholesomeness enabled him to hit the best-seller list in 1958 with *Twist Twelve and Twenty,* a moral and social guide for teenagers that reflected Boone's conservative view of sex and his deeply religious outlook on life. Some teenagers found Boone hopelessly "square," but many others admired his moral rectitude. He was immensely popular in the fifties, perhaps second only to Elvis.

In spite of the existence of clean-cut white performers like Pat Boone, much of the adult world was against the new rock 'n' roll. Many musicians and music critics condemned it on musical grounds, disliking its primitive beat, electrical amplification, witless and repetitive lyrics, loudness, and screams. But most adults opposed it for other reasons. Many objected to its suggestive lyrics and claimed that it fomented rebellion against parents and other authorities, bred immorality, inflamed teenagers to riot, and was un-Christian and unpatriotic. They agreed with Frank Sinatra, who called it "the martial music of every sideburned delinquent on the face of the earth." Others objected to its racial background and content, even claiming, as many southerners did, that rock 'n' roll was a plot jointly sponsored by the Kremlin and the NAACP, and that rock musicians and disc jockeys were dope addicts, communists, integrationists, atheists, and sex fiends. To many whites, North and South, it was "nigger music," and as such was designed to tear down the barriers of segregation and bring about sexual promiscuity, intermarriage, and a decline in the morals of young whites.

The fears of parents and other adults were fed by the isolated incidents of rioting that accompanied rock 'n' roll concerts in Boston, Washington, D.C., and several other cities. As a result of these headline-getting events, rock 'n' roll concerts were banned in many cities or else accompanied by heavy police security and strict regulations as to what the performers could do or say on stage. In many cities, city councils and other local groups also tried to ban rock 'n' roll from record stores or jukeboxes. In San Antonio, Texas, the city council even went so far as to ban the music from the jukeboxes of public swimming pools, claiming that it "attracted undesirable elements given to practicing their gyrations in abbreviated bathing suits." A disc jockey in Buffalo was fired when he played an Elvis Presley record, and across the country disc jockeys were similarly punished for playing the new music or were pressured into boycotting it. Some disc jockeys broke rock 'n' roll records on the air, while radio station WLEV in Erie, Pennsylvania, loaded over 7,000 rock 'n' roll records into a rented hearse and led a funeral procession to Erie Harbor, where the records were "buried at sea." Ministers preached against it, claiming, like the Rev. John Carroll in Boston, that the music corrupted young people and that "rock and roll inflames and excites youth like jungle tom-toms readying warriors for battle," and many churches held public burnings of rock 'n' roll records. Some were even willing to resort to the ugliest kinds of violence to try to stem the advance of rock music. On April 23, 1956, in Birmingham, Alabama, where the White Citizens' Council had succeeded in removing all rock 'n' roll records from jukeboxes, five men connected with the council rushed the stage of the city auditorium and assaulted black ballad singer Nat King Cole, who was badly bruised before the police stopped the attack.

The debate over rock 'n' roll continued through the end of the decade, carried on in the press, over radio and television, in teachers' meetings, pulpits, and city council meeting rooms. By 1960 the debate had begun to die down, with parents coming to see that the music was not going to fade away, that it had not made delinquents of their children, and that all the other dire predictions had not come to pass, either. Some even began to admit grudgingly that they liked some of it, though they wished that it were not played so loudly. Some of the older professional musicians had also come to defend it— Benny Goodman, Sammy Kaye, Paul Whiteman, and Duke Ellington had kind words for the new music from the very beginning, and Whiteman and Kaye publicly recalled that most new musical forms, including their own swing music, had been condemned when it first appeared. And in the May 1959 issue of *Harper's,* critic Arnold Shaw noted that "perhaps it should be added (although it should be self-evident) that just as hot jazz of the twenties (then anathema to our grandparents) did not destroy our parents, and swing (anathema to our parents) did not destroy us, it is quite unlikely that rock 'n' roll will destroy our children."

The spectacular rise of rock 'n' roll should not obscure the fact that the older music continued to thrive. In 1957, when rock 'n' roll claimed seven of the top ten records of the year, the number one song was "Tammy," recorded by both Debbie Reynolds and the Ames Brothers, and Perry Como remained a favorite of young and old throughout the decade. In a 1956 poll by *Woman's Home Companion,* teenage boys and girls chose Como as the best male vocalist, with Presley, Boone, and Sinatra trailing behind. Johnny Mathis, Paul Anka, Pat Boone, Bobby Darin, the Everly Brothers, and many other teen idols also continued to sing fairly traditional love songs, and in the late fifties, building on a tradition established early in the decade by the Weavers, the Kingston Trio brought a revival of folk music to college students with a touch of rock and protest in songs like "Tom Dooley," "Tijuana Jail," and "A Worried Man," paving the way for the folk music explosion in the early 1960s. Rock music dominated from 1956 to 1960, but it did not completely push the older music aside.

In addition to obtaining their own music, movies, television shows, and idols, teenagers of the fifties also acquired their own fashions, and here they followed the trend toward casual dress that was characterizing the rest of society. The favorite dress of high school boys was denim jeans with rolled-up cuffs, sport shirts, baggy pegged pants, pleated rogue trousers with a white side stripe, slacks with buckles in the back, V-neck sweaters, button-down striped shirts, blazers, white bucks, and loafers. In 1955 they also joined older males on college campuses and executive offices in the pink revolution, donning pink shirts, pink striped or polka dot ties, and colonel string ties. Hair styles ranged from the popular flat top or crew cut to the Apache or ducktail (banned at some high schools). "Greasers" of course shunned the Ivy League and pink attire as too effeminate, sticking to their T-shirts (often with sleeves rolled up to hold a cigarette pack), jeans, leather jackets, and ducktails. For girls, the fashions ranged from rolled-up jeans to casual blouses or men's shirts, full dresses with crinolines, skirts and sweaters, blazers, occasional experiments with the tube dress and sack dress and other disasters foisted upon older women by fashion designers, short shorts (with rolled-up cuffs) that got progressively shorter as the decade wore on, two-piece bathing suits (few were bold enough to wear the bikini, imported from France in the late forties), brown and white saddle shoes and loafers, and hair styles from the poodle to the ponytail. Couples who were going steady wore one another's class rings, identification tags, and necklaces or bracelets, and often adopted a unisex look by wearing matching sweaters, blazers, and shirts.

Like the generations before them, the teenagers of the fifties also had their slang. Much of it was concerned, of course, with the great passion of teens, cars. Cars were *wheels,* tires were *skins,* racing from a standing start was called a *drag,* the bumper was *nerf-bar,* a special kind of exhaust system was called *duals,* and a car specially modified for more engine power was a *hot rod* or *souped up car* or *bomb.* A drive-in movie was a *passion pit,* anything or anyone considered dull was a *drag,* and a really dull person was a *square* or a *nosebleed.* An admirable or poised individual or anything worthy of admiration or approval was *cool* or *neat* or *smooth,* someone who panicked or lost his *cool* was accused of *clutching,* and people admonished not to worry were told to *hang loose.* Teenagers also borrowed lingo from the jazz and beatnik world, such as *dig, hip, cat, bread,* and *chick.* A cutting, sarcastic laugh at someone's bad joke was expressed by *a hardeeharhar.* And teenagers also shared the jargon of the rest of society—*big deal, the royal screw* or *royal shaft, up the creek without a paddle, forty lashes with a wet noodle, wild, wicked, crazy, classy, horny, BMOC, looking for action, bad news, out to lunch, gross, fink, loser, creep, dumb cluck, doing the deed, going all the way,* or *coming across.* Many of these colloquialisms were borrowed from earlier generations, sometimes with modifications in meaning, while some had been regionalisms that now became national through the great homogenizing power of television.

By the mid-1950s there were 16.5 million teenagers in the United States. About half of them were crowding the nation's secondary schools, while the rest had entered college or the work world. Wherever they were, they had become, as Gereon Zimmerman would write in *Look* magazine, a "Generation in a Searchlight," a constant subject of media attention and a constant source of anxiety for their parents and the rest of the adult world. As Zimmerman observed, "No other generation has had so such attention, so much admonition, so many statistics."

Zimmerman might also have added that no other young generation had had so much money. One of the most revolutionary aspects of the teenage generation was its effects on the American economy, for by the midfifties teenagers made up a very lucrative consumer market for American manufacturers. By mid-decade teenagers of this affluent era were viewing as necessities goods that their parents, reared during the depression, still saw as luxuries, such as automobiles, televisions, record players, cameras, and the like. By the midfifties, teenagers were buying 43 percent of all records, 44 percent of all cameras, 39 percent of all new radios, 9 percent of all new cars, and 53 percent of movie tickets. By 1959, the amount of money spent on teenagers by themselves and by their parents had reached the staggering total of $10 billion a year. Teenagers were spending around $75 million annually on single popular records, $40 million on lipstick, $25 million on deodorant, $9 million on home permanents, and over $837 million on school clothes for teenage girls. Many teenagers had their own charge accounts at local stores and charge cards issued especially for them, such as Starlet Charge Account, Campus Deb Account, and the 14 to 21 Club. Like their parents, teenagers were being led by the affluence and advertising of the age to desire an ever-increasing diet of consumer goods and services and to buy them even if they had to charge them against future earnings.

Many adults had a distorted image of this affluent young generation, focusing too much on its delinquency, rock 'n' roll, unconventional hair styles and clothing, and dating and sexual practices. Only a very small percentage were delinquents or problem-ridden adolescents. Most were reasonably well-groomed, well-behaved, and active in school and extracurricular functions. Most were interested in sports, automobiles, movies, rock 'n' roll, dating, dancing, hobbies, radio, and television. Their major worries were the typical problems of youth in an affluent age: problems with their parents, their popularity with other teens, their looks and complexions, proper dating behavior, sex, first dates, first kisses, love, bad breath, body odors, posture, body build, friends, schoolwork, college, future careers, money, religion, and the draft.

These teenagers that parents worried so much about were remarkably conservative. Survey after survey of young people in the fifties found that over half of them—and sometimes even larger percentages—believed that censorship of printed materials and movies was justified, that politics was beyond their understanding and was just a dirty game, that most people did not have the ability to make important decisions about what was good for them, that masturbation was shameful and perhaps harmful, that women should not hold public office, and that the theory of evolution was suspect and even dangerous. Like their parents, they were also very religious as a group, tending to believe in the divine inspiration of the Bible, heaven and hell, and a God who answered the prayers of the faithful. They were suspicious of radical groups and were willing to deny them the right to assemble in meetings and to disseminate their ideas, and they saw nothing wrong with denying accused criminals basic constitutional rights, such as the right to know their accuser, to be free from unreasonable search or seizure of their property, or to refuse to testify against themselves. Teenagers were also very conformist: They were very concerned about what their friends thought of their dress, behavior, and ideas, and they tried very hard to be part of the group and not be labeled an oddball or individualist. In short, in this age of corporation man, the country also had corporation teen.

Most teens were also conservative in their approach to dating, sex, and marriage. Religious views, social and peer pressure, and fear of pregnancy all combined to create this conservatism and to ensure that most teens kept their virginity until marriage or at least until the early college years, though heavy petting was certainly prevalent among couples who were engaged or "going steady," a practice reflecting society's emphasis on monogamy. These conservative attitudes toward sexual behavior were reinforced by the authorities teenagers looked to for guidance—parents, teachers, ministers, advice to the lovelorn columnists like Dear Abby and Ann Landers (both of whom began their columns in the midfifties), and books on teenage etiquette by Allen Ludden, Pat Boone, and *Seventeen* magazine. In his book for young men, *Plain Talk for Men Under 21,* Ludden devoted an entire chapter to such things as "That Good Night Kiss"—discussing whether to, how to, and the significance of it if you did. And in the very popular *The Seventeen Book of Young Living* (1957), Enid Haupt, the editor and publisher of *Seventeen* magazine, advised young girls to "keep your first and all your romances on a beyond reproach level" and to save themselves for the one right man in their lives. Acknowledging that "it isn't easy to say no to a persuasive and charming boy," she offered one answer for all potentially compromising situations: " 'No, please take me home. Now.' "

The conservatism of the young would continue over into the college-age population, where it would remain entrenched for the rest of the fifties. The decade witnessed a boom in higher education, as rising prosperity. G.I. benefits, increasing governmental and private financial aid, fear of the draft, and a growing cultural emphasis on higher education all contributed to a great increase in the number of college students, faculty, programs, and buildings. The boom occurred at all levels—undergraduate, graduate, professional, and in the burgeoning junior- and community-college movement. The number of students, which had stood at 1.5 million in 1940 and 2.3 million in 1950, steadily rose in the decade and reached 3.6 million in 1960, and while the population of the country grew by 8 percent in the decade, the college population grew by 40 percent. By the end of the decade, almost 40 percent of the eighteen-to-twenty-one-year-old age group was attending some institution of higher education.

The conservatism of the college students of the 1950s led them to be called the Silent Generation. Why was it so silent? One of the most important reasons was that it mirrored the conservatism of the society at large, a society caught up in the materialistic and Cold War mentality of the decade. Like their elders, students were seeking the good life rather than the examined one, and as the Great Fear spread to the campuses, many were afraid of acquiring a radical reputation that might jeopardize their scholarships and their future careers in private industry, government service, or the military. Many were veterans, and their military experience, especially for those who had served in Korea, had tended to confirm their conservatism. Many others were in college in order to evade or at least defer the draft, and did not want to do or say anything that might endanger their deferred status. And finally, most students were white and drawn from the middle and upper-middle classes of society. The doors of higher education were still closed to most minority groups and to the economically and socially disadvantaged—groups who might have brought questioning or even radical attitudes into the field of higher education had they been part of it. It is not surprising then that most college students were hardworking, conservative, and career-oriented, truly deserving of their Silent Generation label.

The conservatism of the college generation prevailed throughout the decade. In a study of the college generation in 1951, *Time* magazine noted that "the most startling thing about the younger generation is its silence. . . . It does not issue manifestoes, make speeches, or carry posters." Most students,

Time found, were worried about the Korean War and its effects on their plans for careers and marriage, but they pushed these fears into the background and concentrated on earning good grades and landing a good job. They were serious and hardworking, in rebellion against nothing, and had no real heroes or villains. Born during the depression years, they were primarily interested in a good job and security, and they did not want to do or say anything that would jeopardize these goals. "Today's generation," *Time* concluded, "either through fear, passivity, or conviction, is ready to conform."

Soon after the end of the Korean War, *Newsweek* studied college students in seven institutions, and its findings were little different from those of *Time* two years before. In "U.S. Campus Kids of 1953: Unkiddable and Unbeatable," *Newsweek* reported that students were hardworking, ambitious conformists who looked forward to secure jobs and a happy married life. Going steady was more popular then ever before, a sign of the period's emphasis on marriage and of young people's desire for the security that a going-steady relationship brought. Most students, *Newsweek* found, were not very interested in politics or international affairs, and they avoided being linked with unpopular causes. One Vassar girl told the magazine, "We're a cautious generation. We aren't buying any ideas we're not sure of." Another said that "you want to be popular, so naturally you don't express any screwy ideas. To be popular you have to conform." And a Princeton senior said that "the world doesn't owe me a living—but it owes me a job." *Newsweek* also saw a renewed interest in religion, as reflected in increasing enrollments in religion courses and frequent "religious emphasis weeks." The magazine found much to admire in the hardworking materialistic class of 1953, although it did concede that "they might seem dull in comparison with less troubled eras."

Similar collegiate characteristics were reported in a 1955 study by David Riesman, who found that students were ambitious, very sure of what they wanted to do, but also very unadventurous—they wanted secure positions in big companies and were already concerned about retirement plans. As one Princeton senior saw it, "Why struggle on my own, when I can enjoy the big psychological income of being a member of a big outfit?" Most males had already decided that they wanted middle-management jobs—they did not want to rise to the presidential or vice-presidential level because that would require too much drive, take time away from their family life and leisure time, and force them to live in a big city. Most had already decided upon the kind of girl they would marry, how many kids they would have, and which civic clubs and other organizations they would join—and they would be joiners, for they liked the gregarious life and knew it would help their careers. They wanted educated wives who would be intellectually stimulating, yet they wanted them to be dutiful and obedient and to stay at home and raise the kids. Many said they wanted as many as four or five kids, because they felt that a large family would bring happiness, security, contentment. One Harvard senior said that "I'd like six kids. I don't know why I say that—it seems like a minimum production goal." They did not know or care much about politics, but they did like Ike and said that they would probably be Republicans because corporation life dictated that they should be.

These attitudes still seemed to prevail in 1957, when *The Nation* surveyed college and university professors about what their students were reading and thinking. Most reported that their students still read the standard authors—Hemingway, Wolfe, Lawrence, Orwell, Huxley, Faulkner, and Steinbeck—but shied away from fiction or nonfiction that dealt with economic, social, or political protest. One professor lamented that "the only young novelist I have heard praised vociferously is J. D. Salinger, for his discovery of childhood," and complained that "when a liberal and speculative voice is heard in the classroom, it is more likely than not to be the professor's, despite whatever caution the years may have taught him." The director of the Writing Program at Stanford University claimed that students were "hard to smoke out. Sometimes a professor is baited into protest by the rows and circles of their closed, watchful, apparently apathetic faces, and says in effect, 'My God, *feel* something! Get enthusiastic about something, plunge, go boom, look alive!'" A Yale English professor complained that "the present campus indifference to either politics or reform or rebellion is monumental." And most agreed with a University of Michigan professor's claim that to the student of 1957, "college has ceased to be a brightly lighted stage where he discovers who he is. It is rather a processing-chamber where, with touching submissiveness, he accepts the remarks of lecturers and the hard sentences of textbooks as directives that will lead him to a job."

What did the members of the Silent Generation do when they were not studying, planning what company they intended to find a safe niche in, deciding what kind of mate they would marry or how many kids they would have, or planning for retirement? They played sports, drank beer, ate pizzas and hamburgers, went to football games and movies, participated in panty raids, dated, dreamed of the opposite sex, read novels and magazines, watched television, and listened to recordings of jazz, classical music, or the popular crooners of the day. For most, the hottest issues on campus were what to do about a losing football coach or who should be elected homecoming queen or student body president. Both sexes wore conservative preppy clothes, and at many coeducational institutions women were forbidden to wear jeans or shorts to class. Those who could afford to joined one of the fast-growing number of fraternities or sororities in order to party, find identity and security, and form friendships that might later be useful in the business world they hoped to enter after graduation. College students were, indeed, an unrebellious lot.

By the late fifties America's teenagers had acquired a distinct subculture of their own. They had their own money, music, movies, television shows, idols, clothing, and slang. In contrast to previous generations, they were more affluent, better educated, talked more openly about sex, had greater mobility through the widespread ownership of automobiles by their parents or themselves, demanded and received more personal freedom, had more conflicts with their parents, and were the subject of more media and parental concern. But they were not yet in rebellion, for although their life-style had departed from the conventions of their elders, their basic ideas and attitudes were still the conservative ones that mirrored the conservatism of the affluent age in which they grew up.

Still, their parents were worried. As *Look* magazine reported in 1958 in an article entitled "What Parents Say About Teenagers," "many parents are in a state of confusion or despair about their teenagers. And they don't exactly know what to do about it. They would like to sit down with their children and talk over their mutual problems, but often this desire is thwarted by the teenagers themselves." The much-heralded generation gap was coming into view. In the next decade, when the junior high and senior high school students of the fifties crowded the colleges, marched in civil rights demonstrations, protested the Vietnam War, and engaged in unconventional sexual and drug practices, it would take on the temper of a revolution.

POSTSCRIPT

Was Rock and Roll Responsible for Dismantling America's Traditional Family, Sexual, and Racial Customs in the 1950s and 1960s?

Between 1958 and 1963, rock and roll as a distinct form of music nearly disappeared. There were several reasons for this. First were the congressional investigations of 1959–1961 into payoffs to DJs to push certain records on their shows. "Payola" ruined the careers of a number of rock DJs, including Alan Freed, the original rock DJ, who lost his two major jobs in New York, was hounded by the IRS for back taxes, and succumbed to alcoholism in 1965. But Dick Clark of "American Bandstand" fame, was protected by the music establishment even though he became a multimillionaire with interests in a number of record companies whose songs he featured on his own show.

Second, payola McArthyism receded in the early sixties as a result of rock and roll being fused into the mainstream of American popular music. Religious preachers appeared less worried about rock's perversion of the country's sexual moral values, southerners lost the fear of rock's racial mongrelization, and American parents no longer associated rock music with subversives, communists, and other radicals. How could they, when Elvis Presley cut his hair, was drafted into the army, and sang ballads and religious songs that were often integrated into his two dozen forgettable movies? By the time Presley's manager finished reshaping the King's image, Elvis looked more like Pat Boone, a clean-cut handsome wide-toothed singer who "covered" Little Richard's songs for white audiences in the early rock period. At the same time, Dick Clark turned his Philadelphia-based show, "American Bandstand," into an afternoon phenomenon that featured well-groomed teenagers dancing to the latest songs.

In 1963, serious rock was replaced by folk music. Greenwich Village, in the heart of downtown New York City, was its epicenter, Bob Dylan was its creator by writing new folk songs instead of retreading old ones, and the group Peter, Paul, and Mary popularized the music into commercial success. At the same time, folk music became anthems for the civil rights and anti-war protest movements.

Meanwhile, a sixties rock revival came from two sources. First was the British invasion, symbolized by the arrival of the Beatles in 1963, followed by other groups, such as the Rolling Stones, who traced their roots to the early guitar riffs of Chuck Berry. Having come from working-class backgrounds in Liverpool, the Beatles grew up in an environment that challenged authority and poked fun at some of the hypocrisy of middle-class values. Their later songs influenced the protest movements in the United States.

A second source of revival for protest rock music came from the counter-culture movement in San Francisco. Bands such as the Grateful Dead and Jefferson Airplane brought "underground" rock to the forefront. Soon, even the Beatles were imitating the San Francisco underground with their classic album, "Sgt. Pepper's Lonely Hearts Club Band," a style that, according to one writer, combined "a peculiar blend of radical political rhetoric, of allusions to the drug culture, and of the excited sense of imminent, apocalyptic liberation."

Two events in 1969 symbolized the high and low points of sixties rock. In August, 500,000 people converged on a farm in upstate New York for a three-day rock festival. Woodstock became a legendary symbol. There was scant political protest. Music was the common bond that united people sitting in the rain-filled mud, sharing food and drugs while drowning out the fears of participating in an endless war. In December, all the good will of Woodstock was destroyed at a free Rolling Stones concert in Altamont, California. Four people died, one of whom was clubbed, stabbed, and kicked to death by the Hell's Angels, hired as body guards for the Stones on the advice of the Grateful Dead.

Would the sixties "new left" and counterculture movements have taken place without the emergence of rock and roll in the 1950s? Did rock help to reshape America's values, or was it all one big commercial hustle?

The two best overviews of the early history of rock and roll are Glenn C. Altschuler, *All Shook Up: How Rock and Roll Changed America* (Oxford University Press, 2003) and James Miller, *Flowers in the Dustbin: The Rise of Rock and Roll, 1947–1977* (Simon & Schuster, 1999). Four excellent overviews of the 1950s are Douglas T. Miller and Marion Nowak, *The Fifties: The Way We Really Were* (Doubleday, 1975), J. Ronald Oakley, *God's Country: America in the Fifties* (Dembner Books, 1985–1990); David Halberstam, *The Fifties* (Villard, 1993) and William L. O'Neill, *American High: The Years of Confidence, 1945-1960* (Simon & Schuster, 1986). Earlier, O'Neill wrote *Coming Apart: An Informal History of the 1960s* (Times Books, 1971), a classic treatment of the 1960s replete with vignettes that still hold up. David Marcus examines the impact of the 1950s and 1960s upon present-day politics and pop culture in *Happy Days and Wonder Years: The Fifties and Sixties in Contemporary Cultural Politics* (Rutgers University Press, 2004). Between 2000 and 2005, Greenhaven Press has published three readers with great selections on *The 1950s, The 1960s,* and *The 1960s: Examining Pop Culture.*

ISSUE 6

Was President Kennedy Responsible for the Cuban Missile Crisis?

YES: Ronald Steel, from *Imperialists and Other Heroes* (Random House, 1971)

NO: Robert Weisbrot, from *Maximum Danger: Kennedy, the Missiles, and the Crisis of American Confidence* (Ivan R. Dee, 2001)

ISSUE SUMMARY

YES: Political analyst Ronald Steel believes that President Kennedy mishandled the Cuban missile crisis when his hastily organized decision-making committee of 14 experts emphasized military ultimatums over diplomatic solutions.

NO: Historian Robert Weisbrot argues that the new sources uncovered the past 20 years portray Kennedy as a president who had absorbed the values of his time as an anti-Communist, cold warrior who nevertheless acted as a rational leader, who was conciliatory toward his opponent in the Soviet Union in resolving the Cuban missile crisis.

In 1959, the political situation in Cuba changed drastically when dictator Fulgencio Batista y Zaldi'var was overthrown by a 34-year-old revolutionary named Fidel Castro, who led a guerilla band in the Sierra Maestra mountain range. Unlike his predecessors, Castro refused to be a lackey for American political and business interests. The left-wing dictator seized control of American oil refineries and ordered a number of diplomats at the U.S. embassy in Havana to leave the country. President Dwight D. Eisenhower was furious. He imposed economic sanctions on the island and broke diplomatic ties shortly before he left office.

Eisenhower's successor, John F. Kennedy, supported an invasion at the Bay of Pigs in Cuba by a group of disaffected anti-Castro Cuban exiles to foster the overthrow of Castro. However, the April 1961 invasion was a disaster. Castro's army routed the invaders. Many were killed; others were taken prisoner.

The Kennedy administration secured Cuba's removal from the Organization of American States (OAS) in early 1962, imposed an economic embargo on the island, and carried out threatening military maneuvers in the Caribbean.

The isolation and possibility of a second invasion of Cuba probably influenced Soviet premier Nikita Khrushchev to take a more proactive stance to defend Cuba. In the summer of 1962, the Soviet premier sent troops and conventional weapons to the island. In September 1962, launching pads were installed for medium- and intermediate-range nuclear ballistic missiles.

By September 1962, Kennedy was feeling the heat from Republicans such as New York senator Kenneth Keating, who charged that the Russians were bringing not only troops but also nuclear weapons to the island. At first, Kennedy was concerned with the political implications of the charges for the 1962 congressional races. On September 13, 1962, he assured the news reporters that the Cuban military buildup was primarily defensive in nature.

But the situation changed drastically on the morning of October 16, 1962, when National Security Council adviser McGeorge Bundy informed the president that pictures from U-2 flights over Cuba revealed that the Russians were building launching pads for 1,000-mile medium-range missiles as well as 2,200-mile intermediate-range missiles. The president kept the news quiet. He ordered more U-2 flights to take pictures and had Bundy assemble a select group of advisers who became known as the Executive Committee of the National Security Council (Ex-Comm). For six days and nights, the committee met secretly and considered a wide range of options. By the end of the sixth day, the president favored a blockade, or what he called a "quarantine," of the island. On October 22, 1962, Kennedy revealed his plans for the quarantine over national television.

It took six days from the time Kennedy made his announcement for the participants to resolve the crisis. Mark J. White has succinctly summarized the resolution of the Cuban missile crisis in the introduction to his edited collection of documents entitled *The Kennedys and Cuba: The Declassified Documentary History* (Ivan R. Dee, 1999).

Was President Kennedy responsible for the Cuban missile crisis? In the first selection, political analyst Ronald Steel is critical of the Kennedy administration's handling of the crisis on several counts: Military options were emphasized over diplomacy; proper intelligence information was lacking; the Kremlin's motivations for putting the missiles in Cuba were never understood; and the whole decision-making process of the Ex-Comm was flawed.

In the second selection, Professor Robert Weisbrot rejects the earlier portraits of Kennedy partisans as an "effective crisis manager" or the 1970s' critics who discern in his foreign policy "a dismal amalgam of anti-Communist hysteria, reckless posturing, and a disturbing gleeful crisis orientation." Instead, he relies on new evidence that developed over the past 20 years, such as the declassification of various Ex-Comm conversations and the transcripts of several conferences on the missile crisis "in which Soviet and American scholars and former officials (including Cuba's Castro) shared facts and feelings long guarded as official secrets." According to Weisbrot, although President Kennedy embodied the anti-Communist, Cold War values of his time, he acted as a "rational leader" who was conciliatory toward his opponent in the Soviet Union in resolving the Cuban Missile Crisis.

YES

Ronald Steel

Imperialists and Other Heroes:
A Chronicle of the American Empire

Endgame

It was a time, in Khrushchev's memorable phrase, "when the smell of burning hung in the air." Robert Kennedy's account of those Thirteen Days in 1962 from October 16, when he and his brother were presented with proof that the Russians were secretly building long-range missile bases in Cuba, until October 28, when the Kremlin agreed to dismantle them—shows the view from the inside by one of the key participants.

This short, terse memoir—bloated by the publisher with superfluous introductions, photographs, and documents—does not, of course, tell the whole story of the missile crisis. There is a good deal about the events leading up to the crisis that is gone over too lightly or deliberately clouded over. The clash of personalities and ambivalent motives is muted and the tone rather detached. But behind the measured prose we see the spectacle of rational minds swayed by passions and the euphoria of power, governmental machinery breaking down into the struggle of individual wills, and decisions affecting the future of humanity made by a handful of men—the best of whom were not always sure they were right.

We have come to take the balance of terror so much for granted that it is hard to imagine any situation in which the two super-powers would actually use their terrible weapons. Yet more than once during those thirteen days it seemed as though the unthinkable might actually occur. SAC bombers were dispersed to airfields throughout the country and roamed the skies with their nuclear cargoes. At one point President Kennedy, fearful that some trigger-happy colonel might set off the spark, ordered all atomic missiles defused so that the order to fire would have to come directly from the White House.

The first showdown came on the morning of October 24, as Soviet ships approached the 500-mile quarantine line drawn around Cuba. "I felt," Robert Kennedy wrote of those terrible moments, "we were on the edge of a precipice with no way off. . . . President Kennedy had initiated the course of events, but he no longer had control over them." Faced with this blockade, the Russian ships turned back, and the first crisis was surmounted. No more missiles could get into Cuba. But what of the ones already there that Russian technicians were installing with feverish haste? President Kennedy was determined that they had to be removed immediately and on Saturday, October 27, sent his brother to tell Soviet Ambassador Dobrynin "that if they did not remove those bases, we would remove them." The Pentagon prepared for an air strike against the bases and an invasion of Cuba. "The expectation," Robert Kennedy wrote of that fateful Saturday, "was a military confrontation by Tuesday."

We know, of course, how it turned out. On Sunday morning the message came through that Khrushchev would withdraw the missiles in return for a U.S. pledge not to invade Cuba. Kennedy had pulled off the greatest coup of his career—the first, and one hopes the last, military victory of the nuclear era. Not a shot was fired, although we came a good deal closer to war than most people realized at the time, or have cared to think about since.

It was a victory not only over the Soviets, but over many of Kennedy's own advisers who favored a more militant course from the start. The drama was played out among a hastily assembled group, which later took on the formal title of the Executive Committee of the National Security Council, that met several times a day in the White House. The sessions were frequently stormy, although the lines were loosely drawn at first. Several of the participants, according to Robert Kennedy, shifted their opinion "from one extreme to the other—supporting an air attack at the beginning of the meeting and, by the time we left the White House, supporting no action at all." A few, such as Dean Acheson and Douglas Dillon, were hawks from the start, and argued for what they euphemistically called a "surgical strike" against the air bases. They were eventually joined by John McCone, General Maxwell Taylor, Paul Nitze, and McGeorge Bundy. Favoring a more moderate course, which settled around a naval blockage to be "escalated" to an attack on the bases only if absolutely necessary, were the doves, led by Robert Kennedy and Robert McNamara, and including George Ball, Roswell Gilpatric, Llewellyn Thompson, and Robert Lovett.

Dean Rusk, for the most part, avoided taking a stand, or even attending the sessions. The Secretary of State, in Robert Kennedy's caustic words, "had other duties during this period and frequently could not attend our meetings." It would be interesting to know what these duties were. Robert Kennedy does not elaborate, although he does offer the further intriguing aside that "Secretary Rusk missed President Kennedy's extremely important meeting with Prime Minister Macmillan in Nassau because of a diplomatic dinner he felt he should attend." That was the meeting, one will remember, where President Kennedy agreed to help out Harold Macmillan on the eve of the British elections by turning over Polaris missiles to Britain after the Skybolt fiasco that had embarrassed the Tories. De Gaulle, predictably, was furious, declared that Britain still valued her trans-Atlantic ties above her European ones, and vetoed her entry into the Common Market. The Nassau accord was a colossal error of judgment that an astute Secretary of State should have been able to prevent.

Some of the hawks were, of course, predictable. It is not surprising that the Joint Chiefs of Staff were eager to use their expensive hardware. "They seemed always ready to assume," Robert Kennedy wrote, "that a war was in our national interest. One of the Joint Chiefs of Staff once said to me he believed in a preventive attack against the Soviet Union." Nor is it surprising that Dean Acheson, among the most recalcitrant of the cold warriors, should have come down on the side of the military. "I felt we were too eager to liquidate this thing," Elie Abel reports him as saying in *The Missile Crisis*. "So long as we had the thumbscrew on Khrushchev, we should have given it another turn every day. We were too eager to make an agreement with the Russians. They had no business there in the first place." Ever since his crucifixion by Congress during the Alger Hiss affair, Acheson has become increasingly reactionary and eager to prove his toughness toward the communists. His bomb-first-and-talk-later argument found receptive ears in such pillars of the Eastern Republican Establishment as Douglas Dillon, John J. McCloy, and McGeorge Bundy.

Many who were not aware of the drama being played out in the White House during those thirteen days, however, will be surprised to find Robert Kennedy as the leader of the doves and the moral conscience of his brother's administration. Although he does not dramatize his own role, we learn from his account and those of others that he argued against a first strike as contrary to American traditions. "My brother," Abel quotes him as saying, "is not going to be the Tojo of the 1960s." This impassioned plea against a Pearl Harbor in reverse moved even Maxwell Taylor. The general, Abel quotes one of the participants as commenting, "showed what a moral man he is by recommending that we give the Cubans twenty-four hours' advance notice—and then strike the missile bases."

The other outstanding dove of the deliberations was the man in charge of the military establishment, Robert McNamara. The secretary of Defense, in Kennedy's words, "became the blockade's strongest advocate" and argued that "a surgical air strike . . . was militarily impractical." McNamara was not only a consistent dove, fighting off the belligerent advice of his service chiefs, but disputed the prevailing view that the Russians were trying to upset the strategic balance between East and West. "A missile is a missile," Abel and others have quoted him as saying. "It makes no difference whether you are killed by a missile fired from the Soviet Union or from Cuba." Observing that the Russians had ICBMs and that the only effect of the Cuban-based intermediate-range missiles would be to reduce by a few minutes our warning time in case of attack, McNamara's advice, in effect, was to sit tight.

However valid such advice might have been from a military point of view, it was quite unacceptable politically. John F. Kennedy was especially vulnerable on Cuba, having used it as an issue against Nixon during the 1960 campaign, and then having suffered the ignominy of the Bay of Pigs. The Republicans were pressing him hard on his "do-nothing" policy toward Castro, and former Senator Keating of New York was leading a wolf pack in charging that the Russians were turning Cuba into a base for offensive weapons. Kennedy, as Democratic Party leader, could not, tolerate Soviet missiles in Cuba, even if the civilian head of the Pentagon could.

"If the missiles," Roger Hilsman, head of intelligence in the State Department and then Assistant Secretary of State for the Far East, comments in his book, *To Move a Nation,* "were not important enough to justify a confrontation with the Soviet Union, as McNamara initially thought, yet were 'offensive,' then the

United States might not be in mortal danger, but the administration most certainly was." And, according to John Kenneth Galbraith, then ambassador to India, "once they [the missiles] were there, the political needs of the Kennedy administration urged it to take almost any risk to get them out."

Did we, then, nearly go up in radioactive dust to shore up the Kennedy administration's fading image before the November, 1962, elections? Not necessarily, for if the missiles did not upset the strategic balance, even a President less image-conscious than John F. Kennedy could not easily accept such an abrupt change in the status quo—least of all the Caribbean. "To be sure," Theodore Sorenson observed in his *Kennedy*, "these Cuban missiles alone, in view of all the other megatonnage the Soviets were capable of unleashing upon us, did not substantially alter the strategic balance *in fact*. . . . But that balance would have been substantially altered in *appearance* [italics in original]; and in matters of national will and world leadership, as the President said later, such appearances contribute to reality." In fact, Kennedy himself leaned heavily on the prestige argument when he announced the blockade to the nation on October 22.

> This sudden, clandestine decision to station strategic weapons for the first time outside of Soviet soil is a deliberately provocative and unjustified change in the status quo which cannot be accepted by this country, if our courage and our commitments are ever to be trusted again by either friend or foe.

Elevating his rhetoric, as usual, above the needs of the occasion, Kennedy set the stage for a direct military confrontation.

He was acutely conscious of any questioning of his courage, and with the ashes of the Vienna encounter with Khrushchev still in his mouth and another Berlin crisis brewing, he had to get the missiles out of Cuba. But did he have to get them out before the end of October? What would have happened had he negotiated with Khrushchev instead of issuing the ultimatum—delivered to Ambassador Dobrynin on Saturday evening, October 27, by Robert Kennedy— that "we had to have a commitment by tomorrow that those bases would be removed." What would have happened had the negotiations dragged on for a few weeks and some kind of quid pro quo arranged?

The Russians, of course, would have had the already delivered missiles in place by then. But their withdrawal could still be negotiated and, in any case, the continuation of the blockade would have brought Castro to his knees within a few months. Assuming that the missiles had to be removed, was it necessary, in Robert Kennedy's words, "to have a commitment by tomorrow?"

At the time, a good many people believed Kennedy had politics in mind during the missile crisis. General Eisenhower, when informed by McCone about the discovery of the missiles, "took a skeptical view," according to Abel, "suspecting perhaps that Kennedy might be playing politics with Cuba on the eve of Congressional elections." The thought also crossed the mind of Kennedy's old chum, David Ormsby-Gore, then British ambassador to Washington, who felt that "British opinion must somehow be persuaded that the missile crisis was the real thing, not something trumped up by the President for vote-getting purposes." Nor did the elections go unnoticed by the participants in the

Executive Committee. I. F. Stone has pointed out Sorenson's comment that during one of the meetings a Republican member passed him a note saying:

> Ted—have you considered the very real possibility that if we allow Cuba to complete installation and operational readiness of missile bases, the next House of Representatives is likely to have a Republican majority? This would completely paralyze our ability to react sensibly and coherently to further Soviet advances.

It is not to denigrate John F. Kennedy's patriotism to assume that he was aware of such possibilities. Nor is it to question the motives of those who took part in those exhausting, often stormy, meetings during the thirteen days. It would have been political folly for Kennedy to have broached the subject of the elections before the Executive Committee, where it would have fallen on a good many unsympathetic ears, and it is exceedingly unlikely that the question was ever formally raised. Nor did the participants believe they were behaving by the rules of partisan politics when they decided that the missiles had to be removed immediately. But of the fourteen-odd people who participated in most of the meetings, only a few—Sorenson, Robert Kennedy, and, of course, the President—could be considered politicians. As politicians who had to fight elections, as leaders of the party which was about to be tested at the polls, they could not have been oblivious to what was going to happen in early November—even if they never mentioned it in the meetings, or to one another.

To do nothing about the missiles, as McNamara's position would imply, or to take the issue to the United Nations, or to compromise by trading the Soviet missiles in Cuba for the obsolete American missiles in Turkey, would have been bad politics at that particular time. Obsessed by his image, Kennedy feared that Khrushchev would not take him seriously if he again backed down in Cuba. This questioning of "our courage," he believed, could tempt the Russians to a policy of adventurism, perhaps in Central Europe. Indeed, the first reading of the missile crisis was that Khrushchev was prepared to force a Berlin settlement on his own terms. Thus did considerations of high strategy and party politics reinforce one another and convince Kennedy that the Russian withdrawal had to be complete, unilateral, and secured by the end of October.

The question of a quid pro quo revolved around the American missiles in Turkey and Italy. These had been placed there five years earlier during the Eisenhower administration's panic over the Sputnik. Designed to redress the strategic balance during a time when the U.S. had no reliable ICBMs, these relatively primitive liquid-fuel missiles had become in Hilsman's words, "obsolete, unreliable, inaccurate, and very vulnerable." Shortly after his inauguration, Kennedy asked that they be removed and was discouraged by the State Department. He raised the question again in early 1962, and despite objections that the Turks disapproved, instructed Dean Rusk to negotiate the removal of the missiles. "The President," Robert Kennedy has written, barely concealing his contempt for Dean Rusk, "believed he was President and that, his wishes having been made clear, they would be followed and the missiles removed."

But his instructions were not carried out, and Kennedy discovered that the obsolete Turkish missiles had become a bargaining foil for Khrushchev. "We will remove our missiles from Cuba, you will remove yours from Turkey," read the note received from the Kremlin on the morning of Saturday, October 27.". . . . The Soviet Union will pledge not to invade or interfere with the internal affairs of Turkey; the U.S. to make the same pledge regarding Cuba." This note, with its quid pro quo, added a new condition to the emotional message received the night before, in which the Soviet premier indicated he would pull out the missiles in return for a U.S. promise not to invade Cuba.

Adding Turkey to the bargain filled the White House advisers with consternation—not least of all because it appeared perfectly fair. "The proposal the Russians made," in Robert Kennedy's words, "was not unreasonable and did not amount to a loss to the U.S. or to our NATO allies." Categorically to reject such a trade would make the U.S. seem vindictive and threaten the support of its allies—none of whom had any wish to be dragged into nuclear war over the issue of Cuba. But to accept the trade would be to invite accusations of weakness and dishonor by the Republicans. Kennedy, needless to say, was furious at the State Department for putting him in such a vulnerable position.

The Kremlin was not the first to raise the issue of trading the Cuban bases for the Turkish ones. In his column of Thursday, October 25, Walter Lippmann suggested a diplomatic solution to get the missiles out of Cuba:

> There are three ways to get rid of the missiles already in Cuba. One is to invade and occupy Cuba. The second way is to institute a total blockade, particularly of oil shipments, which would in a few months ruin the Cuban economy. The third way is to try, I repeat, to negotiate a face-saving settlement. . . . I am not talking about and do not believe in a "Cuba-Berlin" horse trade. . . . The only place that is truly comparable with Cuba is Turkey. This is the only place where there are strategic weapons right on the frontier of the Soviet Union. . . . The Soviet military base in Cuba is defenseless, and the base in Turkey is all but obsolete. The two bases could be dismantled without altering the world balance of power.

This position had already been argued by Adlai Stevenson who, according to Robert Kennedy, on October 20 "strongly advocated what he had only tentatively suggested to me a few days before—namely, that we make it clear to the Soviet Union that if it withdrew its missiles from Cuba, we would be willing to withdraw our missiles from Turkey and Italy and give up our naval base at Guantanamo Bay." With this suggestion Stevenson went a good deal further than Lippmann, who never included Guantanamo in the trade. This won Stevenson the wrath of several of the participants, including Robert Kennedy, who prevailed upon his brother to send John J. McCloy to the UN to handle the Russians during the missile crisis. But time healed some of Robert Kennedy's wrath, and in *Thirteen Days* he wrote:

> Stevenson has since been criticized publicly for the position he took at this meeting. I think it should be emphasized that he was presenting a point of view from a different perspective than the others, one which was therefore

important for the President to consider. Although I disagreed strongly with his recommendations, I thought he was courageous to make them, and I might add they made as much sense as some others considered during that period.

Stevenson's proposal was not so heretical as it was treated at the time, or as it was in the inside stories that appeared shortly after the crisis. Kennedy was prepared to give up the Turkish bases, but for political reasons could not make it a quid pro quo—although there is some reason to think that he might have done so *in extremis*. On Saturday—when the Russians sent their second note calling for the Turkey-Cuba base trade—Kennedy, according to Abel, told Roswell Gilpatric to prepare a scenario for removing the missiles from Turkey and Italy, and have it ready for the meeting that night. That evening he sent his brother to Ambassador Dobrynin with the demand that the Russians had to promise to withdraw the missiles from Cuba by the following day. The Joint Chiefs of Staff were preparing to bomb the missile sites on Tuesday. Dobrynin, according to Abel, "gave it as his personal opinion that the Soviet leaders were so deeply committed they would have to reject the President's terms."

But while he ruled out an explicit deal, Robert Kennedy told the Soviet ambassador that there need be no problem about the Turkish missiles. "President Kennedy," he said to Dobrynin, "had been anxious to remove those missiles from Turkey and Italy for a long period of time . . . and it was our judgment that, within a short time after this crisis was over, those missiles would be gone." Dobrynin sent on the message to Moscow; President Kennedy, at his brother's suggestion, accepted the more moderate first message from Khrushchev and ignored the second Kremlin note; and an apprehensive Washington awaited the Kremlin's response as plans proceeded for an air strike against the Cuban bases. On Sunday morning the word came through that the missiles would be withdrawn in return for a simple U.S. pledge not to invade Cuba. The worst crisis of the cold war was over. But even at this moment of triumph, some were not satisfied. "On that fateful Sunday morning when the Russians answered they were withdrawing their missiles," Robert Kennedy revealed, "it was suggested by one high military adviser that we attack Monday in any case."

The resolution of the Cuban missile crisis ironically set the stage for a more cooperative policy from Moscow, culminating in the test-ban treaty of 1963. It also contributed to the euphoria of power that led Kennedy's successor, urged on by Kennedy's advisers, to have his little war in Southeast Asia. Had the U.S. been forced to back down in Cuba, or to work out a Cuba-Turkey trade with the Russians, perhaps Washington might have awakened from the dream of American omnipotence before Lyndon Johnson launched his crusade in Vietnam.

Cuba, in Hilsman's words, was "a foreign policy victory of historical proportions," but in the long run the Russians did not come out of it too badly. They lost a certain amount of face, particularly among the Communist parties of Latin America, and they revealed once again that the interests of the Soviet state take precedence over the world revolution. Peking, for its part, lost no time in gloating that it was "sheer adventurism to put missiles into Cuba in the first place, but capitulationism to take them out under American pressure." Perhaps the Cuban setback contributed to Khrushchev's demise, although it is dubious whether that was a net gain for the West. But the blow to Soviet prestige was washed away with passing time, and the Russians, perhaps because they had their fingers burned in Cuba, refrained from exercises in global management of the kind that obsessed President Johnson and ultimately drove him from office.

What was the lesson of the Cuban missile crisis? There were several: first, that diplomacy gave way to military ultimatums; second, that there was a failure of intelligence interpretation; third, that the Kremlin's motives were never adequately understood; and fourth, that there is something basically wrong with the whole process of decision-making.

1. *The suspension of diplomacy.* Kennedy's mistake was not, as former Secretary of State Dean Acheson would have it, in failing to brandish the big stick more quickly. Rather it was in deliberately rejecting diplomatic contact when it might have made unnecessary precisely the kind of confrontation that occurred. Instead of using traditional diplomatic channels to warn the Russians that he knew what they were up to, and thus give them a chance quietly to pull back. Kennedy chose to inform the Kremlin of his discovery by a nation-wide radio-TV hookup. He put them, in other words, in the position where a sub-rosa withdrawal was impossible, and public dismantlement of the bases meant humiliation. In doing so, Kennedy violated the first rule of diplomacy in the nuclear age, a rule he himself expounded in his famous speech at American University in June 1963:

> Above all, while defending our own vital interests, nuclear powers must avert those confrontations which bring an adversary to the choice of either a humiliating retreat or a nuclear war.

To be sure, he did not gloat over the Russian withdrawal, and insisted on treating it as a statesmanlike move. But the Kremlin's withdrawal under a public American ultimatum was a humiliation nonetheless.

President Kennedy certainly had ample opportunity to play it otherwise. There were available not only the Soviet ambassador and the famous "hotline" direct to the Kremlin, recently installed with such fanfare, but also the Soviet Foreign Minister, Andrei Gromyko, who came to visit the President on Thursday afternoon, October 18—three days after Kennedy learned of the secret missile sites, but four days before he announced the blockade. Gromyko's visit had been scheduled some time before the discovery of the missiles, and the wily Soviet diplomat did not, of course, mention them. Instead he insisted that the Russians were furnishing purely "defensive" arms to the Cubans and wanted to relieve tensions with the U.S. over Cuba.

Robert Kennedy reports that his brother "listened, astonished, but also with some admiration for the boldness of Gromyko's position." Why should he have been astonished? Did he expect the Soviet Foreign Minister to confess that his government was secretly setting up long-range missile bases in Cuba? Mastering his astonishment, the President read aloud his statement of September 4, which warned the Russians against putting missiles or offensive weapons in Cuba. Gromyko assured him this would never be done and departed, returning to the Soviet Union a few days later.

The unavoidable question is why didn't President Kennedy tell Gromyko that he knew the truth, and give the Russians a chance to pull back? Robert Kennedy says it was because he hadn't yet decided what course of action to follow and was afraid of giving the Russians a tactical advantage—a judgment, Abel reports, supported by Rusk and Thompson. But Robert Kennedy reports that the President decided on the blockade on Saturday, October 20, two days before his speech to the nation. Why didn't he tell Gromyko on Saturday? The question was raised at the time by Walter Lippmann who, in his column of October 25, warned Kennedy against repeating the mistake of suspending diplomacy that plagued both world wars:

> I see danger of this mistake in the fact that when the President saw Mr. Gromyko on Thursday, and had the evidence of the missile build-up in Cuba, he refrained from confronting Mr. Gromyko with this evidence. This was to suspend diplomacy. If it had not been suspended, the President would have shown Mr. Gromyko the pictures, and told him privately about the policy which in a few days he intended to announce publicly. This would have made it more likely that Moscow would order the ships not to push on to Cuba. But if such diplomatic action did not change the orders, if Mr. Khrushchev persisted in spite of it, the President's public speech would have been stronger. It would not have been subject to the criticism that a great power had issued an ultimatum to another great power without first attempting to negotiate the issue. By confronting Mr. Gromyko privately, the President would have given Mr. Khrushchev what all wise statesmen give their adversaries—the chance to save face.

Roger Hilsman argues that Gromyko somehow erroneously assumed that the President really knew about the missiles all the time. He gleans this from various warnings given to the Russians about putting offensive weapons into Cuba—warnings by Chester Bowles, U.S. Ambassador to Moscow Foy Kohler, and the President himself. With all these lectures the Russians might, perhaps, have assumed that Kennedy knew what they were up to, but was keeping it under his hat until after the elections. "The best explanation for Gromyko's behavior," he writes, "seemed to be that the Soviets were hedging, trying to avoid a direct confrontation with the United States in the hope of leaving their hand free for negotiations or, if faced with extreme danger of war, for withdrawing the missiles with the least loss of face." Yet if the Russians assumed that Kennedy knew, presumably they were not plotting a surprise attack. In any case, Hilsman's argument, while it might excuse Gromyko of duplicity, does not justify Kennedy's behavior, and is not offered as a hypothesis by Robert Kennedy.

2. *The failure of intelligence.* Why were the missile sites not discovered sooner? Discovery of the missiles was a total surprise to the President, Robert Kennedy affirms. "No official within the government had ever suggested to

President Kennedy that the Russian buildup within Cuba would include missiles." The United States Intelligence Board, in its most recent estimate, dated September 19, advised the President "without reservation . . . that the Soviet Union would not make Cuba a strategic base." It based this on the fact that the Russians had never taken such a step in any of their satellites, and that the risk of U.S. retaliation was too great. Although a number of unconfirmed reports had been filtering through the intelligence network. Robert Kennedy maintains "they were not considered substantial enough to pass on to the President or to other high officials within the government."

But the fact is that Washington had been buzzing for weeks with unconfirmed reports that the Russians were secretly introducing long-range missiles into Cuba. According to Abel, as early as August 22, CIA chief John McCone told President Kennedy that the Russians were putting SAMs (surface-to-air missiles) into Cuba to protect offensive missile sites, and urged reconsideration of the September 19 intelligence estimate. Meanwhile reports kept flowing in from agents inside Cuba that missiles much longer than SAMs were being delivered, and Castro's pilot had reportedly boasted "we have everything, including atomic weapons." According to Arthur Krock's *Memoirs,* the French intelligence agent, Thiraud de Vosjoly (the celebrated Topaz) came back with eyewitness evidence for McCone.

Robert Kennedy says "there was no action the U.S. could have taken before the time we actually did act," since no films were available to offer proof to the rest of the world. But why were photographs not made earlier? When McCone returned from his honeymoon in early October, he discovered that the eastern part of Cuba had not been photographed for more than a month. He immediately ordered the entire island photographed, and the U-2s returned from the flight of October 14 with the proof we now know.

What happened was nothing less than a failure of intelligence. Suspicious signs were ignored, Republican charges were dismissed as election year propaganda, and there was a disinclination to probe the evidence. What induced this state of mind? First, the conviction of the analysts that the Russians would never dare do anything so risky. Second, skepticism about charges made by Republican politicians. Third, reluctance to face a new Cuban crisis on the eve of the Congressional elections. Fourth, a personal message from Khrushchev, delivered by Ambassador Dobrynin to Robert Kennedy on September 4, assuring the President that the Soviets would create no trouble for him during the election campaign and would place no offensive weapons in Cuba.

Kennedy had every reason to want to believe Khrushchev, and none of his trusted advisers presented him with any proof to the contrary. There was, of course, McCone. But Kennedy had been burned once over Cuba by the CIA and no doubt was doubly skeptical of its surmises. This skepticism, reinforced by his own desire to accept Khrushchev's assurances, at least until after the elections, and the failure of the intelligence community (and his own advisers) to argue differently, led to the failure to draw the proper inferences from the evidence.

3. *The misreading of the Kremlin's motives.* Why did Khrushchev do it? There is little speculation about this in Robert Kennedy's memoir, for he is concerned with what happened in Washington rather than with Russian motivations. To this

day we do not know why the Soviets took such a colossal gamble. The rewards, one must assume, could only have been commensurate with the risks. The first reaction—that the Russians would try to force the Western allies out of Berlin in return for their withdrawal from Cuba—was unconvincing at the time, and is even more so in retrospect. It showed the New Frontier's vulnerability on the Berlin issue, particularly after the disastrous Vienna meeting. But it offers no reason why Khrushchev could rationally have believed that the Western allies would give up their rights in the former German capital. Perhaps the main reason why the Kennedy administration was caught so flat-footed was that it could never figure out why the Russians might find it advantageous to put missiles in Cuba.

An intriguing explanation has been put forth by Adam Ulam in his study of Soviet foreign policy, *Expansion and Coexistence.* The Russian leaders, he suggests, installed the missiles in Cuba in order to negotiate a package deal to be announced at the UN in November. The deal would include a German peace treaty, with an absolute prohibition on nuclear weapons for Bonn; plus a similar arrangement in the Far East, with a nuclear-free zone in the Pacific and a promise from China not to manufacture atomic weapons. The Chinese, of course, could be expected to balk at such a proposal, but their support might be won by demanding the removal of American protection from Formosa as the final price of withdrawing the Soviet missiles from Cuba. This, Ulam argues, "would add an almost irresistible incentive for the Chinese at least to postpone their atomic ambitions."

This is highly imaginative, and almost certainly an explanation that never occurred to Kennedy and his advisers. It may never have occurred to Khrushchev either, although anything is possible. But without being quite so fanciful, one might speculate that the Russians installed their missiles in Cuba for the purpose of having them there, not in order to withdraw them as part of some future bargain. The placing of the missiles, in short, can be explained as a desperate attempt to compensate for a "missile gap" that put the Soviet Union dangerously far behind the United States.

The so-called "missile gap," it will be recalled, was one of the issues used by John F. Kennedy to club the Eisenhower-Nixon administration in the 1960 campaign. Uncritically accepting the propaganda of the Air Force and the aerospace industry, he charged that the Republicans had allowed the nation to fall hostage to Soviet missiles. Shortly after assuming the Presidency, however, Kennedy discovered that the "missile gap" did not exist. U-2 flights over the Soviet Union and the revelations of Colonel Oleg Penkovsky confirmed that the gap was quite the other way around, with the U.S. possessing a crushing superiority over the Soviet Union.

After returning from Vienna, where Khrushchev reportedly badgered him about the Bay of Pigs and led him to fear a new Berlin crisis was brewing, Kennedy decided to let the Russians know that the missile gap was actually in our favor. About the same time he engineered the bomb-shelter scare to show that he was willing to face nuclear war if necessary. Deputy Secretary of Defense Roswell Gilpatric was chosen to unveil the news to the Russians. In a speech on October 21, 1961, he deliberately revealed that we had penetrated Soviet security and knew where their missile sites were located. "Their Iron Curtain," he declared, "is not so impenetrable as to force us to accept at face value the Kremlin's boasts." For the Russians, the implications were, in Hilsman's words, "horrendous." What frightened them was not that we had military superiority, for they knew that all along—but that *we* knew it.

The U-2s had pin-pointed the Soviet missile sites and Colonel Penkovsky had revealed that they lagged far behind in missile production. Since the Russians at that time had mostly a vulnerable "soft" ICBM system that could be used for retaliation only if the sites were kept secret, the American discovery meant that their entire missile defense system was suddenly obsolete. Had the United States launched a pre-emptive attack, they would have been largely incapable of retaliating. The balance of terror had broken down and the Russians found themselves, for all practical purposes, disarmed.

Naturally this was intolerable to the Soviet leaders (we can imagine the reaction in Washington if the situation were reversed), and perhaps a cheap answer to the problem was installing some of the older missiles in Cuba. This would help redress the strategic imbalance by confronting the U.S. with additional targets to be knocked out. It would also allow the Russians to stretch out the production of the new "hard" ICBMs without putting a further drain on their resources, help satisfy Castro's demands for protection, and strengthen the Soviet position in the Caribbean and Latin America.

Khrushchev made a serious mistake, the folly of "adventurism," as Peking would say. But could he reasonably have assumed that the Kennedy who had been so ineffectual at the Bay of Pigs and unimpressive at Vienna would suddenly become so intransigent? Nothing fails like failure. But in the context of the times, the effort to redress the missile gap seemed like a gamble worth taking. The worst that could have happened, the Russians probably assumed, was that their deception would be discovered and that they would quietly be told to take the missiles out. By immediately escalating the issue to a public confrontation, Kennedy had created a situation that was getting out of hand. In this respect, Khrushchev's message of October 26, when he offered to withdraw the missiles in return for a U.S. pledge not to invade Cuba, is instructive. "If you have not lost your self-control," he wrote,

> and sensibly conceive what this might lead to, then, Mr. President, we and you ought not to pull on the ends of the rope in which you have tied the knot of war, because the more the two of us pull, the tighter the knot will be tied. And a moment may come when that knot will be tied so tight that even he who tied it will not have the strength to untie it, and then it will be necessary to cut that knot, and what that would mean is not for me to explain to you, because you yourself understand perfectly of what terrible forces our countries dispose. Consequently, if there is no intention to tighten that knot, and thereby doom the world to the catastrophe of thermonuclear war, then let us not only relax the forces pulling on the ends of the rope, let us take measures to untie that knot. We are ready for this.

Whatever his motives, Khrushchev certainly did not intend a nuclear confrontation, nor in retrospect did the situation demand it. It seems clear that Russian policy was basically defensive and, as John Kenneth Galbraith has commented, "in the full light of time, it [national safety] doubtless called for a more cautious policy than the one that Kennedy pursued." One of the hallmarks of the New Frontier was a nagging sense of insecurity that manifested itself in inflated rhetoric (the classic being Kennedy's inaugural address) and self-assumed tests of will, such as Cuba and Vietnam. While Kennedy won his victory, he also had Khrushchev to thank, and as Hilsman has observed, "although putting the missiles into Cuba was threatening and irresponsible, the Soviets handled the ensuing crisis with wisdom and restraint." Kennedy showed his skill in throwing down the gauntlet, but it required greater courage for Khrushchev to refuse to pick it up.

4. *The vagaries of decision-making.* The basic decisions of the missile crisis, as we have seen, were reached in the informal group known as the Executive Committee. Most of the members of the Cabinet were excluded from this group, and, indeed, did not even learn about the crisis until a few hours before Kennedy announced it to the nation. Nor were America's NATO allies, who would have been blown up along with us, consulted at any point along the way about plans or strategy. When Dean Acheson arrived in Paris to tell de Gaulle of the blockade, the General asked, "Are you consulting or informing me?" Informing, Acheson confessed. "I am in favor of independent decisions," de Gaulle replied, and remained consistent to that policy.

Some of Kennedy's independent decisions were made in the most curious way. For example, on October 20 it was decided that the U.S. Navy would intercept all ships within an 800-mile radius of the Cuban coast. Three days later David Ormsby-Gore happened to be dining at the White House and observed that 800 miles seemed to be a bit far out. Perhaps, he suggested, the quarantine line could be drawn at 500 miles, thus giving the Russians a bit more time to think. A good idea, replied the President, and on the spot redrew the line—no doubt wisely—over the protests of the Navy. One wonders if any other ambassadors, had they been on as close terms with the President as Ormsby-Gore, might also have had some good suggestions.

We have already learned that the Secretary of State was too busy with other matters to act as chairman of the Executive Committee, or even to attend many of his meetings. It is also instructive to learn how Kennedy, while excluding most of his Cabinet from knowledge of the affair, reached outside the government to tap such venerables as Robert Lovett, John J. McCloy, and the redoubtable Dean Acheson. Recently Acheson, having been bested by Robert Kennedy over the issue of the blockade, has reached into the grave to take a swipe at his old adversary by declaring that the successful outcome of the missile crisis was "plain dumb luck."

In a sense he is right, but for the wrong reasons. He means that President Kennedy was lucky that the Russians didn't make the bases operational before they were discovered. Acheson wouldn't have fiddled around with a blockade or negotiations, but would have joined LeMay in bombing them from the start. As it turns out, there was more time than the participants thought, or accepted, at the time, or that Acheson is willing to admit even today. According to Hilsman, who, as former intelligence chief for the State Department, ought to know, "the two-thousand mile IRBM sites, which were not scheduled for completion until mid-November, never did reach a stage where they were ready to receive the missiles themselves" Kennedy, in other words, had at least two more weeks and could have postponed his ultimatum. Also, it appears that Khrushchev was planning to be true to his word and not make trouble for Kennedy until after the election, when he would unveil the missiles for whatever political purposes he had in mind.

Kennedy was lucky, however, in the sense that Khrushchev chose to withdraw rather than make Cuba a test of national or personal virility. Had Acheson and the other hawks had their way, probably none of us would be here to conduct these post-mortems. Robert Kennedy had something quite interesting to say about this. In an interview given just two days before his death, he commented on the advice given in the Executive Committee during the crisis:

> The fourteen people involved were very significant—bright, able, dedicated people, all of whom had the greatest affection for the U.S.—probably the brightest kind of group that you could get together under those circumstances. If six of them had been President of the U.S., I think that the world might have been blown up.

None of these six is particularly malicious or fanatical, and none is in the government today. Yet if a similar crisis were to occur, would the response of the President's advisers be very different from that given by these six in 1962? The lesson of the *Thirteen Days* is to show us just how slender is the thread of our survival, how the fate of mankind rests in the hands of a few individuals driven by perfectly ordinary fears, anxieties, and rivalries. The Cuban missile crisis was a very close call, and it could have gone the other way.

Were the stakes worth it? Even Robert Kennedy was no longer sure. He intended to complete this memoir by adding a discussion of the ethical question involved: what, if any, circumstances or justification give this government or any government the moral right to bring its people and possibly all people under the shadow of nuclear destruction? It is our common loss that this complex man, who in the last years of his life learned to doubt much of what he had taken for granted, was murdered before he could deal with this question.

Robert Weisbrot

 **NO**

Maximum Danger: Kennedy, the Missiles, and the Crisis of American Confidence

The Missile Crisis in Historical Perspective

In his history of nuclear policy, *Danger and Survival,* McGeorge Bundy acknowledged, "Forests have been felled to print the reflections and conclusions of participants, observers, and scholars" on the Cuban missile crisis. The first great wave of coverage occurred in the mid-1960s, as the nation savored a cold war triumph and saluted a martyred leader of untold promise. A second wave peaked in the 1970s, as critics dissected the episode not to extol President Kennedy's supreme feat but to expose his feet of clay. Beginning in the mid-1980s the deforestation again accelerated, as declassified sources and meetings by former officials from America, Russia, and Cuba provided a wealth of factual corrections to early, long unchallenged recollections. Yet this crisis, perhaps the most intensely scrutinized fortnight in American history, is just beginning to come into historical focus.

1. Early Histories: Kennedy's Matchless "Crisis Management"

Kennedy's admirers were first to the ramparts in the battle over the president's historical reputation. The president's speech writer and special counsel Theodore Sorensen, historian Arthur Schlesinger, Jr., columnists and presidential intimates Joseph Alsop and Charles Bartlett, NBC correspondent Elie Abel, and the president's brother and attorney general, Robert Kennedy (in his posthumously published memoir *Thirteen Days*), all depicted the Soviet placement of missiles in Cuba as a brazen, nuclear-tipped challenge that the president could not decline without compromising credibility and tempting still bolder provocations. Brimming with insiders' revelations of tense national security meetings, their narratives formed a paradigm of successful crisis management that, they suggested, future policymakers should study and emulate.

The early histories lauded President Kennedy for cool judgment "in steering a safe course between war and surrender." Although he had discounted diplomacy alone as inadequate to dislodge the missiles and, in any case, a poor answer to nuclear blackmail, Kennedy had rejected urgings to bomb the missile sites (possibly followed by an invasion of Cuba), which would likely have killed many Russians. According to Robert Kennedy, at least six of twelve top aides, both civilian and military, had pressed this doubtful "surgical" solution, prompting him to muse that had any of them been president, "the world would have been very likely plunged in a catastrophic war."

Kennedy drew further praise for conjuring a diplomatic miracle from an unpromising and increasingly volatile standoff. Elie Abel reported that Khrushchev's public demand that America remove its Jupiter missiles from Turkey was "a doubled sense of shock" to Kennedy, who "distinctly remembered having given instructions, long before" to remove the obsolete Jupiters. Now the president "reflected sadly on the built-in futilities of big government," for "not only were the missiles still in Turkey but they had just become pawns in a deadly chess game." Still, Sorensen observed, "The President had no intention of destroying the Alliance by backing down."

As the story was told: After much wrangling and confusion among Ex Comm members, Robert Kennedy offered "a thought of breathtaking simplicity and ingenuity: why not ignore the second Khrushchev message and reply to the first?" With his brother's approval, he informed the Soviet ambassador that while "there could be no quid pro quo or any arrangement made under this kind of threat or pressure. . . . President Kennedy had been anxious to remove those missiles" and still hoped to do so "within a short time after this crisis was over." The attorney general served this carrot on a stick, adding that either the Soviets must remove the missiles promptly or the Americans would do so. The next morning Khrushchev publicly acceded to these terms.

In the heady aftermath of the crisis, President Kennedy saluted the Soviet premier for his "statesmanlike" decision and privately cautioned aides that there should be "no boasting, no gloating, not even a claim of victory. We had won by enabling Khrushchev to avoid complete humiliation—we should not humiliate him now." Robert Kennedy recalled, "What guided all [the president's] deliberations was an effort not to disgrace Khrushchev," to leave the Soviets a path of graceful retreat.

For a nation emerging from a week of terror of the missile crisis, Henry Pachter wrote in the book *Collision Course,* the "style" and "art" of Kennedy's leadership had "restored America's confidence in her own power." Sorensen, haggard from two weeks of stress and fatigue, recalled pondering the president's achievement as he leafed through a copy of *Profiles in Courage* and read the introductory quotation from Burke's eulogy of Charles James Fox: "He may live long, he may do much. But here is the summit. He never can exceed what he does this day."

2. Revisionist Histories: Reckless Kennedy Machismo

Whether or not history moves in cycles, historians typically do, and by the 1970s the once-standard odes to President Kennedy had given way to hard-edged, often hostile studies. As portrayed by the new histories, the "brief shining moment" of

Kennedy's Camelot was illuminated by nothing more magical than the beacons of modern public relations. From his youth Kennedy had flaunted a reckless self-indulgence encouraged by the family's founding tyrant, Joseph P. Kennedy, who imparted to his male children his own ambition, opportunism, and a shameless *machismo* toward women. A succession of affairs unencumbered by emotional involvement; publication of an intelligent but amateurish senior thesis courtesy of family friends; embellishment of a war record marked by heroism but also by some unexplained lapses in leadership; and reception of a Pulitzer Prize for *Profiles in Courage,* written in significant part by his aide, Sorensen, all reflected a pursuit of expedience more than excellence.

Critics found that Kennedy's performance as president confirmed and extended rather than overcame this pattern of flamboyant mediocrity. They discerned in his conduct of foreign policy a dismal amalgam of anti-Communist hysteria, reckless posturing, and a disturbingly gleeful crisis orientation. The results were accordingly grim, ranging from the early disaster at the Bay of Pigs to the placement—or misplacement—of more than fifteen thousand U.S. military personnel in Vietnam by the time of Kennedy's death. Scarcely learning from his early mistakes, Kennedy ignored legitimate Cuban concerns for defense against American intervention and needlessly flirted with the apocalypse in order to force the removal of missiles that scarcely affected the world military balance. To judge from their skeptical recounting, this harrowing superpower confrontation might better be termed the "misled crisis," for it stemmed from Kennedy's perception of a threat to his personal and political prestige rather than (as Americans were misinformed) to the nation's security.

No crisis existed, then, until Kennedy himself created one by forgoing private diplomacy for a public ultimatum and blockade. Considering that the United States had already planned to remove its obsolete missiles from Turkey, Kennedy should have heeded Adlai Stevenson's advice to propose immediately a trade of bases, rather than rush into a confrontation whose outcome he could neither foresee nor fully control. Instead, "From the first, he sought unconditional surrender and he never deviated from that objective." "He took an unpardonable mortal risk without just cause," Richard J. Walton wrote. "He threatened the lives of millions for appearances' sake."

The prime historical mystery to the revisionists was why any American president would needlessly play Russian roulette in the nuclear age. Critics conceded that the president may have felt "substantial political pressures" over Cuba but blamed him for having largely created those pressures with shrill, alarmist speeches. "He had been too specific about what the United States would and would not tolerate in Cuba, and his statements reduced his options," Louise FitzSimons wrote. Garry Wills also saw Kennedy as a prisoner of his own superheated rhetoric about Khrushchev, Communists, and missiles, which aroused a false sense of crisis; "If he was chained to a necessity for acting, he forged the chains himself. . . . Having fooled the people in order to lead them, Kennedy was forced to serve the folly he had induced."

Revisionist writers detected a sad consistency in Kennedy's anti-Communist hyperbole, so that the missile crisis appeared to be a logical by-product of his style rather than simply a grisly aberration. During his bid for the presidency in 1960 Kennedy had stirred voters by charging his Republican opponent, Vice President Richard Nixon, with failing to "stand up to Castro" and to Khrushchev, or to prevent a potentially lethal "missile gap" with the Soviets (in fact Americans had a vast lead). Such ideological zeal remained evident in the Ex Comm, where, David Detzer claimed, Kennedy was "more Cold Warrior" than many, "worrying about America's reputation (and maybe his own) for toughness. . . ."

Scholars in the rising genre of psychohistory traced the nation's "perilous path" in the missile crisis to "the neuroticism of Kennedy's machismo." According to Nancy Gager Clinch, the president viewed the Cuban missiles "as a personal challenge to [his] courage and status," and "In the Kennedy lexicon of manliness, not being 'chicken' was a primary value." This interpretation radiated to other fields: Sidney Lens, in his study of the military-industrial complex, found in Kennedy's "willingness to gamble with the idea of nuclear war . . . a loss of touch with reality, almost a suicidal impulse."

The more judicious of the new historians, like Richard J. Walton, tempered their personal indictments by depicting the president as "an entirely conventional Cold Warrior." Still, in addition to "his fervent anti-communism, and his acceptance of the basic assumptions of American postwar foreign policy," "the *machismo* quality in Kennedy's character" pushed him to embark on "an anti-communist crusade much more dangerous than any policy Eisenhower ever permitted." Burdened by both personal flaws and political pressures, Kennedy failed during the missile crisis to keep American policy from exhibiting, in his own words, "a collective death-wish for the world."

Like traditional historians of the missile crisis, the revisionists identified a hero, but it was the Soviet premier, Nikita Khrushchev, who withdrew the missiles at risk to his prestige. "Had Khrushchev not done so, there might well have been no later historians to exalt Kennedy," for then Kennedy and his aides, so set on victory at any cost, "would burn the world to a cinder." In effect the new histories inverted the earlier images of Kennedy as a sentry for international order standing firm against a ruthless Soviet Union. To the revisionists, Kennedy's belligerence itself posed the chief threat of global annihilation, and only the belated prudence of his counterpart in the Kremlin salvaged the peace.

3. New Evidence, Old Myths

For more than two decades after the missile crisis, scholarship churned along these two interpretive poles, grinding ever finer a limited cache of primary sources. Denied access to most records of the Ex Comm meetings, historians continued to rely on memoirs by several of President Kennedy's aides. As for the Soviets, a commentator for *Izvestia* later lamented that their press "treated the episode with socialist surrealism," refusing even to concede Khrushchev's placement of nuclear weapons in Cuba. "The word 'missiles' never appeared in the newspapers, though later, in the Kennedy-Khrushchev letters, the phrase 'weapons the United States considers offensive' was used."

As late as 1982 a writer surveying the historical literature could reasonably assert, "There are no new facts about the Kennedys, only new attitudes."

Seldom has an insight aged more rapidly or spectacularly. Beginning in the mid-to-late eighties the volcanic flow of information and inquiry in the era of *glasnost* enabled several conferences on the missile crisis in which Soviet and American scholars and former officials shared facts and feelings long guarded like vital national secrets. These exchanges, coinciding with the declassification of various Ex Comm conversations, overturned much of what both traditional and revisionist scholars had long believed, extending even to shared assumptions about the basic facts of the crisis.

The entire twenty-five-year debate over whether Kennedy was warranted in not pledging to withdraw the Turkish missiles was abruptly exposed as based on a faulty record of events. In 1987 former Secretary of State Dean Rusk revealed that Kennedy had secretly prepared a fallback plan to have UN Secretary General U Thant propose a mutual dismantling of missiles in Cuba and Turkey. This would have let the president appear to comply only with a UN request rather than a Soviet demand. Whether Kennedy would have resorted to this gambit is uncertain, but clearly he had been seeking ways to defuse the risk of war.

Kennedy's back-channel efforts to end the crisis went further still. At a conference in Moscow in 1989, the former Soviet ambassador to the United States, Anatoly Dobrynin, recalled an explicit American agreement to withdraw the missiles from Turkey, not simply a vague expression of hope that this might eventually occur. Robert Kennedy had asked him not to draw up any formal exchange of letters, saying it was important not to publicize the accord, for it could show the administration to be purveying a falsehood to the American public. Sorensen deepened the panelists' astonishment by confirming that Robert Kennedy's diaries, which formed the basis of the posthumously published book *Thirteen Days,* were indeed explicit on this part of the deal. But at the time it was still a secret even on the American side, except for the president and a few officials within the Ex Comm. Sorensen explained that in preparing *Thirteen Days* for publication, "I took it upon myself to edit that out of his diaries."

As a result of Sorensen's editing discretion, Kennedy's conciliatory policy on the Turkish missiles was distorted by histories of the crisis into a symbol of either his valiant resolve or his confrontational bent. Similarly historians had long emphasized the imminent danger of a U.S. attack on the Cuban missile sites, whether to highlight the president's grave choices or to further indict him for war-mongering. Yet McNamara insisted in 1987, "There was no way we were going to war on Monday or Tuesday [October 29 or 30]. No way!" McNamara had suggested in the Ex Comm an intermediate step of tightening the quarantine to include petroleum, oil, and lubricants, and felt "very certain" that the president would have preferred this step to authorizing an attack.

Some of the new evidence is considerably less flattering to President Kennedy's image as a peacemaker. Records of the first day of Ex Comm meetings, October 16, show both John and Robert Kennedy inclined, with most other participants, to a quick air strike. The president's vaunted containment of the risks of war also appears less reassuring than in the idealized portrayals of early histories and memoirs. The perennial boast that he only modestly opened a Pandora's box of nuclear dangers lost much of its luster as scholars inventoried what had nearly escaped. The president never learned that U.S. destroyers might have crippled a Soviet submarine with depth charges near the quarantine line, an episode that could have triggered a wider naval clash. Kennedy also did not know of a series of false nuclear alerts that, in combination with the Strategic Air Command's heightened combat readiness, DEFCON (Defense Condition) 2, posed risks of inadvertent escalation.

Still more alarming, on October 27 a U.S. reconnaissance pilot strayed into Soviet territory, a violation that Khrushchev indignantly likened to a preparation for a preemptive nuclear strike. "There's always some son of a bitch who doesn't get the word," the president said on learning of this provocation. Kennedy would have been still more displeased had he known that because of the heightened military alert, U.S. fighter planes scrambling to protect the lost pilot from Russian MiGs were armed not with conventional weapons but with nuclear missiles. Scott D. Sagan, whose resourceful study *The Limits of Safety* discloses various military miscues and malfunctions during the crisis that might have led to a wider conflict, concludes that while "President Kennedy may well have been prudent," he lacked "unchallenged final control over U.S. nuclear weapons."

Nor did the danger of unwanted escalation stem entirely from U.S. nuclear forces. According to Anatoli Gribkov, who headed operational planning for the Soviet armed forces in 1962, the Russians had placed in Cuba not only medium-range missiles but also twelve *Luna* tactical missiles with nuclear warheads designed for ground combat support. Had Kennedy ordered an invasion, the Soviet commander in Cuba, General Issa Pliyev, in the event he lost contact with Moscow, had authority to fire the *Lunas* at the American landing force. On hearing this in 1992, a stunned McNamara exclaimed, "No one should believe that a U.S. force could have been attacked by tactical nuclear warheads without the U.S. responding with nuclear warheads. And where would it have ended? In utter disaster."

Even Ex Comm veterans who had long exalted the Kennedy administration's "rational crisis management" have renounced the very notion as romantic—and dangerous. President Kennedy's National Security Adviser, McGeorge Bundy, acknowledged, "The most important part of crisis management is not to have a crisis, because there's no telling what will happen once you're in one." McNamara agreed, "'Managing' crises is the wrong term; you don't 'manage' them because you *can't*. . . ." On the twenty-fifth anniversary of the missile crisis, Sorensen, Kennedy's loyal aide and biographer, termed the confrontation "unwise, unwarranted and unnecessary."

The new scholarship has further chipped at the Kennedys' larger-than-life image by crediting the much maligned foreign policy establishment with contributions hitherto unknown or attributed wholly to the president and his brother. Secretary of State Dean Rusk, belying later charges that he was ineffectual in the Ex Comm and nearing a breakdown, originated the contingency plan to have UN Secretary General U Thant request the withdrawal of missiles in both Turkey and Cuba. With the president's approval, Rusk prepared Andrew Cordier, the president of Columbia University and a former UN parliamentarian, to approach U Thant. Had Khrushchev not accepted an earlier

American offer, Rusk's idea might have served as the basis for a settlement under UN auspices.

The administration's celebrated "acceptance" of Khrushchev's tacit proposals on October 26 rather than his sterner public demands the next day—a ploy once credited to Robert Kennedy alone—in fact had a complex patrimony, Llewellyn Thompson, the former ambassador to the Soviet Union, whom Robert Kennedy's memoir credits generously but generally for "uncannily accurate" advice that was "surpassed by none," may have first suggested the outlines of this strategy. Bundy, Assistant Secretary of State for Latin American Affairs Edwin Martin, and others also offered variations on this gambit in informal discussions. Robert Kennedy formally proposed the idea in an Ex Comm meeting and drafted a response with Sorensen. But the view that this was his exclusive brainchild—a view nurtured by his own seemingly definitive account—underscores that memoirs seldom reveal an author's limitations other than a selective memory.

The very machinery of government, long viewed as a cumbersome, bumbling foil to a dynamic chief executive, now appears to have been a responsive (if not fully respected) partner. Contrary to early accounts, the failure to remove American missiles from Turkey before the crisis did not stem from unwitting bureaucratic sabotage of a presidential directive. Rather, Kennedy himself had acquiesced in the delay to avoid embarrassing a Turkish government that had only recently hinged its prestige on accepting the missiles. The president may well have been dismayed by their continued presence, but he was in no way surprised by it in the Ex Comm meetings. Rusk dismissed reports of the president's alleged betrayal by a lazy State Department, saying, "He never expressed any irritation to me because he had been fully briefed by me on that situation."

These and other discoveries all augur a far richer, more precise understanding of Kennedy's role in the missile crisis. But they have yet to produce an interpretive framework to encompass them. Should historians conclude that the president was less militant than once thought because he sanctioned a trade of missile bases? Or more militant because he initially leaned toward bombing Cuba? Does he now appear more adept at crisis management, given his elaborate fallback plans for a possible settlement through the UN? Or simply lucky to survive his own ignorance of swaggering American officers, false nuclear alerts, and nuclear-equipped Soviet forces in Cuba? Was the president more dependent on the Ex Comm in light of contributions by unsung heroes such as Llewellyn Thompson? Or did he treat the Ex Comm as having limited relevance, as in his concealment from most members of the private deal on the Turkish missiles? On these and other issues, the additions to our knowledge have been individually striking but cumulatively chaotic.

A way to make sense of these seemingly disparate and even conflicting pieces of evidence is to view President Kennedy as a moderate leader in a militant age. His vision at all times extended beyond the Ex Comm's deliberations, encompassing the formidable national consensus that the Soviet base in Cuba should be challenged militarily. Honing his policies on the grindstone of political necessity, Kennedy ordered a blockade of the island and considered still bolder action because he knew that Soviet leaders and the American public alike would otherwise view him as fatally irresolute. Yet within his circumscribed political setting, he proved more willing than most Americans, both in and outside his circle of advisers, to limit bellicose displays and to offer the Russians timely, if covert, concessions.

Despite a growing awareness of Kennedy's political constraints, the revisionist image of a man driven by both insecurity and arrogance to rash policies has proven extraordinarily resilient. Thomas G. Peterson, who incisively recounts the covert war against Castro waged by two administrations, judges Kennedy's brand of cold war leadership more dangerous than Eisenhower's. "Driven by a desire for power," Paterson writes, "Kennedy personalized issues, converting them into tests of will." Far from simply continuing "his predecessor's anti-Castro policies," Kennedy "significantly increased the pressures against the upstart island" out of an obsession with Castro. "He thus helped generate major crises, including the October 1962 missile crisis. Kennedy inherited the Cuban problem—and he made it worse."

In *The Dark Side of Camelot* (1997) the award-winning journalist Seymour Hersh cranks up to full strength the assault on Kennedy's character that had stamped revisionist writings of the 1970s. Contrasting Khrushchev's "common sense and dread of nuclear war" with Kennedy's "fanaticism" during the missile crisis, Hersh concludes: "For the first time in his presidency, Kennedy publicly brought his personal recklessness, and his belief that the normal rules of conduct did not apply to him, to his foreign policy. . . . The Kennedy brothers brought the world to the edge of war in their attempts to turn the dispute into a political asset."

Textbooks too have incorporated into their "objective" look at American history the notion that Kennedy's belligerence is the key to understanding his foreign policy. In a leading work, *Promises to Keep: The United States Since World War II* (1999), Paul Boyer finds that "Kennedy's approach to Cold War leadership differed markedly from Eisenhower's. Shaped by an intensely competitive family and a hard-driving father whom he both admired and feared, he eagerly sought to prove his toughness to the Soviet adversary."

The focus on Kennedy's supposed confrontational bent to explain his policies reaches its fullest—and most problematic—development in the aptly titled study by Thomas C. Reeves, *A Question of Character.* Reeves's Kennedy was "deficient in integrity, compassion, and temperance," defects that clearly influenced his Cuban policy, from the decision [in 1961] to ignore the moral and legal objections to an invasion, and through the creation of Operation Mongoose." During the missile crisis too, "Kennedy at times seemed unduly militant, and his aggressive and competitive instincts led him to grant the [diplomatic] initiative to the Soviets at critical points where more skilled diplomacy might have avoided it." Reeves dismisses claims that the president sought never to "challenge the other side needlessly," with the comment, "Neither, of course, were the Kennedys prepared to accept anything short of victory." Faced with the mounting evidence of Kennedy's prudence, Reeves allows that the president's "personal agony over the conflict, his several efforts to avoid bloodshed, and his willingness to make a trade of Turkish for

Cuban missiles, revealed a deeper concern for the nation and the world than many who knew him well might have suspected." But little else leavens Reeves's generally dour portrait of a president whose personal failings compounded the risks of war. Like other revisionist scholars, Reeves dutifully ingests the new scholarship on the missile crisis but cannot easily digest it.

The hazards of treating presidential character as the Rosetta stone to make sense of policies in the missile crisis should by now give pause to even the most confirmed of Kennedy's admirers or detractors. The emergence of contributions by Rusk, Thompson, Bundy, Martin, and other establishment figures has made it more difficult to portray the Kennedys as lonely titans striding across the political stage with ideas and policies uniquely their own. And, granted that Kennedy was "the key decisionmaker," he nonetheless acted within tightly defined parameters that had little to do with the character of the chief executive.

The amplified record of decision-making has also recast or removed issues that long galvanized and framed debates over Kennedy's character. Interpretations of the president's supposedly tough policy on the Jupiter missiles now appear to have rested on accounts that, by embellishment and concealment alike, exaggerated his brinkmanship. The puncturing of those distortions should deflate as well the images of Kennedy as either a surpassingly valiant leader or a Neanderthal cold warrior.

Traditional historians, it is now clear, both sanitized and romanticized the historical record in portraying President Kennedy as an ideal fusion of hawkish resolve and dovish reserve, who forced out the Cuban missiles without making needless concessions or taking heedless risks. In fact Kennedy resolved the crisis not simply through toughness and diplomatic legerdemain but by pledging to remove the missiles from Turkey, a deal he publicly spurned and his partisans long proudly but wrongly denied. And while Kennedy's defenders lauded his rejection of calls for air strikes and invasion, they overlooked the provocation of his actual policies, including the plots against Castro, the push for ever greater American nuclear superiority, and, of course, the blockade of Cuba.

The historical record is even more resistant to revisionist portraits of a president whose psychological deformities impelled him to risk peace for the sake of personal glory or catharsis. These accounts were from the first suspect, whether in drawing tortured connections between Kennedy's womanizing and his foreign policy or deriding him for sharing the beliefs of his own generation rather than a later one. They simply collapse under the weight of evidence that, during the gravest crisis of the cold war, Kennedy repeatedly proved more prudent than many aides, both civilian and military. As he told his brother Robert on October 26, "If anybody is around to write after this, they are going to understand that we made every effort to find peace and every effort to give our adversary room to move. I am not going to push the Russians an inch beyond what is necessary."

Ernest May and Philip Zelikow, editors of an invaluable annotated record of the Ex Comm sessions, marvel that "[Kennedy] seems more alive to the possibilities and consequences of each new development than anyone else."

On October 27, with pressure mounting for decisive action, the president "is the only one in the room who is determined not to go to war over obsolete missiles in Turkey." May and Zelikow acknowledge Kennedy's partial responsibility for this superpower clash but deem it "fortunate" that "[he] was the president charged with managing the crisis."

The most telling dismissal of revisionist rhetoric comes from Kennedy's adversaries themselves. Shortly after the crisis ended, Khrushchev admitted to an American journalist, "Kennedy did just what I would have done if I had been in the White House instead of the Kremlin." In his memoirs the former Soviet leader lamented Kennedy's death as "a great loss," for "he was gifted with the ability to resolve international conflicts by negotiation, as the whole world learned during the so-called Cuban crisis. Regardless of his youth he was a real statesman." As for those "clever people" who "will tell you that Kennedy was to blame for the tensions which might have resulted in war," Khrushchev said, "You have to keep in mind the era in which we live." Castro, for his part, believed Kennedy "acted as he did partly to save Khrushchev, out of fear that any successor would be tougher."

The misrepresentations of Kennedy's leadership go deeper than the debates over whether he was heroic or merely reckless, idealistic or expedient, poised or impulsive. Scholars have so focused on Kennedy's style, aura, temperament, and character as to slight, if not obscure, the crucial framework of national values that he necessarily accommodated and largely shared. The missile crisis, as much as anything, is the story of how Kennedy faithfully reflected a remarkable consensus in political institutions and public opinion regarding America's role as Free World champion in the nuclear age.

Contrary to the impression left by Kennedy's partisans, the Executive Committee he formed to advise him during the missile crisis was never a sealed laboratory for reinventing American policy. Nor was it, as the revisionists later had it, a forum for venting personal demons at public expense. Rather, like any leader in a democracy, Kennedy self-consciously labored under constraints imposed by public opinion, the Congress, the military, the CIA, and a host of civilian constituencies. To argue that he could or should have disdained these pressures is to imply a preference for philosopher kings over accountable presidents. Whatever the appeal of such arguments, they leave little room for either the ideal or the reality of American democracy.

Americans in the early sixties overwhelmingly regarded the prospect of missiles in Cuba as intolerably threatening and judged leaders by their firmness against Soviet encroachments. Whoever occupied the Oval Office would therefore have faced intense pressures to demand removal of the missiles, direct low-level military action against Cuba, and avoid apparent concessions to the Russians. Buffeted by partisan sniping, public opinion, and the force of inherited policies, President Kennedy pursued all of these options. Throughout he sought to minimize confrontation with the Soviet Union to a degree consistent with his political survival.

Accounting for the full political weight of entrenched national attitudes can help resolve the central paradox of Kennedy's policies during the missile crisis, which reflected elements of both recklessness and restraint. Considered against the background of his times, Kennedy appears a rational leader, conciliatory and even empathetic towards his counterpart in the Kremlin. Yet he also represented a political culture marked by fear and bluster, qualities stoked by an uncontrolled arms race and Manichean visions of the East-West divide. To ask which was the "real" Kennedy is to speak of a chimera: a leader somehow extricable from his era.

Kennedy embodied the and-Soviet, anti-Communist values—and obsessions—of his day, though with more skepticism and caution than most contemporaries. His relative detachment from cold war dogmas was not enough to avoid a crisis caused by mutual misjudgments. Still, it allowed for a crucial modicum of flexibility and restraint that helped keep this crisis from spiraling toward war.

It may be tempting to conclude that Kennedy's avoidance of a wider conflict warrants cynicism rather than celebration, as the bare minimum one should expect of any sane leader in the nuclear age. Yet the obstacles to military restraint between states are no less daunting simply because the dangers are so great. Whatever Kennedy's missteps, he proved—together with Soviet Premier Khrushchev—that leaders can resist the lures of unchecked escalation even while mired in a climate of mutual suspicion, fear, and hostility. This achievement may yet gain new luster as nuclear weapons spread to other nations steeped in their own bitter rivalries, a development auguring two, three, many missile crises to come.

POSTSCRIPT

Was President Kennedy Responsible for the Cuban Missile Crisis?

Journalist Ronald Steel used his review of former attorney general, senator, and presidential candidate Robert Kennedy's posthumously published *Thirteen Days* (Norton, 1969) to critically analyze the decisions made by President Kennedy during the Cuban missile crisis. He lists four lessons of the Cuban missile crisis: "first, that diplomacy gave way to military ultimatums; second, that there was a failure of intelligence interpretations; third, that the Kremlin's motives were never adequately understood; and fourth, that there is something basically wrong with the whole process of decision making."

Steel criticizes Kennedy for not using the diplomatic options available to him at the time. Why didn't Kennedy call Premier Khrushchev on the recently installed "hot line"? Or, why didn't he tell Soviet Foreign Minister Gromyko the truth about his knowledge of the missile sites in Cuba at a meeting of the two men four days before he announced the blockade? Couldn't Kennedy have negotiated a settlement? Maybe so, but diplomacy takes time. Steel admits that Kennedy did not "gloat" and treated the Russian exit from Cuba as a "statesmanlike move." Yet, says Steel, "the Kremlin's withdrawal under a public American ultimatum was a 'humiliation' nonetheless." If this were true, how much more difficult would it have been to get the Russians to remove the missiles once they were placed in Cuba? Could Khrushchev have withstood the "humiliation" from Castro and Mao Tse-Tang to not remove the missiles and to stand up to what Mao referred to as "the paper tiger"?

Steel's other criticisms of Kennedy deserve further analysis. What alternative did Kennedy have to forming a non-governmental group of experts to help him make the correct decision? He rejected the State department's advice because many of their policymakers hadn't accepted the split in the Communist world between Russia and China. Steel himself is critical of the role Secretary of State Dean Rusk played on the committee. Kennedy was also suspicious of the intelligence community's analysis. Not only was the CIA late in photographing the entire island in October 1962 because its director had been on his honeymoon, Kennedy himself had distrusted the agency ever since it botched the Bay of Pigs invasion in April 1961 with misleading information.

President Kennedy was probably caught off-guard with Khrushchev's bold actions in Cuba in the fall of 1962. Did Khrushchev want to compensate for the Russian "missile gap"? Did he want to trade Russia's withdrawal from Cuba with the American withdrawal from Berlin? Did Khrushchev wish to provide Cuba with military protection from another U.S. invasion? Forty years later, with much more evidence available from the Cuban and Russian participants in these events, Khrushchev's motives are still the subject of debate. President Kennedy, like most policymakers, had to make his decision to blockade Cuba on the basis of the best available information at the time.

Professor Robert Weisbrot tries to answer some of these questions on the basis of the new information, which has been uncovered during the past 20 years, including declassified government memos, transcriptions of the Ex-Comm meetings, which were taped, and transcriptions of several conferences held in Moscow and Havana where participants and their children recalled the roles they played during the crisis.

Weisbrot concludes that Kennedy was neither the lone crisis hero (which is the way devotees such as his chief speech writer Ted Sorenson portrayed him in *The Kennedy Legacy* (Macmillan, 1969)) nor a macho anti-Communist counterrevolutionary (which is the way revisionists other than Steel pictured him). See, for example, Thomas Paterson's scathing analysis in "Fixation with Cuba: The Bay of Pigs, Missile Crisis and Covert War against Castro," in Thomas Paterson, ed., *Kennedy's Quest for Victory: American Foreign Policy, 1961–1963* (Oxford University Press, 1989).

Weisbrot gives credit for softening the crisis to a number of other participants in the crisis. Secretary of State Dean Rusk, for example, was not the "silent Buddha" as portrayed in the writings of earlier Kennedy admirers. It was Rusk who revealed that Kennedy's fall-back plan was to have U.N. Secretary General U. Thant propose a swap of missiles in Turkey and Cuba. It was Llewellyn Thompson, the former ambassador to the Soviet Union, and not Robert Kennedy who suggested accepting Krushchev's tacit proposals in his October 26, 1962, note and not the harsher terms of the public demands issued the following day.

Future presidents might want to listen to the advice of Kennedy's National Security Adviser McGeorge Bundy, who acknowledged: "The most important part of crisis management is not to have a crisis, because there's no telling what will happen once you're in one." Scott D. Sagan, in *The Limits of Safety: Organizations, Accidents and Nuclear Weapons* (Princeton University, 1985), lists a number of potential disasters, which Professor Weisbrot recounts, that occurred during the Cuban missile crisis, some of which even President Kennedy was not aware of. The real failure of crisis management occurred later. The Kennedy–Johnson team, full of exuberance over their success in Cuba, believed they could manage similar crises in Southeast Asia.

The literature on the Cuban missile crisis is enormous. In addition to the comprehensive footnotes and bibliography in Weisbrot, *op. cit.*, start with Mark J. White, "The Cuban Imbroglio: From the Bay of Pigs to the Missile Crisis and Beyond," in his edited book *Kennedy: The New Frontier Revisited* (New York University Press, 1998). All the essays in this volume strive for an alternative to the Camelot and counter-Camelot interpretations of the Kennedy presidency. The same may be said of White's *Missiles in Cuba: Kennedy, Khrushchev, Castro and the 1962 Crisis* (Ivan R. Dee, 1997).

A superb collection of articles can be found in Robert A. Divine, ed., *The Cuban Missile Crisis* (Quadrangle Books, 1971), which contains older but still useful articles. Divine also reviews a number of books and collections of primary sources, secondary articles, and roundtable discussions in "Alive and

Well: The Continuing Cuban Missile Crisis Controversy," *Diplomatic History* (Fall 1994). James Nathan has edited a collection of articles based on records opened by the American, former Soviet, and Cuban governments and collected by the independent National Security Archive. See the articles by Barton J. Bernstein, Richard Ned Lebow, Philip Brenner, and the editor himself in James A. Nathan, ed., *The Cuban Missile Crisis Revisited* (St. Martin's Press, 1992).

There are a number of primary sources that students can explore without visiting the archives. Mark J. White has edited *The Kennedy's and Cuba: The Declassified History* (Ivan R. Dee, 1999). See also Laurence Chang and Peter Kornbluh, eds., *The Cuban Missile Crisis. 1962: A National Security Archive Documents Reader*, rev. ed. (New Press, 1998). Students are fortunate to have tape recordings of the Ex-Comm meetings. They have been transcribed, along with some other meetings, by Ernest R. May and Philip D. Zelikow and are reprinted in their edited book, *The Kennedy Tapes: Inside the White House During the Cuban Missile Crisis* (Harvard University, 1997). Two excellent summaries of the crisis have appeared in the twenty-first century. In 2001, James A. Nathan provided an up-to-date concise *Anatomy of the Cuban Missile Crisis* in the Greenwood Press Guides Series to Historic Events of the Twentieth Century. Sheldon M. Stern has corrected some of the transcripts of the Ex-Comm meetings and has used these tapes to construct favorable interpretation of JFK, who "often stood virtually alone against war-like council from the Ex-Comm, the Joint Chiefs of Staff and Congress during these historic thirteen days. See *Averting 'The Final Failure': John F. Kennedy and the Secret Cuban Missile Crisis Meetings* (Stanford University Press, 2003) and a shortened paperback version for students, *The Week the World Stood Still: Inside the Secret Cuban Missile Crisis* (Stanford University Press, 2005). Alice L. George's *Awaiting Armageddon: How Americans Faced the Cuban Missile Crisis* (University of North Carolina Press, 2003) points out how unprepared the public was for civil defense in the eight days the public was aware of the crisis. In New Orleans, for example, there was an issue about building segregated bomb shelters.

There are a number of videos for classroom use on the Cuban missile crisis. In 1992, NBC aired a two-hour documentary on *The Cuban Missile Crisis: 30 Years Later*; in the same year, PBS produced a 30-year retrospective in the front-line series on *The Cuban Missile Crisis*.

For Internet sources, see the following:

CNN and BBC produced a 24-hour documentary on the Cold War in 1998. The Web site has valuable interviews, documents, and transcripts of the 50-minute videos, as well as some material not included in the films that aired. The work on the Cuban missile crisis was the tenth in this series. See http://cnn.com/SPECIALS/cold.war/episodes/10/

For transcripts of Ex-Comm meetings in streaming audio, see http://www.hpol.org//jfk/cuban//, and http://www.state.gove/www/about_state/history/frusX/index.html

The Cold War History Project, a joint effort of George Washington University and the National Security Archive, has especially good documents on the Cuban Missile Crisis. See http://cwihp.si.edu/pdj.htm

C-SPAN Online provides RealAudio clips and transcripts from tapes that President Kennedy secretly recorded in the White House, RealAudio newsreels from 1962, an image gallery of the major players and surveillance photos, and RealAudio archives. See http://www.c-spall.org/guide/society/cuba/

The Department of State's definitive volumes relating to the Cuban Missile Crisis are available online: *Foreign Relations of the United States, "Cuba," Vol. X, 1961–1963*; and *Foreign Relations of the United States, "Cuban Missile Crisis and Aftermath," Vol. XI, 1961–1963*. See http://www.state.gov/www/aboucstate/history/frusX/index.htm

Documents Relating to American Foreign Policy: The Cuban Missile Crisis is a Web site maintained by Mount Holyoke College. The collection includes documents, links, and other historical materials concerning the Cuban missile crisis. See http://www.mtholyoke.edu/acad/intrel/cuba.htm

Internet References . . .

National Archives and Records Administration

This site offers access to the "JFK Assassination Records."

http://www.archives.gov

The Papers of Martin Luther King, Jr.

Offers online access to the official and personal papers of Martin Luther King, Jr., which includes material from the projected 14-volume edition at Stanford University of *The Papers of Martin Luther King, Jr.*, five volumes of which are now published.

http://www.kingpapers.org

National Committee to Preserve Social Security and Medicare

The National Committee to Preserve Social Security and Medicare was founded in 1982 to serve as an advocate for the landmark federal programs Social Security and Medicare and for all Americans who seek a healthy, productive, and secure retirement.

http://www.ncpssm.org

Vietnam: Yesterday and Today

The purpose of this Web site, which has been created primarily for students and teachers, is to point those who are interested in studying and teaching about the Vietnam War to materials that will be useful.

http://servercc.oakton.edu/~wittman/

Vietnam War.net

This site offers a variety of educational, entertainment, and research material relevant to the study of the Vietnam War.

http://www.vietnamwar.net

Documents from the Women's Liberation Movement

This site focuses on the radical origins of the women's movement in the United States during the late 1960s and early 1970s.

http://scriptorium.lib.duke.edu/wlm/

The National Women's History Project

The National Women's History Project is a nonprofit corporation, founded in Sonoma County, California, in 1980. The organization provides numerous links to sites on women's history under such categories as The Women's Rights Movement, Politics, African-American Women, and Peace and War.

http://www.nwhp.org

From Liberation through Watergate: 1963–1974

*T**he 1960s have become stereotyped like the roaring twenties. However, there is much truth in the stereotype. John F. Kennedy, the youngest person ever elected president, promised to get the country moving again. After he was assassinated, his successor, Lyndon B. Johnson, attacked poverty by educating and retraining those groups that were left behind by the New Deal, middle-class reforms. At the same time, African Americans and womens rose up and demanded that they be granted their civil, political, and economic rights as first-class citizens.*

Foreign affairs ended the decade on a sour note. "Containment" went berserk in Vietnam. Lyndon Johnson escalated American participation to 550,000 troops by 1968 and then tried to negotiate a peace settlement. His successor, Richard M. Nixon, tried to withdraw American troops and at the same time not lose Vietnam to the Communists. In the long term, Nixon failed on two counts: Vietnam was captured by the Communists in 1975, but Nixon was long gone by then—pressured to resign because of the Watergate fiasco.

- Did Lee Harvey Oswald Kill President Kennedy by Himself?

- Was Martin Luther King, Jr.'s Leadership Essential to the Success of the Civil Rights Revolution?

- Did the Great Society Fail?

- Was the Americanization of the War in Vietnam Inevitable?

- Has the Women's Movement of the 1970s Failed to Liberate American Women?

- Was Richard Nixon America's Last Liberal President?

ISSUE 7

Did Lee Harvey Oswald Kill President Kennedy by Himself?

YES: President's Commission on the Assassination of President John F. Kennedy, from "The Warren Report," *President's Commission on the Assassination of President John F. Kennedy* (September 24, 1964)

NO: Michael L. Kurtz, from *Crime of the Century: The Kennedy Assassination from a Historian's Perspective,* 2d ed. (University of Tennessee Press, 1993)

ISSUE SUMMARY

YES: The President's Commission on the Assassination of President John F. Kennedy argues that Lee Harvey Oswald was the sole assassin of President Kennedy and that he was not part of any organized conspiracy, domestic or foreign.

NO: Professor of history Michael L. Kurtz argues that the Warren commission ignores evidence of Oswald's connections with organized criminals and with pro-Castro and anti-Castro supporters, as well as forensic evidence that points to multiple assassins.

On November 22, 1963, at 12:30 p.m., President John F. Kennedy was shot while riding in a motorcade with his wife, Jacqueline, and Governor and Mrs. John Connally through the western end of downtown Dallas, Texas. After Secret Service agent Roy Kellerman noticed that the president was shot, he ordered the car to proceed as quickly as possible to Parkland Hospital. At one o'clock the president was pronounced dead. A stunned nation mourned for five days. Yet nearly 40 years later many questions remain unanswered. Did Lee Harvey Oswald kill President Kennedy? How many shots were fired? Was there a second or third shooter? Was Oswald set up, or was he part of a grand conspiracy? Did Jack Ruby kill Oswald on the way to his arraignment because he was distraught over the president's death or because he was ordered by the Mafia to kill Oswald?

A belief in conspiracies has been a common thread throughout American history. "The script has become familiar," according to professor of history Robert

Alan Goldberg. "Individuals and groups, acting in secret, move and shape recent American history. Driven by a lust for power and wealth, they practice deceit, subterfuge, and even assassination brazenly executed. Nothing is random or the matter of coincidence."

Popular views on American foreign policy, for example, are strewn with conspiracies. Here is a partial list: munitions makers led America into World War I; President Franklin D. Roosevelt deliberately exposed the fleet at Pearl Harbor to a Japanese attack in order to get the United States into World War II; Roosevelt sold out Eastern Europe to the Soviets at the Yalta Conference because he was pro-Russian; the Communists infiltrated the State Department and foreign service, which permitted the Communists to take over China in 1949; and the "seven sisters"—the big oil companies—deliberately curtailed the flow of oil in 1974 in order to jack up gasoline prices.

Assassinations—the overthrow of an opponent through murder—are not as common in American politics as they have been in other countries. Only four presidents have been assassinated in the United States—Abraham Lincoln, James Garfield, William McKinley and John F. Kennedy. All the assassins were identified as white males who were somewhat delusional or, at best, loners promoting a cause. The best known is John Wilkes Booth, a famous actor who killed Lincoln because the president had destroyed slavery and the Old South. Garfield was murdered by a disappointed office seeker, McKinley by an anarchist, and Kennedy supposedly by a disgruntled Marxist.

The Lincoln and Kennedy assassinations are unique because the deaths of both presidents are linked with conspiracies. Most Lincoln scholars reject the theory that Secretary of War Edward Stanton plotted with Booth to kill the president. But the Kennedy assassination has produced an enormous quantity of literature, if not all of first-rate quality, arguing that Kennedy was the victim of a conspiracy.

In the following selection, the President's Commission on the Assassination of President John F. Kennedy rejects the view that Lee Harvey Oswald was involved with any other person or group in a conspiracy to assassinate the president. The commission denies that Oswald was a foreign agent or was encouraged by any foreign government to kill the president. Nor was Oswald "an agent, employee, or informant of the FBI, CIA or any other governmental agency." In short, Oswald fit the profile of the brooding lone gunmen who killed Garfield and McKinley and set the tone for Arthur Bremmer, Squeaky Frome, and John Hinkley, who tried to kill presidential candidate George Wallace and Presidents Gerald Ford and Ronald Reagan, respectively.

In the second selection, Michael L. Kurtz questions the conclusions of the *Warren Report*. He argues that forensic evidence points to a possible second or third killer located at the grassy knoll in front of the motorcade in addition to the assassin who fired shots from the sixth floor of the Texas School Book Depository Building. Kurtz also contends that Oswald had connections with minor organized crime figures and with both pro-Castro and anti-Castro plotters, supporting the existence of a conspiracy.

YES ↵

The Warren Report

T he Commission has . . . reached certain conclusions based on all the available evidence. No limitations have been placed on the Commission's inquiry; it has conducted its own investigation, and all Government agencies have fully discharged their responsibility to cooperate with the Commission in its investigation. These conclusions represent the reasoned judgment of all members of the Commission and are presented after an investigation which has satisfied the Commission that it: has ascertained the truth concerning the assassination of President Kennedy to the extent that a prolonged and thorough search makes this possible.

1. The shots which killed President Kennedy and wounded Governor Connally were fired from the sixth floor window at the southeast corner of the Texas School Book Depository. This determination is based upon the following:

(a) Witnesses at the scene of the assassination saw a rifle being fired from the sixth floor window of the Depository Building, and some witnesses saw a rifle in the window immediately after the shots were fired.
(b) The nearly whole bullet found on Governor Connally's stretcher at Parkland Memorial Hospital and the two bullet fragments found in the front seat of the Presidential limousine were fired from the 6.5-millimeter Mannlicher-Carcano rifle found on the sixth floor of the Depository Building to the exclusion of all other weapons.
(c) The three used cartridge cases found near the window on the sixth floor at the southeast corner of the building were fired from the same rifle which fired the above-described bullet and fragments, to the exclusion of all other weapons.
(d) The windshield in the Presidential limousine was struck by a bullet fragment on the inside surface of the glass, but was not penetrated.
(e) The nature of the bullet wounds suffered by President Kennedy and Governor Connally and the location of the car at the time of the shots establish that the bullets were fired from above and behind the Presidential limousine, striking the President and the Governor as follows:

(1) President Kennedy was first struck by a bullet which entered at the back of his neck and exited through the lower front portion

From *President's Commission on the Assassination of President John F. Kennedy, The Warren Report: Report of the President's Commission on the Assassination of President John F. Kennedy* (September 24, 1964). Washington, D.C.: U.S. Government Printing Office, 1964.

of his neck, causing a wound which would not necessarily have been lethal. The President was struck a second time by a bullet which entered the right-rear portion of his head, causing a massive and fatal wound.

(2) Governor Connally was struck by a bullet which entered on the right side of his back and traveled downward through the right side of his chest, exiting below his right nipple. This bullet then passed through his right wrist and entered his left thigh where it caused a superficial wound.

(f) There is no credible evidence that the shots were fired from the Triple Underpass, ahead of the motorcade, or from any other location.

2. The weight of the evidence indicates that there were three shots fired.

3. Although it is not necessary to any essential findings of the Commission to determine just which shot hit Governor Connally, there is very persuasive evidence from the experts to indicate that the same bullet which pierced the President's throat also caused Governor Connally's wounds. However, Governor Connally's testimony and certain other factors have given rise to some difference of opinion as to this probability but there is no question in the mind of any member of the Commission that all the shots which caused the President's and Governor Connally's wounds were fired from the sixth floor window of the Texas School Book Depository.

4. The shots which killed President Kennedy and wounded Governor Connally were fired by Lee Harvey Oswald. This conclusion is based upon the following:

(a) The Mannlicher-Carcano 6.5-millimeter Italian rifle from which the shots were fired was owned by and in the possession of Oswald.

(b) Oswald carried this rifle into the Depository Building on the morning of November 22, 1963.

(c) Oswald, at the time of the assassination, was present at the window from which the shots were fired.

(d) Shortly after the assassination, the Mannlicher-Carcano rifle belonging to Oswald was found partially hidden between some cartons on the sixth floor and the improvised paper bag in which Oswald brought the rifle to the Depository was found close by the window from which the shots were fired.

(e) Based on testimony of the experts and their analysis of films of the assassination, the Commission has concluded that a rifleman of Lee Harvey Oswald's capabilities could have fired the shots from the rifle used in the assassination within the elapsed time of the shooting. The Commission has concluded further that Oswald possessed the capability with a rifle which enabled him to commit the assassination.

(f) Oswald lied to the police after his arrest concerning important substantive matters.

(g) Oswald had attempted to kill Maj. Gen. Edwin A. Walker (Resigned, U.S. Army) on April 10, 1963, thereby demonstrating his disposition to take human life.

5. Oswald killed Dallas Police Patrolman J. D. Tippit approximately 45 minutes after the assassination. This conclusion upholds the finding that Oswald fired the shots which killed President Kennedy and wounded Governor Connally and is supported by the following:

(a) Two eyewitnesses saw the Tippit shooting and seven eyewitnesses heard the shots and saw the gunman leave the scene with revolver in hand. These nine eyewitnesses positively identified Lee Harvey Oswald as the man they saw.
(b) The cartridge cases found at the scene of the shooting were fired from the revolver in the possession of Oswald at the time of his arrest to the exclusion of all other weapons.
(c) The revolver in Oswald's possession at the time of his arrest was purchased by and belonged to Oswald.
(d) Oswald's jacket was found along the path of flight taken by the gunman as he fled from the scene of the killing.

6. Within 80 minutes of the assassination and 35 minutes of the Tippit killing Oswald resisted arrest at the theatre by attempting to shoot another Dallas police officer.

7. The Commission has reached the following conclusions concerning Oswald's interrogation and detention by the Dallas police:

(a) Except for the force required to effect his arrest, Oswald was not subjected to any physical coercion by any law enforcement officials. He was advised that he could not be compelled to give any information and that any statements made by him might be used against him in court. He was advised of his right to counsel. He was given the opportunity to obtain counsel of his own choice and was offered legal assistance by the Dallas Bar Association, which he rejected at that time.
(b) Newspaper, radio, and television reporters were allowed uninhibited access to the area through which Oswald had to pass when he was moved from his cell to the interrogation room and other sections of the building, thereby subjecting Oswald to harassment and creating chaotic conditions which were not conducive to orderly interrogation or the protection of the rights of the prisoner.
(c) The numerous statements, sometimes erroneous, made to the press by various local law enforcement officials, during this period of confusion and disorder in the police station, would have presented serious obstacles to the obtaining of a fair trial for Oswald. To the extent that the information was erroneous or misleading, it helped to create doubts, speculations, and fears in the mind of the public which might otherwise not have arisen.

8. The Commission has reached the following conclusions concerning the killing of Oswald by Jack Ruby on November 24, 1963:

(a) Ruby entered the basement of the Dallas Police Department shortly after 11:17 a.m. and killed Lee Harvey Oswald at 11:21 a.m.

(b) Although the evidence on Ruby's means of entry is not conclusive, the weight of the evidence indicates that he walked down the ramp leading from Main Street to the basement of the police department.

(c) There is no evidence to support the rumor that Ruby may have been assisted by any members of the Dallas Police Department in the killing of Oswald.

(d) The Dallas Police Department's decision to transfer Oswald to the county jail in full public view was unsound. The arrangements made by the police department on Sunday morning, only a few hours before the attempted transfer, were inadequate. Of critical importance was the fact that news media representatives and others were not excluded from the basement even after the police were notified of threats to Oswald's life. These deficiencies contributed to the death of Lee Harvey Oswald.

9. The Commission has found no evidence that either Lee Harvey Oswald or Jack Ruby was part of any conspiracy, domestic or foreign, to assassinate President Kennedy. The reasons for this conclusion are:

(a) The Commission has found no evidence that anyone assisted Oswald in planning or carrying out the assassination. In this connection it has thoroughly investigated, among other factors, the circumstances surrounding the planning of the motorcade route through Dallas, the hiring of Oswald by the Texas School Book Depository Co. on October 15, 1963, the method by which the rifle was brought into the building, the placing of cartons of books at the window, Oswald's escape from the building, and the testimony of eyewitnesses to the shooting.

(b) The Commission has found no evidence that Oswald was involved with any person or group in a conspiracy to assassinate the President, although it has thoroughly investigated, in addition to other possible leads, all facets of Oswald's associations, finances, and personal habits, particularly during the period following his return from the Soviet Union in June 1962.

(c) The Commission has found no evidence to show that Oswald was employed, persuaded, or encouraged by any foreign government to assassinate President Kennedy or that he was an agent of any foreign government, although the Commission has reviewed the circumstances surrounding Oswald's defection to the Soviet Union, his life there from October of 1959 to June of 1962 so far as it can be reconstructed, his known contacts with the Fair Play for Cuba Committee and his visits to the Cuban and Soviet Embassies in Mexico City during his trip to Mexico from September 26 to October 3, 1963, and his known contacts with the Soviet Embassy in the United States.

(d) The Commission has explored all attempts of Oswald to identify himself with various political groups, including the Communist Party, U.S.A., the Fair Play for Cuba Committee, and the Socialist Workers Party, and has been unable to find any evidence that the contacts which he initiated were related to Oswald's subsequent assassination of the President.

(e) All of the evidence before the Commission established that there was nothing to support the speculation that Oswald was an agent, employee, or informant of the FBI, the CIA, or any other governmental agency. It has thoroughly investigated Oswald's relationships prior to the assassination with all agencies of the U.S. Government. All contacts with Oswald by any of these agencies were made in the regular exercise of their different responsibilities.

(f) No direct or indirect relationship between Lee Harvey Oswald and Jack Ruby has been discovered by the Commission, nor has it been able to find any credible evidence that either knew the other, although a thorough investigation was made of the many rumors and speculations of such a relationship.

(g) The Commission has found no evidence that Jack Ruby acted with any other person in the killing of Lee Harvey Oswald.

(h) After careful investigation the Commission has found no credible evidence either that Ruby and Officer Tippit, who was killed by Oswald, knew each other or that Oswald and Tippit knew each other.

Because of the difficulty of proving negatives to a certainty the possibility of others being involved with either Oswald or Ruby cannot be established categorically, but if there is any such evidence it has been beyond the reach of all the investigative agencies and resources of the United States and has not come to the attention of this Commission.

10. In its entire investigation the Commission has found no evidence of conspiracy, subversion, or disloyalty to the U.S. Government by any Federal, State, or local official.

11. On the basis of the evidence before the Commission it concludes that Oswald acted alone. Therefore, to determine the motives for the assassination of President Kennedy, one must look to the assassin himself. Clues to Oswald's motives can be found in his family history, his education or lack of it, his acts, his writings, and the recollections of those who had close contacts with him throughout his life. The Commission has presented with this report all of the background information bearing on motivation which it could discover. Thus, others may study Lee Oswald's life and arrive at their own conclusions as to his possible motives.

The Commission could not make any definitive determination of Oswald's motives. It has endeavored to isolate factors which contributed to his character and which might have influenced his decision to assassinate President Kennedy. These factors were:

(a) His deep-rooted resentment of all authority which was expressed in a hostility toward every society in which he lived;

(b) His inability to enter into meaningful relationships with people, and a continuous pattern of rejecting his environment in favor of new surroundings;

(c) His urge to try to find a place in history and despair at times over failures in his various undertakings;

(d) His capacity for violence as evidenced by his attempt to kill General Walker;

(e) His avowed commitment to Marxism and communism, as he understood the terms and developed his own interpretation of them; this was expressed by his antagonism toward the United States, by his defection to the Soviet Union, by his failure to be reconciled with life in the United States even after his disenchantment with the Soviet Union, and by his efforts, though frustrated, to go to Cuba.

Each of these contributed to his capacity to risk all in cruel and irresponsible actions.

12. The Commission recognizes that the varied responsibilities of the President require that he make frequent trips to all parts of the United States and abroad. Consistent with their high responsibilities Presidents can never be protected from every potential threat. The Secret Service's difficulty in meeting its protective responsibility varies with the activities and the nature of the occupant of the Office of President and his willingness to conform to plans for his safety. In appraising the performance of the Secret Service it should be understood that it has to do its work within such limitations. Nevertheless, the Commission believes that recommendations for improvements in Presidential protection are compelled by the facts disclosed in this investigation.

(a) The complexities of the Presidency have increased so rapidly in recent years that the Secret Service has not been able to develop or to secure adequate resources of personnel and facilities to fulfill its important assignment. This situation should be promptly remedied.

(b) The Commission has concluded that the criteria and procedures of the Secret Service designed to identify and protect against persons considered threats to the President, were not adequate prior to the assassination.

(1) The Protective Research Section of the Secret Service, which is responsible for its preventive work, lacked sufficient trained personnel and the mechanical and technical assistance needed to fulfill its responsibility.

(2) Prior to the assassination the Secret Service's criteria dealt with direct threats against the President. Although the Secret Service treated the direct threats against the President adequately, it failed to recognize the necessity of identifying other potential sources of danger to his security. The Secret Service did not develop adequate and specific criteria defining those persons or groups who might present a danger to the President. In effect, the Secret Service largely relied upon other Federal or State agencies to supply the information necessary for it to fulfill its preventive responsibilities, although it did ask for information about direct threats to the President.

(c) The Commission has concluded that there was insufficient liaison and coordination of information between the Secret Service and other Federal agencies necessarily concerned with Presidential protection. Although the FBI, in the normal exercise of its responsibility, had secured considerable information about Lee Harvey Oswald, it had no official responsibility, under the Secret Service criteria existing at the time of the President's trip to Dallas, to refer to the Secret Service the information it had about Oswald. The Commission has concluded, however, that the FBI took an unduly restrictive view of its role in preventive intelligence work prior to the assassination. A more carefully coordinated treatment of the Oswald case by the FBI might well have resulted in bringing Oswald's activities to the attention of the Secret Service.

(d) The Commission has concluded that some of the advance preparations in Dallas made by the Secret Service, such as the detailed security measures taken at Love Field and the Trade Mart, were thorough and well executed. In other respects, however, the Commission has concluded that the advance preparations for the President's trip were deficient.

(1) Although the Secret Service is compelled to rely to a great extent on local law enforcement officials, its procedures at the time of the Dallas trip did not call for well-defined instructions as to the respective responsibilities of the police officials and others assisting in the protection of the President.

(2) The procedures relied upon by the Secret Service for detecting the presence of an assassin located in a building along a motorcade route were inadequate. At the time of the trip to Dallas, the Secret Service as a matter of practice did not investigate, or cause to be checked, any building located along the motorcade route to be taken by the President. The responsibility for observing windows in these buildings during the motorcade was divided between local police personnel stationed on the streets to regulate crowds and Secret Service agents riding in the motorcade. Based on its investigation the Commission has concluded that these arrangements during the trip to Dallas were clearly not sufficient.

(e) The configuration of the Presidential car and the seating arrangements of the Secret Service agents in the car did not afford the Secret Service agents the opportunity they should have had to be of immediate assistance to the President at the first sign of danger.

(f) Within these limitations, however, the Commission finds that the agents most immediately responsible for the President's safety reacted promptly at the time the shots were fired from the Texas School Book Depository Building.

Michael L. Kurtz

NO

Some Questions

When a historian investigates a past event, he usually begins by asking questions about that event. Innumerable questions about the Kennedy assassination have been raised. Some of them are worth considering, for they touch upon the most critical features of the assassination mysteries. The available evidence does not permit definitive answers to all those questions, but they do deserve attention.

1. Who killed President Kennedy?

This, of course, remains the central mystery in the entire assassination saga. Unfortunately, we do not know the answer. That more than one individual fired shots at the president cannot seriously be doubted. Their identities, however, are unknown.

2. Did Lee Harvey Oswald fire any of the shots?

The evidence against Oswald is impressive: the discovery of his rifle bearing his palmprint on the sixth floor of the Book Depository building; the testimony of eyewitness Howard Brennan; Oswald's prints on the cartons and paper sack at the window; the discovery of three cartridge cases from his rifle by the window; the discovery of two bullet fragments fired from his rifle in the limousine; his departure from the building soon after the shooting.

On the other side of the coin, the evidence in Oswald's favor is equally impressive: eyewitness identification of him on the second floor of the Depository building fifteen minutes before the assassination and two minutes after it; the lack of his prints on the outside of the rifle; the questions as to whether the cartridge cases had actually been fired from the rifle during the assassination; the extremely difficult feat of marksmanship an assassin firing from the window faced; the lack of corroboration for Brennan's contradictory and confused identification.

3. How did Lee Harvey Oswald escape the scene of the assassination?

There is no evidence to support the claim of the Warren Commission that Oswald walked out through the front door of the Book Depository building at 12:33. With the exception of the bus transfer allegedly found in Oswald's pocket, neither is there any evidence to support the commission's claim that Oswald caught a bus and a taxi. Replete with contradictions, the testimony of Mary Bledsoe and William Whaley hardly prove that the bus and taxi ride took place.

In contrast, the eyewitness and photographic evidence strongly supports Deputy Sheriff Roger Craig's testimony that he saw Oswald run from the rear of the building about fifteen minutes after the assassination and enter a station wagon driven by a dark-skinned man. Eyewitness Helen Monaghan saw Oswald in an upper floor of the building five to ten minutes after the shots. Eyewitnesses Helen Forrest and James Pennington corroborated Craig's story, for they, too, saw Oswald flee the building and enter the station wagon. While not conclusive, this evidence very solidly supports the conspiracy theory.

4. Was Oswald's gun fired at President Kennedy and Governor Connally?

The fact that two large bullet fragments, ballistically proven traceable to Oswald's rifle, were found in the front seat of the presidential limousine supplies very strong evidence that the rifle was fired once, although the possibility that the fragments were planted in the car cannot be disproven.

No other evidence proves that the rifle was fired more than once. Even if they could be proven beyond question to have been fired from Oswald's rifle, the three empty cartridge cases found on the floor by the sixth-floor window of the Depository building provide no indication that they were fired from the weapon on 22 November 1963. Obviously, the possibility exists that they were fired previously and dropped there to implicate Oswald. Even if the rifle was one of the assassination weapons, there is no proof that Oswald fired it.

5. Are the backyard photographs of Oswald holding a rifle authentic?

Because of several apparent discrepancies between the man pictured in the photographs and known pictures of the real Oswald, many Warren Commission critics questioned the authenticity of the backyard photographs. The panel of photographic experts appointed by the House Select Committee did exhaustive tests on the photographs and negatives and concluded that they were authentic.

For all of the commotion about the photographs, their relevance to the assassination is obscure. They were taken in April 1963, seven months before the assassination. Photographs of Oswald holding a weapon at that time hardly prove or disprove that he discharged that weapon seven months later.

6. How many shots were fired?

The Warren Commission based its three-shot theory primarily on the three cartridge cases, and the House Committee based its four-shot theory primarily on the Dallas police tape. The earwitnesses provide little assistance, for their accounts of the number of shots range from none to seven. Nor do the wounds on Kennedy and Connally provide an answer. Connally's wounds could have been caused by as few as one and as many as three shots, while Kennedy's may have been caused by from two to four shots. The bulk of the evidence points to four shots, three from the rear and one from the front.

7. How many shots struck President Kennedy?

On the surface, the two bullet wounds in the rear of Kennedy's body and the two in front suggest four as the answer to the question. However, the possibility that the two front holes were exit wounds for the rear holes demands close analysis. The rear holes of entrance in the head and back are positive evidence of two shots. As we have seen, the huge, gaping wound in the right front of the president's head could not simply have been an exit hole from one of Oswald's bullets. Almost certainly, it was also an entrance wound caused by a "dum-dum" or exploding bullet fired from the Grassy Knoll. The front wound in Kennedy's throat was probably *not* caused by a separate bullet. The answer, therefore, is at least three.

8. What caused the tiny bullet hole in President Kennedy's throat?

The Warren Commission's and House Committee's claim that this hole was the exit hole for the bullet that entered Kennedy's back is not supported by the evidence. The wound in the president's throat was round, clean, and encircled by a ring of bruising. Moreover, it was extremely small, smaller than the diameter of most bullets. The Forensic Pathology Panel's assertion that the buttoned collar of Kennedy's shirt caused his skin to stretch taut, thus resulting in a small exit wound, appears erroneous. Ordinarily, bullets exiting through taut skin cause large exit wounds because the bullets push tissue and matter through the skin causing it to explode outward, much as a paper bag filled with air will expand and rupture in an uneven, jagged manner as the air rushes out.

If the throat wound were an entrance wound, as some critics have charged, there would have to be some evidence of its path through the body. Since there is none, this explanation can likewise be discounted.

The most plausible explanation for the wound is that it was caused by a fragment of bone or bullet from the head shot. No hole in the neck is visible in enlargements of individual frames of the Zapruder film and in other visual records. This virtually eliminates both the exit and entrance wound theories. The most reasonable explanation, then, is that a fragment was forced through the skull cavity by the tremendous cranial pressure of the head shot and exited through the president's neck.

9. Was Bullet 399 a genuine assassination bullet?

The overwhelming weight of the evidence indicates that Bullet 399 played no role in the Kennedy assassination. The bullet's almost intact condition precludes it as the cause of Governor Connally's wounds. The removal of bullet fragments from the governor's wrist, the extensive damage to his rib and wrist, and the wounds ballistics tests results all argue persuasively against Bullet 399 as having caused any of Connally's injuries.

A bullet was discovered on a hospital stretcher that had no connection with the assassination. Darrell Tomlinson and O. P. Wright, the only two witnesses who saw the bullet on the stretcher, refused to believe that Bullet 399 was the one they saw. Nor would the two Secret Service officials who handled the stretcher bullet agree that Bullet 399 was the one they handled.

Although Bullet 399 was fired from Oswald's rifle, there is no evidence whatsoever to suggest that it caused any of the wounds on Kennedy and Connally. The Warren Commission and the House Committee assumed that Bullet 399 was the infamous single bullet, primarily because it could be traced to Oswald's rifle. Both bodies, however, failed to investigate the possibility that the bullet was planted in order to implicate Oswald.

It is possible that Bullet 399 entered Kennedy's back, penetrated only a couple of inches into the body, and did not exit—later falling out during external cardiac massage. This, in fact, was the original impression of the autopsy pathologists. If this is the case, we do not know how it wound up on a hospital stretcher that had no connection with the assassination.

Because of the incomplete information available, we still do not know when Bullet 399 was fired or how it came into the possession of the FBI as an item of ballistic evidence.

10. Did an assassin fire shots from the Grassy Knoll?

Yes. The huge, gaping hole in the right front of President Kennedy's head was almost certainly caused by an exploding bullet fired from the knoll. The rapid backward and leftward movement of Kennedy's head, as well as the backward and leftward spray of brain tissue, skull bone, and blood are very strong indicators of a shot from the right front. Assuming that it is authentic, the acoustical tape actually recorded the sound of a knoll shot.

Eye and earwitness testimony furnishes further evidence of a shot from the knoll. Almost three-quarters of the witnesses who testified heard shots from the knoll during the shooting, and three people saw a flash of light there. Five witnesses smelled gunpowder in the knoll area. A witness saw a man fleeing the knoll immediately after the shooting, and two law enforcement officials encountered phony "Secret Service" men in the parking lot behind the knoll within minutes after the gunfire.

11. If a shot came from the Grassy Knoll, why was no physical evidence of it discovered?

The answer to this question, so frequently asked by defenders of the *Warren Report,* is as simple as it is obvious. Common sense should be sufficient to explain that anyone taking the risk of killing the President of the United States would also have taken the precautions necessary to avoid leaving physical evidence of his guilt. The peculiar part of this aspect of the assassination case is not the lack of physical evidence on the knoll, but the plethora of evidence scattered all over the sixth floor of the Book Depository building. The two government investigations insist that Lee Harvey Oswald did not even bother to pick up the three cartridge cases and paper bag near the sixth-floor window but, in the process of descending the building stairs, paused for the refreshment of a Coke before departing the building.

An assassin with even the slightest concern with making a successful escape would hardly have selected the sixth floor of the Depository Building for his firing site. He would have been trapped on an upper floor of the building.

His only means of escape would have been to descend six flights of stairs and then weave his way through the crowd of spectators and police to freedom.

The Grassy Knoll, on the other hand, provided a natural and ideal sniper's position. The six-foot-high wooden fence and the abundance of shrubbery concealed him from the crowd, yet gave him an undisturbed line of fire at the president. The parking lot right behind the knoll gave him quick access to a getaway vehicle.

12. Who were the "Secret Service" men encountered on the knoll right after the shots?

We know that they were not genuine Secret Service agents since all agents remained with the motorcade during its dash to Parkland Hospital. The men who flashed "Secret Service" credentials to Officer Smith and Constable Weizman, therefore, were imposters, and their identities have never been discovered. It need hardly be mentioned that the Warren Commission made no attempt to investigate this obviously serious matter.

13. Who were the three "tramps" arrested in the railroad yards behind the Grassy Knoll?

The theory that two of the three men were E. Howard Hunt and Frank Sturgis may be dismissed as unwarranted speculation. However, their true identities have never been determined. The Dallas police must have had some reason for arresting them but destroyed the records of the arrest. It is unlikely that the police would have suspended their search for the president's assassin to look for vagrants. However, as with so many other aspects of this case, the incomplete evidence does not permit an answer to the question.

14. Were two men seen together on an upper floor of the Texas School Book Depository building?

Yes. Witnesses Carolyn Walther, Richard Carr, Ruby Henderson, Arnold Rowland, and Johnny L. Powell saw two men, one of them dark-complected, together on the sixth floor. The Hughes and Bronson films of the assassination apparently show two men near the sixth-floor window.

15. Why did the Secret Service fail to respond to the initial gunshots and attempt to protect President Kennedy?

The Zapruder and other films and photographs of the assassination clearly reveal the utter lack of response by Secret Service agents Roy Kellerman and James Greer, who were in the front seat of the presidential limousine. After the first two shots, Greer actually slowed the vehicle to less than five miles an hour. Kellerman merely sat in the front seat, seemingly oblivious to the shooting. In contrast, Secret Service Agent Rufus Youngblood responded instantly to the first shot, and before the head shots were fired, had covered Vice-President Lyndon Johnson with his body.

Trained to react instantaneously, as in the attempted assassinations of President Gerald Ford by Lynette Fromme and Sara Jane Moore and of President Ronald Reagan by John Warnock Hinckley, the Secret Service agents assigned to protect President Kennedy simply neglected their duty. The reason for their neglect remains one of the more intriguing mysteries of the assassination.

16. Why have so many important witnesses in the assassination case met strange deaths?

It is true that certain key individuals in the Kennedy assassination case have met with sudden death under rather unusual circumstances. Among these are Lee Harvey Oswald, David Ferrie, and Jimmy Hoffa. Oswald was gunned down by Jack Ruby in the presence of seventy armed policemen. Ferrie died of natural causes after typing two suicide notes. Hoffa mysteriously disappeared.

The deaths of these and other persons connected with the case have prompted some assassination researchers to speculate that certain sinister forces responsible for Kennedy's murder are responsible for these deaths. However, there is no concrete evidence linking any of the deaths with the assassination itself. Unless such evidence is produced, all attempts to establish such a connection must remain in the realm of conjecture.

17. Was a paper bag found on the floor by the sixth-floor window?

The *Warren Report* claims that it was. However, the bag was not photographed in place, and Dallas law enforcement officers Luke Mooney, Roger Craig, and Gerald Hill, the first three policemen to reach the "sniper's nest," testified that they did *not* see the 38-inch-long sack, which, according to the *Report,* lay only two feet from the window. Three officers who arrived later remember seeing a bag there.

Once again, we are faced with conflicting evidence, and the reader has to decide for himself which appears more reliable.

18. Were all the eyewitnesses to the assassination interviewed?

No. Incredibly, the Dallas police did not seal off Dealey Plaza right after the assassination. They permitted traffic to proceed on Elm Street, just as if nothing had happened there. Over half the eyewitnesses simply left and went home without ever being questioned. Many inmates in the Dallas County Jail watched the motorcade from their prison cells. Even though these men literally constituted a captive audience, none was ever interrogated.

19. Did the Dallas police mishandle the physical evidence?

Yes. The paper bag allegedly found near the sixth-floor window was not photographed in place. The three empty cartridge cases were placed in an envelope, with no indication of the precise location in which each case was found. The police mishandled the book cartons around the window so badly that while only three of Oswald's prints were found on the nineteen cartons, twenty-four prints of policemen were found. The police permitted the press to enter the Depository building shortly after the discovery of the rifle. Before a thorough search of the building had taken place, the press roamed all over it, conceivably destroying evidence. The Dallas police neglected to mark and seal each item of physical evidence, e.g., the rifle, the revolver, the cartridge cases, thus separating each from the others. Instead, they put all the evidence in a large box, an action that resulted in their needlessly touching each other. The police, moreover, gave the Warren Commission three separate and contradictory versions of the transcription of the police radio calls at the time of the assassination. The Dallas police also produced four different, contradictory versions of the way in which the boxes by the window were stacked.

20. Why did the authorities change the motorcade route?

The original route, published in the *Dallas Morning-News* on 22 November 1963, called for the motorcade to proceed directly on Main Street through the triple underpass, *without* making the cumbersome turns onto Houston and Elm streets. The motorcade, however, did make the turn onto Elm, so it could take the Elm Street ramp to Stemmons Freeway. This was not the most direct route to President Kennedy's destination, the Trade Mart building. It would have been quicker and safer for the caravan to go straight on Main Street to Industrial Boulevard, where the Trade Mart is located. We do not know why the change was made.

21. Why did Officer Tippit stop Oswald?

It is difficult to accept the Warren Commission's claim that Tippit stopped Oswald because Oswald fitted the description of the suspect in the Kennedy assassination. That description was so general that it could have described thousands of individuals. Since Tippit had a view only of Oswald's rear, one wonders how he could have matched him with the suspect. Furthermore, if Tippit really suspected Oswald, he almost surely would have drawn his revolver against such a dangerous suspect. Yet, according to the commission's star eyewitness, Helen Markham, Tippit not only made no attempt to make the arrest of a lifetime, he engaged him in friendly conversation.

Neither the Warren Commission nor the House Select Committee on Assassinations tried to explore the unusual circumstances surrounding Tippit's presence in the area. Almost every other police officer in Dallas was ordered to proceed to Dealey Plaza, Parkland Hospital, or Love Field Airport. Tippit alone received instructions to remain where he was, in the residential Oak Cliffs section, where no suspicion of criminal activity had been raised. The police dispatcher also ordered Tippit to "be at large for any emergency that comes in," most unusual instructions, since the primary duty of all policemen is to "be at large" for emergencies.

22. Did Oswald murder J. D. Tippit?

The evidence against Oswald is strong. Eyewitness Helen Markham identified Oswald as the murderer. The House Select Committee located another eyewitness, Jack Tatum, who also identified Oswald as the killer. Six other witnesses saw

Oswald fleeing the murder scene, and four cartridge cases fired from Oswald's revolver were found at the scene.

On the other hand, eyewitnesses Aquila Clemmons and Frank Wright saw two men kill Tippit. A witness, questioned by the FBI but never called before the Warren Commission, saw a man who did not resemble Oswald kill Tippit. The bullets removed from Tippit's body were too mutilated to permit identification of them with Oswald's revolver. Moreover, the cartridge cases and the bullets did not match, the cases coming from different manufacturers than the bullets.

Clearly, the proper channel for resolving this conflicting evidence was a court of law, but Oswald's death made this impossible. As noted, neither the commission nor the committee conducted its inquiry under the adversary process to help settle such issues. The question, therefore, must remain unanswered.

23. Why was Officer Tippit patrolling an area outside his assigned district when he was shot?

Only J. D. Tippit could answer that question, and he is dead. At 12:45 P.M., fifteen minutes after the assassination, the Dallas police dispatcher ordered Tippit to proceed to the "central Oak Cliffs area," which is outside his regularly assigned district. The original Dallas police version of the police tape contains no reference to Tippit. The second version, transcribed five months later, contains the order to Tippit. J. D. Tippit was the only policeman in Dallas who was given instructions to patrol a quiet residential area, where no crime had been committed. Every available police officer was ordered to proceed immediately to Dealey Plaza or to Parkland Hospital. The last known location of Officer Tippit was Lancaster and Eighth, about eight blocks from the murder scene. Tippit reported this location at 12:54, twenty-one minutes before he was shot. The Warren Commission would have us believe that Tippit was so careful and methodical in his duties that it took him twenty-one minutes to travel eight blocks. This is a speed of about two miles an hour, slower than a normal walking pace. Obviously, this is yet another matter requiring further investigation.

24. Why did it take Oswald thirty minutes to run from the scene of the Tippit murder to the Texas theater only five blocks away?

Officer Tippit was killed at 1:15 P.M. and Oswald ran into the Texas Theater at 1:45. Clearly, it did not take him a half-hour to run five blocks. Neither the Warren Commission nor the House Select Committee produced any evidence to indicate what Oswald did during that time span.

25. How many shots were fired at Officer Tippit?

The official Tippit autopsy report states that four bullets were recovered from Tippit's body. Four bullets now form part of the physical evidence in the case. Yet, as with so many other parts of the Kennedy assassination, some of the circumstances underlying the discovery of this evidence appear strange and indeed mysterious.

The original Dallas police inventory of evidence turned over to the FBI lists "bullet [*sic*] recovered from body of Officer J. D. Tippit." The other three bullets did not turn up until four months after the murder, when they were discovered in a file cabinet at Dallas police headquarters (the same cabinet that contained the tape?).

On 11 December 1963, Secret Service agents Edward Moore and Forrest Sorrels reported their conversation with Dallas medical examiner Dr. Earl Rose: "only three of the four bullets penetrated into Tippit's body. The fourth apparently hit a button on the officer's coat. . . . When the examination [autopsy] was performed, three bullets were removed from the body and turned over to the Police Crime Lab." The police homicide report confirms this. According to that report, Tippit was shot "once in the right temple, once in the right side of the chest, and once in center of stomach." The actual autopsy, however, states that three bullets struck Tippit in the chest and one struck him in the head. A letter from J. Edgar Hoover to J. Lee Rankin notifies the commission that the FBI did not receive the "three [*sic*] bullets until late March 1964, four months after the assassination. Yet Secret Service agents Moore and Sorrels reported on 11 December, only three weeks after the murder, that the bullets "are now in the possession of the FBI."

The obvious contradictions in the evidence leave unanswered the questions of whether three or four shots struck Tippit and what happened to the bullets. Considering the fact that three of the bullets were Remingtons and one was a Winchester, while two of the cartridge cases found at the Tippit murder scene were Remingtons and two were Winchesters, it is not unreasonable to conclude that the Tippit murder requires clarification.

26. Why did Jack Ruby kill Lee Harvey Oswald?

The Warren Commission's claim that Ruby wanted to spare Mrs. Kennedy the personal ordeal of a trial seems flimsy. When Earl Warren interviewed Ruby in the Dallas jail, Ruby pleaded with the chief justice to let him testify in Washington, where he would tell the real story behind the whole assassination controversy. Inexplicably, Warren denied Ruby's request.

While it is possible to imagine numerous motives for Ruby's act, there is no reliable, independent evidence to substantiate such speculation. Whatever Ruby's reasons, they remain unknown.

27. How did Ruby gain access to the heavily guarded basement of Dallas police headquarters?

The House Select Committee on Assassinations uncovered evidence that indicated the likelihood that a Dallas police officer assisted Ruby in entering the basement.

The fact that Ruby managed to walk past seventy armed law enforcement officials and gun down Oswald obviously raises suspicions of a conspiracy in this murder. The available evidence, however, does not permit a conclusive determination either of the nature or extent of that conspiracy.

28. Did Jack Ruby and Lee Harvey Oswald know each other?

Over a dozen reliable witnesses claim to have seen the two men together during the four months prior to the assassination. Six separate eyewitnesses saw Ruby and Oswald in Ruby's Carousel Club in November 1963. Those witnesses included three employees and three patrons of the club. The author has interviewed a journalist who saw a photograph of Ruby and Oswald together.

The other witnesses included a lady who saw Ruby and Oswald together in New Orleans in the summer of 1963. While the FBI dismissed her account, Ruby, in fact, did visit New Orleans during that period.

Again, the evidence is not conclusive, but it does strongly suggest that Ruby and Oswald may very well have known each other before the assassination.

29. Did the Dallas police violate Lee Harvey Oswald's legal rights while they held him in custody?

Despite the Warren Commission's disclaimer, the answer is a decided affirmative. At his midnight press conference on 22 November, Oswald told newsmen that he was "not allowed legal representation" and requested "someone to come forward to give me legal assistance." The Dallas police chief, Jesse Curry, admitted that "we were violating every principle of interrogation." . . . [T]he police lineups appeared rigged to make identification of Oswald almost certain. He was the only suspect with a bruised and cut face and with disheveled clothing. He was dressed differently from the other men in the lineup. He was put in a lineup with three teenagers. At least one witness was persuaded by the police to sign an affidavit identifying Oswald *before* he viewed the lineup. The search warrant authorizing the search of Oswald's room did not specify the objects being sought by the police.

30. Did Oswald drive an automobile?

The Warren Commission claims that he did not, but there is substantial evidence to the contrary. Albert Bogard, a Dallas new car salesman, swore that he took Oswald for a test drive of a car less than two weeks before the assassination. Edith Whitworth and Gertrude Hunter saw Oswald driving a blue 1957 Ford about two weeks before the assassination. One of the lodgers in Oswald's rooming house at 1026 North Beckley Avenue let him drive his blue Ford sedan. Two service station operators recalled Oswald's driving a car and having it serviced. Journalists attempting to trace Oswald's route from Laredo, Mexico, to Dallas interviewed numerous service station operators, cafe owners, and other proprietors who recalled Oswald's stopping at their establishments.

31. With whom did Oswald associate during his stay in New Orleans in the spring and summer of 1963?

Although the Warren Commission concluded that Oswald's Marxist, pro-Castro views led him to various activities promoting those views, it failed to demonstrate that Oswald contacted even one individual of similar views during his New Orleans stay. The evidence, in fact, demonstrated that *all* of Oswald's known associations were with individuals of right-wing persuasion. The author's extensive research into this topic has produced much new evidence of Lee Harvey Oswald's right-wing activities in New Orleans.

On numerous occasions, Oswald associated with Guy Bannister, an ex-FBI official and a private investigator. Militantly anti-Castro and rabidly segregationist, Bannister was well known in the New Orleans area for his extremist views. Twice, Bannister and Oswald visited the campus of Louisiana State University in New Orleans and engaged students in heated discussions of federal racial policies. During these discussions, Oswald vehemently attacked the civil rights policies of the Kennedy administration.

Another right-wing extremist with whom Oswald associated was David William Ferrie. A defrocked Eastern Orthodox priest, an expert pilot, a research chemist, and a sexual deviate, Ferrie also actively participated in anti-Castro organizations and smuggled supplies to anti-Castro rebels in Cuba. Once, Ferrie and Oswald attended a party, where they discussed the desirability of a *coup d'état* against the Kennedy administration. On another occasion, Oswald and Ferrie were seen at Ponchartrain Beach, a New Orleans amusement park. Oswald and Ferrie also frequented the Napoleon House bar, a popular hangout for college students. There they often debated Kennedy's foreign policy with the students. Accompanied by two "Latins," Ferrie and Oswald were observed in Baton Rouge, where they openly denounced Kennedy's foreign and domestic policies.

One of the most significant eyewitness observations was of Ferrie, Oswald, and numerous Cubans, all dressed in military fatigues and carrying automatic rifles, conducting what appeared to be a "military training maneuver." This event took place near Bedico Creek, a swampy inland body of water near Lake Ponchartrain, about fifty miles north of New Orleans. This occurred in early September 1963, two months after the final government raid on anti-Castro guerrilla camps in the United States.

The night of 22 November, David Ferrie drove 250 miles from New Orleans to Galveston, Texas, in a blinding thunderstorm. At Galveston, Ferrie received and made several long-distance telephone calls. The following day, he drove to Houston, then Alexandria, Louisiana, and then to Hammond, where he spent the night in the dormitory room of a friend who was a student at a local college. Then he returned to New Orleans, where he underwent questioning by the FBI. Shortly after the assassination, Ferrie deposited over seven thousand dollars in his bank account, even though he did not have a steady job.

Obviously, these New Orleans activities of Oswald's warrant further investigation. The House Select Committee on Assassinations appreciated the significance of Oswald's New Orleans activities but failed to investigate them properly. Instead, it devoted much attention to such irrelevant matters as Ferrie's tenuous link to Carlos Marcello and the bookmaking activities of Oswald's uncle.

What relationship these matters have to the assassination of President Kennedy is unclear. As we have seen, the evidence does not permit a definitive statement about Oswald's role in the Kennedy murder. As far as David Ferrie and Guy Bannister are concerned, there is no evidence at all to link them to the crime. The New Orleans evidence, however, does demonstrate that Oswald's public image as a pro-Castro Marxist was a facade masking the anti-Castro and anti-Communist agitator beneath.

32. How significant was the Garrison investigation?

In February 1967, New Orleans District Attorney Jim Garrison announced that his office was investigating the assassination. This sensational news aroused a storm of controversy and publicity. The Garrison investigation resulted in the arrest and trial of New Orleans businessman Clay Shaw for conspiracy to murder John F. Kennedy. The 1969 trial resulted in Shaw's acquittal.

During the two-year investigation, Garrison made many irresponsible statements about the FBI, CIA, and other government agencies and about assassins firing from manholes and escaping through underground sewers. However, he did reveal the large extent to which the federal government had suppressed evidence about the assassination, demonstrated the relationship between Oswald and Bannister and Ferrie, and brought out much new information about the Zapruder film, the Kennedy autopsy, and ballistics evidence.

33. Did Oswald work for an intelligence agency of the United States government?

No. The evidence clearly shows that Oswald had no direct relationship with United States intelligence. After his defection to the Soviet Union, both the FBI and CIA maintained dossiers on Oswald, but these files contain no information pertinent to the assassination. Those writers who have suggested that Oswald's sojourn in the U.S.S.R., his trip to Mexico City, or his contacts with FBI Agent James Hosty proved significant to the assassination have failed to substantiate their theories.

34. Was an imposter buried in Lee Harvey Oswald's grave?

Differences of up to three inches in reports of Oswald's height, plus minor variations in the reports of certain physical marks on Oswald's body (wrist scars, mastoidectomy scar, etc.) have led some critics, most notably Michael Eddowes, a British investigator, to call for a disinterrment of Oswald's coffin and an exhumation autopsy on the body in it.

Eddowes's theory that while he was in the Soviet Union, Oswald was eliminated by the KGB and his place taken by a trained imposter is far-fetched. Oswald lived with his wife for over a year after they left the U.S.S.R. Oswald's mother, brother, and other relatives all saw him and had close contact with him and did not notice anything unusual about him.

35. Is vital evidence in the Kennedy assassination missing from the National Archives collection of assassination materials?

Numerous items of critical significance are indeed missing: the president's brain, tissue slides of his wounds, several autopsy photographs and X-rays, some bullet fragments originally tested by the FBI, and miscellaneous documents and other materials. The lack of these materials obviously presents a formidable obstacle to any attempt to answer some of the key questions about the assassination. Why they are missing is not known.

36. Why did the FBI and CIA withhold information from the Warren Commission?

As far as the FBI is concerned, it seems that the main reason was J. Edgar Hoover's precipitous decision that there was no assassination conspiracy and his almost paranoid desire not to tarnish the bureau's public image. Hoover tried to dissuade Lyndon Johnson from appointing a presidential commission to investigate the assassination, but Johnson bowed to public pressure. One of Hoover's top assistants, William Sullivan, stated that Hoover regarded the Warren Commission as an adversary and even periodically leaked information to the press to force the commission to conduct its inquiry along the lines of the already completed FBI report. The acting attorney general Nicholas deB. Katzenbach, testified that if the FBI had come across evidence of a conspiracy, "what would have happened to that information, God only knows." The 125,000 pages of FBI assassination files, many of them marked by Hoover himself, contain much information that the bureau never shared with the commission.

The CIA, too, failed to share all of its information with the Warren Commission. But its refusal to do so stemmed from the nature of the agency itself. The purpose of the CIA is to gather intelligence, a function that requires secrecy. The agency investigated the assassination only as it related to foreign activities. It appointed Richard Helms as its liaison with the Warren Commission, and Helms gave the commission only information that did not compromise the CIA's extensive network of agents. It is true that the CIA did not inform the Warren Commission about various matters, but in almost all instances, the information withheld had only an indirect connection with the assassination.

37. In his book Best Evidence, *David Lifton asserted that the body of President Kennedy was altered to conceal evidence of shots from the front. How valid is Lifton's theory?*

In his book, Lifton asserted that an unidentified group of conspirators planned, executed, and concealed the assassination of President Kennedy. Even though the Zapruder film and certain other evidence indicated gunfire from the Grassy Knoll, the "best evidence" in the case and the evidence that would be given the most credence in a court of law was the official autopsy. Therefore, the conspirators altered the body of President Kennedy to make it appear he had been shot from behind.

When the president was rushed into the emergency room at Parkland Hospital, the doctors noticed a tiny hole in the throat. They all believed that this hole was clearly a wound of entrance, as the remarks to the press by the Parkland physicians indicated. Furthermore, the Dallas doctors stated, both in their written medical reports and in their testimony before the Warren Commission, that there was a very large wound of exit in the rear of the president's head. These observations were substantiated by those of laboratory and X-ray technicians, photographers, and physicians at Bethesda Naval Hospital who saw the body before the autopsy began.

To assure the success of their scheme, the plotters had to change the nature of the wounds on the body in order to make it appear that it contained only evidence of rear-entry wounds. The conspirators, therefore, carried out an elaborate plot of what Lifton calls "deception and disguise," a fantastic plot that entailed altering the body of John Kennedy.

From interviews with witnesses at Bethesda and from other sources, Lifton concludes that the body was removed from its bronze coffin while the presidential party was aboard Air Force One on the trip from Dallas to Washington. As the television cameras focused on the removal of the bronze coffin from the plane, the conspirators put the body in a helicopter and flew it to Bethesda. There they arranged various means, including two ambulances, to deceive the official party awaiting the arrival of the bronze coffin.

As this deception took place, his body was altered to give it the appearance of having been struck from the rear. The conspirators removed the brain and "reconstructed" the skull, eradicating all signs of the massive exit hole in the back of the head. They also placed small entrance holes in the upper back and in the rear of the head. When the actual autopsy was performed, the pathologists inspected a body that gave the appearance of being hit twice from behind. Lifton quotes the Sibert-O'Neill FBI autopsy report that "surgery of the head area" had been performed prior to the start of the postmortem. This, Lifton believes, was the alteration done on the original head wounds.

David Lifton's theory is not only novel, but it presents a startling account of an assassination plot conceived, executed, and disguised by the executive branch of the federal government. David Lifton has a reputation as one of the most thorough assassination researchers. His work is well documented and displays a careful attention to detail. For these reasons, and because of the sensational nature of Lifton's theory, an analysis of his main points will now be presented.

The documentary record substantiates Lifton's contention that medical descriptions of the Kennedy head wounds vary widely. Most of the Dallas doctors did testify that they saw a large exit wound in the back of the head, whereas the autopsy describes a small entrance wound in the back of the head and a large exit wound to the front. Lifton, however, ignored the fact that not all the Dallas doctors saw a large wound in the rear of the head. Dr. Charles Baxter stated that he saw a wound in the "temporal parietal plate of bone" in the side of the head. Dr. Adolph Giesecke noted the absence of skull from the top of the head to the ear, and from the browline to the back of the head. Dr. Kenneth Salyer observed a wound of the right temporal region on the side of the head. And Dr. Marion Jenkins mentioned "a great laceration of the right side of the head." Lifton quoted only those Dallas physicians who saw the large hole in the rear of the head and thus presented a misleading impression to his readers.

More significantly, Lifton ignored a vital aspect of the evidence. Throughout the emergency room treatment, President Kennedy lay on his back, with the back of his head resting on the mattress of the emergency cart. As Dr. Malcolm Perry told the Warren Commission, "He was lying supine [on his back] on the emergency cart." At no time was he turned over. If there was one point on which all the Dallas doctors agreed, it was that they never saw the president's back, including the rear of his head.

During the twenty minutes in which they worked to save President Kennedy's life, the Parkland physicians did not even attempt to treat the head wound. Their efforts at resuscitation centered on the tracheotomy and on closed chest massage. Busy with these emergency measures, the doctors did not examine the head wound closely. During the time in which they were in the emergency room, the Dallas doctors glanced at the head wound and saw blood and brain tissue oozing out and two large flaps of scalp covering much of the hair and exposing the cranial cavity. They did not see the head after it was cleaned, and they took no measurements to record the exact nature of the wounds. As one of the Dallas physicians remarked to the author, the reason he and his colleagues mentioned a large wound in the rear of the head is that from their brief glances at the head, it looked like a rear wound. However, after seeing the Zapruder film and the autopsy drawings, he was perfectly satisfied that the would was indeed in the right front of the head.

Another omission in Lifton's theory is his belief that the conspirators inflicted wounds on the body over six hours after the assassination. Although he claims to have read widely in textbooks on forensic pathology, Lifton apparently did not notice one of the most elementary principles of autopsy procedure: damage inflicted on a body after death is easily distinguishable from that inflicted on a living body. If the conspirators had reconstructed Kennedy's skull and produced two entrance wounds on the body, the Bethesda pathologists would have recognized the postmortem changes. By the time of the autopsy, the body was in the beginning stages of rigor mortis and exhibited signs of livor mortis and algor mortis (three of the stages a corpse undergoes after death). Any damage inflicted on that body would have displayed definite pathological signs of alteration, and the entrance wounds in the back and the head would not have shown microscopic indications of "coagulation necrosis," since the blood had long since ceased circulating.

Lifton claims that John Kennedy was shot in the front of the head by gunfire from the Grassy Knoll, thus causing the large exit wound in the rear observed by the Dallas doctors. Yet he fails to account for the fact that no one at Dallas or Bethesda saw an entrance wound in the front of the head. If the Dallas doctors were so observant as to see an exit wound in the rear of the head while the president lay face-up on the cart, why did they not see the entrance wound also?

Instead of the contradictory recollections of the Dallas doctors, we possess the objective evidence of the Zapruder film. Frames Z314–335 clearly depict the very large wound on the right front side of John Kennedy's head. The film also shows that the rear of the head remains intact throughout the assassination. Lifton argues that the CIA must have "doctored" the film to produce a false image. In addition to producing no evidence whatsoever to support this speculation, Lifton ignored the fact that the film graphically shows the violent backward movement of the head, hardly evidence of a rear-entering shot.

The autopsy X-rays and photographs depict the entrance holes in the back and in the rear of the head and also the huge, gaping wound in the right front of the head. According to Lifton, the photographs and X-rays were taken after the reconstruction of the body, so they would corroborate the autopsy findings. As we have seen, the photographs and X-rays do not provide irrefutable evidence of wounds inflicted only from the rear. The very large wound on the right side of the head depicted in these visual records could have been made by the explosion of a "dum-dum" bullet fired from the right front. In addition, through dental identification and precise comparisons of certain anatomical features, experts hired by the House Select Committee on Assassinations positively identified the X-rays and photographs as authentic and the body depicted in them as that of John F. Kennedy. If the skull were "reconstructed," as Lifton claims, the X-rays would not contain the anatomical features essential to proper authentication.

In his work, Lifton quotes extensively from the FBI agents present at the autopsy and from laboratory technicians. FBI Agents Sibert and O'Neill, for example, stated that "surgery of the head area" had been performed prior to the autopsy. To Lifton, this is proof that the conspirators had reconstructed the skull. In fact, the Sibert-O'Neill report was written by the agents the day after the autopsy. It is neither a verbatim record of the proceedings nor a detailed medical recounting of the events that took place. The laboratory technicians and other witnesses to the autopsy provided widely divergent accounts of the wounds. By quoting only those that supported his thesis, Lifton provided a very misleading account to his readers, as he did with the Dallas doctors.

Another of Lifton's arguments is that during the autopsy, Dr. Humes removed the brain from the cranial vault without recourse to the surgical procedures normally required. To Lifton, this was evidence that the brain had been removed prior to the autopsy by the conspirators in order to alter it. This argument has little basis. The autopsy protocol, as well as the testimony of the pathologists, attest to the enormous damage done to the head. The skull was shattered. Almost three-quarters of the right half of the brain had been blown out of the head. When Dr. Humes began his examination of the head, pieces of the skull came apart in his hands, vivid testimony to the explosive impact of the bullet. All of the damage to the head that Lifton details as unusual can be explained as the result of an exploding bullet literally blowing the head apart.

Lifton believes that the autopsy photographs showing the large, gaping wound in the right front of President Kennedy's head were deliberately altered to make the wound appear as an exit wound. That it was an exit wound is precisely what the autopsy pathologists believed and what all subsequent medical inspections of the photographs concluded. However, the wound is not necessarily one of exit. An exploding bullet fired from the right front could have caused that wound. In the first volume of the House Select Committee on Assassinations hearings on the murder of Martin Luther King, drawings made from autopsy photographs of Dr. King clearly show a huge hole almost four inches long and two inches wide on the lower right side of the face, just above the jaw. According to the committee's Forensic Pathology Panel, this huge wound in Dr. King's face was an *entrance* wound caused by the explosion of a soft-nosed 30.06 bullet. Dr. Michael Baden, the chairman of the panel, told the committee that "the injuries seen on Dr. King with the bursting explosive-like injury to the face" were "entirely consistent" with an entrance wound of an exploding bullet.

David Lifton's theory, as sensational as it may appear, simply does not stand verified by the objective evidence. As detailed here, the autopsy left much room for criticism, and the fact that certain items of the medical evidence are missing obviously raises suspicions of a possible cover-up. The questions surrounding the death of President Kennedy are numerous, many of them still unanswered. Those posed by David Lifton, however, do not fall into this category.

POSTSCRIPT

Did Lee Harvey Oswald Kill President Kennedy by Himself?

Since the Kennedy assassination, more than 3,000 books, articles, films (both fictional and documentaries), plays, television programs, and newsletters have been released. The two best books that summarize and critically analyze the literature, give their own interpretation of the assassination, and contain the most extensive bibliographical listings are Michael L. Kurtz, *Crime of the Century: the Kennedy Assassination from a Historian's Perspective*, 2nd ed. (University of Tennessee Press, 1993) and Robert Alan Goldberg, *Enemies Within: The Culture of Conspiracy in Modern America* (Yale University Press, 2001). Readers will enjoy Bob Callahan, *Who Shot JFK? A Guide to Major Conspiracy Theories* (Simon Schuster, 1993) because of Mark Zigarelli's pointed and humorous illustrations in addition to a lively text that provides welcome relief for the more sober accounts.

In early 1964, President Lyndon Johnson appointed a seven-man commission to investigate the assassination of President Kennedy. On September 24, 1964, Earl Warren, chief justice of the United States Supreme Court, and chairman, presented the Commission's Report. The product was impressive. It includes 26 volumes of hearing transcripts and exhibits based on testimony from more than 500 witnesses and 26,500 FBI interviews. The summary volume was over 900 pages with more than 2,600 footnotes. The conclusion was direct and simple: Oswald alone killed Kennedy. There was no conspiracy involved.

In spite of apparent thoroughness, *The Warren Report* was flawed from its inception. President Johnson had appointed seven established figures to come up with a preordained conclusion that Oswald acted alone. At least one member of the Commission, Senator Richard Russell of Georgia, was reluctant to sign the report. Johnson himself was conspiracy conscious: "[W]ho would they shoot next? And what was going on in Washington? And when would the missiles be coming? . . . . I was fearful that the Communists were trying to take over."

President Johnson had hoped the Commission's conclusions would calm the American public. For a short time, the media elite—*The New York Times*, influential CBS newscaster Walter Cronkite, and others—accepted the findings. The FBI had provided the Commission with tons of evidence in its own report to support the lone gunman theory in order to cover up its own investigative failings.

But within 3 years, *The Warren Report* was thoroughly discredited. Criticisms fall into several categories. First, a number of writers questioned the Commission's scientific evidence of a lone gunman. Second, if you could establish the case for a second or third gunman, the motives for killing the president lead to a conspiracy. Who was involved? Was it a governmental agency such as the CIA or FBI, an anti-Castro or pro-Castro group, or organized crime? There is enough evidence to support a number of realistic and plausible conspiracy theories. Third, the Kennedy assassination has produced a number of implausible conspiracy theories that all too often have emerged in numerous books, films, and television series.

There is an abundance of conflicting scientific evidence to challenge if not refute the lone gunman theory. The police mishandled the book cartons around the window of the sixth floor of the Texas Depository where Oswald supposedly shot Kennedy. While three prints of Oswald were found on the cartons, 24 prints of policemen were found. The press were also allowed to roam the building before a thorough search had taken place. Three empty cartridges from Oswald's gun were placed in an envelope before their location was marked. The evidence was not precisely marked but was all lumped together in one box. Professor Kurtz admits that although "the evidence makes Oswald a prime suspect," he may have been set up.

Could Oswald, an average marksman in the Marines, have fired three shots in five to eight seconds, which was the time allotted in the films of the assassination? The answer is yes, although elaborate marksmanship tests by three U.S. Army expert marksmen conducted for the Commission could not duplicate the accuracy of Oswald's supposed three shots.

Could a single bullet have wounded Governor Connally and killed President Kennedy by penetrating the back of his neck? Dennis Brio supports the single bullet theory in a series of articles in the *Journal of American Medical Association* (May and October 1992). Critics wrote dissenting letters in the October 1992 issues with response from Dr. John Lattimer in the March 1993 issue of *JAMA*. The single bullet theory is supported by Gerald Posner in chapter 14 of *Case Closed: Lee Harvey Oswald and the Assassination of JFK* (Random House, 1993), which relies on computer enhancements of the Zapruder film (the only one to record the entire period of the shooting) by Dr. Michel West and the Failure Analysis Associates, a firm specializing in computer reconstruction for lawsuits. But Dr. John Nichols, a forensic pathologist, and Charles Wilber, a forensic scientist, have conducted studies that demonstrate that major bullet #399 could not have inflicted all the damage to Governor Connally. See their presentations in the video *Reasonable Doubt: The Single Bullet Theory* (White Star Productions, 1998).

Professor Kurtz believes that a second assassin fired at least one shot from the grassy knoll in front of President Kennedy's head. Although no bullets were found at the scene, eye-witnesses heard shots, smelled gunpowder, and saw a flash of light, and two Dallas officials "encountered phony 'Secret Service' men in the parking lot behind the knoll within minutes after the gunfire."

Conspiracy theories about Kennedy's assassination abound. Organized crime had vendettas for a number of reasons. Attorney General Robert Kennedy continued to investigate racketeering by President James Hoffa in the Teamster's Union, which he had begun for a Senate Committee in the

1950s. Author John Davis claims in *The Kennedy Contract* (Harper's, 1993) and *Mafia Kingfish,* 2nd ed. (Signet, 1989) that New Orleans mafia chieftain Carlos Marcello ordered a hit on the president because Kennedy had reneged on his promise to go easy on organized crime after the mob delivered the deciding vote from Illinois from the west side of Chicago in the close presidential election of 1960.

Right-wing extremists also had reason to kill Kennedy. A number were angry with the president for his failure to use air cover to support the failed Bay of Pigs invasion against Castro in April 1961. Southern segregationists were also angry with a president whose civil rights program threatened to mongrelize the nation. Kurtz demonstrated that Oswald, a proclaimed Marxist, had numerous contacts with right-wing extremists during his stay in New Orleans in the spring and summer of 1963.

But Kurtz gives evidence to support the opposite view in the introduction to the revised edition of the *Crime of the Century.* He argues that Castro most likely masterminded the assassination because he wanted to kill Kennedy before the president assassinated the Cuban dictator. In 1975, Senator Frank Church's Committee revealed the numerous assassination plans hatched by the CIA to remove Castro from power during the Eisenhower/Kennedy years. Both the president's brother Robert and vice president Lyndon Johnson knew of these attempts against Castro at the time JFK was killed. While Professor Kurtz admits the evidence is thin and the theory may be wrong, he nevertheless argues:

> . . . Lee Harvey Oswald was recruited as a decoy, a "patsy," to distract attention from the real assassins. The actual gunmen in Dealey Plaza situated themselves for a perfectly executed crossfire with two firings from the Book Depository Building, and one from the Grassy Knoll. In the mass confusion following the shooting , they easily made their escapes, with one crossing into Mexico, then flying to the safety of Havana, and the others simply leaving Dealy Plaza in automobiles. With Marcello's permission (his territory covered Texas), Trafficante's men recruited Jack Ruby for the purpose of silencing Oswald to ensure the embarrassing revelations would not leak out at a trial. With the cover-up of the case by the United States government, the real assassins and those who put them up to it got away scot-free.

Since this postscript was first written, a number of new books and articles have been written about the Kennedy assassination. Support for the conspiracy view came from "Study [that] backs theory of 'Grassy Knoll'," *The Washington Post,* March 26, 2001, which summarizes an article by D.B. Thomas in *Science and Justice,* a peer-reviewed quarterly publication of Britain's Forensic Science Society; Joan Mellen, *A Farewell to Justice: Jim Garrison, JFK's Assassination, and the Case That Should Have Changed History* (Potomac Books, 2005); and Michael L. Kurtz's more recent *The JFK Assassination Debates* (University of Kansas Press, 2006), which argues the reason we can't answer the "Who killed JFK?" question is because the Dallas public, the FBI, and the Warren Commission mishandled the evidence so poorly, "They would have been laughed off the air if they had been portrayed on TV's popular 'CSI' series." Gerald McKnight's *Breach of Trust: How the Warren Commissions Failed the Nation and Why* (University of Kansas Press, 2006) maintains that the Warren Commission embraced the one-gunman theory and ignored all evidence to the contrary. See McKnight's arguments summarized in "Time for the Truth" (*The Baltimore Sun,* November 2, 2003).

Support for the lone-gunman theory comes from Max Holland "The Key to the Warren Report," *American Heritage* (1995), who argues that Cold War national security concerns caused the Commissions to not tell the "whole" truth about what certain government agencies were up to. Holland has edited *The Presidential Recordings: Lyndon B. Johnson: The Kennedy Assassination and the Transfer of Power, November 1963–January 1964, Volume One* (Norton, 2005), which argues conclusively that President Johnson was not involved with any conspiracy. See also Max Holland, ed., *The Kennedy Assassination Tapes: The White House Conversations of Lyndon B. Johnson Regarding the Assassination, the Warren Commission, and the Aftermath* (Knopf, 2004). A live exchange between LBJ and FBI Chief J. Edgar Hoover can be found on reporter Ted Koeppel's Nightline show, *The LBJ Tapes* on VHS (Films for the Humanities, 1998). Two student-oriented collections that tend to report the lone-gunman theory are Charles Carey, ed., *The Kennedy Assassination* (Greenhaven Press, 2004), which includes excerpts from the press government reports and early pro and con articles about *The Warren Commission Report.* Gary Mack gives a David Letterman assessment on the "Top Ten Myths of the Kennedy Assassination," *American History* (December 2003), whose entire issue is devoted to articles commemorating the fortieth anniversary of the assassination.

ISSUE 8

Was Martin Luther King, Jr.'s Leadership Essential to the Success of the Civil Rights Revolution?

YES: **Adam Fairclough,** from "Martin Luther King, Jr. and the Quest for Nonviolent Social Change," *Phylon* (Spring 1986)

NO: **Clayborne Carson,** from "Martin Luther King, Jr.: Charismatic Leadership in a Mass Struggle," *Journal of American History* (September 1987)

ISSUE SUMMARY

YES: Professor of history Adam Fairclough argues that Martin Luther King, Jr., was a pragmatic reformer who organized nonviolent direct action protests in strategically targeted local communities, which provoked violence from his opponents, gaining publicity and sympathy for the civil rights movement.

NO: Professor of history Clayborne Carson concludes that the civil rights struggle would have followed a similar course of development even if King had never lived because its successes depended upon mass activism, not the actions of a single leader.

$\mathbf{T}$he modern civil rights movement goes back to the Reconstruction era (1865–1877), when blacks were granted freedom, citizenship, and voting rights. By the end of the nineteenth century, however, black Americans had been legally segregated in public facilities, which included schools, parks, swimming pools, and municipal and state offices. At the same time the southern states had disenfranchised blacks or intimidated them into not voting. The black middle class, led by Booker T. Washington, had accepted legal segregation as a trade-off for limited economic opportunities in their segregated communities.

The black community entered the twentieth century determined to regain its rights as American citizens. During the opening years of the twentieth century, a group of northern black professionals, led by its most prominent intellectual W.E.B Du Bois, joined with white progressives and formed the National Association for the Advancement of Colored People (NAACP). The main objective of the NAACP was to eradicate the accommodationist policies of Booker T. Washington and the acceptance of segregation through the "separate but equal principle," which the Supreme Court had written into the legal system. This was accomplished in 1896 when the Court ruled in *Plessy v. Ferguson* that segregating blacks and whites into separate railroad cars was permissible provided both facilities were equal.

Realizing that no civil rights legislation could pass through the committee chaired in Congress by southern white conservatives, the NAACP decided to attack the separate but equal principle established in the *Plessy* case through the courts. The concept of separate but equal was challenged in a series of court cases in which it was argued that segregation violated the equal protection clause of the Fourteenth Amendment.

The legal system moves very slowly, but protest movements often speed up changes. As early as the 1930s blacks picketed stores in Harlem when they were refused service. In 1947 there were protests at Palisades Amusement Park in northern New Jersey when blacks were not allowed to purchase tickets to the swimming pool.

The first big step in the nonviolence resistance phase of the civil rights movement came in 1956 with the Montgomery Bus Boycott. On December 1, 1955, Rosa Parks, a middle-aged black seamstress, refused to give up her seat to a white passenger as required by Alabama law. E. B. Nixon, an officer with the all-black Brotherhood of Sleeping Car Porters and local head of the NAACP, bailed his friend and fellow worker Parks out of jail. She then gave Nixon permission to use her arrest to mount a one-day bus boycott.

On the day of the boycott Nixon asked Martin Luther King, Jr., a 27-year-old son of a prominent Atlanta minister and a newcomer to Montgomery, to deliver the keynote address at a mass rally of the Montgomery Improvement Association (MIA). King appeared an unlikely candidate to challenge the status quo on race relations. He grew up comfortably, was middle class, was educated at the black Atlanta University complex, and received a master's degree at Crozier Theological Seminary at Boston University. Though King had never been politically active before, he delivered a memorable address to an overflow audience at a local Baptist church.

The Montgomery Bus Boycott led to a Supreme Court ruling that declared unconstitutional a Montgomery ordinance that required segregated city buses. The boycott provided a number of lessons for civil rights leaders. First, it made many black southerners more assertive in their demands for full citizenship in spite of a white backlash of bomb threats and Ku Klux Klan (KKK) rallies. Second, it propelled King into the spotlight. Third, it captured the attention of the nation's news media and gained sympathetic coverage of its causes. Finally, the boycott produced a new set of tactics, which speeded up the pace of desegregation for the black community.

In the selections that follow, Adam Fairclough demonstrates the importance of King's leadership to the civil rights movement, while Clayborne Carson plays down the mythical image of King, arguing that King is a product of a movement that would have occurred even if King had never lived.

Adam Fairclough

Martin Luther King, Jr. and the Quest for Nonviolent Social Change

The Alabama cities of Birmingham and Selma have given their names to the most effective campaigns of nonviolent protest in recent history. The Birmingham demonstrations paved the way for the 1964 Civil Rights Act, which swept away segregation in public accommodations. The Selma protests of 1965 engendered the Voting Rights Act, a measure that cut away the political basis of white supremacy by ending the disfranchisement of blacks. Together, this legislation amounted to a "Second Reconstruction" of the South, restoring to black Southerners rights that had been formally granted after the Civil War but stripped away after the Compromise of 1877.

Understanding of this historical breakthrough, however, is far from perfect. It is beyond doubt that the man who led the Birmingham and Selma protests, Martin Luther King, Jr., made a mighty contribution. But more needs to be known about the dynamics of social change in the 1960s and about the political world in which King and his followers operated. King's biography, much of it hagiographic in character, has tended to simplify these dynamics and neglect the wider political context. There has been inadequate appreciation, too, of the hard-headed calculation that entered into King's strategy, the political sophistication of his advisers, and the importance of his organizational base, the Southern Christian Leadership Conference (SCLC). Nevertheless, some historians and political scientists have begun to analyze critically the campaigns of nonviolent direct action undertaken by King and SCLC. Implicitly or explicitly, their work has cast doubt on many commonly held assumptions about the civil rights movement and raised important questions. Why, if most whites disapproved of it so strongly, could nonviolent protest succeed in generating political support for the civil rights movement? Was nonviolent direct action a means of persuasion, or did it depend for its effectiveness upon pressure and coercion? To what extent, if any, did King seek deliberately to provoke violence by whites? How much support did King's tactics command among blacks? Did he create a truly "mass" movement, or were his victories achieved in spite of limited backing? This essay explores the evolution, execution, and political impact of King's methods in an attempt to explain the dynamics of nonviolent direct action.

In the most systematic study of King's techniques to date, political scientist David J. Garrow argued that the evolution of King's strategy fell into two phases. During the first, from his emergence as a leader in 1956 to the Albany protests of 1961–62, King conceived of direct action as a means of persuading Southern whites of the moral injustice of segregation and discrimination. When the Albany campaign failed, however, King abandoned this approach as unrealistic and, according to Garrow, adopted a strategy of "nonviolent coercion." Instead of trying to convince their adversaries of the rightness of their goals, King and SCLC sought to pressure the federal government into curbing white supremacists through legislation. Implemented with great success in Birmingham and Selma, this new strategy mobilized Northern public opinion behind the civil rights movement through dramatic confrontations that publicized segregationist violence. Since it invited violent opposition, this strategy, Garrow believes, "bordered on nonviolent provocation."

Garrow is not alone in detecting a distinct shift from persuasion to coercion in the way King conducted nonviolent direct action, with the coercive elements very much to the fore by the time of the 1963 Birmingham campaign. Elliott M. Zashin earlier had advanced a similar argument in his study, *Civil Disobedience and Democracy* (1972). Their experience in the deep South, Zashin contended, convinced most black activists that nonviolent protest had virtually no effect on white racists: its only value lay in its utility as a pressure tactic. By 1964, few entertained the notion that direct action could change the values of the adversary. King, Zashin believed, came to a similar conclusion and although, for reasons of diplomacy, he downplayed the coercive nature of his tactics, SCLC's leader "clearly . . . recognized the pressure involved in direct action." As he admitted in his celebrated "Letter From Birmingham City Jail," nonviolent protest sought to "create such a crisis and foster such a tension that a community which has constantly refused to negotiate is forced to confront the issue."

Before examining this argument, it is necessary to recognize that the historical analysis of King's thought presents a number of problems. First, King never expounded his theory of nonviolence in a systematic way, nor did he record a detailed account of his tactics. In addition, many of his books, articles and speeches were partly or wholly "ghosted," and it is not always easy to determine exactly what King did write. Third it must be borne in mind that King's writings and speeches were public statements designed to persuade and convince, and many of them were tailored to white audiences. Finally, King did not live in an intellectual vacuum: he had a wide circle of friends, colleagues and advisers with whom he debated tactics and strategy. His thinking was never fixed and rigid. Indeed, it would be astonishing if King's perception of the world remained static in view of the turbulent era in which he lived. Without doubt, he became more hard-headed and politically astute as a result of age and experience. In "Letter From Birmingham City Jail," for example, he expressed profound disappointment that the civil rights movement had failed to attract more support from white Southerners. There is no reason to suppose that this disillusionment was insincere.

It is doubtful, however, that King's strategy underwent a basic shift in emphasis of the kind posited by Zashin and Garrow. There is little evidence that

King ever believed that nonviolent protest functioned solely, or even mainly, as a form of moral persuasion. Quite the contrary; in his earliest public writings he equated nonviolence with struggle and resistance organized through a militant mass movement. Philosophically and in practice, he explicitly rejected the notion that oppressed groups could overcome their subjection through ethical appeals and rational argument; they also needed an effective form of pressure. The assertion that King failed to appreciate the necessity for "black power" is simply erroneous. "A mass movement exercising nonviolence," he wrote in 1957, "is an object lesson in power under discipline." Having recently led a successful year-long economic boycott supported by 50,000 black people, he surely knew what he was talking about. A *New York Times* profile in March, 1956 noted that King stressed the Hegelian concept of "struggle as a law of growth," and that he regarded the bus boycott "as just one aspect of a world-wide revolt of oppressed peoples."

The intentions of the people who created SCLC underline this point. Bayard Rustin, Stanley Levison and Ella Baker were seasoned political activists who moved in the circles of the New York Left. Steeped in Marxist and socialist ideas, they regarded nonviolent direct action in political, not moral, terms. "The basic conception of SCLC," said Baker, "was that it would capitalize on what was developed in Montgomery in terms of mass action." In Levison's words, the subject was "to reproduce that pattern of mass action, underscore mass, in other cities and communities." It is unlikely that King viewed SCLC in any other way.

To emphasize King's political realism is not to deny his underlying idealism. For him, nonviolence was an ethical imperative, and his commitment to it was absolute and consistent. Moreover, he did sometimes imply that nonviolent protest worked partly through persuasion, by "awakening a sense of moral shame in the opponent." Nonviolent resisters, he explained, touched the hearts and consciences of their adversaries, converting oppressors into friends. But the significance of such statements should not be exaggerated. He admitted that "when the underprivileged demand freedom, the privileged first react with bitterness and resistance;" nonviolence could not change the "heart" of the oppressor until the social structure that perpetuated injustice and false ideology had been destroyed. His verbal characterizations of nonviolence must also be read in context. In sermons, for example, he frequently likened nonviolence to a kind of supranatural power—a "Soul Force" that could defeat physical force. Of course, such descriptions were not meant to be taken literally: King was simplifying complex ideas and communicating them in a way that black Southerners—poorly educated, politically inexperienced, but imbued with a deep religious sensibility—could grasp easily. King's belief that some adversaries might still be touched by the suffering and goodwill of nonviolent resisters was genuine, although in Bayard Rustin's opinion it "was often very confusing—and frustrating—to his followers." But this belief was marginal to his strategy of protest. When King spoke of "converting" oppressors, he was thinking of a long-term historical process rather than an immediate personal response.

There was, therefore, an underlying continuity in King's conception of nonviolent direct action. It envisaged a mass movement opposed to white supremacy and which operated primarily through direct pressure. It assumed that racism was a Southern anachronism and that a growing majority of whites sympathized with the goal of integration and equality. It regarded the federal government as a potential ally, and it believed that the nonviolent protesters attracted support if their opponents responded with violence. The notion of a pre-1963 "persuasive" strategy aimed at winning over Southern whites and a post-1963 "coercive" strategy designed to provoke federal intervention is misleading. King consistently followed the two-pronged strategy of exerting pressure on Southern whites and seeking to involve the federal government.

Federal involvement comprised a crucial element in SCLC's strategy as early as 1961, when King called upon President Kennedy to issue a "Second Emancipation Proclamation"—an Executive Order banning segregation and discrimination. King was not alone, of course, in appreciating the importance of federal action: with the election of a Democratic President whose platform included a strong civil-rights plank, black leaders sensed a golden opportunity to mobilize federal support for their goals. They knew that political considerations made Kennedy reluctant to meddle in the South's "local" affairs. But the daring Freedom Rides of May–August 1961 demonstrated that nonviolent protest could spur the government to action, even against its will, by creating a crisis of law and order to which it had to respond.

SCLC's protests in Albany, Georgia, represented King's first major effort to implement the two-pronged strategy outlined above. On the one hand he exerted pressure on local whites, through demonstrations, sit-ins and economic boycotts, to negotiate over the demands of blacks. On the other hand, by creating a serious local crisis and generating public concern, he tried to induce the federal government to intervene in some way. That he failed on both counts does not mean that the strategy was unsound or that it differed in essentials from the one successfully pursued in Birmingham. King failed in Albany for tactical reasons, notably inadequate planning and poor choice of target, rather than over-reliance on "nonviolent persuasion." The significance of Birmingham is not that King finally discovered the necessity for pressure, but that he at last discovered how to make that pressure effective.

If the strategy was clear, the tactics had to be developed and refined through trial and error and the experience of others. From the founding of SCLC in 1957 to the Birmingham campaign of 1963, King was speculating, experimenting and learning, attempting to adapt a theory that both to political realities and to the practical considerations that constrained black Southerners.

King learned two vital tactical lessons during these years. The first was that he would have to make do with limited numbers. SCLC's architects had anticipated that the Montgomery bus boycott would spark a wave of similar protests throughout the South. For a variety of reasons, however, this did not happen. Many blacks were skeptical of boycotts. More radical tactics like sit-ins and demonstrations evoked still deeper misgivings: they set back orderly progress; they alienated white moderates and provoked a "backlash;" they were wasteful and ineffective. Jail often spelt economic disaster, and individuals thought twice about volunteering for arrest if their families might suffer as a consequence. True, the sit-in movement of 1960 showed that students and young people, free from the economic burdens and family responsibilities that constrained their elders, would willingly act as "foot soldiers" in direct action campaigns. The sit-ins also demonstrated how direct action itself tended to promote unity and support among blacks, rendering the conservatism of older leaders less troublesome. Even so, the number of "foot soldiers" was limited; the concept, much in vogue in 1960–1964, of a "nonviolent army" that would steamroll the opposition through sheer weight of numbers turned out to be unrealistic. Albany taught King that no more than 5 percent of a given black population could be persuaded to volunteer for jail. He learned to frame his tactics accordingly.

The second tactical lesson was that, to quote Bayard Rustin, "protest becomes an effective tactic to the degree that it elicits brutality and oppression from the power structure." The government's conduct during the Freedom Rides—intervening in Alabama, where Klan mobs had been permitted to run amok, but adopting a "hands-off" policy towards Mississippi, where the police had kept order and carried out "peaceful" arrests—sent a coded but clear message to Southern segregationists; federal intervention could be avoided if the authorities kept violence in check. Albany's Chief of Police, Lauri Pritchett, applied this lesson with intelligence and skill, out-maneuvering the protesters. First, he trained his men to arrest demonstrators courteously and without unnecessary force. "For a period of four to five months," he reported to the city commission, "members of the Albany Police Department was [sic] indoctrinated to this plan of nonviolence. . . . At each roll call [they] were lectured and shown films on how to conduct themselves." Second, anticipating a "jail-in," Pritchett secured ample prison space in the surrounding counties. Finally, to protect the City's legal flank he charged demonstrators with such offenses as breach of the peace and unlawful assembly rather than with violation of the segregation laws. His plan worked to perfection: blacks went to jail by the thousands—King himself went three times—but the City adamantly refused to negotiate and the federal government did virtually nothing.

However much King and SCLC deplored Pritchett's self-serving definition of "nonviolence," they had to accept that victory had eluded them. Clearly, SCLC needed to be much more careful in its choice of target. In Birmingham, King elected to confront an adversary with a clear record of brutality, gambling on a violent response which, publicized by a violence-fixated press, would galvanize public opinion and jolt the federal government into action. In 1951 the reporter Carl Rowan had described Birmingham as "the world's most race-conscious city . . . a city of gross tensions, a city where the color line is drawn in every conceivable place [and where] Eugene "Bull" Connor, white-supremacist police commissioner, sees that no man, white or black, crosses the line." Connor was still police commissioner in 1963, and SCLC calculated that this man, notorious for his Klan connections and violence toward blacks, would react to nonviolent protests in a manner very different from Pritchett's. It disclaimed any intent to "provoke" violence. Nevertheless, as local black leader Fred Shuttlesworth put it, "the idea of facing 'Bull' Connor was the thing." Acting as predicted by SCLC, Connor's response to the protests of early May—the mass arrest of children, the use of fire-hoses and police-dogs—was publicized the world over.

But did the protests really achieve anything? The desegregation agreement which King won with the help of federal mediators has often been denigrated. One of the most widely read texts on black history describes it as "token concessions that were later not carried out." At the time, Southern whites argued that orderly change was already on the way; the protests merely hindered that process. It is surely no coincidence, however, that the first small steps in the direction of desegregation occurred precisely when King's campaign climaxed. Few blacks believed that the city's businessmen would have accepted desegregation but for the double pressure of the demonstrations and the economic boycott of downtown stores. Conservative blacks like A. G. Gaston, who had initially opposed direct action, changed their minds when they saw that the white merchants were bending: "The demonstrations gave us a wedge we never had before to use at the bargaining table." Narrow as it was, the agreement of May 10, 1963, represented the city's first substantive break with its white supremacist past. In the most thorough available study of the negotiations, historian Robert Corley concluded that "the end of segregation was dramatically hastened because King and his demonstrators threatened chaos in a city whose leaders were now desperate for order."

What of its impact on federal policy: did Birmingham produce the Civil Rights Act, as King and Shuttlesworth liked to claim? Garrow thinks not, pointing to the gap between SCLC's protests and the introduction of the Bill, as well as the long delay in its becoming law. He suggests that the lack of a clear goal in Birmingham, plus the black rioting of early May, might explain why there was "no widespread national outcry, no vocal reaction by the nation's clergy, and no immediate move by the administration to propose salutary legislation." Birmingham, he concludes, was far less successful than SCLC's later campaign in Selma.

Comparisons between Birmingham and Selma, however, must be treated with caution. It is true, as Garrow notes, that Birmingham produced a relatively muted response from Congress; Selma prompted nearly two hundred sympathetic speeches, Birmingham a mere seventeen. But a simple statistical comparison is misleading for the political context in 1963 was very different from that of 1965. Congressmen were far more wary about speaking out on civil rights in 1963. Most regarded it as a sure "vote-loser," and Northern Democrats were anxious to avoid a damaging intra-party dispute that would redound to the benefit of the Republican party. But in 1965, with the Republicans routed in the elections of the previous year, Northern Democrats felt politically less inhibited. In addition, by 1965 the nation had become more accustomed to the idea that the government should combat racial discrimination; far fewer people still maintained that the South's racial problems could be solved through local, voluntary action. Finally, by 1965 the civil rights movement enjoyed greater legitimacy and respectability. To compare the Congressional response to Birmingham with the reaction to Selma two years later is to compare like with unlike.

The impact of Birmingham should not be judged by its effect on Congress: the initiative for the Civil Rights Bill came from the Executive, not the

Legislative branch. And by all accounts, SCLC's protests were pivotal in persuading the Kennedy administration to abandon its executive-action strategy in favor of legislation. Robert Kennedy was the driving force behind the Bill. For two years he had tried to deal with each racial crisis on an ad hoc basis. However, Birmingham convinced him that crises would recur, with increasing frequency and magnitude, unless the government adopted a more radical approach. According to Edwin Guthman, who served under Attorney General Kennedy, the violence in Birmingham "convinced the President and Bob that stronger federal civil rights laws were needed."

Did the rioting in Birmingham detract from the effectiveness of SCLC's campaign? SCLC did everything possible to minimize the likelihood of counterviolence by blacks. But King and his advisers realized that the Kennedy administration was not simply responding to the moral outrage evoked by Connor's tactics; it was far more perturbed by the threat of chaos and bloodshed. Birmingham raised the specter of retaliation by blacks and the prospect of a violent revolt by them, leading to uncontrollable racial warfare, began to haunt John and Robert Kennedy. Much as he deplored violence by his followers, King consciously exploited this anxiety for the sake of furthering his goals. In "Letter From Birmingham City Jail" he buttressed his appeal for support by whites by warning that without major concessions "millions of Negroes will . . . seek solace in black-nationalist ideologies—a development that would inevitably lead to a frightening racial nightmare." Thus did he redefine nonviolence as an alternative to, or defense against, violence by blacks. This argument reached its target: the Civil Rights Bill was in large measure designed to get blacks off the streets, to obviate the threat of violence, and to strengthen the influence of "responsible" black leaders.

In Birmingham, King broke the political logjam and delivered a hammer-blow against white supremacy. Mass movements did not come made-to-order, however; their success hinged upon sound planning, intelligent leadership, and a fortuitous situation. King had the advantage in Birmingham of a strong local base created by Fred Shuttlesworth, meticulous planning by Wyatt Walker, and a civic elite that was amenable to change. His next campaign, in St. Augustine, Florida (March–July 1964), went awry because the local movement was weak, the planning poor, and opposition by whites intransigent. Largely ineffective, the St. Augustine protests also suffered from lack of clarity in goals; because of this confusion, SCLC's tactics tended to cancel out each other. It is easy to see why King targeted St. Augustine. Heavily dependent on the tourist industry, the city's economy could be seriously damaged by demonstrations. Second, SCLC's chances of engineering a dramatic confrontation were excellent: Northern Florida was Ku Klux Klan country. A branch had been organized in the St. Augustine area in the summer of 1936, and it had close ties with the city and county police. From King's point of view, the Klan presence made St. Augustine doubly attractive. Demonstrations would flush the Klan into the open, thus compelling the state authorities or, failing these, the federal government to suppress it. The nature of SCLC's strategy was evident from its use of the night march. Adopted at the instance of Hosea Williams, who had pioneered this tactic in Savannah, the night march invited attack. The resulting Klan violence showed the police in their true colors, exposing the inadequacy of local law enforcement.

By publicizing the Klan menace King did succeed, with help from U.S. District Judge Bryan Simpson, in making Governor Farris Bryant crack down on white troublemakers. The strategy of forcing the Klan out of the woodwork, however, hampered the achievement of desegregation, SCLC's publicly stated goal. Moreover, in light of the imminent passage of the Civil Rights Bill, SCLC's demonstrations against segregated motels and restaurants seemed pointless. King reasoned that when whites accepted desegregation under legal compulsion they could avoid making any admission that blacks were not treated fairly. "This is morally wrong," he insisted. "We want them to admit that segregation is evil and take it upon themselves to rid this city of it." Yet it made little difference in practice if they abandoned segregation under the pressure of direct action rather than the compulsion of the law, and in any event, the Civil Rights Act, backed up by legal action from the NAACP Legal Defense Fund, desegregated St. Augustine's public accommodations.

In the Selma campaign (January–April 1965), everything went right. The local movement, built up by The Student Nonviolent Coordinating Committee (SNCC), was solidly entrenched. The strategy of the protests had been carefully thought out by James Bevel. SCLC's preparatory staff work was thorough. Above all, the campaign had a single clear, attainable goal—federal voting rights legislation—to which both the target and the tactics were directly relevant. With justice, Selma has been singled out as the most effective application of nonviolent direct action in the history of the civil rights movement.

The notes which he penned in Selma jail give a fascinating insight into King's tactics. In detailed written instructions to Andrew Young, SCLC's executive director, King orchestrated the protests from his cell with masterly finesse. Perhaps the most telling lines were those chiding Young for cancelling a demonstration in response to a favorable court decision. "Please don't be too soft," he wrote his lieutenant. "We have the offensive. It was a mistake not to march today. In a crisis we must have a sense of drama. . . . We may accept the restraining order as a partial victory, but we can't stop." Not until SCLC triggered the violent confrontation of March 7—"Bloody Sunday"—did King feel his goal securely within reach.

The efficacy of King's tactics at Selma flowed from the fact that, to quote Zashin, "people were shocked by the segregationists' violence, not because the self-suffering of the demonstrators was saliently impressive." Garrow came to the same conclusion, adding that the non-controversial nature of SCLC's goal, the right to vote, and the complete absence of violence by blacks both helped to make the campaign a success.

The fact that SCLC designed its tactics to elicit violence might appear callous and irresponsible. Yet the assertion that SCLC deliberately "provoked" violence by whites has to be qualified. If their nonviolent efforts to secure basic Constitutional rights met with violence from racist whites, King argued, then law, logic and morality required society to punish the perpetrators of violence, not condemn its victims. It might seem paradoxical that King invited racist violence but denied in any sense provoking it. But he could also argue that violence was intrinsic to white supremacy and that nonviolent protesters merely brought that violence to the public's attention. In some notes he prepared for a press conference, he anticipated the question "Does your movement depend on violence?" by writing, "When you give witness to an evil you do not cause that evil but you oppose it so it can be cured." The violence of March 7, he added, "brought into every home the terror and brutality that Negroes face every day."

Nevertheless, SCLC's tactics exposed King to the charge that he manipulated local blacks, offering his followers as targets for the aggression of whites. Although undeniably manipulative, nobody could justifiably accuse SCLC of disguising to its followers the dangers they faced. "There can be no remission of sin without the shedding of blood," wrote King. SCLC's claim to leadership rested on the fact that its staff shared the same risks as the rank-and-file demonstrators. Thus King came under the sharpest criticism when he seemed to be avoiding the perils that he asked his followers to brave.

By staging its protests in carefully contrived, highly publicized situations, SCLC tried to evoke violence by whites while keeping casualties to a minimum. The news media played a crucial, if unwitting, role in this strategy. "The presence of reporters," wrote Paul Good, "not only publicized their cause but also acted as a deterrent in places where officials feared bad publicity." Television crews and photographers had an especially inhibiting effect; as Bayard Rustin put it, "Businessmen and chambers of commerce across the South dreaded the cameras." Even in Birmingham, and to some extent in Selma as well, extensive press coverage caused law enforcement officials to proceed with caution. As another of King's advisers, Stanley Levison, pointed out, "the fact that the demonstrations focused public attention from all over the country . . . restrained even the most vicious elements from moving out too freely." When the police did resort to violence, they usually stopped short of lethal force; in all of SCLC's demonstrations in the South, only two deaths resulted from police attacks. SCLC realized moreover, that the news value of racist violence depended as much on the ability of the press to report it as on the gravity of the violence itself. Snarling German Shepherds, gushing firehoses, and club-wielding state troopers could have a greater impact on the public consciousness than murders and bombings if reporters and film crews were present at the scene. Nonviolent protest, wrote King, "dramatized the essential meaning of the conflict and in magnified strokes made clear who was the evildoer and who was the undeserving victim." SCLC tried to evoke dramatic violence rather than deadly violence, and King, as August Meier pointed out in 1965, constantly retreated "from situations that might result in the deaths of his followers."

Despite his enormous popularity and prestige, King learned never to take support of blacks for granted. Leadership and tactics, not numbers, were the key ingredients in King's successes. In the teeming cities of the North, one-twentieth of the black population amounted to a small army. The potential for nonviolent direct action seemed immense. If the team that had organized Selma were turned loose on Chicago, Andrew Young speculated, SCLC would have numbers enough—perhaps 100,000—to bring the city to a standstill. The sheer power of numbers in the North was "awesome," he thought. "I tremble to think what might happen if it is not organized and disciplined in the interests of positive social change." Even as Young spoke, a devastating riot was unfolding in Los Angeles, which, after five days of violence, left thirty-one blacks and three whites dead. On the heels of the Watts riot King, previously so cautious about leaving the South, insisted that SCLC move North and move fast; "The present mood dictates that we cannot wait." Thus it was with a mixture of self-confidence and pessimistic urgency that SCLC embarked on its first Northern campaign.

The anticipated numbers, however, failed to materialize. Chicago had a black population of a million, but it stayed on the sidelines. Barely 50,000 people attended the biggest mass rally: King's demonstrations attracted, at most, twenty-five hundred, at least half of whom were white. King, it has been argued, was out of tune with the mood, culture, and problems of the Northern ghetto. The product of a cocooned middle-class environment, he was not attuned to the cynicism and defeatism that so often prevailed among the black urban poor. His bourgeois emphasis on thrift and self-help obscured him to the realities of their plight; his goal of integration (expressed in Chicago by the demand for "open housing") was marginal, at best, to their immediate concerns. There is a scintilla of truth in this argument. Yet there were many sound reasons for attacking housing segregation, the most visible and far-reaching expression of white racism. Exposure to the Chicago slums, moreover, soon brought home to King the poverty and degradation of the urban ghetto, rapidly disabusing him of his more simplistic assumptions about the efficacy of "bootstrap" economics.

The fact remained, nevertheless, that only a tiny minority acted on King's message. By 1966, in fact, King was becoming increasingly isolated as an advocate of nonviolent direct action. The concept of independent action by blacks in opposition to the white majority—a concept popularized by SNCC's slogan, "Black Power"—was fast gaining ground among intellectuals and activists. But the opposite strategy of seeking political change in coalition with whites was also winning converts. Articulated most persuasively by Bayard Rustin, the coalition strategy envisaged little role for nonviolent direct action on the grounds that economic problems simply were not susceptible to marches and demonstrations. Indeed, Rustin argued that in the post-Watts era, with rioting and repression feeding off each other, direct action had become counterproductive, alienating whites and "breeding despair and impotence" among blacks. Reflecting on SCLC's decline from the perspective of the mid-1970s, Rustin concluded that King persisted in the tactics of protest long after their usefulness had been exhausted.

The disturbed political climate of the late 1960s made doubtful the success of any strategy of blacks. King assessed "Black Power" as a confused, impractical doctrine, and he deplored its connotations of violence and separatism. Yet Rustin's coalitionism struck him as only slightly less unrealistic. In practice, it boiled down to giving blanket support to the Johnson administration—a line rendered both morally repugnant and politically futile by Johnson's growing obsession with the war in Vietnam. The defeat of the 1966 Civil Rights Bill and the Republicans gains in the November elections signalled the disintegration of the informal, bi-partisan "coalition of conscience" which had sustained the civil rights movement in 1963–65. King accurately sensed that it would be impossible—and, in light of the conservatism and hawkishness of most trade unions, undesirable—to resurrect it. Yet he could offer no alternative strategy with any conviction. Indeed, political trends plus his own experiences in Chicago persuaded him that he had badly underestimated the force of white racism. Blacks were not confronting a regional minority but a national majority. It was a shattering conclusion and it drove him to despair.

During the last two years of his life, King was torn between his old faith in the capacity of liberal democracy for enlightened reform, and a Marxian view of the state as an engine of capitalist exploitation. That he became more radical is certain; the need for a thoroughgoing redistribution of wealth and power was a consistent theme of his public and private statements. Occasionally, in his darkest moments, he feared that America was drifting irreversibly toward facsism. Yet King could never forget that the federal government had been his ally. He wanted to believe the current reactionary trend was a passing phase, the irrational spin-off of rioting and war. Although shaken by Chicago and alienated from the President, he convinced himself that public opinion was malleable and the government still susceptible to the right kind of pressure. Nonviolent protest could still work, he insisted to his somewhat skeptical staff. "If it hasn't worked in the North, it just hasn't been tried enough."

King's last project, the "Poor People's Campaign," is sometimes described as revolutionary. To some it recalled the "nonviolent army" idea of the early 1960s. King himself spoke of "class struggle" and threatened massive civil disobedience on a scale that could bring Washington to a grinding halt. Behind the radical rhetoric, however, the strategy and tactics of the campaign closely resembled the pattern of Birmingham and Selma. Although he spoke of creating a new radical coalition, the groups King looked to for support were, by and large, the same that had comprised the "coalition of conscience" in the earlier period. He envisaged a "Selma-like movement" which, if "powerful enough, dramatic enough, and morally appealing enough," would mobilize "the churches, labor, liberals, intellectuals," as well as the new breed of "Black Power" militants and "New Left" white radicals. Far from raising a "nonviolent army," King planned to bring only three thousand demonstrators to Washington—about the number who had gone to jail in Birmingham and Selma. "We aren't going to close down the Pentagon," he told SCLC's board of directors. "Anybody talking about closing down the Pentagon is just talking foolishness. We can't close down Capitol Hill." The aim was not to "coerce" the federal government, but to generate a sympathetic response from the people of the nation. King's demands were moderate, he believed, and he wanted to promote consensus, not conflict.

Had he lived, King might well have achieved at least a partial success. The political situation in 1968 was volatile and fluid; the election of Richard Nixon, and the years of "benign neglect," was not a foregone conclusion. Perhaps King would have cancelled or postponed the Poor People's Campaign, reasoning that a Hubert Humphrey or Robert Kennedy presidency would give him more room for maneuver. In terms of influence and accomplishment, King outstripped all other black leaders and would-be leaders. His capacity to adapt to rapidly changing circumstances would surely have been tested to the limit, but a healthy and astute pragmatism had always been part of his outlook. "I am still searching myself," he told his staff. "I don't have all the answers, and I certainly have no claim to omniscience." There was no magic formula for social change; the dynamics of direct action could only be discovered in struggle, in resistance, even in defeat.

Clayborne Carson  **NO**

Martin Luther King, Jr.: Charismatic Leadership in a Mass Struggle

The legislation to establish Martin Luther King, Jr.'s birthday as a federal holiday provided official recognition of King's greatness, but it remains the responsibility of those of us who study and carry on King's work to define his historical significance. Rather than engaging in officially approved nostalgia, our remembrance of King should reflect the reality of his complex and multi-faceted life. Biographers, theologians, political scientists, sociologists, social psychologists, and historians have given us a sizable literature of King's place in Afro-American protest tradition, his role in the modern black freedom struggle, and his electic ideas regarding nonviolent activism. Although King scholars may benefit from and may stimulate the popular interest in King generated by the national holiday, many will find themselves uneasy participants in annual observances to honor an innocuous, carefully cultivated image of King as a black heroic figure.

The King depicted in serious scholarly works is far too interesting to be encased in such a didactic legend. King was a controversial leader who challenged authority and who once applauded what he called "creative maladjusted nonconformity." He should not be transformed into a simplistic image designed to offend no one—a black counterpart to the static, heroic myths that have embalmed George Washington as the Father of His Country and Abraham Lincoln as the Great Emancipator.

One aspect of the emerging King myth has been the depiction of him in the mass media, not only as the preeminent leader of the civil rights movement, but also as the initiator and sole indispensible element in the southern black struggles of the 1950s and 1960s. As in other historical myths, a Great Man is seen as the decisive factor in the process of social change, and the unique qualities of a leader are used to explain major historical events. The King myth departs from historical reality because it attributes too much to King's exceptional qualities as a leader and too little to the impersonal, large-scale social factors that made it possible for King to display his singular abilities on a national stage. Because the myth emphasizes the individual at the expense of the black movement, it not only exaggerates King's historical importance but also distorts his actual, considerable contribution to the movement.

A major example of this distortion has been the tendency to see King as a charismatic figure who single-handedly directed the course of the civil rights movement through the force of his oratory. The charismatic label however, does not adequately define King's role in the southern black struggle. The term *charisma* has traditionally been used to describe the godlike, magical qualities possessed by certain leaders. Connotations of the term have changed, of course, over the years. In our more secular age, it has lost many of its religious connotations and now refers to a wide range of leadership styles that involve the capacity to inspire—usually through oratory—emotional bonds between leaders and followers. Arguing that King was not a charismatic leader, in the broadest sense of the term, becomes somewhat akin to arguing that he was not a Christian, but emphasis on King's charisma obscures other important aspects of his role in the black movement. To be sure, King's oratory was exceptional and many people saw King as a divinely inspired leader, but King did not receive and did not want the kind of unquestioning support that is often associated with charismatic leaders. Movement activists instead saw him as the most prominent among many outstanding movement strategists, tacticians, ideologues, and institutional leaders.

King undoubtedly recognized that charisma was one of many leadership qualities at his disposal, but he also recognized that charisma was not a sufficient basis for leadership in a modem political movement enlisting numerous self-reliant leaders. Moreover, he rejected aspects of the charismatic model that conflicted with his sense of his own limitations. Rather than exhibiting unwavering confidence in his power and wisdom, King was a leader full of self-doubts, keenly aware of his own limitations and human weaknesses. He was at times reluctant to take on the responsibilities suddenly and unexpectedly thrust upon him. During the Montgomery bus boycott, for example, when he worried about threats to his life and to the lives of his wife and child, he was overcome with fear rather than confident and secure in his leadership role. He was able to carry on only after acquiring an enduring understanding of his dependence on a personal God who promised never to leave him alone.

Moreover, emphasis on King's charisma conveys the misleading notion of a movement held together by spellbinding speeches and blind faith rather than by a complex blend of rational and emotional bonds. King's charisma did not place him above criticism. Indeed, he was never able to gain mass support for his notion of nonviolent struggle as a way of life, rather than simply a tactic. Instead of viewing himself as the embodiment of widely held Afro-American racial views, he willingly risked his popularity among blacks through his steadfast advocacy of nonviolent strategies to achieve radical social change.

He was a profound and provocative public speaker as well as an emotionally powerful one. Only those unfamiliar with the Afro-American clergy would assume that his oratorical skills were unique, but King set himself apart from other black preachers through his use of traditional black Christian idiom to advocate unconventional political ideas. Early in his life King became disillusioned with the unbridled emotionalism associated with his father's religious fundamentalism, and, as a thirteen year old, he questioned the bodily resurrection of Jesus in his Sunday school class. His subsequent search for an intellectually satisfying religious faith conflicted with the emphasis on emotional expressiveness that pervades evangelical religion. His preaching manner was rooted in the traditions of the black church, while his subject matter, which often reflected his wide-ranging philosophical interests, distinguished him from other preachers who relied on rhetorical devices that manipulated the emotions of the listeners. King used charisma as a tool for mobilizing black communities, but he always used it in the context of other forms of intellectual and political leadership suited to a movement containing many strong leaders.

Recently, scholars have begun to examine the black struggle as a locally based mass movement, rather than simply a reform movement led by national civil rights leaders. The new orientation in scholarship indicates that King's role was different from that suggested in King-centered biographies and journalistic accounts. King was certainly not the only significant leader of the civil rights movement, for sustained protest movements arose in many southern communities in which King had little or no direct involvement.

In Montgomery, for example, local black leaders such as E. D. Nixon, Rosa Parks, and Jo Ann Robinson started the bus boycott before King became the leader of the Montgomery Improvement Association. Thus, although King inspired blacks in Montgomery and black residents recognized that they were fortunate to have such a spokesperson, talented local leaders other than King played decisive roles in initiating and sustaining the boycott movement.

Similarly, the black students who initiated the 1960 lunch counter sit-ins admired King, but they did not wait for him to act before launching their own movement. The sit-in leaders who founded the Student Nonviolent Coordinating Committee (SNCC) became increasingly critical of King's leadership style, linking it to the feelings of dependency that often characterize the followers of charismatic leaders. The essence of SNCC's approach to community organizing was to instill in local residents the confidence that they could lead their own struggles. A SNCC organizer failed if local residents became dependent on his or her presence; as the organizers put it, their job was to work themselves out of a job. Though King influenced the struggles that took place in the Black Belt regions of Mississippi, Alabama, and Georgia, those movements were also guided by self-reliant local leaders who occasionally called on King's oratorical skills to galvanize black protestors at mass meetings while refusing to depend on his presence.

If King had never lived, the black struggle would have followed a course of development similar to the one it did. The Montgomery bus boycott would have occurred, because King did not initiate it. Black students probably would have rebelled—even without King as a role model—for they had sources of tactical and ideological inspiration besides King. Mass activism in southern cities and voting rights efforts in the deep South were outgrowths of large-scale social and political forces, rather than simply consequences of the actions of a single leader. Though perhaps not as quickly and certainly not as peacefully nor with as universal a significance, the black movement would probably have achieved its major legislative victories without King's leadership, for the southern Jim Crow system was a regional anachronism, and the forces that undermined it were inexorable.

To what extent, then, did King's presence affect the movement? Answering that question requires us to look beyond the usual portrayal of the black struggle. Rather than seeing an amorphous mass of discontented blacks acting out strategies determined by a small group of leaders, we would recognize King as a major example of the local black leadership that emerged as black communities mobilized for sustained struggles. If not as dominant a figure as sometimes portrayed, the historical King was nevertheless a remarkable leader who acquired the respect and support of self-confident, grass-roots leaders, some of whom possessed charismatic qualities of their own. Directing attention to the other leaders who initiated and emerged from those struggles should not detract from our conception of King's historical significance; such movement-oriented research reveals King as a leader who stood out in a forest of tall trees.

King's major public speeches—particularly the "I Have a Dream" speech—have received much attention, but his exemplary qualities were also displayed in countless strategy sessions with other activists and in meetings with government officials. King's success as a leader was based on his intellectual and moral cogency and his skill as a conciliator among movement activists who refused to be simply King's "followers" or "lieutenants."

The success of the black movement required the mobilization of black communities as well as the transformation of attitudes in the surrounding society, and King's wide range of skills and attributes prepared him to meet the internal as well as the external demands of the movement. King understood the black world from a privileged position, having grown up in a stable family within a major black urban community; yet he also learned how to speak persuasively to the surrounding white world. Alone among the major civil rights leaders of his time, King could not only articulate black concerns to white audiences, but could also mobilize blacks through his day-to-day involvement in black community institutions and through his access to the regional institutional network of the black church. His advocacy of nonviolent activism gave the black movement invaluable positive press coverage, but his effectiveness as a protest leader derived mainly from his ability to mobilize black community resources.

Analyses of the southern movement that emphasize its nonrational aspects and expressive functions over its political character explain the black struggle as an emotional outburst by discontented blacks, rather than recognizing that the movement's strength and durability came from its mobilization of black community institutions, financial resources, and grass-roots leaders. The values of southern blacks were profoundly and permanently transformed not only by King, but also by involvement in sustained protest activity and community-organizing efforts, through thousands of mass meetings, workshops, citizenship classes, freedom schools, and informal discussions. Rather than merely accepting guidance from above, southern blacks were resocialized as a result of their movement experiences.

Although the literature of the black struggle has traditionally paid little attention to the intellectual content of black politics, movement activists of the 1960s made a profound, though often ignored, contribution to political thinking. King may have been born with rare potential, but his most significant leadership attributes were related to his immersion in, and contribution to, the intellectual ferment that has always been an essential part of Afro-American freedom struggles. Those who have written about King have too often assumed that his most important ideas were derived from outside the black struggle—from his academic training, his philosophical readings, or his acquaintance with Gandhian ideas. Scholars are only beginning to recognize the extent to which his attitudes and those of many other activists, white and black, were transformed through their involvement in a movement in which ideas disseminated from the bottom up as well as from the top down.

Although my assessment of King's role in the black struggles of his time reduces him to human scale, it also increases the possibility that others may recognize his qualities in themselves. Idolizing King lessens one's ability to exhibit some of his best attributes or, worse, encourages one to become a debunker, emphasizing King's flaws in order to lessen the inclination to exhibit his virtues. King himself undoubtedly feared that some who admired him would place too much faith in his ability to offer guidance and to overcome resistance, for he often publicly acknowledged his own limitations and mortality. Near the end of his life, King expressed his certainty that black people would reach the Promised Land whether or not he was with them. His faith was based on an awareness of the qualities that he knew he shared with all people. When he suggested his own epitaph, he asked not to be remembered for his exceptional achievements—his Nobel Prize and other awards, his academic accomplishments; instead, he wanted to be remembered for giving his life to serve others, for trying to be right on the war question, for trying to feed the hungry and clothe the naked, for trying to love and serve humanity. "I want you to say that I tried to love and serve humanity." Those aspects of King's life did not require charisma or other superhuman abilities.

If King were alive today, he would doubtless encourage those who celebrate his life to recognize their responsibility to struggle as he did for a more just and peaceful world. He would prefer that the black movement be remembered not only as the scene of his own achievements, but also as a setting that brought out extraordinary qualities in many people. If he were to return, his oratory would be unsettling and intellectually challenging rather than remembered diction and cadences. He would probably be the unpopular social critic he was on the eve of the Poor People's Campaign rather than the object of national homage he became after his death. His basic message would be the same as it was when he was alive, for he did not bend with the changing political winds. He would talk of ending poverty and war and of building a just social order that would avoid the pitfalls of competitive capitalism and repressive communism. He would give scant comfort to those who condition their activism upon the appearance of another King, for he recognized the extent to which he was a product of the movement that called him to leadership.

The notion that appearances by Great Men (or Great Women) are necessary preconditions for the emergence of major movements for social change reflects not only a poor understanding of history, but also a pessimistic view of the possibilities for future social change. Waiting for the Messiah is a human weakness that is unlikely to be rewarded more than once in a millennium. Studies of King's life offer support for an alternative optimistic belief that ordinary people can collectively improve their lives. Such studies demonstrate the capacity of social movements to transform participants for the better and to create leaders worthy of their followers.

POSTSCRIPT

Was Martin Luther King, Jr.'s Leadership Essential to the Success of the Civil Rights Revolution?

Fairclough delivers an important portrait of King. He challenges not only the mythical views about King but also the portraits that a number of his biographers have written. First of all, he places King within the context of the dynamics of the social changes of the 1960s. Fairclough disagrees with those who see King primarily as a great orator and a symbolic leader of the movement. He argues that King was a flexible and practical revolutionary who understood that power, not moral suasion, lay at the heart of the civil rights protest movements. Consequently, Fairclough disputes David J. Garrow's contention in *Bearing the Cross: Martin Luther King, Jr. and the Southern Christian Leadership Conference* (Morrow/Avon, 1999) that King's belief about nonviolence was originally viewed as a form of moral suasion. When the demonstrations failed to convert white southerners or even attract white moderates, says Garrow, King finally realized that mass protests would only work as a pressure tactic that was needed to evoke a violent response from the oppressors.

Fairclough denies that King ever made such an ideological shift. King, in his view, was a realist who understood that nonviolence was a tactic used in a struggle to achieve power. While he may have been disappointed that only a few white southerners converted to the movement, the Montgomery Bus Boycott of 1956 was only the first phase of a worldwide revolt of oppressed people.

Carson might seem to underestimate the uniqueness of King. He admits that King could speak persuasively to the white community and at the same time "mobilize black community resources." These ideas were first articulated by the historian August Meier, who described King as a conservative militant in his widely reprinted article "On the Role of Martin Luther King," *New Politics* (Winter 1965). King not only bridged the black and white power structures, but he also acted as a broker between the more militant protest groups, such as the Student Nonviolent Coordinating Committee (SNCC) and the more conservative, legal-oriented NAACP.

The literature on King is enormous. An interpretive short biography is Adam Fairclough, *Martin Luther King, Jr.* (University of Georgia Press, 1995). Older interpretations are nicely summarized in C. Eric Lincoln, ed., *Martin Luther King, Jr.: A Profile* (Hill & Wang, 1970), which includes Meier's classic essay. Peter J. Albert and Ronald Hoffman have edited a more recent symposium, *We Shall Overcome: Martin Luther King, Jr. and the Black Freedom Struggle* (Da Capo Press, 1990). Stephen B. Oates, *Let the Trumpet Sound: The Life of Martin Luther King, Jr.* (Harper & Row, 1982) uses King's papers but is mainly descriptive. Also see Oates, "Trumpet of Conscience: A Portrait of Martin Luther King, Jr.," *American History Illustrated* (April 1988); David Garrow, "Martin Luther King, Jr. and the Cross of Leadership," *Peace and Change* (Fall 1987); and "The Intellectual Development of Martin Luther King, Jr.: Influences and Commentaries," *Union Seminary Quarterly* (vol. 40, 1986), pp. 5–20. A well-written early biography is David L. Lewis, *King: A Critical Biography* (Praeger, 1970). See also Lewis's "Martin Luther King, Jr. and the Promise of Nonviolent Populism," in John Hope Franklin and August Meier, eds., *Black Leaders of the Twentieth Century* (University of Illinois Press, 1982). Two volumes that defy description are Taylor Branch's sprawling *Parting the Waters* (Simon & Schuster, 1988) and *Pillar of Fire* (Simon & Schuster, 1998), which takes the reader through the King years up to 1965. A third volume has yet to be published.

The literature of the civil rights movement is also enormous. Two of the best overviews written for students are John A. Salmond, *My Mind Set on Freedom: A History of the Civil Rights Movement, 1954–1968* (Ivan R. Dee, 1997), a survey in the American Ways series; and Peter B. Levy, *The Civil Rights Movement* (Greenwood Press, 1998), which is part of the Greenwood Press Guides to Historic Events of the Twentieth Century series. Two excellent collections of essays are Charles W. Eagles, ed., *The Civil Rights Movement in America* (University Press of Mississippi, 1986), a symposium held at the University of Mississippi in 1985 among several of the most important civil rights historians, and Paul Winters, ed., *The Civil Rights Movement* (Greenhaven Press, 2000), which contains a number of useful topical articles. Three more detailed studies are Jack M. Bloom's theoretical *Class, Race, and the Civil Rights Movement* (Indiana University Press, 1987); Harvard Sitkoff, *The Struggle for Black Equality, 1954–1992*, rev. ed. (Hill & Wang, 1993); and David R. Goldfield, *Black, White, and Southern: Race Relations and Southern Culture, 1940 to the Present* (Louisiana State University Press, 1990). The best film series on the civil rights movement is Henry Hampton's 14-hour *Eyes on the Prize: America's Civil Rights Years, 1954–1965*. Two excellent primary source anthologies came from this series: Clayborne Carson et al., eds., *Eyes on the Prize: Civil Rights Reader* (Penguin Books, 1991) and Henry Hampton and Steve Fayer, eds., *Voice of Freedom: An Oral History of the Civil Rights Movement From the 1950s Through the 1980s* (Bantam Books, 1990).

Local studies that de-emphasize the national movement covered so well by the contemporary press and most American history texts include William Chafe, *Civilities and Civil Rights: Greensboro, North Carolina, and the Black Struggle for Freedom* (Oxford University Press, 1981), which castigates the white moderates for using southern charm to avoid the racial divide; Adam Fairclough, *Race and Democracy: The Civil Rights Struggle in Louisiana, 1915–1972* (University of Georgia Press, 1995); Charles M. Payne, *I've Got the Light of Freedom: The Organizing Tradition and the Mississippi Freedom Struggle* (University of California Press, 1995); and John Dittmer, *Local People: The Struggle for Civil Rights in Mississippi* (University of Illinois, 1994).

ISSUE 9

Did the Great Society Fail?

YES: Charles Murray, from *Losing Ground: American Social Policy, 1950–1980* (Basic Books, 1984)

NO: Joseph A. Califano, Jr., from "The Ship Sails On," in Thomas W. Cowger and Sherwin J. Markman, eds., *Lyndon Johnson Remembered* (Rowman & Littlefield, 2003)

ISSUE SUMMARY

YES: Conservative social critic Charles Murray argues that the Great Society removed the stigma of poverty, blamed the system instead of the individual for being unemployed and created a permanent underclass of inner-city African-American welfare recipients.

NO: Joseph A. Califano, Jr., a former aide to President Johnson, maintains that the Great Society programs brought about possible revolutionary changes in the area of civil rights, education, health care, the environment, and consumer protection.

Now that the twentieth century has ended, historians can look back at the era's three major political reform movements: Progressivism (1900–1917), the New Deal (1933–1938), and the Great Society (1963–1965). There were a number of similarities among the three movements. They were allied by activist, Democratic presidents—Woodrow Wilson, Franklin Roosevelt, and Lyndon Johnson. Top-heavy Democratic congressional majorities were created, which allowed the reform-minded presidents to break through the gridlock normally posed by an unwieldy Congress and to pass an unusual amount of legislation in a short time span. Finally, all three reform currents came to a sudden stop when America's entrance into war diverted the nation's physical and emotional resources from reform efforts at home.

Progressivism, the New Deal, and the Great Society also had to grapple with the social and economic problems of a nation where the majority of people lived in cities with populations of 100,000 or more and worked for large corporations. In order to solve these problems, government could no longer be a passive observer of the Industrial Revolution. Reformers believed that government would have to intervene in order to make capitalism operate fairly.

Two approaches were used: (1) regulating the economy from the top down and (2) solving social problems from the bottom up.

World War II, the subsequent Cold War, a world economy that was dominated by the United States until the late 1960s, and a general prosperity that prevailed in the economic cycle kept reform efforts at a minimum during the Truman (1945–1953) and Eisenhower (1953–1961) presidencies.

In 1960, when Democrat John F. Kennedy defeated Republican Richard Nixon, there were two major social and economic problems that remained unresolved by the New Deal: (1) the failure to integrate blacks into the mainstream of American society and (2) the failure to provide a decent standard of living for the hard-core poor, the aged, the tenant farmers, the migrant workers, the unemployed coal miners and mill workers, and the single mothers of the inner city. Early in Kennedy's administration, Congress passed the Area Redevelopment Act of 1961, which provided close to $400 million in federal loans and grants for help to 675 "distressed areas" of high unemployment and low economic development. The president had plans for a more comprehensive attack on poverty, but his assassination on November 22, 1963, prevented implementation.

Kennedy's successor, Lyndon Johnson, took advantage of the somber mood of the country after Kennedy's assassination and his landslide election victory in 1964, which created top-heavy Democratic congressional majorities of 295 to 140 in the House of Representatives and 68 to 32 in the Senate. Johnson believed that the Great Society and its programs were to be the completion of the New Deal. The Civil Rights Act of 1964 and the Voting Rights Act of 1965 introduced blacks into the mainstream of American society. Medicare and Medicaid tied health care for the elderly and poor people to the social security system, and the Elementary Secondary Education and the Higher Education Acts of 1965 provided funds for low-income local school districts and scholarships and subsidized low-interest loans for needy college students.

In January 1964, Johnson called for an "unconditional war on poverty." Later that year, the Economic Opportunity Act was passed. This created an Office of Economic Opportunity (OEO), which set up a variety of community action programs for the purpose of expanding the educational, health care, housing, and employment opportunities in poor neighborhoods. Between 1965 and 1970, the OEO operated on the cheap, establishing such community action programs (CAPs) as the Job Corps, which trained lower-class teenagers and young adults for employment, and Head Start, whose purpose was to give underprivileged preschool children skills that they could use when they attended regular elementary schools.

In the first of the following selections, social critic Charles Murray argues that the Great Society removed the stigma of poverty, blamed the system instead of the individual for being unemployed, and related a permanent underclass of inner-city African-American welfare recipients. But Joseph A. Califano, Jr., a former domestic aide to President Johnson, maintains that the Great Society programs brought about possible revolutionary change in the areas of civil rights, education, healthcare, the environment, and consumer protection.

YES

Charles Murray

Losing Ground: American Social Policy, 1950–1980

The Civil Rights Movement Moves North

Speaking to an interviewer in 1967, Daniel Patrick Moynihan summed up in a few sentences the toils in which the social welfare experiment had wound itself when the civil rights movement moved north.

> In the South . . . there were a great many outcomes—situations, customs, rules—which were inimical to Negro rights, which violated Negro rights and which were *willed* outcomes. Intended, planned, desired outcomes. And it was, therefore, possible to seek out those individuals who were willing the outcomes and to coerce them to cease to do so.
>
> Now, you come to New York City, with its incomparable expenditures on education; and you find that, in the twelfth grade, Negro students are performing at the sixth grade level in mathematics. Find for me the man who wills *that* outcome. Find the legislator who has held back money, the teacher who's held back his skills, the school superintendent who's deliberately discriminating, the curriculum supervisor who puts the wrong books in, the architect who builds the bad schools. He isn't there!

By and large—not perfectly by any means, but by and large—the legal system outside the southern states had rid itself of designed-in racism. There were no voter "literacy" tests to get rid of, no Jim Crow laws to repeal. While northern racism might simply be more subtle, as many black leaders claimed, it provided few specific, reified targets to hit out against.

And yet equality of rights under the law had not been accompanied by equality of outcome. Blacks in the North as in the South lived in worse housing than whites, had less education, ate less nutritious food, and so on down the list of indicators that were used to measure well-being. On virtually every one, a large difference between black and white remained, and it was always to the disadvantage of the blacks. Whites were made aware of this by accounts such as Kenneth Clark's "Youth in the Ghetto," passed everywhere in mimeograph by poverty planners long before it was published. Blacks who lived in the ghetto did not need to read about it. Their response followed a pattern that could be used as a textbook example of a revolution of rising expectations.

The first phase of the civil rights movement culminated in the passage of the Civil Rights Act of 1964 on 3 July. For all practical purposes, the national legislative struggle for equality was over. The Voting Rights Bill remained to be enacted a year later, but the generalized legal clout granted in the 1964 act was enormous: No one could with impunity deny someone *access* to the institutions of this country because of race without being liable to criminal penalties or inviting a nasty and probably losing lawsuit. The civil rights movement had triumphed—and thirteen days later came the first of the race riots, in Harlem.

The riots continued that summer in Rochester, Paterson, Philadelphia, and Dixmoor, a suburb of Chicago. They quieted during the winter, then erupted again in Watts, in August 1965, with a violence that dwarfed the disturbances of the preceding year. They would crescendo in 1967, with riots in more than thirty cities.

The riots changed, or coincided with a change in, what had until then been a movement of legal challenges, nonviolent demonstrations, and coalition-building. Writing from a Marxist perspective, some observers saw this as the trigger for the explosion in social spending that occurred during the same period: The white power structure needed to control the restiveness of blacks, and the shift from "a hand, not a handout" to income transfers was in the nature of a bribe.

A careful review of what bills passed when, with what support, casts doubt on this argument, though it retains intuitive plausibility. But the post-1964 militancy unquestionably had another and arguably more pernicious long-term effect. It tightly restricted the permissible terms of debate within academia and the government on issues involving blacks—which is to say, virtually every issue associated with social policy.

Specifically, the riots and the militancy adjoined the moral monopoly that the civil rights movement of 1964 still enjoyed. The year 1964 was not only the year when the Civil Rights Act passed and the first riots occurred. It was also the year when Martin Luther King, Jr., won the Nobel Peace Prize. It was the year when Chaney, Goodman, and Schwerner were tortured and killed in Mississippi. It was, in short, the year in which all that created the moral monopoly was most in evidence.

Black leaders blamed the riots on whites—or, coextensively, The System. Stokely Carmichael and Rap Brown said it with a rhetoric as bloodyminded and as unapologetic as the rioters. Martin Luther King said it with more elegance, thoughtfulness, and political astuteness, but said it nonetheless. "A profound judgment of today's riots," King told a convention of social scientists, "was expressed by Victor Hugo a century ago. He said, 'If a soul is left in darkness, sins will be committed. The guilty one is not he who commits the sin, but he who causes the darkness.'"

As a statement about ultimate causes, the black interpretation was nearly unarguable. But history was not the issue. The exigent question was: What do we do now, today, in response to people rioting in the streets? Devising an answer put whites in a terrible moral bind—not one that blacks were likely to have much sympathy with, but a bind nonetheless. A white who had supported the simple, purely "good" civil rights movement against the nasty southerners and now said, "Wait a minute, that doesn't mean you can start burning northern cities" was exposed as a summer soldier. Manifestly, racial discrimination continued to exist; manifestly, it was a moral perversity. Therefore. . . . And that was the hard part. What came after the "therefore"?

Whites who saw themselves as friends of the civil rights movement had to agree that the riots were regrettable but not the fault of blacks. The inevitability of the riots, even their reasonableness, had to be accepted, not as a matter of historical causation but as the basis for the white policy reaction. Of course the civil rights legislation had not forestalled violence, *Newsweek* told us. After all, "The promises of the present could not undo in a day the ugly legacy of the Negro past," the magazine wrote in its lead paragraph on the Watts riot. "A summer ago, that past exploded in a bloody war of rioting across the urban North. And last week, on a steamy, smoggy night in Los Angeles, it exploded again." A few pages later, a poll of whites' reactions to the riots divided the discussion into two paragraphs—the "intelligent" reactions, meaning those who understood that the riots were an understandable manifestation of past injustice, and those who were "less perceptive," meaning the people who said that the rioters were breaking the law and ought to be punished. The two stands were widely perceived as being mutually exclusive.

Not everybody agreed. "White backlash" was a phrase coined at about the same time as "black power." The year 1966 saw the election of an ideologically adamant conservative governor in California, Ronald Reagan, and widely publicized campaigns by racial hardliners like Boston's Louise Day Hicks. But even on Main Street, well into the riot years, a majority remained in favor of taking new steps to remedy black grievances.

Within the Establishment (for lack of a better term), a much narrower, circumscribing mindset took hold: The blame is embedded in the structure of the system, and the system must be made right.

The most vocal advocates for sweeping reform were from the left, but it would be mistaken to treat the sense of guilt as "liberal" versus "conservative." The *mea culpa* resounded everywhere, including the most unlikely places. For example:

> [W]e are creating a monster within our midst, a people being alienated from the mainstream of American life . . . [We must] cease thinking of racial relations as a nice and good thing, as one important national and local task—*among many others*—to do. American race relations today, like religion and basic ideologies historically, must have an absolute priority or we are as a nation lost! [Emphasis in the original]

Strong words—not from a political rostrum, but from the lead article in the January 1967 issue of *The American Journal of Economics and Sociology*, a sober academic journal. But they were no more unexpected than an angry editorial, entitled "Cry of the Ghetto," complaining bitterly of "white society's stubborn refusal to admit that the ghetto is a problem it must solve, that its promises, broken and inadequate, are no longer tolerable." It appeared in *The Saturday Evening Post*—the staid, middle-American, Norman-Rockwell-covered *Saturday Evening Post*—during that bloody August of 1967.

The National Commission on Civil Disorders, headed by an ex-governor of Illinois and comprising a distinguished selection of Americans from the business and professional worlds as well as from public life, put the imprimatur of the federal government on the explanation for the riots, concluding that "[w]hite racism is essentially responsible for the explosive mixture which has been accumulating in our cities since the end of World War II." The report presented no proof for this statement, but few objected. Its truth was self-evident.

Whether the Establishment view of the black condition in the last half of the 1960s was right or wrong is not the issue that concerns us. The fact that this view was so widely shared helped force the shift in assumptions about social welfare. White America owed black America; it had a conscience to clear.

The moral agonizing among whites was strikingly white-centered. *Whites* had created the problem, it was up to *whites* to fix it, and there was very little in the dialogue that treated blacks as responsible actors. Until July 1964 most whites (and most blacks) thought in terms of equal access to opportunity. Blacks who failed to take advantage were in the same boat with whites who failed to take advantage. By 1967 this was not an intellectually acceptable way to conceive of the issue. Blacks were exempted. Once more, in a new and curious fashion, whites had put up the "Whites Only" sign.

White confusion and guilt over the turn of events in the civil rights movement created what Moynihan has called "a near-obsessive concern to locate the 'blame' for poverty, especially Negro poverty, on forces and institutions outside the community concerned." The structuralists, with their view of poverty as embedded in the American economic and social system, provided a ready-made complement to this impulse. If society were to blame for the riots, if it were to blame for the economic and social discrepancies between whites and blacks, if indeed it were to blame for poverty itself among all races, and *if society's responsibility were not put right by enforcing a formalistic legal equality*, then a social program could hardly be constructed on grounds that simply guaranteed equality of opportunity. It must work toward equality of *outcome*. A "hand" was not enough.

Hard Noses and Soft Data

The riots and black militancy constituted one of the two empirical developments that made the structural view of poverty attractive. The second was the early realization, within the ranks of the Johnson administration as well as among its critics, that the antipoverty programs were not working as expected.

For this part of the story, we return to the fall of 1964, when the first antipoverty bill had just been passed and the Office of Economic Opportunity (OEO) was being organized. Our focus shifts from the academicians, the journalists, the cabinet officers and congressional leaders to the people who did the work—the middle- and lower-echelon officials who designed and implemented the programs that constituted the War on Poverty.

They were an assortment of New Frontiersmen (Sargent Shriver at OEO being the most conspicuous example) and people who came into the bureaucracy especially to play a role in the great social reform that Johnson had launched. Few were bureaucrats, few were from the social-work tradition. They tended to see themselves as pragmatic idealists. "Hardnosed" was a favorite self-descriptor in the Kennedy years, and it carried over. The first poverty warriors did not intend to get bogged down in interminable debates about doctrine. They had a job to do and, from the accounts of people who participated in those early years of the Great Society, it was an exciting job. The recountings have the flavor of war stories—of allnight sessions preparing for crucial Senate hearings; of small, sweaty working groups designing new programs on impossibly short schedules; of meetings in Newark or Chicago or Biloxi where the people across the table were not mayors and city planners, but the heads of tenants' associations and ghetto churches and street gangs. Speaking of his staff, the director of one of the early programs wrote:

> All were the antithesis of the stereotyped bureaucrat cautiously protecting his career. Their approach right down the line was: "What needs to be done? How can we do it best, and faster?" When the answers were clear, they were all willing to risk their careers and their health and sacrifice their personal lives, to get the job done well and quickly. Something happened to us all . . . that created a rare combination of shared dedication, excitement, and satisfaction.

Such people characterized the early years both in Washington and in the field offices. They had no serious doubts that they would have an impact on the poverty problem. It seemed obvious to them (as it did to many observers at the time) that the only reason we continued to have poverty at a time of such manifest national affluence was that nobody had really been trying to get rid of it. Once the effort was made, so their assumption went, progress would surely follow.

Their optimism had two bases. One was that the programs depended on human responses that seemed natural and indeed nearly automatic to them. The gloomy implications of the "culture of poverty" argument did not carry much weight at OEO in 1964 and 1965. A sensible, hard-working poor person would find much to work with in the opportunities offered by the initial antipoverty programs. Or to put it another way, if the people who ran the programs had suddenly found themselves poor, they probably would have been quite successful in using the antipoverty programs to rescue themselves. The early programs put chips on the table; as their advocates had promised, they did indeed give some of the poor a chance at a piece of the action, with the operative word being "chance." The staff at OEO and its companion agencies scattered around Washington did not think that the loan programs or the community development programs would transform the ghetto instantaneously, but they had no doubt that such programs would be individually successful—steps in the right direction.

In the case of the training programs such as the Job Corps, success seemed to be still more natural. The logistics of providing training were straightforward. The educational technology was adequate and in place. There were plenty of welfare recipients who said they wanted jobs and who acted as though they wanted jobs. During the 1960s, and especially after the Vietnam

War heated up, jobs were available for people with the kinds of skills that could be acquired in the training programs. The training programs would work, without question. What was to stop them?

It would be important to document the successes that were about to emerge. In the spirit of cost-effectiveness that McNamara had taken to the Pentagon, the early poverty warriors were prepared to be judged on the hardest of hard-nosed measures of success. The programs would be removing enough people from the welfare rolls, from drug addiction, and from crime to provide an economically attractive return on the investment.

But how was this information to be obtained? Social scientists who had been at the periphery of the policy process—sociologists, psychologists, political scientists—had the answer: scientific evaluation. The merits of doing good would no longer have to rest on faith. We would be able to *prove* that we had done good, as objectively as a scientist proves an hypothesis.

In the space of a few years, applied social science and especially program evaluation became big business. In Eisenhower's last year in office, 1960, the Department of Health, Education, and Welfare (HEW) spent $46 million on research and development other than health research. It took three more years for the budget to reach $90 million, followed by sizable jumps in 1964 and 1965. Then, in a single year, 1966, the budget doubled from $154 million to $313 million. Similar patterns prevailed at the other departments, agencies, institutes, and bureaus engaged in the antipoverty struggle.

The product of all this activity and money was a literature describing what was being accomplished by the antipoverty programs. It is what scholars call a "fugitive" literature, with most reports being printed in editions of a few dozen photocopies submitted to the government sponsor. The release of a major evaluation might get a column or two on a back page of a few of the largest newspapers. But otherwise, the work of the evaluators went unread by the outside world.

Within those governmental circles where the reports were read, they led to a rapid loss of innocence about what could be expected from the efforts to help people escape from welfare dependency. Starting with the first evaluation reports in the mid-sixties and continuing to the present day, the results of these programs have been disappointing to their advocates and evidence of failure to their critics.

The War on Poverty had originally struck on two fronts: For depressed neighborhoods and entire communities, "community action" programs were funded in profusion, to further all sorts of objectives; for individuals, manpower programs provided training or job opportunities. We shall be discussing the substance of what the evaluators found, not only in 1964–67 but subsequently, when we examine explanations for the breakdown in progress. For now, a few examples will convey the tenor of the findings.

The Community Action Programs

The community action programs fared worst. A number of histories and case studies are available to the public at large, Moynihan *Maximum Feasible*

Misunderstanding being the best known. With the advantage of hindsight, it is not surprising that the community development programs so seldom got off the ground. Faith in spontaneity and in *ad hoc* administrative arrangements were traits of the sixties that met disillusionment in many fields besides the antipoverty programs. Surprising or not, the record they compiled was dismal. For every evaluation report that could document a success, there was a stack that told of local groups that were propped up by federal money for the duration of the grant, then disappeared, with nothing left behind.

Each project had its own tale to tell about why it failed—an ambitious city councilman who tried to horn in, a balky banker who reneged on a tentative agreement, and so on. There were always villains and heroes, dragons and maidens. But failure was very nearly universal.

The course of the projects followed a pattern. To see how this worked in practice, we have the example of the Economic Development Administration's major employment and urban development program in Oakland, the subject of a scholarly case study. This was the sequence:

The story broke with considerable fanfare. *The Wall Street Journal* of 25 April 1966 had it on page one, under the headline "URBAN AID KICKOFF: ADMINISTRATION SELECTS OAKLAND AS FIRST CITY IN REBUILDING PROGRAM." The governor of California and the assistant secretary of commerce for economic development held a press conference announcing a program of $23 million in federal grants and loans. The program was an assortment of community-run economic development projects bankrolled by the government. Various incentives were designed to prompt private business to invest in the ghetto. In the short term, 2,200 jobs were to be provided, and more were to follow from "spinoffs." These jobs would go to the unemployed residents of the inner city.

As far as its national publicity told the story, the program was a great success. A book (*Oakland's Not for Burning*) was in the bookstores by 1968, claiming that the program "may have made the difference" in preventing a riot in Oakland. *The New Yorker* told its readers that the program had "managed to break a longtime deadlock between the Oakland ghetto and the local business and government Establishment." Oakland was a showcase of the War on Poverty.

It was not until a year after these stories had appeared that the *Los Angeles Times* printed a follow-up story revealing that the activities described in the book and in *The New Yorker* had in actuality never gotten beyond the planning stage. All told, only twenty jobs had been created. The program was bogged down in bureaucratic infighting. The authors of the case study, writing from the perspective of four years later, concluded that the effect of the project on "despair and disillusionment" among blacks was probably to have made matters worse.

The Oakland project was not chosen for study as an example of failure; the study began while hopes were still high. The Oakland experience was representative, not exceptional, and the gradual realization of this by those connected with the poverty programs was one source of their dampened hopes for the "hand, not a handout" approach. Few of them reacted by giving up; through the rest of the 1960s and well into the 1970s, it was argued that the community action programs were slowly learning from their failures and would do better next time. But if their proponents did not give up, neither did they speak so boldly about the imminent end of the dole.

The Training Programs

The failure of the training programs was a greater surprise still. These of all programs were expected to be a sure bet. They dealt with individuals, not institutions, and teaching a person who wants to learn is something we know how to do. But starting with the first evaluation reports in the mid-sixties and continuing to the present day, the results failed to show the hoped-for results, or anything close to them. The programs were seldom disasters; they simply failed to help many people get and hold jobs that they would not have gotten and held anyway.

As with the community development programs, the findings varied in detail but not in pattern. In one of the most recent and technically precise studies of the Manpower Development and Training Act (MDTA), the linchpin of Kennedy's original program and one that eventually grew to a multibillion dollar effort, the final conclusion is that male trainees increased their earnings between $150 and $500 *per year* immediately after training, "declining to perhaps half this figure after five years." For the females, the study found a continuing effect of $300 to $600 per year. A panel study of the effects of vocational training found a wage increase of 1.5 percent that could be attributed to the training. The early studies of Job Corps trainees found effects of under $200 per year, and these early findings have been repeated in subsequent work. Effects of this magnitude were far from the results that had been anticipated when the programs began.

Even as the program designers and evaluators debated what to do next and how to do it better, they could not avoid recognizing some discomfiting realities. It was quickly learned that people on welfare do not necessarily enroll in job training programs once they become available. Those who enroll do not necessarily stick it through to the end of the program. Those who stick it through do not necessarily get jobs. And, of those who find jobs, many quickly lose them. Sometimes they lose them because of their lack of seniority when layoffs occur. Sometimes they lose them because of discrimination. Sometimes they lose them because they fail to show up for work or don't work very hard when they do show up. And—more often than anyone wanted to admit—people just quit, disappearing from the evaluator's scorecard.

Unable to point to large numbers of trainees who were escaping from welfare dependency, the sponsors of the training programs turned to other grounds for their justification. They found two. First, a cost-effectiveness case could be wrenched even from small increments in income. If the average trainee's earnings increase even by a few hundred dollars, sooner or later the increase will add up to more than the cost of the training, and it was this type of calculation to which the sponsors were reduced. "The average effect [on earnings] for all enrollees is quite large," we find in one evaluation of Job Corps, then read on to the next sentence, where it is revealed that the "quite large" effect amounted to $3.30 per week. It was a statistically significant gain.

Second, the training programs lent themselves to upbeat anecdotes about individual success stories: John Jones, an ex-con who had never held a job in his life, became employed because of program X and is saving money to send his child to college. Such anecdotes, filmed for the evening news, were much more interesting than economic analyses. They also were useful in hearings before congressional appropriations committees. Tacit or explicit, a generalization went with the anecdote: John Jones's story is typical of what this project is accomplishing or will accomplish for a large number of people. That such success stories were extremely rare, and that depressingly often John Jones would be out of his job and back in jail a few months after his moment in the spotlight—these facts were not commonly publicized. The anecdotes made good copy. Thus the training programs continued to get a good press throughout the 1970s. They were the archetypal "hand, not a handout" programs, and they retained much of the intellectual and emotional appeal that had made them popular in the early 1960s. To some extent, whether they worked or not was irrelevant.

We have been scanning a record that has accumulated over the years since the first antipoverty projects in the early 1960s. But the loss of innocence came early. It soon became clear that large numbers of the American poor were not going to be moved off the welfare rolls by urban development schemes or by training programs.

At another time, that might have been the end of the attempt. Or, at another time, perhaps we would have done a better job of learning from our mistakes and have developed less ambitious, more effective programs. But the demands for urban renewal programs and jobs programs and training programs were growing, not diminishing, as the disappointing results began to come in. We were not in a position to back off, and, in fact, funding for such programs continued to grow for years. Neither, however, could we depend on such programs to solve the poverty problem.

The forces converged—not neatly, not at any one point that we can identify as the crucial shift. But the intellectual analysis of the nature of structural poverty had given a respectable rationale for accepting that it was not the fault of the poor that they were poor. It was a very small step from that premise to the conclusion that it is not the fault of the poor that they fail to pull themselves up when we offer them a helping hand. White moral confusion about the course of the civil rights movement in general and the riots in particular created powerful reasons to look for excuses. It was the system's fault. It was history's fault. Tom Wicker summed up the implications for policy toward the poor:

> Really compassionate and effective reforms to do something about poverty
> in America would have to recognize, first, that large numbers of the poor are
> always going to have to be helped. Whether for physical or mental reasons,
> because of environmental factors, or whatever, they cannot keep pace. . . .
> Thus the aim of getting everyone off welfare and into "participation in our
> affluent society" is unreal and a pipe dream. . . . [A] decent standard of living
> ought to be made available not just to an eligible few but to everyone, and
> without degrading restrictions and policelike investigations.

The column ran on the day before Christmas, 1967. It followed by only a few months an announcement from the White House. Joseph Califano, principal aide to Lyndon Johnson, had called reporters into his office to tell them that a government analysis had shown that only 50,000 persons, or *1 percent* of the 7,300,000 people on welfare, were capable of being given skills and training to make them self-sufficient. The repudiation of the dream—to end the dole once and for all—was complete.

✦

An Elite Wisdom

In speaking of the paradigm shift of the reform period, it is important to specify who did the shifting. The mid- and late-1960s did not see a revolution in American opinion. The analogy to the reform period in the sixties is not the New Deal, which enjoyed broad, often enthusiastic public support. Rather, the 1964-67 reform period reminded Daniel Patrick Moynihan of the English suffrage reform of 1867, "most especially in the degree to which neither was the result of any great popular agitation on behalf of the measures that were eventually adopted." For the blue-collar and white-collar electorate, not much changed. For them, the welfare cheats and loafers still loomed large, and sturdy self-reliance was still a chief virtue. For them, criminals ought to be locked up, students ought to shut up and do what the teacher says, demonstrators ought to go home and quit interrupting traffic.

The shift in assumptions occurred among a small group relative to the entire population, but one of enormous influence. The group is, with no perjorative connotations, best labeled the intelligentsia—a broad and diffuse group in late-twentieth-century America, but nonetheless identifiable in a rough fashion. It includes the upper echelons of (in no particular order of importance) academia, journalism, publishing, and the vast network of foundations, institutes, and research centers that has been woven into partnership with government during the last thirty years. An important and little-recognized part of the intelligentsia is also found in the civil service, in the key positions just below the presidential appointment level, where so much of the policy formation goes on. Politicians and members of the judiciary (Senator J. William Fulbright and Justice William O. Douglas are examples from the sixties) and bankers and businessmen and lawyers and doctors may be members of the intelligentsia as well, though not all are. I do not mean to provide a tightly constructed definition, but a sense of the population: people who deal professionally in ideas.

For purposes of understanding the nature of the shift in assumptions, the salient feature of the intelligentsia is not that it holds power—though many of its members occupy powerful positions—but that at any given moment it is the custodian of the received wisdom. It originates most of the ideas in the dialogue about policy, writes about them, publishes them, puts them on television and in the magazines and in memoranda for presidential assistants. Most of all, it confers respectability on ideas. I do not mean to trivialize the seriousness of the process, but it is akin to fashion. Ideas are "in" and ideas are "out," for reasons having something to do with their merit but also with being au courant. We may recall the fashionability of being thought "liberal" in the early sixties (and, for that matter, the unfashionability of being thought "a liberal" in the early eighties).

My thesis is that the last half of the 1960s saw remarkably broad agreement on the directions in which a just and effective social policy must move, and this agreement—this "elite wisdom"—represented an abrupt shift with the past.

The shift in assumptions first became apparent in 1964. By the end of 1967—probably earlier—the nature of the political dialogue had been altered unrecognizably. It was not just that by the end of 1967 certain types of legislation had more support than formerly, but the premises—the unconscious, "everybody-knows-that" premises—shifted in the minds of the people who were instrumental in making policy.

The New Premises

We may debate the list of new premises and their order of priority. Theodore White (among many others) describes the shift from "equality of opportunity" to "equality of outcome" as a fundamental change. The sponsors of the Civil Rights Act of 1964, with Hubert Humphrey in the lead, had come down adamantly on the side of equality of opportunity—the nation was to be made color-blind. The wording of the legislation itself expressly dissociated its provisions from preferential treatment. Yet only a year later, speaking at Howard University commencement exercises, Lyndon Johnson was proclaiming the "next and most profound stage of the battle for civil rights," namely, the battle "not just [for] equality as a right and theory but equality as a fact and equality as a result." A few months later, Executive Order 11246 required "affirmative action." By 1967, people who opposed preferential measures for minorities to overcome the legacy of discrimination were commonly seen as foot-draggers on civil rights if not closet racists.

A number of writers have pointed to a combination of two events: the ascendency of legal stipulations as the only guarantor of fair treatment and the contemporaneous Balkanization of the American population into discrete "minorities." Before 1964, blacks were unique. They constituted the only group suffering discrimination so pervasive and so persistent that laws *for that group* were broadly accepted as necessary. By 1967, blacks were just one of many minorities, each seeking equal protection as a group. Each assumed that express legislation and regulation spelling out its rights was—of course—the only way to secure fair treatment of the individual member of the group. For minorities such as juveniles and the mentally handicapped, the remedy was access to legal due process. Before 1964, it was assumed that their interests were best looked after by parents and relatives, with a limited role for the court. Even when the court did become involved, it was in a parental role. After 1967, it was assumed (by Supreme Court decision) that due process was the only adequate protection for anyone. For populations such as the elderly, women, and the physically handicapped, the change meant regulatory intervention. Why should they be less protected from discrimination than blacks?

Too many things were going on too fast during the 1960s for us to identify the nuclear change in the elite wisdom with certainty. But the new stances just described, though important in themselves, were enabled by a deeper change in the perception of how American society works. There was a reason why they made sense when only a few years earlier they had not. I suggest that this more primitive change was the one described in the last chapter: from a view of the American system as benign and self-correcting to the pervasive assumption that if something was wrong, the system was to blame. *Why* was it necessary to use the government to promote equality of outcome? Because, left alone, the system would perpetuate unacceptable inequality. *Why* was it necessary to spell out the prohibitions against any form of discrimination against any group and to buttress them with enforcing agencies? Because, left alone, the system would tolerate discriminatory behavior. Ultimately, the rationale for the sweeping changes in practice that occurred in the last half of the 1960s had to fall back upon a belief that the system as it existed prior to 1964 was deeply flawed and tended to perpetuate evils.

Joseph A. Califano, Jr.  **NO**

Lyndon Johnson Remembered: An Intimate Portrait of a Presidency

The Ship Sails On

"Somehow you never forget what poverty and hatred can do when you see its scars on the hopeful face of a young child." With those words President Lyndon Johnson recalled his year as a teacher of poor Mexican children in Cotulla, Texas, as he spoke to a joint session of Congress proposing the Voting Rights Act. It was the evening of March 15, 1965. He continued,

> I never thought then, in 1928, that I would be standing here in 1965. It never even occurred to me in my fondest dreams that I might have the chance to help the sons and daughters of those students and to help people like them all over this country. But now I do have that chance—and I'll let you in on a secret—I mean to use it. And I hope that you will use it with me.

We who shared that opportunity with Lyndon Johnson have vivid recollections of how he drove us to use every second of his presidency: the 5 A.M. calls waking us to ask about a front-page story in the *New York Times* that had not yet been delivered to our homes; the insatiable appetite for a program to cure every ill he saw, or to solve a problem that some Oval Office visitor or wire service story had just brought to his attention; the complaint that we weren't getting Senator Margaret Chase Smith or a conservative southern House Democrat like Eddie Herbert to vote with us to kill a motion to recommit; the demand for an explanation why the *Washington Post*, or Huntley, Brinkley, or Cronkite, didn't cast their lead stories the way he wanted; the insistence that hearings begin only one day after we sent a bill up to Congress; the pressure to get more seniors enrolled in Medicare, more blacks registered to vote, more schools desegregated, more kids signed up for Head Start, more Mexican-Americans taking college scholarships or loans—and more ugly billboards torn down, faster, for Lady Bird.

His perpetual hunt for simpler, more dramatic ways to explain new programs in shorter sentences led Harry McPherson and me, on one occasion, to write a mock message to Congress, composed completely of three-word sentences; it almost went to Capitol Hill by mistake. Perhaps most disconcerting were the notes from George Christian during a press briefing that conveyed a presidential order to contradict a comment I'd made just a few minutes

From *Lyndon Johnson Remembered,* by Joseph A. Califano, Jr. (2003), pp. 167–183. Copyright © 2003 by Rowman & Littlefield. Reprinted by permission.

before; or a presidential command to find some individual out of his past, whose name LBJ could only partially remember, and invite that person to a signing ceremony the next day. Up in heaven, LBJ is probably ordering members of his administration who have passed away to spend more time with deceased senators and representatives to muster support for some celestial program of his. And with every order came Johnson's signature admonition, "Do it now. Not next week. Not tomorrow. Not later this afternoon. Now."

We who served him knew that Lyndon Johnson could be brave and brutal, compassionate and cruel, incredibly intelligent and infuriatingly insensitive. We came to know his shrewd and uncanny instinct for the jugulars of both allies and adversaries. We learned that he could be altruistic and petty, caring and crude, generous and petulant, bluntly honest and calculatingly devious— all within the same few minutes. That his determination to succeed ran over or around whoever and whatever got in his way. That, as allies and enemies around him slumped in exhaustion, his prodigious energy produced second, third, and fourth winds to mount a social revolution and to control everyone and everything around him.

Well, all of that pent-up energy cajoling, driving, and, yes, inspiring each of us to do more than we thought possible did change life in America. In recent years, it is hailed as an accomplishment when a president persuades Congress to pass a few significant bills—even just one, like welfare reform—over an entire congressional session. In today's media world, the voracious quest for television sound bites—or the need to divert attention from scandal—prompts a president routinely to announce initiatives once considered appropriate only for subcabinet officials, mayors, and county commissioners; grants to a few dozen schools or police departments; or release of a new pamphlet issued by the Department of Health and Human Services.

What a contrast. In those tumultuous Great Society years, the president submitted and Congress enacted more than a hundred major proposals in each of the eighty-ninth and ninetieth Congresses! In those years of do-it-now optimism, presidential speeches were about redistributing wealth, overhauling our economic system, reshaping the balance between the consumer and big business, articulating the concept of affirmative action, rebuilding our cities, and eliminating poverty and hunger in our nation.

The complaint heard from Capitol Hill in those years was that the president was promoting too many big ideas at one time.

Well, he was. Why? Because Lyndon Johnson was a revolutionary. He refused to accept pockets of poverty in the richest nation in history. He saw a nation so hell bent on industrial growth and amassing wealth that greed threatened to destroy its natural resources. He saw cities deteriorating and municipal political machines unresponsive to the early migration of Hispanics and the masses of blacks moving north. He saw racial justice as a moral issue, not just a political one. To him government was neither a bad man to be tarred and feathered nor a bagman to collect campaign contributions, but an instrument to help the most vulnerable among us.

The measure of Lyndon Johnson's presidency is how he spent his popu- larity, not how he accumulated it. For LBJ, popularity—or more properly, his mandate—was something to be disbursed to help the weakest and neediest in our society, not to be husbanded for self-protection. High poll ratings were chips to be shoved into the political pot to pass laws ending segregation and opening voting booths and housing to African Americans and Hispanics.

He had the politician's hunger to be loved. But more than that, he had the courage to fall on his sword if that's what it took to move us closer to a society where "the meaning of our lives matches the marvelous products of our labor." He did just that when, in an extraordinary act of abnegation, he withdrew from the political arena to calm the roiling seas of strife and end the war in Vietnam.

In his view, "The Great Society [asked] not how much, but how good; not only how to create wealth, but how to use it; not only how fast we are going, but where we are headed."

His ambition knew no horizons. He wanted it all. He wanted to be the education president, the health president, the environmental president, the consumer president, the president who eliminated poverty, who gave to the poor the kind of education, health, and social support that most of us get from our parents.

Lyndon Johnson was as much an American revolutionary as George Washington and Thomas Jefferson. Just as their innovations irrevocably reshaped America, his changes set the federal government on a course that it continues to steer to this day despite the conservative, even reactionary, waves that have washed over its bow. Medicare sails on. Student loans and grants sail on. Consumer and environmental protection sails on. His ship—our ship—sails on.

In education, LBJ passed the Elementary and Secondary Education Act, which for the first time committed the federal government to help local school districts. His higher education legislation, with its scholarships, grants, and work-study programs, opened college to any American with the necessary brains and ambition, however thin daddy's wallet or empty mommy's purse. He anticipated the needs of Hispanics with bilingual education, which today serves a million children a year. Special-education legislation bearing his stamp brought help to millions of children with learning disabilities.

Thanks to those Great Society programs, since 1965 the federal government has provided more than 120 billion dollars for elementary and secondary schools; more than a quarter of a trillion dollars in eighty-six million college loans to twenty-nine million students; more than fourteen billion dollars in eighteen million work-study awards to six million students. Today nearly 60 percent of full-time undergraduate students receive federal financial aid under Great Society programs and their progeny. The ship sails on.

What are the fruits for our economy and our society? These programs ensure a steady supply of educated people who enable our industries to lead the world; they provide the human cornerstones for our economic prosperity.

When Lyndon Johnson took office, only 41 percent of Americans had completed high school; only 8 percent held college degrees. By 2000, more than 81 percent had finished high school and 24 percent had completed college. If Johnson's revolution had not established the federal government's responsibility to finance this educational surge, would we have had the trained human resources to be the world's greatest industrial power today? The leading power in computer and information technology? The leading military and communications power? These phenomenal achievements didn't just happen. He moved the fulcrum to offer the opportunity to every American—based on brains, not bucks—to develop his or her talents to the fullest.

And let's not forget Head Start. More than sixteen million preschoolers have been through Head Start programs in just about every city and county in the nation. Today this program serves eight hundred thousand children a year.

How many people remember the battles over Head Start? Conservatives opposed such early-childhood education as an attempt by government to interfere with parental control of their children. In the 1960s those were code words to conjure up images of the Soviet Union wrenching children from their homes to convert them to atheistic communism. But LBJ knew that the rich had kindergartens and nursery schools; why not, he asked, the same benefits for the poor?

And health care. In 1963, most elderly Americans had no health insurance. Few retirement plans provided any such coverage. The poor had little access to medical treatment until they were in critical condition. Only wealthier Americans could get the finest care, and then only by traveling to a few big cities, like Boston or New York.

Is revolution too strong a word? Since 1965, seventy-nine million Americans have signed up for Medicare. In 1966, nineteen million were enrolled; in 1998, thirty-nine million. Since 1966, Medicaid has served more than two hundred million needy Americans. In 1967, it served ten million poor citizens; in 1997, thirty-nine million. The 1968 heart, cancer, and stroke legislation has provided funds to create centers of medical excellence in just about every major city—from Seattle to Houston, Miami to Cleveland, New Orleans to St. Louis and Pittsburgh. To staff these centers, the 1965 Health Professions Educational Assistance Act provided resources to double the number of doctors graduating from medical schools, from eight thousand to sixteen thousand. That act also increased the pool of specialists and researchers, nurses, and paramedics. LBJ's commitment to fund basic medical research lifted the National Institutes of Health to unprecedented financial heights, seeding a harvest of medical miracles.

Closely related to LBJ's Great Society health programs were his programs to reduce malnutrition and hunger. Today, the Food Stamp program helps feed more than twenty million men, women, and children in more than eight million households. Since it was launched in 1967, the school breakfast program has provided daily breakfasts to nearly a hundred million schoolchildren.

The Great Society has played a pivotal role in the stunning recasting of America's demographic profile. When Johnson took office, life expectancy was 66.6 years for men and 73.1 years for women (69.7 years overall). In a single generation, by 1997, life expectancy jumped 10 percent: for men, to 73.6 years; for women, to 79.2 years (76.5 years overall). The jump was most dramatic among the less advantaged, suggesting that better nutrition and access to health care have played an even larger role than medical miracles. Infant mortality stood at twenty-six deaths for each thousand live births when Johnson took office; today it stands at only 7.3 deaths per thousand live births, a reduction of almost 75 percent. The ship sails on.

It is fair to ask the question, without his programs, would our nation be the world's leader in medical research? In pharmaceutical invention? In creation of surgical procedures and medical machinery to diagnose our diseases, breathe for us, clean our blood, and transplant our organs? Would so much have come about without the basic research fueled by Great Society investments in the National Institutes of Health and in the training of scientific specialists?

Those of us who worked with Lyndon Johnson would hardly characterize him as a patron of the arts. I remember him squirming restlessly, pulling on his ears and rubbing the back of his neck, as he sat at UN Ambassador Arthur Goldberg's Waldorf Towers apartment on the evening before he was scheduled to become the first American president to meet with a pope. Anna Moffo was singing opera—and with each encore I thought Johnson would crawl out of his suit.

Yet one historian—Irving Bernstein, in his book *Guns or Butter: The Presidency of Lyndon Johnson*—titles a chapter, "Lyndon Johnson, Patron of the Arts." Think about it. What would cultural life in America be like without the Kennedy Center for the Performing Arts, the programs of which entertain three million people each year and are televised to millions more; or without the Hirshhorn Museum and Sculpture Garden, which attracts more than seven hundred thousand visitors annually? Both are Great Society accomplishments.

The National Endowments for the Arts and Humanities are fulfilling a dream Johnson expressed when he asked Congress to establish them and have, for the first time, the federal government provide financial support for the arts: "To create conditions under which the arts can flourish; through recognition of achievements, through helping those who seek to enlarge creative understanding, through increasing the access of our people to the works of our artists, and through recognizing the arts as part of the pursuit of American greatness. That is the goal of this legislation."

Johnson used to say that he wanted fine theater and music available throughout the nation and not just on Broadway and at the Metropolitan Opera in New York. In awarding nearly four billion dollars in grants since 1965, the Endowment for the Arts has spawned art councils in all fifty states and more than 420 playhouses, 120 opera companies, four hundred dance companies, and 230 professional orchestras. Since 1965, the Endowment for the Humanities has awarded more than three billion dollars in fifty-six thousand fellowships and grants.

Johnson established the Corporation for Public Broadcasting to create public television and public radio, which have given the nation countless hours of fine arts, superb in-depth news coverage, and educational programs, like *Sesame Street*, that teach as they entertain generations of children. Public television, in fact, invented educational programming for preschool children. Now some say there is no need for public radio and television, with so many cable channels and radio stations. But when you surf with your TV remote or twist your radio dial, you are not likely to find the kind of quality broadcasting that marks the 350 public television and 699 public radio stations that the Corporation for Public Broadcasting supports today. The ship sails on.

Johnson's main contribution to the environment was not the passage of laws but the establishment of a principle that to this day guides the environmental movement. The old principle was simply to conserve resources that had not been touched. Lyndon Johnson was the first president to put forth a larger idea—that we must not only protect the pristine but undertake the additional responsibility of restoring what we had damaged or defiled in the name of development and industrialization. His words in 1965 set the ideological footing for today's environmental movement:

> The air we breathe, our water, our soil and wildlife, are being blighted by the poisons and chemicals which are the by-products of technology and industry? The same society which receives the rewards of technology, as a cooperating whole, take responsibility for control. To deal with these new problems will require a new conservation. We must not only protect the countryside and save it from destruction, we must restore what has been destroyed and salvage the beauty and charm of our cities. Our conservation must be not just the classic conservation of protection and development, but a creative conservation of restoration and innovation.

That new environmental commandment—that we have an obligation to restore as well as preserve, and that those who reap the rewards of modern technology must also pay the price of their industrial pollution—inspired a legion of Great Society laws: the Clear Air, Water Quality and Clean Water Restoration Acts and amendments, the 1965 Solid Waste Disposal Act, the 1965 Motor Vehicle Air Pollution Control Act, the 1968 Aircraft Noise Abatement Act. It also provided the rationale for later laws creating the Environmental Protection Agency and the Superfund.

Johnson wanted parks close enough for people to enjoy them. Of the thirty-five national parks that he pushed through Congress, thirty-two are within easy driving distance of large cities. The 1968 Wild and Scenic Rivers Act today protects 155 river segments in thirty-seven states. The 1968 National Trail System Act established more than eight hundred recreation, scenic, and historic trails covering forty thousand miles. No wonder *National Geographic* calls Johnson "our greatest conservation president."

Above all else, Johnson was consumed with creating racial justice and eliminating poverty. Much of the legislation I have mentioned was aimed at those two objectives. But he directly targeted these areas with laserlike intensity.

The social system LBJ faced as he took office featured segregated movie theaters and public accommodations; separate toilets and water fountains for blacks; restaurants and hotels restricted to whites only. Job discrimination was rampant. With the 1964 Civil Rights Act Johnson tore down, all at once, the "whites only" signs. That law ended segregated public accommodations. No longer would employers be able to discriminate against blacks. In 1968, one day after the assassination of Martin Luther King, Johnson sought, characteristically, to find some good even in tragedy. He pressed House speaker John McCormack to pass the Fair Housing Act, a bill LBJ had been pushing since 1966. In the wake of that assassination, Johnson finally got fair housing written into law.

But LBJ knew that laws were not enough. In one of his most moving speeches, the 1965 Howard University commencement address, entitled, "To

Fulfill These Rights" he said, "But freedom is not enough. You do not take a person who, for years, has been hobbled by chains and liberate him, bring him to the starting line of a race and then say, 'You are free to compete with all the others.' And still justly believe that you have been completely fair. . . . This is the next and the more profound stage of the battle for civil rights."

Thus was born the concept of affirmative action, Johnson's conviction that it is essential as a matter of social justice to provide the tutoring, the extra help, even the preference if necessary, to those who had suffered generations of discrimination in order to give them a fair chance to share in the American dream. Perhaps even more controversial today than when LBJ set it forth, affirmative action has provided opportunity to millions of blacks and has been a critical element of creating a substantial black middle class, an affluent black society, in a single generation.

That Howard University speech provided another insight that this nation unfortunately ignored. In a catalogue of the long suffering of blacks, Johnson included this passage:

> Perhaps most important—its influence radiating to every part of life—is the breakdown of the Negro family structure. It flows from centuries of oppression and persecution of the Negro man. . . . And when the family collapses it is the children that are usually damaged. When it happens on a massive scale the community itself is crippled. So, unless we work to strengthen the family, to create conditions under which most parents will stay together—all the rest, schools, and playgrounds, and public assistance, and private concern, will never be enough to cut completely the circle of despair and deprivation.

If only we had listened to that advice thirty-eight years ago. If only Congress had heeded his recommendation that welfare benefits no longer be conditioned on the man leaving the house. What grief we might have saved millions of children and our nation.

In civil rights, indeed in the entire treasury of Great Society measures, the jewel of which the president was proudest—and believed would have the greatest value—was the Voting Rights Act of 1965. That law opened the way for black Americans to strengthen their voices at every level of government. In 1964 there were seventy-nine black elected officials in the South and three hundred in the entire nation. By 1998, there were some nine thousand elected black officials across the nation, including six thousand in the South. In 1965 there were five black members of the House. In 2000 there were thirty-nine.

LBJ's contributions to racial equality were not only civic and political. In 1960, black life expectancy was 63.6 years, not even long enough to benefit from the Social Security taxes that black citizens paid during their working lives. By 1997, black life expectancy was 71.2 years, thanks almost entirely to Medicaid, community health centers, job training, Food Stamps, and other Great Society programs. In 1960, the infant mortality rate for blacks was 44.3 for each thousand live births; in 1997, that rate had plummeted by two-thirds, to 14.7. In 1960, only 20 percent of blacks completed high school and only

3 percent college; in 1997, 75 percent completed high school and more than 13 percent earned college degrees. The ship sails on.

Most of the laws I have noted were part of LBJ's War on Poverty. He used every tool at his disposal to wage this war, the war on which he had set his heart. Though he found the opposition too strong to pass an income-maintenance law, he took advantage of the biggest automatic cash machine available—Social Security. He proposed, and Congress enacted, whopping increases in the minimum benefits that lifted 2.5 million Americans sixty-five and over above the poverty line, in "the greatest stride forward since Social Security was launched in 1935." In 1996, Social Security lifted twelve million senior citizens above the poverty line. The ship sails on.

The combination of that Social Security increase, Medicare, and the coverage of nursing home care under Medicaid (which funds care for 68 percent of nursing home residents) has had a defining impact on American families. Millions of middle-aged Americans, freed from the burden of providing medical and nursing home care for their elderly parents, suddenly were able to buy homes and (often with an assist from Great Society higher education programs) send their children to college. This salutary and pervasive impact has led many scholars to cite Medicare and Social Security as the most significant social programs of the twentieth century.

Johnson's relationship with his pet project—the Office of Economic Opportunity—was that of a proud father often irritated by an obstreperous child. For years conservatives have raged about the OEO programs. Yet Johnson's War on Poverty was founded on the most conservative of principles—put the power in the local community, not in Washington; give people at the grass-roots the ability to stand on their own two feet, and to stand tall, off the federal welfare dole.

Conservative claims to have killed the OEO poverty programs are preposterous—as fanciful as Ronald Reagan's quip that Lyndon Johnson declared war on poverty and poverty won. As of the year 2000, eleven of the twelve programs that OEO launched are alive, well, and funded at an annual rate exceeding ten billion dollars. They have grown by almost 1,000 percent since their inception in 1965. Head Start, Job Corps, Community Health Centers, Foster Grandparents, Upward Bound (now part of the Trio Program in the Department of Education), Green Thumb (now Senior Community Service Employment), Indian Opportunities (now in the Labor Department), and Migrant Opportunities (now Seasonal Worker Training and Migrant Education) were all designed to do what they have been doing—empowering individuals to stand tall on their own two feet.

Community Action, VISTA Volunteers, and Legal Services were designed to put power in the hands of individuals—down at the grassroots. The grassroots that these programs fertilize don't produce just the manicured laws that conservatives prefer. Of all the Great Society programs started in the Office of Economic Opportunity, only the Neighborhood Youth Corps has been abandoned—in 1974, after enrolling more than five million individuals. Despite the political rhetoric, every president has urged Congress to fund these OEO programs or approved substantial appropriations for them. The ship sails on.

When LBJ took office, 22.2 percent of Americans were living in poverty. When he left, only 13 percent were living below the poverty line. By the year 2000, the poverty level stood at 13.3 percent, still disgraceful in the context of what was the greatest economic boom in our history. But what if the Great Society had not achieved that dramatic reduction in poverty? What if the nation had not maintained that reduction? There would today be twenty-four million more Americans living below the poverty level.

Johnson confronted two monumental shifts in America: the urbanization of the population and the nationalization of commercial power.

For urban America, he drove through Congress the Urban Mass Transit Act. Among other things, that law gave San Franciscans BART, Washingtonians the Metro, Atlantans MARTA, and cities across America thousands of buses and modernized transit systems. His 1968 Housing Act has provided housing for more than seven million families. He created Ginnie Mae, which has added more than a million dollars to the supply of affordable mortgage funds. He privatized Fannie Mae, which has helped more than thirty million families purchase homes. He established the Department of Housing and Urban Development, naming the first black cabinet member to be its secretary. And he put financial muscle in the National Trust for Historic Preservation to preserve historic, including urban, treasures.

Johnson also faced the rise of the national grocery and retail chains and enormous corporate enterprises—a nationalization of commercial power that had the potential to disadvantage the individual American consumer. As he took office, superstores and super-corporations were rapidly shoving aside the corner grocer, local banker, and independent drug store. Automobiles were complex and dangerous, manufactured by giant corporations with deep pockets to protect themselves. Banks had the most sophisticated accountants and lawyers to draft their loan agreements. Sellers of everyday products—soaps, produce, meats, appliances, clothing, cereals, and canned and frozen foods—packaged their products with the help of the shrewdest marketers and designers. The individual was outflanked at every position.

Sensing that mismatch, Johnson pushed through Congress a bevy of laws to level the playing field for consumers: auto and highway safety legislation for the car buyer and motorist; truth in packaging for the housewife; truth in lending for the home buyer, small businessman, and individual borrower; meat and wholesome poultry laws to enhance food safety. He created the Product Safety Commission to ensure that toys and other products would be safe for users; he had passed the Flammable Fabrics Act to reduce the incendiary characteristics of clothing and blankets. To keep kids out of the medicine bottle he proposed the Child Safety Act.

The revolution in transportation and its importance to the nation led to Johnson's decision to ram through Congress the Department of Transportation and the National Transportation Safety Board, combining more than thirty independent agencies to help rationalize the nation's transportation system.

By the numbers, the legacy of Lyndon Johnson is monumental. It exceeds in domestic impact even the New Deal of his idol, Franklin Roosevelt. But I believe that LBJ's legacy is far more profound and lasting. He recognized that laws and programs were written not in stone but on a blackboard of history that can be changed or erased. LBJ's most enduring legacy is not in the numbers and the statistics of programs but in the fundamental tenets of public responsibility that he espoused. Those tenets influence and shape the nation's public policy and political dialogue to this day.

Until the New Deal, the federal government had been regarded as a regulatory power, protecting the public health and safety with the Food and Drug Administration, and enforcing antitrust and commercial fraud laws to rein in concentrations of economic power. With the creation of the Securities and Exchange and Interstate Commerce Commissions and the other "alphabet" agencies, FDR took the government into deeper regulatory waters. He also put the feds into the business of cash handouts to the needy: welfare payments, railroad retirement, and Social Security.

Johnson converted the federal government into a far more energetic, proactive force for social justice—striking down discriminatory practices, offering a hand up with education, health care, and job training. These functions had formerly been the preserves of private charities and the states. Before the Johnson administration, for example, the federal government was not training a single worker. He vested the federal government with responsibility to soften the sharp elbows of capitalism and give it a human, beating heart; to redistribute opportunity as well as wealth. In education, Johnson postulated a new right—the right of all individuals to all the education they needed to develop their talents, regardless of their economic circumstances.

He had a penetrating prescience. He saw the frightful implications of savaging "the Negro family"; He called "the welfare system in America outmoded and in need of a major change" and pressed Congress to create "a work incentive program, incentives for earning, day care for children, child and maternal health and family planning services."

He saw the threat posed by the spread of guns and proposed, in 1968, national registration of all guns and national licensing of all gun owners. Congress rejected his proposals. But he did convince Capitol Hill to close the loophole of mail-order guns, prohibit sales to minors, and end the import of "Saturday-night specials."

He spotted the "for sale" signs of political corruption going up in the nation's capital. Accordingly, he proposed public financing of presidential campaigns, full disclosure of contributions and expenses by all federal candidates, limits on the amount of contributions, and closure of lobbying loopholes. In 1967, he warned of the problems that plague our political life today:

> More and more, men and women of limited means may refrain from running for public office. Private wealth increasingly becomes an artificial and unrealistic arbiter of qualifications, and the source of public leadership is thus severely narrowed. The necessity of acquiring substantial funds to finance campaigns diverts a candidate's attention from his public obligations and detracts from his energetic exposition of the issues.

To me, Johnson's greatest quality was one not often mentioned as an LBJ trait—his courage. His means were often Machiavellian, but he was a true believer. He believed, and he fought for what he believed in, no matter how it hurt him politically. He fought for racial equality even when it hurt him and clobbered his party in the South. He fought to end poverty, even when it hurt him and subjected him to ridicule. And yes, he fought the war in Vietnam—and that hurt.

He was wiling to fall upon his sword for what he thought was right. He viewed his soaring popularity, in the wake of his landslide against Barry Goldwater, not as something to be hoarded but as something to be poured out on behalf of those who didn't have shoes to pound the pavements of power. Lyndon Johnson didn't talk the talk of legacy; he walked the walk. He lived the life. He didn't have much of a profile—but he did have courage.

Why then does current history, along with Democratic politicians, so ignore him? Why did Bill Clinton, presidential candidate, come to the LBJ Library during the 1992 campaign and never speak the name of Lyndon Johnson? Why do Democratic House and Senate leaders rarely invoke his name even as they battle to preserve and build on his legacy?

The answers lie in their fear of being called "Liberal," and in the Vietnam War.

In contemporary America, politicians want to be called anything but liberal; they are paralyzed by fear of the liberal label that comes with the heritage of Lyndon Johnson. Democrats rest their hopes on promises to preserve and expand Great Society programs like Medicare and aid to education, but they tremble at the thought of linking those programs to the liberal Lyndon. The irony is that they seek to distance themselves from the president who once said that the difference between liberals and cannibals is that cannibals eat only their enemies.

Democratic officeholders also assign Johnson the role of "stealth president," because of the Vietnam War. Most contemporary observers put the war down as a monumental blunder. Only a handful—most of them Republicans—defend Vietnam as part of a half-century bipartisan commitment to contain communism with American blood and money. Seen in that context, Vietnam was a tragic losing battle in a long, winning war—a war that began with Truman's ordeal in Korea, the Marshall Plan, and the 1948 Berlin airlift, and ended with the collapse of communism at the end of the Reagan administration.

Let everyone think what they will about Vietnam—and let the politicians shrink from the liberal label. But let us all recognize the reality of this revolutionary's remarkable achievements. When Lyndon Johnson surveyed history, he observed that World War II had killed Roosevelt's New Deal and that the Korean War killed Harry Truman's Fair Deal. The Vietnam War slowed Johnson's domestic crusade—but it did not kill it.

Indeed, the tension that marked Johnson's presidency arose from his refusal to let Vietnam destroy his Great Society. His concentration on domestic progress amid the incredible sound and fury of those years was phenomenal. His determination was fierce, and it was articulated most powerfully in his 1966 State of the Union message:

> We will continue to meet the needs of our people by continuing to develop
> the Great Society. . . . There are men who cry out: We must sacrifice. Well,

let us rather ask them: Who will they sacrifice? Are they going to sacrifice the children who seek the learning, or the sick who need medical care, or the families who dwell in squalor now brightened by the hope of a home? Will they sacrifice opportunity for the distressed, the beauty of our land, the hope of our poor? . . . I believe that we can continue the Great Society while we fight in Vietnam. But if there are some who do not believe this, then, in the name of justice, let them call for the contribution of those who live in the fullness of our blessing, rather than try to strip it from the hands of those that are most in need.

Johnson's critics derided this as a profligate call for "guns and butter." But it was vintage LBJ—and it too reflected his unquenchable courage and determination.

The sharpest attacks on LBJ's Vietnam policies came from George McGovern, the South Dakota senator and antiwar Democratic presidential candidate in 1972. In 1999, McGovern placed Johnson alongside Woodrow Wilson and Franklin Roosevelt as one of the greatest presidents since Abraham Lincoln. "Johnson did more than any other president to advance civil rights, education, and housing, to name just three of his concerns," McGovern wrote. Citing Johnson's opposition, when he was majority leader, to any U.S. involvement in Vietnam, McGovern concluded; "If it had been up to Lyndon Johnson we would have not gone to Vietnam in the first place. It would be a historic tragedy if his outstanding domestic record remained forever obscured by his involvement in a war he did not begin and did not know how to stop."

As the century ended, another critic of LBJ on the Vietnam War, John Kenneth Galbraith—Harvard University economist, ambassador to India, and liberal activist—placed Lyndon Johnson "next only to Franklin D. Roosevelt as a force for a civilized and civilizing social policy essential for human well-being and for peaceful co-existence between the economically favored (or financially fortunate) and the poor. . . . Next only to Roosevelt, and in some respects more so, Lyndon Johnson was the most effective advocate of humane social change in the United States in this century."

At his best, Lyndon Johnson put the thumb of government forcefully on the scale for the vulnerable among us. He hauled and dragooned talented people into public service, a calling he considered the highest an individual could have. At the risk of nagging, he reminded the American people that God and history would judge us not just on how much our gross national product grew but on how we spent it; not simply on how many millionaires a booming economy produced but on how many millions of people it lifted out of poverty.

In the last speech of his life, when his civil rights papers were opened to the public, Lyndon Johnson had this to say: "Well, this cry of 'Never' I've heard since I was a little boy, all my life. And what we commemorate this great day is some of the work which has helped to make 'never' now."

Through it all—the war, the hurt, the sometimes devious and crude behavior, the haunting ghosts of the Kennedys, the ambition for his country and himself, during what LBJ called "the most serious" times "confronted by the nation in the course of my lifetime"—he never lost his concentration on trying "to make 'never' now." He left us plenty of achievements to build on—achievements that in my judgment far out-weigh the mistakes he left us.

It is time now for his heirs to recognize—and, yes, for history to recognize—that no president ever cared more, tried harder, or helped more needy Americans.

The waves of his critics may crash against the bow of his efforts and his record. But the record is there. The ship—his ship, our ship—sails on.

POSTSCRIPT

Did the Great Society Fail?

Charles Murray's *Losing Ground* became required reading for the domestic policy makers of the Reagan administration in the early 1980s. In this selection, the author documents the view of the Kennedy/Johnson domestic advisers, who believed that by juggling tax and interest rates under an economic management program known as Keynesian economics, the country would avoid major recessions and depression. Influenced by books such as Michael Harrington's *The Other America: Poverty in the United States* (Macmillan, 1962) and Edward R. Murrow's televised documentary, *Harvest of Shame* about the plight of the migrant worker, the "poverty warriors" of the Kennedy/Johnson administration decided to attack structural roots of poverty and elevate the bottom fifth of the population into the middle class.

President Johnson had a gut level understanding of poverty. While not poor himself, he grew up in the hill country of Texas, served as a congressional aide and member of Congress during the 1930s, ran a government retraining programming in Texas, and was a devoted supporter of FDR's New Deal. As president, Johnson believed that he was completing FDR's New Deal by eliminating segregation and discrimination against American's poorest minorities.

Murray argues that the community action and retraining programs did not work because the administration tried to attack structural poverty by shifting the responsibility of poverty onto society instead of onto the individual. Even the Johnson administration's own statistics, he argued, demonstrated the failure on very limited success of the programs.

Murray's book was written in the 1980s when the American votes had shifted from center-left to center-right. The intellectual attack on poverty on the early 1960s was short lived. The urban riots of 1965–1968 and the escalation of the war in Vietnam led to a backlash against soft cures for the poverty of the ghetto.

Murray himself was supported by think tanks such as the Manhattan Institute, the Hoover Institute, the Heritage Foundation, the CATO Institute, and most importantly the American Enterprise Institute (AEI), which titled the debate about managing the economy away from Keynesian into a less governmental free-market orientation. In another controversial book written in 1994 with Richard J. Herrnstein, *The Bell Curve: Intellectual and Class Structure in American Life* (Free Press), Murray challenged the intellectual capacity of certain minority groups to compete in American society. While *The Bell Curve* came in for some severe criticism; it demonstrated how far right the debate about poverty had shifted. Murray himself tried to defuse the racial attacks with his lengthy article "The Coming White Underclass" (*The Wall Street Journal*, October 29, 1993).

As a special assistant for Domestic Affairs from 1965 through early 1969, Joseph Califano got to view LBJ and the Great Society programs from the inside of the White House. The president, says Califano, worked his aides seven days a week, 24 hours a day. He possessed a manic personality displaying fits of anger and deviousness, warmth and generosity, all within a matter of minutes. A true believer, LBJ would often use "Machiavellian" means to pass his legislation.

Califano sees Johnson as a revolutionary and a liberal, a word that all politicians including Democrats shy away from today. The 100-plus pieces of legislation that the president named through the eighty-ninth and ninetieth sessions of Congress represented an attempt to complete the social and economic change started but left unfinished by FDR's New Deal. The war on poverty included passage of the Civil Rights Act of 1964 and 1965, which outlawed discrimination in public places against African Americans and secured their voting rights. The passage of Medicare, the coverage of nursing home care under Medicaid, and the increases in Social Security payments were of great benefit to American families. Passage of the Elementary and Secondary Education Act and the student loan programs for college students dramatically increased the number of students graduating from high school and college.

Johnson was also the most important environmental president since Theodore Roosevelt. His administration created the Environmental Protection Agency (EPA), passed a number of antipollution laws, and created 35 national parks, mostly within easy driving distance of large cities. His wife Lady Bird Johnson was also instrumental in cleaning up the nation's highways and landscapes.

Unlike Professor Murray, who concentrates on the failures to cure the problems of welfare dependency and anticity crime, Califano takes a macroeconomic look at the success of the war on poverty. The statistics reflect major changes in American society. When Johnson took office in 1964, 41 percent of Americans graduated from high school, and only 8 percent graduated from college. By 2000, more than 81 percent completed high school and 24 percent finished college.

Demographic changes reflected the positive effects of the war on poverty. Better nutrition and health care increased life expectancies for men and women, African Americans as well as whites. "When Johnson took office," says Califano, "life expectancy was 66.6 years for men and 73.1 for women (69.7 years overall). In a single generation, by 1997, life expectancy jumped 10 percent: for men, to 73.6 years; for women, to 79.2 years (76.5 years overall)."

Califano's analysis can be faulted in several grounds. Most of the programs of the Great Society benefited the middle class. These include clean air, highway beautification, federal subsidies for the arts, and affirmative action programs for minorities. Even Social Security and Medicare became supplements to the retirement and health care benefits of a more affluent middle class.

Califano makes a good case for the substantial reduction of the number of people below the poverty level. He even admits that 13 percent is a disgrace for such a wealthy nation. But several problems remain that Califano does not discuss in this essay. First of all are the costs for an aging population with a higher standard of living. Can the nation afford the medical costs to take care of its elderly? Will choices have to be made to determine who lives and who dies? Secondly, there was always a problem with the implementation of so many programs being passed so quickly. Was Murray correct in arguing that the community action and retraining programs didn't work? Does the free market provide better job opportunities than government programs or even governmental regulation of the economy? (See Issue 14 on what happened to the economy in the 1980s.) Thirdly, Califano does not effectively answer the guns and butter argument. His defense of Vietnam as part of the foreign policy of containment from Truman through Reagan is weak. Nor does Califano deal with the conservative backlash after 1966 as a result of the urban riots in northern cities and the emergence of conservative politicians such Ronald Reagan, who was elected governor of California in 1966.

Johnson believed that he would never get a favorable or fair evaluation from historians. But he was wrong. Califano wrote an informal, humorous yet revealing insider's account of *The Triumph and Tragedy of Lyndon Johnson: The White House Years* (Simon and Schuster, 1991), where he argues that Johnson wanted to have guns and butter simultaneously as he escalated the wars in Vietnam and on poverty at home. His *Inside: A Public and Private Life* (Perseus Books, 2004) takes us through his years as a Washington power broker, lawyer, and Secretary of Health, Education and Welfare fired by President Jimmy Carter.

The two most recent bibliographies on the Johnson years are found in the introductory essays in Thomas W. Cowger et al., *Lyndon Johnson Remembered: An Intimate Portrait of a President* (Rowman & Littlefield, 2003) and Sidney M. Milkis et al., *The Great Society and the High Tide of Liberalism* (University of Amherst Press, 2005). All the essays in these books deserve to be read. Critically from the left is Allen J. Matusow's *The Unraveling of America: A History of Liberalism in the 1960s* (Perennial, 1985). John A. Andrews III has written a student-friendly work on *Lyndon Johnson and the Great Society* (Ivan R. Dee, 1998), which examines programs that failed (e.g., the housing initiative) and those that succeeded (e.g., beautification projects, consumer rights and—some may question—crime control laws).

Johnson's two most recent biographers, Robert Dalleck and Randall Woods, are much more sympathetic—even when critical—than Robert Caro's magisterial, overwritten, overly critical and probably-never-to-be-completed multivolume portrait. See Roner Dallek, *One Star Rising: Lyndon Johnson and His Times, 1908–1960* (Oxford, 1991), *Flawed Giant: Lyndon Johnson and His Time, 1961–1973* (Oxford, 1998), Randal B. Woods, *LBJ: Architect of American Ambition* (Free Press, 2006), Robert Caro, *The Years of Lyndon Johnson: The Path to Power* (Knopf, 1982), and *The Year of Lyndon Johnson: Means of Assent* (Knopf, 2002).

Publication of some of Johnson's White House tapes provided an incredible glimpse into his personality and management style. See the two volumes edited with commentary by Michael R. Beschlorss, *Taking Charge: The Johnson White House Tapes, 1963–1964* (Simon and Schuster, 1997) and

Reaching for Glory: Lyndon Johnson's Secret White House Tapes, 1964–1965 (Simon & Schuster, 2001).

Ted Koppel did a 21-minute nighttime show that plays portions of *The LBJ Tapes* (Films for the Humanities, 1991), which is the correct length for classroom use. The three-part American Experience Biography of LBJ (WGBH, Boston, 1991) is superb.

ISSUE 10

Was the Americanization of the War in Vietnam Inevitable?

YES: Brian VanDeMark, from *Into the Quagmire: Lyndon Johnson and the Escalation of the Vietnam War* (Oxford University Press, 1991)

NO: H. R. McMaster, from *Dereliction of Duty: Lyndon Johnson, Robert McNamara, the Joint Chiefs of Staff, and the Lies That Led to Vietnam* (HarperCollins, 1997)

ISSUE SUMMARY

YES: Professor of history Brian VanDeMark argues that President Lyndon Johnson failed to question the viability of increasing U.S. involvement in the Vietnam War because he was a prisoner of America's global containment policy and because he did not want his opponents to accuse him of being soft on communism or endanger support for his Great Society reforms.

NO: H. R. McMaster, an active-duty army tanker, maintains that the Vietnam disaster was not inevitable but a uniquely human failure whose responsibility was shared by President Johnson and his principal military and civilian advisers.

$\mathbf{A}$t the end of World War II, imperialism was coming to a close in Asia. Japan's defeat spelled the end of its control over China, Korea, and the countries of Southeast Asia. Attempts by the European nations to reestablish their empires were doomed. Anti-imperialist movements emerged all over Asia and Africa, often producing chaos.

The United States faced a dilemma. America was a nation conceived in revolution and was sympathetic to the struggles of Third World nations. But the United States was afraid that many of the revolutionary leaders were Communists who would place their countries under the control of the expanding empire of the Soviet Union. By the late 1940s the Truman administration decided that it was necessary to stop the spread of communism. The policy that resulted was known as *containment.*

Vietnam provided a test of the containment doctrine in Asia. Vietnam had been a French protectorate from 1885 until Japan took control of it during

255

World War II. Shortly before the war ended, the Japanese gave Vietnam its independence, but the French were determined to reestablish their influence in the area. Conflicts emerged between the French-led nationalist forces of South Vietnam and the Communist-dominated provisional government of the Democratic Republic of Vietnam (DRV), which was established in Hanoi in August 1945. Ho Chi Minh was the president of the DRV. An avowed Communist since the 1920s, Ho had also become the major nationalist figure in Vietnam. As the leader of the anti-imperialist movement against French and Japanese colonialism for over 30 years, Ho managed to tie together the communist and nationalist movements in Vietnam.

A full-scale war broke out in 1946 between the communist government of North Vietnam and the French-dominated country of South Vietnam. After the Communists defeated the French at the battle of Dien Bien Phu in May 1954, the latter decided to pull out. At the Geneva Conference that summer, Vietnam was divided at the 17th parallel, pending elections.

The United States became directly involved in Vietnam after the French withdrew. In 1955 the Republican president Dwight D. Eisenhower refused to recognize the Geneva Accord but supported the establishment of the South Vietnamese government. In 1956 South Vietnam's leader, Ngo Dinh Diem, with U.S. approval, refused to hold elections, which would have provided a unified government for Vietnam in accordance with the Geneva Agreement. The Communists in the north responded by again taking up the armed struggle. The war continued for another 19 years.

Both President Eisenhower and his successor, John F. Kennedy, were anxious to prevent South Vietnam from being taken over by the Communists, so economic assistance and military aid were provided. Kennedy's successor, Lyndon Johnson, changed the character of American policy in Vietnam by escalating the air war and increasing the number of ground forces from 21,000 in 1965 to a full fighting force of 550,000 at its peak in 1968.

The next president, Richard Nixon, adopted a new policy of "Vietnamization" of the war. Military aid to South Vietnam was increased to ensure the defeat of the Communists. At the same time, American troops were gradually withdrawn from Vietnam. South Vietnamese president Thieu recognized the weakness of his own position without the support of U.S. troops. He reluctantly signed the Paris Accords in January 1973 only after being told by Secretary of State Henry Kissinger that the United States would sign them alone. Once U.S. soldiers were withdrawn, Thieu's regime was doomed. In spring 1975 a full-scale war broke out, and the South Vietnamese government collapsed.

In the following selection, Brian VanDeMark argues that President Johnson failed to question the viability of increasing U.S. involvement in Vietnam because he was a prisoner of America's global containment policy and because he did not want his opponents to accuse him of being soft on communism. In the second selection, H. R. McMaster argues that the Vietnam disaster was not inevitable but a uniquely human failure whose responsibility was shared by Johnson and his civilian and military advisers.

YES

Brian VanDeMark

Into the Quagmire

Vietnam divided America more deeply and painfully than any event since the Civil War. It split political leaders and ordinary people alike in profound and lasting ways. Whatever the conflicting judgments about this controversial war—and there are many—Vietnam undeniably stands as the greatest tragedy of twentieth-century U.S. foreign relations.

America's involvement in Vietnam has, as a result, attracted much critical scrutiny, frequently addressed to the question, "Who was guilty?"—"Who led the United States into this tragedy?" A more enlightening question, it seems, is "How and why did this tragedy occur?" The study of Vietnam should be a search for explanation and understanding, rather than for scapegoats.

Focusing on one important period in this long and complicated story—the brief but critical months from November 1964 to July 1965, when America crossed the threshold from limited to large-scale war in Vietnam—helps to answer that question. For the crucial decisions of this period resulted from the interplay of longstanding ideological attitudes, diplomatic assumptions and political pressures with decisive contemporaneous events in America and Vietnam.

Victory in World War II produced a sea change in America's perception of its role in world affairs. Political leaders of both parties embraced a sweepingly new vision of the United States as the defender against the perceived threat of monolithic communist expansion everywhere in the world. This vision of American power and purpose, shaped at the start of the Cold War, grew increasingly rigid over the years. By 1964–1965, it had become an iron-bound and unshakable dogma, a received faith which policymakers unquestionably accepted—even though the circumstances which had fostered its creation had changed dramatically amid diffused authority and power among communist states and nationalist upheaval in the colonial world.

Policymakers' blind devotion to this static Cold War vision led America into misfortune in Vietnam. Lacking the critical perspective and sensibility to reappraise basic tenets of U.S. foreign policy in the light of changed events and local circumstances, policymakers failed to perceive Vietnamese realities accurately and thus to gauge American interests in the area prudently. Policymakers, as a consequence, misread an indigenous, communist-led nationalist movement as part of a larger, centrally directed challenge to world order and stability; tied American fortunes to a non-communist regime of slim popular legitimacy and effectiveness; and intervened militarily in the region far out of proportion to U.S. security requirements.

An arrogant and stubborn faith in America's power to shape the course of foreign events compounded the dangers sown by ideological rigidity. Policymakers in 1964–1965 shared a common postwar conviction that the United States not only should, but could, control political conditions in South Vietnam, as elsewhere throughout much of the world. This conviction had led Washington to intervene progressively deeper in South Vietnamese affairs over the years. And when—despite Washington's increasing exertions—Saigon's political situation declined precipitously during 1964–1965, this conviction prompted policymakers to escalate the war against Hanoi, in the belief that America could stimulate political order in South Vietnam through the application of military force against North Vietnam.

Domestic political pressures exerted an equally powerful, if less obvious, influence over the course of U.S. involvement in Vietnam. The fall of China in 1949 and the ugly McCarthyism it aroused embittered American foreign policy for a generation. By crippling President Truman's political fortunes, it taught his Democratic successors, John Kennedy and Lyndon Johnson [LBJ], a strong and sobering lesson: that another "loss" to communism in East Asia risked renewed and devastating attacks from the right. This fear of reawakened McCarthyism remained a paramount concern as policymakers pondered what course to follow as conditions in South Vietnam deteriorated rapidly in 1964–1965.

～◦◉◦～

Enduring traditions of ideological rigidity, diplomatic arrogance, and political vulnerability heavily influenced the way policymakers approached decisions in Vietnam in 1964–1965. Understanding the decisions of this period fully, however, also requires close attention to contemporary developments in America and South Vietnam. These years marked a tumultuous time in both countries, which affected the course of events in subtle but significant ways.

Policymakers in 1964–1965 lived in a period of extraordinary domestic political upheaval sparked by the civil rights movement. It is difficult to overstate the impact of this upheaval on American politics in the mid-1960s. During 1964–1965, the United States—particularly the American South—experienced profound and long overdue change in the economic, political, and social rights of blacks. This change, consciously embraced by the liberal administration of Lyndon Johnson, engendered sharp political hostility among conservative southern whites and their deputies in Congress—hostility which the politically astute Johnson sensed could spill over into the realm of foreign affairs, where angry civil rights opponents could exact their revenge should LBJ stumble and "lose" a crumbling South Vietnam. This danger, reinforced by the memory of McCarthyism, stirred deep political fears in Johnson, together with an abiding aversion to failure in Vietnam.

LBJ feared defeat in South Vietnam, but he craved success and glory at home. A forceful, driving President of boundless ambition, Johnson sought to harness the political momentum created by the civil rights movement to enact a far-reaching domestic reform agenda under the rubric of the Great Society. LBJ would achieve the greatness he sought by leading America toward justice and opportunity for all its citizens, through his historic legislative program.

Johnson's domestic aspirations fundamentally conflicted with his uneasy involvement in Vietnam. An experienced and perceptive politician, LBJ knew his domestic reforms required the sustained focus and cooperation of Congress. He also knew a larger war in Vietnam jeopardized these reforms by drawing away political attention and economic resources. America's increasing military intervention in 1964–1965 cast this tension between Vietnam and the Great Society into sharp relief.

Johnson saw his predicament clearly. But he failed to resolve it for fear that acknowledging the growing extent and cost of the war would thwart his domestic reforms, while pursuing a course of withdrawal risked political ruin. LBJ, instead, chose to obscure the magnitude of his dilemma by obscuring America's deepening involvement as South Vietnam began to fail. That grave compromise of candor opened the way to Johnson's eventual downfall.

Events in South Vietnam during 1964–1965 proved equally fateful. A historically weak and divided land, South Vietnam's deeply rooted ethnic, political, and religious turmoil intensified sharply in the winter of 1964–1965. This mounting turmoil, combined with increased communist military attacks, pushed Saigon to the brink of political collapse.

South Vietnam's accelerating crisis alarmed American policymakers, driving them to deepen U.S. involvement considerably in an effort to arrest Saigon's political failure. Abandoning the concept of stability in the South *before* escalation against the North, policymakers now embraced the concept of stability *through* escalation, in the desperate hope that military action against Hanoi would prompt a stubbornly elusive political order in Saigon.

This shift triggered swift and ominous consequences scarcely anticipated by its architects. Policymakers soon confronted intense military, political, and bureaucratic pressures to widen the war. Unsettled by these largely unforeseen pressures, policymakers reacted confusedly and defensively. Rational men, they struggled to control increasingly irrational forces. But their reaction only clouded their attention to basic assumptions and ultimate costs as the war rapidly spun out of control in the spring and summer of 1965. In their desperation to make Vietnam policy work amid this rising tide of war pressures, they thus failed ever to question whether it could work—or at what ultimate price. Their failure recalls the warning of a prescient political scientist, who years before had cautioned against those policymakers with "an infinite capacity for making ends of [their] means."

The decisions of 1964–1965 bespeak a larger and deeper failure as well. Throughout this period—as, indeed, throughout the course of America's Vietnam involvement—U.S. policymakers strove principally to create a viable noncommunist regime in South Vietnam. For many years and at great effort and cost, Washington had endeavored to achieve political stability and competence in Saigon. Despite these efforts, South Vietnam's political disarray persisted and deepened, until, in 1965, America intervened with massive military force to avert its total collapse.

Few policymakers in 1964–1965 paused to mull this telling fact, to ponder its implications about Saigon's viability as a political entity. The failure to reexamine this and other fundamental premises of U.S. policy—chief among them Vietnam's importance to American national interests and Washington's ability to forge political order through military power—proved a costly and tragic lapse of statesmanship. . . .

⋖❀⋗

The legacy of Vietnam, like the war itself, remains a difficult and painful subject for Americans. As passions subside and time bestows greater perspective, Americans still struggle to understand Vietnam's meaning and lessons for the country. They still wonder how the United States found itself ensnared in an ambiguous, costly, and divisive war, and how it can avoid repeating such an ordeal in the future.

The experience of Lyndon Johnson and his advisers during the decisive years 1964–1965 offers much insight into those questions. For their decisions, which fundamentally transformed U.S. participation in the war, both reflected and defined much of the larger history of America's Vietnam involvement.

Their decisions may also, one hopes, yield kernels of wisdom for the future; the past, after all, can teach us lessons. But history's lessons, as Vietnam showed, are themselves dependent on each generation's knowledge and under-standing of the past. So it proved for 1960s policymakers, whose ignorance and misperception of Southeast Asian history, culture, and politics pulled America progressively deeper into the war. LBJ, [Secretary of State Dean] Rusk, [Robert] McNamara, [McGeorge] Bundy, [Ambassador Maxwell] Taylor—most of their generation, in fact—mistakenly viewed Vietnam through the simplistic ideologi-cal prism of the Cold War. They perceived a deeply complex and ambiguous regional struggle as a grave challenge to world order and stability, fomented by communist China acting through its local surrogate, North Vietnam.

This perception, given their mixture of memories—the West's capitulation to Hitler at Munich, Stalin's postwar truculence, Mao's belligerent rhetoric—appears altogether understandable in retrospect. But it also proved deeply flawed and oblivious to abiding historical realities. Constrained by their memo-ries and ideology, American policymakers neglected the subtle but enduring force of nationalism in Southeast Asia. Powerful and decisive currents—the deep and historic tension between Vietnam and China; regional friction among the Indochinese states of Vietnam, Laos, and Cambodia; and, above all, Hanoi's fanatical will to unification—went unnoticed or unweighed because they failed to fit Washington's worldview. Although it is true, as Secretary of State Rusk once said, that "one cannot escape one's experience," Rusk and his fellow policymakers seriously erred by falling uncritical prisoners of their experience.

Another shared experience plagued 1960s policymakers like a ghost: the ominous specter of McCarthyism. This frightful political memory haunted

LBJ and his Democratic colleagues like a barely suppressed demon in the national psyche. Barely ten years removed from the traumatic "loss" of China and its devastating domestic repercussions, Johnson and his advisers remembered its consequences vividly and shuddered at a similar fate in Vietnam. They talked about this only privately, but then with genuine and palpable fear. Defense Secretary McNamara, in a guarded moment, confided to a newsman in the spring of 1965 that U.S. disengagement from South Vietnam threatened "a disastrous political fight that could . . . freeze American political debate and even affect political freedom."

Such fears resonated deeply in policymakers' minds. Nothing, it seemed, could be worse than the "loss" of Vietnam—not even an intensifying stalemate secured at increasing military and political risk. For a President determined to fulfill liberalism's postwar agenda, Truman's ordeal in China seemed a powerfully forbidding lesson. It hung over LBJ in Vietnam like a dark shadow he could not shake, an agony he would not repeat.

McCarthyism's long shadow into the mid-1960s underscores a persistent and troubling phenomenon of postwar American politics: the peculiar vulnerability besetting liberal Presidents thrust into the maelstrom of world politics. In America's postwar political climate—dominated by the culture of anti-communism—Democratic leaders from Truman to Kennedy to Johnson remained acutely sensitive to the domestic repercussions of foreign policy failure. This fear of right-wing reaction sharply inhibited liberals like LBJ, narrowing what they considered their range of politically acceptable options, while diminishing their willingness to disengage from untenable foreign commitments. Thus, when Johnson did confront the bitter choice between defeat in Vietnam and fighting a major, inconclusive war, he reluctantly chose the second because he could not tolerate the domestic consequences of the first. Committed to fulfilling the Great Society, fearful of resurgent McCarthyism, and afraid that disengagement meant sacrificing the former to the latter, LBJ perceived least political danger in holding on.

But if Johnson resigned never to "lose" South Vietnam, he also resigned never to sacrifice his cherished Great Society in the process. LBJ's determination, however understandable, nonetheless led him deliberately and seriously to obscure the nature and cost of America's deepening involvement in the war during 1964–1965. This decision bought Johnson the short-term political maneuverability he wanted, but at a costly long-term political price. As LBJ's credibility on the war subsequently eroded, public confidence in his leadership slowly but irretrievably evaporated. And this, more than any other factor, is what finally drove Johnson from the White House.

It also tarnished the presidency and damaged popular faith in American government for more than a decade. Trapped between deeply conflicting pressures, LBJ never shared his dilemma with the public. Johnson would not, or felt he dare not, trust his problems with the American people. LBJ's decision, however human, tragically undermined the reciprocal faith between President and public indispensable to effective governance in a democracy. Just as tragically, it fostered a pattern of presidential behavior which led his successor, Richard Nixon, to eventual ruin amid even greater popular political alienation.

Time slowly healed most of these wounds to the American political process, while reconfirming the fundamental importance of presidential credibility in a democracy. Johnson's Vietnam travail underscored the necessity of public trust and support to presidential success. Without them, as LBJ painfully discovered, Presidents are doomed to disaster.

Johnson, in retrospect, might have handled his domestic dilemma more forthrightly. An equally serious dilemma, however, remained always beyond his—or Washington's—power to mend: the root problem of political disarray in South Vietnam. The perennial absence of stable and responsive government in Saigon troubled Washington policymakers profoundly; they understood, only too well, its pivotal importance to the war effort and to the social and economic reforms essential to the country's survival. Over and over again, American officials stressed the necessity of political cooperation to their embattled South Vietnamese allies. But to no avail. As one top American in Saigon later lamented, "[Y]ou could tell them all 'you've got to get together [and stop] this haggling and fighting among yourselves,' but how do you make them do it?" he said. "How do you make them do it?"

Washington, alas, could not. As Ambassador Taylor conceded early in the war, "[You] cannot order good government. You can't get it by fiat." This stubborn but telling truth eventually came to haunt Taylor and others. South Vietnam never marshaled the political will necessary to create an effective and enduring government; it never produced leaders addressing the aspirations and thus attracting the allegiance of the South Vietnamese people. Increasing levels of U.S. troops and firepower, moreover, never offset this fundamental debility. America, as a consequence, built its massive military effort on a foundation of political quicksand.

The causes of this elemental flaw lay deeply imbedded in the social and political history of the region. Neither before nor after 1954 was South Vietnam ever really a nation in spirit. Divided by profound ethnic and religious cleavages dating back centuries and perpetuated under French colonial rule, the people of South Vietnam never developed a common political identity. Instead, political factionalism and rivalry always held sway. The result: a chronic and fatal political disorder.

Saigon's fundamental weakness bore anguished witness to the limits of U.S. power. South Vietnam's shortcomings taught a proud and mighty nation that it could not save a people in spite of themselves—that American power, in the last analysis, offered no viable substitute for indigenous political resolve. Without this basic ingredient, as Saigon's turbulent history demonstrated, Washington's most dedicated and strenuous efforts will prove extremely vulnerable, if not futile.

This is not a happy or popular lesson. But it is a wise and prudent one, attuned to the imperfect realities of an imperfect world. One of America's sagest diplomats, George Kennan, understood and articulated this lesson well when he observed: "When it comes to helping people to resist Communist pressures, . . . no assistance . . . can be effective unless the people themselves have a very high degree of determination and a willingness to help themselves. The moment they begin to place the bulk of the burden on us," Kennan warned, "the whole situation is lost." This, tragically, is precisely what befell America in South Vietnam during 1964–1965. Hereafter, as perhaps always before—*external* U.S. economic, military, and political support provided the vital elements of stability and strength in South Vietnam. Without that *external* support, as events following America's long-delayed withdrawal in 1973 showed, South Vietnam's government quickly failed.

Washington's effort to forge political order through military power spawned another tragedy as well. It ignited unexpected pressures which quickly overwhelmed U.S. policymakers, and pulled them ever deeper into the war. LBJ and his advisers began bombing North Vietnam in early 1965 in a desperate attempt to spur political resolve in South Vietnam. But their effort boomeranged wildly. Rather than stabilizing the situation, it instead unleashed forces that soon put Johnson at the mercy of circumstances, a hostage to the war's accelerating momentum. LBJ, as a result, began steering with an ever looser hand. By the summer of 1965, President Johnson found himself not the controller of events but largely controlled by them. He had lost the political leader's "continual struggle," in the words of Henry Kissinger, "to rescue an element of choice from the pressure of circumstance."

LBJ's experience speaks powerfully across the years. With each Vietnam decision, Johnson's vulnerability to military pressure and bureaucratic momentum intensified sharply. Each step generated demands for another, even bigger step—which LBJ found increasingly difficult to resist. His predicament confirmed George Ball's admonition that war is a fiercely unpredictable force, often generating its own inexorable momentum.

Johnson sensed this danger almost intuitively. He quickly grasped the dilemma and difficulties confronting him in Vietnam. But LBJ lacked the inner strength—the security and self-confidence—to overrule the counsel of his inherited advisers.

Most of those advisers, on the other hand—especially McGeorge Bundy and Robert McNamara—failed to anticipate such perils. Imbued with an overweening faith in their ability to "manage" crises and "control" escalation, Bundy and McNamara, along with Maxwell Taylor, first pushed military action against the North as a lever to force political improvement in the South. But bombing did not rectify Saigon's political problems; it only exacerbated them, while igniting turbulent military pressures that rapidly overwhelmed these advisers' confident calculations.

These advisers' preoccupation with technique, with the application of power, characterized much of America's approach to the Vietnam War. Bundy and McNamara epitomized a postwar generation confident in the exercise and efficacy of U.S. power. Despite the dark and troubled history of European intervention in Indochina, these men stubbornly refused to equate America's situation in the mid-1960s to France's earlier ordeal. To them, the United States possessed limitless ability, wisdom, and virtue; it would therefore prevail where other western powers had failed.

This arrogance born of power led policymakers to ignore manifest dangers, to persist in the face of ever darkening circumstances. Like figures in Greek tragedy, pride compelled these supremely confident men further into disaster.

They succumbed to the affliction common to great powers throughout the ages—the dangerous "self-esteem engendered by power," as the political philosopher Hans Morgenthau once wrote, "which equates power and virtue, [and] in the process loses all sense of moral and political proportion."

Tradition, as well as personality, nurtured such thinking. For in many ways, America's military intervention in Vietnam represented the logical fulfillment of a policy and outlook axiomatically accepted by U.S. policymakers for nearly two decades—the doctrine of global containment. Fashioned at the outset of the Cold War, global containment extended American interests and obligations across vast new areas of the world in defense against perceived monolithic communist expansion. It remained the lodestar of America foreign policy, moreover, even as the constellation of international forces shifted dramatically amid diffused authority and power among communist states and nationalist upheaval in the post-colonial world.

Vietnam exposed the limitations and contradictions of this static doctrine in a world of flux. It also revealed the dangers and flaws of an undiscriminating, universalist policy which perceptive critics of global containment, such as the eminent journalist Walter Lippmann, had anticipated from the beginning. As Lippmann warned about global containment in 1947:

> Satellite states and puppet governments are not good material out of which to construct unassailable barriers [for American defense]. A diplomatic war conducted as this policy demands, that is to say conducted indirectly, means that we must stake our own security and the peace of the world upon satellites, puppets, clients, agents about whom we can know very little. Frequently they will act for their own reasons, and on their own judgments, presenting us with accomplished facts that we did not intend, and with crises for which we are unready. The "unassailable barriers" will present us with an unending series of insoluble dilemmas. We shall have either to disown our puppets, which would be tantamount to appeasement and defeat and loss of face, or must support them at an incalculable cost. . . .

Here lay the heart of America's Vietnam troubles. Driven by unquestioning allegiance to an ossified and extravagant doctrine, Washington officials plunged deeply into a struggle which itself dramatized the changed realities and complexities of the postwar world. Their action teaches both the importance of re-examining premises as circumstances change and the costly consequences of failing to recognize and adapt to them.

Vietnam represented a failure not just of American foreign policy but also of American statesmanship. For once drawn into the war, LBJ and his advisers quickly sensed Vietnam's immense difficulties and dangers—Saigon's congenital political problems, the war's spiraling military costs, the remote likelihood of victory—and plunged in deeper nonetheless. In their determination to preserve America's international credibility and protect their domestic political standing, they continued down an ever costlier path.

That path proved a distressing, multifaceted paradox. Fearing injury to the perception of American power, diminished faith in U.S. resolve, and a conservative political firestorm, policymakers rigidly pursued a course which ultimately injured the substance of American power by consuming exorbitant lives and resources, shook allied confidence in U.S. strategic judgment, and shattered liberalism's political unity and vigor by polarizing and paralyzing American society.

Herein lies Vietnam's most painful but pressing lesson. Statesmanship requires judgment, sensibility, and, above all, wisdom in foreign affairs—the wisdom to calculate national interests prudently and to balance commitments with effective power. It requires that most difficult task of political leaders: "to distinguish between what is desireable and what is possible, . . . between what is desireable and what is essential."

This is important in peace; it is indispensable in war. As the great tutor of statesmen, Carl von Clausewitz, wrote, "Since war is not an act of senseless passion but is controlled by its political object, the value of this object must determine the sacrifices to be made for it in *magnitude* and also in *duration*. Once the expenditure of effort exceeds the value of the political object," Clausewitz admonished, "the object must be renounced. . . ." His maxim, in hindsight, seems painfully relevant to a war which, as even America's military commander in Vietnam, General William Westmoreland, concluded, "the vital security of the United States was not and possibly could not be clearly demonstrated and understood. . . ."

LBJ and his advisers failed to heed this fundamental principle of statesmanship. They failed to weigh American costs in Vietnam against Vietnam's relative importance to American national interests and its effect on overall American power. Compelled by events in Vietnam and, especially, coercive political pressures at home, they deepened an unsound, peripheral commitment and pursued manifestly unpromising and immensely costly objectives. Their failure of statesmanship, then, proved a failure of judgment and, above all, of proportion.

Dereliction of Duty

T he Americanization of the Vietnam War between 1963 and 1965 was the product of an unusual interaction of personalities and circumstances. The escalation of U.S. military intervention grew out of a complicated chain of events and a complex web of decisions that slowly transformed the conflict in Vietnam into an American war.

Much of the literature on Vietnam has argued that the "Cold War mentality" put such pressure on President Johnson that the Americanization of the war was inevitable. The imperative to contain Communism was an important factor in Vietnam policy, but neither American entry into the war nor the manner in which the war was conducted was inevitable. The United States went to war in Vietnam in a manner unique in American history. Vietnam was not forced on the United States by a tidal wave of Cold War ideology. It slunk in on cat's feet.

Between November 1963 and July 1965, LBJ made the critical decisions that took the United States into war almost without realizing it. The decisions, and the way in which he made them, profoundly affected the way the United States fought in Vietnam. Although impersonal forces, such as the ideological imperative of containing Communism, the bureaucratic structure, and institutional priorities, influenced the president's Vietnam decisions, those decisions depended primarily on his character, his motivations, and his relationships with his principal advisers.

Most investigations of how the United States entered the war have devoted little attention to the crucial developments which shaped LBJ's approach to Vietnam and set conditions for a gradual intervention. The first of several "turning points" in the American escalation comprised the near-contemporaneous assassinations of Ngo Dinh Diem and John F. Kennedy. The legacy of the Kennedy administration included an expanded commitment to South Vietnam as an "experiment" in countering Communist insurgencies and a deep distrust of the military that manifested itself in the appointment of officers who would prove supportive of the administration's policies. After November 1963 the United States confronted what in many ways was a new war in South Vietnam. Having deposed the government of Ngo Dinh Diem and his brother Nhu, and having supported actions that led to their deaths, Washington assumed responsibility for the new South Vietnamese leaders. Intensified Viet Cong activity added impetus to U.S. deliberations, leading Johnson and his advisers to conclude that the situation in South Vietnam demanded action beyond military advice and support. Next, in the spring of 1964, the Johnson administration adopted graduated pressure as its strategic concept for the Vietnam War. Rooted in Maxwell Taylor's national security strategy of flexible response, graduated pressure evolved over the next year, becoming the blueprint for the deepening American commitment to maintaining South Vietnam's independence. Then, in August 1964, in response to the Gulf of Tonkin incident, the United States crossed the threshold of direct American military action against North Vietnam.

The Gulf of Tonkin resolution gave the president carte blanche for escalating the war. During the ostensibly benign "holding period" from September 1964 to February 1965, LBJ was preoccupied with his domestic political agenda, and McNamara built consensus behind graduated pressure. In early 1965 the president raised U.S. intervention to a higher level again, deciding on February 9 to begin a systematic program of limited air strikes on targets in North Vietnam and, on February 26, to commit U.S. ground forces to the South. Last, in March 1965, he quietly gave U.S. ground forces the mission of "killing Viet Cong." That series of decisions, none in itself tantamount to a clearly discernable decision to go to war, nevertheless transformed America's commitment in Vietnam.

Viewed together, those decisions might create the impression of a deliberate determination on the part of the Johnson administration to go to war. On the contrary, the president did not want to go to war in Vietnam and was not planning to do so. Indeed, as early as May 1964, LBJ seemed to realize that an American war in Vietnam would be a costly failure. He confided to McGeorge Bundy, ". . . looks like to me that we're getting into another Korea. It just worries the hell out of me. I don't see what we can ever hope to get out of this." It was, Johnson observed, "the biggest damn mess that I ever saw. . . . It's damn easy to get into a war, but . . . it's going to be harder to ever extricate yourself if you get in." Despite his recognition that the situation in Vietnam demanded that he consider alternative courses of action and make a difficult decision, LBJ sought to avoid or to postpone indefinitely an explicit choice between war and disengagement from South Vietnam. In the ensuing months, however, each decision he made moved the United States closer to war, although he seemed not to recognize that fact.

The president's fixation on short-term political goals, combined with his character and the personalities of his principal civilian and military advisers, rendered the administration incapable of dealing adequately with the complexities of the situation in Vietnam. LBJ's advisory system was structured to achieve consensus and to prevent potentially damaging leaks. Profoundly insecure and distrustful of anyone but his closest civilian advisers, the president viewed the JCS [Joint Chiefs of Staff] with suspicion. When the situation in Vietnam seemed to demand military action, Johnson did not turn to his military advisers to determine how to solve the problem. He turned instead to his civilian advisers to determine how to postpone a decision. The relationship between the president, the secretary of defense, and the Joint Chiefs led to the curious situation in which the nation went to war without the benefit of effective military advice from the organization having the statutory responsibility to be the nation's "principal military advisers."

⋅୧◉ഉ⋅

What Johnson feared most in 1964 was losing his chance to win the presidency in his own right. He saw Vietnam principally as a danger to that goal. After the election, he feared that an American military response to the deteriorating situation in Vietnam would jeopardize chances that his Great Society would pass through Congress. The Great Society was to be Lyndon Johnson's great domestic political legacy, and he could not tolerate the risk of its failure. McNamara would help the president first protect his electoral chances and then pass the Great Society by offering a strategy for Vietnam that appeared cheap and could be conducted with minimal public and congressional attention. McNamara's strategy of graduated pressure permitted Johnson to pursue his objective of not losing the war in Vietnam while postponing the "day of reckoning" and keeping the whole question out of public debate all the while.

McNamara was confident in his ability to satisfy the president's needs. He believed fervently that nuclear weapons and the Cold War international political environment had made traditional military experience and thinking not only irrelevant, but often dangerous for contemporary policy. Accordingly, McNamara, along with systems analysts and other civilian members of his own department and the Department of State, developed his own strategy for Vietnam. Bolstered by what he regarded as a personal triumph during the Cuban missile crisis, McNamara drew heavily on that experience and applied it to Vietnam. Based on the assumption that carefully controlled and sharply limited military actions were reversible, and therefore could be carried out at minimal risk and cost, graduated pressure allowed McNamara and Johnson to avoid confronting many of the possible consequences of military action.

⋅୧◉ഉ⋅

Johnson and McNamara succeeded in creating the illusion that the decisions to attack North Vietnam were alternatives to war rather than war itself. Graduated pressure defined military action as a form of communication, the object of which was to affect the enemy's calculation of interests and dissuade him from a particular activity. Because the favored means of communication (bombing fixed installations and economic targets) were not appropriate for the mobile forces of the Viet Cong, who lacked an infrastructure and whose strength in the South was political as well as military, McNamara and his colleagues pointed to the infiltration of men and supplies into South Vietnam as proof that the source and center of the enemy's power in Vietnam lay north of the seventeenth parallel, and specifically in Hanoi. Their definition of the enemy's source of strength was derived from that strategy rather than from a critical examination of the full reality in South Vietnam—and turned out to be inaccurate.

Graduated pressure was fundamentally flawed in other ways. The strategy ignored the uncertainty of war and the unpredictable psychology of an activity that involves killing, death, and destruction. To the North Vietnamese, military action, involving as it did attacks on their forces and bombing of their territory, was not simply a means of communication. Human sacrifices in war evoke strong emotions, creating a dynamic that defies systems analysis quantification. Once the United States crossed the threshold of war against North Vietnam with covert raids and the Gulf of Tonkin "reprisals," the future course of events depended not only on decisions made in Washington but also on enemy responses and actions that were unpredictable. McNamara, however, viewed the war as another business management problem that, he assumed, would ultimately succumb to his reasoned judgment and others' rational calculations. He and his assistants thought that they could predict with great precision what amount of force applied in Vietnam would achieve the results they desired and they believed that they could control that force with great precision from halfway around the world. There were compelling contemporaneous arguments that graduated pressure would not affect Hanoi's will sufficiently to convince the North to desist from its support of the South, and that such a strategy would probably lead to an escalation of the war. Others expressed doubts about the utility of attacking North Vietnam by air to win a conflict in South Vietnam. Nevertheless, McNamara refused to consider the consequences of his recommendations and forged ahead oblivious of the human and psychological complexities of war.

⋅◉⋅

Despite their recognition that graduated pressure was fundamentally flawed, the JCS were unable to articulate effectively either their objections or alternatives. Interservice rivalry was a significant impediment. Although differing perspectives were understandable given the Chiefs' long experience in their own services and their need to protect the interests of their services, the president's principal military advisers were obligated by law to render their best advice. The Chiefs' failure to do so, and their willingness to present single-service remedies to a complex military problem, prevented them from developing a comprehensive estimate of the situation or from thinking effectively about strategy.

When it became clear to the Chiefs that they were to have little influence on the policy-making process, they failed to confront the president with their objections to McNamara's approach to the war. Instead they attempted to work within that strategy in order to remove over time the limitations to further action. Unable to develop a strategic alternative to graduated pressure, the Chiefs became fixated on means by which the war could be conducted and pressed for an escalation of the war by degrees. They hoped that graduated pressure would evolve over time into a fundamentally different strategy, more in keeping with their belief in the necessity of greater force and its more resolute application. In so doing, they gave tacit approval to graduated pressure during the critical period in which the president escalated the war. They did not recommend the total force they believed would ultimately be required in Vietnam and accepted a strategy they knew would lead to a large but inadequate commitment of troops, for an extended period of time, with little hope for success.

⸙⟐⸙

McNamara and Lyndon Johnson were far from disappointed with the joint Chiefs' failings. Because his priorities were domestic, Johnson had little use for military advice that recommended actions inconsistent with those priorities. McNamara and his assistants in the Department of Defense, on the other hand, were arrogant. They disparaged military advice because they thought that their intelligence and analytical methods could compensate for their lack of military experience and education. Indeed military experience seemed to them a liability because military officers took too narrow a view and based their advice on antiquated notions of war. Geopolitical and technological changes of the last fifteen years, they believed, had rendered advice based on military experience irrelevant and, in fact, dangerous. McNamara's disregard for military experience and for history left him to draw principally on his staff in the Department of Defense and led him to conclude that his only real experience with the planning and direction of military force, the Cuban missile crisis, was the most relevant analogy to Vietnam.

While they slowly deepened American military involvement in Vietnam, Johnson and McNamara pushed the Chiefs further away from the decision-making process. There was no meaningful structure through which the Chiefs could voice their views—even the chairman was not a reliable conduit. NSC meetings were strictly *pro forma* affairs in which the president endeavored to build consensus for decisions already made. Johnson continued Kennedy's practice of meeting with small groups of his most trusted advisers. Indeed he made his most important decisions at the Tuesday lunch meetings in which Rusk, McGeorge Bundy, and McNamara were the only regular participants. The president and McNamara shifted responsibility for real planning away from the JCS to ad hoc committees composed principally of civilian analysts and attorneys, whose main goal was to obtain a consensus consistent with the president's pursuit of the middle ground between disengagement and war. The products of those efforts carried the undeserved credibility of proposals that had been agreed on by all departments and were therefore hard to oppose. McNamara and Johnson endeavored to get the advice they wanted by placing conditions and qualifications on questions that they asked the Chiefs. When the Chiefs' advice was not consistent with his own recommendations, McNamara, with the aid of the chairman of the Joint Chiefs of Staff, lied in meetings of the National Security Council about the Chiefs' views.

Rather than advice McNamara and Johnson extracted from the JCS acquiescence and silent support for decisions already made. Even as they relegated the Chiefs to a peripheral position in the policy-making process, they were careful to preserve the facade of consultation to prevent the JCS from opposing the administration's policies either openly or behind the scenes. As American involvement in the war escalated, Johnson's vulnerability to disaffected senior military officers increased because he was purposely deceiving the Congress and the public about the nature of the American military effort in Vietnam. The president and the secretary of defense deliberately obscured the nature of decisions made and left undefined the limits that they envisioned on the use of force. They indicated to the Chiefs that they would take actions that they never intended to pursue. McNamara and his assistants, who considered communication the purpose of military action, kept the nature of their objective from the JCS, who viewed "winning" as the only viable goal in war. Finally, Johnson appealed directly to them, referring to himself as the "coach" and them as "his team." To dampen their calls for further action, Lyndon Johnson attempted to generate sympathy from the JCS for the great pressures that he was feeling from those who opposed escalation.

The ultimate test of the Chiefs' loyalty came in July 1965. The administration's lies to the American public had grown in magnitude as the American military effort in Vietnam escalated. The president's plan of deception depended on tacit approval or silence from the JCS. LBJ had misrepresented the mission of U.S. ground forces in Vietnam, distorted the views of the Chiefs to lend credibility to his decision against mobilization, grossly understated the numbers of troops General Westmoreland had requested, and lied to the Congress about the monetary cost of actions already approved and of those awaiting final decision. The Chiefs did not disappoint the president. In the days before the president made his duplicitous public announcement concerning Westmoreland's request, the Chiefs, with the exception of commandant of the Marine Corps Greene, withheld from congressmen their estimates of the amount of force that would be needed in Vietnam. As he had during the Gulf of Tonkin hearings, Wheeler lent his support to the president's deception of Congress. The "five silent men" on the Joint Chiefs made possible the way the United States went to war in Vietnam.

⁕

Several factors kept the Chiefs from challenging the president's subterfuges. The professional code of the military officer prohibits him or her from engaging in political activity. Actions that could have undermined the administration's credibility and derailed its Vietnam policy could not have been undertaken lightly. The Chiefs felt loyalty to their commander in chief. The Truman-MacArthur controversy during the Korean War had warned the Chiefs about the dangers of overstepping the bounds of civilian control. Loyalty to their services also weighed against opposing the president and the secretary of defense. Harold Johnson, for example, decided against resignation because he thought he had to remain in office to protect the Army's interests as best he could. Admiral McDonald and Marine Corps Commandant Greene compromised their views on Vietnam in exchange for concessions to their respective services. Greene achieved a dramatic expansion of the Marine Corps, and McDonald ensured that the Navy retained control of Pacific Command. None of the Chiefs had sworn an oath to his service, however. They had all sworn, rather, to "support and defend the Constitution of the United States."

General Greene recalled that direct requests by congressmen for his assessment put him in a difficult situation. The president was lying, and he expected the Chiefs to lie as well or, at least, to withhold the whole truth. Although the president should not have placed the Chiefs in that position, the flag officers should not have tolerated it when he had.

Because the Constitution locates civilian control of the military in Congress as well as in the executive branch, the Chiefs could not have been justified in deceiving the peoples' representatives about Vietnam. Wheeler in particular allowed his duty to the president to overwhelm his obligations under the Constitution. As cadets are taught at the United States Military Academy, the JCS relationship with the Congress is challenging and demands that military officers possess a strong character and keen intellect. While the Chiefs must present Congress with their best advice based on their professional experience and education, they must be careful not to undermine their credibility by crossing the line between advice and advocacy of service interests.

Maxwell Taylor had a profound influence on the nature of the civil-military relationship during the escalation of American involvement in Vietnam. In contrast to Army Chief of Staff George C. Marshall, who, at the start of World War II, recognized the need for the JCS to suppress service parochialism to provide advice consistent with national interests, Taylor exacerbated service differences to help McNamara and Johnson keep the Chiefs divided and, thus, marginal to the policy process. Taylor recommended men for appointment to the JCS who were less likely than their predecessors to challenge the direction of the administration's military policy, even when they knew that that policy was fundamentally flawed. Taylor's behavior is perhaps best explained by his close personal friendship with the Kennedy family; McNamara; and, later, Johnson. In contrast again to Marshall, who thought it important to keep a professional distance from President Franklin Roosevelt, Taylor abandoned an earlier view similar to Marshall's in favor of a belief that the JCS and the president should enjoy "an intimate, easy relationship, born of friendship and mutual regard."

The way in which the United States went to war in the period between November 1963 and July 1965 had, not surprisingly, a profound influence on the conduct of the war and on its outcome. Because Vietnam policy decisions were made based on domestic political expediency, and because the president was intent on forging a consensus position behind what he believed was a middle policy, the administration deliberately avoided clarifying its policy objectives and postponed discussing the level of force that the president was willing to commit to the effort. Indeed, because the president was seeking domestic political consensus, members of the administration believed that ambiguity in the objectives for fighting in Vietnam was a strength rather than a weakness. Determined to prevent dissent from the JCS, the administration concealed its development of "fall-back" objectives.

Over time the maintenance of U.S. credibility quietly supplanted the stated policy objective of a free and independent South Vietnam. The principal civilian planners had determined that to guarantee American credibility, it was not necessary to win in Vietnam. That conclusion, combined with the belief that the use of force was merely another form of diplomatic communication, directed the military effort in the South at achieving stalemate rather than victory. Those charged with planning the war believed that it would be possible to preserve American credibility even if the United States armed forces withdrew from the South, after a show of force against the North and in the South in which American forces were "bloodied." After the United States became committed to war, however, and more American soldiers, airmen, and Marines had died in the conflict, it would become impossible simply to disengage and declare America's credibility intact, a fact that should have been foreseen. The Chiefs sensed the shift in objectives, but did not challenge directly the views of civilian planners in that connection. McNamara and Johnson recognized that, once committed to war, the JCS would not agree to an objective other than imposing a solution on the enemy consistent with U.S. interests. The JCS deliberately avoided clarifying the objective as well. As a result, when the United States went to war, the JCS pursued objectives different from those of the president. When the Chiefs requested permission to apply force consistent with their conception of U.S. objectives, the president and McNamara, based on their goals and domestic political constraints, rejected JCS requests, or granted them only in part. The result was that the JCS and McNamara became fixated on the means rather than on the ends, and on the manner in which the war was conducted instead of a military strategy that could connect military actions to achievable policy goals.

Because forthright communication between top civilian and military officials in the Johnson administration was never developed, there was no reconciliation of McNamara's intention to limit the American military effort sharply and the Chiefs' assessment that the United States could not possibly win under such conditions. If they had attempted to reconcile those positions, they could not have helped but recognize the futility of the American war effort.

The Joint Chiefs of Staff became accomplices in the president's deception and focused on a tactical task, killing the enemy. General Westmoreland's "strategy" of attrition in South Vietnam, was, in essence, the absence of a strategy. The result was military activity (bombing North Vietnam and killing the enemy in South Vietnam) that did not aim to achieve a clearly defined objective. It was unclear how quantitative measures by which McNamara interpreted the success and failure of the use of military force were contributing to an end of the war. As American casualties mounted and the futility of the strategy became apparent, the American public lost faith in the effort. The Chiefs did not request the number of troops they believed necessary to impose a military solution in South Vietnam until after the Tet offensive in 1968. By that time, however, the president was besieged by opposition to the war and was unable even to consider the request. LBJ, who had gone to such great lengths to ensure a crushing defeat over Barry Goldwater in 1964, declared that he was withdrawing from the race for his party's presidential nomination.

Johnson thought that he would be able to control the U.S. involvement in Vietnam. That belief, based on the strategy of graduated pressure and McNamara's confident assurances, proved in dramatic fashion to be false. If the president was surprised by the consequences of his decisions between November 1963 and July 1965, he should not have been so. He had disregarded the advice he did not want to hear in favor of a policy based on the pursuit of his own political fortunes and his beloved domestic programs.

⌒⌒

The war in Vietnam was not lost in the field, nor was it lost on the front pages of the *New York Times* or on the college campuses. It was lost in Washington, D.C., even before Americans assumed sole responsibility for the fighting in 1965 and before they realized the country was at war; indeed, even before the first American units were deployed. The disaster in Vietnam was not the result of impersonal forces but a uniquely human failure, the responsibility for which was shared by President Johnson and his principal military and civilian advisers. The failings were many and reinforcing: arrogance, weakness, lying in the pursuit of self-interest, and, above all, the abdication of responsibility to the American people.

POSTSCRIPT

Was the Americanization of the War in Vietnam Inevitable?

The book from which VanDeMark's selection was excerpted is a detailed study of the circumstances surrounding the decisions that President Lyndon Johnson made to increase America's presence in Vietnam via the bombing raids of North Vietnam in February 1965 and the introduction of ground troops the following July. VanDeMark agrees with McMaster that Johnson did not consult the Joint Chiefs of Staff about the wisdom of escalating the war. In fact, Johnson's decisions of "graduated pressure" were made in increments by the civilian advisers surrounding Secretary of Defense Robert McNamara. The policy, if it can be called such, was to prevent the National Liberation Front and its Viet Cong army from taking over South Vietnam. Each service branch fought its own war without coordinating with one another or with the government of South Vietnam. In VanDeMark's view, U.S. intervention was doomed to failure because South Vietnam was an artificial and very corrupt nation-state created by the French and later supported by the Americans. It was unfortunate that the nationalist revolution was tied up with the Communists led by Ho Chi Minh, who had been fighting French colonialism and Japanese imperialism since the 1920s—unlike Korea and Malaysia, which had alternative, noncommunist, nationalist movements.

Why did Johnson plunge "into the quagmire"? For one thing, Johnson remembered how previous democratic presidents Franklin D. Roosevelt and Harry S. Truman had been charged with being soft on communism and accused of losing Eastern Europe to the Russians after the Second World War and China to the Communists in the Chinese Civil War in 1949. In addition, both presidents were charged by Senator Joseph McCarthy and others of harboring Communists in U.S. government agencies. If Johnson was tough in Vietnam, he could stop communist aggression. At the same time, he could ensure that his Great Society social programs of Medicare and job retraining, as well as the impending civil rights legislation, would be passed by Congress.

As an army officer who fought in the Persian Gulf War, McMaster offers a unique perspective on the decision-making processes used by government policymakers. McMaster spares no one in his critique of what he considers the flawed Vietnam policy of "graduated pressure." He says that McNamara, bolstered by the success of America during the Cuban Missile Crisis, believed that the traditional methods of fighting wars were obsolete. Johnson believed in McNamara's approach, and the president's own need for consensus in the decision-making process kept the Joint Chiefs of Staff out of the loop.

Unlike other military historians, who generally absolve the military from responsibility for the strategy employed during the war, McMaster argues that the Joint Chiefs of Staff were responsible for not standing up to Johnson and telling him that his military strategy was seriously flawed. McMaster's views are not as new as some reviewers of his book seem to think. Bruce Palmer, Jr., in *The Twenty-Five Year War: America's Military Role in Vietnam* (University Press of Kentucky, 1984), and Harry G. Summers, Jr., in *On Strategy: A Critical Analysis of the Vietnam War* (Presidio Press, 1982), also see a flawed strategy of war. Summers argues that Johnson should have asked Congress for a declaration of war and fought a conventional war against North Vietnam.

One scholar has claimed that over 7,000 books about the Vietnam War have been published. The starting point for the current issue is Lloyd Gardner and Ted Gittinger, eds., *Vietnam: The Early Decisions* (University of Texas Press, 1997). See also Larry Berman, *Planning a Tragedy: The Americanization of the War in Vietnam* (W. W. Norton, 1982) and *Lyndon Johnson's War* (W. W. Norton, 1989); David Halberstam, *The Best and the Brightest* (Random House, 1972); and Lloyd C. Gardner, *Pay Any Price: Lyndon Johnson and the Wars for Vietnam* (Ivan R. Dee, 1995). Primary sources can be found in the U.S. Department of State's two-volume *Foreign Relations of the United States, 1964-1968: Vietnam* (Government Printing Office, 1996) and in the relevant sections of one of the most useful collections of primary sources and essays, *Major Problems in the History of the Vietnam War*, 2d ed., by Robert J. McMahon (Houghton Mifflin, 2000).

The bureaucratic perspective can be found in a series of essays by George C. Herring entitled *LBJ and Vietnam: A Different Kind of War* (University of Texas Press, 1995). Herring is also the author of the widely used text *America's Longest War: the United States and Vietnam* (Alfred A. Knopf, 1986). A brilliant article often found in anthologies is by historian and former policymaker James C. Thomson, Jr., "How Could Vietnam Happen? An Autopsy," *The Atlantic Monthly* (April 1968). An interesting comparison of the 1954 Dien Bien Phu and 1965 U.S. escalation decisions is Fred I. Greenstein and John P. Burke, "The Dynamics of Presidential Reality Testing: Evidence From Two Vietnam Decisions," *Political Science Quarterly* (Winter 1989–1990). A nice review essay on Vietnam's impact on today's military thinking is Michael C. Desch's "Wounded Warriors and the Lessons of Vietnam," *Orbis* (Summer 1998).

The literature on the Vietnam War, like the war on terror, seems endless. Errol Morris' documentary *The Fog of War* (2004) is an extended interview with former Secretary of Defense Robert McNamara, who blames the escalation of the war, contrary to his advice, on President Johnson. But see a roundtable critique of this film in *Passport: The Newsletter for Historians of American Foreign Relations* (April 2005) and Gareth Porter, *Perils of Dominance: Imbalance of Power and the Road to War in Vietnam* (University of California Press, 2004), which blames McNamara and not Johnson for escalating the war. Two important roundtables on the war that emphasize new approaches such as the international view, Vietnamese responses, modernization theory, and analogies to their way such as Iraq can be found in the following: Carl Abbott et. al., "Vietnam in Historical Thinking," *Pacific Historical Review*

(August 2005) and David Anderson et. al., "Interchange: Legacies of the Vietnam War," *The Journal of American History* (September 2006). Anderson, a Vietnam veteran, has edited two student-friendly anthologies on the war: *Shadow on the White House: Presidents and the Vietnam War 1945–1973* (University of Kansas Press, 1993) and *The Human Tradition in the Vietnam Era* (Scholarly Resources, 2000).

ISSUE 11

Has the Women's Movement of the 1970s Failed to Liberate American Women?

YES: F. Carolyn Graglia, from *Domestic Tranquility: A Brief Against Feminism* (Spence, 1998)

NO: Sara M. Evans, from "American Women in the Twentieth Century," in Harvard Sitkoff, ed., *Perspectives on Modern America: Making Sense of the Twentieth Century* (Oxford University Press, 2001)

ISSUE SUMMARY

YES: Writer and lecturer F. Carolyn Graglia argues that women should stay at home and practice the values of "true motherhood" because contemporary feminists have discredited marriage, devalued traditional homemaking, and encouraged sexual promiscuity.

NO: According to Professor Sara M. Evans, despite class, racial, religious, ethnic, and regional differences, women in America experienced major transformations in their private and public lives in the twentieth century.

In 1961, President John F. Kennedy established the Commission on the Status of Women to examine "the prejudice and outmoded customs that act as barriers to the full realization of women's basic rights." Two years later, Betty Friedan, a closet leftist from suburban Rockland County, New York, wrote about the growing malaise of the suburban housewife in her best-seller *The Feminist Mystique* (W.W. Norton, 1963).

The roots of Friedan's "feminine mystique" go back much earlier than the post–World War II "baby boom" generation of suburban America. Women historians have traced the origins of the modern family to the early nineteenth century. As the nation became more stable politically, the roles of men, women, and children became segmented in ways that still exist today. Dad went to work, the kids went to school, and Mom stayed home. Women's magazines, gift books, and the religious literature of the period ascribed to these women a role that Professor Barbara Welter has called the "Cult of True

Womanhood." She describes the ideal woman as upholding four virtues—piety, purity, submissiveness, and domesticity.

In nineteenth-century America, most middle-class white women stayed home. Those who entered the workforce as teachers or became reformers were usually extending the values of the Cult of True Womanhood to the outside world. This was true of the women reformers in the Second Great Awakening and the peace, temperance, and abolitionist movements before the Civil War. The first real challenge to the traditional values system occurred when a handful of women showed up at Seneca Falls, New York, in 1848 to sign the Women's Declaration of Rights.

It soon became clear that if they were going to pass reform laws, women would have to obtain the right to vote. After an intense struggle, the Nineteenth Amendment was ratified on August 26, 1920. Once the women's movement obtained the vote, there was no agreement on future goals. The problems of the Great Depression and World War II overrode women's issues.

World War II brought about major changes for working women. Six million women entered the labor force for the first time, many of whom were married. "The proportion of women in the labor force," writes Lois Banner, "increased from 25 percent in 1940 to 36 percent in 1945. This increase was greater than that of the previous four decades combined." Many women moved into high-paying, traditionally men's jobs as policewomen, firefighters, and precision toolmakers. Steel and auto companies that converted over to wartime production made sure that lighter tools were made for women to use on the assembly lines. The federal government also erected federal childcare facilities.

When the war ended in 1945, many of these women lost their nontraditional jobs. The federal day-care program was eliminated, and the government told women to go home even though a 1944 study by the Women's Bureau concluded that 80 percent of working women wanted to continue in their jobs after the war.

Most history texts emphasize that women did return home, moved to the suburbs, and created a baby boom generation, which reversed the downward size of families in the years from 1946 to 1964. What is lost in this description is the fact that after 1947 the number of working women again began to rise, reaching 31 percent in 1951. Twenty-two years later, at the height of the women's liberation movement, it reached 42 percent.

When Friedan wrote *The Feminine Mystique* in 1963, both working-class and middle-class college-educated women experienced discrimination in the marketplace. When women worked, they were expected to become teachers, nurses, secretaries, and airline stewardesses—the lowest-paying jobs in the workforce. In the turbulent 1960s, this situation was no longer accepted.

In the following selection, F. Carolyn Graglia defends the traditional role of women in contemporary America. Women, she contends, should stay at home and practice the values of "true womanhood." Contemporary feminists, she argues, have devalued traditional homemaking, encouraged sexual promiscuity, and discredited marriage as a career for women. In the second selection, Sara M. Evans argues that in spite of class, racial, religious, ethnic, and regional differences, women in America experienced major transformations in their private and public lives in the twentieth century.

YES

F. Carolyn Graglia

Domestic Tranquility

Introduction

Since the late 1960s, feminists have very successfully waged war against the traditional family, in which husbands are the principal breadwinners and wives are primarily homemakers. This war's immediate purpose has been to undermine the homemaker's position within both her family and society in order to drive her into the work force. Its long-term goal is to create a society in which women behave as much like men as possible, devoting as much time and energy to the pursuit of a career as men do, so that women will eventually hold equal political and economic power with men. . . .

Feminists have used a variety of methods to achieve their goal. They have promoted a sexual revolution that encouraged women to mimic male sexual promiscuity. They have supported the enactment of no-fault divorce laws that have undermined housewives' social and economic security. And they obtained the application of affirmative action requirements to women as a class, gaining educational and job preferences for women and undermining the ability of men who are victimized by this discrimination to function as family breadwinners.

A crucial weapon in feminism's arsenal has been the status degradation of the housewife's role. From the journalistic attacks of Betty Friedan and Gloria Steinem to Jessie Bernard's sociological writings, all branches of feminism are united in the conviction that a woman can find identity and fulfillment only in a career. The housewife, feminists agree, was properly characterized by Simone de Beauvoir and Betty Friedan as a "parasite," a being something less than human, living her life without using her adult capabilities or intelligence, and lacking any real purpose in devoting herself to children, husband, and home.

Operating on the twin assumptions that equality means sameness (that is, men and women cannot be equals unless they do the same things) and that most differences between the sexes are culturally imposed, contemporary feminism has undertaken its own cultural impositions. Revealing their totalitarian belief that they know best how others should live and their totalitarian willingness to force others to conform to their dogma, feminists have sought to modify our social institutions in order to create an androgynous society in which male and female roles are as identical as possible. The results of the feminist juggernaut now engulf us. By almost all indicia of well-being, the institution of the American family has become significantly less healthy than it was thirty years ago.

Certainly, feminism is not alone responsible for our families' sufferings. As Charles Murray details in *Losing Ground,* President Lyndon Johnson's Great Society programs, for example, have often hurt families, particularly black families, and these programs were supported by a large constituency beyond the women's movement. What distinguishes the women's movement, however, is the fact that, despite the pro-family motives it sometimes ascribes to itself, it has actively sought the traditional family's destruction. In its avowed aims and the programs it promotes, the movement has adopted Kate Millett's goal, set forth in her *Sexual Politics,* in which she endorses Friedrich Engels's conclusion that "the family, as that term is presently understood, must go"; "a kind fate," she remarks, in "view of the institution's history." This goal has never changed: feminists view traditional nuclear families as inconsistent with feminism's commitment to women's independence and sexual freedom.

Emerging as a revitalized movement in the 1960s, feminism reflected women's social discontent, which had arisen in response to the decline of the male breadwinner ethic and to the perception—heralded in Philip Wylie's 1940s castigation of the evil "mom"—that Western society does not value highly the roles of wife and mother. Women's dissatisfactions, nevertheless, have often been aggravated rather than alleviated by the feminist reaction. To mitigate their discontent, feminists argued, women should pattern their lives after men's, engaging in casual sexual intercourse on the same terms as sexually predatory males and making the same career commitments as men. In pursuit of these objectives, feminists have fought unceasingly for the ready availability of legal abortion and consistently derogated both motherhood and the worth of full-time homemakers. Feminism's sexual teachings have been less consistent, ranging from its early and enthusiastic embrace of the sexual revolution to a significant backlash against female sexual promiscuity, which has led some feminists to urge women to abandon heterosexual sexual intercourse altogether.

Contemporary feminism has been remarkably successful in bringing about the institutionalization in our society of the two beliefs underlying its offensive: denial of the social worth of traditional homemakers and rejection of traditional sexual morality. The consequences have been pernicious and enduring. General societal assent to these beliefs has profoundly distorted men's perceptions of their relationships with and obligations to women, women's perceptions of their own needs, and the way in which women make decisions about their lives.

Traditional Homemaking Devalued

The first prong of contemporary feminism's offensive has been to convince society that a woman's full-time commitment to cultivating her marriage and rearing her children is an unworthy endeavor. Women, assert feminists, should treat marriage and children as relatively independent appendages to their life of full-time involvement in the workplace. To live what feminists assure her is the only life worthy of respect, a woman must devote the vast bulk of her time and energy to market production, at the expense of marriage and children. Children, she is told, are better cared for by surrogates, and marriage, as these feminists perceive it, neither deserves nor requires much attention; indeed, the very idea of a woman's "cultivating" her marriage seems ludicrous. Thus spurred on by the women's movement, many women have sought to become male clones.

But some feminists have appeared to modify the feminist message; voices—supposedly of moderation—have argued that women really are different from men. In this they are surely right: there are fundamental differences between the average man and woman, and it is appropriate to take account of these differences when making decisions both in our individual lives and with respect to social issues. Yet the new feminist voices have not conceded that acknowledged differences between the sexes are grounds for reexamining women's flight from home into workplace. Instead, these new voices have argued only that these differences require modification of the terms under which women undertake to reconstruct their lives in accordance with the blueprint designed by so-called early radicals. The edifice erected by radical feminism is to remain intact, subject only to some redecorating. The foundation of this edifice is still the destruction of the traditional family. Feminism has acquiesced in women's desire to bear children (an activity some of the early radicals discouraged). But it continues steadfast in its assumption that, after some period of maternity leave, daily care of those children is properly the domain of institutions and paid employees. The yearnings manifested in women's palpable desire for children should largely be sated, the new voices tell us, by the act of serving as a birth canal and then spending so-called quality time with the child before and after a full day's work.

Any mother, in this view, may happily consign to surrogates most of the remaining aspects of her role, assured that doing so will impose no hardship or loss on either mother or child. To those women whose natures make them less suited to striving in the workplace than concentrating on husband, children, and home, this feminist diktat denies the happiness and contentment they could have found within the domestic arena. In the world formed by contemporary feminism, these women will have status and respect only if they force themselves to take up roles in the workplace they suspect are not most deserving of their attention. Relegated to the periphery of their lives are the home and personal relationships with husband and children that they sense merit their central concern.

Inherent in the feminist argument is an extraordinary contradiction. Feminists deny, on the one hand, that the dimension of female sexuality which engenders women's yearning for children can also make it appropriate and satisfying for a woman to devote herself to domestic endeavors and provide her children's full-time care. On the other hand, they plead the fact of sexual difference to justify campaigns to modify workplaces in order to correct the effects of male influence and alleged biases. Only after such modifications, claim feminists, can women's nurturing attributes and other female qualities be adequately expressed in and truly influence the workplace. Manifestations of these female qualities, feminists argue, should and can occur in the workplace once it has been modified to blunt the substantial impact of male aggression and competitiveness and take account of women's special requirements.

Having launched its movement claiming the right of women—a right allegedly denied them previously—to enter the workplace on an *equal* basis with men, feminism then escalated its demands by arguing that female differences require numerous changes in the workplace. Women, in this view, are insufficiently feminine to find satisfaction in rearing their own children but too feminine to compete on an equal basis with men. Thus, having taken women out of their homes and settled them in the workplace, feminists have sought to reconstruct workplaces to create "feminist playpens" that are conducive to female qualities of sensitivity, caring, and empathy. Through this exercise in self-contradiction, contemporary feminism has endeavored to remove the woman from her home and role of providing daily care to her children—the quintessential place and activity for most effectively expressing her feminine, nurturing attributes.

The qualities that are the most likely to make women good mothers are thus redeployed away from their children and into workplaces that must be restructured to accommodate them. The irony is twofold. Children—the ones who could benefit most from the attentions of those mothers who do possess these womanly qualities—are deprived of those attentions and left only with the hope of finding adequate replacement for their loss. Moreover, the occupations in which these qualities are now to find expression either do not require them for optimal job performance (often they are not conducive to professional success) or were long ago recognized as women's occupations—as in the field of nursing, for example—in which nurturing abilities do enhance job performance.

Traditional Sexual Morality Traduced

The second prong of contemporary feminism's offensive has been to encourage women to ape male sexual patterns and engage in promiscuous sexual intercourse as freely as men. Initially, feminists were among the most dedicated supporters of the sexual revolution, viewing female participation in casual sexual activity as an unmistakable declaration of female equality with males. The women in our society who acted upon the teachings of feminist sexual revolutionaries have suffered greatly. They are victims of the highest abortion rate in the Western world. More than one in five Americans is now infected with a viral sexually transmitted disease which at best can be controlled but not cured and is often chronic. Sexually transmitted diseases, both viral and bacterial, disproportionately affect women because, showing fewer symptoms, they often go untreated for a longer time. These diseases also lead to pelvic infections that cause infertility in 100,000 to 150,000 women each year.

The sexual revolution feminists have promoted rests on an assumption that an act of sexual intercourse involves nothing but a pleasurable physical sensation, possessing no symbolic meaning and no moral dimension. This is an understanding of sexuality that bears more than a slight resemblance to sex as depicted in pornography: physical sexual acts without emotional involvement. In addition to the physical harm caused by increased sexual promiscuity, the denial that sexual intercourse has symbolic importance within a framework of moral accountability corrupts the nature of the sex act. Such denial necessarily makes sexual intercourse a trivial event, compromising the act's ability to fulfill its most important function after procreation. This function is to bridge the gap between males and females who often seem separated by so many differences, both biological and emotional, that they feel scarcely capable of understanding or communicating with each other.

Because of the urgency of sexual desire, especially in the male, it is through sexual contact that men and women can most easily come together. Defining the nature of sexual intercourse in terms informed by its procreative potentialities makes the act a spiritually meaningful event of overwhelming importance. A sexual encounter so defined is imbued with the significance conferred by its connection with a promise of immortality through procreation, whether that connection is a present possibility, a remembrance of children already borne, or simply an acknowledgment of the reality and truth of the promise. Such a sex act can serve as the physical meeting ground on which, by accepting and affirming each other through their bodies' physical unity, men and women can begin to construct an enduring emotional unity. The sexual encounter cannot perform its function when it is viewed as a trivial event of moral indifference with no purpose or meaning other than producing a physical sensation through the friction of bodily parts.

The feminist sexual perspective deprives the sex act of the spiritual meaningfulness that can make it the binding force upon which man and woman can construct a lasting marital relationship. The morally indifferent sexuality championed by the sexual revolution substitutes the sex without emotions that characterizes pornography for the sex of a committed, loving relationship that satisfies women's longing for romance and connection. But this is not the only damage to relationships between men and women that follows from feminism's determination to promote an androgynous society by convincing men and women that they are virtually fungible. Sexual equivalency, feminists believe, requires that women not only engage in casual sexual intercourse as freely as men, but also that women mimic male behavior by becoming equally assertive in initiating sexual encounters and in their activity throughout the encounter. With this sexual prescription, feminists mock the essence of conjugal sexuality that is at the foundation of traditional marriage.

Marriage as a Woman's Career Discredited

Even academic feminists who are considered "moderates" endorse doctrines most inimical to the homemaker. Thus, Professor Elizabeth Fox-Genovese, regarded as a moderate in Women's Studies, tells us that marriage can no longer be a viable career for women. But if marriage cannot be a woman's career, then despite feminist avowals of favoring choice in this matter, homemaking cannot be a woman's goal, and surrogate child-rearing must be her child's destiny. Contrary to feminist claims, society's barriers are not strung tightly to inhibit women's career choices. Because of feminism's very successful efforts, society encourages women to pursue careers, while stigmatizing and preventing their devotion to child-rearing and domesticity.

It was precisely upon the conclusion that marriage cannot be a viable career for women that *Time* magazine rested its Fall 1990 special issue on "Women: The Road Ahead," a survey of contemporary women's lives. While noting that the "cozy, limited roles of the past are still clearly remembered, sometimes fondly," during the past thirty years "all that was orthodox has become negotiable." One thing negotiated away has been the economic security of the homemaker, and *Time* advised young women that "the job of full-time homemaker may be the riskiest profession to choose" because "the advent of no-fault and equitable-distribution divorce laws" reflect, in the words of one judge, the fact that "[s]ociety no longer believes that a husband should support his wife."

No-fault divorce laws did not, however, result from an edict of the gods or some force of nature, but from sustained political efforts, particularly by the feminist movement. As a cornerstone of their drive to make women exchange home for workplace, and thereby secure their independence from men, the availability of no-fault divorce (like the availability of abortion) was sacrosanct to the movement. *Time* shed crocodile tears for displaced home-makers, for it made clear that women must canter down the road ahead with the spur of no-fault divorce urging them into the workplace. Of all *Time*'s recommendations for ameliorating women's lot, divorce reform—the most crying need in our country today—was not among them. Whatever hardships may be endured by women who would resist a divorce, *Time*'s allegiance, like that of most feminists, is clearly to the divorce-seekers who, it was pleased to note, will not be hindered in their pursuit of self-realization by the barriers to divorce that their own mothers had faced.

These barriers to divorce which had impeded their own parents, however, had usually benefited these young women by helping to preserve their parents' marriage. A five-year study of children in divorcing families disclosed that "the overwhelming majority preferred the unhappy marriage to the divorce," and many of them, "despite the unhappiness of their parents, were in fact relatively happy and considered their situation neither better nor worse than that of other families around them." A follow-up study after ten years demonstrated that children experienced the trauma of their parents' divorce as more serious and long-lasting than any researchers had anticipated. *Time* so readily acquiesced in the disadvantaging of homemakers and the disruption of children's lives because the feminist ideological parameters within which it operates have excluded marriage as a *proper* career choice. Removing the obstacles to making it a *viable* choice would, therefore, be an undesirable subversion of feminist goals.

That *Time* would have women trot forward on life's journey constrained by the blinders of feminist ideology is evident from its failure to question any feminist notion, no matter how silly, or to explore solutions incompatible with the ideology's script. One of the silliest notions *Time* left unexamined was that young women want "good careers, good marriages and two or three kids, and they don't want the children to be raised by strangers." The supposed realism of this expectation lay in the new woman's attitude that "I don't want to work 70 hours a week, but I want to be vice president, and *you* have to change." But even if thirty hours were cut from that seventy-hour workweek, the new woman would still be working the normal full-time week, her children would still be raised by surrogates, and the norm would continue to be the feminist version of child-rearing that *Time* itself described unflatteringly as "less a preoccupation than an improvisation."

The illusion that a woman can achieve career success without sacrificing the daily personal care of her children—and except among the very wealthy, most of her leisure as well—went unquestioned by *Time*. It did note, however, the dissatisfaction expressed by Eastern European and Russian women who had experienced as a matter of government policy the same liberation from home and children that our feminists have undertaken to bestow upon Western women. In what *Time* described as "a curious reversal of Western feminism's emphasis on careers for women," the new female leaders of Eastern Europe would like "to reverse the communist diktat that all women have to work." Women have "dreamed," said the Polish Minister of Culture and Arts, "of reaching the point where we have the choice to stay home" that communism had taken away. But blinded by its feminist bias, *Time* could only find it "curious" that women would choose to stay at home; apparently beyond the pale of respectability was any argument that it would serve Western women's interest to retain the choice that contemporary feminism—filling in the West the role of communism in the East—has sought to deny them.

Nor was its feminist bias shaken by the attitudes of Japanese women, most of whom, *Time* noted, reject "equality" with men, choosing to cease work after the birth of a first child and later resuming a part-time career or pursuing hobbies or community work. The picture painted was that of the 1950s American suburban housewife reviled by Betty Friedan, except that the American has enjoyed a higher standard of living (particularly a much larger home) than has the Japanese. In Japan, *Time* observed, being "a housewife is nothing to be ashamed of." Dishonoring the housewife's role was a goal, it might have added, that Japanese feminists can, in time, accomplish if they emulate their American counterparts.

Japanese wives have broad responsibilities, commented *Time,* because most husbands leave their salaries and children entirely in wives' hands; freed from drudgery by modern appliances, housewives can "pursue their interests in a carefree manner, while men have to worry about supporting their wives and children." Typically, a Japanese wife controls household finances, giving her husband a cash allowance, the size of which, apparently, dissatisfies one-half of the men. Acknowledging that Japanese wives take the leadership in most homes, one husband observed that "[t]hings go best when the husband is swimming in the palm of his wife's hand." A home is well-managed, said one wife, "if you make your men feel that they're in control when they are in front of others, while in reality you're in control." It seems like a good arrangement to me.

Instead of inquiring whether a similar carefree existence might appeal to some American women, *Time* looked forward to the day when marriage would no longer be a career for Japanese women, as their men took over household and child-rearing chores, enabling wives to join husbands in the workplace. It was noted, however, that a major impediment to this goal, which would have to be corrected, was the fact that Japanese day-care centers usually run for only eight hours a day. Thus, *Time* made clear that its overriding concern was simply promoting the presence of women in the work force. This presence is seen as a good *per se,* without any *pro forma* talk about the economic necessity of a second income and without any question raised as to whether it is in children's interest to spend any amount of time—much less in excess of eight hours a day—in communal care. . . .

The Awakened Brünnhilde

. . . Those who would defend anti-feminist traditionalism today are like heretics fighting a regnant Inquisition. To become a homemaker, a woman may need the courage of a heretic. This is one reason that the defense of traditional women is often grounded in religious teachings, for the heretic's courage usually rests on faith. The source of courage I offer is the conviction, based on my own experience, that contemporary feminism's stereotypical caricature of the housewife did not reflect reality when Friedan popularized it, does not reflect reality today, and need not govern reality.

Feminists claimed a woman can find identity and fulfillment only in a career; they are wrong. They claimed a woman can, in that popular expression, "have it all"; they are wrong—she can have only some. The experience of being a mother at home is a different experience from being a full-time market producer who is also a mother. A woman can have one or the other experience, but not both at the same time. Combining a career with motherhood requires a woman to compromise by diminishing her commitment and exertions with respect to one role or the other, or usually, to both. Rarely, if ever, can a woman adequately perform in a full-time career if she diminishes her commitment to it sufficiently to replicate the experience of being a mother at home.

Women were *never* told they could *not* choose to make the compromises required to combine these roles; within the memory of all living today there were always some women who did so choose. But by successfully degrading the housewife's role, contemporary feminism undertook to force this choice upon all women. I declined to make the compromises necessary to combine a career with motherhood because I did not want to become like Andrea Dworkin's spiritual virgin. I did not want to keep my being intact, as Dworkin puts it, so that I could continue to pursue career success. Such pursuit would have required me to hold too much of myself aloof from husband and children: the invisible "wedge-shaped core of darkness" that Virginia Woolf described as being oneself would have to be too large, and not enough of me would have been left over for them.

I feared that if I cultivated that "wedge-shaped core of darkness" within myself enough to maintain a successful career, I would be consumed by that career, and that thus desiccated, too little of me would remain to flesh out my roles as wife and mother. Giving most of myself to the market seemed less appropriate and attractive than reserving myself for my family. Reinforcing this decision was my experience that when a woman lives too much in her mind, she finds it increasingly difficult to live through her body. Her nurturing ties to her children become attenuated; her physical relationship with her husband becomes hollow and perfunctory. Certainly in my case, Dr. James C. Neely spoke the truth in *Gender: The Myth of Equality:* "With too much emphasis on intellect, a woman becomes 'too into her head' to function in a sexual, motherly way, destroying by the process of thought the process of feeling her sexuality."

Virginia Woolf never compromised her market achievements with motherhood; nor did the Brontë sisters, Jane Austen, or George Eliot. Nor did Helen Frankenthaler who, at the time she was acknowledged to be the most prominent living female artist, said in an interview: "We all make different compromises. And, no, I don't regret not having children. Given my painting, children could have suffered. A mother must make her children come first: young children are helpless. Well, paintings are objects but they're also helpless." I agree with her; that is precisely how I felt about the briefs I wrote for clients. Those briefs were, to me, like helpless children; in writing them, I first learned the meaning of complete devotion. I stopped writing them because I believed they would have been masters too jealous of my husband and my children.

Society never rebuked these women for refusing to compromise their literary and artistic achievements. Neither should it rebuke other kinds of women for refusing to compromise their own artistry of motherhood and domesticity. Some women may agree that the reality I depict rings truer to them than the feminist depiction. This conviction may help them find the courage of a heretic. Some others, both men and women, may see enough truth in the reality I depict that they will come to regret society's acquiescence in the status degradation of the housewife. They may then accept the currently unfashionable notion that society should respect and support women who adopt the anti-feminist perspective.

It is in society's interest to begin to pull apart the double-bind web spun by feminism and so order itself as not to inhibit any woman who *could* be an awakened Brünnhilde. Delighted and contented women will certainly do less harm—and probably more good—to society than frenzied and despairing ones. This is not to suggest that society should interfere with a woman's decision to follow the feminist script and adopt any form of spiritual virginity that suits her. But neither should society continue to validate destruction of the women's pact by the contemporary feminists who sought to make us all follow their script. We should now begin to dismantle our regime that discourages and disadvantages the traditional woman who rejects feminist spiritual virginity and seeks instead the very different delight and contentment that she believes best suits her.

American Women in the Twentieth Century

In 1900, our foremothers predicted that the twentieth century would be the "century of the child." It might be more accurate, however, to call it the "century of women." Among the many dramatic changes in American society, it is hard to find an example more striking than the changes in women's lives on every level.

At the beginning of the twentieth century, women were challenging the confines of an ideology that relegated them to the private realm of domesticity. Despite the reality that thousands of women could be found in factories, offices, and fields—not to mention in a wide variety of political and reform activities—those ideas still held powerful sway both in law and in dominant notions of propriety. Over the course of the twentieth century, however, women in America emerged fully (though still not equally) into all aspects of public life—politics, labor force participation, professions, mass media, and popular culture. As they did so, they experienced a transformation in the fundamental parameters of their private lives as well—marriage, family, fertility, and sexuality. In complex ways, women transformed the landscapes of both public and private life so that at century's end we are left with a deeply puzzling conundrum about just what we mean by the terms *public* and *private*.

Women, of course, are part of every other social group. Deeply divided by race, class, religion, ethnicity, and region, they don't always identify with one another, and as a result women's collective identity—their sense of solidarity as women—has waxed and waned. Twice in this century, however, there has been a massive wave of activism focused on women's rights. We can trace the surges of change in women's status that accompanied each of these, one at the beginning and another near the end of the century.

Changes in women's lives were certainly driven by large structural forces such as the emergence of the postindustrial service economy, rising levels of education, and the exigencies of two world wars. Yet they have also been due to women's own self-organized activism in two great waves and in numerous ripples in between. In some instances women fought for the right to participate in public life. In other instances, already present in public spaces, they struggled for equity. As a result of these struggles, American political and public life has undergone a series of fundamental transformations. Not only are women in different places at the end of the century then they were at the beginning, but also all Americans enter a new century shaped by the complexities of women's journey.

1900—Dawn of the Twentieth Century

At the beginning of the twentieth century, women's lives were defined primarily by their marital status, linked to race and class. If we take a snapshot (understanding that we are capturing a moment in a dynamic process of change), the normative adult woman—both statistically and in the images that pervaded popular culture—was married, middle class, and white. On average, women lived to 48.3 years; they married around age 22 and bore approximately four children. The vast majority of households consisted of male-headed married couples and their children.

In 1900 women's legal standing was fundamentally governed by their marital status. They had very few rights.

- A married woman had no separate legal identity from that of her husband.
- She had no right to control of her reproduction (even conveying information about contraception, for example, was illegal); and no right to sue or be sued, since she had no separate standing in court.
- She had no right to own property in her own name or to pursue a career of her choice.
- Women could not vote, serve on juries, or hold public office. According to the Supreme Court, Women were not "persons" under the Fourteenth Amendment to the Constitution that guarantees equal protection under the law.

These realities reflected an underlying ideology about women and men that allocated the public realms of work and politics to men and defined the proper place of women in society as fundamentally domestic. Confined to the realm of the home, women's duty to society lay in raising virtuous sons (future citizens) and dutiful daughters (future mothers). Over the course of the nineteenth century, however, women had pushed at the boundaries of their domestic assignment, both by choice and by necessity. They invented forms of politics outside the electoral arena by forming voluntary associations and building institutions in response to unmet social needs. In the 1830s, when women like Sarah and Angelina Grimké began to speak publicly against slavery, the mere appearance of a woman as a public speaker was considered scandalous. By 1900, however, women appeared in all manner of public settings, setting the stage for change in the twentieth century.

Signs of Change

A closer look at women's status in 1900 reveals trends that signal imminent change particularly in the areas of education, labor force participation, and sexuality. The coexistence of new possibilities alongside ongoing restrictions and discrimination laid the groundwork for challenges to the norms of female subordination.

Education   Women in 1900 had achieved a high degree of literacy. In fact, more girls than boys actually graduated from high school, probably because boys had access to many jobs that did not require significant education. When it came to higher education, however, women were seriously disadvantaged. They were overtly excluded from most professional education: only about 5 percent of medical students were women, and women's exclusion from legal education shows up in the fact that in 1920 only 1.4 percent of lawyers in the United States were female.

It is crucial to note, however, that in 1900 women constituted about 30 percent of students in colleges and universities, including schools for the growing female professions of nursing, teaching, librarianship, and social work. In the long run, this was a potent mix, as thousands of middle-class women embraced the opportunity to pursue higher education, which in turn generated new expectations. Education was a crucial force in creating the key leadership as well as a highly skilled constituency for the feminist mobilizations at either end of the century.

Labor Force Participation   In 1900, though wage labor was defined as a fundamentally male prerogative, women could be found in many parts of the labor force. Women's work outside the home, however, was framed by their marital status and overt discrimination based on race as well as sex.

- Approximately one in five women worked outside the home, a figure that was sharply distinguished by race: 41 percent nonwhite; 17 percent white.
- The average working woman was single and under age 25.
- Only 11 percent of married women worked outside the home (up to 15% by 1940), though the proportion among black women (26%) was considerably higher because discrimination against black men made it much harder for blacks to secure a livable income from a single wage.
- Available occupations were sharply limited. Most women who worked for wages served as domestics, farm laborers, unskilled factory operatives, or teachers. In fact, one in three women employed in nonagricultural pursuits worked in domestic service.
- Some new female-dominated professions, such as nursing, social work, and librarianship, were emerging. In addition, the feminization of clerical work, linked to the new technology of the typewriter and the record-keeping needs of growing corporate bureaucracies, signaled a dramatic trend that made the "working girl" increasingly respectable. By 1920 the proportion of women engaged in clerical work (25.6%) had surpassed the number in manufacturing (23.8), domestic service (18.2%), and agriculture (12.9%).

Sexuality and the Body   Late Victorians presumed (if they thought about it at all) that female sexuality should be confined entirely to marriage. Compared with today, there was very little premarital sex, and women were understood not to have much in the way of sexual desire. It was illegal to transmit information about contraception, though women clearly conveyed it anyway through networks of rumor and gossip. Within the dominant middle class even the simplest acknowledgments of female sexuality were suppressed into euphemism and other forms of denial. Body parts could not be named in polite company, so chicken "legs" and "breast," for example, became "dark meat" and "white meat." Female attire covered women's bodies with clothing that revealed some shape but very little skin.

Yet, as the twentieth century dawned with its emerging consumer culture, sexuality could no longer be so easily contained. Popular culture included vaudeville, dance halls, and a growing variety of public amusements (such as the brand-new movie theaters). In the past, women who frequented such places risked having a "bad reputation." Yet the growing popularity of public amusements within the "respectable middle class" was beginning to challenge such perceptions.

Women's bodies were also finding new visibility in athletics. In the wildly popular arenas of public competition such as baseball and boxing, athletics were virtually synonymous with masculinity. And yet women were beginning to play lawn tennis, field hockey, and gymnastics. Some even rode bicycles.

Race, Class, and Gender Ideals   Within the gender ideology of the urban middle class that emerged over the course of the nineteenth century, the "good woman" (and her antithesis) took on distinct characteristics associated with race and class. "Good" (white, Protestant, middle class) women embodied private virtues. They were chaste, domestic, pious, and submissive. "Bad" women were "low class"—immigrants, racial minorities—presumed to be promiscuous, bad mothers, and improper housewives largely on the basis of their presence in previously male-only public spaces (factories, saloons, dance halls). Such perceptions multiplied in the case of southern black women subjected to a regime of racial/sexual domination that included the constant threat of rape and the public humiliations of segregation. Yet, the denigration of lower-class and minority women on the basis of their presence in public was getting harder to sustain as growing numbers of supposedly "respectable" women showed up in the same, or similar, spaces.

The First Wave

This brief sketch of women's condition at the beginning of the century points to several forces for change that would bear fruit in the first few decades. The growth in women's education, their move into a wide variety of reform efforts as well as professions, laid the groundwork for a massive suffrage movement that demanded the most basic right of citizenship for women. The claim of citizenship was in many ways a deeply radical challenge to the ideology of separate spheres for men and women. It asserted the right of the individual woman to stand in direct relation to the state rather than to be represented through the participation of her husband or father. The growing power of the women's suffrage movement rested both on women's collective consciousness, born in female associations, and on increased individualism among women in an urbanizing industrializing economy.

While a small but crucial number of upper-middle-class women attended college, where they developed a transformed awareness of their own potential as women both individually and collectively, working-class immigrant and African-American women experienced both individualism and collectivity in very different ways. Forced to work outside the home in the least-skilled, lowest paying jobs, both they and their employers presumed that women's labor force participation was temporary. Unions objected to their presence and blocked them from apprenticeship and access to skilled jobs. Despite these obstacles, when wage-earning women organized their own unions, often in alliance with middle-class reformers, they exhibited awesome courage and militancy. In the garment district of New York, for example, the "uprising of the twenty thousand" in 1909 confounded the garment industry and led to a new kind of industrial unionism.

By 1910, middle-class white reformers had formed increasingly effective alliances with black and working-class women around the issue of women's suffrage. The massive mobilization of American women in the decade before the Nineteenth Amendment was ratified in 1920 included rallies of thousands of "working girls" and the organization of numerous African-American women's suffrage clubs. Shared exclusion from the individual right of civic participation symbolized their common womanhood. Following their victory, leaders of the National American Woman Suffrage Association joyfully dismantled their organization and reassembled as the newly formed League of Women Voters. Their new task, as they defined it, was to train women to exercise their individual citizenship rights.

Such a reorientation seemed congruent with the popular culture of the 1920s, which emphasized individual pleasures along with individual rights. The development of a consumer economy, emphasizing pleasure and using sexuality to sell, offered women other paths out of submissive domesticity and into more assertive forms of individualism, paths that did not require solidarity, indeed undermined it. The female subculture that relied on a singular definition of "woman" eroded. Female reform efforts remained a powerful force in American politics—laying much of the groundwork for the emergence of a welfare state—but a broad-based movement for women's rights no longer existed after 1920. The pace of change in areas like education and labor force participation also reached a plateau and remained relatively unchanged for several decades after 1920. Modern women were individuals. And "feminism" became an epithet.

The loss of female solidarity meant that women's organizations in subsequent decades drew on narrow constituencies with very different priorities. Professional women, lonely pioneers in many fields, felt the continuing sting of discrimination and sought to eradicate the last vestiges of legal discrimination with an Equal Rights Amendment (ERA). The National Women's Party, one of the leading organizations in the struggle, first proposed the ERA in 1923 for the vote. But they were opposed by former allies, social reformers who feared that the protections for working women, which they had won during the Progressive era, would be lost. Though fiercely opposed to the ERA, reformers continued to advocate a stronger role for government in responding to social welfare. Many of them—with leaders like Eleanor Roosevelt—assumed key positions in the 1930s and shaped the political agenda known as the New Deal. In particular, their influence on the Social Security Act laid the foundations of the welfare state. Even among female reformers, however, alliances across racial lines remained rare and fraught with difficulty. As the progressive female reform tradition shaped an emergent welfare state, African-American voices remained muted, the needs of working women with children unaddressed.

The Second Wave

By mid-century the conditions for another surge of activism were under way. During the Second World War women joined the labor force in unprecedented numbers. Most significant, perhaps, married women and women over age 35 became normative among working women by 1950. Yet cold war culture, in the aftermath of World War II, reasserted traditional gender roles. The effort to contain women within the confines of the "feminine mystique" (as Betty Friedan later labeled this ideology), however, obscured but did not prevent rising activism among different constituencies of women. Under the cover of popular images of domesticity, women were rapidly changing their patterns of labor force and civic participation, initiating social movements for civil rights and world peace, and flooding into institutions of higher education.

The President's Commission on the Status of Women, established in 1961, put women's issues back on the national political agenda by recruiting a network of powerful women to develop a set of shared goals. They issued a report in 1963, the same year that Friedan published The Feminine Mystique. That report documented in meticulous detail the ongoing realities of discrimination in employment and in wages, numerous legal disabilities such as married women's lack of access to credit, and the growing problems of working mothers without adequate child care. In 1964, Title VII of the Civil Rights Act gave women their most powerful legal weapon against employment discrimination. An opponent of civil rights introduced Title VII, and many members of Congress treated it as a joke. But Title VII passed because the small number of women then in Congress fiercely and effectively defended the need to prohibit discrimination on the basis of "sex" as well as race, religion, and national origin.

The second wave emerged simultaneously among professional women and a younger cohort of social activists. Professionals, with the leadership of women in labor unions, government leaders, and intellectuals like Friedan, created the National Organization for Women (NOW) in 1966 to demand enforcement of laws like Title VII. A second branch of feminist activism emerged from younger women in the civil rights movement and the student new left. Civil rights offered a model of activism, an egalitarian and visionary language, an opportunity to develop political skills, and role models of courageous female leaders. Young women broke away in 1967 to form consciousness-raising groups and build on the legacy of the movements that had trained them.

The slogan, "the personal is political," became the ideological pivot of the second wave of American feminism. It drove a variety of challenges to gendered relations of power, whether embodied in public policy or in the most intimate personal relationships. The force of this direct assault on the public/private dichotomy has left deep marks on American politics, American society, and the feminist movement itself. Issues like domestic violence, child care, abortion, and sexual harassment have become central to the American political agenda, exposing deep divisions in American society that are not easily subject to the give-and-take compromises of political horse-trading.

From 1968 to 1975, the "Women's Liberation Movement," using the techniques of consciousness-raising in small groups, grew explosively. The synergy between different branches of feminist activism made the 1970s a very dynamic era. Feminist policymakers dubbed the years 1968 to 1975 "the golden years" because of their success in courtrooms and legislatures. These included the Equal Rights Amendment, which passed Congress in 1972 and went to the states; the 1973 Supreme Court decision legalizing abortion (*Roe* v. *Wade*); Title IX of the Higher Education Act, which opened intercollegiate athletics to women; the Women's Equity Education Act; and the Equal Credit Opportunity Act.

Women formed caucuses and organizations in most professional associations and in the labor movement. By the mid-1970s there were feminist organizations representing a broad range of racial groups as well—African-American women, Chicanas and Hispanic women, Asian-American women, Native American women. Women also built new organizations among clerical workers to challenge the devaluation and limited opportunities of traditional women's work.

With their new strength, women challenged barriers to the professions (law, medicine), to ordination within mainstream Protestant and Jewish denominations, and to the full range of traditionally male blue-collar occupations, from carpenters to firefighters and police. They filed thousands of complaints of discrimination, mounted hundreds of lawsuits, and also built thousands of new institutions—day-care centers, shelters for battered women, bookstores, coffeehouses, and many others. The new feminism drew on women's stories to rethink the most intimate personal aspects of womanhood including abortion rights, sexual autonomy, rape, domestic violence, and lesbian rights.

The second wave of feminism also changed the American language both through its own publications (of which there were hundreds, the largest of them being *Ms.*, first published in 1972) and through pressure on commercial publishing houses and mass media. New words entered the American lexicon—"Ms.," "firefighter," "sexism"—while uses of the generic masculine (mankind, brotherhood, policeman) suddenly seemed exclusive. In Women's Studies programs, which grew rapidly in the early 1970s, young scholars rethought the paradigms of their disciplines and initiated new branches of knowledge.

The second wave provoked a strong reaction, of course, revealing not only male hostility but also deep fissures among women themselves. Antifeminism became a strong political force by the late 1970s with the mobilization of Phyllis Schlafley's Stop-ERA and antiabortion forces. In the face of widespread cultural anxiety about equality for women and changing gender roles, the Equal Rights Amendment stalled after 1975 and went down to defeat in 1982 despite an extension of the deadline for ratification. Antifeminism drew on the insecurities of a declining economy in the wake of the Vietnam War and on the growing political power of the New Right which made cultural issues (abortion, the ERA, "family values," and homophobia) central. The

1980s, framed by the hostile political climate of the Reagan administration, nourished a growing backlash against feminism in the media, the popular culture, and public policy. As public spending shifted away from social programs and toward the military, female poverty increased sharply. The Reagan boom after 1983 did not touch the poorest, disproportionately female and racial minority, segments of the population.

At the same time, the 1980s witnessed the continued growth of women's presence in positions of public authority: Supreme Court justice, astronaut, arctic explorer, military officer, truck driver, carpenter, Olympic star, bishop, rabbi. Mainstream religious denominations began to rewrite liturgies and hymn books to make them more "inclusive." Despite regular announcements of the "death" of feminism, it would be more accurate to say that in the 1980s feminism entered the mainstream with new levels of community activism, sophisticated political fundraisers like EMILY's List, and broad political alliances on issues like comparable worth. Experimental "counterinstitutions" started in the 1970s (battered women's shelters, health clinics, bookstores, etc.) survived by adopting more institutionalized procedures, professionalized staff, and state funding. Women's Studies took on the trappings of an academic discipline.

Feminism was broad, diffuse, and of many minds in the 1980s. Legal and cultural issues grew more complex. Feminist theorists wrestled with the realities of differences such as race, class, age, and sexual preference, asking themselves whether the category "woman" could withstand such an analysis. The multifaceted activities that embraced the label "feminist"—policy activism, research think tanks, literary theory, music, art, spirituality—signaled the fact that the women's movement had lost some cohesiveness.

The testimony of Anita Hill during the 1991 hearings on the nomination of Clarence Thomas to the Supreme Court, however, catalyzed a new round of national conversation, complicated by the deep fissures of race and sex. The sight of a genteel black woman being grilled by a committee of white men who made light of this "sexual harassment crap" mobilized thousands of women to run for office and contribute to campaigns. In 1992 an unprecedented number of women were elected to public office.

2000—Dawn of a New Millennium

If we return to our original categories to describe women's situation at the end of the twentieth century, the contrast with 1900 could hardly be more dramatic. The average woman now can expect to live 79.7 years (65% longer than her great-grandmother in 1900), marry at age 24.5, and bear only about two children (if any at all). There are now decades in women's lives—both before and after the years of childbearing and child care—which earlier generations never experienced. As a result of the second wave of women's rights activism in the final decades of the twentieth century, in politics and law, labor force participation, education, and sexuality women live in a truly different world. Yet, in each instance equity remains an elusive goal, suggesting the need for continued and revitalized activism in the twenty-first century.

Politics and Law

No longer defined by their marital status, women enjoy virtually the full range of formal legal rights. In addition to winning the right to vote in 1920, they achieved equal pay (for the same work) in 1963 and guarantees against discrimination in housing and employment in 1964 (Title VII of the Civil Rights Act). Since 1970 women have won the right to a separate legal identity; privacy rights regarding reproduction and bodily integrity; and rights to sue for discrimination in employment, to work when pregnant, to equal education, and to equal access to athletics. Whole new bodies of law have developed since the 1970s on issues like domestic violence and sexual harassment. Nonetheless, the failure of the Equal Rights Amendment (ERA) in 1982 means that women still have no constitutional guarantee of equality.

In the last twenty-five years we have also seen a dramatic growth in the numbers of female elected officials. In 1997 there were 60 women in Congress (11.2%)—14 of them women of color; 81 statewide executive officials (25%); 1,597 state legislators (21.5%); and 203 mayors of cities with population over 30,000 (20.6%). There are two women on the Supreme Court, 30 female circuit court judges (18.6%), and 107 female district court judges (17.2%).

Education

At the end of the twentieth century, 88 percent of young women ages 25 to 34 are high-school graduates. The transformations in primary and secondary education for girls cannot be captured in graduation numbers, however. They also reside in the admission of girls to shop and other vocational classes (and boys to cooking and sewing courses), in girls' participation in athletics, in curricula that—at least sometimes—emphasize women's achievements in the past, and in school counselors who no longer single-mindedly socialize girls for domesticity and/or nonskilled stereotypically female jobs.

In the arena of higher education women are closing in on equity. Today, 54 percent of all bachelor of arts degrees go to women; 25 percent of women aged 25 to 34 are college graduates. Most striking, the proportion of women in professional schools is now between 36 and 43 percent. The revolution of the late twentieth century is evident in these figures, as most of the change occurred in the last three decades. Compare current numbers with those of 1960, when the proportion of women in law school was 2 percent (today 43%); medicine 6 percent (today 38%); MBA programs 4 percent (today 36%); Ph.D. programs 11 percent (today 39%), and dentistry 1 percent (today 38%).

Labor Force Participation

In stark contrast to a century ago, more than 61 percent of all women are in the labor force, including two-thirds of women with preschoolers and three-fourths of women with school-age children. Though African-American women continue to work at a higher rate than average (76% overall), the gap is clearly shrinking as the patterns that they pioneered are becoming the norm. With overt discrimination now outlawed, women practice virtually every occupation on the spectrum from blue collar to professional.

Yet alongside change, older patterns persist. Women remain concentrated in female-dominated, low-paid service occupations despite their presence in many professions and in traditionally male blue-collar occupations such as construction or truck driving. Although the exceptions are highly visible (tracked in the popular media frequently as interesting and unusual phenomena), 70 percent of women work either in the services industry (health and education) or in wholesale or retail trade. Women's median weekly earnings are still only 75 percent those of men—though there has been a dramatic gain since 1970 when they were 62.2 percent. (Note, however, that this change represents a combined gain for women of 17% and a 3% decline for men.)

Sexuality, Fertility, and Marriage

The late twentieth century has witnessed a sharp increase in single motherhood even as overall fertility has declined. One birth in three is to an unmarried woman; in 1970, that proportion was only one in ten. Sixty-nine percent of children live with two parents; 23.5 percent with mother only (for African Americans this is 52%).

Some of this single parenthood is due to divorce, something that was relatively rare in 1900 and today affects nearly one in every two marriages. The divorce rate seems to have peaked in 1980, however, and has declined somewhat since that time (in 1980 there were 5.2 divorces/1,000 population; today there are 4.4). Single motherhood is not the source of shame that it was in 1900, but it remains highly correlated with poverty.

If female sexuality was suppressed in 1900 (even though incompletely), at the end of the century sexual references and images saturate American culture. It was not until the 1930s that birth control became legal in most states. In 1961 the birth control pill introduced the possibility of radically separating sexual experience from the likelihood of procreation. Then in 1973, the Supreme Court's Roe v. Wade decision legalized abortion. Today, premarital sex is common, even normative. According to the Alan Guttmacher Institute, in the early 1990s 56 percent of women and 73 percent of men had sex by age 18.

As dramatic, homosexuality has become an open subject of public discourse, and lesbians—once completely hidden, even to one another—are creating new public spaces and organizations, fields of intellectual inquiry and theory, and families that rely on voluntary ties in the absence of any legal sanction. Lesbians have been a major constituency and source of leadership in the second feminist wave. Twenty years of visibility, however, is just a beginning. American society remains deeply, and emotionally, divided on the issue of homosexuality. Opposition to gay rights marks a key issue for the religious right, and open violence against lesbians and gay men continues.

Race and Class

The second wave grew directly from and modeled itself on the civil rights movement in the 1950s and 1960s. That movement, itself, relied heavily on the grass-roots (if relatively invisible) leadership of African-American women. In the last decades of the century, the voices of minority women have become increasingly distinct and powerful. Diversity among women, as in the society at large, has taken on new dimensions with a surge of immigration since the 1960s from Southeast Asia, East Africa, Central America, and other parts of the Third World. Predictions based on immigration and fertility suggest that by the middle of the next century whites will be only half the U.S. population. Women of color will become the new norm. Women remain deeply divided on racial grounds, but race is no longer defined as black and white.

Challenges to traditional conceptions of gender have also shaken the previous consensus on what constitutes a "good woman" (except perhaps to the right-wing traditionalists who still hold to a set of ideals quite similar to those that dominated American culture a century ago). Yet discomfort with women's move into public life is still widespread, and race and class stigmas remain. The massive growth of a welfare system whose clients are disproportionately women and children combines racial and gender stereotypes to create a new category of "bad women": single, minority, poor mothers. And wherever women appear in previously male-dominated environments, they remain suspect. In particular, the sharply polarized emotional response to Hillary Rodham Clinton during her time as first lady illustrates the undercurrent of anger at powerful, professional women. Radio talk shows have filled thousands of hours with hosts and callers venting their hostility toward this woman who, in their view, did not stay "in her place." But, of course, that is the open question at century's end: just what is "woman's place"?

Conclusion

This brief discussion of women in the twentieth century does not trace a smooth arc from the beginning of the century to the end. It is not simply about "progress" toward "equality." But it is, indeed, about a kind of sea change with unanticipated consequences and with dramatic acceleration in the last thirty years.

In the nineteenth century women created much of what today we call civil society. In the twentieth century they used that layer of society—which lies between formal governmental structures and private familial life—in an amazing variety of ways to reshape the landscape of American life. Virtually all of the public spaces previously presumed to belong properly to men—paid labor, higher education, electoral politics and public office, athletics—now incorporate a large and visible proportion of women. This theme of participation in public life, and the concomitant politicization of issues previously considered personal, runs through the entire century.

Such spectacular shifts have clearly been driven by large structural forces: the emergence of a postindustrial service economy, rising levels of education, two cataclysmic world wars, global power and national wealth on a level never imagined, changing patterns of marriage, fertility, and longevity. Yet the most dramatic changes can clearly be traced in equal measure to two large waves of women's activism.

The suffrage movement, by the 1910s, involved hundreds of thousands of women, branching out both tactically with the use of massive public parades and street corner speeches (females occupying public, political spaces) and in composition as it reached out to working women, immigrants, and minorities. That movement won for women the fundamental right of citizenship, the right to vote. And the Progressive movement on which it built laid the groundwork and provided many key players for the subsequent emergence of the welfare state. The impact of the second wave shows up in the astonishing acceleration of change in the last three decades of the century.

Each of these waves continued to surge forward in the decades after cresting. But each was also followed by a period in which the multiplicity of women's voices reasserted itself along with debates over the real meaning of equality. And each left much work undone for subsequent generations that face new issues and new dilemmas.

In the twenty-first century women will have choices that have never before been available, but they will not be easy. The twentieth century challenged our very definitions of male and female. Many of the signs of manhood and womanhood no longer function effectively. Work is no longer a manly prerogative and responsibility. Families are no longer constituted around a male breadwinner, a wife, and their children. More often they are two-income households (same or different sexes) or single-parent households. Large numbers of single men and women live alone. Yet "family values" have become a political code for attacks on welfare mothers, homosexuals, and nontraditional families (which, in fact, far outnumbered traditional ones). In the absence of significant societal or governmental support for women's traditional responsibilities, women assume a double burden. They participate in the labor force almost to the same degree as men, and yet work outside the home is still organized as though workers had wives to take care of household work, child care, and the myriad details of private life. Work outside the home makes few accommodations to the demands and priorities of family life.

The pioneering work of the twentieth century—as women made their way into hostile, male-dominated public spaces—remains unfinished. Most of the barriers have been broken at least once. But equity remains a distant goal. Achieving that goal is complicated by the fact that for the moment women are not a highly unified group. The contemporary struggles within feminism to deal with the differences among women are the essential precursor to any future social movement that claims to speak for women as a group. The very meanings of masculinity and femininity and their multiple cultural and symbolic references are now overtly contested throughout the popular culture.

Another legacy of the feminist movement that proclaimed that "the personal is political" is an unresolved ambiguity about just where the boundary between the personal and the political properly lies, and the dilemmas resulting from politicizing private life. At the end of the century, Americans faced a constitutional crisis rooted in the strange career of personal politics. For an entire year virtually everyone in the United States was riveted by the scandal concerning President Clinton, Monica Lewinsky, Kenneth Starr, and the American Congress. Behaviors that once would have been considered purely private (and gone unremarked by political reporters, for example) became the basis for impeachment. Who defended the distinction between public and private and who assaulted it? The tables seem to have turned with a vengeance as the right wing pried into intimate details about the president's sexual activities in a consensual relationship while the liberals (including feminist leaders) protested. The politicization of private life is indeed a double-edged sword. This should be no surprise, as conservative backlash since the 1970s has evidenced a clear willingness to use the power of the state to enforce its vision of proper private relationships on issues such as abortion, homosexuality, divorce, prayer in the schools, and the content of textbooks.

The recent history of feminism calls to our attention a number of dimensions in this crisis that should not go unnoticed. First, there have always been many members of society (racial and sexual minorities, welfare recipients, and women, to name only the most obvious) whose private behaviors have been scrutinized and regulated by those in power. By forcing these issues into public debate and evolving laws that might protect such groups (for example laws against sexual harassment) feminists have also removed the cover of silence that protected powerful men from public scrutiny for their private behaviors. That such laws were subsequently used in a campaign to unseat a president whose election was directly due to the votes of politically mobilized women resonates with irony.

Women's solidarity has waxed and waned across the twentieth century. It will certainly continue to do so in the twenty-first. The next wave of feminist activism will no doubt take a shape we cannot envision, just as no one at the dawn of the twentieth century could have imagined the battles that awaited them. That there will be another wave, however, is a safe prediction, given the unfinished agendas of the last century and the still unforeseen contradictions that future changes will create. The next wave will shape the new century.

Bibliography

William H. Chafe, *The American Woman: Her Changing Social, Economic, and Political Roles, 1920–1970* (New York: Oxford University Press, 1972), laid the groundwork for subsequent studies of twentieth-century women. Peter Filene examines the implications of changing definitions of womanliness and manliness on both sexes in *Him/Her Self: Sex Roles in Modern America*, 2nd ed. (Baltimore: Johns Hopkins University Press, 1986). Sara M. Evans, *Born for Liberty: A History of Women in America*, 2nd ed. (New York: Free Press, 1996) provides a general overview of women in American history.

The "first wave" of women's rights activism in the twentieth century is chronicled by Nancy F. Cott, *The Grounding of Modern Feminism* (New Haven, Conn.: Yale University Press, 1987), and Mari Jo Buhle and Paul Buhle, eds., *The Concise History of Woman Suffrage: Selections from the Classic Work of Stanton, Anthony, Gage, and Harper* (Urbana: University of Illinois Press, 1978). On women's role in the New Deal see Susan Ware, *Beyond Suffrage: Women in the New Deal* (Cambridge, Mass.: Harvard University Press, 1981). The critical eras of the 1940s and the cold war are examined in Susan Hartmann, *The Homefront and Beyond: American Women in the 1940s* (Boston: Twayne Publishers, 1982) and Elaine Tyler May, *Homeward Bound: American Families in the Cold*

War Era (New York: Basic Books, 1988). There is a growing literature on the "second wave" of feminism. Some starting points would be Sara Evans, *Personal Politics: The Roots of Women's Liberation in the Civil Rights Movement and the New Left* (New York: Vintage, 1980); Alice Echols, *Daring to Be Bad: Radical Feminism in America, 1967–1975* (Minneapolis: University of Minnesota Press, 1989); and Donald Mathews and Jane De Hart, *Sex, Gender, and the Politics of ERA* (New York: Oxford University Press, 1990).

For more depth on the history of sexuality see John D'Emilio and Estelle B. Freedman, *Intimate Matters: A History of Sexuality in America* (New York: Harper & Row, 1988); on education see Barbara Solomon, *In the Company of Educated Women: A History of Women and Higher Education in America* (New Haven, Conn.: Yale University Press, 1985); on women in the labor force see Julia Blackwelder, *Now Hiring: The Feminization of Work in the United States: 1900–1995* (College Station: Texas A&M University Press, 1997. Some excellent starting points on racial minority and immigrant ethnic women include Vicki L. Ruíz, *From Out of the Shadows: Mexican Women in Twentieth-Century America* (New York: Oxford University Press, 1999); on African-American women see Jacqueline Jones, *Labor of Love, Labor of Sorrow: Black Women, Work, and the Family from Slavery to the Present* (New York: Basic Books, 1985), and on Chinese women Judy Yung, *Unbound Feet: A Social History of Chinese Women in San Francisco* (Barkeley: University of California Press, 1995); Donna Gabaccia, *From the Other Side: Women, Gender, and Immigrant Life in the U.S., 1920–1990* (Bloomington: Indiana University Press, 1994),

For the most recent descriptions of women's status in all aspects of American life, see the series sponsored by the Women's Research and Education Institute in Washington, D.C., *The American Woman* (New York: W. W. Norton). This series has been updated biannually from its inception in 1987.

POSTSCRIPT

Has the Women's Movement of the 1970s Failed to Liberate American Women?

F. Carolyn Graglia's critique of contemporary feminism is a throwback to women of the late nineteenth and early twentieth century who opposed the women social workers and suffragettes who entered the man's world. Her book is a modern restatement of Barbara Welter's classic and widely reprinted article, "The Cult of True Womanhood," *American Quarterly* (Summer 1996).

Graglia argues that contemporary feminism ignores women's primary role in raising the children and preserving the moral character of the family. She blames contemporary feminism along with the Great Society's social programs for promoting a sexual revolution that has destroyed the American family by fostering sexually transmitted diseases and a high divorce rate.

Historian Sara M. Evans takes a long-range view of the women's liberation movement. By comparing the political, legal, and domestic situation of women in 1900 with today, Evans charts the successes and failures that were achieved by the two waves of feminist protest movements in the twentieth century.

At the beginning of the twentieth century, a number of middle-class women from elite colleges in the northeast were in the vanguard of a number of progressive reform movements—temperance, anti-prostitution, child labor, and settlement houses. Working in tandem with the daughters of first-generation immigrants employed in the garment industry, the early feminists realized that laws affecting women could be passed only if women had the right to vote. The suffragettes overcame the arguments of male and female antisuffragists who associated women voters with divorce, promiscuity, and neglect of children and husbands with the ratification of the Nineteenth Amendment in 1920.

The women's movement stalled between the two wars for a variety of reasons: Women pursued their own individual freedom in a consumer-oriented society in the 1920s, and the Great Depression of the 1930s placed the economic survival of the nation at the forefront. But the Second World War had long-range effects on women. Minorities—African Americans and Hispanics—worked for over 3 years in factory jobs traditionally reserved for white males at high wages. So did married white females, often in their thirties. Although the majority of these women returned to the home or took more traditional low-paying "women's" jobs after the war, the consciousness of the changing role of women during the Second World War would reappear during the 1960s.

Evans points out the two streams that formed the women's liberation movement from the mid-1960s. First were the professional women like Betty Freidan, who created the National Organization for Women (NOW) in 1966, who worked with women leaders in labor unions, government, and consciousness-raising groups to demand enforcement of Title VII of the 1965 Civil Rights Act, which banned discrimination in employment and wages. A second wing of feminist activists came from the civil rights and anti-war new left protest groups from the elite universities. Many of these women felt like second-class citizens in these movements and decided they had their own issues that they had to deal with.

Evans dubbed the years 1968 to 1975 "the golden years" because of the following successes: "Passage of the Equal Rights Amendment in Congress in 1972; the 1973 Supreme Court decision (*Roe* v. *Wade*) legalizing abortion; Title IX of the Higher Education Act which opened intercollegiate athletics to women; the Women's Equity Education Act; and the Equal Credit Opportunity Act."

Evans points out that the women's movement suffered a "backlash" in the 1980s as America became much more conservative. The new right blamed the increases in divorce, single parenthood, out-of-wedlock births, abortions, and open homosexuality on the cultural values of the 1960s. But by the beginning of the twenty-first century, middle-class women made substantial gains in the professions compared with 1960: Law school today 43 percent, 1960 2 percent; medicine today 38 percent, 1960 6 percent; MBA programs today 35 percent, 1960 4 percent; dentistry today 38 percent, 1960 1 percent; and Ph.D. programs today 39 percent, 1960 11 percent. Working-class women, however, have been much less successful in breaking into traditional blue collar jobs such as truck driving and construction.

Both the antifeminist Graglia and to a much less extent the pro-feminist Evans have been critiqued by moderate feminists like Elizabeth Fox-Genovese and Cathy Young, who contend that contemporary feminists have not spoken to the concerns of married women, especially women from poor to lower-middle-class families who must work in order to help support the family. Fox-Genovese's *Feminism Is Not the Story of My Life: How Today's Feminist Elite Have Lost Touch With the Real Concerns of Women* (Doubleday, 1996) is peppered with interviews of white, African American, and Hispanic Americans of different classes and gives a more complex picture of the problems women face today. Young, author of *Cease Fire! Why Women and Men Must Join Forces to Achieve True Equality* (Free Press, 1999), asserts that Graglia denies the real discrimination women faced in the job market in the 1950s. Furthermore, Graglia's critique of the sexual revolution is an attempt to restore a view of female sexuality as essentially submissive.

In 1998 Harvard University Press reprinted Betty Friedan's two later books—*The Second Stage* and *It Changed My Life*, both with new introductions with suggestions for the twenty-first century—which are critical of some of the directions that the women's movement took.

Important books and articles by activists with a historical perspective include Sara Evans, *Personal Politics: The Roots of Women's Liberation in the Civil Rights Movement and the New Left* (Vintage, 1979). This book is nicely summarized in "Sources of the Second Wave: The Rebirth of Feminism," in Alexander Bloom, ed., *Long Time Gone: Sixties America Then and Now* (Oxford, 2001). For a general overview of women's history, see Evans, *Born for Liberty: A History of*

Women in America, 2nd ed. (Free Press, 1996), and Roger Adelson's *"Interview with Sara Margaret Evans,"* *The Historian* (vol. 63, Fall 2000); Donna Gabaccia, *From the Other Side: Women, Gender and Immigrant Life in the U.S., 1920–1990* (Indiana University Press, 1994); and John D'Emilio and Estelle B. Freedman, *Intimate Matters: A History of Sexuality in America* (Harper & Row, 1988).

Review essays from various journals reflect the continuous battle over the importance of the women's movement. The neo-conservative magazine *Commentary* is constantly critical of feminism. See Elizabeth Kristol, "The Sexual Revolution" (April 1996) and Elizabeth Powers, "Back to Basics" (March 1999). Also critical is Daphne Patai, "Will the Real Feminists in Academe Stand Up," *The Chronicle of Higher Education* (October 6, 2000 pp. B6–9). Sympathetic to the movement is Christine Stansell, "Girlie Interrupted: The Generational Progress of Feminism," *The New Republic* (January 15, 2001); Andrew Hacker, "How Are Women Doing," *The New York Review of Books* (Fall 2000). See also Jo Freeman, "The Women's Liberation Movement: Its Origins, Structure, Activities, and Ideas," in Jo Freeman, ed., *Women: A Feminist Perspective*, 3rd ed. (Mayfield, 1984); Estelle B. Freedman, *No Turning Back: The History of Feminism and the Future of Women* (Balantine, 2001); and Susan Brownmiller, *In Our Time: Memoir of a Revolution* (Dial Press, 2000).

The best starting point is Ruth Rosen, *The World Split Open: How the Modern Woman's Movement Changed America* (Viking, 2000), written by a former Berkley activist for her students who were born in the 1980s.

Books that deal with the impact of the movement on specific groups include Johnnetta B. Cole and Beverly Gray-Sheftall, *Gender Talk: The Struggle for Women's Equality in African American Communities* (Balantine, 2003); Jacqueline Jones, *Labor of Love, Labor of Sorrow: Black Women, Work, and the Family from Slavery to the Present* (Basic Books, 1985); Vicki L. Ruiz, *From out of the Shadows: Mexican Women in Twentieth-Century Books* (April 11, 2002); and Kim France's review of Phyllis Chesler, *Letters to a Young Feminist* (Four Walls Eight Windows, 1998) in *The New York Times Book Review* (April 26, 1998 pp. 10–11).

ISSUE 12

Was Richard Nixon America's Last Liberal President?

YES: Joan Hoff-Wilson, from "Richard M. Nixon: The Corporate Presidency," in Fred I. Greenstein, ed., *Leadership in the Modern Presidency* (Harvard University Press, 1988)

NO: Bruce J. Schulman, from *The Seventies: The Great Shift in American Culture, Society, and Politics* (The Free Press/Simon & Schuster, 2001)

ISSUE SUMMARY

YES: According to professor of history Joan Hoff-Wilson, the Nixon presidency reorganized the executive branch and portions of the federal bureaucracy and implemented domestic reforms in civil rights, welfare, and economic planning, despite its limited foreign policy successes and the Watergate scandal.

NO: According to Professor Bruce J. Schulman, Richard Nixon was the first conservative president of the post–World War II era who undermined the Great Society legislative program of President Lyndon Baines Johnson and built a new Republican majority coalition of white, northern, blue-collar workers, and southern and sunbelt conservatives.

Richard Milhous Nixon was born in Yorba Linda in Orange County, California, on January 9, 1913. When he was nine, his family moved to Whittier, California. He attended Whittier College, where he excelled at student politics and debating. He earned a tuition-paid scholarship to Duke University Law School and graduated third out of a class of 25 in 1937. He returned to Whittier and for several years worked with the town's oldest law firm.

Nixon had hopes of joining a bigger law firm, but World War II intervened. He joined the navy as a lieutenant, junior grade, where he served in a Naval Transport Unit in the South Pacific for the duration of the war. Before his discharge from active duty, Republicans asked him to run for a seat in California's 12th congressional district in the House of Representatives. He won the primary and defeated Jerry Vorhees, a New Deal Democratic incumbent, in the general election of 1946. In that year, the Republicans gained control of Congress for the first time since 1930.

During Nixon's campaign against Vorhees, he accused Vorhees of accepting money from a communist-dominated political action committee. This tactic, known as "red-baiting," was effective in the late 1940s and early 1950s because the American public had become frightened of the communist menace. In 1950, Nixon utilized similar tactics in running for the U.S. Senate against Congresswoman Helen Gahaghan Douglas. He won easily.

Young, energetic, a vigorous campaign orator, and a senator from the second largest state in the Union with impeccable anticommunist credentials, Nixon was chosen by liberal Republicans to become General Dwight D. Eisenhower's running mate in the 1952 presidential election. In the election, Eisenhower and Nixon overwhelmed the Democrats. Nixon became the second-youngest vice president in U.S. history and actively used the office to further his political ambitions.

The 1960 presidential campaign was one of the closest in modern times. Nixon, who was considered young for high political office at that time, lost to an even younger Democratic senator from Massachusetts, John F. Kennedy. Out of 68 million votes cast, less than 113,000 votes separated the two candidates.

In 1962, Nixon was persuaded to seek the governorship of California on the premise that he needed a power boost to keep his presidential hopes alive for 1964. Apparently, Nixon was out of touch with state politics. Governor Pat Brown defeated him by 300,000 votes.

Nixon then left for New York City and became a partner with a big-time Wall Street legal firm. He continued to speak at Republican dinners, and he supported Barry Goldwater of Arizona for the presidency in March 1968. After Goldwater's decisive defeat by Lyndon B. Johnson, Nixon's political fortunes revived yet again. In March 1965, Johnson announced that he was not going to run again for the presidency. Nixon took advantage of the opening and won the Republican nomination.

During the 1968 presidential campaign, Nixon positioned himself between Democratic Vice President Hubert Humphrey, the liberal defender of the Great Society programs, and the conservative, law-and-order, third-party challenger Governor George Wallace of Alabama. Nixon stressed a more moderate brand of law and order and stated that he had a secret plan to end the war in Vietnam. He barely edged Humphrey in the popular vote, but Nixon received 301 electoral votes to 191 for Humphrey. Wallace received nearly 10 million popular votes and 46 electoral college votes.

This background brings us to Nixon's presidency. Was Nixon an effective president? In the following sections, Joan Hoff-Wilson argues that Nixon achieved a number of domestic policy successes in the areas of civil rights, welfare, and economic planning, and in the reorganization of the executive branch and some federal agencies. But Professor Bruce J. Schulman disagrees. He believes that President Nixon was the first conservative president of the post–World War II era who undermined the Great Society legislative programs of Lyndon Baines Johnson and built a new Republican majority coalition of northern white blue-collar workers and southern white conservatives and sunbelt space-age employees and its retirement communities.

YES

Joan Hoff-Wilson

Richard M. Nixon:
The Corporate Presidency

Richard Milhous Nixon became president of the United States at a critical juncture in American history. Following World War II there was a general agreement between popular and elite opinion on two things: the effectiveness of most New Deal domestic policies and the necessity of most Cold War foreign policies. During the 1960s, however, these two crucial postwar consensual constructs began to break down; and the war in Indochina, with its disruptive impact on the nation's political economy, hastened their disintegration. By 1968 the traditional bipartisan, Cold War approach to the conduct of foreign affairs had been seriously undermined. Similarly, the "bigger and better" New Deal approach to the modern welfare state had reached a point of diminishing returns, even among liberals.

In 1968, when Richard Nixon finally captured the highest office in the land, he inherited not only Lyndon Johnson's Vietnam war but also LBJ's Great Society. This transfer of power occurred at the very moment when both endeavors had lost substantial support among the public at large and, most important, among a significant number of the elite group of decision makers and leaders of opinion across the country. On previous occasions when such a breakdown had occurred within policy- and opinion-making circles—before the Civil and Spanish American Wars and in the early years of the Great Depression—domestic or foreign upheavals had followed. Beginning in the 1960s the country experienced a similar series of failed presidents reminiscent of those in the unstable 1840s and 1850s, 1890s, and 1920s.

In various ways all the presidents in these transitional periods failed as crisis managers, often because they refused to take risks. Nixon, in contrast, "[couldn't] understand people who won't take risks." His proclivity for risk taking was not emphasized by scholars, journalists, and psychologists until after he was forced to resign as president. "I am not necessarily a respecter of the status quo," Nixon told Stuart Alsop in 1958; "I am a chance taker." Although this statement was made primarily in reference to foreign affairs, Nixon's entire political career has been characterized by a series of personal and professional crises and risky political policies. It is therefore not surprising that as president he rationalized many of his major foreign and domestic

Reprinted by permission of the publisher from "Richard M. Nixon: The Corporate Presidency" by Joan Hoff-Wilson in LEADERSHIP IN THE MODERN PRESIDENCY, edited by Fred I. Greenstein, pp. 164–167, 189–198, Cambridge, Mass.: Harvard University. Notes omitted.

initiatives as crises (or at least as intolerable impasses) that could be resolved only by dramatic and sometimes drastic measures.

A breakdown in either the foreign or domestic policy consensus offers both opportunity and danger to any incumbent president. Nixon had more opportunity for risk-taking changes at home and abroad during his first administration than he would have had if elected in 1960 because of the disruptive impact of war and domestic reforms during the intervening eight years. Also, he inherited a wartime presidency, with all its temporarily enhanced extralegal powers. Although the Cold War in general has permanently increased the potential for constitutional violations by presidents, only those in the midst of a full-scale war (whether declared or undeclared) have exercised with impunity what Garry Wills has called "semi-constitutional" actions. Although Nixon was a wartime president for all but twenty months of his five and one-half years in office, he found that impunity for constitutional violations was not automatically accorded a president engaged in an undeclared, unsatisfying, and seemingly endless war. In fact, he is not usually even thought of, or referred to, as a wartime president.

Periods of war and reform have usually alternated in the United States, but in the 1960s they burgeoned simultaneously, hastening the breakdown of consensus that was so evident by the time of the 1968 election. This unusual situation transformed Nixon's largely unexamined and rather commonplace management views into more rigid and controversial ones. It also reinforced his natural predilection to bring about change through executive fiat. Thus a historical accident accounts in part for many of Nixon's unilateral administrative actions during his first term and for the events leading to his disgrace and resignation during his second.

The first few months in the Oval Office are often intoxicating, and a new president can use them in a variety of ways. But during the socioeconomic confusion and conflict of the late 1960s and early 1970s, some of the newly appointed Republican policy managers (generalists) and the frustrated holdover Democratic policy specialists (experts) in the bureaucracy unexpectedly came together and began to consider dramatic policy changes at home and abroad. Complex interactions between these very different groups produced several significant shifts in domestic and foreign affairs during the spring and summer of 1969. A radical welfare plan and dramatic foreign policy initiatives took shape.

The country had elected only one other Republican president since the onset of FDR's reform administrations thirty-six years earlier. Consequently, Nixon faced not only unprecedented opportunities for changing domestic policy as a result of the breakdown in the New Deal consensus, but also the traditional problems of presidential governance, exacerbated in this instance by bureaucratic pockets of resistance from an unusual number of holdover Democrats. Such resistance was not new, but its magnitude was particularly threatening to a distrusted (and distrustful) Republican president who did not control either house of Congress. Nixon's organizational recommendations for containing the bureaucracy disturbed his political opponents and the liberal press as much as, if not more than, their doubts about the motivation behind many of his substantive and innovative suggestions on other domestic issues such as welfare and the environment.

Because much of the press and both houses of Congress were suspicious of him, Nixon naturally viewed administrative action as one way of obtaining significant domestic reform. Moreover, some of his initial accomplishments in administratively redirecting U.S. foreign policy ultimately led him to rely more on administrative actions at home than he might have otherwise. In any case, this approach drew criticism from those who already distrusted his policies and priorities. Nixon's covert and overt expansion and prolongation of the war during this period reinforced existing suspicions about his personality and political ethics. In this sense, liberal paranoia about his domestic programs fueled Nixon's paranoia about liberal opposition to the war, and vice versa. By 1972, Nixon's success in effecting structural and substantive change in foreign policy through the exercise of unilateral executive power increasingly led him to think that he could use the same preemptive administrative approach to resolve remaining domestic problems, especially following his landslide electoral victory. . . .

Foreign Policy Scorecard

It was clearly in Nixon's psychic and political self-interest to end the war in Vietnam as soon as possible. Although he came to office committed to negotiate a quick settlement, he ended up prolonging the conflict. As a result, he could never build the domestic consensus he needed to continue the escalated air and ground war (even with dramatically reduced U.S. troop involvement) and to ensure passage of some of his domestic programs. For Nixon (and Kissinger) Vietnam became a symbol of influence in the Third World that, in turn, was but one part of their geopolitical approach to international relations. Thus the war in Southeast Asia had to be settled as soon as possible so as not to endanger other elements of Nixonian diplomatic and domestic policy.

Instead, the president allowed his secretary of state to become egocentrically involved in secret negotiations with the North Vietnamese from August 4, 1969, to January 25, 1972 (when they were made public). As a result, the terms finally reached in 1973 were only marginally better than those rejected in 1969. The advantage gained from Hanoi's agreement to allow President Nguyen Van Thieu to remain in power in return for allowing North Vietnamese troops to remain in South Vietnam can hardly offset the additional loss of twenty thousand American lives during this three-year-period—especially given the inherent weaknesses of the Saigon government by 1973. On the tenth anniversary of the peace treaty ending the war in Vietnam, Nixon admitted to me that "Kissinger believed more in the power of negotiation than I did." He also said that he "would not have temporized as long" with the negotiating process had he not been "needlessly" concerned with what the Soviets and Chinese might think if the United States pulled out of Vietnam precipitately. Because Nixon saw no way in 1969 to end the war quickly except through overt massive bombing attacks, which the public demonstrated in 1970 and 1971 it would not tolerate, there was neither peace nor honor in

Vietnam by the time that war was finally concluded on January 27, 1973; and in the interim he made matters worse by secretly bombing Cambodia.

The delayed ending to the war in Vietnam not only cast a shadow on all Nixon's other foreign policy efforts but also established secrecy, wiretapping, and capricious personal diplomacy as standard operational procedures in the conduct of foreign policy that ultimately carried over into domestic affairs. Despite often duplicitous and arbitrary actions, even Nixon's strongest critics often credit him with an unusual number of foreign policy successes.

Although fewer of his foreign policy decisions were reached in a crisis atmosphere than his domestic ones, Nixon's diplomatic legacy is weaker than he and many others have maintained. For example, the pursuit of "peace and honor" in Vietnam failed; his Middle Eastern policy because of Kissinger's shuttling ended up more show than substance; his Third World policy (outside of Vietnam and attempts to undermine the government of Allende in Chile) were nearly nonexistent; détente with the USSR soon foundered under his successors; and the Nixon Doctrine has not prevented use of U.S. troops abroad. Only rapprochement with China remains untarnished by time because it laid the foundation for recognition, even though he failed to achieve a "two China" policy in the United Nations. This summary is not meant to discredit Richard Nixon as a foreign policy expert both during and after his presidency. It is a reminder that the lasting and positive results of his diplomacy may be fading faster than some aspects of his domestic policies.

Outflanking Liberals on Domestic Reform

Presidents traditionally achieve their domestic objectives through legislation, appeals in the mass media, and administrative actions. During his first administration Nixon offered Congress extensive domestic legislation, most of which aimed at redistributing federal power away from Congress and the bureaucracy. When he encountered difficulty obtaining passage of these programs, he resorted more and more to reform by administrative fiat, especially at the beginning of his second term. All Nixonian domestic reforms were rhetorically linked under the rubric of the New Federalism. Most competed for attention with his well-known interest in foreign affairs. Most involved a degree of the boldness he thought necessary for a successful presidency. Most increased federal regulation of nondistributive public policies. Most were made possible in part because he was a wartime Republican president who took advantage of acting in the Disraeli tradition of enlightened conservatism. Most offended liberals (as well as many conservatives), especially when it came to implementing certain controversial policies with legislation. Many were also undertaken in a crisis atmosphere, which on occasion was manufactured by individual members of Nixon's staff to ensure his attention and action.

In some instances, as political scientist Paul J. Halpern has noted, Nixon's long-standing liberal opponents in Congress "never even bothered to get the facts straight" about these legislative and administrative innovations; the very people who, according to Daniel Moynihan, formed the "natural constituency" for most of Nixon's domestic policies refused to support his programs. It may well have been that many liberals simply could not believe that Nixon would ever do the right thing except for the wrong reason. Thus they seldom took the time to try to determine whether any of his efforts to make the 1970s a decade of reform were legitimate, however politically motivated. Additionally, such partisan opposition made Nixon all the more willing to reorganize the executive branch of government with or without congressional approval.

My own interviews with Nixon and his own (and others') recent attempts to rehabilitate his reputation indicate that Nixon thinks he will outlive the obloquy of Watergate because of his foreign policy initiatives—not because of his domestic policies. Ultimately, however, domestic reform and his attempts at comprehensive reorganization of the executive branch may become the standard by which the Nixon presidency is judged.

Environmental Policy

Although Nixon's aides cite his environmental legislation as one of his major domestic achievements, it was not high on his personal list of federal priorities, despite polls showing its growing importance as a national issue. White House central files released in 1986 clearly reveal that John Ehrlichman was initially instrumental in shaping the president's views on environmental matters and conveying a sense of crisis about them. Most ideas were filtered through him to Nixon. In fact Ehrlichman, whose particular expertise was in land-use policies, has been described by one forest conservation specialist as "the most effective environmentalist since Gifford Pinchot." Ehrlichman and John Whitaker put Nixon ahead of Congress on environmental issues, especially with respect to his use of the permit authority in the Refuse Act of 1899 to begin to clean up water supplies before Congress passed any "comprehensive water pollution enforcement plan."

"Just keep me out of trouble on environmental issues," Nixon reportedly told Ehrlichman. This proved impossible because Congress ignored Nixon's recommended ceilings when it finally passed (over his veto) the Federal Water Pollution Control Act amendments of 1972. Both Ehrlichman and Whitaker agreed then and later that it was "budget-busting" legislation designed to embarrass the president on a popular issue in an election year. Statistics later showed that the money appropriated could not be spent fast enough to achieve the legislation's stated goals. The actual annual expenditures in the first years after passage approximated those originally proposed by Nixon's staff.

Revamping Welfare

Throughout the 1968 presidential campaign Nixon's own views on welfare remained highly unfocused. But once in the Oval Office he set an unexpectedly fast pace on the issue. On January 15, 1969, he demanded an investigation by top aides into a newspaper allegation of corruption in New York City's Human Resources Administration. Nixon's extraordinary welfare legislation originated in a very circuitous fashion with two low-level Democratic holdovers from the Johnson administration, Worth Bateman and James Lyday.

These two bureaucrats fortuitously exercised more influence on Robert Finch, Nixon's first secretary of health, education and welfare, than they had been able to on John W. Gardner and Wilbur J. Cohn, Johnson's two appointees. Finch was primarily responsible for obtaining Nixon's approval of what eventually became known as the Family Assistance Program (FAP).

If FAP had succeeded in Congress it would have changed the emphasis of American welfare from providing services to providing income; thus it would have replaced the Aid to Families with Dependent Children (AFDC) program, whose payments varied widely from state to state. FAP called for anywhere from $1,600 (initially proposed in 1969) to $2,500 (proposed in 1971) for a family of four. States were expected to supplement this amount, and in addition all able-bodied heads of recipient families (except mothers with preschool children) would be required to "accept work or training." However, if a parent refused to accept work or training, only his or her payment would be withheld. In essence, FAP unconditionally guaranteed children an annual income and would have tripled the number of children then being aided by AFDC.

A fundamental switch from services to income payments proved to be too much for congressional liberals and conservatives alike, and they formed a strange alliance to vote it down. Ironically, FAP's final defeat in the Senate led to some very impressive examples of incremental legislation that might not have been passed had it not been for the original boldness of FAP. For example, Supplementary Security Income, approved on October 17, 1972, constituted a guaranteed annual income for the aged, blind, and disabled.

The demise of FAP also led Nixon to support uniform application of the food stamp program across the United States, better health insurance programs for low-income families, and an automatic cost-of-living adjustment for Social Security recipients to help them cope with inflation. In every budget for which his administration was responsible—that is, from fiscal 1971 through fiscal 1975—spending on all human resource programs exceeded spending for defense for the first time since World War II. A sevenfold increase in funding for social services under Nixon made him (not Johnson) the "last of the big spenders" on domestic programs.

Reluctant Civil Rights Achievements

Perhaps the domestic area in which Watergate has most dimmed or skewed our memories of the Nixon years is civil rights. We naturally tend to remember that during his presidency Nixon deliberately violated the civil rights of some of those who opposed his policies or were suspected of leaking information. Nixon has always correctly denied that he was a conservative on civil rights, and indeed his record on this issue, as on so many others, reveals as much political expediency as it does philosophical commitment. By 1968 there was strong southern support for his candidacy. Consequently, during his campaign he implied that if elected he would slow down enforcement of federal school desegregation policies.

Enforcement had already been painfully sluggish since the 1954 *Brown v. Board of Education* decision. By 1968 only 20 percent of black children in the

South attended predominantly white schools, and none of this progress had occurred under Eisenhower or Kennedy. Moreover, the most dramatic improvement under Johnson's administration did not take place until 1968, because HEW deadlines for desegregating southern schools had been postponed four times since the passage of the 1964 Civil Rights Act. By the spring of 1968, however, a few lower court rulings, and finally the Supreme Court decision in *Green v. Board of Education,* no longer allowed any president the luxury of arguing that freedom-of-choice plans were adequate for rooting out racial discrimination, or that de facto segregation caused by residential patterns was not as unconstitutional as *de jure* segregation brought about by state or local laws.

Despite the real national crisis that existed over school desegregation, Nixon was not prepared to go beyond what he thought the decision in *Brown* had mandated, because he believed that de facto segregation could not be ended through busing or cutting off funds from school districts. Nine days after Nixon's inauguration, his administration had to decide whether to honor an HEW-initiated cutoff of funds to five southern school districts, originally scheduled to take place in the fall of 1968 but delayed until January 29, 1969. On that day Secretary Finch confirmed the cutoff but also announced that the school districts could claim funds retroactively if they complied with HEW guidelines within sixty days. This offer represented a change from the most recent set of HEW guidelines, developed in March 1968, which Johnson had never formally endorsed by signing.

At the heart of the debate over various HEW guidelines in the last half of the 1960s were two issues: whether the intent of the Civil Rights Act of 1964 had been simply to provide freedom of choice or actually to compel integration in schools; and whether freedom-of-choice agreements negotiated by HEW or lawsuits brought by the Department of Justice were the most effective ways of achieving desegregation. Under the Johnson administration the HEW approach, based on bringing recalcitrant school districts into compliance by cutting off federal funding, had prevailed. Nixon, on the other hand, argued in his First Inaugural that the "laws have caught up with our consciences" and insisted that it was now necessary "to give life to what is in the law." Accordingly, he changed the emphasis in the enforcement of school desegregation from HEW compliance agreements to Justice Department actions—a legal procedure that proved very controversial in 1969 and 1970, but one that is standard now.

Nixon has been justifiably criticized by civil rights advocates for employing delaying tactics in the South, and particularly for not endorsing busing to enforce school desegregation in the North after the April 20, 1971, Supreme Court decision in *Swann v. Charlotte-Mecklenburg Board of Education.* Despite the bitter battle in Congress and between Congress and the executive branch after *Swann,* the Nixon administration's statistical record on school desegregation is impressive. In 1968, 68 percent of all black children in the South and 40 percent in the nation as a whole attended all-black schools. By the end of 1972, 8 percent of southern black children attended all-black schools, and a little less than 12 percent nationwide. A comparison of budget outlays is equally revealing. President Nixon spent $911 million on civil rights activities, including $75 million for civil rights enforcement in fiscal 1969. The Nixon administration's budget for fiscal 1973 called for $2.6 billion in total civil rights outlays, of which $602 million was earmarked for enforcement through a substantially strengthened Equal Employment Opportunity Commission. Nixon supported the civil rights goals of American Indians and women with less reluctance than he did school desegregation because these groups did not pose a major political problem for him and he had no similar legal reservations about how the law should be applied to them.

Mixing Economics and Politics

Nixon spent an inordinate amount of time on domestic and foreign economic matters. Nowhere did he appear to reverse himself more on views he had held before becoming president (or at least on views others attributed to him), and nowhere was his aprincipled pragmatism more evident. Nixon's failure to obtain more revenue through tax reform legislation in 1969, together with rising unemployment and inflation rates in 1970, precipitated an effort (in response to a perceived crisis) to balance U.S. domestic concerns through wage and price controls and international ones through devaluation of the dollar. This vehicle was the New Economic Policy, dramatically announced on August 15, 1971, at the end of a secret Camp David meeting with sixteen economic advisers. Largely as a result of Treasury Secretary Connally's influence, Nixon agreed that if foreign countries continued to demand ever-increasing amounts of gold for the U.S. dollars they held, the United States would go off the gold standard but would at the same time impose wage and price controls to curb inflation. The NEP perfectly reflected the "grand gesture" Connally thought the president should make on economic problems, and the August 15 television broadcast dramatized economic issues that most Americans, seldom anticipating long-range consequences, found boring.

When he was not trying to preempt Congress on regulatory issues, Nixon proposed deregulation based on free-market assumptions that were more traditionally in keeping with conservative Republicanism. The administration ended the draft in the name of economic freedom and recommended deregulation of the production of food crops, tariff and other barriers to international trade, and interest rates paid by various financial institutions. Except for wage and price controls and the devaluation of the dollar, none of these actions was justified in the name of crisis management. In general, however, political considerations made Nixon more liberal on domestic economic matters, confounding both his supporters and his opponents.

Nixon attributes his interest in international economics to the encouragement of John Foster Dulles and his desire as vice-president in the 1950s to create a Foreign Economic Council. Failing in this, he has said that his travels abroad in the 1950s only confirmed his belief that foreign leaders understood economics better than did American leaders, and he was determined to remedy this situation as president. Nixon faced two obstacles in this effort: Kissinger (because "international economics was not Henry's bag"), and State

Department officials who saw "economic policy as government to government," which limited their diplomatic view of the world and made them so suspicious or cynical (or both) about the private sector that they refused to promote international commerce to the degree that Nixon thought they should. "Unlike the ignoramuses I encountered among economic officers at various embassies in the 1950s and 1960s," Nixon told me, "I wanted to bring economics to the foreign service."

Because of Nixon's own interest in and knowledge of international trade, he attempted as president to rationalize the formulation of foreign economic policy. After 1962, when he was out of public office and practicing law in New York, he had specialized in international economics and multinational corporations—definitely not Henry Kissinger's areas of expertise. In part because they were not a "team" on foreign economic policy and in part because Nixon bypassed the NSC almost entirely in formulating his New Economic Policy, Nixon relied not on his national security adviser but on other free-thinking outsiders when formulating foreign economic policy.

Next to John Connally, Nixon was most impressed with the economic views of Peter G. Peterson, who, after starting out in 1971 as a White House adviser on international economic affairs, became secretary of commerce in January 1972. Although Connally and Peterson appeared to agree on such early foreign economic initiatives as the NEP and the "get tough" policy toward Third World countries that nationalized U.S. companies abroad, as secretary of commerce Peterson ultimately proved much more sophisticated and sensitive than the secretary of the treasury about the United States' changed economic role in the world. In a December 27, 1971, position paper defending Nixon's NEP, Peterson remarked that the new global situation in which the United States found itself demanded "shared leadership, shared responsibility, and shared burdens. . . . The reform of the international monetary systems," he said, must fully recognize and be solidly rooted in "the growing reality of a genuinely interdependent and increasingly competitive world economy whose goal is mutual, shared prosperity—not artificial, temporary advantage." At no point did Peterson believe, as Connally apparently did, that "the simple realignment of exchange rates" would adequately address the economic realignment problems facing the international economy.

In 1971 Nixon succeeded in establishing an entirely new cabinet-level Council on International Economic Policy (CIEP), headed by Peterson. This was not so much a reorganization of functions as it was an alternative to fill an existing void in the federal structure and to provide "clear top-level focus on international economic issues and to achieve consistency between international and domestic economic policy." For a variety of reasons—not the least of which was Kissinger's general lack of interest in, and disdain for, the unglamorous aspects of international economics—the CIEP faltered and finally failed after Nixon left office. Its demise seems to have been hastened by Kissinger's recommendation to the Congressional Commission on Organization of Foreign Policy that it be eliminated, despite the fact that others, including Peterson, testified on its behalf. The CIEP was subsequently merged with the Office of the Special Trade Representative.

Even with Nixon's impressive foreign and domestic record, it cannot be said that he would have succeeded as a managerial or administrative president had Watergate not occurred. Entrenched federal bureaucracies are not easily controlled or divested of power even with the best policy-oriented management strategies. That his foreign policy management seems more successful is also no surprise: diplomatic bureaucracies are smaller, more responsive, and easier to control than their domestic counterparts. Moreover, public concern (except for Vietnam) remained minimal as usual, and individual presidential foreign policy initiatives are more likely to be remembered and to appear effective than domestic ones. Nonetheless, the real importance of Nixon's presidency may well come to rest not on Watergate or foreign policy, but on his attempts to restructure the executive branch along functional lines, to bring order to the federal bureaucracy, and to achieve lasting domestic reform. The degree to which those Nixonian administrative tactics that were legal and ethical (and most of them were) became consciously or unconsciously the model for his successors in the Oval Office will determine his final place in history.

Although Nixon's corporate presidency remains publicly discredited, much of it has been privately preserved. Perhaps this is an indication that in exceptional cases presidential effectiveness can transcend popular (and scholarly) disapproval. What Nixon lacked in charisma and honesty, he may in the long run make up for with his phoenixlike ability to survive disaster. Nixon has repeatedly said: "No politician is dead until he admits it." It is perhaps an ironic commentary on the state of the modern presidency that Richard Nixon's management style and substantive foreign and domestic achievements look better and better when compared with those of his immediate successors in the Oval Office.

Bruce J. Schulman

 **NO**

"Down to the Nut-Cutting": The Nixon Presidency and American Public Life

. . . Nixon's ambitious and cunning policy agenda would poison American politics and fragment American society. His presidency, often deliberately, sometimes unintentionally, drilled a deep well of cynicism about national politics—about the possibilities for community and communication, about the capacity of government to address the nation's needs, about the dignity and necessity of public service itself. In the process, Nixon shifted the balance of power in American politics and the terms of debate in American culture. . . .

Tricky Dick

. . . Nixon's resentments persisted as well: his crude disregard for Jews, his contempt for African Americans, his hatred of the press. But most of all he hated the establishment, for its wealth and connections, its intellectual and cultural hauteur, its exclusiveness. "In this period of our history, the leaders and the educated class are decadent," President Nixon instructed his chief of staff, H. R. Haldeman. The educated become "brighter in the head, but weaker in the spine." The nation's elite, in Nixon's mind, no longer possessed any character. Nixon would prove it to them, and prove it in the most cunning of ways.

Nixon's presidency presented more than just a fascinating, and baffling, psychological profile. It even accomplished more than the unprecedented abuse of power Americans have too narrowly labeled "Watergate." His administration also posed a crucial historical problem about the evolution of contemporary American politics and public policy. Was Nixon the last of the liberals, or the first of the conservatives? Did his domestic presidency mark the last gasp of postwar liberalism—of energetic, activist government? Or did it mark the onset of a new, more cautious era—of small government, fiscal conservatism, diverting resources and initiative from the public to the private sector?

In some ways, Nixon did seem like the last interventionist liberal. He doubled the budgets for the National Endowment for the Arts (NEA) and the

National Endowment for the Humanities (NEH). He proposed a guaranteed income for all Americans, signed the nation's principal environmental protection laws, and expanded affirmative action for racial minorities. Under Nixon's watch, the regulatory state swelled; federal agencies began monitoring nearly every aspect of American life. The Nixon administration created the Occupational Health and Safety Administration and instituted the first peacetime wage and price controls in U.S. history.

Nixon even conceded that "I am now a Keynesian in economics." He embraced the idea that a humming economy was the responsibility of the federal government and that the White House should actively intervene in economic affairs, carefully calibrating the policy controls, to ensure robust growth and low unemployment. Nixon even dispensed with the gold standard, that most reassuring symbol of conservative fiscal orthodoxy.

By the middle of his first term, Nixon's seeming unwillingness to crush liberalism and disband social programs angered many committed conservatives. Patrick Buchanan, the president's in-house right-wing fire-eater, warned that conservatives felt Nixon had betrayed them. "They are the niggers of the Nixon administration," Buchanan fumed in a scathing seven-page memo.

On the other hand, the Nixon era seemed to initiate a new, more conservative era in American politics. Nixon intervened on behalf of southern school districts, supporting efforts to curtail busing and slow the pace of school desegregation. He attacked the Warren Court, replacing such liberal icons as Abe Fortas and Earl Warren with Warren Burger and William Rehnquist (and even unsuccessfully attempted to appoint two southern conservatives to the Supreme Court). He dismantled, or at least attempted to eliminate, the principal agencies of 1960s liberalism, such as the Office of Economic Opportunity (which ran Lyndon Johnson's war on poverty) and the legal services program. While he signed the popular legislation restricting air and water pollution, Nixon also established procedures for economic cost-benefit review of all environmental regulations. And he made it clear that officials should scrap or water down any pollution control that might slow the economy or antagonize business.

Nixon also pioneered what came to be called devolution—transferring authority from the federal government to state and local governments and from the public sector to the private sphere. Through a complicated series of initiatives—a combination of block grants, revenue sharing, and the like—Nixon consigned to the states policy areas that had been the responsibility of the federal government. He also took problems and programs that had been thought to require public attention and shifted them to business and the private sector. Indeed, when Nixon left office in August 1974, CBS Evening News commentator Rod MacLeish described devolution as Nixon's major achievement. "As president," MacLeish told a national television audience, "Mr. Nixon made serious policy efforts to disburse responsibility as well as money for the alleviation of our domestic problems."

By the end of his first term, Nixon had embraced small government as his campaign theme. Concluding that cutting government could become a winning strategy, Nixon declared in his second inaugural address that "government must learn to take less from people so that people can do more for themselves." Reversing John F. Kennedy's famous call for collective sacrifice, Nixon instructed, "In our own lives, let each of us ask—not just what will government do for me, but what can I do for myself?"

Faced with such a contradictory record, Nixon watchers have been tempted to split the difference. But Nixon the president did more than combine economic liberalism with social conservatism. He was no mere transitional president, a passage from one era to another that embraced elements of both, although many scholars have portrayed him as such. Others have dismissed Nixon as nothing more than opportunistic, swaying with the prevailing political winds. Primarily interested in foreign affairs, Nixon viewed domestic policy as a nuisance; he would do anything so long as it would not cost him votes.

Splitting the difference, however, mistakes not only Nixon's character, but his presidency's decisive influence on American political culture. Although Nixon was both a transitional president and an opportunist, those assessments miss his historical significance—the ways that the man (the psychological puzzle) and the policies (the historical problem) intertwined.

Not for nothing did Nixon earn the nickname Tricky Dick. Nixon was indeed the first of the conservatives. He fooled many observers, then and now, because he pursued this conservative agenda—this assault on public life—in a particularly devious sort of way. Unlike Barry Goldwater before him and Ronald Reagan after him, Nixon never took on big government directly. He rarely assailed the liberal establishment he so furiously hated and so openly resented. He did not attack liberal programs or the agencies and political networks that undergirded them. Rather, he subtly, cunningly undermined them. Nixon wanted to destroy the liberal establishment by stripping it of its bases of support and its sources of funds. . . .

Toward a Guaranteed Income?

Of all Richard Nixon's domestic policies, the most celebrated and the most controversial proposal never actually materialized: the Family Assistance Plan (FAP). In August 1969, Nixon appeared before the nation with a radical scheme, a far-reaching program the federal government had never before even contemplated—a minimum guaranteed income for every American family. Nixon proposed to abolish the existing welfare system with its labyrinthine series of benefits: AFDC (Aid to Families with Dependent Children), food stamps, housing subsidies, furniture grants. Nixon also promised to eliminate the army of social workers who ran the system and the mountains of paperwork they produced—to get rid of all that and simply replace it with direct cash grants to the poor.

"We face an urban crisis, a social crisis—and at the same time, a crisis of confidence in the capacity of government to do its job," Nixon explained when he announced the program. "Our states and cities find themselves sinking in a welfare quagmire, as case loads increase, as costs escalate, and as the welfare system stagnates enterprise and perpetuates dependency." The system, he complained, "created an incentive for fathers to desert their families," it spawned grossly unequal variations in benefits levels, it forced poor children to begin "life in an atmosphere of handout and dependency."

An ominous "welfare crisis" loomed by the time Nixon took command of the war on poverty. Between 1960 and 1975 the number of relief recipients doubled, from 7 to 14 million people. Including in-kind assistance—food stamps, Medicaid, public housing—more than 24 million Americans received means-tested benefits by the end of the Nixon years. By highlighting the problems of poverty, Lyndon Johnson's Great Society and the agencies it created had focused attention on the impoverished. Daniel Patrick Moynihan, the former Kennedy-Johnson poverty warrior who ran Nixon's Urban Affairs Council, became especially concerned with the explosion of AFDC costs in New York City. Although the economy hummed and unemployment had actually decreased, New York's welfare caseload had tripled in only five years. Moynihan and Nixon became convinced (wrongly) that New York's troubles portended the imminent collapse of the national welfare system.

Most observers, across the American political spectrum, agreed that something had to be done about welfare. On the far left, welfare radicals like the National Welfare Rights Organization (NWRO) sought to empower the poor. A group representing mostly single mothers, the NWRO encouraged poor people to apply for public assistance—to demand welfare as a right, not to accept it reluctantly and shamefully. And in fact, the vast expansion in caseloads during the 1960s stemmed not from growing numbers of people eligible for welfare but from a huge increase in the number of already eligible poor people who applied for welfare. In 1960, only about one-third of the Americans eligible for welfare actually received it; by the early 1970s, the figure had climbed to 90 percent, thanks in part to the agitation of advocates like the NWRO.

At the other end of the spectrum, free market economist Milton Friedman, a leading conservative guru, promoted his plan for a negative income tax. The grab-bag of welfare programs, Friedman asserted, served only the interests of the legislators who enacted them and the bureaucrats who administered them. Poverty resulted not from failed institutions, broken homes, or the legacy of slavery, but from a pure and simple shortage of cash. Government could cure poverty by dispensing money directly to the needy through the tax system; Americans earning less than an established minimum would receive money from the Internal Revenue Service (IRS) just as those above the threshold paid in their taxes. The negative income tax would allow poor citizens to purchase the goods and services they needed rather than the ones their congressmen and social workers insisted they should have.

Friedman was no great ally of public assistance, and he wanted to get government out of the welfare business. That sentiment appealed to Nixon. "Nixon didn't like welfare workers," his aide Martin Anderson recalled in a television documentary. A shift to cash grants would undermine the entire welfare establishment, circumventing the bureaucrats, the psychologists, and the social workers.

Nixon embraced the radical analyses of Friedman and the NWRO, rejecting the proposals for moderate, incremental welfare reform circulating on Capitol Hill and within the social service agencies. He would replace the entire AFDC system with a national minimum standard, available to the welfare poor and working poor alike. "What I am proposing," Nixon announced, "is that the Federal Government build a foundation under the income of every American family with dependent children that cannot care for itself—and wherever in America that family may live." A federal minimum would support all such families, intact or "broken," working or on welfare. The program would include work incentives (to encourage earnings, benefits would be reduced by only fifty cents for every dollar earned) and work requirements (every recipient except mothers of preschool children would have to accept employment or job training). "A guaranteed income," Nixon explained, distinguishing his plan from rival proposals, "establishes a right without any responsibilities. Family assistance recognizes a need and establishes a responsibility."

Nixon seemingly pressed for a liberal goal: one that would expand welfare and extend benefits to millions of working poor. A guaranteed income for all Americans truly aimed to unite the fractured nation, to make every citizen a member of a national community with national standards. Assistance for every family seemed to envision everyone as part of the same national family. But however extravagant the hopes of FAP supporters, Nixon's guaranteed income plan pursued an authentically conservative objective. Nixon sought to dismantle the welfare system and the agencies and programs that administered it, eliminate the social workers who ran them, and starve the liberal networks they nourished.

Certainly Nixon cared more about undercutting his liberal opposition than about putting FAP into effect. While analysts disagreed then and today about Nixon's commitment to welfare reform, he certainly made little effort to secure its passage. Despite Moynihan's urging that he spend political capital to secure congressional approval, the president remained on the sidelines, allowing his most far-reaching policy proposal to wither and die.

And expire it did. Congressional Democrats and their liberal allies denounced Nixon's guaranteed minimum as too low. Demanding a much higher income floor—roughly four times the level Nixon offered—the NWRO urged supporters to "Zap FAP." The NWRO also encouraged Americans to "Live Like a Dog" on the proposed budget, which they computed to just nineteen cents a meal per person. Mainstream liberal organizations like the National Association for the Advancement of Colored People, the American Friends Service Committee, and the Methodist church also denounced Nixon's plan. Meanwhile, conservatives opposed FAP because it would extend public assistance to millions more Americans and add billions of dollars to the federal budget.

Representative Wilbur Mills (D, Arkansas), chairman of the Ways and Means Committee, steered FAP through the House, adding sweeteners for the states that offered low benefits. But the Senate Finance Committee, largely controlled by southern and rural legislators, buried the plan. Nixon resubmitted FAP three times but never worked to secure its passage. In 1972, when Democratic presidential candidate George McGovern announced his own proposed "demogrant" of a thousand dollars for every man, woman, and child in the United States, the FAP passed into oblivion. The very idea of replacing the welfare system with cash grants became the stuff of derisive jokes.

Denounced by both left and right, FAP ended up on the ash heap of history, but it was no failure for Richard Nixon. By introducing the guaranteed income program, Nixon divided his opponents and torpedoed more generous proposals for welfare reform. His apparent boldness in meeting the welfare crisis insulated Nixon from criticism; no one could claim that he fiddled while New York and other cities burned (or at least went broke). At the same time, the president's solicitude for the working poor, antipathy to the welfare bureaucracy, and stringent work requirements appealed to blue-collar voters and appeased the Republican right wing. Even in defeat, Nixon had pulled off a remarkable tactical victory.

The Silent Majority

Nixon's indirect, underhanded strategy with regard to welfare, environmental protection, housing, and the arts represented more than a career politician's cunning or a pathological liar's need to be devious. Every one of these maneuvers advanced Nixon's larger political objective: his ambition to transform American politics by creating a new majority coalition in the United States.

Nixon had long envisioned such a realignment. His 1968 campaign had hinged on winning over two sets of voters that normally remained loyal Democrats but appeared ready to switch parties. First, Nixon targeted white southerners. By hinting he would slow the pace of desegregation, Nixon's "southern strategy" drew Dixie's yellow-dog Democrats and prosperous new migrants to the metropolitan South into the emerging Republican majority. Second, Nixon went after blue-collar northerners—white ethnics who for generations had voted their pocketbooks and supported liberal Democrats, but had recently become alarmed about the social issues—crime, drugs, loose morals, streets filled with antiwar protestors and black militants.

In 1968, white southerners seemed ripe for this strategy. Many had opposed the civil rights revolution and resented the northern liberals they felt had imposed on them an odious second Reconstruction. In 1964, many southerners had abandoned the Democrats—the "Party of the Fathers"—and cast votes for Senator Barry Goldwater, an outspoken opponent of the Civil Rights Act. Goldwater won five Deep South states.

Nixon certainly welcomed the votes of disgruntled segregationists. The campaign enlisted South Carolina senator Strom Thurmond, the former Dixiecrat leader and recent convert to the GOP, to rally white southerners. Thurmond promised that Nixon would support local control of public schools. Nixon even hired a Thurmond protégé to coordinate his campaign in the South and bombarded the region with advertisements warning against wasted votes for Alabama governor George Wallace, the hero of massive resistance running a third-party campaign for president.

Still, in 1968 Nixon carefully chose not to tread in Thurmond or Goldwater's footsteps. The campaign recognized that Wallace had locked up the Deep South. Nixon understood that overt racial appeals for the Wallace vote would alienate moderates, and even many conservatives, in the burgeoning suburbs of the metropolitan South. So Nixon largely conceded the segregationist, rural

Deep South that Goldwater had won and constructed a plurality connecting the Sunbelt with blue-collar Rustbelt neighborhoods.

In a very close race, Nixon's strategists focused on middle-class white voters in the industrializing subdivisions of the peripheral South. The population of the South's major metropolises, Nixon recognized, had doubled or even tripled in the 1950s and 1960s. New suburbs were crowded with professionals and skilled workers from outside the South and young families who had come of age after the *Brown* decision and found massive resistance self-defeating.

In September 1968, Nixon launched a campaign swing through Dixie in Charlotte, North Carolina. There, he addressed a polite, well-dressed, middle class crowd. He made his familiar stump appeal to forgotten Americans, never even mentioning race. Pressed later by an interviewer, he staked out a middle ground, affirming support for *Brown* but criticizing the Democrats and the courts for pushing too hard, too fast. Nixon cleverly laid out a moderate approach, neither championing minority rights like Hubert Humphrey nor defending segregation and states' rights like Goldwater and Wallace. He simultaneously endorsed local desegregation efforts—the nominally color-blind freedom-of-choice plans that had enrolled a few black students in formerly all-black schools across the South and Southwest—and opposed openly race-conscious remedies like busing that threatened dramatic changes in the status quo.

That strategy appealed to crucial swing voters in the 1968 election, helping the Republican standard-bearer win Virginia, the Carolinas, Florida, Tennessee, and Kentucky. Nixon's southern strategy offered more than a short-term political prize. It was premised on the fundamental demographic and political shifts that would continue throughout the Seventies and would give a new shape to American life.

A young political consultant named Kevin Phillips diagnosed this power shift in a series of position papers for the Nixon campaign and in a 1969 book, *The Emerging Republican Majority.* Phillips identified a new locus of power in national politics, a region he called the Sunbelt that connected the booming subdivisions of the metropolitan South, the sun country of Florida and southern California, and the desert Southwest. Phillips described the Sunbelt's conservative leanings and its potential as the foundation for a political realignment. The "huge postwar white middle class push to the Florida-California sun country" seemed to be forging a new political era. "The persons most drawn to the new sun culture are the pleasure-seekers, the bored, the ambitious, the space-age technicians and the retired—a super-slice of the rootless, socially mobile group known as the American middle class." The region's politics, he concluded, "is bound to cast a lengthening national shadow."

Nixon and his top advisers recognized the growing influence of the Sunbelt South in national politics. Shortly after becoming president, Nixon changed his voting residence from New York to Florida. "The time has come," he declared in 1970, "to stop kicking the South around." He detected not only the rise of the Sunbelt but the growing influence of a Sunbelt mind-set in American life generally. The South and Southwest seemed to embody a new set of cultural attitudes about race, taxation, defense, government spending, and social mores—Sunbelt attitudes that might eventually spread into the suburbs and working-class neighborhoods of the old North.

In August 1970, while vacationing in San Clemente, Pat Buchanan alerted Nixon to *The Real Majority,* a political manual for the coming decade by Richard M. Scammon and Ben J. Wattenberg. Hoping to revive their own party, these two disaffected Democrats mapped the political landscape in Nixonian terms. The voter in the center, they asserted, the key to assembling a winning coalition, was a "47 year old Catholic housewife in Dayton, Ohio whose husband is a machinist." Since the 1930s, she and her blue-collar husband had always voted Democratic. According to Scammon and Wattenberg, they had voted their pocketbooks, looking to liberal Democrats for strong unions, high wages, cheap mortgages, and college loans for their children. But now, at the end of the 1960s, they might defect to the Republicans and vote conservative on social issues. "To know that the lady in Dayton is afraid to walk the streets alone at night," Scammon and Wattenberg explained, "to know that she has a mixed view about blacks and civil rights because before moving to the suburbs she lived in a neighborhood that became all black, to know that her brother-in-law is a policeman, to know that she does not have the money to move if her new neighborhood deteriorates, to know that she is deeply distressed that her son is going to a community junior college where LSD was found on campus—to know all this is the beginning of contemporary political wisdom."

The book thrilled Nixon. If he did nothing to deny blue-collar workers their fat pay envelopes and hit hard on rioters, protesters, and drugs, he could forge a new conservative majority. "P [the president] talked about Real Majority and need to get that thinking over to all our people," Haldeman reported. "Wants to hit pornography, dope, bad kids." Nixon himself asserted that the Republicans needed to "preempt the Social Issue in order to get the Democrats on the defensive. We should aim our strategy primarily at disaffected Democrats, at blue-collar workers, and at working-class white ethnics. We should," the president concluded, "set out to capture the vote of the forty-seven-year-old Dayton housewife."

Nixon made wooing these voters—Americans he famously named the Silent Majority in a 1969 speech—the subject of concerted effort. Indeed for several years, Nixon envisioned creating a new political party—he usually called it the Independent Conservative party—to foster a wholesale realignment of American politics. This new party would unite white southerners, the Silent Majority, and traditionally Republican rural and suburban conservatives around social issues. It would ostracize the socially liberal, economically conservative eastern establishment—Wall Street and business Republicans like Nelson Rockefeller who had long dominated Republican party affairs—and attack liberal Democrats for playing so heavily to "the fashionable, but unrepresentative constituencies of the young, the poor, the racial minorities, and the students."

Nixon envisioned a new party that would appeal to the "Okie from Muskogee," the hero of Merle Haggard's 1969 country and western hit. "I'm proud to be an Okie from Muskogee," Haggard declared, "a place where even squares can have a ball." Nixon admired Haggard's anthem as the authentic voice of the Silent Majority; Haggard's Oklahoma town honored the values of millions of worried, disgruntled Americans. "We don't smoke marijuana in Muskogee," the singer explained. "We don't take our trips on LSD. We don't burn our draft cards down on Main Street. We like livin' right and bein' free." The song so impressed the president that Nixon invited Haggard to perform at the White House.

To build this new political agenda, Nixon not only inflamed the Silent Majority about social issues and appealed to the national pride of working Americans. He also took a number of concrete steps. First, he reached out to organized labor. Recognizing the social conservatism and deep-rooted patriotism of union Democrats, Nixon believed he could pry their votes away from the party of FDR. After National Guardsmen shot and killed antiwar marchers at Kent State University, 150,000 hard hats paraded for flag and country down New York's Broadway. Outraged that New York's liberal mayor had dropped the flag on city hall to half-staff in honor of the slain antiwar protesters, the construction workers denounced (and even beat up a handful of) hippies and student radicals, defended the war in Vietnam, and supported their president in the White House. Nixon deeply appreciated the construction workers' show of support, and the march reinforced his determination to incorporate labor into his New American Majority. The president offered generous loopholes for organized labor in his wage and price controls, horrifying Wall Street and business interests.

Second, Nixon named Texas governor John Connally, a former protégé of Lyndon Johnson, as his secretary of the treasury. By naming Connally to his cabinet and grooming him as his successor, Nixon hoped to entice conservative southern Democrats into his new majority. The president also understood that Connally would happily dispense with Republican economic orthodoxy and keep working people happy about their paychecks while Nixon stung the Democrats on social issues.

Nixon also valued Connally's Lone Star state charisma. Henry Kissinger thought that "there was no American public figure Nixon held in such awe. Connally's swaggering self-assurance," Kissinger reflected, "fulfilled Nixon's image of how a leader should act; he found it possible to emulate this conduct only in marginal comments on memoranda, never face to face." And Nixon never denigrated Connally behind his back, "a boon not granted to many."

In August 1971, under Connally's leadership, Nixon reversed field on economic policies. He adopted wage and price controls to cool inflation, a series of tax cuts to stimulate the economy in time for the 1972 elections, and he closed the gold window and allowed the dollar to float against other currencies, ending the Bretton Woods monetary system that had stabilized the international currency markets since World War II.

His mission accomplished, Connally returned to his native Texas in 1972 and took control of "Democrats for Nixon." The president imagined Connally as his natural successor. "By structuring it right," Haldeman recalled Nixon's ruminations in his diary, "we could develop a new majority party. Under a new name. Get control of the Congress without an election, simply by realignment, and make a truly historic change in the entire American political structure." From this coalition, with Nixon and Connally as "the strong men," Connally "clearly would emerge as the candidate for the new party in '76, and the P would strongly back him in that."

As the 1972 election approached, Nixon made little use of traditional party labels, touting his connections to Democrats like Connally and downplaying his own Republican affiliation. "Use the new American Majority," he told Haldeman, "not Republican majority." Nixon would seek the "election of Congressman and Senators who will support the P[resident], not who are Republicans."

Nixon even trumpeted his frequent escapes to La Casa Pacifica, his seaside retreat in San Clemente, California, as an assault on the establishment. Appealing to his new conservative majority, Nixon instructed his staff to tout his San Clemente home as the "Western White House." White House communications director Herb Klein informed reporters that the "San Clemente operation gives Westerners a symbolic share in the business of government. . . ." It proved that "Government is not an exclusively Eastern institution."

Nixon recognized by 1971 that the center of the American political spectrum had shifted toward the right. The archetypal Dayton housewife and her machinist husband were becoming fed up with liberals, bureaucracy, and big government. Many of them had moved to southern California, the outskirts of Houston, the suburbs of Charlotte and Atlanta. Increasingly these one-time loyal Democrats and millions of others like them believed that government programs helped only other people, not themselves. "We've had enough social programs: forced integration, education, housing," Nixon told his chief of staff as the 1972 election approached. "People don't want more on welfare. They don't want to help the working poor, and our mood has to be harder on this, not softer."

Nixon instructed his staff to adopt a tougher, more openly conservative stance. Attorney General John Mitchell launched a furious attack against black militants and student protesters in *Women's Wear Daily*. Mitchell tore into "these stupid kids" on college campuses and "the professors are just as bad if not worse. They don't know anything. Nor do these stupid bastards who are ruining our educational institutions." This country, Mitchell warned, "is going so far right you are not even going to recognize it." Nixon applauded his attorney general's hard line. "John—Good Job," he wrote. "Don't back off."

Nixon's strategy paid rich dividends in November 1972. He won reelection by a landslide over Democratic challenger George McGovern, in the process assembling the new majority of his fondest political dreams. Both organized labor and the white South went heavily for Nixon in 1972.

After winning reelection, Nixon decided to promote what he called a conservative revolution. "Now I planned to give expression to the more conservative values and beliefs of the New Majority throughout the country," Nixon recalled in his memoirs, "and use my power to put some teeth in my new American Revolution." Sounding his new conservative theme, Nixon declared in his second inaugural address, "Let us remember that America was not built by government but by people; not by welfare, but by work."

Still, the president understood that although Americans opposed expansive government in principle, in practice they demanded many specific public programs. Nixon understood, as he put it in a cabinet meeting, that "government spending is a lousy issue. People are for spending." The only way to slash popular programs was to portray cuts as "the only way to avoid inflation and higher taxes. . . . You never win," the president explained, "on the question of screwing up rich kids. You have to hit on higher taxes. You never debate the programs. By cutting the budget back, we are avoiding more taxes, and that's the line we have to use."

The budget thus became the instrument of Nixon's conservative revolution. The president set stringent targets for the fiscal year ending June 1973; to reach them, he refused to spend more than $12 billion that the Congress had already appropriated. This infuriated the Congress, which soon would debate whether these "impoundments" merited impeachment.

The impoundments were just the beginning. Having sundered the liberal policy networks and collapsed the liberal electoral coalition, Nixon next aimed to slash domestic spending. In February 1973, he proposed a shocking budget for the 1974 fiscal year, featuring deep cuts in government programs. Nixon proposed to eliminate urban renewal, impacted-area aid for school districts near military bases, hospital construction grants, soil management payments to farmers, and the Rural Electrification Administration. He slashed spending on milk for schoolchildren, mental health facilities, compensatory education for poor students. He meant to reverse the Great Society, calling for the abolition of the Office of Economic Opportunity, the vanguard of Lyndon Johnson's war on poverty.

Nixon would see neither his new American revolution nor his new majority politics through to completion. By the time he unveiled his rightward shift and his harsh budgets, the nation had become obsessed with the unfolding story of scandal in the White House. But, oddly, Nixon's personal failures—a scandal so large that he would become the first (and thus far only) president driven from office—would only aid his larger agenda. In trusting too much in government," Nixon intoned, "we have asked more of it than we can deliver." The time has come to turn away from activist government and replace it with "a new feeling of self-discipline."

In retrospect, most observers have read Nixon's declaration ironically; Watergate certainly proved that Americans had trusted too much in Nixon's government. But although the scandals brought down a Republican conservative and helped to elect the only Democratic president of the era, their principal effect was to discredit government itself. Watergate only intensified Americans' alienation from public life: their contempt for the secrecy, inefficiency, and failures of "big government.". . .

⋅◦⟨◉⟩◦⋅

In fact, Watergate impressed many contemporary observers as a bizarre series of events presided over by a singular villain; it had been "historic but irrelevant." A year after Nixon left office, CBS News correspondent Bruce Morton concluded that "the fact is Watergate didn't change much." A decade later, many pundits echoed Morton's assessment. "Most experts," the *Los Angeles Times* reported on the tenth anniversary of Nixon's ouster, "find no evidence that the traumatic ousting of a U.S. President has caused any basic change in public attitudes about either the American system of government or the persons who occupy public positions." Sure, public confidence in government waned after Watergate, but it had been declining since the race riots and anti-war protests of the mid-1960s.

Still, Nixon's presidency, and its dramatic end, nourished a profound unease with a direction that American life had taken. And the scandal's most conspicuous and enduring effect ironically realized some of Richard Nixon's most grandiose objectives. Watergate gave a boost to conservatism and conservative Republican politicians. That effect did not immediately appear; in the first blip after Nixon's ruin, the Republicans took a bath as the Democrats won big in the 1974 midterm elections. In 1976, enough resentment persisted that Gerald Ford, Nixon's pardoner, narrowly lost the presidency to an unknown whose platform consisted of a fairly convincing promise that he would never lie to the American people.

But the general trends bolstered conservatives. The ultimate lesson of Watergate remained "you can't trust the government." The scandal reinforced a generalized antigovernment passion whose main effect worked against Democrats and liberals and for Republicans and conservatives. Even President Jimmy Carter represented a more conservative faction of the Democratic party: southern, fiscally responsible, suspicious of labor unions and government regulation.

When convicted felon and former attorney general John Mitchell left Washington, reporters mocked his earlier prediction. "In the next ten years," Mitchell had prophesied, "this country will go so far to the right you won't recognize it." Reporters shook their heads, but John Mitchell would have the last laugh.

And perhaps his chief would enjoy it. In retirement, Nixon would witness his enemies in disarray, their conception of government as the instrument of national purpose discredited, their vision of an inclusive national community debased. . . .

POSTSCRIPT

Was Richard Nixon America's Last Liberal President?

J oan Hoff-Wilson is one of the few professional historians to render a positive evaluation of President Nixon. She places him in the context of the late 1960s and early 1970s, when support for big government, New Deal, Great Society programs had dimmed, and the bipartisan, anticommunist foreign policy consensus had been shattered by the Vietnam War. She gives him high marks for vertically restructuring the executive branch of the government and for attempting a similar reorganization of the federal bureaucracy.

Unlike most defenders of Nixon, Hoff-Wilson considers Nixon's greatest achievement to be domestic. Although Nixon was a conservative, the welfare state grew during his presidency. In the area of civil rights, between 1968 and 1972, affirmative action programs were implemented, and schools with all black children in the southern states declined from 68 percent to 8 percent. Even on such Democratic staples as welfare, the environment, and economic planning, Nixon outflanked the liberals.

Hoff-Wilson has fleshed out her ideas in much greater detail in *Nixon Reconsidered* (Basic Books, 1994). British conservative cabinet minister and historian Jonathan Aitken has also written a favorable and more panoramic view of the former president entitled *Nixon: A Life* (Regnery Gateway, 1993).

Historian Stephen E. Ambrose's three-volume biography on Nixon (Simon & Schuster, 1987–1991) also substantiates Hoff-Wilson's emphasis on Nixon's domestic successes. Ambrose's evaluation is even more remarkable because he was a liberal historian who campaigned for George McGovern in 1972 and had to be talked into writing a Nixon biography by his publisher. In domestic policy, Ambrose told *The Washington Post* on November 26, 1989, Nixon "was proposing things in '73 and '74 he couldn't even make the front pages with—national health insurance for all, a greatly expanded student loan operation, and energy and environmental programs." With regard to foreign policy, both Ambrose and Aitken disagree with Hoff-Wilson; they consider Nixon's foreign policy substantial and far-sighted. In the second volume of his biography, *Nixon: The Triumph of a Politician, 1962–1972* (Simon & Schuster, 1989), Ambrose concludes that the president was "without peer in foreign relations where 'profound pragmatic' vision endowed him with the potential to become a great world statesman."

Professor Bruce Schulman disagrees with historians like Hoff-Wilson who see Nixon as the last liberal or with others who view him as a mere political opportunist. Schulman makes a strong case that Nixon pretended to support liberal measures in his first term such as increased national funding for the arts and humanities, enforcement of environmental laws, more public housing and a guaranteed annual income for poverty-ridden citizens. But as Schulman points out, many of these programs would be passed to private agencies or state and local governments through the use of block grants and revenue-sharing mechanisms. In the case of Family Assistance Program, Schulman believes Nixon expected Congress to kill the idea because it was too extreme for conservatives and didn't guarantee enough income to appease the radicals.

Schulman makes a strong case that Nixon spent the 1968 and 1972 presidential campaigns building a new conservative Republican majority. An avid reader, Nixon absorbed the ideas of Kevin Phillips, *The Emerging Republican Majority* (1969) and Richard M. Scammon and Ben J. Wattenberg's *The Real Majority* (1970). These authors suggested that the president could fashion a majority coalition of white southern Democratic conservatives, who disliked the civil rights acts; northern blue-collar workers who were more concerned about riots, increased crime, and use of illegal drugs than economic issues; and finally, migrants to the sunbelt states of Florida, Arizona, and southern California who retired or worked in space-age technological industries. Critics like veteran *The Washington Post* columnist David Broder disagree with this analysis. Because Nixon was obsessed with his reelection campaign in 1972, the president funneled all the money into his personal reelection campaign organization known as CREEP and defunded the money that the Republican National Committee could have used to support state and local candidates. The result was a 49-state electoral college victory for Nixon over his anti-war Democratic opponent George McGovern while the Democrats maintained strong majorities in the House of Representatives and the United States Senate. Had Nixon expended his political capital on state and local races, perhaps the Watergate burglary might not have happened. For Broder's comments, see the PBS 3-hour production on *Nixon: The American Experience* (1991) available on videotape or DVD.

Schulman believes that Watergate did not reinforce the belief that the system worked to curb an abuse of presidential power. Instead, it reinforced the negative attitude toward government that the American public had experienced with Lyndon Johnson's credibility gap in managing the Vietnam War. Nixon's former attorney general and campaign manager John Mitchell had it right in 1974 when he told a group of disbelieving reporters: "In the next ten years, this country will go so far to the right you won't recognize it." Reporters shook their heads but Reagan was elected for two terms in the 1980s, and in 1994, the Republicans swept the Democrats out of the House and controlled both houses of Congress for the first time since 1946.

In addition to the books mentioned, students should begin their research with Melvin Small's *The Presidency of Richard Nixon* (1999), a fair and balanced study in the University Press of Kansas' American Presidency series complete with footnotes and bibliography. David Greenberg has a fascinating study of *Nixon's Shadow: The History of an Image* (Norton, 2003), which chronicles the life and career of his images in search of the real Nixon. Jeff Hay has edited a series of secondary interpretations of *Richard Nixon* (2001) in the Greenhaven Press series on *Presidents and Their Decisions*. Interestingly, Hay neglects the domestic side, which Professor Hoff-Wilson claims were Nixon's major successes. This gap is filled by Allen J. Matusow's critical *Nixon's Economy: Booms, Busts, Dollars & Votes* (University of Kansas Press, 1998). Other biographies worth consulting include the liberal historian Herbert Parmet's panoramic *Richard Nixon and His America* (Little, Brown, 1990), the first to be based on Nixon's pre-presidential papers. Less thoroughly researched in primary sources but more insightful is *The New York Times* reporter Tom Wicker's *One of Us: Richard Nixon and the American Dream* (Random House, 1991).

In order to gain a real feel for the Nixon years, you should consult contemporary or primary accounts. Nixon himself orchestrated his own rehabilitation in *RN: The Memoirs of Richard Nixon* (Grosset & Dunlop, 1978); *The Real War* (Warner Books, 1980); *Real Peace* (Little, Brown, 1984); *No More Vietnams* (Arbor House, 1985); and *In the Arena: A Memoir of Victory, Defeat and Renewal* (Simon & Schuster, 1990). Nixon's own accounts should be compared with former national security adviser Henry Kissinger's memoirs *White House Years* (Little, Brown, 1979). *The Haldeman Diaries: Inside the Nixon White House* (Putnam, 1994), which is the subject of Kutler's review essay, is essential for any undertaking of Nixon. Haldeman's account fleshes out the daily tensions of life in the Nixon White House and adds important details to the Nixon and Kissinger accounts. Other primary accounts include Kenneth W. Thompson, ed., *The Nixon Presidency: Twenty-Two Intimate Perspectives of Richard M. Nixon, Portraits of American Presidents series,* vol. 6 (University Press of America, 1987), which contains a series of discussions with former officials of the Nixon administration conducted by the White Burkett Miller Center for the Study of Public Affairs at the University of Virginia.

Three of the best review essays on the new historiography about America's thirty seventh president are "Theodore Draper: Nixon, Haldeman, and History," *The New York Review of Books* (July 14, 1994); Sydney Blumenthal, "The Longest Campaign," *The New Yorker* (August 8, 1994); and Stanley I. Kutler, "Et tu, Bob?" *The Nation* (August 22–29, 1994), a critical review of *The Haldeman Diaries* that also contains a CD version, available on Sony Imagesoft, which contains 60 percent more of the original text than the book, as well as home movies, photos, and biographical information on the Nixon staff.

Researchers who want a first-hand glimpse of Nixon should take a trip to the National Archives and listen to some of the 4,000 hours of tape, many of which have been declassified and released earlier than the papers of other presidents because of the Watergate scandal. Stanley I. Kutler has edited some of them in *The Abuse of Power: The New Nixon Tapes* (Touchstone Books, 1998). Nixon's view can be compared with Haldeman's *Diaries* as well as *The Kissinger Transcripts* (New Press, 1998), edited by William Burr. Nixon's presidential papers, after several court suits, have also ended up in the National Archives. A sample of some of these papers can be found in Bruce Oudes, ed., *From the President: Richard Nixon's Secret Files* (Harper & Row, 1989).

Internet References . . .

The Gulf War

This FRONTLINE page is a comprehensive and critical analysis of the 1990–1991 Persian Gulf crisis.

http://pbs.org/wgbh/pages/frontline/gulf/

American Immigration Resources on the Internet

This site contains many links to American immigration resources on the Internet. It includes a site on children's immigration issues, the Immigration and Naturalization Service home page, and a forum on immigration.

http://www.immigration-usa.com/resource.html

Sebago Associates: Notes on the Florida Vote in the 2000 Election

Sebago Associates, Inc., undertook a variety of preliminary analyses on the Florida vote immediately following the November 7, 2000, presidential election. Three notes resulting from these analyses are presented on this site, along with links to other analyses.

http://www.sbgo.com/election.htm

National Council for Science and the Environment

The National Council for Science and the Environment (NCSE) has been working since 1990 to improve the scientific basis for environmental decision making. NCSE is supported by almost 500 academic, scientific, environmental, and business organizations.

http://www.cnie.org

POTUS: George W. Bush

This is the George W. Bush page of POTUS: Presidents of the United States, a publication of the Internet Public Library. It features biographical information on Bush, information on many members of his presidential staff, his inaugural addresses, and audio files of the president himself.

http://www.ipl.org/div/potus/GWBush.html

The White House

Visit the home page of the White House for direct access to information about commonly requested federal services, the White House Briefing Room, and the presidents and vice presidents. The "Virtual Library" allows you to search White House documents, listen to speeches, and view photos. See in particular George W. Bush, "Remarks at the 2002 Graduation Exercise of the United States Military Academy," West Point, New York, June 1, 2002 (http://www. whitehouse.gov/news/releases/2002/06/20020601-3.html [accessed March 2005]) and The National Security Strategy of the United States, Washington, D.C., September 2002 (http://www.whitehouse.gov/nsc/nss.html [accessed March 2005]).

http://www.whitehouse.gov/

Postindustrial America and the End of the Cold War: 1974–2007

*A*merica continued to experience a series of highs and lows during the last quarter of the twentieth century. President Ronald Reagan's tax cuts and increased defense spending stimulated the economy but created an enormous budget deficit. Historians will continue to debate whether supply-side economics ended the Cold War by forcing the Russians to spend themselves into bankruptcy or whether the United States could have become prosperous with less defense spending and more attention paid to those groups left out of the "new prosperity." The reputations of President Reagan, the two George Bushes, and Bill Clinton are heavily dependent on whether or not the United States remains or declines as the dominant power in the world in the twenty-first century. Three recurring problems are left from the last half of the twentieth century. One problem is whether or not the creation of Israel in 1948 has permanently destabilized the Middle East. Will the United States have to fight a second Gulf War to stabilize the balance of power in the area and to maintain a steady supply of oil? Second, can America remain a nation of immigrants and still retain its core culture as well as be secure from terrorism? Finally, is a prosperous growing economy compatible with a healthy environment? Is the earth in danger of extinction or can humankind solve any present or future environmental problems?

- Did President Reagan Win the Cold War?

- Were the 1980s a Decade of Affluence for the Middle Class?

- Is George W. Bush the Worst President in American History?

- Should America Remain a Nation of Immigrants?

- Is the Environmental Crisis "An Inconvenient Truth"?

ISSUE 13

Did President Reagan Win the Cold War?

YES: John Lewis Gaddis, from *The Cold War: A New History* (Penguin Press, 2005)

NO: Daniel Deudney and G. John Ikenberry, from "Who Won the Cold War?" *Foreign Policy* (Summer 1992)

ISSUE SUMMARY

YES: Professor of history John Lewis Gaddis argues that President Reagan combined a policy of militancy and operational pragmatism that perplexed his hard-line advisers when he made the necessary compromises to bring about the most significant improvement in Soviet-American relations since the end of World War II.

NO: Professors of political science Daniel Deudney and G. John Ikenberry contend that the cold war ended only when Soviet President Gorbachev accepted Western liberal values and the need for global cooperation.

$\mathbf{T}$he term *cold war* was first coined by the American financial whiz and presidential adviser Bernard Baruch in 1947. Cold War refers to the extended but restricted conflict that existed between the United States and the Soviet Union from the end of World War II in 1945 until 1990. Looking back, it appears that the conflicting values and goals of a democratic/capitalist United States and a communist Soviet Union reinforced this state of affairs between the two countries. Basically, the Cold War ended when the Soviet Union gave up its control over the Eastern European nations and ceased to be a unified country itself.

The Nazi invasion of Russia in June 1941 and the Japanese attack on America's Pacific outposts in December united the United States, Great Britain, and the Soviet Union against the Axis powers during World War II. Nevertheless, complications ensued during the top-level Allied discussions to coordinate war strategy. The first meeting between the big three took place in Teheran in 1943 followed by another at Yalta in February 1945. These high-level negotiations were held under the assumption that wartime harmony among Great Britain, the United States, and the Soviet Union would continue; that Stalin, Churchill, and Roosevelt would lead the postwar world as they had conducted the war; and that the details of the general policies and agreements would be resolved at a less pressing time.

But none of these premises were fulfilled. By the time the Potsdam Conference (to discuss possible action against Japan) took place in July 1945, Churchill had been defeated in a parliamentary election, Roosevelt had died, and President Harry S. Truman had been thrust, unprepared, into his place. Of the big three, only Stalin remained as a symbol of continuity. Details about the promises at Teheran and Yalta faded into the background. Power politics, nuclear weapons, and mutual fears and distrust replaced the reasonably harmonious working relationships of the three big powers during World War II.

By 1947 the Truman administration had adopted a conscious policy of containment toward the Russians. This meant maintaining the status quo in Europe through various U.S. assistance programs. The NATO alliance of 1949 completed the shift of U.S. policy away from its pre–World War II isolationist policy and toward a commitment to the defense of Western Europe.

In the 1960s the largest problem facing the two superpowers was controlling the spread of nuclear weapons. The first attempt at arms control took place in the 1950s. After Stalin died in 1953, the Eisenhower administration made an "open-skies" proposal. This was rejected by the Russians, who felt (correctly) that they were behind the Americans in the arms race. In the summer of 1962 Soviet premier Nikita Khrushchev attempted to redress the balance of power by secretly installing missiles in Cuba that could be employed to launch nuclear attacks against U.S. cities. This sparked the Cuban Missile Crisis, the high point of the Cold War, which brought both nations to the brink of nuclear war before the Russians agreed to withdraw the missiles.

During the Leonid Brezhnev–Richard Nixon years, the policy of détente (relaxation of tensions) resulted in a series of summit meetings. Most important was the SALT I agreement, which outlawed national antiballistic missile defenses and placed a five-year moratorium on the building of new strategic ballistic missiles.

Soviet-American relations took a turn for the worse when the Soviets invaded Afghanistan in December 1979. In response, President Jimmy Carter postponed presenting SALT II to the Senate and imposed an American boycott of the 1980 Olympic Games, which were held in Moscow.

Détente remained dead during President Ronald Reagan's first administration. Reagan not only promoted a military budget of $1.5 trillion over a five-year period, he also was the first president since Truman to refuse to meet the Soviet leader. Major changes, however, took place during Reagan's second administration. In the following selections, John Lewis Gaddis argues that President Reagan combined a policy of militancy and operational pragmatism to bring about significant improvements in Soviet-American relations, while Daniel Deudney and G. John Ikenberry credit Soviet President Mikhail Gorbachev with ending the cold war because he accepted Western liberal values and the need for global cooperation.

YES

John Lewis Gaddis

The Cold War: A New History

Soon to declare his own candidacy for the presidency of the United States, [Ronald] Reagan had already made it clear what *he* thought of détente: "[I]sn't that what a farmer has with his turkey—until thanksgiving day?" His rise to power, like that of Deng, Thatcher, and John Paul II, would also have been difficult to anticipate, but at least his acting skills were professionally acquired. His fame as a film star predated the Cold War, even World War II, and gave him a head start when he went into politics. It also caused his opponents—sometimes even his friends—to underestimate him, a serious mistake, for Reagan was as skillful a politician as the nation had seen for many years, and one of its sharpest grand strategists ever. His strength lay in his ability to see beyond complexity to simplicity. And what he saw was simply this: that because détente perpetuated—and had been meant to perpetuate—the Cold War, only killing détente could end the Cold War.

Reagan came to this position through faith, fear, and self-confidence. His faith was that democracy and capitalism would triumph over communism, a "temporary aberration which will one day," he predicted in 1975, "disappear from the earth because it is contrary to human nature." His fear was that before that happened human beings would disappear as the result of a nuclear war. "[W]e live in a world," he warned in 1976, "in which the great powers have aimed . . . at each other horrible missiles of destruction . . . that can in minutes arrive at each other's country and destroy virtually the civilized world we live in." It followed that neither communism nor nuclear weapons should continue to exist, and yet détente was ensuring that both did. "I don't know about you," he told a radio audience in 1977, "but I [don't] exactly tear my hair and go into a panic at the possibility of losing détente." It was that jaunty self-confidence—Reagan's ability to threaten détente without seeming threatening himself—that propelled him to a landslide victory over Carter in November, 1980, thereby bringing him to power alongside the other great contemporaries, and the other great actors, of his age.

There was one more—as it happened, another Pole—whose name few people would have known only a few months earlier. A short, squat man with a drooping mustache and jerky Charlie Chaplin like movements, he had seen the shootings at the Gdansk shipyard in 1970, and had been sacked from his job there in 1976 for trying to organize the workers. Now, on August 14, 1980, with protests mounting once again, the shipyard director was trying to calm an angry crowd. Lech Wałęsa scrambled up on an excavator behind him, tapped him on the shoulder, and said: "Remember me?" Two weeks later— after lots of scrambling to rally his supporters from atop excavators, trucks, and the shipyard gate—Wałęsa announced the formation of the first independent and self-governing trade union ever in the Marxist-Leninist world. The pen with which he co-signed the charter for *Solidarność* (Solidarity) bore the image of John Paul II. And from Rome the pontiff let it be known, quietly but unmistakably, that he approved.

It was a moment at which several trends converged: the survival of a distinctive Polish identity despite the attempts of powerful neighbors, over several centuries, to try to smother it; the church's success in maintaining its autonomy through decades of war, revolution, and occupation; the state's incompetence in managing the post–World War II economy, which in turn discredited the ruling party's ideology. But trends hardly ever converge automatically. It takes leaders to make them do so, and here the actor-priest from Kraków and the actor-electrician from Gdansk played to each other's strengths—so much so that plans began to be made to remove them both from the stage.

The agent was Mehmet Ali Agca, a young Turk who may have plotted to kill Wałęsa on a January, 1981, visit to Rome, and who did shoot and almost kill the pope in St. Peter's Square on May 13, 1981. Agca's ties to Bulgarian intelligence quickly became clear. Soviet complicity was more difficult to establish, but it strains credulity to suggest that the Bulgarians would have undertaken an operation of this importance without Moscow's approval. The Italian state prosecutor's official report hinted strongly at this: "In some secret place, where every secret is wrapped in another secret, some political figure of great power . . . mindful of the needs of the Eastern bloc, decided that it was necessary to kill Pope Wojtyla." The pope's biographer put it more bluntly: "The simplest and most compelling answer . . . [is that] the Soviet Union was not an innocent in this business."

John Paul II recovered, attributing his survival to divine intervention. But Solidarity found its survival increasingly at risk as Kremlin leaders, alarmed that any communist government would share power with anybody, pressed the Polish authorities to suppress it. "Our friends listen, agree with our recommendations, but do practically nothing," Brezhnev fumed, "[a]nd the counterrevolution is advancing on every front." It could even take hold within the U.S.S.R. itself: what was happening in Poland was "having an, influence . . . in the western oblasts of our country," K.G.B. chief Yuri Andropov warned. "Additionally, . . . spontaneous demonstrations have flared up in parts of Georgia, [with] groups of people shouting anti-Soviet slogans . . . So we have to take strict measures here as well."

Apart from warning the Poles and cracking down on its own dissidents, however, it was not at all clear what the Soviet Union could do about the challenge Solidarity posed. Reagan's election ensured that any occupation of Poland would provoke an even harsher response than Carter's to the invasion of Afghanistan; meanwhile the Red Army was bogged down in that latter country with costs and casualties mounting and no exit strategy in sight. The

Soviet economy could hardly stand the strain of supporting Eastern Europe, something it would have to do if, as seemed certain in the event of military action against Poland, the West imposed still further sanctions. Moreover, the Polish situation was not like the one in Czechoslovakia in 1968. General Anatoly Gribkov recalls warning his superiors:

> In Czechoslovakia, events developed beginning with the highest echelons of power. In Poland, on the other hand, it is the people rising up who have all stopped believing in the government of the country and the leadership of the Polish United Workers Party . . . The Polish armed forces arc battle-ready and patriotic. They will not fire on their own people.

By December, 1981, the Politburo had decided *not* to intervene: "[E]ven if Poland falls under the control of 'Solidarity,' that is the way it will be," Andropov told his colleague. "If the capitalist countries pounce on the Soviet Union, . . . that will be very burdensome for us. We must be concerned above all with our own country." The Kremlin's top ideologist, Mikhail Suslov, agreed: "If troops are introduced, that will mean a catastrophe. I think we have reached a unanimous view here on this matter, and there can be no consideration at all of introducing troops."

This was a remarkable decision in two respects. It meant, first, the end of the Brezhnev Doctrine, and hence of the Soviet Union's willingness—extending all the way back through Hungary in 1956 and East Germany in 1953—to use force to preserve its sphere of influence in Eastern Europe. But it also acknowledged that the world's most powerful Marxist-Leninist state no longer represented proletarians beyond its borders, for in Poland at least the workers themselves had rejected that ideology. Had these conclusions become known at the time, the unraveling of Soviet authority that took place in 1989 might well have occurred eight years earlier.

But they did not become known: in a rare instance of successful dramatization, the Politburo convinced the new Polish leader, General Wojciech Jaruzelski, that the U.S.S.R. was *about* to intervene. Desperate to avoid that outcome, he reluctantly imposed martial law on the morning of December 13, 1981, imprisoned the organizers of Solidarity, and abruptly ended the experiment of granting workers autonomy Within a workers' state. Ever the actor, Lech Wałęsa had his line ready for the occasion. "This is the moment of your defeat," he told the men who came to arrest him. "These are the last nails in the coffin of Communism."

⠀ৼ⦿ৡ⠀

On March 30, 1981, six weeks before the attempt on the pope's life, another would-be assassin shot and almost killed Reagan. The Soviet Union had nothing to do with this attack: it was the effort, rather, of a demented young man, John W. Hinckley, to impress his own movie star idol, the actress Jodie Foster. The improbable motive behind this near-fatal act suggests the importance and vulnerability of individuals in history, for had Reagan's vice president, George

H. W. Bush, succeeded him at that point, the Reagan presidency would have been a historical footnote and there probably would not have been an American challenge to the Cold War status quo. Bush, like most foreign policy experts of his generation, saw that conflict as a permanent feature of the international landscape. Reagan, like Wałęsa, Thatcher, Deng, and John Paul II, definitely did not.

He shared their belief in the power of words, in the potency of ideas, and in the uses of *drama* to shatter the constraints of conventional wisdom. He saw that the Cold War itself had become a convention: that too many minds in too many places had resigned themselves to its perpetuation. He sought to break the stalemate—which was, be believed, largely psychological—by exploiting Soviet weaknesses and asserting western strengths. His preferred weapon was public oratory.

The first example came at Notre Dame University on May 17, 1981, only a month and a half after Reagan's brush with death. The pope himself had been shot five days earlier, so this could have been an occasion for somber reflections on the precariousness of human existence. Instead, in the spirit of John Paul II's "be not afraid," a remarkably recovered president assured his audience "[t]hat the years ahead are great ones for this country, for the cause of freedom and the spread of civilization." And then he made a bold prediction, all the more striking for the casualness with which he delivered it:

> The West won't contain communism, it will transcend communism. It won't bother to . . . denounce it, it will dismiss it as some bizarre chapter in human history whose last pages are even now being written.

This was a wholly new tone after years of high-level pronouncements about the need to learn to live with the U.S.S.R. as a competitive superpower. Now Reagan was focusing on the *transitory* character of Soviet power, and on the certainty with which the West could look forward to its demise.

The president developed this theme in an even more dramatic setting on June 8, 1982. The occasion was a speech to the British Parliament, delivered at Westminster with Prime Minister Thatcher in attendance. Reagan began by talking about Poland, a country which had "contributed mightily to [European] civilization" and was continuing to do so "by being magnificently unreconciled to oppression." He then echoed Churchill's 1946 "Iron Curtain" speech by reminding his audience:

> From Stettin in the Baltic to Varna on the Black Sea, the regimes planted by totalitarianism have had more than 30 years to establish their legitimacy. But none—not one regime—has yet been able to risk free elections. Regimes planted by bayonets do not take root.

Karl Marx, Reagan acknowledged, had been right: "We are witnessing today a great revolutionary crisis, . . . where the demands of the economic order are conflicting directly with those of the political order." That crisis was happening, though, not in the capitalist West, but in the Soviet Union, a country "that runs against the tides of history by denying human freedom and human dignity," while "unable to feed its own people." Moscow's nuclear capabilities could not shield it from these facts: "Any system is inherently unstable that has no peaceful means to legitimize its leaders." It followed then, Reagan concluded—pointedly paraphrasing Leon Trotsky—that "the march of freedom and democracy . . . will leave Marxism-Leninism on the ash-heap of history."

The speech could not have been better calculated to feed the anxieties the Soviet leadership already felt. Martial law had clamped a lid on reform in Poland, but that only fueled resentment there and elsewhere in Eastern Europe. Afghanistan had become a bloody stalemate. Oil prices had plummeted, leaving the Soviet economy in shambles. And the men who ran the U.S.S.R. seemed literally to exemplify its condition: Brezhnev finally succumbed to his many ailments in November, 1982, but Andropov, who succeeded him, was already suffering from the kidney disease that would take his life a year and a half later. The contrast with the vigorous Reagan, five years younger than Brezhnev but three years older than Andropov, was too conspicuous to miss.

Then Reagan deployed religion. "There is sin and evil in the world," he reminded the National Association of Evangelicals on March 8, 1983, in words the pope might have used, "and we're enjoined by Scripture and the Lord Jesus to oppose it with all our might." As long as communists "preach the supremacy of the state, declare its omnipotence over individual man, and predict its eventual domination of all peoples on Earth, they are the focus of evil in the modern world." Therefore:

> I urge you to speak out against those who would place the United States in a position of military and moral inferiority . . . I urge you to beware the temptation of Juride—the temptation of blithely declaring yourselves above it all and label[ing] both sides equally at fault, [of ignoring] the facts of history and the aggressive impulses of an evil empire.

Reagan chose the phrase, he later admitted, "with malice aforethought. . . . I think it worked." The "evil empire" speech completed a rhetorical offensive designed to expose what Reagan saw as the central error of détente: the idea that the Soviet Union had earned geopolitical, ideological, economic, and moral legitimacy as an equal to the United States and the other western democracies in the post–World War II international system.

The onslaught, however, was not limited to words. Reagan accelerated Carter's increase in American military spending: by 1985 the Pentagon's budget was almost twice what it had been in 1980. He did nothing to revive the SALT II treaty, proposing instead START—Strategic Arms *Reduction* Talks—which both his domestic critics and the Russians derided as an effort the kill the whole arms control process. The reaction was similar when Reagan suggested *not* deploying Pershing II and cruise missiles if the Soviet Union would dismantle *all* of its SS-20S. After Moscow contemptuously rejected this "zero-option," the installation of the new NATO missiles went ahead, despite a widespread nuclear freeze movement in the United States and vociferous anti-nuclear protests in western Europe.

But Reagan's most significant deed came on March 23, 1983, when he surprised the Kremlin, most American arms control experts, and many of his own advisers by repudiating the concept of Mutual Assured Destruction. He had never thought that it made much sense: it was like two Old West gunslingers "standing in a saloon aiming their guns to each other's head—permanently." He had been shocked to learn that there were no defenses against incoming missiles, and that in the curious logic of deterrence this was supposed to be a good thing. And so he asked, in a nationally televised speech: "What if . . . we could intercept and destroy strategic ballistic missiles before they reached our own soil or that of our allies?" It was an "emperor's new clothes" question, which no one else in a position of responsibility in Washington over the past two decades had dared to ask.

The reason was that *stability* in Soviet-American relations had come to be prized above all else. To attempt to build defenses against offensive weapons, the argument ran, could upset the delicate equilibrium upon which deterrence was supposed to depend. That made sense if one thought in static terms—if one assumed that the nuclear balance defined the Cold War and would continue to do so indefinitely. Reagan, however, thought in evolutionary terms. He saw that the Soviet Union had lost its ideological appeal, that it was losing whatever economic strength it once had, and that its survival as a superpower could no longer be taken for granted. That made stability, in his view, an outmoded, even immoral, priority. If the U.S.S.R. was crumbling, what could justify continuing to hold East Europeans hostage to the Brezhnev Doctrine—or, for that matter, continuing to hold Americans hostage to the equally odious concept of Mutual Assured Destruction? Why not hasten the disintegration?

That is what the Strategic Defense Initiative was intended to do. It challenged the argument that vulnerability could provide security. It called into question the 1972 Anti-Ballistic Missile Treaty, a center-piece of SALT I. It exploited the Soviet Union's backwardness in computer technology, a field in which the Russians knew that they could not keep up. And it undercut the peace movement by framing the entire project in terms of *lowering* the risk of nuclear war: the ultimate purpose of SDI, Reagan insisted, was not to freeze nuclear weapons, but rather to render them "impotent and obsolete."

This last theme reflected something else about Reagan that almost everybody at the time missed: he was the only nuclear abolitionist ever to have been president of the United States. He made no secret of this, but the possibility that a right-wing Republican anti-communist promilitary chief executive could also be an anti-nuclear activist defied so many stereotypes that hardly anyone noticed Reagan's repeated promises, as he had put it in the "evil empire" speech, "to keep America strong and free, while we negotiate real and verifiable reductions in the world's nuclear arsenals and one day, with God's help, their total elimination."

Reagan was deeply committed to SDI: it was not a bargaining chip to give up in future negotiations. That did not preclude, though, using it as a bluff: the United States was years, even decades, away from developing a missile defense capability, but Reagan's speech persuaded the increasingly frightened Soviet leaders that this was about to happen. They were convinced,

Dobrynin recalled, "that the great technological potential of the United States had scored again and treated Reagan's statement as a real threat." Having exhausted their country by catching up in offensive missiles, the suddenly faced a new round of competition demanding skills they had no hope of mastering. And the Americans seemed not even to have broken into a sweat.

The reaction, in the Kremlin, approached panic. Andropov had concluded, while still head of the K.G.B., that the new administration in Washington might be planning a surprise attack on the Soviet Union. "Reagan is unpredictable," he warned. "You should expect anything from him." There followed a two-year intelligence alert, with agents throughout the world ordered to look for evidence that such preparations were under way. The tension became so great that when a South Korean airliner accidentally strayed into Soviet airspace over Sakhalin on September 1, 1983, the military authorities in Moscow assumed the worst and ordered it shot down, killing 269 civilians, 63 of them Americans. Unwilling to admit the mistake, Andropov maintained that the incident had been a "sophisticated provocation organized by the U.S. special services."

Then something even scarier happened that attracted no public notice. The United States and its NATO allies had for years carried out fall military exercises, but the ones that took place in November—designated "Able Archer 83"—involved a higher level of leadership participation than was usual. The Soviet intelligence agencies kept a close watch on these maneuvers, and their reports caused Andropov and his top aides to conclude—briefly—that a nuclear attack was imminent. It was probably the most dangerous moment since the Cuban missile crisis, and yet no one in Washington knew of it until a well-placed spy in the K.G.B.'s London headquarters alerted British intelligence, which passed the information along to the Americans.

That definitely got Reagan's attention. Long worried about the danger of a nuclear war, the president had already initiated a series of quiet contacts with Soviet officials—mostly unreciprocated—aimed at defusing tensions. The Able Archer crisis convinced him that he had pushed the Russians far enough, that it was time for another speech. It came at the beginning of Orwell's fateful year, on January 16, 1984, but Big Brother was nowhere to be seen. Instead, in lines only he could have composed, Reagan suggested placing the Soviet-American relationship in the capably reassuring hands of Jim and Sally and Ivan and Anya. One White House staffer, puzzled by the hand-written addendum to the prepared text, exclaimed a bit too loudly: "Who wrote this shit?"

Once again, the old actor's timing was excellent. Andropov died the following month, to be succeeded by Konstantin Chemenko, an enfeebled geriatric so zombie-like as to be beyond assessing intelligence reports, alarming or not. Having failed to prevent the NATO missile deployments, Foreign Minister Gromyko soon grudgingly agreed to resume arms control negotiations. Meanwhile Reagan was running for re-election as both a hawk and a dove: in November he trounced his Democratic opponent, Walter Mondale. And when Chemenko died in March, 1985, at the age of seventy-four, it seemed an all-too-literal validation of Reagan's predictions about "last pages" and historical "ash-heaps." Seventy-four himself at the time, the president had another line ready: "How am I supposed to get anyplace with the Russians, if they keep dying on me?"

⋅◈⋅

"We can't go on living like this," Mikhail Gorbachev recalls saying to his wife, Raisa, on the night before the Politburo appointed him, at the age of fifty-four, to succeed Chernenko as general secretary of the Communist Party of the U.S.S.R. That much was obvious not just to Gorbachev but even to the surviving elders who selected him: the Kremlin could not continue to be run as a home for the aged. Not since Stalin had so young a man reached the top of the Soviet hierarchy. Not since Lenin had there been a university-educated Soviet leader. And never had there been one so open about his country's shortcomings, or so candid in acknowledging the failures of Marxist-Leninist ideology.

Gorbachev had been trained as a lawyer, not an actor, but he understood the uses of personality at least as well as Reagan did. Vice President Bush, who represented the United States at Chernenko's funeral, reported back that Gorbachev "has a disarming smile, warm eyes, and an engaging way of making an unpleasant point and then bouncing back to establish real communication with his interlocutors." Secretary of State George Shultz, who was also there, described him as "totally different from any Soviet leader I've ever met." Reagan himself, on meeting Gorbachev at the November, 1985, Geneva summit, found "warmth in his face and style, not the coldness bordering on hatred I'd seen in most other senior Soviet leaders I'd met until then."

For the first time since the Cold War began the U.S.S.R. had a ruler who did not seem sinister, boorish, unresponsive, senile—or dangerous. Gorbachev was "intelligent, well-educated, dynamic, honest, with ideas and imagination," one of his closest advisers, Anatoly Chernyaev, noted in his private diary. "Myths and taboos (including ideological ones) are nothing for him. He could flatten any of them." When a Soviet citizen congratulated him early in 1987 for having replaced a regime of "stonefaced sphinxes," Gorbachev proudly published the letter.

What would replace the myths, taboos, and sphinxes, however, was less clear. Gorbachev knew that the Soviet Union could not continue on its existing path, but unlike John Paul II, Deng, Thatcher, Reagan, and Wałęsa, he did not know what the new path should be. He was at once vigorous, decisive, and adrift: he poured enormous energy into shattering the status quo without specifying how to reassemble the pieces. As a consequence, he allowed circumstances—and often the firmer views of more far-sighted contemporaries—to determine his own priorities. He resembled, in this sense, the eponymous hero of Woody Allen's movie *Zelig*, who managed to be present at all the great events of his time, but only by taking on the character, even the appearance, of the stronger personalities who surrounded him.

Gorbachev's malleability was most evident in his dealings with Reagan, who had long insisted that he could get through to a Soviet leader if he could ever meet one face-to-face. That had not been possible with Brozhnev, Andropov, or

Chernenko, which made Reagan all the keener to try with Gorbachev. The new Kremlin boss came to Geneva bristling with distrust: the president, he claimed, was seeking "to use the arms race . . . to weaken the Soviet Union. . . . But we can match any challenge, though you might not think so." Reagan responded that "we would prefer to sit down and get rid of nuclear weapons, and with them, the threat of war." SDI would make that possible: the United States would even share the technology with the Soviet Union. Reagan was being emotional, Gorbachev protested: SDI was only "one man's dream." Reagan countered by asking why "it was so horrifying to seek to develop a defense against this awful threat." The summit broke up inconclusively.

Two months later, though, Gorbachev proposed publicly that the United States and the Soviet Union commit themselves to ridding the world of nuclear weapons by the year 2000. Cynics saw this as an effort to test Reagan's sincerity, but Chernyaev detected a deeper motive. Gorbachev, he concluded, had "really decided to end the arms race no matter what. He is taking this 'risk' because, as he understands, it's no risk at all—because nobody would attack us even if we disarmed completely." Just two years earlier Andropov had thought Reagan capable of launching a surprise attack. Now Gorbachev felt confident that the United States would never do this. Reagan's position had not changed: he had always asked Soviet leaders to "trust me." After meeting Reagan, Gorbachev began to do so.

A nuclear disaster did, nevertheless, occur—not because of war but as the result of an explosion at the Chernobyl nuclear power plant on April 26, 1986. This event also changed Gorbachev. It revealed "the sicknesses of our system . . . the concealing or hushing up of accidents and other bad news, irresponsibility and carelessness, slipshod work, wholesale drunkenness." For decades, he admonished the Politburo, "scientists, specialists, and ministers have been telling us that everything was safe. . . . [Y]ou think that we will look on you as gods. But now we have ended up with a fiasco." Henceforth there would have to be *glasnost* (publicity) and *perestroika* (restructuring) within the Soviet Union itself. "Chernobyl," Gorbachev acknowledged, "made me and my colleagues rethink a great many things."

The next Reagan-Gorbachev summit, held the following October in Reykjavik, Iceland, showed how far the rethinking had gone. Gorbachev dismissed earlier Soviet objections and accepted Reagan's "zero option," which would eliminate all intermediate-range nuclear missiles in Europe. He went on to propose a 50 percent cut in Soviet and American strategic weapons, in return for which the United States would agree to honor the Anti-Ballistic Missile Treaty for the next decade while confining SDI to laboratory testing. Not to be outdone, Reagan suggested phasing out all intercontinental ballistic missiles within that period and reiterated his offer to share SDI. Gorbachev was skeptical, leading Reagan to wonder how anyone could object to "defenses against non-existent weapons." The president then proposed a return to Reykjavik in 1996:

> He and Gorbachev would come to Iceland, and each of them would bring the last nuclear missile from each country with them. Then they would

give a tremendous party for the whole world. . . . The President . . . would be very old by then and Gorbachev would not recognize him. The President would say "Hello, Mikhail." And Gorbachev would say, "Ron, is it you?" And then they would destroy the last missile.

It was one of Reagan's finest performances, but Gorbachev for the moment remained unmoved: the United States would have to give up the right to deploy SDI. That was unacceptable to Reagan, who angrily ended the summit.

Both men quickly recognized, though, the significance of what had happened: to the astonishment of their aides and allies, the leaders of the United States and the Soviet Union had found that they shared an interest, if not in SDI technology, then at least in the principle of nuclear abolition. The logic was Reagan's, but Gorbachev had come to accept it. Reykjavik, he told a press conference, had not been a failure: "[I]t is a breakthrough, which allowed us for the first time to look over the horizon."

The two men never agreed formally to abolish nuclear weapons, nor did missile defense come anywhere close to feasibility during their years in office. But at their third summit in Washington in December, 1987, they did sign a treaty providing for the dismantling of all intermediate-range nuclear missiles in Europe. *"Dovorey no provorey,"* Reagan insisted at the signing ceremony, exhausting his knowledge of the Russian language: "Trust but verify." You repeat that at every meeting," Gorbachev laughed. "I like it," Reagan admitted. Soon Soviet and American observers were witnessing the actual destruction of the SS-20, Pershing II, and cruise missiles that had revived Cold War tensions only a few years before—and pocketing the pieces as souvenirs. If by no means "impotent," certain categories of nuclear weapons had surely become "obsolete." It was Reagan, more than anyone else, who made that happen.

Gorbachev's impressionability also showed up in economics. He had been aware, from his travels outside the Soviet Union before assuming the leadership, that "people there . . . were better off than in our country." It seemed that "our aged leaders were not especially worried about our undeniably lower living standards, our unsatisfactory way of life, and our falling behind in the field of advanced technologies." But he had no clear sense of what to do about this. So Secretary of State Shultz, a former economics professor at Stanford, took it upon himself to educate the new Soviet leader.

Shultz began by lecturing Gorbachev, as early as 1985, on the impossibility of a closed society being a prosperous society: "People must be free to express themselves, move around, emigrate and travel if they want to. . . . Otherwise they can't take advantage of the opportunities available. The Soviet economy will have to be radically changed to adapt to the new era." "You should take over the planning office here in Moscow," Gorbachev joked, "because you have more ideas than they have." In a way, this is what Shultz did. Over the next several years, he used his trips to that city to run tutorials for Gorbachev and his advisers, even bringing pie charts to the Kremlin to illustrate his argument that as long as it retained a command economy, the Soviet Union would fall further and further behind the rest of the developed world.

Gorbachev was surprisingly receptive. He echoed some of Shultz's thinking in his 1987 book, *Perestroika:* "How can the economy advance," he asked, "if it creates preferential conditions for backward enterprises and penalizes the foremost ones?" When Reagan visited the Soviet Union in May, 1988, Gorbachev arranged for him to lecture at Moscow State University on the virtues of market capitalism. From beneath a huge bust of Lenin, the president evoked computer chips, rock stars, movies, and the "irresistible power of unarmed truth." The students gave him a standing ovation. Soon Gorbachev was repeating what he had learned to Reagan's successor, George H. W. Bush: "Whether we like it or not, we will have to deal with a united, integrated, European economy. . . . Whether we want it or not, Japan is one more center of world politics. . . . China . . . is [another] huge reality. . . . All these, I repeat, are huge events typical of a regrouping of forces in the world."

Most of this, however, was rhetoric: Gorbachev was never willing to leap directly to a market economy in the way that Deng Xiaoping had done. He reminded the Politburo late in 1988 that Franklin D. Roosevelt had saved American capitalism by "borrow[ing] socialist ideas of planning, state regulation, [and] . . . the principle of more social fairness. "The implication was that Gorbachev could save socialism by borrowing from capitalism, but just how remained uncertain. "[R]epeated incantations about 'socialist values' and 'purified ideas of October,'" Chernyaev observed several months later, "provoke an ironic response in knowing listeners. . . . [T]hey sense that there's nothing behind them." After the Soviet Union collapsed, Gorbachev acknowledged his failure. "The Achilles heel of socialism was the inability to link the socialist goal with the provision of incentives for efficient labor and the encouragement of initiative on the part of individuals. It became clear in practice that a market provides such incentives best of all."

There was, however, one lesson Reagan and his advisers tried to teach Gorbachev that he did not need to learn: it had to do with the difficulty of sustaining an unpopular, overextended, and antiquated empire. The United States had, since Carter's final year in office, provided covert and sometimes overt support to forces resisting Soviet influence in Eastern Europe, Afghanistan, Central America, and elsewhere. By 1985 there was talk in Washington of a "Reagan Doctrine": a campaign to turn the forces of nationalism against the Soviet Union by making the case that, with the Brezhnev Doctrine, it had become the last great imperialist power. Gorbachev's emergence raised the possibility of convincing a Kremlin leader himself that the "evil empire" was a lost cause, and over the next several years Reagan tried to do this. His methods included quiet persuasion, continued assistance to anti-Soviet resistance movements, and as always dramatic speeches: the most sensational one came at the Brandenburg Gate in West Berlin on June 12, 1987, when—against the advice of the State Department—the president demanded: "Mr. Gorbachev, tear down this wall!"

For once, a Reagan performance fell flat the reaction in Moscow was unexpectedly restrained. Despite this challenge to the most visible symbol of Soviet authority in Europe, planning went ahead for the Intermediate-Range Nuclear Forces Treaty and the Washington summit later that year. The reason, it is now clear, is that the Brezhnev Doctrine had died when the Politburo decided, six years earlier, against invading Poland. From that moment on Kremlin leaders depended upon *threats* to use force to maintain their control over Eastern Europe—but they knew that they could not actually use force. Gorbachev was aware of this, and had even tried to signal his Warsaw Pact allies, in 1985, that they were on their own: "I had the feeling that they were not taking it altogether seriously." So he began making the point openly.

One could always "suppress, compel, bribe, break or blast," he wrote in his book *Perestroika*, "but only for a certain period. From the point of view of long-term, big-time politics, no one will be able to subordinate others. . . . Let everyone make his own choice, and let us all respect that choice." Decisions soon followed to begin withdrawing Soviet troops from Afghanistan and to reduce support for Marxist regimes elsewhere in the "third world." Eastern Europe, though, was another matter: the prevailing view in Washington as well as in European capitals on both sides of the Cold War divide was that the U.S.S.R. would never voluntarily relinquish its sphere of influence there. "Any Soviet yielding of the area," one western analyst commented in 1987, "not only would undermine the ideological claims of Communism . . . and degrade the Soviet Union's credentials as a confident global power, but also would gravely jeopardize a basic internal Soviet consensus and erode the domestic security of the system itself."

For Gorbachev, though, any attempt to *maintain* control over unwilling peoples through the use of force would degrade the Soviet system by over-stretching its resources, discrediting its ideology, and resisting the irresistible forces of democratization that, for both moral and practical reasons, were sweeping the world. And so he borrowed a trick from Reagan by making a dramatic speech of his own: he announced to the United Nations General Assembly, on December 7, 1988, that the Soviet Union would *unilaterally* cut its ground force commitment to the Warsaw Pact by half a million men. "It is obvious," he argued, "that force and the threat of force cannot be and should not be an instrument of foreign policy. . . . Freedom of choice is . . . a universal principle, and it should know no exceptions."

The speech "left a huge impression," Gorbachev boasted to the Politburo upon his return to Moscow, and "created an entirely different background for perceptions of our policies and the Soviet Union as a whole." He was right about that. It suddenly became apparent, just as Reagan was leaving office, that the Reagan Doctrine had been pushing against an open door. But Gorbachev had also made it clear, to the peoples and the governments of Eastern Europe, that the door was now open.

Daniel Deudney and
G. John Ikenberry

 **NO**

Who Won the Cold War?

The end of the Cold War marks the most important historical divide in half a century. The magnitude of those developments has ushered in a wide-ranging debate over the reasons for its end—a debate that is likely to be as protracted, controversial, and politically significant as that over the Cold War's origins. The emerging debate over why the Cold War ended is of more than historical interest: At stake is the vindication and legitimation of an entire world view and foreign policy orientation.

In thinking about the Cold War's conclusion, it is vital to distinguish between the domestic origins of the crisis in Soviet communism and the external forces that influenced its timing and intensity, as well as the direction of the Soviet response. Undoubtedly, the ultimate cause of the Cold War's outcome lies in the failure of the Soviet system itself. At most, outside forces hastened and intensified the crisis. However, it was not inevitable that the Soviet Union would respond to this crisis as it did in the late 1980s—with domestic liberalization and foreign policy accommodation. After all, many Western experts expected that the USSR would respond to such a crisis with renewed repression at home and aggression abroad, as it had in the past.

At that fluid historic juncture, the complex matrix of pressures, opportunities, and attractions from the outside world influenced the direction of Soviet change, particularly in its foreign policy. The Soviets' field of vision was dominated by the West, the United States, and recent American foreign policy. Having spent more than 45 years attempting to influence the Soviet Union, Americans are now attempting to gauge the weight of their country's impact and, thus, the track record of U.S. policies.

In assessing the rest of the world's impact on Soviet change, a remarkably simplistic and self-serving conventional wisdom has emerged in the United States. This new conventional wisdom, the "Reagan victory school," holds that President Ronald Reagan's military and ideological assertiveness during the 1980s played the lead role in the collapse of Soviet communism and the "taming" of its foreign policy. In that view the Reagan administration's ideological counter-offensive and military buildup delivered the knock-out punch to a system that was internally bankrupt and on the ropes. The Reagan Right's perspective is an ideologically pointed version of the more broadly held conventional wisdom on the end of the Cold War that emphasizes the success of the "peace-through-strength" strategy manifest in four decades of Western containment. After decades of waging a costly "twilight struggle," the West now celebrates the triumph of its military and ideological resolve.

The Reagan victory school and the broader peace-through-strength perspectives are, however, misleading and incomplete—both in their interpretation of events in the 1980s and in their understanding of deeper forces that led to the end of the Cold War. It is important to reconsider the emerging conventional wisdom before it truly becomes an article of faith on Cold War history and comes to distort the thinking of policymakers in America and elsewhere.

The collapse of the Cold War caught almost everyone, particularly hardliners, by surprise. Conservatives and most analysts in the U.S. national security establishment believed that the Soviet-U.S. struggle was a permanent feature of international relations. As former National Security Council adviser Zbigniew Brzezinski put it in 1986, "the American-Soviet contest is not some temporary aberration but a historical rivalry that will long endure." And to many hardliners, Soviet victory was far more likely than Soviet collapse. Many ringing predictions now echo as embarrassments.

The Cold War's end was a baby that arrived unexpectedly, but a long line of those claiming paternity has quickly formed. A parade of former Reagan administration officials and advocates has forthrightly asserted that Reagan's hardline policies were the decisive trigger for reorienting Soviet foreign policy and for the demise of communism. As former Pentagon officials like Caspar Weinberger and Richard Perle, columnist George Will, neoconservative thinker Irving Kristol, and other proponents of the Reagan victory school have argued, a combination of military and ideological pressures gave the Soviets little choice but to abandon expansionism abroad and repression at home. In that view, the Reagan military buildup foreclosed Soviet military options while pushing the Soviet economy to the breaking point. Reagan partisans stress that his dramatic "Star Wars" initiative put the Soviets on notice that the next phase of the arms race would be waged in areas where the West held a decisive technological edge.

Reagan and his administration's military initiatives, however, played a far different and more complicated role in inducing Soviet change than the Reagan victory school asserts. For every "hardening" there was a "softening": Reagan's rhetoric of the "Evil Empire" was matched by his vigorous anti-nuclearism; the military buildup in the West was matched by the resurgence of a large popular peace movement; and the Reagan Doctrine's toughening of containment was matched by major deviations from containment in East-West economic relations. Moreover, over the longer term, the strength marshaled in containment was matched by mutual weakness in the face of nuclear weapons, and efforts to engage the USSR were as important as efforts to contain it.

The Irony of Ronald Reagan

Perhaps the greatest anomaly of the Reagan victory school is the "Great Communicator" himself. The Reagan Right ignores that his anti-nuclearism was as strong as his anticommunism. Reagan's personal convictions on nuclear weapons were profoundly at odds with the beliefs of most in his administration.

Staffed by officials who considered nuclear weapons a useful instrument of statecraft and who were openly disdainful of the moral critique of nuclear weapons articulated by the arms control community and the peace movement, the administration pursued the hardest line on nuclear policy and the Soviet Union in the postwar era. Then vice president George Bush's observation that nuclear weapons would be fired as a warning shot and Deputy Under Secretary of Defense T. K. Jones's widely quoted view that nuclear war was survivable captured the reigning ethos within the Reagan administration.

In contrast, there is abundant evidence that Reagan himself felt a deep antipathy for nuclear weapons and viewed their abolition to be a realistic and desirable goal. Reagan's call in his famous March 1983 "Star Wars" speech for a program to make nuclear weapons impotent and obsolete was viewed as cynical by many, but actually it expressed Reagan's heartfelt views, views that he came to act upon. As *Washington Post* reporter Lou Cannon's 1991 biography points out, Reagan was deeply disturbed by nuclear deterrence and attracted to abolitionist solutions. "I know I speak for people everywhere when I say our dream is to see the day when nuclear weapons will be banished from the face of the earth," Reagan said in November 1983. Whereas the Right saw anti-nuclearism as a threat to American military spending and the legitimacy of an important foreign policy tool, or as propaganda for domestic consumption, Reagan sincerely believed it. Reagan's anti-nuclearism was not just a personal sentiment. It surfaced at decisive junctures to affect Soviet perceptions of American policy. Sovietologist and strategic analyst Michael MccGwire has argued persuasively that Reagan's anti-nuclearism decisively influenced Soviet-U.S. relations during the early Gorbachev years.

Contrary to the conventional wisdom, the defense buildup did not produce Soviet capitulation. The initial Soviet response to the Reagan administration's buildup and belligerent rhetoric was to accelerate production of offensive weapons, both strategic and conventional. That impasse was broken not by Soviet capitulation but by an extraordinary convergence by Reagan and Mikhail Gorbachev on a vision of mutual nuclear vulnerability and disarmament. On the Soviet side, the dominance of the hardline response to the newly assertive America was thrown into question in early 1985 when Gorbachev became general secretary of the Communist party after the death of Konstantin Chernenko. Without a background in foreign affairs, Gorbachev was eager to assess American intentions directly and put his stamp on Soviet security policy. Reagan's strong antinuclear views expressed at the November 1985 Geneva summit were decisive in convincing Gorbachev that it was possible to work with the West in halting the nuclear arms race. The arms control diplomacy of the later Reagan years was successful because, as *Washington Post* journalist Don Oberdorfer has detailed in *The Turn: From the Cold War to a New Era* (1991), Secretary of State George Shultz picked up on Reagan's strong convictions and deftly side-stepped hard-line opposition to agreements. In fact, Schultz's success at linking presidential unease about nuclear weapons to Soviet overtures in the face of rightwing opposition provides a sharp contrast with John Foster Dulles's refusal to act on President Dwight Eisenhower's nuclear doubts and the opportunities presented by Nikita Khrushchev's détente overtures.

Reagan's commitment to anti-nuclearism and its potential for transforming the U.S-Soviet confrontation was more graphically demonstrated at the October 1986 Reykjavik summit when Reagan and Gorbachev came close to agreeing on a comprehensive program of global denuclearization that was far bolder than any seriously entertained by American strategists since the Baruch Plan of 1946. The sharp contrast between Reagan's and Gorbachev's shared skepticism toward nuclear weapons on the one hand, and the Washington security establishment's consensus on the other, was showcased in former secretary of defense James Schlesinger's scathing accusation that Reagan was engaged in "casual utopianism." But Reagan's anomalous anti-nuclearism provided the crucial signal to Gorbachev that bold initiatives would be reciprocated rather than exploited. Reagan's anti-nuclearism was more important than his administration's military buildup in catalyzing the end of the Cold War.

Neither anti-nuclearism nor its embrace by Reagan have received the credit they deserve for producing the Soviet-U.S. reconciliation. Reagan's accomplishment in this regard has been met with silence from all sides. Conservatives, not sharing Reagan's anti-nuclearism, have emphasized the role of traditional military strength. The popular peace movement, while holding deeply antinuclear views, was viscerally suspicious of Reagan. The establishment arms control community also found Reagan and his motives suspect, and his attack on deterrence conflicted with their desire to stabilize deterrence and establish their credentials as sober participants in security policy making. Reagan's radical anti-nuclearism should sustain his reputation as the ultimate Washington outsider.

The central role of Reagan's and Gorbachev's anti-nuclearism throws new light on the 1987 Treaty on Intermediate-range Nuclear Forces, the first genuine disarmament treaty of the nuclear era. The conventional wisdom emphasizes that this agreement was the fruit of a hard-line negotiating posture and the U.S. military buildup. Yet the superpowers' settlement on the "zero option" was not a vindication of the hard-line strategy. The zero option was originally fashioned by hardliners for propaganda purposes, and many backed off as its implementation became likely. The impasse the hard line created was transcended by the surprising Reagan-Gorbachev convergence against nuclear arms.

The Reagan victory school also overstates the overall impact of American and Western policy on the Soviet Union during the 1980s. The Reagan administration's posture was both evolving and inconsistent. Though loudly proclaiming its intention to go beyond the previous containment policies that were deemed too soft, the reality of Reagan's policies fell short. As Sovietologists Gail Lapidus and Alexander Dallin observed in a 1989 *Bulletin of the Atomic Scientists* article, the policies were "marked to the end by numerous zigzags and reversals, bureaucratic conflicts, and incoherence." Although rollback had long been a cherished goal of the Republican party's right wing, Reagan was unwilling and unable to implement it.

The hard-line tendencies of the Reagan administration were offset in two ways. First, and most important, Reagan's tough talk fueled a large peace movement in the United States and Western Europe in the 1980s, a movement that put significant political pressure upon Western governments to pursue far reaching arms control proposals. That mobilization of Western opinion created a political climate in which the rhetoric and posture of the early Reagan administration was a significant political liability. By the 1984 U.S. presidential election, the administration had embraced arms control goals that it had previously ridiculed. Reagan's own anti-nuclearism matched that rising public concern, and Reagan emerged as the spokesman for comprehensive denuclearization. Paradoxically, Reagan administration policies substantially triggered the popular revolt against the nuclear hardline, and then Reagan came to pursue the popular agenda more successfully than any other postwar president.

Second, the Reagan administration's hard-line policies were also undercut by powerful Western interests that favored East-West economic ties. In the early months of Reagan's administration, the grain embargo imposed by President Jimmy Carter after the 1979 Soviet invasion of Afghanistan was lifted in order to keep the Republican party's promises to Midwestern farmers. Likewise, in 1981 the Reagan administration did little to challenge Soviet control of Eastern Europe after Moscow pressured Warsaw to suppress the independent Polish trade union Solidarity, in part because Poland might have defaulted on multibillion dollar loans made by Western banks. Also, despite strenuous opposition by the Reagan administration, the NATO allies pushed ahead with a natural gas pipeline linking the Soviet Union with Western Europe. That a project creating substantial economic interdependence could proceed during the worst period of Soviet-U.S. relations in the 1980s demonstrates the failure of the Reagan administration to present an unambiguous hard line toward the Soviet Union. More generally, NATO allies and the vocal European peace movement moderated and buffered hardline American tendencies.

In sum, the views of the Reagan victory school are flawed because they neglect powerful crosscurrents in the West during the 1980s. The conventional wisdom simplifies a complex story and ignores those aspects of Reagan administration policy inconsistent with the hardline rationale. Moreover, the Western "face" toward the Soviet Union did not consist exclusively of Reagan administration policies, but encompassed countervailing tendencies from the Western public, other governments, and economic interest groups.

Whether Reagan is seen as the consummate hardliner or the prophet of anti-nuclearism, one should not exaggerate the influence of his administration, or of other short-term forces. Within the Washington beltway, debates about postwar military and foreign policy would suggest that Western strategy fluctuated wildly, but in fact the basic thrust of Western policy toward the USSR remained remarkably consistent. Arguments from the New Right notwithstanding, Reagan's containment strategy was not that different from those of his predecessors. Indeed, the broader peace-through-strength perspective sees the Cold War's finale as the product of a long-term policy, applied over the decades.

In any case, although containment certainly played an important role in blocking Soviet expansionism, it cannot explain either the end of the Cold War or the direction of Soviet policy responses. The West's relationship with the Soviet Union was not limited to containment, but included important elements of mutual vulnerability and engagement. The Cold War's end was not simply a result of Western strength but of mutual weakness and intentional engagement as well.

Most dramatically, the mutual vulnerability created by nuclear weapons overshadowed containment. Nuclear weapons forced the United States and the Soviet Union to eschew war and the serious threat of war as tools of diplomacy and created imperatives for the cooperative regulation of nuclear capability. Both countries tried to fashion nuclear explosives into useful instruments of policy, but they came to the realization—as the joint Soviet-American statement issued from the 1985 Geneva summit put it—that "nuclear war cannot be won and must never be fought." Both countries slowly but surely came to view nuclear weapons as a common threat that must be regulated jointly. Not just containment, but also the overwhelming and common nuclear threat brought the Soviets to the negotiating table. In the shadow of nuclear destruction, common purpose defused traditional antagonisms.

A second error of the peace-through-strength perspective is the failure to recognize that the West offered an increasingly benign face to the communist world. Traditionally, the Soviets' Marxist-Leninist doctrine held that the capitalist West was inevitably hostile and aggressive, an expectation reinforced by the aggression of capitalist, fascist Germany. Since World War II, the Soviets' principal adversaries had been democratic capitalist states. Slowly but surely Soviet doctrine acknowledged that the West's behavior did not follow Leninist expectations, but was instead increasingly pacific and cooperative. The Soviet willingness to abandon the Brezhnev Doctrine in the late 1980s in favor of the "Sinatra Doctrine"—under which any East European country could sing, "I did it my way"—suggests a radical transformation in the prevailing Soviet perception of threat from the West. In 1990, the Soviet acceptance of the de facto absorption of communist East Germany into West Germany involved the same calculation with even higher stakes. In accepting the German reunification, despite that country's past aggression, Gorbachev acted on the assumption that the Western system was fundamentally pacific. As Russian foreign minister Andrei Kozyrev noted subsequently, that Western countries are pluralistic democracies "practically rules out the pursuance of an aggressive foreign policy." Thus the Cold War ended despite the assertiveness of Western hardliners, rather than because of it.

The War of Ideas

The second front of the Cold War, according to the Reagan victory school, was ideological. Reagan spearheaded a Western ideological offensive that dealt the USSR a death blow. For the Right, driving home the image of the Evil Empire was a decisive stroke rather than a rhetorical flourish. Ideological warfare was such a key front in the Cold War because the Soviet Union was, at its core, an ideological creation. According to the Reagan Right, the supreme vulnerability of the Soviet Union to ideological assault was greatly underappreciated by Western leaders and publics. In that view, the Cold War was won by the West's uncompromising assertion of the superiority of its values and its complete denial of the moral legitimacy of the Soviet system during the 1980s. Western military strength could prevent defeat, but only ideological breakthrough could bring victory.

Underlying that interpretation is a deeply ideological philosophy of politics and history. The Reagan Right tended to view politics as a war of ideas, an orientation that generated a particularly polemical type of politics. As writer Sidney Blumenthal has pointed out, many of the leading figures in the neoconservative movement since the 1960s came to conservatism after having begun their political careers as Marxists or socialists. That perspective sees the Soviet Union as primarily an ideological artifact, and therefore sees struggle with it in particularly ideological terms. The neoconservatives believe, like Lenin, that "ideas are more fatal than guns."

Convinced that Bolshevism was quintessentially an ideological phenomenon, activists of the New Right were contemptuous of Western efforts to accommodate Soviet needs, moderate Soviet aims, and integrate the USSR into the international system as a "normal" great power. In their view, the *realpolitik* strategy urged by George Kennan, Walter Lippmann, and Hans Morgenthau was based on a misunderstanding of the Soviet Union. It provided an incomplete roadmap for waging the Cold War, and guaranteed that it would never be won. A particular villain for the New Right was Secretary of State Henry Kissinger, whose program of détente implied, in their view, a "moral equivalence" between the West and the Soviet Union that amounted to unilateral ideological disarmament. Even more benighted were liberal attempts to engage and co-opt the Soviet Union in hopes that the two systems could ultimately reconcile. The New Right's view of politics was strikingly globalist in its assumption that the world had shrunk too much for two such different systems to survive, and that the contest was too tightly engaged for containment or Iron Curtains to work. As James Burnham, the ex-communist prophet of New Right anticommunism, insisted in the early postwar years, the smallness of our "one world" demanded a strategy of "rollback" for American survival.

The end of the Cold War indeed marked an ideological triumph for the West, but not of the sort fancied by the Reagan victory school. Ideology played a far different and more complicated role in inducing Soviet change than the Reagan school allows. As with the military sphere, the Reagan school presents an incomplete picture of Western ideological influence, ignoring the emergence of ideological common ground in stimulating Soviet change.

The ideological legitimacy of the Soviet system collapsed in the eyes of its own citizens not because of an assault by Western ex-leftists, but because of the appeal of Western affluence and permissiveness. The puritanical austerity of Bolshevism's "New Soviet Man" held far less appeal than the "bourgeois decadence" of the West. For the peoples of the USSR and Eastern Europe, it was not so much abstract liberal principles but rather the Western way of life—the material and cultural manifestations of the West's freedoms—that subverted the Soviet vision. Western popular culture—exemplified in rock and roll, television, film, and blue jeans—seduced the communist world far more effectively than ideological sermons by anticommunist activists. As journalist William Echikson noted in his 1990 book *Lighting the Night: Revolution in Eastern Europe*, "instead of listening to the liturgy of Marx and Lenin, generations of would-be socialists tuned into the Rolling Stones and the Beatles."

If Western popular culture and permissiveness helped subvert communist legitimacy, it is a development of profound irony. Domestically, the New Right battled precisely those cultural forms that had such global appeal. V. I. Lenin's most potent ideological foils were John Lennon and Paul McCartney, not Adam Smith and Thomas Jefferson. The Right fought a two-front war against communism abroad and hedonism and consumerism at home. Had it not lost the latter struggle, the West may not have won the former.

The Reagan victory school argues that ideological assertiveness precipitated the end of the Cold War. While it is true that right-wing American intellectuals were assertive toward the Soviet Union, other Western activists and intellectuals were building links with highly placed reformist intellectuals there. The Reagan victory school narrative ignores that Gorbachev's reform program was based upon "new thinking"—a body of ideas developed by globalist thinkers cooperating across the East-West divide. The key themes of new thinking—the common threat of nuclear destruction, the need for strong international institutions, and the importance of ecological sustainability—built upon the cosmopolitanism of the Marxist tradition and officially replaced the Communist party's class-conflict doctrine during the Gorbachev period.

It is widely recognized that a major source of Gorbachev's new thinking was his close aide and speechwriter, Georgi Shakhnazarov. A former president of the Soviet political science association, Shakhnazarov worked extensively with Western globalists, particularly the New York-based group known as the World Order Models Project. Gorbachev's speeches and policy statements were replete with the language and ideas of globalism. The Cold War ended not with Soviet ideological capitulation to Reagan's anticommunism but rather with a Soviet embrace of globalist themes promoted by a network of liberal internationalists. Those intellectual influences were greatest with the state elite, who had greater access to the West and from whom the reforms originated.

Regardless of how one judges the impact of the ideological struggles during the Reagan years, it is implausible to focus solely on recent developments without accounting for longer-term shifts in underlying forces, particularly the widening gap between Western and Soviet economic performance. Over the long haul, the West's ideological appeal was based on the increasingly superior performance of the Western economic system. Although contrary to the expectation of Marx and Lenin, the robustness of capitalism in the West was increasingly acknowledged by Soviet analysts. Likewise, Soviet elites were increasingly troubled by their economy's comparative decline.

The Reagan victory school argues that the renewed emphasis on free-market principles championed by Reagan and then British prime minister Margaret Thatcher led to a global move toward market deregulation and privatization that the Soviets desired to follow. By rekindling the beacon of laissez-faire capitalism, Reagan illuminated the path of economic reform, thus vanquishing communism.

That view is misleading in two respects. First, it was West European social democracy rather than America's more free-wheeling capitalism that attracted Soviet reformers. Gorbachev wanted his reforms to emulate the Swedish model. His vision was not of laissez-faire capitalism but of a social democratic welfare state. Second, the Right's triumphalism in the economic sphere is ironic. The West's robust economies owe much of their relative stability and health to two generations of Keynesian intervention and government involvement that the Right opposed at every step. As with Western popular culture, the Right opposed tendencies in the West that proved vital in the West's victory.

There is almost universal agreement that the root cause of the Cold War's abrupt end was the grave domestic failure of Soviet communism. However, the Soviet response to this crisis—accommodation and liberalization rather than aggression and repression—was significantly influenced by outside pressures and opportunities, many from the West. As historians and analysts attempt to explain how recent U.S. foreign policy helped end the Cold War, a view giving most of the credit to Reagan-era assertiveness and Western strength has become the new conventional wisdom. Both the Reagan victory school and the peace-through-strength perspective on Western containment assign a central role in ending the Cold War to Western resolve and power. The lesson for American foreign policy being drawn from those events is that military strength and ideological warfare were the West's decisive assets in fighting the Cold War.

The new conventional wisdom, in both its variants, is seriously misleading. Operating over the last decade, Ronald Reagan's personal anti-nuclearism, rather than his administration's hardline, catalyzed the accommodations to end the Cold War. His administration's effort to go beyond containment and on the offensive was muddled, counter-balanced, and unsuccessful. Operating over the long term, containment helped thwart Soviet expansionism but cannot account for the Soviet domestic failure, the end of East-West struggle, or the direction of the USSR'S reorientation. Contrary to the hard-line version, nuclear weapons were decisive in abandoning the conflict by creating common interests.

On the ideological front, the new conventional wisdom is also flawed. The conservatives' anticommunism was far less important in delegitimating the Soviet system than were that system's internal failures and the attraction of precisely the Western "permissive culture" abhorred by the Right. In addition, Gorbachev's attempts to reform communism in the late-1980s were less an ideological capitulation than a reflection of philosophical convergence on the globalist norms championed by liberal internationalists. And the West was more appealing not because of its laissez-faire purity, but because of the success of Keynesian and social welfare innovations whose use the Right resisted.

Behind the debate over who "won" the Cold War are competing images of the forces shaping recent history. Containment, strength, and confrontation—the trinity enshrined in conventional thinking on Western foreign policy's role in ending the Cold War—obscure the nature of these momentous changes. Engagement and interdependence, rather than containment, are the ruling trends of the age. Mutual vulnerability, not strength, drives security politics. Accommodation and integration, not confrontation, are the motors of change.

That such encouraging trends were established and deepened even as the Cold War raged demonstrates the considerable continuity underlying the West's support today for reform in the post-Soviet transition. Those trends also expose as one-sided and self-serving the New Right's attempt to take credit for the success of forces that, in truth, they opposed. In the end, Reagan partisans have been far more successful in claiming victory in the Cold War than they were in achieving it.

POSTSCRIPT

Did President Reagan
Win the Cold War?

Now that the cold war is over, historians must assess why it ended so suddenly and unexpectedly. Did President Reagan's military buildup in the 1980s force the Russians into economic bankruptcy? Gaddis gives Reagan high marks for ending the cold war. By combining a policy of militancy and operational pragmatism, says Gaddis, Reagan brought about the most significant improvement in Soviet-American relations since the end of World War II. Deudney and Ikenberry disagree. In their view the cold war ended only when the Russians saw the need for international cooperation in order to end the arms race, prevent a nuclear holocaust, and liberalize their economy. It was Western global ideas and not the hard-line containment policy of the early Reagan administration that caused Gorbachev to abandon traditional Russian communism, according to Deudney and Ikenberry.

Gaddis has established himself as the leading diplomatic historian of the cold war period. His assessment of Reagan's relations with the Soviet Union is balanced and probably more generous than that of most contemporary analysts. It is also very useful because it so succinctly describes the unexpected shift from a hard-line policy to one of détente. Gaddis admits that not even Reagan could have foreseen the total collapse of communism and the Soviet empire. While he allows that Reagan was not a profound thinker, Gaddis credits him with the leadership skills to overcome any prior ideological biases toward the Soviet Union and to take advantage of Gorbachev's offer to end the arms race. While many of the present hard-liners could not believe that the collapse of the Soviet Union was for real, Reagan was consistent in his view that the American arms buildup in the early 1980s was for the purpose of ending the arms race. Reagan, says Gaddis, accomplished this goal.

Gaddis's view of Reagan has not changed from his earlier assessment in *The United States and the End of the Cold War: Implications, Reconsiderations, Provocations* (Oxford University Press, 1992). See the eleventh edition of *Taking Sides . . . American History,* volume two. But Gaddis builds upon the new Russian sources now available from the Cold War International History Project at the Woodrow Wilson International Center as well as the published works of Gorbachev and his aides. Turning the tables on those historians who see Reagan as an "empty vessel," an actor who read a script, Gaddis compares Gorbachev to Woody Allen's movie character Zelig, "who managed to be present at all the great events of his time, but only by taking the character, even the appearance, of the stronger personalities who surrounded him." Unlike Reagan, the Russian leader knew Russia needed a new direction but did not know what the direction for his economy and foreign policy should be. Finally, Gaddis speculates that if

Reagan was assassinated in 1991, his successor George Bush might not have ended the cold war.

Deudney and Ikenberry give less credit to Reagan than to global influences in ending the cold war. In their view, Gorbachev softened his hard-line foreign policy and abandoned orthodox Marxist economic programs because he was influenced by Western European cosmopolitans who were concerned about the "common threat of nuclear destruction, the need for strong international institutions, and the importance of ecological sustainability." Deudney and Ikenberry agree that Reagan became more accommodating toward the Russians in 1983, but they maintain that the cold war's end "was not simply a result of Western strength but of mutual weakness and intentional engagement as well."

There is a considerable bibliography about both the Reagan administration and the Soviet Union in assessing their roles in ending the cold war. Three *Washington Post* reporters have provided early accounts of the Reagan years. Lou Cannon's *President Reagan: the Role of a Lifetime* (Simon & Schuster, 1991) is a remarkably objective, detailed, and interesting account by a reporter who followed Reagan's career during his California gubernatorial years. Haynes Johnson's *Sleepwalking through History: America in the Reagan Years* (W.W. Norton, 1991) is more critical than Cannon but readable. Don Oberdorfer, a former Moscow correspondent for *The Washington Post,* has revised *From Cold War to a New Era: the United States and the Soviet Union, 1983–1991* (Updated edition, Johns Hopkins University Press, 1998). Oberdorfer credits Secretary of State George P. Schultz with Reagan's turnaround from a hard-line to détente approach to foreign policy. The former Stanford economics professor and policymaker weighs in with his own perceptive assessment of the Reagan administration in *Turmoil and Triumph: My Years as Secretary of State* (Scribner's, 1993).

A number of conservatives have published books and articles arguing that American foreign policy hard-liners won the cold war. Two of the most articulate essays written early from the "Reagan victory school" point of view are Arch Puddington, "The Anti-Cold War Brigade," *Commentary* (August 1990) and Owen Harries, "The Cold War and the Intellectuals," *Commentary* (October 1991). Michael Howard reviews five books on the end of the cold war in "Winning the Peace: How Both George Kennan and Gorbachev Were Right," *Times Literary Supplement* (January 8, 1993). President Reagan's death from Alzheimer's in June, 2004, also produced an outpouring of favorable assessments of America's most popular president since Eisenhower in newspapers, magazines, and television.

In some ways President Reagan is best viewed through his own writings. His *An American Life: the Autobiography* (Simon and Schuster, 1990) contains his views but is stilted and doesn't capture his essence. More successful is *The Greatest Speeches of Ronald Reagan* (NewsMax.com, 2001) compiled by his conservative son Michael Reagan. Between his acting career and his presidency Reagan wrote a lot of speeches and newspaper and radio editorials. To prove he was not an "amiable dunce," Kiron K. Skinner, et al., edited *Reagan, In His Own Hand* (Free Press, 2001).

With the opening of some of the Russian and Eastern European country's archives, we are getting a better picture, if not a more balanced view, of the cold war. The Cold War International History Project at the Woodrow Wilson International Center for scholars has collected many of these documents and its journal, the *Cold War International History Project Bulletin*, publishes important scholarly articles utilizing its archives. Mikhail Gorbachev has weighted in the fray with his own *Memoirs* (Doubleday, 1995) and *Perestroika: New Thinking for Our Country and the World* (Harper & Row, 1987). See also his latest reflections in Gorbachev and Zdenek Mlynar, *Conversations with Gorbachev: On Perestroika, the Prague Spring, and the Crossroads of Socialism,* translated by George Schriver (Columbia University Press, 2002). Earlier, historian Michael R. Beschloss and *Time Magazine,* and later, Clinton adviser Strobe Talbot interviewed Gorbachev for *At the Highest Levels: the Inside Story of the End of the Cold War* (Little, Brown, 1993), which carries the story from 1987 through the presidency of the first George Bush.

Political scientists have weighed in the controversy. In addition to the classic Deudney and Ikenberry essay, Coral Bell analyzes the *Reagan Paradox: U.S. Foreign Policy in the 1980s* (Rutgers University Press, 1989). The Mershon Center at Ohio State University has recently run a conference at which former Russian and American participants were interviewed via round table discussions. Two of the scholars, Richard K. Hermann and Richard Ned Lebow, have edited *Ending the Cold War: Interpretations, Causation and the Study of International Relations* (Palgrave/Macmillan, 2004), which raises a number of interesting counterfactual propositions even if at times the essays become overly theoretical.

The historians also weighed in as soon as Reagan left office. Both David E. Kyvig, ed., *Reagan and the World* (Greenwood Press, 1990), and Michael J. Hogan, *The End of the Cold War: Its Meaning and Implications* (Cambridge University Press, 1992), were generally unable to forecast future events. The most insightful account because of its broader perspective is Raymond Garthoff, *Détente and Confrontation: American Soviet Relations from Nixon to Reagan* (Brookings Institution, 1994).

Two interesting perspectives on the nuclear war issue are Paul Lettow, *Ronald Reagan and His Quest to Abolish Nuclear Weapons* (Random House, 2005), which supports Gaddis and Stephen J. Zaloga, *The Kremlin's Nuclear Sword: The Rise and Fall of Russia's Strategic Nuclear Forces, 1945–2000* (Smithsonian Institution, 2002).

Reagan is best assessed through the media. After all he was an actor before he became a politician. Two good starting points are PBS's *The American Experience* series two-part biography of President Ronald Reagan (2001), and CNN's *Cold War* television documentary (1998).

ISSUE 14

Were the 1980s a Decade of Affluence for the Middle Class?

YES: J. David Woodard, from *The America That Reagan Built* (Praeger, 2006)

NO: Thomas Byrne Edsall, from "The Changing Shape of Power: A Realignment in Public Policy," in Steve Fraser and Gary Gerstle, *The Rise and Fall of the New Deal Order, 1930–1980* (Princeton University Press, 1980)

ISSUE SUMMARY

YES: According to Professor J. David Woodard, supply-side economics unleashed a wave of entrepreneurial and technological innovation that transformed the economy and restored America's confidence in the Golden Age from 1983 to 1992.

NO: Political journalist Thomas B. Edsall argues that the Reagan revolution brought about a policy realignment that reversed the New Deal and redistributed political power and economic wealth to the top 20 percent of Americans.

In 1939, after 6 years of the New Deal, unemployment in the United States remained at an unacceptably high rate of 17 percent. World War II bailed America out of the Great Depression. When 20 million workers entered the armed forces, married American women, along with African-American and Hispanic males and females, filled the void in the higher-paying factory jobs. Everyone not only made money but poured it into war bonds and traditional savings accounts. Government and business cemented their relationship with "cost plus" profits for the defense industries.

By the end of 1945, Americans had stashed away $134 billion in cash, savings accounts, and government securities. This pent-up demand meant there would be no depression akin to the end of World War I or the 1930s. Following initial shortages before industry completed its conversion to peacetime production, Americans engaged in the greatest spending spree in the country's history. Liberals and conservatives from both political parties had developed a consensus on foreign and domestic policies.

The president's Council of Economic Advisers was composed of Keynesians, who believed that government spending could increase employment even if it meant that budget deficits would be temporarily created. For nearly 25 years, they used fiscal and monetary tools to manipulate the economy so that inflation would remain low while employment would reach close to its maximum capacity.

Around 1968, the consensus surrounding domestic and foreign policy broke down for three reasons: (1) the Vietnam imbroglio, (2) the oil crises of 1974 and 1979, and (3) the decline of the smokestack industries.

Lyndon Johnson's presidency was ruined by the Vietnam War. He believed that he could escalate the war and his Great Society programs at the same time. His successor, Richard Nixon, attempted to solve the Vietnam dilemma by bringing the American troops home and letting Asians fight Asians. The process of withdrawal was slow and costly. Also expensive were many of the Great Society programs, such as Social Security, Aid to Families with Dependent Children, environmental legislation, and school desegregation, which Nixon continued to uphold. In August 1971, Nixon acknowledged that he had become a Keynesian when he imposed a 90-day wage and price control freeze and took the international dollar off the gold standard and allowed it to float. With these bold moves, Nixon hoped to stop the dollar from declining in value. He was also faced with a recession that included both high unemployment and high inflation. "Stagflation" resulted, leading to the demise of Keynesian economics.

In early 1974, shortly before Nixon was forced to resign from office, the major oil-producing nation of the world—primarily in the Middle East—agreed to curb oil productions and raise oil prices. The OPEC cartel, protesting the pro-Israeli policies of the Western nations, brought these countries to their knees. In the United States, gasoline went from $0.40 to $2.00 per gallon in a matter of days. In the early 1980s, President Jimmy Carter implored the nation to conserve energy, but he appeared helpless as the unemployment rate approached double digits and as the Federal Reserve Board raised interest rates to 18 percent in a desperate attempt to stem inflation.

The Reagan administration introduced a new economic philosophy: supply-side economics. Its proponents, led by economists Martin Anderson and Arthur Laffer, believed that if taxes were cut and spending on frivolous social programs were reduced—even while military spending increases—businesses will use the excess money to expand. More jobs would result, consumers would increase spending, and the multiplying effect would be a period of sustained growth and prosperity. Did it work?

Professor J. David Woodward answers this question with an arousing yes. Supply-side economics, he says in the first essay, unleashed a wave of entrepreneurial and technological innovation that transformed the economy and restored America's confidence in the Golden Age from 1983 to 1992. But political journalist Thomas B. Edsall disagrees with this analysis. Yes, there was prosperity in the 1980s, but only for a few groups. The Reagan revolution, he says, brought about a policy realignment as well as a political one that redistributed political and economic wealth to the top 20 percent of Americans.

YES

A Rising Tide

The Reagan Revolution, as the times came to be called, followed the economic growth in real income from 1983 through the end of the president's second term in 1988, to the recession that concluded the Bush presidency in 1992. During this time the gross domestic product (GDP) doubled. In the expansion through the two Reagan terms, "real-after-tax income per person rose by 15.5 percent, [and] the real median income of families, before taxes, went up 12.5 percent." Measured in constant 1990 dollars, the percentage of families earning between $15,000 and $50,000 fell by 5 points, and the percentage earning more than $50,000 in constant dollars rose by 5 points. Millions of families moved up the ladder from the lower class to the middle class. America had gone from "stagflation" and the highest prices in thirty years to galloping capitalism, and everyday citizens were investing in the stock market.

The middle-class market sought the deposits of ordinary savers and young people just beginning to accumulate assets. Wall Street had previously ignored these customers, but now it sought them out. Prudential-Bache, an aggressive firm, was quoted in *Barron's* as saying it "sees its clients as the $40,000-a-year young professional on the fast track." As the market expanded, more individuals placed their money in funds to balance risk and profit. Suddenly the stock market report was of interest to everyone.

Stockbrokers assured investors that their money was safe, but in late 1987 they discovered the real meaning of risk. The market was doing quite well for the first nine months of the year; it was up more than 30 percent and reaching unprecedented heights. Then, in the days between October 14 and October 19, the market fell off a cliff. On October 19, subsequently known as "Black Monday," the Dow Jones Industrial Average plummeted 508 points, losing 22.6 percent of its total value. This was the greatest loss Wall Street had ever suffered on a single day, even worse than the crash of 1929. It took two years for the Dow to recover completely; not until September of 1989 did it regain all the value it lost in the 1987 crash.

One important lesson came out of the crash: investors who sold took a bath. Those who held on and continued a disciplined and systematic program received rewards. The American economy continued as the greatest wealth producer the world had ever seen. The consequence of all this was a standard of living beyond the comprehension of the rest of the world, and a cause for

From *The America that Built Reagan*, by J. David Woodard (Praeger, 2006), pp. 63–77. Copyright © 2006 by Greenwood Publishing Group. Reprinted by permission.

envy by peer nations. While $200,000 was enough to make the top 1 percent of American income in 1980, a family might need well over $300,000 to be in that category a decade later. The Congressional Budget Office estimated that it would take more than $550,000 to be in the top 1 percent in 1992. No sooner had a survivor of the 1970s comprehended what was happening than he became obsolete. Reagan's supply-side ideas unleashed a wave of entrepreneurial and technological innovation that transformed the economy and restored the country's self-confidence. Economic prosperity had been the impossible dream of youth, and now it was everywhere.

The vast majority of the population experienced substantial gains in real income and wealth. With millions of people earning more money, much higher incomes were required to make it to the top 5 percent, or the top 1 percent of the nation's income bracket. At the time, the rising tide of economic prosperity lifted at least 90 percent of the American family boats. For those who lived through it, the 1983–1992 period would be remembered as an uncomplicated golden time, mourned as lost, and remembered as cloudless.

The spending began at home, where people purchased new homes and remodeled older ones. Declining interest rates made mortgages affordable, and the number of single-family homes expanded each year from 1980 to 1988. Consumers also had more cars to drive as the two-income, two-car family became the norm. From 1980 to 1988, the number of new car models increased by half, the most popular being the minivans for suburban families. Lower air fares and discount packages allowed passengers to travel to previously unheard-of places, and the number of people flying overseas rose by 40 percent during the 1980s.

Much of this expense for the new lifestyle was charged to credit cards. Americans took three-, four-, and five-day trips and the amount of credit card debt more than doubled. Specialty chain stores like the Gap, Limited, and Banana Republic targeted upscale, professional customers who wanted to take advantage of their new standing and credit to add the latest styles to their wardrobes. Shopping malls proliferated in suburban settings, and the consumption ethic gave birth to Wal-Mart, destined in the next decade to become the nation's largest company. While American life was becoming more affluent, it was also becoming more complex.

Of course there were critics, and for them the era was never that splendid; it was derided for its inbred conformity, flatulent excesses, and materialistic binges. The "me" decade of the 1970s turned into the "my" decade of the 1980s. The faultfinders saw the surge of abundance as a joyless vulgarity. In 1987, filmmaker Oliver Stone released the movie *Wall Street*. The story involved a young stockbroker, Bud Fox, who becomes involved with his hero, Gordon Gekko, an extremely successful, but corrupt, stock trader. In the most memorable scene of the movie. Gekko makes a speech to the shareholders of a company he was planning to take over. Stone used the scene to give Gekko, and by extension corporate America at the time, the characteristic trait of economic success.

Gekko: Teldar Paper, Mr. Cromwell, Teldar Paper has 33 different vice presidents, each making over 200 thousand dollars a year. Now, I have spent the last two months analyzing what all these guys do, and I still can't figure it out. One thing I do know is that our paper company lost 110 million dollars last year, and I'll bet that half of that was spent in all the paperwork going back and forth between all these vice presidents.

The new law of evolution in corporate America seems to be survival of the unfittest. Well, in my book you either do it right or you get eliminated.

In the last seven deals that I've been involved with, there were 2.5 million stockholders who had made a pretax profit of 12 billion dollars. Thank you.

I am not a destroyer of companies. I am a liberator of them!

The point is, ladies and gentlemen, is that greed—for lack of a better word—is good.

Greed is right.

Greed works.

Greed clarifies, cuts through, and captures the essence of the evolutionary spirit.

Greed in all its forms—greed for life, for money, for love, knowledge—has marked the upward surge of mankind.

And greed—you mark my words—will not only save Teldar Paper, but that other malfunctioning corporation called the USA.

Thank you very much.

The same theme was addressed in literature. In 1990, one of America's foremost writers, Tom Wolfe, released a blockbuster bestseller entitled *The Bonfire of the Vanities*. The book dealt with what Wolfe called the "big, rich slices of contemporary life," in this case the heady materialism of the 1980s. The plot followed the life of Sherman McCoy, a prodigiously successful bond trader at a prestigious Wall Street firm. One night Sherman, accompanied by his mistress, fatally injures a black man in a car accident. As a result of this accident, all the ennui of metropolitan life, race relations, instant affluence and gratification, and the class structure of the city afflict the lead character.

As a member of the new ruling class, Sherman McCoy and other bond traders were allied with opportunistic politicians in speculative excesses. Sherman was supremely confident that he would escape his fate. The 1980s were critiqued as the epitome of American decline and the triumph of finance capitalism spurred by Wall Street bond and stock manipulators, like McCoy's employer, Eugene Lopwitz. Sherman McCoy had to pay for his greed and irresponsibility; he lost his job, his wife and his child, his mistress, his home, and his class standing. But in the end he lied to escape prosecution, and got even with every institution—the courts, the media, and the economic system—which were also built on a foundation of lies.

American capitalism, and its excesses, had long been a topic of intellectual and literary criticism. Theodore Dreiser wrote the novel *An American Tragedy* in 1925 as a critique of business practices at the time. The story followed a bellboy who sets out to gain success and fame, only to slip into murder and death by execution. Dreiser declared that the materialistic society was as much to blame as the murderer himself. What was new in the *Bonfire* plot was that the perpetrators escaped capture and conviction. In the new world people could be evil and—if they had enough money—bear no consequences for their actions.

During the 1980s, the power and influence of American corporations expanded to exorbitant heights. General Motors had revenues greater than 90 percent of the world's nations. The Reagan administration eased restrictions on the stock market and on antitrust laws so some of the more massive corporate takeovers in American history happened in the decade. The largest one was between R. J. Reynolds, the tobacco company, and Nabisco, the maker of cookies, crackers, and cereals, for $24.9 billion.

Other companies were taken over in what was known as a leveraged buyout, where investors joined forces with the managers of a company to buy it. The funds came from the managers themselves, but most were borrowed. The money for takeovers was raised through the sale of so-called junk bonds. Junk bonds were high-risk investments by securities rating agencies, such as Standard and Poor's and Moody's, marked as such because they had a potential for higher yield and failure. If the people who bought the bonds were successful in the takeover, then they were handsomely rewarded; but if they failed, then there was the possibility that the bonds would not be repaid.

Companies with low debt loads were attractive targets for leveraged buyouts, which meant that successful businessmen found themselves the object of "corporate raiders." Benjamin Franklin's age-old virtues of thrift and frugality resulted in business success, so much so that the entrepreneurial founders lost control of their companies. Sometimes, to prevent these unwanted effects, recently acquired companies bought back their stock at higher than market prices—in effect, paying raiders to go away. The practice was known as "greenmail," for its resemblance to blackmail. More than $12 billion in greenmail was paid by corporations such as Texaco, Warner, and Quaker State in the first few months of 1984.

The business of mergers required dozens of brokers, lawyers, and bankers. A new class of business people known as "young, urban professionals," or "yuppies," emerged as experts in the takeover game. They were stereotyped as college-educated men and women, who dressed well, lived in expensive apartments, drove expensive cars, exercised in gyms, and worked twelve-hour days. "An MBA (Masters of Business Administration), a condo and a BMW" became the mantra of the age. One woman interviewed on television unabashedly declared, "I aspire to materialism." "Big spender" became a term of approbation. A writer at the time described it this way: "People saw money as power . . . [they went to] 'power lunches' while wearing fashionable 'power suits' . . . designer fashions bloated egos and fattened the cash registers of swank stores." The spenders were living on credit and buying on margin, but they did not seem to mind. Spending and mergers were fueling the boom, and any tendency to go slow was seen as alarming.

Leveraged buyouts were risky, but legal, transactions. As in any business, a few successful corporate raiders operated outside the law. On May 12, 1986, Dennis Levine, who had made $12.6 million on insider-trading deals, implicated two well-known Wall Street traders: Michael Milken and Ivan Boesky. Both men were charged with violations of federal securities law. Boesky agreed to pay $100 million in forfeitures and penalties, and Michael Milken admitted to six felonies and agreed to pay $600 million in fines. The amount of the fines was staggering, but more revealing was the corporate raider lifestyle the investigations uncovered. In the early 1980s Milken was reportedly making $550 million a year.

Overall, the freeing of the market for corporate control had important benefits for women in the workforce. College-educated women moved into fields like business, engineering, medicine, and law. "The result was that women as a whole, whose average earnings had been 58 percent of those of men in 1979, earned 68 percent ten years later." Professional women began moving into managerial positions where they soon faced the problem of how to combine motherhood and career. In the 1980s work itself was changing. The computer and instant communication enabled more people to work at home, and women soon learned that part-time, or maternity leave, arrangements allowed them to close the income gap with their male counterparts.

The boom arose from numerous springs: the new government economic philosophy, technological innovation, an altered world economy, and a changing labor market. The latter trend would have political consequences well into the next century. For example, immigration had a dramatic influence on the labor pool and the expansion of entry-level jobs. In the 1970s, 4.5 million immigrants were legally admitted into the country, and many more came illegally. In the 1980s legal immigration swelled to 7.4 million, with additional millions of illegal entrants. The vast majority of immigrants from Central and South America, who made up about half the total, had considerably lower levels of schooling than native-born Americans. Their presence resulted in higher wages for college graduates and depressed wages for those who had lower levels of schooling.

The immigration trends caused increases in wage and income inequality, because of the demand for skilled labor due to technological changes and new trade patterns. Sophisticated new technologies flourished in the aerospace, defense, electronics, and computer industries. Sprawling scientific complexes raised the standard of living for millions of Americans. Research funds for technology, or R & D (research and development), which were practically insignificant in the 1950s, amounted to an estimated $100 billion a year at the end of the 1980s. Americans were making money with their minds, and not on the assembly line.

Little of this was new. Sociologist Daniel Bell wrote in 1973 that there was a natural progression from a traditional society, based on agriculture, to an industrial one based on manufacturing. Then there was a subsequent transition from an industrial to a postindustrial society, which culminated in a service economy. This progression to a postindustrial society occurred when the emphasis on the production of goods was overtaken by a service economy. The postindustrial society meant an extension of scientific rationality into the economic, social, and political spheres. By the late 1970s only 13 percent of American workers were involved in the manufacture of goods, whereas a full 60 percent were engaged in the production of information. The new "knowledge society" was run by university-trained employers. In this society technical skill was the base of power, and education the means of access to power. Individuals who exercised authority through technical competence, called "technocrats," dominated society.

The birth years of the postindustrial society were in the 1950s, but it came to fruition in the 1980s. The 1950s saw great technological developments such as the atomic bomb and the digital computer, but the character of knowledge itself began to change thirty years later. Workers had to be taught how to think, not how to do routine tasks. Change was so prevalent that knowledge of any specific task was quickly washed away by a new wave of innovation. Theoretical knowledge of abstract principles was central in the postindustrial society, and the key organization of the future was the university, along with think tanks and research centers.

During the 1980s the academy itself was changing. The number of professors at American universities in 1980 was four times what it was in 1960. As faculties grew, so too did the specialization of their disciplines. Student enrollments in fields like business, computer science, engineering, and mathematics soared, while the liberal arts and social sciences lost out in comparison. It was the age of the computer chip, which made everything smaller and faster.

Universities were only the tip of the iceberg of culture producers that included not only the creators of the new society, but also its transmitters. Labor in the postindustrial context involved those in journalism, publishing, magazines, broadcast media, theater, and museums and anyone who was involved in the influence and reception of serious cultural products. The growth of cultural output was a fact in the knowledge industry. Consider what happened to those Daniel Bell called "the cultural mass" of art producers. New York had only a handful of galleries in 1945, and no more than a score of known artists; by the 1980s the city had some 680 galleries and more than 150,000 artists. Add to these artists producers of books, printers, serious music recordings, writers, editors, movie makers, musicians, and so forth and the size of just one part of the mass culture was exposed.

Bell argued that the postindustrial society would change politics, as well as culture and economics. In his view, government would increasingly become instrumental in the management of the economy; less control would be left to market forces. Instead of relying on the invisible hand, Bell saw that the postindustrial society would work toward directing and engineering society. He could not have been more wrong. The spirit of the 1980s was against the command decision views of Daniel Bell. Conservatives had long denounced Keynesian economics as a fraud, and expanding government as a threat, but their ideas were unpopular in the period of post–World War II prosperity. When liberalism's troubles began to mount in the 1970s, free market alternatives re-emerged.

Milton and Rose Friedman effectively rebutted the government as manager thesis, and replaced it with the free market–rational actor model. Their book, *Free to Choose*, was as clear an exposition of free market economics as anything since Adam Smith, and it showed how good intentions in Washington often had deplorable results in practice. Friedman made conservative economic ideas available and attractive to the mass public. To quote their thesis on the power of a free market idea: "If an exchange between two parties is voluntary, it will not take place unless both believe that they will benefit from it," or "the price system is the mechanism that performs this task without central direction, without requiring people to speak to one another or like one another." This was the book that explained how freedom had been eroded, and prosperity undermined, by the runaway spending and growth of government in Washington. *Free to Choose* was very influential on the thinking of Ronald Reagan and millions of ordinary Americans.

As strange as it may seem, by the 1980s the modern postindustrial society was itself becoming old fashioned. The period after World War II was characterized by three things: (1) the power of reason over ignorance, (2) the power of order over disorder, and (3) the power of science over superstition. These features were regarded as universal values, and were inculcated into the fabric of American culture. They were also the basis for Ronald Reagan's view of the world. His time with General Electric convinced him that American technology was second to none, and he wedded that faith to the national experience. After he left office he said, "There are no such things as limits to growth, because there are no limits on the human capacity for intelligence, imagination and wonder."

In the decade of the 1980s, the faith in reason, order, and the power of science, so dear to Reagan, was coming in for criticism. The command and control center for the criticism was the universities, the very postindustrial leaders Daniel Bell had identified years earlier. Much of Reagan's initial political success in his California gubernatorial race was based on criticism of antagonistic college students and their teachers, and his belief that America was a nation of technological might that outproduced and advanced knowledge to win a rightful place on the world stage. For example, Reagan regularly recalled American production in World War II, and his belief that the nation was a "bastion of freedom," and "a city set on a hill."

The problem was that universities were questioning everything Reagan said and stood for. The best known of these criticisms was labeled as deconstruction, a French import that questioned rationality and definitions. Deconstruction held that written words could never have fixed meanings, and, as a result, any text revealed ambiguities, contradictions, hidden meanings, and repressive political relationships. The modern world, according to these new thinkers, had expanded industrial capitalism and scientific thinking, but it also brought the world Auschwitz, the possibility of nuclear war, the horrors of Nazism and Stalinism, neocolonialism, racism, and world hunger. The critics believed that modernism had run its course, and society had entered a new age—the age of postmodernism.

Postmodernism is a complicated term because the concept appears in a wide variety of disciplines and areas of study, including art, architecture, music, film, literature, fashion, and technology. In general, postmodernism rejects the uncritical acceptance of the power of reason, order, and science. According to postmodernists, the assumption that there is such a thing as objective truth is at base a modern fallacy. For them there is no linear progress in society, no ideal social order, and no standardization of knowledge. Instead the world was a picture of fragmentation, indeterminacy, and chaos. Postmodernists held that culture should affirm this fragmented reality, and consider order to be only provisional and varying from person to person.

The contrast between modern and postmodern is seen in a comparison of professions. In several of them, such as medicine, law, and engineering, mastery of a specific body of knowledge and the application of an intrinsic logic led to something known as progress. When a doctor diagnosed and treated a disease, or when an engineer designed a bridge, their work assumed a rational understanding of the world and a logical means of dealing with it. In short, these professions presupposed an objective order in existence. Different medical doctors, using the same objective science and trained in a standard methodology, could examine the same patient and arrive at an identical diagnosis and course of treatment. They exemplify modernism.

A host of new professions arose by the 1980s that had no universally recognized body of knowledge, and no generally accepted methods, although they invoked the jargon of science. The social sciences were shining examples of new postmodern professions. For example, someone in need of "mental health" could be treated by a Freudian, a Jungian, a humanist, or a behaviorist. A political scientist could be a behaviorist, a formal theorist, one trained in classical political thought, or an area specialist with no training other than language skills, and then there were those who believed politics could not be a science. The philosophies behind the psychological analysis and the political analysis were incompatible, and the methodologies conflicted and were oftentimes incomplete and sometimes untested. They exemplify postmodern professions.

The conflict between modern and postmodern surfaced in Reagan's appointment of William Bennett as chairman of the National Endowment for the Humanities. Bennett had a Ph.D. in philosophy from the University of Texas and a law degree from Harvard. He was a conservative academic who spoke movingly about the threat deconstruction and postmodernism posed to the teaching of the Western classics. "We must give greater attention to a sound common curriculum emphasizing English, history, geography, math, and science . . . [and] we have to understand why these subjects were thrown out or weakened in the cultural deconstruction of our schools of the last twenty-five years." The very thing Bennett warned against was taking place at one of America's premier universities. The curriculum of Stanford became an issue in 1988, when the faculty voted to reform the Western Civilization course away from a "European-Western and male bias." The revision became an issue for discussion not only on college campuses, but also in newspapers and television talk shows across the country.

The education debate was part of a national one on the modernist/ postmodernist divide. The society had not moved beyond modernity; there were still plenty of people who thought America was the hope of the world and believed in its technological future as well. But there were others who had their doubts, and they delighted in the period of transition. The character of the change was seen in the new pop culture.

The baby boomers, usually defined as those born between 1946 and 1964, left the world a legacy of rock and roll. In the 1980s "rock became a reference point for a splintered culture." The most important outlet for 1980s music was MTV, or Music Television, that began broadcasting on August 1, 1981. It brought music videos into American homes, and criticism of the dominant modern culture to a new generation. Some immediately saw that the new medium, which exulted in "fast cuts, slow motion, and artsy black-and-white photography—all selling sex and violence—defined the visual style of the decade, spreading to movies, prime time series, advertising and magazines."

The end of the peace and love generation of music came on December 8, 1980, when John Lennon was shot seven times outside the Dakota, an apartment building where he lived in New York City. Lennon's murder, by twenty-five-year-old Mark David Chapman, was made more horrifying because the assassin was a self-confessed fan. The paranoid fear by pop starts of their audiences was epitomized in Lennon's death, which was a prelude to the era's approaching fragmentation and cult of personality.

Michael Jackson was the most important pop rock star of the decade. When Jackson recorded *Off the Wall* with Quincy Jones as producer in 1979, it sold 6 million copies. That achievement made it the best-selling album ever recorded by an African American. His next album, *Thriller,* entered the Billboard Top Ten on January 3, 1983, where it stayed for seventy-eight weeks, remaining at number one for thirty-seven weeks. At the end of the decade, *Thriller* had sold over 40 million copies, making it the best-selling record album of all time.

By the mid-1980s, African American artists dominated the Top Ten music list. Lionel Richie, Tina Turner, Rick James, Billy Ocean, and Stevie Wonder all had number one hits in 1984. The most flamboyant artist of the time was Prince Rogers Nelson, whose shocking lyrics on the album *Dirty Mind* (1980) led Tipper Gore to form the Parents Music Resource Center in 1984 to protest sexually explicit lyrics. That protest would eventually result in "Parental Advisory" labels on album covers. Prince's flamboyant style led to questions about his personal life, especially if he was gay or bisexual. His response was classically postmodern: "Who cares?"

The popularity of rock music, and musicians, became a global experience in the 1980s. Renowned rock figures embarked on world tours, and the performances were experienced through enormous video screens and television broadcasts. Technology blurred the distinction between live events and reproduced videos and recordings. "From rock music to tourism to television and even education, advertising imperatives and consumer demand are no longer for goods, but for experiences." A rock music concert became the ultimate postmodern experience, proof with manufactured reality that all claims to truth—and even truth itself—were socially constructed.

In July 1985, one of the biggest events in rock history, the Live Aid concert, was held simultaneously in London and Philadelphia. The concert was attended by 160,000 fans while another 1.5 billion watched it on television or listened on the radio in 130 countries. The two simultaneous all-day concerts involved pretty much anybody who was anybody in the rock-and-roll world, and Phil Collins caught the supersonic Concord to play in both cities on two different continents. Hundreds of thousands of people raised their voices together to end the show by singing, "We are the World." The Live Aid concert raised over

$80 million in foreign aid that went to seven African nations: Ethiopia, Mozambique, Chad, Burkina Faso, Niger, Mali, and Sudan.

MTV opened opportunities for women to flaunt their personality and sexuality on the screen in ways, and at an age, their parents could never have imagined. Tina Turner, Cyndi Lauper, and Madonna Ciccone emerged as singing, sexual icons of the time. The latter's album *Like a Virgin* created a stir when she took the woman-as-sex-object ploy to new public heights. She found herself singing to prepubescent audiences dressed in layered gypsy blouses, bangled necklaces, and an exposed midriff. In true postmodern style, Madonna changed her public image many times, going from dance queen to "boy toy," to the "Material Girl," to trashy on-stage exhibitionist. Each time, she influenced popular fashion and the style of pop music.

Rock music was becoming an index of cultural capital, and a telltale revelation of social change. Older Americans, who had invented the youth culture, stood by speechless as their children adopted rebellious fashions at increasingly younger ages. Girls as young as eleven or twelve found themselves on the cover of beauty magazines. A 1989 article in the *New York Times* described a new marketing drive of cosmetics for little girls, six years old, "painted to the hilt." Preadolescent dieting was rampant in the fourth and fifth grades, and in a survey of schoolgirls in San Francisco, more than half described themselves as overweight, while only 15 percent were so by medical standards.

American adolescence in the 1980s was prolonged, enjoyed, and catered to by a host of advertisers offering instant gratification. None of this was new, but the scale of the assault was unprecedented. The television suggested a morality far different from what most Americans were used to. Little girls wore leg warmers and wanted to be like Jennifer Beals, the dancing heroine in *Flashdance*. Patrick Swayze crossed the line from courtship to seduction in *Dirty Dancing*. The top movie in 1986 was *Top Gun* starring Tom Cruise as Lt. Pete "Maverick" Mitchell, a U.S. Navy fighter pilot who seduces his flight instructor. At some time every kid saw, or played with, a *Ghostbuster* product. The 1984 science fiction comedy starred three parapsychologists who were fired from New York University and started up their own business investigating and eliminating ghosts.

The 1980s were a time when the "Cola Wars" between Coke and Pepsi reached new heights—or lows, depending on your perspective. Coke was losing market share to its competitor, so on April 23, 1985, "New Coke," a sweeter variant on the original, was released with great fanfare, By the middle of June, people were saying "no" to New Coke. The reaction was nationwide, with the recent product called "furniture polish" and "sewer water." Within weeks "Coke Classic" returned to the market, and the company stock jumped 36 percent. Only in America could a marketing disaster turn into company profit. For entertainment, Americans fooled with Rubik's Cube, a plastic square with its surface subdivided so that each face consisted of nine squares. Rotation of each face allowed the smaller cubes to be arranged in different ways. The challenge, undertaken by millions of addicts, was to return the cube from any given state to its original array with each face consisting of nine squares of the same color.

Kids still rode bicycles around the neighborhood, swam in local pools, and used little CB radios to talk to each other. Schools were discussing twelve-month sessions, but summer for most was still from Memorial Day to Labor Day. They did not yet have 100 channels to flip through on television, or cell phones to flip open, email, or instant messengers. If they wanted to visit with friends they still went home and gave them a call.

Television aired a number of shows with black stars, the most successful of which was the *Bill Cosby Show*. It was the top-rated show of the decade, and showed African Americans as economically successful, middle-class professionals. *Miami Vice* made a star of Don Johnson. *The Golden Girls* made its premier in 1985 and featured stars well into their fifties and sixties. The best night on television from 1984 to 1986 was Thursday, when *The Cosby Show, Family Ties, Cheers, Night Court,* and *Hill Street Blues* dominated. *St. Elsewhere*, along with shows like *Hill Street Blues, L.A. Law,* and *Thirtysomething* were a result of demographic programming at a time when cable television was experiencing spectacular growth. The shows earned comparatively low ratings, but were kept on the air because they delivered highly desirable audiences of young affluent viewers whom advertisers wanted to reach. In 1987, a fourth network, Fox, went on the air to compete with CBS, NBC, and ABC. Before the end of the decade, 90 percent of American homes were able to tune into Fox.

Talk shows flooded onto the airways in the 1980s. David Letterman got his start in 1982, and by 1989 Oprah Winfrey, Geraldo Rivera, Sally Jessey Raphael, Pat Sajak, Arsenio Hall, and Larry King hosted popular shows. The Reagan appointees on the Federal Communications Commission (FCC) revolutionized broadcasting when they voted to abolish the agency's long-standing fairness doctrine, which required broadcasters to provide a balanced presentation of public issues. With FM radio stations given over to rock and country music, older, more conservative listeners turned to AM radio, where right-wing hosts like Rush Limbaugh, Pat Buchanan, and G. Gordon Liddy entertained them with criticisms of women, liberals, Democrats, and environmentalists.

In the burgeoning suburbs, kids collected and traded Garbage Pail Kids, and had to have as many Cabbage Patch Kids as possible. They wore Swatch watches and Izod shirts, and spent time in shopping malls where they found their every need: music stores, clothing stores, fast food courts, movie theaters, and all their friends. On their first kiss they heard "Take Your Breath Away" on the radio, they danced like an Egyptian, and they did the "moonwalk," The Challenger explosion was broadcast live, and a viewer never heard a curse word used on television.

The combination of technological change and more consumer outlets led to a growth in pornography. Cheap video technology allowed the industry to grow to an estimated $7 billion in 1984, as three-quarters of the nation's video stores carried the tapes for rental. In May of 1985, Attorney General Ed Meese appointed a commission to study the effects of pornography and suggest ways to control it. The recommendations had little effect because the individualistic ethic of the time valued choice and consumption over any standard of government control of cultural morality.

For most Americans, the return of economic prosperity was tacit proof that an improvement of black and white relations was imminent. An expanding economy meant gains for everyone. Discussions of race revolved around the place of affirmative action, but the nation was occasionally treated to sensational stories of scandal, and introduced to new leaders. In November 1987, a black teenager covered in dog excrement with racial slurs written on her body was discovered crawling in the garbage of a town south of Poughkeepsie, New York. The girl, Tawana Brawley, was soon represented by the Reverend Al Sharpton of New York City and two lawyers. Sharpton had no congregation, but did have a reputation as a community activist and spokesman for dissident causes. Brawley claimed to have been abducted by several white men who held her for four days and repeatedly raped her while in captivity. The Sharpton team turned the sensational incident into a national media feeding frenzy.

Before the press, Sharpton claimed that Brawley was the victim of a racist judicial system, and the legal team recommended she not cooperate with the police conducting the investigation. Eventually, Tawana Brawley's story fell apart, and an official examination found that she had never been assaulted and had smeared the excrement and written the epithets herself. Once the truth came out, the two lawyers were subject to legal discipline, but Al Sharpton suffered no repercussions and continued his race-baiting activities. He ran for the New York Senate seat in 1992 and 1994, for mayor of New York City in 1997, and for the Democratic presidential nomination in 2004. Throughout his career he never apologized or explained his activities in the Tawana Brawley case.

The Brawley case showed the power of the new mass media. The "age of publicity," as Louis Kronenberger called it, began in the 1920s when flagpole sitting and goldfish swallowing became ways to get attention. Conspicuous ballyhoo became fashionable after World War II, when couples took their marriage vows on carnival carousels and spent their honeymoons in department store windows. As television grew, so too did the Barnum spirit. World records were set for domino toppling, frankfurter eating, and kazoo playing, and all of it was seen on television. The problem was that no one could predict what was likely to become news or why it would occupy public attention or for how long. More importantly, fame in America not only lasted for just fifteen minutes; it often left devastating results in its wake.

In October of 1987 the country fixated on the rescue of "Baby Jessica" McClure, who fell down an eight-inch-wide, twenty-two-foot-deep hole in her backyard in Midland, Texas. For the next fifty-eight hours the country watched spellbound as rescuers left jobs and worked nonstop to save the baby. On the evening of October 16, paramedics Steve Forbes and Robert O'Donnell wriggled into a passageway drilled through rock to save "Baby Jessica."

When it was over, the gifts sent to her would provide a million-dollar trust fund. Twenty years later, hardened West Texas roughnecks would wipe tears from their cheeks as they talked about the rescue and the media coverage it inspired. The child's parents, Chip and Cissy McClure, subsequently divorced, and one of the rescuers, Robert O'Donnell, killed himself in 1995. His brother, Ricky, said O'Donnell's life fell apart because of the stress of the rescue. In the new media age fame was fleeting and suffocating at the same time.

In 1941 Henry Luce wrote an article for *Life* magazine entitled "The American Century." Luce was the most powerful and innovative mass communications person of his era, and the purpose of his essay was twofold: (1) to urge American involvement in World War II, and (2) to put forth the idea that the American principles of democracy and free enterprise would eventually come to dominate the world. The idea of American preeminence was dangerous in the eyes of some, but the basis of the piece bespoke what most people acknowledged whether they liked Luce's formulation or not.

"We have some things in this country which are infinitely precious and especially American," wrote Luce, "a love of freedom, a feeling for the equality of opportunity, a tradition of self-reliance and independence." Forty-two years later, the editors of *Time* magazine, the sister publication to *Life*, updated Luce's vision with an essay entitled "What Really Mattered." In the essay the *Time* editors evaluated the meaning of America and what values were most precious to its citizens in 1983. They concluded the fundamental idea America represented was freedom, but it was different from what Luce had in mind: "America was merely free: it was freed unshackled. . . . To be free was to be modern: to be modern was to take chances. . . . The American Century was to be the century of unleashing."

During the 1980s the limits of freedom were explored in the political, social, and personal realm. In the 1930s, scientists freed the atom, and fifty years later doctors were trying to free the body from its genetic dictates. Could organ transplants, sex change operations, and genetic manipulation make us immortal? Could the nation be free of superstition, so that Americans could indulge their passions for personal peace and affluence? Freedom was one of the prime conditions of postmodernity, and the cultural preoccupation with it a prelude for change. The advent of a global communications system meant that the world was coming together at one level, and falling apart at another. At the end of the decade the United States was the world's only superpower, yet it would be held captive by countries with only a fraction of its political power, but united by television to worldwide religious followers across the globe.

Postmodernism came of age in this climate in the decade of the 1980s. The election and re-election of ex-actor Ronald Reagan put a new gloss on the possibility of politics shaped by images alone. The convictions of the president were a throwback to an earlier time, but his style of image politics, carefully crafted and orchestrated for mass consumption, was of a newer era. The world was changing, and the older language of genres and forms was becoming obsolete.

 **NO**

The Changing Shape of Power: A Realignment in Public Policy

The past twenty years in America have been marked by two central political developments. The first is the continuing erosion of the political representation of the economic interests of those in the bottom half of the income distribution. The second is the growing dominance of the political process by a network of elites that includes fund-raisers, the leadership of interest groups, specialists in the technology and manipulation of elections, and an army of Washington lobbyists and law firms—elites that augment and often overshadow political officeholders and the candidates for office themselves.

This shift in the balance of power has not been accompanied by realignment of the electorate, although the shape and relative strength of the Republican and Democratic Parties have changed dramatically.

Twice during the past twenty years, the Republican party has had the opportunity to gain majority status: in the early 1970s, and again after the 1980 election. The first opportunity emerged when the fragile Democratic coalition was fractured by the independent presidential bid of Alabama governor George G. Wallace in 1968. The Democratic party then amplified its own vulnerability four years later with the nomination of Sen. George S. McGovern, Democrat of South Dakota, whose candidacy alienated a spectrum of traditional Democrats from Detroit to Atlanta. This potential Republican opportunity crumbled, however, when the web of scandals known as Watergate produced across-the-board setbacks for the GOP in campaigns ranging from city council contests to the presidency in the elections of 1974 and 1976.

The period from 1978 to 1981 offered even more fertile terrain for the Republican party. Not only had Democratic loyalties dating back to the depression of the 1930s been further weakened during the presidency of Jimmy Carter, with the emergence of simultaneous inflation and high unemployment, but the candidacy of Ronald Reagan provided the Republican party with its first substantial opportunity to heal the fissures that had relegated the GOP to minority status for two generations. In Reagan, the party long identified with the rich found a leader equipped to bridge divisions between the country club and the fundamentalist church, between the executives of the Fortune 500 and the membership of the National Rifle Association. Just as Watergate halted Republican momentum in the early 1970s, however, the severe recession of 1981–82 put the brakes on what had the earmarks of a potential Republican takeover, for the first time since 1954, of both branches of Congress. In the first two years of the Reagan administration, the Republican party captured the Senate by a six-vote margin and, with a gain of thirty-two House seats, acquired de facto control of the House in an alliance with southern Democratic conservatives. The recession, however, resulted in the return of twenty-six House seats to the Democrats in 1982, and with those seats went the chance to establish Republican dominance of the federal government.

As the two parties have gained and lost strength, the underlying alteration of the balance of political power over the past decade has continued in a shift of power among the rich, the poor, and the middle class; among blacks and whites; among regions in the country; and among such major competitors for the federal dollar as the defense and social services sectors.

The past twenty years have, in effect, produced a policy realignment in the absence of a political realignment. The major beneficiaries of this policy realignment are the affluent, while those in the bottom half of the income distribution, particularly those whose lives are the most economically marginal, have reaped the fewest rewards or have experienced declines in their standard of living.

A major factor contributing to this development is the decline of political parties: In the United States, as well as in most democratic countries, parties perform the function of representing major interests and classes. As parties erode, the groups that suffer most are those with the fewest resources to protect themselves. In other words, the continued collapse of the broad representation role of political parties in the United States has direct consequences for the distribution of income.

As the role of parties in mobilizing voters has declined, much of the control over both election strategy and issue selection—key functions in defining the national agenda—has shifted to a small, often interlocking, network of campaign specialists, fund-raisers, and lobbyists. While this element of politics is among the most difficult to quantify, there are some rough measures. For example, there are approximately thirty Republican and Democratic consultants and pollsters, almost all based in Washington, who at this writing are the principal strategists in almost every presidential and competitive Senate race, in addition to playing significant roles in gubernatorial, House, and local referenda contests.

At another level, the years from 1974 to 1984 show a steady growth in the financial dependence of House and Senate candidates on political action committees (PACS), vehicles through which money is transferred from organized interest groups to elected officeholders. In that decade, the PAC share of the total cost of House campaigns went from 17 percent to 36 percent, while individual contributions fell from 73 percent to 47 percent, with the remainder coming from parties, loan, and other sources. For House Democratic incumbents, 1984 marked the first year in which PACS were the single most important source of cash; they provided 47 percent of the total, compared with 45 percent from individuals.

This shift has, in turn, magnified the influence of a group of lobbyists who organize Washington fund-raisers for House and Senate incumbents, among whom are Thomas Hale Boggs, Jr., whose clients include the Trial Lawyers Association, the Chicago Board of Options Exchange, and Chrysler; Edward H. Forgotson, whose clients include Enserch Corp., the Hospital Corp. of America, and the Texas Oil and Gas Corp.; Robert J. Keefe, whose clients include Westinghouse and the American Medical Association; and J. D. Williams, whose clients include General Electric Co. and the National Realty Committee. The Washington consulting-lobbying firm of Black, Manafort, Stone, Kelly and Atwater provides perhaps the best example of the range of political and special interests one firm can represent. In 1987, one partner, Charles Black, managed the presidential bid of Rep. Jack Kemp (R–N.Y.); another, Lee Atwater, managed the campaign of Vice-President George Bush; and a third, Peter Kelly, was a principal fund-raiser for the campaign of Sen. Albert Gore (D–Tenn.). At the same time, the firm's clients have included the Dominican Republic, the anti-Communist insurgency in Angola run by Jonas Savimbi, Salomon Brothers, the government of Barbados, the Natural Gas Supply Association, and, briefly, the Marcos government in the Philippines. In addition, the firm has served as principal political consultant to the Senate campaigns of Phil Gramm (R–Tex.), Jesse Helms (R–N.C.), and Paula Hawkins (formerly R–Fla.).

A few general indicators of the scope of lobbying and political party bureaucracies point to the sizable influence small elites can exercise over public policy. In 1986, there were almost 10,000 people employed as registered Washington lobbyists, with 3,500 of these serving as officers of 1,800 trade and professional organizations, including labor unions; another 1,300 were employed by individual corporations, and approximately 1,000 represented organizations ranging from the National Right to Life Association to the Sierra Club. The six major political party committees headquartered in Washington now employ roughly 1,200 people. The creation and expansion of such ideological think tanks as the Heritage Foundation, the Center for National policy, the Urban Institute, the American Enterprise Institute, the Cato Institute, and the Hoover Institution have established whole networks of influential public policy entrepreneurs specializing in media relations and in targeted position papers. Within a general framework of increasingly monopolized American mass media—both print and electronic—the growth of the Gannett and Los Angeles Times—Mirror chains are examples of an ever greater concentration of power within the media, just as the acquisition of NBC by General Electric has functioned to submerge a major network within the larger goals of the nation's sixth biggest corporation. Staffers acquiring expertise and influence on Capitol Hill, in the executive branch, and throughout the regulatory apparatus routinely travel to the private sector—and sometimes back again—through the so-called revolving door. In effect, an entire class of public and private specialists in the determination of government policy and political strategy has been created—a process replicated in miniature at the state level.

The rise to authority of elites independent of the electorate at large, empowered to make decisions without taking into direct account the economic interests of voters, is part of a much larger shift in the balance of power involving changed voting patterns, the decline of organized labor, a restructuring of the employment marketplace, and a transformed system of political competition. This power shift, in turn, has produced a policy realignment most apparent in the alteration of both the *pre-tax* distribution of income and the *after-tax* distribution of income. In both cases, the distribution has become increasingly regressive. The alteration of the pretax distribution of income is the subject of a broad debate in which there are those, particularly critics on the left, who argue that growing regressivity emerges from government policies encouraging weakened union representation and a proliferation of low-wage service industry jobs. On the other side, more conservative analysts contend that changes in the pre-tax distribution result from natural alterations of the marketplace and the workplace, as the United States adjusts to a changing economic and demographic environment. The figures in table 1, derived from Census Bureau data, indicate changes in the distribution of pretax household income from 1980 through 1985, the most recent year for which data from the census is available.

The data clearly show a growing disparity in the distribution of income. Of the five quintiles, all but those in the top 20 percent have seen their share of household income decline. In addition, most of the gains of the top 20 percent have, in fact, been concentrated in the top 5 percent of the income distribution. The gain of 1.1 percent for the top 5 percent translates into a total of $38.8 billion (in 1987 dollars) more for this segment of the population than if the income distribution had remained constant after 1980. These regressive trends were, moreover, intensified by the tax policies enacted between 1980 and 1985, as demonstrated in table 2, based on Census Bureau data.

Table 1

Shares of Pre-Tax Household Income, by Income Distribution

	Year	
Income group	1980 (%)	1985 (%)
Quintile[a]		
Bottom	4.1	3.9
Second	10.2	9.7
Third	16.8	16.3
Fourth	24.8	24.4
Top	44.2	45.7
Top 5%	16.5	17.6

Sources: Bureau of the Census, *Estimating After-Tax Money Income Distribution*, Series P-23, no. 126, issued August 1983; and ibid., *Household After-Tax Income: 1985*, Series P-23, no. 151, issued June 1987.

[a]A quintile is a block of 20% of the population.

Table 2

Shares of After-Tax Household Income, by Income Distribution

	Year	
Income group	1980 (%)	1985 (%)
Quintile[a]		
Bottom	4.9	4.6
Second	11.6	11.0
Third	17.9	17.2
Fourth	25.1	24.7
Top	40.6	42.6
Top 5%	14.1	15.5

Sources: Bureau of the Census, *Estimating After-Tax Money Income Distribution,* Series P-23, no. 126, issued August 1983; and ibid., *Household After-Tax Income: 1985,* Series P-23, no. 151, issued June 1987.

[a]A quintile is a block of 20% of the population.

What had been a $38.8 billion improvement in the status of the top 5 percent in pre-tax income over these six years becomes a $49.5 billion gain in after-tax income, while the bottom 80 percent of the population saw larger losses in its share of after-tax income between 1980 and 1985 than it had seen in the case of pre-tax income. These findings are even more sharply delineated in a November 1987 study by the Congressional Budget Office showing that from 1977 to 1988, 70 percent of the population experienced very modest increases in after-tax income or, for those in the bottom 40 percent, net drops, when changes over that period in the federal income tax, the Social Security tax, corporate tax, and excise taxes are taken into account. In contrast, those in the seventy-first to ninetieth percentiles experienced a modest improvement, and those in the top 10 percent significantly improved their standard of living. For those at the very top, the gains have been enormous. Table 3, developed from Congressional Budget Office data, shows that distribution.

What these tables point to is a major redistribution of economic power in the private marketplace and of political power in the public sector, which, in turn, has been reflected in very concrete terms in family income patterns. One of the major characteristics, then, of the post–New Deal period in American politics has been a reversal of the progressive redistribution of income that underlay the policies of the administrations of Franklin Roosevelt and Harry Truman.

In the competition between the defense and social welfare sectors, the outcome of a parallel, although more recent, shift in the balance of power can be seen in the years from 1980 through 1987. During this period, the share of the federal budget going to national defense grew from 22.7 percent in 1980 to 28.4 percent in 1987. At the same time, the share of federal dollars collectively

Table 3

Changes in Estimated Average After-Tax Family Income, by Income Distribution (In 1987 Dollars)

Income group	1977 average income ($)	1988 average income ($)	Percentage change (+ or −)	Dollar change (+ or −)
Decile[a]				
First (poor)	3,528	3,157	−10.5	−371
Second	7,084	6,990	−1.3	−94
Third	10,740	10,614	−1.2	−126
Fourth	14,323	14,266	−0.4	−57
Fifth	18,043	18,076	+0.2	+33
Sixth	22,009	22,259	+1.1	+250
Seventh	26,240	27,038	+3.0	+798
Eighth	31,568	33,282	+5.4	+1,718
Ninth	39,236	42,323	+7.9	+3,087
Tenth (rich)	70,459	89,783	+27.4	+19,324
Top 5%	90,756	124,651	+37.3	+33,895
Top 1%	174,498	303,900	+74.2	+129,402
All groups	22,184	26,494	+9.6	+2,310

Source: Congressional Budget Offices, *The Changing Distribution of Federal Taxes: 1975–1990*, October 1987.

[a]A decile is a block of 10% of the population.

going to education, training, employment, social services, health, income security, and housing dropped from 25.5 percent in 1980 to 18.3 percent in 1987.

In many respects, these policy changes reflect the rising strength of the Republican party. In terms of tax policy and the balance of spending between defense and social programs, the Republican party under Ronald Reagan has been the driving force pushing the country to the right. During the past ten years, the Republican party has made substantial gains in the competition for the allegiance of voters, gaining near parity by 1987, reducing what had been a 20- to 25-point Democratic advantage in terms of self-identification to a six- or seven-point edge.

The income distribution trends and the shifts in budget priorities began, however, before the Republican party took over the presidency and the U.S. Senate in 1980. The emergence of a vital, competitive Republican party is less a cause of the changed balance of power in the country than a reflection of the underlying forces at work in the post–New Deal phase of American politics.

Together, these forces—which include the deterioration of organized labor, the continued presence of divisive racial conflict, the shift from manufacturing to service industries, the slowing rates of economic growth, the threat of international competition to domestic production, the replacement of political organization with political technology, and the growing class-skew of voter turnout—have severely undermined the capacity of those in the bottom half of the income distribution to form an effective political coalition.

In tracing the erosion of the left wing of the Democratic party in the United States, it is difficult to overestimate the importance of the collapse of the labor movement. In 1970, the continuing growth in the number of labor union members came to a halt. Unions represented 20.7 million workers that year, or 27.9 percent of the nonagricultural work force. Through 1980, the number of workers represented by unions remained roughly the same, dropping slightly to 20.1 million employees by 1980. At the same time, however, the total work force had grown, so that the percentage of workers who were represented by unions fell to 23 percent in 1980. With the election of Ronald Reagan, however, the decline of organized labor began to accelerate sharply, a process encouraged by Reagan's firing of 11,500 striking PATCO air traffic controllers, and by the appointment of pro-management officials to the National Labor Relations Board and to the Department of Labor. From 1980 to 1986, not only did the share of the work force represented by unions drop from 23 percent to 17.5 percent, but the number of workers in unions began to fall precipitously for the first time in fifty years, dropping by 3.1 million men and women, from 20.1 million to 17 million, in 1986. During the first half of the 1980s, almost all the decline in union membership was among whites employed in private industry.

The decline of organized labor dovetailed with a continuing shift from traditional manufacturing, mining, and construction employment to work in the technology and service industries. From 1970 to 1986, the number of jobs in goods-producing industries, which lend themselves to unionization, grew only from 23.8 million to 24.9 million, while employment in the service industries, which are much more resistant to labor organizing, shot up from 47.3 million to 75.2 million.

The difficulties of organized labor were compounded by the unexpected decision on the part of many of the major corporations in the early 1970s to abandon what had been a form of tacit détente between labor and management, in which Fortune 500 companies kept labor peace through agreements amounting to a form of profit sharing by means of automatic cost-of-living pay hikes. Faced with growing competition from foreign producers—in 1968, car imports exceeded exports for the first time in the nation's history, an unmistakable signal that domestic producers of all goods faced serious foreign competition—major American companies dropped the fundamentally cordial relations that had characterized the largest part of postwar union negotiations. Catching the leaders of organized labor entirely unprepared, these corporations adopted a tough, adversarial approach regarding both pay and fringe benefits, willing to break union shops and to relocate facilities either abroad or in nonunion communities in the South and Southwest.

The decline of organized labor was particularly damaging to the Democratic party because unions represent one of the few remaining institutional links between working-class voters and the Democratic party. The decline of political parties has resulted in the end of the clubhouse tie between the party of Franklin Delano Roosevelt and the blue-collar voters of row- and tract-house neighborhoods throughout the Northeast and Midwest. In addition, it is among these white, blue-collar workers that the racial conflicts within the Democratic party have been the most divisive. Interviews with whites in Dearborn, Michigan, the west-side suburbs of Birmingham, Chicago, Atlanta, and New Orleans—all communities that have suffered major industrial layoffs and that are either part of or adjoin cities now run by Democratic black mayors—reveal voters who are disenchanted with the unions that failed to protect their jobs, and with a local Democratic party no longer controlled by whites. Race, which previously severed the tie between the white South and the Democratic party, has, in cities with black mayors, served to produce white Republican voting, not only for president but for local offices that once were unchallenged Democratic bastions.

These developments, in the 1970s, contributed significantly to the creation of a vacuum of power within the Democratic party, allowing the party to be taken over, in part, by its most articulate and procedurally sophisticated wing: affluent, liberal reformers. This faction capitalized first on the public outcry against police violence at the Chicago presidential convention in 1968, and then on the Watergate scandals in the mid-1970s, to force priority consideration of a series of reforms involving campaign finance, the presidential nominating process, the congressional seniority system, the congressional code of ethics—and an expansion of the federal role in regulating the environment, through creation of the Environmental Protection Agency and new water- and air-pollution standards. The strength of this wing of the Democratic party subsided during the 1980s, although its leverage within the party has been institutionalized through the creation of a host of primaries and caucuses in the presidential selection process, giving disproportionate influence to middle- and upper-middle-class voters and interests in a party that claims to represent the nation's working and lower-middle classes. The turnout in primaries and in caucuses is skewed in favor of the affluent and upper-middle class. In addition, these delegate selection processes have been contributing factors in the acceleration of the decline of political organizations in working-class communities.

The Democratic agenda set in the 1970s by the reform wing of the party was, however, more important for what it omitted and neglected than for what was included. The ascendancy of the reformers took place just when the fissures within the Democratic party had become most apparent. In 1968, 9.9 million mostly Democratic voters turned to George C. Wallace, the segregationist-populist governor of Alabama, and they strayed off the Democratic reservation in 1972 when Nixon beat McGovern by a margin of 47.2 million votes to 29.2 million. The cultural and ideological gulf that had steadily widened between these voters and the wings of the Democratic party supporting the antiwar movement, gay rights, women's rights, and civil rights had reached such proportions in the early and mid 1970s that rapprochement between warring factions was difficult, if not impossible.

The rise to prominence within the Democratic party of a well-to-do liberal-reform wing worked in other ways to compound the divisions in the party. Relatively comfortable in their own lives, reformers failed to recognize the growing pressure of marginal tax rates on working- and lower-middle-class voters. The progressive rate system of the federal income tax remained effectively unchanged from the early 1950s through the 1970s, so that the series of sharply rising marginal tax rates that had originally been designed to affect only the upper-middle class and rich, began to directly impinge on regular Democratic voters whose wages had been forced up by inflation. By neglecting to adjust the marginal rate system to account for inflation, in combination with repeated raising of the highly regressive Social Security tax, Democrats effectively encouraged the tax revolt of the 1970s which, in turn, provided a critically important source of support to the conservative movement and to the rise of the Republican party. . . .

On the Republican side, the same developments that debilitated the Democratic coalition served to strengthen ascendant constituencies of the Right. For a brief period in the late 1970s and early 1980s, the constituencies and interests underpinning the Republican party had the potential to establish a new conservative majority in the electorate. The tax revolt, the rise of the religious right, the mobilization of much of the business community in support of the Republican party, renewed public support for defense spending, the political-financial mobilization of the affluent, and the development of a conservative economic theory promising growth through lower taxes—all combined to empower the political right to a degree unprecedented since the 1920s.

Proposed tax cuts provided an essential common ground for the right-of-center coalition that provided the core of the Reagan revolution. The combination of corporate tax reductions and individual tax cuts embodied in the 1981 tax bill served to unify a divided business community by providing a shared legislative goal, to strengthen the commitment of the affluent to the Republican party, and to attract white working- and lower-middle-class former Democrats who had seen their paychecks eaten away by inflation-driven higher marginal rates. The tax cut theme was adopted as a central element of the speeches of such religious-right figures as the Rev. Jerry Falwell of the Moral Majority, Ed McAteer of the Religious Roundtable, and the Rev. Marion G. (Pat) Robertson of the Christian Broadcast Network. . . .

This growing political tilt in favor of the affluent is further reflected in voting turnout patterns over the past twenty years. During this period, the class-skewing of voting in favor of the affluent has grown significantly. In the presidential election year of 1964, the self-reported turnout among members of professions associated with the middle and upper classes was 83.2 percent, compared with 66.1 percent among those employed in manual jobs, including skilled crafts, a difference of 17.1 points; by 1980, the spread between the two had grown to 25 points, 73 percent to 48 percent. In the off-year election of

1966, the percentage-point spread in terms of voter turnout between middle-to-upper-class job holders and those employed in manual jobs was 18.1 percent; by 1978, this had grown to a 23.8-percent spread. While overall turnout has been declining, the drop has been most severe among those in the bottom third of the income distribution.

For the Republican party, these turnout trends were a political bonanza, accentuated by trends in the correlation between income and both voting and partisan commitment. Through the 1950s, 1960s, and into the early 1970s, the sharp class divisions that characterized the depression-era New Deal coalition structure gave way to diffuse voting patterns with relatively little correlation between income and allegiance to the Democratic or Republican party. By 1980 and 1982, with the election of Reagan and then the enactment of the budget and tax bills of 1981, the correlation between income and voting began to reemerge with a vengeance. By 1982, the single most important determinant of probable voting, aside from membership in either the Republican or Democratic party, became income, with the Democratic margin steadily declining as one moved up the ladder. . . .

In other words, the Reagan years polarized the electorate along sharp income lines. While income made almost no difference in the partisan loyalties of 90 percent of the population in 1956, by 1984 income became one of the sharpest dividing lines between Democrats and Republicans. In 1956, the very poor were only 5 percentage points more likely to be Democratic than the upper-middle class, and 40 points more likely than the affluent top 10 percent of the income distribution. By 1984, however, the spread between the poor and the upper-middle class reached 36 points, and between the poor and affluent, 69 points. . . .

These figures accurately describe an electorate polarized by income, but what they mask are the effects of black and white voter participation on the figures. The civil rights movement, and civil rights legislation enacted in the 1960s, enfranchised millions of blacks who, in 1956, were barred from voting. During the twenty-eight years from 1956 to 1984, roughly 4.2 million blacks entered the electorate. During the same period, blacks' allegiance to the Democratic party, which in 1956 held their loyalty by a 34-percentage-point edge, increased to provide an overwhelming 72-percentage-point Democratic edge in 1984. This infusion of black Democratic support sharply increased the low-income tilt of the party: in 1984, the median family income for whites was $28,674, while for blacks it was $15,982.

The Reagan revolution was, at its core, a revolution led by the affluent. The class polarization of voters . . . cut across the country, but nowhere were the trends stronger than in the South, where a realignment in miniature took place among the white elite. In the 1950s, Democratic allegiance in the South was strongest among the most well-to-do whites, for whom the Democratic party was the vehicle for maintaining the pre–civil rights social structure of the Confederate states. These voters gave the Democratic party their support by a 5 to 1 margin, higher than that of any other income group in the South. By the 1980s, in the aftermath of a civil rights movement supported by the Democratic party, these same voters had become the most Republican in the

South. "The class cleavage had reversed itself," John R. Petrocik, of UCLA, noted. Whites, particularly white men, have become increasingly Republican as blacks have become the most consistent source of Democratic votes. In the five presidential elections from 1968 to 1984, only one Democrat, Jimmy Carter, received more than 40 percent of the white vote, and by 1984, white, male Protestants voted for Reagan over Mondale by a margin of 74 to 26.

The Reagan revolution would, however, have been a political failure if it had not gained extensive support from voters outside the upper-middle class. In addition to the deep inroads made in previously Democratic working-class communities in northern urban areas, perhaps the single most important source of new support for the Republican party has been the religious Right.

In a far shorter period, voters identifying themselves as born-again Christians radically shifted their voting in presidential elections. Between 1976 and 1984, these voters went from casting a 56-to-44 margin for the Democratic candidate, Jimmy Carter, to one of the highest levels of support of any group for the reelection of President Reagan in 1984: 81 to 19, according to *New York Times*/CBS exit polls. This shift represents, in effect, a gain of eight million voters for the GOP.

As a political resource, support among born-again Christians represents not only a loyal core of voters, but a growing core. In contrast with such mainline churches as the United Methodist Church, the United Church of Christ, and the United Presbyterians, which experienced membership losses from 1970 to 1980, the fundamentalist, evangelical, and charismatic churches have seen their congregations grow at an explosive rate: the Southern Baptist Convention by 16 percent, the Assemblies of God by 70 percent, and Seventh Day Adventists by 36 percent.

The Republican party has, in turn, been the major beneficiary of an internal power struggle taking place within the Southern Baptist Convention, now the largest Protestant denomination. During a ten-year fight, the denomination has been taken over by its conservative wing, believers in the "absolute inerrancy" of the Bible. This wing of the denomination, in turn, has been a leading force within the broader religious Right, as such pastors as Adrian Rogers, James T. Draper, Jr., and Charles F. Stanley—all outspoken conservatives—have won the denomination's presidency. The move to the right has been reflected in the ranks of the denomination, producing what amounts to a realignment of the ministry of the Southern Baptist Convention. James L. Guth, of Furman University, found that in just three years, surveys of Southern Baptist ministers showed a remarkable shift from a strong majority in 1981 favoring the Democratic party 41 to 29, to nearly 70 percent in 1984 favoring the GOP, 66 to 26.

The growth of Republican strength is not, however, confined to evangelical and charismatic Christians, and the party appears to be developing a much broader religious base as part of its core constituency. In one of the most interesting recent analyses of voting trends, Frederick T. Steeper, of Market Opinion Research, and John Petrocik, of UCLA, have found that since 1976, one of the sharpest partisan cleavages emerging among white voters in the electorate is between those who attend church regularly and those who never go to church. This represents a major change from past findings. In the period from 1952 to 1960, there was no statistical difference between the Democratic and Republican loyalties of white churchgoers and nonchurchgoers. By the elections of 1972 and 1976, a modest difference began to appear, with non-churchgoers 7 percentage points more likely to be Democrats than regular churchgoers. By 1986, however, the spread had grown to a striking 35-point difference, with regular churchgoers identifying themselves as Republicans by a 22-point margin, and with nonchurchgoers identifying themselves as Demo-crats by a 13-point edge. The partisan spread between churchgoers and non-churchgoers was most extreme among white Northern Protestants (51 points) and Catholics (52 points). These findings dovetail with studies showing that the memberships of such Establishment, nonevangelical denominations as the Methodists, Episcopalians, Lutherans, and Presbyterians were significantly more supportive of the election of Ronald Reagan than the electorate at large. . . .

Cumulatively, developments over the past twenty years—the deteriora-tion of the labor movement; economically polarized partisanship; the skew-ing of turnout patterns by income; stagnation of the median family income; the rising importance of political money; the emergence of a Republican core composed of the well-to-do and the religious; the globalization of the econ-omy; and competition from foreign producers—have combined to disperse constituencies and groups seeking to push the country to the left, and to con-solidate those on the right. The consequences of that shift are most readily seen in the figures in table 3, which show that 80 percent of the population has experienced a net loss in after-tax income between 1977 and 1988, while the top 5 percent has seen average family income grow by $26,134, and the top 1 percent, by $117,222.

In the long run the prospects are for the maintenance of a strong, conserva-tive Republican party, continuing to set the national agenda on basic distribu-tional issues, no matter which party holds the White House. Barring a major economic catastrophe, or a large-scale international conflict, the basic shift from manufacturing to service industry jobs is likely to continue to undermine the political left in this country, not only for the reasons outlined earlier in this essay, but also by weakening economically—and therefore politically—those in the bottom 40 percent of the income distribution.

In the thirty-year period spanning 1949 to 1979, the number of manufac-turing jobs grew by an average of three million a decade, from 17.6 million in 1949, to 20.4 million in 1959, to 24.4 million in 1969, and finally to a high of 26.5 million in 1979. This growth in no way kept pace with the increase in ser-vice industry jobs, which shot up from 26.2 million in 1949 to 63.4 million in 1979, but the continuing, if modest, manufacturing expansion provided a par-tial cushion in an economy going through a major restructuring—a restructur-ing involving the loss of 950,000 jobs in steel and other metals industries, automobiles, food production, and textiles from 1972 to 1986. From 1979 to 1986, however, the absolute number of manufacturing jobs began to decline, dropping from 26.5 million to 24.9 million, a loss of 1.6 million jobs.

These employment shifts have been particularly damaging to blacks and Hispanics. From 1970 to 1984, in major northern cities, there has been a massive

Table 4

Changes in the Combined Number of Jobs, by Employee Education Level, in New York, Philadelphia, Boston, Baltimore, St. Louis, Atlanta, Houston, Denver, and San Francisco, 1970 and 1984

	Number of Jobs		
Mean level of employee education	1970	1984	Change, 1970–84
Less than high school	3,068,000	2,385,000	−683,000
Some higher education	2,023,000	2,745,000	+722,000

Source: Computed from William Julius Wilson, *The Truly Disadvantaged: The Inner City, the Underclass, and Public Policy* (Chicago: University of Chicago Press, 1987), table 2.6, p. 40. The table, in turn, is taken from John D. Kasarda, "The Regional and Urban Redistribution of People and Jobs in the U.S." (Paper presented to the National Research Council Committee on National Urban Policy, National Academy of Sciences, 1986).

decline in the number of jobs requiring relatively little education—the kind of jobs that provide entry into the employment marketplace for the poor—and a sharp increase in the number of jobs requiring at least some higher education: "Demographic and employment trends have produced a serious mismatch between the skills of inner-city blacks and the opportunities available to them . . . substantial job losses have occurred in the very industries in which urban minorities have the greatest access, and substantial employment gains have occurred in the higher-education-requisite industries that are beyond the reach of most minority workers," according to William Julius Wilson, of the University of Chicago (see table 4).

While blacks and Hispanics will, at least for the time being, disproportionately bear the burden of this shift in job requirements, the altered structure of the marketplace will work to the disadvantage of the poorly educated of all races. In 1985, there were 30.6 million whites over the age of twenty-five without a high school education—five times the number of blacks without high school degrees (5.9 million) and seven times the number of poorly educated Hispanics (4.4 million). These job market trends will intensify throughout the rest of this century. According to estimates by the Department of Labor, 21.4 million jobs will be created between 1986 and the year 2000, all of which will be in service industries or government, as losses in traditional goods manufacturing industries are unlikely to be fully offset by gains in the technology manufacturing sector. In terms of educational requirements, there will be a significant increase in the proportion of jobs requiring at least one year of college education, no change in the proportion of jobs requiring a high school degree, and a sharp decline in the percentage of jobs requiring no high school education.

In effect, trends in the job market through the next ten years will in all likelihood exacerbate the regressive distribution of income that has taken place over the past decade. Under American democracy, those who are unemployed or marginally employed are weakest politically. The decline of traditional political organizations and unions has made significantly more difficult the political mobilization of the working poor, the working class, and the legions of white-collar workers making from $10,000 to $25,000 a year—a universe roughly containing 24.6 million white households, 3.4 million black households, and 2 million Hispanic households. Within this group, providing a political voice becomes even more difficult for those workers with poor educations who have been dispersed from manufacturing employment into cycles of marginal work. While most of those who have lost manufacturing jobs have found full-time employment, such workers have, in the main, seen wages fall and fringe benefits, often including medical coverage, decline or disappear, leaving them even further outside of the American mainstream and even less well equipped to ensure adequate educational levels for their children. When combined with the declining voter turnout rates associated with falling income, these workers have fallen into what amounts to a new political underclass.

The major forces at work in the last two decades of the post–New Deal period are, then, cumulatively functioning to weaken the influence and power of those in the bottom half of the income distribution, while strengthening the authority of those in the upper half, and particularly the authority of those at elite levels. Trends in political competition and pressures in the private marketplace have combined to create a whipsaw action, reversing New Deal policies that empowered the labor movement and reduced disparities between rich and poor. Recent forces, both in the marketplace and in the political arena, have not produced a realignment of the electorate, but, in terms of outcomes, there has been a realignment in public policy—with few forces, short of a downturn in the business cycle, working against the continuing development of a political and economic system in which the dominant pressures will be toward increased regressivity in the distribution of money and in the ability to influence the outcome of political decisions.

POSTSCRIPT

Were the 1980s a Decade of Affluence for the Middle Class?

Professor J. David Woodard takes a broader view of the 1980s. He notes with approval the increased participation of the middle class in the stock market. He also points out the risks taken by the new investors who saw a 22 percent dip in the market in mid-October 1987. While disapproving of the insider trading tactics that landed multimillionaire Wall Street dealers Michael Milken and Ivan Boesky in jail, Woodard approves of the free-market rational actor model espoused by Milton and Rose Friedman in their book *Free to Choose* (Avon Books, 1985), which "effectively" rebutted the government-as-manager thesis.

While Woodard argues that "a rising tide" raised the income level of 90 percent of Americans, he does not counter the statistical arguments of Edsall, who believes the boat leaked for those blue collar urban whites and minorities who found themselves in the poverty and lower middle class. Woodard admits that inequalities existed between "the knowledge practitioners" who controlled the new economy and the non-educated blue collar worker who saw their well-paid union protected jobs in steel, automobile and the oil industry disappear, victims of automation or outsourced to foreign countries.

Woodard is somewhat critical of the movie industry, which dispensed anti-capitalist movies such as *Wall Street* and *Bonfire of the Vanities*. He also shows a mild distaste for the non-rational "deconstructionist" views of the social science and humanities at America's elite universities. He also sees MTV as an opportunity to flaunt the sexuality of rock and roll music, now dominated by African-American artists, in ways previously denied to earlier rock pioneers like Elvis Presley whose gyrating pelvis was not shown on the Ed Sullivan Sunday-night variety show in 1956. Ironically, Woodard views President Ronald Reagan as both a premodern and postmodern figure. While his convictions were of an earlier time, "his style of image politics, [were] carefully crafted and orchestrated for mass consumption." Two books that explain the rise of the post–World War II conservative movement in which Reagan became the major player are Lee Edwards' sympathetic *The Conservative Revolution: The Movement That Remade America* (Free Press, 1999) and Godfrey Hodgson's more critical *The World Turned Right Side Up: A History of the Conservative Ascendancy in America* (Houghton Mifflin, 1996). Gregory L. Schneider's essay on "Conservatives and the Reagan Presidency," in Richard S. Conley, ed., *Reassessing the Reagan Presidency* (University Press of America, 2003) is a sympathetic objective account with a full bibliography.

Written nearly two decades ago, political journalist Thomas B. Edsall's analysis on the changing landscape of political and economic power in the

1970s and 1980s remains the same in 2007. Political parties have declined in influence. Members of Congress continue receiving the bulk of their money from economic interest groups and political action committees (PACs). Reforms in the 1970s and 2004 have not significantly changed their influence. Presidential candidates and presidential office holders continue to operate their campaign and policy operations independent of Congress.

Edsall believes that the Republican party attained power because of the defection of the white male working class, both in the South and the North. He argues that the Wallace third-party movement in 1968 and 1972 capitalized on the civil rights and women's movement, which led to affirmative action jobs for women and minorities in areas previously held by white males. The erosion of well-paid union jobs in steel, coal, automobiles, and clothing manufacturing to foreign countries also contributed to the income decline of the noncollege educated white male, who had to settle for low-wage jobs in the service industries.

Edsall's major thesis is that in the 1980s, a policy rather than a political realignment was led by the upper middle and upper classes, whose tax reform bills in the 1980s caused a redistribution of income to these classes. This view is supported by Frederick Strobel, a former senior business economist at the Federal Reserve, Bank of Atlanta, in *Upward Dreams, Downward Mobility: The Economic Decline of the American Middle Class* (Rowman & Littlefield, 1993).

The reasons that Strobel gives for the economic decline include an increased supply of workers (baby boomers, housewives, and immigrants), a decline in union membership, a strong dollar, an open import dollar that destroyed many U.S. manufacturing jobs, corporate merger mania, declining government jobs, energy inflation, high interest rates, and the corporate escape for federal, state, and local taxes.

Unexpected criticism also comes from President Reagan's own director of the Office of Management and Budget, David A. Stockman. His *Triumph of Politics: Why the Revolution Failed* (Harper & Row, 1986) details the "ideological hubris" that surrounded Reagan's advisers, who, in conjunction with a spendthrift Congress beholden to outside interest groups, ran up massive budget deficits by implementing a theory known as supply-side economics. More critical from the left are a series of academic articles in *Understanding America's Economic Decline*, edited by Michael A. Bernstein and David E. Adler (Cambridge University Press, 1994). Also critical are the writings of Kevin Phillips, especially *The Politics of Rich and Poor: Wealth and the American Electorate in the Reagan Afermath* (Random House, 1990) and Joseph J. Hogan, "Reaganomics and Economic Policy," in Dilys M. Hill et-al., eds., *The Reagan Presidency: An Incomplete Revolution?* (St. Martin's Press, 1990), which argues, "while constantly disavowing government interventionism and proclaiming the virtues of a free market economy, the Reagan administration continually pursued economic expansionist policies based upon massive government deficits, periods of maintained monetary expansionism and unprecedented high levels of international borrowing."

For dissenting views that support supply-side economics as the key policy leading to America's economy since the early 1980s, see almost any issue of *Commentary, The National Review, The Weekly Standard, Barron's,* and editorial pages of *The Wall Street Journal.* For example, see "The Real Reagan Record," *The National Review* (August 31, 1992, pp. 25–62); in particular, the essays by Alan Reynolds in "Upstarts and Downstarts," who asserts that all income groups experienced significant gains in income during the 1980s; and Paul Craig Roberts, "What Everyone 'Knows' about Reaganomics," *Commentary* (February 1991), which is critical of the Keynesian explanation for the economic downturn in the early 1990s.

Two books that fully support Reagan's positive contribution to the prosperity of the 1980s (in addition to Woodard) are John Ehrman, *The Eighties: America in the Age of Reagan* (Yale University Press, 2005) and Cato Institute economist Richard B. McKenzie, *What Went Right in the 1980s* (Pacific Research Institute for Public Policy, 1994). Karl Zinsmeister, "Summing Up the Reagan Era," *Wilson Quarterly* (Winter 1990) is similar to Woodard and Ehrman in its interpretation.

James D. Torr, editor, provides balanced treatments in *Ronald Reagan* (Thomson Gale, 2001) and *The 1980s: America's Decades* (Greenhaven Press, 2000). The two most recent and important collection of essays by historians and political scientists are Richard S. Conley, ed., *Reassuring the Reagan Presidency* (University Press of America, 2003) and W. Eliot Brownlee and Hugh David Graham, eds., *The Reagan Presidency: Pragmatic Conservatism and Legacies* (University Press of Kansas, 2003), which lives up to its title. In the essay on taxation, authors Brownlee and C. Eugene Steuerle argue that Reagan's commitment to the extreme version of the Laffer curve came in 1977, two or three years earlier than the version given by David Stockman, just before his victory in the 1980 New Hampshire primaries where supposedly Laffer drew his famous curve on a dinner napkin. The two authors claim that Reagan had been reading economist Jude Wanniski's *Wall Street Journal* editorials supporting Laffer's ideas. Finally worth consulting for the worldwide perspective is Bruce J. Schulman, "The Reagan Revolution in International Perspective: Conservative Assaults on the Welfare State across the Industrialized World in the 1980s," in Richard Steven Conley, ed., *Reassessing the Reagan Presidency.* For Reagan's impact on the 2008 presidential race, see Karen Tumulty, "How the Right Went Wrong: What Would Ronnie Do? And Why the Republican Candidates Need to Reclaim the Reagan Legacy," *Time* (March 26, 2007).

ISSUE 15

Is George W. Bush the Worst President in American History?

YES: Sean Wilentz, from "The Worst President in History?" *Rolling Stone* (May 4, 2006)

NO: Conrad Black, from "George W. Bush, FDR, and History," *The American Spectator* (April 2005)

ISSUE SUMMARY

YES: Bancroft prize–winning historian Sean Wilentz argues that the current president ranks with Presidents James Buchanan, Andrew Johnson, and Herbert Hoover in having divided the nation, governed erratically, and left the nation worse off than when he came into office.

NO: FDR biographer Conrad Black believes that President Bush is, with the exception of FDR, the most important president since Lincoln in accomplishing a highly successful domestic and foreign policy.

The American president is the most powerful political figure in the world. The modern presidency achieved this stature in two ways. First was the dominance of America's military power in World War II. Our government also developed and used, with the help of its scientific and military establishments, the first atomic weapons. The ultimate decision to drop the two atomic bombs on Japan was made by President Truman.

A second way in which the modern president transcended the early presidency was the responsibility for managing the economy assumed by the national government in the 1930s. This started incrementally with the alphabet soup agencies in charge of the New Deal programs, but the Employment Act of 1946 created the Council of Economic Advisers and charged the national government with the responsibility for maintaining economic conditions that allowed individuals to find jobs.

The president of the United States wears two hats: ceremonial and political. As *chief of state,* the president is expected to attend special events commemorating the anniversaries of our major holidays—Christmas, Memorial Day, Independence Day, Labor Day, Thanksgiving—as well as to respond to a national emergency such as Roosevelt's address to the nation declaring war on December 8, 1941, the day after the Pearl Harbor attack; Johnson's address to Congress in 1965 exhorting the nation that "We Shall Overcome" in support of the struggle for civil rights; and Bush's address to the nation after the September 11 attacks on New York City and Washington, D.C., in 2001.

Other countries divide the roles. In England, Queen Elizabeth is the ceremonial leader and Tony Blair, the prime minister, is the political. In Japan, a similar division takes place between the emperor and the prime minister of the Japanese diet.

In the twentieth century, the president of the United States spent the majority of his time in office dealing with foreign affairs. As *chief diplomat,* Woodrow Wilson led the negotiations ending World War I by the Treaty of Versailles even though he was unable to get the United States to sign the treaty and join the League of Nations. FDR negotiated numerous agreements with the Allied powers during the war and was instrumental in creating the current United Nations international organization. His successor, Harry S. Truman, was responsible for financing the regional economic alliances in Western Europe such as the Marshall Plan, and for forming the North Atlantic Treaty Organization (NATO), whose purpose was to "contain" Russian expansion during the Cold War. Presidents Eisenhower, Kennedy, Johnson, Nixon, Carter, and Reagan expended an enormous amount of energy trying to diffuse an arms race between the two superpowers. Gorbachev and Reagan virtually ended the Cold War, but post–Cold War presidents Clinton and the two Bushes encountered other problems in Eastern Europe, Africa, and the Middle East.

The major difference between the early and modern presidency can be found in the role of *commander-in-chief.* The first president, George Washington, who traveled by stagecoach from his plantation in Washington, D.C., to be inaugurated in New York City, could hardly imagine being in charge of the decision to use nuclear weapons in war with the power to blow up the world a thousand times over. Presidents have played a dominant role in determining military strategy since the Civil War when Lincoln fired a multitude of generals until he found one—Grant—who relentlessly pursued the enemy. Presidents Wilson, FDR, Truman, and LBJ were important decision makers during the two world wars, Korea, and Vietnam. A classic case of the clash between the president and his military commander occurred during the Korean War when President Truman, with the support of the Joint Chiefs of Staff, relieved the popular General Douglas McArthur of his command of the United Nations' forces during the Korean War. It was a very unpopular decision and Truman suffered a severe drop in the public opinion polls, but the president was determined to uphold his authority as commander-in-chief.

Is it possible to use these roles to evaluate our current leader? How much time must pass before we can dispense with partisanship and attempt to view any president from a detached and objective point of view? In the first essay, Pulitzer Prize–winning historian Sean Wilentz argues that the current president ranks with Presidents James Buchanan, Andrew Johnson, and Herbert Hoover in having divided the nation, governed erratically, and left the nation worse off than when he came into office. But FDR biographer Conrad Black believes that President Bush is, with the exception of FDR, the most important president since Lincoln in accomplishing a highly successful domestic and foreign policy.

YES

Sean Wilentz

The Worst President in History?

George W. Bush's presidency appears headed for colossal historical disgrace. Barring a cataclysmic event on the order of the terrorist attacks of September 11th, after which the public might rally around the White House once again, there seems to be little the administration can do to avoid being ranked on the lowest tier of U.S. presidents. And that may be the best-case scenario. Many historians are now wondering whether Bush, in fact, will be remembered as the very worst president in all of American history.

From time to time, after hours, I kick back with my colleagues at Princeton to argue idly about which president really was the worst of them all. For years, these perennial debates have largely focused on the same handful of chief executives whom national polls of historians, from across the ideological and political spectrum, routinely cite as the bottom of the presidential barrel. Was the lousiest James Buchanan, who, confronted with Southern secession in 1860, dithered to a degree that, as his most recent biographer has said, probably amounted to disloyalty—and who handed to his successor, Abraham Lincoln, a nation already torn asunder? Was it Lincoln's successor, Andrew Johnson, who actively sided with former Confederates and undermined Reconstruction? What about the amiably incompetent Warren G. Harding, whose administration was fabulously corrupt? Or, though he has his defenders, Herbert Hoover, who tried some reforms but remained imprisoned in his own outmoded individualist ethic and collapsed under the weight of the stock-market crash of 1929 and the Depression's onset? The younger historians always put in a word for Richard M. Nixon, the only American president forced to resign from office.

Now, though, George W. Bush is in serious contention for the title of worst ever. In early 2004, an informal survey of 415 historians conducted by the nonpartisan History News Network found that eighty-one percent considered the Bush administration a "failure." Among those who called Bush a success, many gave the president high marks only for his ability to mobilize public support and get Congress to go along with what one historian called the administration's "pursuit of disastrous policies." In fact, roughly one in ten of those who called Bush a success was being facetious, rating him only as the best president since Bill Clinton—a category in which Bush is the only contestant.

The lopsided decision of historians should give everyone pause. Contrary to popular stereotypes, historians are generally a cautious bunch. We assess the past from widely divergent points of view and are deeply concerned about being viewed as fair and accurate by our colleagues. When we make historical judgments, we are acting not as voters or even pundits, but as scholars who must evaluate all the evidence, good, bad or indifferent. Separate surveys, conducted by those perceived as conservatives as well as liberals, show remarkable unanimity about who the best and worst presidents have been.

Historians do tend, as a group, to be far more liberal than the citizenry as a whole—a fact the president's admirers have seized on to dismiss the poll results as transparently biased. One pro-Bush historian said the survey revealed more about "the current crop of history professors" than about Bush or about Bush's eventual standing. But if historians were simply motivated by a strong collective liberal bias, they might be expected to call Bush the worst president since his father, or Ronald Reagan, or Nixon. Instead, more than half of those polled—and nearly three-fourths of those who gave Bush a negative rating—reached back *before* Nixon to find a president they considered as miserable as Bush. The presidents most commonly linked with Bush included Hoover, Andrew Johnson and Buchanan. Twelve percent of the historians polled—nearly as many as those who rated Bush a success—flatly called Bush the worst president in American history. And these figures were gathered before the debacles over Hurricane Katrina, Bush's role in the Valerie Plame leak affair and the deterioration of the situation in Iraq. Were the historians polled today, that figure would certainly be higher.

Even worse for the president, the general public, having once given Bush the highest approval ratings ever recorded, now appears to be coming around to the dismal view held by most historians. To be sure, the president retains a considerable base of supporters who believe in and adore him, and who reject all criticism with a mixture of disbelief and fierce contempt—about one-third of the electorate. (When the columnist Richard Reeves publicized the historians' poll last year and suggested it might have merit, he drew thousands of abusive replies that called him an idiot and that praised Bush as, in one writer's words, "a Christian who actually acts on his deeply held beliefs.") Yet the ranks of the true believers have thinned dramatically. A majority of voters in forty-three states now disapprove of Bush's handling of his job. Since the commencement of reliable polling in the 1940s, only one twice-elected president has seen his ratings fall as low as Bush's in his second term: Richard Nixon, during the months preceding his resignation in 1974. No two-term president since polling began has fallen from such a height of popularity as Bush's (in the neighborhood of ninety percent, during the patriotic upswell following the 2001 attacks) to such a low (now in the midthirties). No president, including Harry Truman (whose ratings sometimes dipped below Nixonian levels), has experienced such a virtually unrelieved decline as Bush has since his high point. Apart from sharp but temporary upticks that followed the commencement of the Iraq war and the capture of Saddam Hussein, and a recovery during the weeks just before and after his re-election, the Bush trend has been a profile in fairly steady disillusionment.

How does any president's reputation sink so low? The reasons are best understood as the reverse of those that produce presidential greatness. In almost every survey of historians dating back to the 1940s, three presidents have emerged as supreme successes: George Washington, Abraham Lincoln and Franklin D. Roosevelt. These were the men who guided the nation through what historians consider its greatest crises: the founding era after the ratification of the Constitution, the Civil War, and the Great Depression and Second World War. Presented with arduous, at times seemingly impossible circumstances, they rallied the nation, governed brilliantly and left the republic more secure than when they entered office.

Calamitous presidents, faced with enormous difficulties—Buchanan, Andrew Johnson, Hoover and now Bush—have divided the nation, governed erratically and left the nation worse off. In each case, different factors contributed to the failure: disastrous domestic policies, foreign-policy blunders and military setbacks, executive misconduct, crises of credibility and public trust. Bush, however, is one of the rarities in presidential history: He has not only stumbled badly in every one of these key areas, he has also displayed a weakness common among the greatest presidential failures—an unswerving adherence to a simplistic ideology that abjures deviation from dogma as heresy, thus preventing any pragmatic adjustment to changing realities. Repeatedly, Bush has undone himself, a failing revealed in each major area of presidential performance.

The Credibility Gap

No previous president appears to have squandered the public's trust more than Bush has. In the 1840s, President James Polk gained a reputation for deviousness over his alleged manufacturing of the war with Mexico and his supposedly covert pro-slavery views. Abraham Lincoln, then an Illinois congressman, virtually labeled Polk a liar when he called him, from the floor of the House, "a bewildered, confounded and miserably perplexed man" and denounced the war as "from beginning to end, the sheerest deception." But the swift American victory in the war, Polk's decision to stick by his pledge to serve only one term and his sudden death shortly after leaving office spared him the ignominy over slavery that befell his successors in the 1850s. With more than two years to go in Bush's second term and no swift victory in sight, Bush's reputation will probably have no such reprieve.

The problems besetting Bush are of a more modern kind than Polk's, suited to the television age—a crisis both in confidence and credibility. In 1965, Lyndon Johnson's Vietnam travails gave birth to the phrase "credibility gap," meaning the distance between a president's professions and the public's perceptions of reality. It took more than two years for Johnson's disapproval rating in the Gallup Poll to reach fifty-two percent in March 1968—a figure Bush long ago surpassed, but that was sufficient to persuade the proud LBJ not to seek re-election. Yet recently, just short of three years after Bush buoyantly declared "mission accomplished" in Iraq, his disapproval ratings have been running considerably higher than Johnson's, at about sixty percent. More than half the country now considers Bush dishonest and untrustworthy, and a decisive plurality consider him less trustworthy than his predecessor, Bill Clinton—a figure still attacked by conservative zealots as "Slick Willie."

Previous modern presidents, including Truman, Reagan and Clinton, managed to reverse plummeting ratings and regain the public's trust by shifting attention away from political and policy setbacks, and by overhauling the White House's inner circles. But Bush's publicly expressed view that he has made no major mistakes, coupled with what even the conservative commentator William F. Buckley Jr. calls his "high-flown pronouncements" about failed policies, seems to foreclose the first option. Upping the ante in the Middle East and bombing Iranian nuclear sites, a strategy reportedly favored by some in the White House, could distract the public and gain Bush immediate political capital in advance of the 2006 midterm elections—but in the long term might severely worsen the already dire situation in Iraq, especially among Shiite Muslims linked to the Iranians. And given Bush's ardent attachment to loyal aides, no matter how discredited, a major personnel shake-up is improbable, short of indictments. Replacing Andrew Card with Joshua Bolten as chief of staff—a move announced by the president in March in a tone that sounded more like defiance than contrition—represents a rededication to current policies and personnel, not a serious change. (Card, an old Bush family retainer, was widely considered more moderate than most of the men around the president and had little involvement in policy-making.) The power of Vice President Dick Cheney, meanwhile, remains uncurbed. Were Cheney to announce he is stepping down due to health problems, normally a polite pretext for a political removal, one can be reasonably certain it would be because Cheney actually did have grave health problems.

Bush at War

Until the twentieth century, American presidents managed foreign wars well—including those presidents who prosecuted unpopular wars. James Madison had no support from Federalist New England at the outset of the War of 1812, and the discontent grew amid mounting military setbacks in 1813. But Federalist political overreaching, combined with a reversal of America's military fortunes and the negotiation of a peace with Britain, made Madison something of a hero again and ushered in a brief so-called Era of Good Feelings in which his Jeffersonian Republican Party coalition ruled virtually unopposed. The Mexican War under Polk was even more unpopular, but its quick and victorious conclusion redounded to Polk's favor—much as the rapid American victory in the Spanish-American War helped William McKinley overcome anti-imperialist dissent.

The twentieth century was crueler to wartime presidents. After winning re-election in 1916 with the slogan "He Kept Us Out of War," Woodrow Wilson oversaw American entry into the First World War. Yet while the doughboys returned home triumphant, Wilson's idealistic and politically disastrous campaign for American entry into the League of Nations presaged a resurgence of the opposition Republican Party along with a redoubling of American isolationism that lasted until Pearl Harbor.

Bush has more in common with post-1945 Democratic presidents Truman and Johnson, who both became bogged down in overseas military conflicts with no end, let alone victory, in sight. But Bush has become bogged down in a singularly crippling way. On September 10th, 2001, he held among the lowest ratings of any modern president for that point in a first term. (Only Gerald Ford, his popularity reeling after his pardon of Nixon, had comparable numbers.) The attacks the following day transformed Bush's presidency, giving him an extraordinary opportunity to achieve greatness. Some of the early signs were encouraging. Bush's simple, unflinching eloquence and his quick toppling of the Taliban government in Afghanistan rallied the nation. Yet even then, Bush wasted his chance by quickly choosing partisanship over leadership.

No other president—Lincoln in the Civil War, FDR in World War II, John F. Kennedy at critical moments of the Cold War—faced with such a monumental set of military and political circumstances failed to embrace the opposing political party to help wage a truly national struggle. But Bush shut out and even demonized the Democrats. Top military advisers and even members of the president's own Cabinet who expressed any reservations or criticisms of his policies—including retired Marine Corps Gen. Anthony Zinni and former Treasury Secretary Paul O'Neill—suffered either dismissal, smear attacks from the president's supporters or investigations into their alleged breaches of national security. The wise men who counseled Bush's father, including James Baker and Brent Scowcroft, found their entreaties brusquely ignored by his son. When asked if he ever sought advice from the elder Bush, the president responded, "There is a higher Father that I appeal to."

All the while, Bush and the most powerful figures in the administration, Vice President Dick Cheney and Defense Secretary Donald Rumsfeld, were planting the seeds for the crises to come by diverting the struggle against Al Qaeda toward an all-out effort to topple their pre-existing target, Saddam Hussein. In a deliberate political decision, the administration stampeded the Congress and a traumatized citizenry into the Iraq invasion on the basis of what has now been demonstrated to be tendentious and perhaps fabricated evidence of an imminent Iraqi threat to American security, one that the White House suggested included nuclear weapons. Instead of emphasizing any political, diplomatic or humanitarian aspects of a war on Iraq—an appeal that would have sounded too "sensitive," as Cheney once sneered—the administration built a "Bush Doctrine" of unprovoked, preventive warfare, based on speculative threats and embracing principles previously abjured by every previous generation of U.S. foreign policy-makers, even at the height of the Cold War. The president did so with premises founded, in the case of Iraq, on wishful thinking. He did so while proclaiming an expansive Wilsonian rhetoric of making the world safe for democracy—yet discarding the multilateralism and systems of international law (including the Geneva Conventions) that emanated from Wilson's idealism. He did so while dismissing intelligence that an American invasion could spark a long and bloody civil war among Iraq's fierce religious and ethnic rivals, reports that have since proved true. And he did so after repeated warnings by military officials such as Gen. Eric

Shinseki that pacifying postwar Iraq would require hundreds of thousands of American troops—accurate estimates that Paul Wolfowitz and other Bush policy gurus ridiculed as "wildly off the mark."

When William F. Buckley, the man whom many credit as the founder of the modern conservative movement, writes categorically, as he did in February, that "one can't doubt that the American objective in Iraq has failed," then something terrible has happened. Even as a brash young iconoclast, Buckley always took the long view. The Bush White House seems incapable of doing so, except insofar as a tiny trusted circle around the president constantly reassures him that he is a messianic liberator and profound freedom fighter, on a par with FDR and Lincoln, and that history will vindicate his every act and utterance.

THE BIGGEST FAILURES

James Buchanan

Like Bush, Buchanan left the country more divided and acrimonious. As a Pennsylvania Democrat with friendly feelings for Southerners, Buchanan believed he could contain the mounting controversies over slavery by playing an even hand. Yet at crucial moments—the notorious Dred Scott decision and the bloody battles over slavery in Kansas—Buchanan tilted heavily to the South. When Lincoln's election in 1860 provoked Southern states to secede, Buchanan insisted the government lacked the power to stop them. His inaction verged on disloyalty—and handed his successor a nation already torn asunder.

Andrew Johnson

Johnson's efforts during Reconstruction were as disastrous as the rebuilding of Iraq. A Democrat from Tennessee who assumed the presidency after Lincoln's assassination, Johnson proved bitterly hostile to newly freed slaves. His opposition to the Civil Rights Act of 1866, which promoted civil and political rights for former slaves, prompted Congress to override a presidential veto of a major bill for the first time in history. Johnson's friendliness with ex-Confederates and defiance of Congress led to his impeachment in 1868; he escaped removal from office by a single vote after his trial in the Senate.

Herbert Hoover

The failure of Bush's domestic agenda is unmatched since Hoover. Running for president in 1928, Hoover declared that America had come closer to "the final triumph over poverty than ever before in the hisotry of any land." A year later, when the stock-market crash sparked the Great Depression, he oversaw loans to business and modest expansion of public works—but emphasized that caring for the unfortunate must remain primarily a local and voluntary effort. His upbeat insistence that "prosperity is just around the corner" backfired, resulting in a landslide for FDR.

Bush at Home

Bush came to office in 2001 pledging to govern as a "compassionate conserva-tive," more moderate on domestic policy than the dominant right wing of his party. The pledge proved hollow, as Bush tacked immediately to the hard right. Previous presidents and their parties have suffered when their actions have belied their campaign promises. Lyndon Johnson is the most conspicu-ous recent example, having declared in his 1964 run against the hawkish Republican Barry Goldwater that "we are not about to send American boys nine or ten thousand miles away from home to do what Asian boys ought to be doing for themselves." But no president has surpassed Bush in departing so thoroughly from his original campaign persona.

The heart of Bush's domestic policy has turned out to be nothing more than a series of massively regressive tax cuts—a return, with a vengeance, to the discredited Reagan-era supply-side faith that Bush's father once ridiculed as "voodoo economics." Bush crowed in triumph in February 2004, "We cut taxes, which basically meant people had more money in their pocket." The claim is bogus for the majority of Americans, as are claims that tax cuts have led to impressive new private investment and job growth. While wiping out the solid Clinton-era federal surplus and raising federal deficits to staggering record levels, Bush's tax policies have necessitated hikes in federal fees, state and local taxes, and co-payment charges to needy veterans and families who rely on Medicaid, along with cuts in loan programs to small businesses and college students, and in a wide range of state services. The lion's share of ben-efits from the tax cuts has gone to the very richest Americans, while new busi-ness investment has increased at a historically sluggish rate since the peak of the last business cycle five years ago. Private-sector job growth since 2001 has been anemic compared to the Bush administration's original forecasts and is chiefly attributable not to the tax cuts but to increased federal spending, especially on defense. Real wages for middle-income Americans have been dropping since the end of 2003: Last year, on average, nominal wages grew by only 2.4 percent, a meager gain that was completely erased by an average inflation rate of 3.4 percent.

The monster deficits, caused by increased federal spending combined with the reduction of revenue resulting from the tax cuts, have also placed Bush's administration in a historic class of its own with respect to government borrowing. According to the Treasury Department, the forty-two presidents who held office between 1789 and 2000 borrowed a combined total of $1.01 trillion from foreign governments and financial institutions. But between 2001 and 2005 alone, the Bush White House borrowed $1.05 trillion, more than all of the previous presidencies *combined*. Having inherited the largest federal surplus in American history in 2001, he has turned it into the largest deficit ever—with an even higher deficit, $423 billion, forecast for fiscal year 2006. Yet Bush—sounding much like Herbert Hoover in 1930 predicting that "prosperity is just around the corner"—insists that he will cut federal deficits in half by 2009, and that the best way to guarantee this would be to make permanent his tax cuts, which helped cause the deficit in the first place!

The rest of what remains of Bush's skimpy domestic agenda is either failed or failing—a record unmatched since the presidency of Herbert Hoover. The No Child Left Behind educational-reform act has proved so unwieldy, draconian and poorly funded that several states—including Utah, one of Bush's last remaining political strongholds—have fought to opt out of it entirely. White House proposals for immigration reform and a guest-worker program have succeeded mainly in dividing pro-business Republicans (who want more low-wage immigrant workers) from paleo-conservatives fearful that hordes of Spanish-speaking newcomers will destroy American culture. The paleos' call for tougher anti-immigrant laws—a return to the punitive spirit of exclusion that led to the notorious Immigration Act of 1924 that shut the door to immigrants from Southern and Eastern Europe—has in turn deeply alienated Hispanic voters from the Republican Party, badly undermining the GOP's hopes of using them to build a permanent national electoral majority. The recent pro-immigrant demonstrations, which drew millions of marchers nationwide, indicate how costly the Republican divide may prove.

The one noncorporate constituency to which Bush has consistently deferred is the Christian right, both in his selections for the federal bench and in his implications that he bases his policies on premillennialist, prophetic Christian doctrine. Previous presidents have regularly invoked the Almighty. McKinley is supposed to have fallen to his knees, seeking divine guidance about whether to take control of the Philippines in 1898, although the story may be apocryphal. But no president before Bush has allowed the press to disclose, through a close friend, his startling belief that he was ordained by God to lead the country. The White House's sectarian positions—over stem-cell research, the teaching of pseudoscientific "intelligent design," global population control, the Terri Schiavo spectacle and more—have led some to conclude that Bush has promoted the transformation of the GOP into what former Republican strategist Kevin Phillips calls "the first religious party in U.S. history."

Bush's faith-based conception of his mission, which stands above and beyond reasoned inquiry, jibes well with his administration's pro-business dogma on global warming and other urgent environmental issues. While forcing federally funded agencies to remove from their Web sites scientific information about reproductive health and the effectiveness of condoms in combating HIV/AIDS, and while peremptorily overruling staff scientists at the Food and Drug Administration on making emergency contraception available over the counter, Bush officials have censored and suppressed research findings they don't like by the Environmental Protection Agency, the Fish and Wildlife Service and the Department of Agriculture. Far from being the conservative he said he was, Bush has blazed a radical new path as the first American president in history who is outwardly hostile to science—dedicated, as a distinguished, bipartisan panel of educators and scientists (including forty-nine Nobel laureates) has declared, to "the distortion of scientific knowledge for partisan political ends."

The Bush White House's indifference to domestic problems and science alike culminated in the catastrophic responses to Hurricane Katrina. Scientists had long warned that global warming was intensifying hurricanes, but Bush ignored them—much as he and his administration sloughed off warnings from the director of the National Hurricane Center before Katrina hit. Reorganized under the Department of Homeland Security, the once efficient Federal Emergency Management Agency turned out, under Bush, to have become a nest of cronyism and incompetence. During the months immediately after the storm, Bush traveled to New Orleans eight times to promise massive rebuilding aid from the federal government. On March 30th, however, Bush's Gulf Coast recovery coordinator admitted that it could take as long as twenty-five years for the city to recover.

Karl Rove has sometimes likened Bush to the imposing, no-nonsense President Andrew Jackson. Yet Jackson took measures to prevent those he called "the rich and powerful" from bending "the acts of government to their selfish purposes." Jackson also gained eternal renown by saving New Orleans from British invasion against terrible odds. Generations of Americans sang of Jackson's famous victory. In 1959, Johnny Horton's version of "The Battle of New Orleans" won the Grammy for best country & western performance. If anyone sings about George W. Bush and New Orleans, it will be a blues number.

Presidential Misconduct

Virtually every presidential administration dating back to George Washington's has faced charges of misconduct and threats of impeachment against the president or his civil officers. The alleged offenses have usually involved matters of personal misbehavior and corruption, notably the payoff scandals that plagued Cabinet officials who served presidents Harding and Ulysses S. Grant. But the charges have also included alleged usurpation of power by the president and serious criminal conduct that threatens constitutional government and the rule of law—most notoriously, the charges that led to the impeachments of Andrew Johnson and Bill Clinton, and to Richard Nixon's resignation.

Historians remain divided over the actual grievousness of many of these allegations and crimes. Scholars reasonably describe the graft and corruption around the Grant administration, for example, as gargantuan, including a kickback scandal that led to the resignation of Grant's secretary of war under the shadow of impeachment. Yet the scandals produced no indictments of Cabinet secretaries and only one of a White House aide, who was acquitted. By contrast, the most scandal-ridden administration in the modern era, apart from Nixon's, was Ronald Reagan's, now widely remembered through a haze of nostalgia as a paragon of virtue. A total of twenty-nine Reagan officials, including White House national security adviser Robert McFarlane and deputy chief of staff Michael Deaver, were convicted on charges stemming from the Iran-Contra affair, illegal lobbying and a looting scandal inside the Department of Housing and Urban Development. Three Cabinet officers—HUD Secretary Samuel Pierce, Attorney General Edwin Meese and Secretary of Defense Caspar Weinberger—left their posts under clouds of scandal. In contrast, not a single official in the Clinton administration was even indicted over his or her White House duties, despite repeated high-profile investigations and a successful, highly partisan impeachment drive.

The full report, of course, has yet to come on the Bush administration. Because Bush, unlike Reagan or Clinton, enjoys a fiercely partisan and loyal majority in Congress, his administration has been spared scrutiny. Yet that mighty advantage has not prevented the indictment of Vice President Dick Cheney's chief of staff, I. Lewis "Scooter" Libby, on charges stemming from an alleged major security breach in the Valerie Plame matter. (The last White House official of comparable standing to be indicted while still in office was Grant's personal secretary, in 1875.) It has not headed off the unprecedented scandal involving Larry Franklin, a high-ranking Defense Department official, who has pleaded guilty to divulging classified information to a foreign power while working at the Pentagon—a crime against national security. It has not forestalled the arrest and indictment of Bush's top federal procurement official, David Safavian, and the continuing investigations into Safavian's intrigues with the disgraced Republican lobbyist Jack Abramoff, recently sentenced to nearly six years in prison—investigations in which some prominent Republicans, including former Christian Coalition executive director Ralph Reed (and current GOP aspirant for lieutenant governor of Georgia) have already been implicated, and could well produce the largest congressional corruption scandal in American history. It has not dispelled the cloud of possible indictment that hangs over others of Bush's closest advisers.

History may ultimately hold Bush in the greatest contempt for expanding the powers of the presidency beyond the limits laid down by the U.S. Constitution. There has always been a tension over the constitutional roles of the three branches of the federal government. The Framers intended as much, as part of the system of checks and balances they expected would minimize tyranny. When Andrew Jackson took drastic measures against the nation's banking system, the Whig Senate censured him for conduct "dangerous to the liberties of the people." During the Civil War, Abraham Lincoln's emergency decisions to suspend habeas corpus while Congress was out of session in 1861 and 1862 has led some Americans, to this day, to regard him as a despot. Richard Nixon's conduct of the war in Southeast Asia and his covert domestic-surveillance programs prompted Congress to pass new statutes regulating executive power.

By contrast, the Bush administration—in seeking to restore what Cheney, a Nixon administration veteran, has called "the legitimate authority of the presidency"—threatens to overturn the Framers' healthy tension in favor of presidential absolutism. Armed with legal findings by his attorney general (and personal lawyer) Alberto Gonzales, the Bush White House has declared that the president's powers as commander in chief in wartime are limitless. No previous wartime president has come close to making so grandiose a claim. More specifically, this administration has asserted that the president is perfectly free to violate federal laws on such matters as domestic surveillance and the torture of detainees. When Congress has passed legislation to limit those assertions, Bush has resorted to issuing constitutionally dubious "signing statements," which declare, by fiat, how he will interpret and execute the law in question, even when that interpretation flagrantly violates the will of Congress. Earlier presidents, including Jackson, raised hackles by offering their own view of the Constitution in order to justify vetoing congressional acts. Bush doesn't bother with that: He signs the legislation (eliminating any risk that Congress will overturn a veto), and then governs how he pleases— using the signing statements as if they were line-item vetoes. In those instances when Bush's violations of federal law have come to light, as over domestic surveillance, the White House has devised a novel solution: Stonewall any investigation into the violations and bid a compliant Congress simply to rewrite the laws.

Bush's alarmingly aberrant take on the Constitution is ironic. One need go back in the record less than a decade to find prominent Republicans railing against far more minor presidential legal infractions as precursors to all-out totalitarianism. "I will have no part in the creation of a constitutional double-standard to benefit the president," Sen. Bill Frist declared of Bill Clinton's efforts to conceal an illicit sexual liaison. "No man is above the law, and no man is below the law—that's the principle that we all hold very dear in this country," Rep. Tom DeLay asserted. "The rule of law protects you and it protects me from the midnight fire on our roof or the 3 A.M. knock on our door," warned Rep. Henry Hyde, one of Clinton's chief accusers. In the face of Bush's more defini-tive dismissal of federal law, the silence from these quarters is deafening.

The president's defenders stoutly contend that war-time conditions fully justify Bush's actions. And as Lincoln showed during the Civil War, there may be times of military emergency where the executive believes it imperative to take immediate, highly irregular, even unconstitutional steps. "I felt that mea-sures, otherwise unconstitutional, might become lawful," Lincoln wrote in 1864, "by becoming indispensable to the preservation of the Constitution, through the preservation of the nation." Bush seems to think that, since 9/11, he has been placed, by the grace of God, in the same kind of situation Lincoln faced. But Lincoln, under pressure of daily combat on American soil against fellow Americans, did not operate in secret, as Bush has. He did not claim, as Bush has, that his emergency actions were wholly regular and constitutional as well as necessary; Lincoln sought and received Congressional authorization for his suspension of habeas corpus in 1863. Nor did Lincoln act under the amorphous cover of a "war on terror"—a war against a tactic, not a specific nation or political entity, which could last as long as any president deems the tactic a threat to national security. Lincoln's exceptional measures were intended to survive only as long as the Confederacy was in rebellion. Bush's could be extended indefinitely, as the president sees fit, permanently endan-gering rights and liberties guaranteed by the Constitution to the citizenry.

THE GREATEST SUCCESSES

George Washington

Unlike Bush, whose contested election sharply divided the country, the greatest hero of the American Revolution was named the nation's first presi-dent nearly by acclamation, which gave the new national government imme-diate credibility. During Washington's presidency, the federal machinery sketched out by the Constitution took shape. Although criticized for his administration's pomp. Washington renounced the role of Patriot King that many Americans would have gladly given him and stepped down after his second term.

Abraham Lincoln

Lincoln, under pressure of daily combat on American soil, did not flout the law in secret, as Bush has. He welcomed rival voices in his own cabinet, and his unconstitutional actions were ultimately approved by Congress and intended to survive only as long as the Confederacy was in rebellion. Although he came to office as moderate Republican willing to accept slavery where it already existed, he responded to Southern secession by deftly keeping border states in the Union—and by issuing his famous Emancipation Proclamation of 1863, turning the war for the Union into a war to free the slaves.

Franklin Delano Roosevelt

While Bush adheres to a simplistic ideology in the face of changing realities, Roosevelt fought the Great Depression by engaging in relentless experimentation. His sweeping new programs aided businesses and the unemployed, created jobs, and improved public housing and the nation's infrastucture, notably with the Tennessee Valley Authority. After his election to an unprecedented third term, when the Japanese attack on Pearl Harbor precipitated American entry into the Second World War, Roosevelt again altered course, changing, as he put it, from "Dr. New Deal" to "Dr. Win the War."

Much as Bush still enjoys support from those who believe he can do no wrong, he now suffers opposition from liberals who believe he can do no right. Many of these liberals are in the awkward position of having supported Bush in the past, while offering little coherent as an alternative to Bush's policies now. Yet it is difficult to see how this will benefit Bush's reputation in history.

The president came to office calling himself "a uniter, not a divider" and promising to soften the acrimonious tone in Washington. He has had two enormous opportunities to fulfill those pledges: first, in the noisy aftermath of his controversial election in 2000, and, even more, after the attacks of September 11th, when the nation pulled behind him as it has supported no other president in living memory. Yet under both sets of historically unprecedented circumstances, Bush has chosen to act in ways that have left the country less united and more divided, less conciliatory and more acrimonious— much like James Buchanan, Andrew Johnson and Herbert Hoover before him. And, like those three predecessors, Bush has done so in the service of a rigid ideology that permits no deviation and refuses to adjust to changing realities. Buchanan failed the test of Southern secession, Johnson failed in the face of Reconstruction, and Hoover failed in the face of the Great Depression. Bush has failed to confront his own failures in both domestic and international affairs, above all in his ill-conceived responses to radical Islamic terrorism.

Having confused steely resolve with what Ralph Waldo Emerson called "a foolish consistency . . . adored by little statesmen," Bush has become entangled in tragedies of his own making, compounding those visited upon the country by outside forces.

No historian can responsibly predict the future with absolute certainty. There are too many imponderables still to come in the two and a half years left in Bush's presidency to know exactly how it will look in 2009, let alone in 2059. There have been presidents—Harry Truman was one—who have left office in seeming disgrace, only to rebound in the estimates of later scholars. But so far the facts are not shaping up propitiously for George W. Bush. He still does his best to deny it. Having waved away the lessons of history in the making of his decisions, the present-minded Bush doesn't seem to be concerned about his place in history. "History. We won't know," he told the journalist Bob Woodward in 2003. "We'll all be dead."

Another president once explained that the judgments of history cannot be defied or dismissed, even by a president. "Fellow citizens, *we* cannot escape history," said Abraham Lincoln. "We of this Congress and this administration, will be remembered in spite of ourselves. No personal significance, or insignificance, can spare one or another of us. The fiery trial through which we pass, will light us down, in honor or dishonor, to the latest generation."

Conrad Black

 **NO**

George W. Bush, FDR, and History

The American, and to an extent the international media, many rubbing their eyes with disbelief, are starting to contemplate the possibility that George W. Bush may be a president of great historical significance. Disparaged by opponents as an accidental president, or even the beneficiary of a stolen election, and regarded even by many of his supporters as a man of insufficient intellect for his office, the ambitions he has revealed for his second term have prompted comparisons (in the *Financial Times* and elsewhere) with Franklin D. Roosevelt, who, the President says, "fascinates" him.

These comparisons with FDR are overdone. Unlike Roosevelt, George W. Bush did not enter office with unemployment at 33 percent, a collapsed banking system and farm prices, nearly half the homes in the country threatened by foreclosure and eviction. Nor will he likely have to face any such prospect as a Nazi takeover of Europe. He is unlikely to have to lead the nation to victory in the greatest war in history, and he doesn't have to conduct his office from a wheelchair, while disguising from the public the extent of his infirmity.

Some Republican traditionalists and liberal alarmists have invoked Roosevelt by predicting that Bush will now try to undo what is left of the New Deal. There is no truth in this, unless he succumbs to second term dementia and tries to abolish the FDIC guarantee of bank deposits, and to restore Prohibition.

President Bush was obliged to focus on foreign crises in his first term, and is moving to domestic reform in his second. Roosevelt dealt with the economic emergency in his first year, structural reforms such as Social Security in his second year, cranked up his workfare programs as required for the next three years, eliminated remaining unemployment with defense production and conscription in the two years before Pearl Harbor, and concluded the New Deal with the GI Bill of Rights in 1944. Prior to World War II, there wasn't much American foreign policy.

Roosevelt did say in the 1940 election campaign that "we are going to build a country in which no one is left out," but there is no evidence that President Bush thought he was paraphrasing him when he took up the same theme. President Bush has neither the regal bearing, nor the oratorical powers, nor the protean qualities of FDR.

From *The American Spectator*, April 2005, pp. 26–30, 32–33. Copyright © 2005 by American Spectator, LLC. Reprinted by permission.

Yet, with a completely different style and timetable, George W. Bush could come closer to replicating FDR's importance as both a foreign and domestic policy president than all Roosevelt's other successors in that office.

❧

Electoral facts invite a reassessment by those who did not take the president seriously before. Bill Clinton and George W. Bush are the first successive presidents of opposing parties to win two consecutive terms in American history, and the first consecutive two-term presidents since Madison and Monroe (1809–1825). The President is only the sixteenth of 42 holders of that office to win two terms, the fifteenth to win two consecutive terms, the thirteenth to win two consecutive contested terms, and, if he serves out this term in good health, he will be only the sixth president since the emergence of the modern party and electoral system (in the Jackson era) to do so. Of his five predecessors in this category, only U. S. Grant and Franklin D. Roosevelt led parties that controlled both houses of Congress in their second terms. Grant, though he rendered immense service to the country, was a largely ineffectual president. Hence the frequent current comparisons with FDR.

Incredulous media commentators endlessly repeat that George W. Bush's poll ratings are ten points below those of Ronald Reagan and Bill Clinton when they started their second terms. (They are also 20 percent below Roosevelt's when he began his third term.) This isn't really relevant. Bush and his advisers have mastered the technique of concentrating adequate political force at strategic legislative points. In the 2004 election they brought out conservative voters by putting referenda on the emotive issue of same-sex marriage on ballots in eleven states, eliciting the margin of victory in a number of those states. Bush is adequately, though not overwhelmingly, popular, but he is overwhelmingly tactically agile.

Reagan's and Clinton's partisans did not control both houses of Congress when they were re-elected. Neither did the Republicans when Dwight D. Eisenhower and Richard Nixon won landslide reelection victories. There is more of a comparison with Lyndon Johnson when he won a crushing victory in 1964 to a full term after succeeding the assassinated John F. Kennedy. President Johnson did have an ambitious program and a friendly Congress, and great legislative aptitudes, but most of his Great Society program, apart from his immense contribution to civil rights, has been a debatable legacy.

LBJ's term swiftly became mired in Vietnam. Some Democrats and media skeptics have tried to claim that the same fate awaits President Bush, but this is nonsense. Congress has fully authorized the action in Iraq, which it did not in Vietnam, the forces committed are scarcely a quarter of those at their highest point in Vietnam, and the American casualty rates are at less than 5 percent of the Vietnam level through most of that war. Despite the impositions on the National Guard, this is still essentially a volunteer military; the enemy is not being fed by overt foreign intervention on the lines of the North Vietnamese, nor by great power suppliers, as the Soviets and Chinese stoked up the enemy in Vietnam. Where Ho Chi Minh was a widely respected figure, almost no one disputes that the world is better off without Saddam Hussein, and the Iraqi election is an unanswerable legitimization of the efforts to promote power-sharing and reasonable wealth-distribution in the Middle East.

The debate over weapons of mass destruction, like the arguments that the United States should first have tracked down Osama bin Laden or secured a permanent resolution of the Israeli-Palestinian dispute before removing Saddam, was a side-show (and pretexts for doing nothing). George W. Bush prevented the United Nations, against the wishes of its own secretary general and most of the corrupt despotisms that compose much of its membership, from becoming a toothless talking society like the League of Nations, as he promised in 2003 to the General Assembly that he would (after Saddam had ignored 17 Security Council resolutions).

More importantly, he has discovered and proclaimed the only method of reversing 13 centuries of retreat by the Arab world. Though most Arabs would not spontaneously put it this way, Arab power and influence have been in retreat since the defeat of the Moors at the Battle of Tours (or Poitiers) in 732. The Arab armies were driven out of France and slowly expelled from Europe, and almost all the Arabs were eventually colonized. To conventional modern Arab opinion, their final humiliation was the establishment of the State of Israel in what Arabs claim to be Arab land, as an apparent consolation by the Great Powers for the crimes the Jews had suffered in Europe in the 1930s and '40s. The existence of Israel has been a hairshirt for the Arabs for nearly 60 years, the ultimate, constant demonstration of their enfeeblement.

If Iraq develops some plausible institutions of power-sharing and popular consultation and wealth distribution, even stopping well short of the highest standards of electoral and social democracy in the West, it will give the Arab masses a model for government that they will eventually judge to be preferable to the tyrannies in the major Arab powers that oppress their peoples, steal and squander their money, and distract them with what should be the red herring of Israel.

There were certainly some serious intelligence shortcomings before September 11, 2001, and before the invasion of Iraq. There were also costly mistakes in the early occupation phase. But these are overshadowed by the potential benefit of a reformed Iraq.

The congratulations on the Iraqi election from the president of Egypt and the head of the Arab League; the virtual Thatcherization of the Egyptian economy and Hosni Mubarak's promise of "freer" elections, the cross-community reconciliations in Lebanon in defiance of the Syrians despite the recent assassination of the leading advocate of conciliation, the self-redemption of Qaddafi, and the emergence among the Palestinians of an authentically elected leadership that is apparently prepared to discourage terrorism and seek a two-state permanent agreement with Israel, are all, at least in part, early manifestations of the impact of the Bush policy.

This is the rationale for the nation-building effort in Iraq, and the only possible method of eliminating the danger of endless Muslim, and especially Arab Muslim, disaffection on a scale that could be a menace to the whole world. If successful, this will be as great a strategic achievement as any

American president's except for Lincoln's victory in the Civil War, Franklin Roosevelt's contribution to victory in World War II and his engagement of the United States durably in Europe and the Far East, and Harry Truman's championship of NATO and the Marshall Plan, and his resistance to communism in Korea and Greece and Turkey. It would rank with Richard Nixon's normalization of relations with China and pursuit of nuclear arms limitations with the Soviet Union; and with Ronald Reagan's ultimate bloodless victory in the Cold War. (The Louisiana Purchase was also an epochal event, but the United States would eventually have seized that territory if Napoleon had not sold it to Jefferson.) This would put the current President in far more distinguished company than his detractors could imagine with any equanimity.

~◉~

The President's detractors are fond of claiming that he doesn't understand all these issues. But he has sketched out his motives much more clearly than Franklin D. Roosevelt described his plans, even to intimates, for assuring the defeat of the Berlin-Tokyo Axis in the world and the isolationists at home, and the renaissance of France, Germany, Italy, and Japan as democratic allies of the Americans and British. Roosevelt has justly received the credit for that inspired policy. President Bush cannot be denied the credit and responsibility for his ambitious plan to reorient the Arab world.

He has already had an immense success in discouraging terrorism. The tepid responses of the Clinton administration to the Kobar Towers, USS *Cole*, and Nairobi and Dar es Salaam embassy bombings invited the escalation that climaxed on September 11, 2001. The Bush administration should have been better prepared than it was for the assault. But since then, despite the belligerent videos of bin Laden and others, the terrorists managed only a few incidents, serious though the attacks in Madrid and Bali, in particular, were. There have been no further attacks on the United States. The cumulative effects of the international terror campaign have not amounted to 15 percent of the human devastation of 9/11/01. At the same time, thousands of terrorists and of their more promising recruits have been killed or captured. Large numbers of them have been attracted to Iraq and eliminated there, and their methods have been thoroughly discredited. No government in the world would now openly promote or assist terrorism in the way Afghanistan, Iraq, Yemen, Syria, Iran, and some other countries had been routinely doing prior to the President's response to the World Trade Center and Pentagon outrages.

The President and his advisers recognized that much of the professed solidarity with America after the 9/11 attacks was an attempt by fundamentally irresolute governments to gain leverage on the American official response to the attacks. There was also, behind the genuine sadness of all civilized people at the murder of thousands of innocent civilians, and the general respect for the bravery of New York's firemen and for the spirit of that city generally, an unspoken consolability at the novel thought of America as a victim. The President made it clear on the evening of the attacks that the United States would not remain a victim for long, that it would make no distinction between terrorists and countries that harbored or assisted terrorists, and that other governments would be judged by their conduct, as for or against the United States.

Though these positions could have been more subtly implemented at times, especially with traditional allies, they were the right policy. Anything less would have yielded to the collegiality sought by the rest of the world: that the United States is like a great St. Bernard that will do the work and take the risks, while foreigners, especially Europeans, hold the leash and give the orders. There was an informal attempt to divide the anti-terrorist world between the wronged country which had the power to resolve the problem by imposition of its military might, and the more "moderate" allies, who substituted moral shilly-shallying and even spitefulness for the strength they did not possess (because of their own lassitude and not a lack of resources).

Modern American foreign and security policy was established by President Roosevelt in 1941 in two speeches to the Congress. In January of that year, he warned that the country "must always be wary of those who with 'sounding brass and tinkling cymbal' would preach the 'ism' of appeasement." In December, in calling for a declaration of war after the attack on Pearl Harbor, he promised that the nation would "make very certain that this form of treachery never again endangers us." Ever since, the United States has not been an appeasement power and it has possessed and deployed sufficient deterrent strength to assure that no other state overtly attacked it.

On September 11, 2001, elements that thought they had found a way around American deterrence directly attacked the American civil population for the first time in history (other than, in hindsight, the first attack on the World Trade Center in 1993). Nothing less than President Bush's immediate and continuing response was necessary for the retention of the strength of American deterrence, which administrations of both parties have maintained for 60 years. No other country remotely possesses such deterrent capacity, and no ally, no matter how genuine, could be relied upon to advocate what was necessary to uphold this cornerstone of American national security.

Franklin D. Roosevelt, behind the façade of the United Nations, sought and achieved an imbalance of power in favor of the United States. The Soviet Union managed a serious military and subversive (and even in some misguided circles, intellectual) threat for 45 years before collapsing under the weight of the competition. The imbalance of power in America's favor that Roosevelt sought now exists and cannot be disguised. Many governments and intelligent people in the world are uncomfortable with American preeminence. But instead of reviling President Bush, they shall either have to accommodate to America's position, as Tony Blair does, or develop the strength and coherence to earn a greater voice in the world, as the Chinese seem to be trying to do.

The effort of the French and Germans and Russians to stand on each others' shoulders and obstruct the United States' Iraq policy, in the name of misplaced self-righteousness, was contemptible, and Bush was right to respond to it accordingly. And now he is right to mend his fences with those countries, having made his point that America will not compromise where its own security is at stake.

If this had been George W. Bush's only major foreign policy accomplishment, it would have been an entitlement to a serious position among foreign policy presidents. Assisting the Arab world to slough its tendency to corruption, despotism, and political failure; to evolve from a source of instability in the world to a justified recovery of the pride of an ancient people with a once-distinguished history, will, if he is successful, make him an outstanding foreign policy president.

⋅◦❀◦⋅

In domestic policy, the President has defeated what had threatened to become a severe recession, introduced tax cuts as important as those of Coolidge, Kennedy-Johnson, or Reagan and launched the most comprehensive educational reform in decades. He has pledged to overhaul, partially privatize, and preemptively rescue Social Security from actuarial problems, and make medical care more accessible and efficient, partly through tort reform. If he is largely successful in achieving his domestic goals, Bush would be, next to FDR, the most important domestic policy president in the country's history (excluding Lincoln's conduct of the Civil War, which does not meet normal criteria for domestic policy).

President Truman had limited success and not a great deal of originality in domestic affairs. President Nixon had more success than his legions of frenzied enemies concede, but his record was obscured and durably diminished by the Watergate debacle, even allowing for the subsidence of cant and emotionalism he attracted over much of his career. President Reagan's domestic achievements consisted mainly of his tax cuts and simplifications, the economic boom, and his genius for inspiriting the nation after Vietnam, Watergate, and the dreariness of the Carter interregnum.

The other presidents of living memory, even so elegant a leader as John F. Kennedy, so revered a president as Dwight D. Eisenhower, the obviously very able Bill Clinton, and this president's own father, were, in domestic policy terms, more or less capable caretakers. The great achievements of the Clinton administration—apart from good fiscal order, which didn't require tax increases on the scale of those that he inflicted—such as welfare reform and the Crime Bill, were largely the work of the Republican leaders in the Congress.

Theodore Roosevelt's domestic claim to greatness consists of a bout of trust-busting, and heightened railway regulation, meat-packing, and food and drug labeling legislation, and hortatory encouragements to conservation. Woodrow Wilson's rests on the Federal Reserve Act, the Clayton Anti-Trust Act, and the establishment of the Federal Trade Commission. Andrew Jackson is remembered for promoting federal government assistance to public works and suppressing secessionism, as well as decentralizing banking (causing a severe recession that swamped his hand-chosen successor). These are all significant, and TR and Wilson and Jackson were all important presidents, but George W. Bush is well placed to surpass them in the significance of his legislation.

No one expects that President Bush will easily enact his imaginative proposals for Social Security, Medicare, tort reform, durable tax reduction and simplification, and education. The partisan antagonism in the Congress is severe. But though the Republicans have only slender majorities in both houses and their party discipline is not infallible, the President is stirring public desire for action on these issues. The President has the initiative over the dazed and listless Democrats. He will have to make some concessions, but it is a reasonable supposition that he will achieve a large part of what he seeks. Even if he does not, his historical claims will rest on his foreign policy record, his tax reductions, and his education reforms. This would still be a defensible performance that would bear comparison with most of his predecessors.

His fiscal policy remains fuzzy and his pledge of spending and deficit reductions is not entirely plausible. A $650 billion current account deficit is obviously intolerable. It is not quite as grim as it appears, because about a third of it is foreign operations of American companies selling back into the United States to the ultimate profit of American shareholders. A legitimate modernization of calculation methods would deal with this. Another third is excessive oil prices and imports. This could at least be moderated by pursuing exploration and alternate energy sources more aggressively and by selling infrastructure to more consensually governed oil-exporting countries, starting with Iraq. Most of the rest of the current account deficit is effectively dumping, especially by the Chinese. This too can be combated, as some Democrats are already demanding. But it will require subtlety and perseverance to do it without provoking serious economic and strategic friction, so addicted have China and some other countries become to their ability to export on a massive and exploitive scale to the United States. Waiting for the development of an electric automobile is not an adequate response to the trade deficit.

Bush's Treasury secretaries have not had the weight of such recent holders of that office as John Connolly, George Shultz, William Simon, James Baker, Lloyd Bentsen, and Robert Rubin. He never should have signed Sarbanes-Oxley, which mires all public companies in an almost impenetrable thicket of compliance rules (see Robert L. Bartley, "No Profit: The Craze to Reform Corporate Accounting Gets Things Exactly Backward," *TAS*, December 2003-January 2004). And in addition to taking credit in his State of the Union message for prosecuting corporate criminals, the President should also discourage the arraignment of the entire corporate executive class of the country as embezzlers by his enemies in the media and overzealous prosecutors. There are now signs that this onslaught of what at times approached corporate McCarthyism is subsiding.

∼◉∼

The group of so-called value issues represents core beliefs certainly, but they are also rallying points to the President's natural supporters on specific issues, as with the same-sex marriage question. Where Bill Clinton confused the Republicans by stealing certain natural Republican issues, as in adding 100,000 policemen, George W. Bush presses the seven values buttons to produce irresistible support for measures only slightly related to the values invoked.

President Bush could not seriously imagine that he will get a constitutional amendment about the nature of marriage, any more than Ronald Reagan thought he would get one about abortion or school prayer. That he wishes a distinction between marriage and a homosexual union of equivalent legal standing is reasonable. The stem-cell research controversy is a harder sell. The moral issues this leads to are serious and troubling, but the scientific possibilities for longer and healthier lives may not be met by his present position. Some fine-tuning should be possible and sincere Christians should be able to accept the sort of research advocated by Ronald Reagan Jr. at last year's Democratic convention.

Complaints about Bush's excessive religiosity are hard to take seriously. Franklin D. Roosevelt referred to God so often that Molotov asked Averell Harriman how an intelligent man could be so preoccupied with religion. In his first Inaugural Address he said: "Our problems, thank God, concern only material things." All his major speeches had some reference to God in them and his address on D-Day, one of the greatest of his career, was ostensibly a prayer. Dwight Eisenhower, unlike Roosevelt, was not a particularly religious man, but he began his first Inaugural Address with a prayer. Ronald Reagan wasn't a great publicly observant religious communicant either, but he began his acceptance speech of his first presidential nomination with a minute of silence in prayer for the country. All presidents bandy God about. The tastefulness of doing so is open to legitimate discussion, but the incumbent should not be unfairly singled out.

At a strictly tactical level, when the United States' most visible foreign enemy is a group of fanatical Muslim terrorists and terrorist-sponsors, it is helpful to make the point that America is not only a center of commercialization, glitz, permissiveness, and self-indulgence. The world should know that it is also a brave country that acts on belief, including a variety of widely and strongly held religious beliefs, and that the bin Laden theory that it is soft, decadent, and cowardly is a dangerous misperception.

The United States had to overcome the political legacy of Vietnam, the Beirut bombing, and Mogadishu: that it had no staying power and could not endure the sight of body bags, no matter what the cause. Every American death in Iraq is a great sadness (that much of the media mawkishly amplifies), but each is also a sacrifice in a noble cause and a reaffirmation of American moral strength. There is little evidence that the President is pandering more than rhetorically to the religious right, in judicial appointments or otherwise. To be a traditionalist is not to be a toady to a faction.

George W. Bush does not have the heroic qualities of Andrew Jackson, drummer-boy in the Revolutionary war, victorious general, champion of the frontier and of the Common Man. He has none of the panache or urbanity of the Roosevelts, the intellect or articulation of Woodrow Wilson. He does not possess the hypnotic oratorical powers or (as far as we know) the human qualities of Ronald Reagan that enabled him, with a bullet in his chest and a collapsed lung, to stroll into the hospital operating room and say that he hoped the assembled doctors and nurses were all Republicans. I doubt that even Karl Rove, brilliant political operator though he undoubtedly is, would claim that

President Bush has the prepossessing personal stature of Lincoln, Washington, or Jefferson.

If he has a precedent, it could be James Knox Polk, who was rather color-less and somewhat overshadowed by such contemporaries as Henry Clay, Daniel Webster, and John C. Calhoun. But as president, he settled relations with Britain, especially the northern border, won the Mexican war, adding Texas, California, and New Mexico to the country, reduced tariffs, and restored an independent treasury system. Polk is generally reckoned by histo-rians to be one of the country's ten best presidents. Everything is to scale. These are much more complicated times, the United States is an unprecedent-edly formidable world power, and George W., unlike Polk (who did not seek re-election), is a two-term president.

The substantial achievement of his foreign and domestic objectives would install George W. Bush as the most important president since FDR, and, except for FDR, possibly the most important president since Lincoln. What he and his advisers recognize, even if most of the media do not, is that he can be a great president by concentrating his great tactical political ability on spe-cific ambitious goals. The general perception of him may continue to lag his objective accomplishments, for a time. This doesn't affect a president's perfor-mance or historical standing and has been the lot of many other presidents, including Truman, Eisenhower, and Nixon.

At the mid-point in his administration, George W. Bush has been a suc-cessful president. He has indisputable aptitudes for leadership, unquestion-able courage and integrity, and a chance to be one of America's great leaders. All who wish America and its enduring values well, should wish him well, including millions of people in the United States and throughout the world who now profess to dislike, disparage, or fear him.

POSTSCRIPT

Is George W. Bush the Worst President in American History?

Conrad Black, a well-to-do conservative publisher, recently wrote a massive and surprisingly favorable biography of *Franklin Delano Roosevelt: Champion of Freedom* (Public Affair, 2003). In the article reprinted in this reader, he argues that President George W. Bush is "the most important president since FDR, and except for FDR, possibly the most important president since Lincoln." This is high praise for a president whose public polling ratings in the spring of 2006 are in the mid- to low-thirtieth percentile.

But Black takes the long view. He compares Bush's 9/11 response to the terrorist attacks on the World Trade Center's twin towers, in New York City to FDR's response to the isolationists and appeasers of Hitler and the Japanese before and after the Pearl Harbor attack on December 7, 1941. Like FDR, says Black, President Bush sought to take advantage of America's paramount position in the world by strengthening the enfeebled United Nations in his own response to the defiance by Saddam Hussein of the organization's resolutions.

Black delivers a spirited defense of both foreign and domestic policies of the president. He defends nation-building in Iraq, arguing rather nastily "that Arab power and influence have been in retreat with the exception of Israel since the defeat of the Moors at the Battle of Tours in 732." He also argues that the president's tax cut, and his attempts to overhaul Social Security, reform Medicare, and engage in a comprehensive "no child left behind" education reform will surpass the domestic achievements of all other twentieth-century presidents, with the exception of FDR.

Contrary to his critics on the left, Black downplays Bush's right-wing agenda, arguing that he does not want to undo the New Deal, he appoints conservatives and not religious zealots to office, and uses "values" issues to rally his supporters. Furthermore, Bush's religious views are no different from that of previous presidents, especially FDR who invoked God's name on innumerable occasions.

Professor Wilentz believes that Bush will be ranked among the lowest presidents long after he leaves office. Instead of comparing him with FDR and Lincoln as Black does, Wilentz compares Bush's failures to those of Buchanan, who failed to stop the Southern secession from the union; of Andrew Johnson, who made a debacle of Reconstruction; and of Hoover, who was inflexible in his responses to the Great Depression. Both authors compare Bush with the reticent Polk, with Black crediting him for successful expansionist acquisitions in the Southwest after the Mexican War.

Wilentz believes that President Bush has abused the power of the presidency with policies that permit the torture of detainees and the wiretapping of phone calls by the National Security Agency (NSA) without obtaining a court order. He also argues that he is waging "an unlimited war" on terror and refuses to follow Lincoln's example of consulting dissenting opinions from his cabinet. Bush, he argues, never consulted with the Democratic leadership and shut down dissenting voices of military generals like retired General Andrew Zunni, General Eric Shinseki, and his own father's National Security Chief Brent Scocroft, who pointed out potential problems in rebuilding Iraq once Hussein was overthrown.

Wilentz also sees President Bush as much more radical in his religious views than Black. Not even FDR ever said, as Bush has, that he was ordained by God to lead the country. Bush's positions on stem-cell research, global population control, intelligent design as replacement for evolution, the Terri Shiavo fiasco, and his appointments to the federal bench appear to be more than a mere nod and a wink to the Christian right. For a critical view of Bush's religious views, see Peter Singer, *The President of Good and Evil: The Ethics of George W. Bush* (Dutton, 2004). But Stephen Mansfield defends *The Faith of George W. Bush* (Penguin Group, Inc., 2003).

Where Black and Wilentz differ the most is on the consequences of Bush's economic policies. Conservatives like Black see the tax cuts as a stimulus and the deficits a matter of correcting the bookkeeping methods. Wilentz believes that Bush has geared tax cuts to the richest while real wages for middle-income Americans have been dropping since the end of 2003. In short, Bush took a Clinton surplus and raised "the federal deficits to staggering record levels."

Will the indictment of Dick Cheney's Chief of Staff Lewis "Scooter" Libby for a security breach in outing a CIA agent or the intrigues of convicted lobbyist Jack Abramoff with prominent Republicans tarnish the Bush administration in the verdict of history? Will the lowest sustained polls in history for an incumbent president matter? Or is President Bush correct when he responded to reporter Bob Woodward about his historical reputation? "History," Bush said, "we won't know. We'll all be dead."

The bibliography on the American presidency is enormous. The renowned diplomatic historian Thomas A. Bailey's older *Presidential Greatness: The Image and the Man from George Washington to the Present* (Appleton-Century, 1966) discusses the political biases in the Schlesinger surveys, the importance of fortuities, temperament, personalities, as well as the roles of the presidency. Bailey also gives his summary reassessments from George Washington through Lyndon Johnson. Lewis L. Gould argues that *The Modern American Presidency* (University Press of Kansas, 2003) began in the McKinley administration, whose presidential secretary George Cortelyou made the administration of the office more efficient in dealing with reporters and issues that needed immediate action. In *The American Presidency: An Intellectual History* (University Press of Kansas, 1994), conservative historian Forrest McDonald concentrates on the eighteenth- and nineteenth-century roots and establishment of the presidency before deploring its institutional decline by the late twentieth century. Liberal pundit Eric Altman also deplores the lies told during the Yalta Conference, the Cuban Missile Crisis, the Gulf of Tonkin incidents, the Iran-Contra scandal, and George W. Bush's "post-truth" presidency in *When Presidents Lie: A History of Official Deception and Its Consequences* (Viking, 2004). A more balanced approach in line with Bailey's book is Max J. Skidmore, *Presidential Performance: A Comprehensive Review* (McFarland & Co., 2004), whose introduction contains footnotes of all the major polls but questions the validity of presidential rankings. Skidmore's sketches of each president are similar to those found in other collections written by top-notch historians. Two of the best are Alan Brinkley and Davis Dyer, eds., *Readers Companion to the American Presidency* (Houghton Mifflin, 2000) and Melvin I. Urofsky, ed., *The American Presidents* (Garland Publishing Group, 2000).

The presidential ratings game began in 1948 when Arthur Schlesinger, Sr., polled 55 prominent historians for *Life* magazine, updated in 1962 with a second poll for *The New York Times* magazine, followed in 1996 for the same magazine by his son Arthur Schlesinger, Jr. In between, at least a half dozen other polls have been conducted by historians, political scientists, and journalists. What is interesting about these polls is the agreement that Lincoln, Washington, and FDR are America's three greatest presidents.

Conservative critics complain that the criteria are biased toward activist presidents who pursued an assertive domestic program and an internationalist foreign policy with FDR as the role model. The discrepancies in the ratings are best seen in the table below, which compares the liberal historians surveyed by Schlesinger, Jr., in 1996, with the results from the conservative Intercollegiate Studies Institute from 1997. Most controversial in the Schlesinger poll is the ranking of Carter ahead of Reagan, a conservative icon as witnessed by the endless memorial services when he died in June 1994.

The presidential ratings game is rightly criticized for its liberal and conservative biases, its questionable classification schemes by some political scientists and psychologists, and the inability to locate some of the presidents in the context of their times.

The best summary of bibliography and articles is from the 1999 conference at Hofstra University on the rankings of presidents "Special Issue: The

Table 1

Discrepancies in Ratings

President	Schlesinger 1996	ISI 1997
Clinton	low average	failure
Reagan	low average	near great
Carter	low average	failure
Nixon	failure	below average
Johnson	high average	failure
Kennedy	high average	below average
Eisenhower	high average	near great

Uses and Abuses of Presidential Ratings," *White House Studies*, Volume 3, Number 1, 2003, a journal edited by Professor Robert P. Watson of Florida Atlantic University.

An interesting sidebar but relevant to this issue is Nathan Miller's *Star-Spangled Men: America's Ten Worst Presidents* (Scribner, 1998). Miller's top-ten list, like late-night host David Letterman's, includes from the bottom to the top—Carter, Taft, Harrison, Coolidge, Grant, A. Johnson, Pierce, Buchanan, Harding, and Nixon. This list is similar to the below average and failure of the other presidential polls with the exception of John Tyler, who is credited with the annexation of Texas, and Millard Filmore, who helped form the Compromise of 1850, which forestalled the Civil War for a decade.

Most likely, President Bush's reputation will rise and fall with the way the nation-building experiment works out in Iraq. Books that defend America's informal empire include British historian Niall Ferguson, *Colossus: The Price of America's Empire* (Penguin Press, 2004) and conservative journalist Max Boot, *The Savage Wars of Peace: Small Wars and the Rise of American Power* (Basic Books, 2002). Both have written numerous articles summarizing their views. See Niall Ferguson, "The Empire Slinks Back: Why Americans Don't Really Have What It Takes to Rule the World," *The New York Times Magazine* (April 27, 2003) and Max Boot, "Guess What? We're Winning [In Iraq]," *The American Interest* (Spring 2006). *Washington Times* senior White House correspondent Bill Salmon is a defendant of the president's policies in *Fighting Back: The War on Terrorism from Inside the Bush White House* (Regnery, 2002) and *Misunderestimated: The President Battles Terrorism, John Kerry and the Bush Haters* (Regan Books, 2004). Finally, Stephen Hayes tries to make the case for links between Al Qaeda and Iraq in "Case Closed," *The Weekly Standard*, November 24, 2003, though most commentators argue against this.

The bibliography about an incumbent president is very incomplete and continuous. The earliest assessments are highly partisan pro and con and are written by political scientists, journalists, and second-tier policymakers. Important assessments from cabinet officials and high-level policymakers such as Condoleezza Rice, Colin Powell, Vice President Richard Cheney, Donald Rumsfeld, and close confidant Karl Rowe will be written shortly after President Bush leaves office. Hopefully scholars will have access to the president's official papers once a presidential library is established at a major Texas university. Three of the earliest memoirs are negative. Paul O'Neill (with *New York Times* writer Ron Suskind), Bush's secretary of the treasury, criticizes the president's indifference to economic policy in *The Price of Loyalty* (Simon & Schuster, 2004), a complaint more recently aired by the conservative Bruce Bartlett, *Imposter: How George W. Bush Bankrupted America and Betrayed the Reagan Legacy* (Doubleday, 2006), which cost him his job as a policy analyst at a conservative think tank in Dallas. Richard Clarke, the former counterterrorism czar for both Bill Clinton and George W. Bush, argues that the current president "squandered the opportunity to eliminate Al Qaeda," which "has emerged and is growing stronger in part because of our actions and inactions." See *Against All Odds: Inside America's War on Terror* (Simon & Schuster, 2004). More favorable but still critical is David Frum, *The*

Right Man: The Surprise Presidency of George Bush (Random House, 2003). Frum is a former White House aide.

Freelance *Washington Post* writer Bob Woodward, the man who with his partner Carl Bernstein broke the Watergate scandal, now gets Washington policymakers to spill their guts. *Bush at War* (Simon & Schuster, 2002) and *Plan of Attack* (Simon & Schuster, 2004) are based upon lengthy interviews with top officials including President Bush. Primary source documents can be accessed on the Internet sources listed in the Unit 3 opener. Two important documents are the December 2002, "U.S. National Security: A New Era," which spells out the preemption policy and National Security Council (November, 2005), "National Strategy for Victory in Iraq."

Most of the information about current politics can be gleaned from the newspapers, magazines, radio, television, and the Internet. On the liberal side are *The Washington Post, The Los Angeles Times, The Nation, The Progressive, Mother Jones, The New Republic* (increasingly less liberal), and the articles by Sy Hersh on the Washington policymakers and John Anderson on Iraq in *The New Yorker*. Conservatives also control the *Washington Times*, the editorial pages of *The Wall Street Journal, The Weekly Standard, National Review, Commentary*, and *The* (neo-isolationist) *American Conservative*. Conservatives dominate AM talk radio led by hosts Rush Limbaugh, Sean Hannity, and former White House aide and felon G. Gordon Liddy. The liberal *Air America* station struggles with a much smaller but devoted audience. Conservatives also dominate the cable news market with Ruppert Murdoch's "fair and balanced" *Fox* network. Mainstream journalism (criticized as biased by both liberals and conservatives) include *The New York Times, Time, Newsweek, U.S. News & World Report, USA Today*, cable news networks (CNN, CNBC, MSNBC), and the three major networks ABC, NBC, and CBS (Dan Rather notwithstanding).

Bush's case for preemption as a strategy of the neoconservatives is critiqued in a number of books. The fullest and most critical account is *Washington Post* reporter James Mann, *The Rise of the Vulcans: The History of Bush's War Cabinet* (Penguin Books, 2004). John B. Judis takes on nation-building in *The Folly of Empire: What George W. Bush Could Learn from Theodore Roosevelt and Woodrow Wilson* (Oxford University Press, 2004). A good summary of Judis's argument is "Imperial America," *Foreign Policy* (July/August, 2004).

Bush's military strategy has also taken some heavy hits. James Risen, "Captives Deny Qaeda worked with Baghdad," *The New York Times* (June 9, 2003); Seymour Hersh, "Selective Intelligence," *The New Yorker* (May 12, 2003); and Michael Isikoff and Mark Hosenball's response to Stephen Hayes, "Case Decidedly Not Closed," *Newsweek Web Exclusive*, November 19, 2003. *New York Times'* military correspondent Michael R. Gordon and retired General Bernard E. Trainor have followed up their critique of *The Generals War: The Inside Story of the (First) Conflict in the Gulf* (Little, Brown, 1995) with *Cobra II: The Inside Story of the Invasion and Occupation of Iraq* (Pantheon, 2006), a detailed critique of how both sides planned and fought the war.

Fred Greenstein has edited *The George W. Bush Presidency: An Early Assessment* (Johns Hopkins University Press, 2003). Jon Kraus et al. have also edited *Transformed by Crisis: The Presidency of George W. Bush and American*

Politics (Palgrave MacMillan, 2004). Extremely useful is Ivo H. Daulder and James M. Lindsay, *America Unbound: The Bush Revolution in Foreign Policy, Revised and Updated* (Wiley, 2005), which makes the Bush foreign policy understandable to its supporters and critics.

A wide-ranging analysis with historical analogies similar to the works of Niall Ferguson are two books by Kevin Phillips, *American Dynasty: Aristocracy, Fortune, and the Politics of Deceit in the House of Bush* (Viking, 2004) and *American Theocracy: The Peril and Politics of Radical Religion, Oil and Borrowed Money in the 21st Century* (Viking, 2006), whose titles say it all. More temperate and favorable to the president is John Lewis Gaddis's *Surprise Security and the American Experience* (Harvard University Press, 2004), which traces Bush's policies of "preemption," "unilateralism," and "isolationism" back to the policies of John Quincy Adams, Andrew Jackson, and James K. Polk. Gaddis comes in for criticism in his discussion with Paul Kennedy in *The New York Times Book Review* (July 25, 2004), page 23, and also by Andrew J. Rotter et al. in "John Gaddis's *Surprise, Security and the American Experience: A Roundtable Critique," Passport: the Newsletter of the Society for Historians of American Foreign Relations* 36/2 (August, 2005). Gaddis modified his support for Bush's policies, suggesting in "Grand Strategy in the Second Term," *Foreign Affairs* (January/February 2005) that the president should speak more softly and obtain international help in restoring security in a more dangerous world.

There is substantial agreement between Nathan Miller and Jay Tolson, "The Ten Worst Presidents," *U.S. News & World Report* (February 26, 2007). Tolson chooses Tyler, Taylor, and Hoover, while Miller's are Taft, Coolidge, and Carter. Fifteen historians, political scientists, and public commentors weigh in on George Bush from various perspectives in "The (Unfinished) Legacy of George W. Bush," *Texas Monthly* (March 2007).

ISSUE 16

Should America Remain a Nation of Immigrants?

YES: Tamar Jacoby, from "Immigrant Nation," *Foreign Affairs* (November/December 2006)

NO: Patrick J. Buchanan, from *The Death of the West: How Dying Populations and Immigrant Invasions Imperil Our Country and Civilization* (Thomas Dunne Books, 2002)

ISSUE SUMMARY

YES: Social scientist Tamar Jacoby believes that legal immigration quotas should be increased to over 400,000 per year because the newest immigrants keep America's economy strong because they work harder and take jobs that native-born Americans reject.

NO: Syndicated columnist Patrick J. Buchanan argues that America is no longer a nation because immigrants from Mexico and other Third World Latin American and Asian countries have turned America into a series of fragmented multicultural ethnic enclaves that lack a common culture.

Historians of immigration tend to divide the forces that encouraged voluntary migrations from one country to another into push-and-pull factors. Historically, the major reason why people left their native countries was the breakdown of feudalism and the subsequent rise of a commercially oriented economy. Peasants were pushed off the feudal estates of which they had been a part of for generations. In addition, religious and political persecution for dissenting groups and the lack of economic opportunities for many middle-class émigrés also contributed to the migrations from Europe to the New World.

America was attractive to settlers long before the American Revolution took place. While the United States may not have been completely devoid of feudal traditions, immigrants perceived the United States as a country with a fluid social structure where opportunities abounded for everyone. By the mid-nineteenth century, the Industrial Revolution had provided opportunities for jobs in a nation that had always experienced chronic labor shortages.

There were four major periods of migration to the United States: 1607–1830, 1830–1890, 1890–1925, and 1968 to the present. In the seventeenth and eighteenth centuries, the white settlers came primarily, although not entirely, from the British Isles. They were joined by millions of African slaves. Both groups lived in proximity to several hundred thousand Native Americans. In those years, the cultural values of Americans were a combination of what history professor Gary Nash has referred to as "red, white, and black." In the 30 years before the Civil War, a second phase began when immigrants came from other countries in northern and western Europe and China. Two European groups dominated. Large numbers of Irish Catholics emigrated in the 1850s because of the potato famine. Religious and political factors were as instrumental as economic factors in pushing the Germans to America. Chinese immigrants were also encouraged to come during the middle and later decades of the nineteenth century in order to help build the western portion of America's first transcontinental railroad and to work in low-paying service industries like laundries and restaurants.

By 1890, a third period of immigration had begun. Attracted by the unskilled jobs provided by the Industrial Revolution and the cheap transportation costs of fast-traveling, steam-powered ocean vessels, immigrants poured in at a rate of close to 1 million a year from Italy, Greece, Russia, and other countries of southern and eastern Europe. This flood continued until the early 1920s, when fears of a foreign takeover led Congress to pass legislation restricting the number of immigrants into the United States to 150,000 per year.

For the next 40 years, America was ethnically frozen. The restriction laws of the 1920s favored northern and western European groups and were biased against southern and eastern Europeans. The depression of the 1930s, World War II in the 1940s, and minimal changes in the immigration laws of the 1950s kept migrations to the United States at a minimum level.

In the 1960s, the immigration laws were drastically revised. The civil rights acts of 1964 and 1965, which ended legal discrimination against African Americans, were also the impetus for immigration reform. The 1965 Immigration Act represented a turning point in U.S. history. But it had unintended consequences. In conjunction with the 1990 Immigration Act, discrimination against non-European nations was abolished and preferences were given to family-based migrants over refugees and those with special skills. Immigrants from Latin American and Asian countries have dominated the fourth wave of migration and have used the loophole in the legislation to bring into the country "immediate relatives," such as spouses, children, and parents of American citizens who are exempt from the numerical ceilings of the immigration laws.

Should the United States allow the current flow of immigrants into the country to continue? In the following selection, Tamar Jacoby asserts that legal immigrant quotas should be increased to 400,000 annually because the newest immigrants keep America's economy strong because they work harder and take jobs that native-born workers reject. Jacoby also maintains that the newest immigrants will assimilate into mainstream culture as earlier generations did once the immigrant laws provide permanence and stability. In the second selection, Patrick J. Buchanan argues that the new immigrants from Mexico, other parts of Latin America, and Asia who have been entering America since 1968 are destroying the core culture of the United States.

YES

Tamar Jacoby

Immigrant Nation

The Road to Reform

As recently as 18 months ago, a visitor could have spent a week in the United States, watching television and reading the newspapers, and come away with virtually no clue that immigration was a major issue. Today, it is at or near the top of most voters' lists of problems facing the nation—one that, in many people's minds, outweighs every other threat save international terrorism. This shift has been driven in large part by politicians and the media. The U.S. immigration system has been broken for a long time, and little—including the number of immigrants arriving in the country—has changed dramatically in recent years. There is little doubt that the system needs fixing. But just how big a problem is immigration? Is it in fact a crisis that threatens the United States' security and identity as a nation? And does it, as today's bitter debate suggests, raise so many fundamental questions as to be all but unsolvable?

As of this writing, Congress appears to be at an impasse, after nine months of intense debate and the passage of two major bills (one in each chamber) still unable to agree on a piece of legislation. The president has made clear that immigration reform is his top domestic priority, and legislators from both camps spent the summer insisting on the need for change. And yet, as the 109th Congress draws to a close, it seems unlikely that members will make a serious effort to resolve their differences before going home to face voters in November.

In fact, the nation is far less divided on immigration, legal or illegal, than the current debate suggests. In the last six months, virtually every major media outlet has surveyed public attitudes on the issue, and the results have been remarkably consistent. Americans continue to take pride in the United States' heritage as a nation of immigrants. Many are uneasy about the current influx of foreigners. But an overwhelming majority—between two-thirds and three-quarters in every major poll—would like to see Congress address the problem with a combination of tougher enforcement and earned citizenship for the estimated 12 million illegal immigrants already living and working here. A strange-bedfellow coalition—of business associations, labor unions, and the Catholic Church, among others—has endorsed this position. In Washington, the consensus behind it is even more striking, with supporters spanning the

Reprinted by permission of *Foreign Affairs*, vol. 85, no. 6, November/December 2006, pp. 50-65.

spectrum from conservative President George W. Bush to left-leaning Senator Edward Kennedy (D-Mass.), from mavericks like Senator John McCain (R-Ariz.) to party regulars like Senator Bill Frist (R-Tenn.) and all but a handful of congressional Democrats. But even this broad agreement may not produce a solution this fall.

Congress' failure to act is largely a product of political circumstances. The high-stakes midterm elections in November put an unusual premium on the opinions of the 20–25 percent of voters who depart from the emerging national consensus. Mostly male, white, and lacking college degrees, these naysayers believe immigrants are bad for the economy; they want to build a wall along the southern border and adamantly oppose allowing illegal immigrants to become citizens. Only about half are Republicans, and they account for no more than a quarter of the GOP. But many Republicans in Congress, particularly in the House, are convinced that this group is more intense—more concerned, more motivated, more likely to vote on the basis of this single issue—than anyone else likely to go to the polls. So the naysayers have become the tail wagging the dog of the immigration debate, and they may succeed in blocking a solution this year.

Still, such circumstances will not last forever. The political stars will realign, perhaps sooner than anyone expects, and when they do, Congress will return to the task it has been wrestling with: how to translate the emerging consensus into legislation to repair the nation's broken immigration system.

Reality Check

The term of art for what the consensus favors is "comprehensive immigration reform." But the shared understanding is far more than a grab bag or a horse traders' deal with a little something for everyone. The president and Senator Kennedy, for example, are both convinced that far from being a threat or a crisis, immigration is a boon to the United States—that the newcomers bring a welcome vitality, and that openness and optimism are a critical part of the nation's character. Neither man sees danger in the growing role immigrants play in the economy; both see today's influx as a force to be harnessed for the United States' benefit. And although troubled by the illegality currently associated with immigration, both believe that reform must go beyond reasserting existing law in the face of lawlessness. Any effective overhaul must also bring the immigration system more into line with the changing realities of a global world.

The most important of those new realities is the global integration of labor markets. Today's immigrant influx—second in volume only to the wave that arrived a hundred years ago—is not some kind of voluntary experiment that Washington could turn off at will, like a faucet. On the contrary, it is the product of changing U.S. demographics, global development, and the increasingly easy international communications that are shrinking the planet for everyone, rich and poor. Between 2002 and 2012, according to the Bureau of Labor Statistics, the U.S. economy is expected to create some 56 million new jobs, half of which will require no more than a high school education. More than 75 million baby boomers will retire in that period. And declining native-born fertility rates will be approaching replacement level. Native-born workers, meanwhile, are becoming more educated with every decade. Arguably the most important statistic for anyone seeking to understand the immigration issue is this: in 1960, half of all American men dropped out of high school to look for unskilled work, whereas less than ten percent do so now.

The resulting shortfall of unskilled labor—estimated to run to hundreds of thousands of workers a year—is showing up in sector after sector. The construction industry creates some 185,000 jobs annually, and although construction workers now earn between $30,000 and $50,000 a year, employers in trades such as masonry and dry-walling report that they cannot find enough young Americans to do the work. The prospects for the restaurant business are even bleaker. With 12.5 million workers nationwide, restaurants are the nation's largest private-sector employer, and their demand for labor is expected to grow by 15 percent between 2005 and 2015. But the native-born work force will grow by only ten percent in that period, and the number of 16- to 24-year-old job seekers—the key demographic for the restaurant trade—will not expand at all. So unless the share of older Americans willing to bus tables and flip hamburgers increases—and in truth, it is decreasing—without immigrants, the restaurant sector will have trouble growing through the next decade.

Fortunately for the United States, economic changes south of the border are freeing up a supply of unskilled labor to meet these growing needs in a timely way. Some of the circumstances generating the flow are positive (the move from subsistence agriculture to economies that require investment capital, including at the family level); others are not (the failure of Mexico to provide enough jobs for its working-age population). But even if Mexico were to become Switzerland overnight, the fact is that the United States would still lack unskilled laborers and would have to find them elsewhere.

The market mechanisms that connect U.S. demand with foreign supply, particularly from Latin America, are surprisingly efficient. Immigrants already here communicate to their compatriots still at home that the job market in, say, Detroit is flat, while that in Las Vegas is booming—and this produces a just-in-time delivery of workers wherever they are most needed. The vast majority of the immigrants who make the trip to the United States do so in order to work: if you are going to be unemployed, it is better to be unemployed at home in Mexico than in New York or Chicago. Not even legal immigrants, who account for about two-thirds of the total influx, are eligible, during their first five to ten years in the United States, for the kind of welfare transfers that could sustain them without work. Illegal immigrants receive virtually no transfers. Labor-force participation among foreign-born men exceeds that of the native born: the figure for illegal immigrant men is the highest of any group—94 percent. And immigrants are less likely than natives to be unemployed.

These facts are stark, and those who buy into the comprehensive vision see no point in quarreling with them. Rather than seeking to repeal the laws of supply and demand—or trying futilely to block them, as current policy does—reformers want an immigration policy that acknowledges and makes the most of these realities.

Competition or Complementarity?

Critics of the comprehensive model dispute these fundamental economic assumptions, and some of their questions are serious enough to require answers. Do immigrants lower American wages, as the naysayers contend? Would Americans fill these jobs, at a higher wage, if foreigners were not available? Is it only employers who profit from the influx? And do the fiscal costs associated with immigration outweigh any macroeconomic benefit? If the answer to any of those questions were yes, the case for comprehensive reform would be far less compelling than it is. (Why change the law to accommodate a market reality if that reality is not good for the United States?) But the critics' case does not stand up.

Of all the economic consequences of immigration, the easiest to calculate is the fiscal effect—whether immigrants consume more in government benefits than they contribute in taxes. Although this is one of the most disputed and emotional aspects of the immigration debate, in fact the net effect in most states is close to a wash. True, much of the immigrant population is poor and unskilled, which inevitably reduces their tax contribution. But most nonetheless pay as much to the government as comparable poor and unskilled native-born workers do, and even illegal immigrants pay sales and property taxes, thus contributing toward their childrens' schooling. To be sure, in states with lots of newcomers, the burden on native-born taxpayers can still add up: according to one estimate, in California in the mid-1990s the bite was $1,178 per native-born household. But in most states today, the cost per native household is no more than a couple of hundred dollars a year. And on average, this is offset by what immigrants pay in federal taxes. According to estimates, two-thirds of illegal immigrants have income tax withheld from their paychecks, and the Social Security Administration collects some $7 billion a year that goes unclaimed, most of it thought to come from unauthorized workers.

Immigrants' overall contribution to U.S. economic growth is harder to measure, although there is no doubt among economists that newcomers enlarge the economic pie. Foreign workers emerging at the end of the day from the meatpacking plant or the carpet factory buy groceries and shoes for their children; on Saturday, they buy washing machines and then hire plumbers to install them. The companies where they work are more likely to stay in the United States, rather than move operations to another country where labor is cheaper. Readily available immigrant workers allow these businesses to expand, which keeps other Americans on the job and other U.S. businesses, both up- and downstream, afloat. Economists call this shifting the demand curve outward, and no one disputes that it results in a bigger, more productive economy.

Just how much do immigrants expand the economy? One conventional way to measure this would be to calculate their spending power, but it is difficult to isolate immigrant purchases. And even if we could, that would not reflect the growth that occurs when, say, suppliers of irrigation equipment, fertilizer, and trucks sell more of their products to a farmer whose business is expanding thanks to immigrant workers. Still another way to quantify the immigrant contribution is to look at the percentage of new jobs they fill. Over the last decade, it was more than half of the total—and two-thirds in regions such as the Midwest and the Southwest—making them effectively responsible for half of the nation's economic expansion in that period.

Some of the best efforts to measure the elusive immigrant growth dividend look at states or regions rather than the nation as a whole. A recent report on immigrants in North Carolina—which has one of the fastest-growing foreign-born populations in the country—estimated their contribution to economic expansion and compared it with the more easily measured fiscal consequences. The bottom line: newcomers filled one-third of North Carolina's new jobs in the past decade, and they were responsible for $9.2 billion in consumer spending and $1.9 billion in saved wages—a total growth dividend of $11 billion, which dwarfed the $61 million (or $102 per native-born taxpayer) that the newcomers cost the state when taxes and services were netted out.

But even these calculations may significantly underestimate the immigrant contribution to the U.S. economy. Economists disagree on whether economic growth is in fact good or bad for a society. Many believe that it produces economies of scale and overall strength, both economic and other kinds, for the nation. Others feel it burdens and clogs the economy. The critical question is whether growth makes life better for individual workers, augmenting their productivity and increasing their incomes. And according to most economists, this is what happens when immigrants complement, rather than substitute for, native-born workers. In other words, the more different the foreigners are—the less interchangeable with Americans—the more they add. This, too, has yet to be adequately measured. A much-cited nine-year-old estimate by the National Academy of Sciences suggests that complementarity could add as much as $10 billion a year to U.S. incomes. But according to some economists, immigrants may be even more different (and thus account for even more added income) than many realize.

Think about a typical company. If all the employees were the same, adding more would expand the business but not—once maximum economies of scale were achieved—make other workers better off. But the picture changes dramatically if the employees have different skills. Then, adding more low-level workers would mean not only more opportunities for foremen but also that these supervisors would be more productive and earn more. In the case of immigration, this benefit comes not just within companies but also across the economy.

Immigrants are different from native-born workers in myriad ways. Roughly a quarter are more skilled and a third less skilled. On the whole, they are younger and more mobile (think of the construction workers who raced to New Orleans in the wake of Hurricane Katrina). They generally know the language less well and are less familiar with the culture. (Remember, complementarity is beneficial even when the added workers are less productive.) They often work harder and for longer hours, and in some cases they take jobs many Americans no longer want to do. But rather than undercut the native born, immigrants who are genuinely different make Americans better off. More low-skilled construction workers mean more jobs and higher wages for plumbers, electricians, and architects. More service workers allow skilled Americans to spend more of their time doing more productive work: instead of staying home to cut the grass, the brain surgeon has time for more brain surgeries. And over time, the higher return for higher-level work creates incentives for more Americans to become plumbers, electricians, and architects, thus making the entire economy more productive.

Complementarity also affects wage levels. Opponents of immigration ask why employers do not simply pay American workers more and avoid the need for foreign labor. But many industries cannot pay more, because they would be undercut by imports from abroad. Even in sectors such as construction and hospitality, in which the work must be done in the United States, it hardly makes sense to lure an American to a less productive job than he or she is capable of by paying more for less-skilled work. Meanwhile, because they complement rather than compete with most native-born workers (and this in turn attracts additional capital), immigrants raise rather than lower most Americans' wages.

Immigrants do compete with one category of American workers: native-born high school dropouts. But not even the most pessimistic economists think that the resulting downward pressure on wages affects more than ten percent of the U.S. labor force or that the drop in those American workers' earnings has been more than five percent over the last 20 years. Moreover, these unskilled native workers benefit in other ways from immigrant complementarity, because they pay less for goods such as food and housing.

Finally, rather than taking jobs from Americans, immigrants often create jobs where none existed before: look at the explosion of lawn-care businesses or the proliferation of manicure parlors in recent decades. (This is the new, complementary labor force attracting capital and making it productive in new ways.) And even if there were fewer immigrants in the United States, wages for low-skilled work would not necessarily rise. On the contrary, in many instances the jobs would simply disappear as the capital that created and sustained them dried up or the companies mechanized their production.

So how big is the real growth dividend? No one knows, in large part because it is so difficult to measure the extent and effects of immigrant complementarity. A back-of-the-envelope calculation suggests that eight million laborers working 2,000 hours a year at $9 an hour—an average wage based on employers' reports—would generate $144 billion worth of economic activity. Add the National Academy of Sciences' conservative estimate of the native-born income these immigrants make possible because they are different—an additional $10 billion—and the total contribution comes to $154 billion, or more than the gross state product of Kentucky and 1.2 percent of what is now a $13 trillion U.S. economy. A similar estimate of all immigrants' contributions—legal and illegal—comes to $700 billion, or 5.4 percent of GDP. And neither of these figures takes the full measure of the way the newcomers complement American workers.

Perhaps the most telling way to assess the immigrant contribution is to ask what would happen if the influx stopped or if those already here left the country. Those who favor comprehensive reform believe this would be disastrous—in some regions, they say, whole sectors of the economy could collapse. Restrictionist opponents counter that a cutoff would mean at most a temporary inconvenience for a few employers, who would soon wean themselves from their dependence on foreign workers. Perhaps. But even if some businesses could adjust somewhat, there would be no averting the demographic nosedive to come—the ever-slowing growth of the native-born work force. And either way, there is no reason to forfeit immigrant-driven economic expansion or the improved standard of living that comes with it for all Americans. Whether the nation benefits a great deal or just a modest amount, the newcomers still make life in the United States better—and not just with the work they do. They also renew and reinvigorate the country's spirit with their energy, hard work, and old-fashioned values. Surely, rather than go without all of this, it makes sense to find a better way to manage the immigrant influx, so that Americans reap more benefits with fewer costs.

Control Without a Crackdown

Comprehensive reformers start with these assumptions about the economic benefits of immigration and build out from there to design policy. Their basic idea is that the U.S. immigration system should be market-based. For the past decade or so, market forces have brought some 1.5 million immigrants, skilled and unskilled, to work in the United States each year. But annual quotas admit only about a million, or two-thirds of the total. Enforcement of these limits is poor in part because the nation is ambivalent about how much it wants to control immigration and also because it is all but impossible to make unrealistic laws stick. And as a result, some half a million foreign workers, most of them unskilled and from Latin America, breach the border every year or overstay their visas to remain on a job. It is as if American cars were made with imported steel but the government maintained such restrictive steel quotas that a third of what was needed had to be smuggled in. The only plausible remedy is more generous quotas combined with more effective enforcement.

Reformers understand the need to retake control, both on the border and in the workplace. Restrictionist opponents maintain that the way to do this is simply to crack down harder, enforcing the laws already on the books. The problem is that the United States has already tried that, tripling the size of the Border Patrol and quintupling its budget over the past decade, to virtually no avail: roughly the same number of immigrants still manages to enter the country each year, albeit by different methods and in different locations. Reinforced efforts and new, more creative tools, particularly in the workplace, can have some effect, as the Department of Homeland Security has shown in recent months. And if immigration were truly harmful for the United States, the government probably could shut it down with enforcement alone. But the cost would be the creation of a virtual police state, with an electric fence and armed guards on the border, roadblocks on every highway, regular raids on all U.S. businesses, a Big Brother-like national tracking system, and extensive use of ethnic profiling. Short of such drastic measures, which still might not succeed in stemming supply and demand, it makes more sense to revise the law to make it more realistic and then use modest enforcement means to ensure it holds.

This is the paradox at the heart of the comprehensive consensus. The best way to regain control is not to crack down but to liberalize—to expand quotas, with a guest-worker program or some other method, until they line up with labor needs. The analogy is Prohibition: an unrealistic ban on alcohol was all but impossible to enforce. Realistic limits, in contrast, are relatively easy to implement.

Not only is such reform the only way to restore the rule of law; it is also one of the best ways to improve border security. As one veteran Border Patrol agent in Arizona put it, "What if another 9/11 happens, and it happens on my watch? What if the bastards come across here in Arizona and I don't catch them because I'm so busy chasing your next busboy or my next gardener that I don't have time to do my real job—catching terrorists?" The government needs to take the busboys and the gardeners out of the equation by giving them a legal way to enter the country, so that the Border Patrol can focus on the smugglers and the terrorists who pose a genuine threat.

The third leg of the comprehensive vision—legalizing the illegal immigrants already here—is the most controversial, and without it, reform legislation would undoubtedly pass much more easily. But this, too, is an essential ingredient. It makes no sense to build a new immigration policy on an illegal foundation; neither new quotas nor new enforcement will stick as long as there are 12 million illegal immigrants living and working in the country.

Some opponents of reform insist that the government deport these unauthorized residents. Others maintain that more strenuous law enforcement would persuade them to leave voluntarily, by making it difficult or impossible for them to work, secure loans, attend school, or obtain driver's licenses. In fact, neither of these approaches is likely to succeed. Many of these people have lived in the United States for years, if not decades. Many own homes and businesses and have given birth to children who, because they were born in the United States, are U.S. citizens. A drive to deport them would cost billions and strike much of the public as unacceptably draconian. As for an attrition strategy, it would only drive immigrants further underground, deeper into the arms of smugglers and document forgers.

The only practical solution is to give these unauthorized workers and their families a way to earn their way onto the right side of the law. This should be done not just for their sake but also because it is the only way to restore the integrity of the immigration code, bring the underground economy onto the tax rolls, and eliminate the potential security threat posed by millions of illegal immigrants whose real names no one knows and who have never undergone security checks.

This, then, is the essential architecture of comprehensive reform: more immigrant worker visas, tougher and more effective enforcement, and a one-time transitional measure that allows the illegal immigrants already here to earn their way out of the shadows. Together, these three elements add up to a blueprint, not a policy, and many questions and disagreements remain. But on one thing everyone who shares the vision agrees: all three elements are necessary, and all three must be implemented together if the overhaul is to be successful. Think of them as the three moving parts of a single engine. There is no tradeoff between enforcement and legalization or between enforcement and higher visa limits. On the contrary, just as enforcement is pointless if the law is unrealistic, so even the best crafted of laws will accomplish little if it has no teeth, and neither one will work unless the ground is prepared properly.

After the Impasse

The bill passed in the Senate last May reflects the essential architecture of comprehensive reform. The critical question for the future is how to protect the design as it makes its way through the political process—particularly in the House. Debate is sure to center on five key issues.

Arguments about immigration inevitably come down to numbers, and this one is no exception. The goal of comprehensive reform is not to increase the total number of immigrants who enter the country each year, nor to open up new sources of supply (new sending countries); it is merely to replace the current illegal flow with a comparable lawful influx. Still, when the issue came up in the Senate, fear of higher numbers led legislators to set a new quota well below the size of the existing flow: not the half million or so who now arrive illegally each year, but only 200,000 workers. This may sound like a trivial matter, or the limit may even seem wise: Why not start the experiment prudently? But few mistakes could do more to undermine reform. There is little point in overhauling the system if the new ceilings are not realistic—a halfway reform that would result in more hypocrisy and more failed enforcement. (That would be like repealing Prohibition for those over 40 years old but not for the rest of the drinking-age population.) The definition of a realistic immigration system is one in which the annual legal intake is more or less equal to the flow generated by supply and demand: not the 5,000 visas currently issued to year-round unskilled workers but something closer to the 400,000–500,000 needed to keep the economy growing.

Second, some legislators, particularly House Republicans, insist that any new slots be strictly temporary: workers would be admitted, perhaps without family, for a period of two or three or six years and would then go home, with no possibility of appeal or adjustment. The Senate legislation, in contrast, although nominally a temporary-worker program, would allow workers to stay permanently if, at the end of their temporary stints, they went through a second round of processing to adjust their status. The Senate approach is the sounder of the two, although perhaps the misleading label "temporary" should be reconsidered. Some migrants want to work in the United States for a short time, earning cash for their families, and then return home. Others know from the start that they want to settle permanently. Still others start out as short-timers and change their minds along the way. The bottom line: in this case, too, no policy can hope to work if it is not realistic. A successful program must accommodate the ways real people behave, not ignore human nature. That means a policy that creates incentives for migrants to return home when their temporary-worker visas expire—and also incentives for them to become citizens if they decide to settle in the United States.

A third issue sure to come up—one of the most misunderstood in the immigration debate—is the balance between high-skilled and low-skilled workers. In fact, there is no reason to choose between the two categories: both are needed. Remember the theory of complementarity: depending on the circumstances, more busboys may do as much as more engineers to make the economy more productive. Today, the United States is short on both, and this means that more of both would make American workers better off. As is, perhaps 25 percent of the annual intake is moderately or highly skilled and the rest are unskilled, and conventional wisdom holds that Congress should recalibrate this balance. But there need be no tradeoff between the two groups—each should be considered independently—and no arbitrary limits in either case. What is important is that the quota for each category be consistent with the flow generated by supply and demand.

Fourth, some of the most charged disagreements of the past year were about enforcement issues: whether or not to build a fence, whether to make felons of unauthorized workers or of those who provide them with humanitarian assistance. But in fact, of the three essential elements of comprehensive reform, enforcement is the least controversial, at least among policymakers serious about fixing the system. It is well known what works best on the border: little can be done that is not done already, although it could be augmented by more technology. And it is well known what is needed in the workplace: a national, mandatory, electronic employment-verification system that informs employers in a timely way whether the job applicants standing before them are authorized to work in the United States or not. Such a system need not be Orwellian: the basic elements are biometric identity cards and a computer database. And the process should operate much like ordinary credit card verification but be backed up by significantly stepped-up sanctions against employers who fail to use the system or who abuse it.

The only real question about enforcement is how exactly to introduce it. Many conservatives do not believe the Bush administration is serious about retaking control, either on the border or in the workplace, and as a result they want the enforcement provisions of any bill to be implemented before the temporary-worker program or the legalization drive. This is not an ideal solution—comprehensive reform will succeed only if all three arms coexist and complement one another. But if it is politically necessary—and carefully designed—an enforcement "trigger" could be incorporated into a workable reform package. As for workplace enforcement, the challenge there is to get a workable system up and running in a timely way, rather than rushing to implement something that does not work.

The fifth issue on the table, sure to be the most bitterly argued of all, is whether the illegal immigrants already here should be allowed to become citizens. House hard-liners will insist not. "It is bad enough," they will say, "that we are letting these lawbreakers remain in the United States. We must draw the line somewhere—we must not reward them with citizenship." The problem with this approach, principled as it may seem, is that it would create a permanent caste of second-class workers, people trusted to cook Americans' food and tend their children but not to call themselves Americans or participate in politics. They would live in permanent limbo, at risk of deportation if they lost their jobs, afraid of bargaining with employers, and unlikely to make the all-important emotional leap that is essential for assimilation. Surely, this is not the answer for a proud democracy such as the United States. Indeed, it is hard to imagine anything worse, for the immigrants or for American values.

What then should be required of those who wish to become citizens? Reasonable people can disagree about conditions and criteria. Some, taking their cue from the Senate bill, will argue that it is enough to ask applicants to come forward and register with the government, pay a fine and all back taxes, then continue to work and take English classes while they wait in line behind other would-be immigrants. Other reformers will maintain that this is not stringent enough—that those already in the United States should be required to return to their home countries and reenter legally. But surely, once policy-makers agree that it is unthinkable to deport these workers or allow them to remain here in legal limbo, it should be possible to agree on a compromise—one that signals the nation's seriousness about enforcing its laws but does not preclude long-term residents from earning citizenship.

At the current impasse, it may be hard to imagine that such a moment will ever come. But immigration is not, and should not be thought of as, an unsolvable issue. If the influx is good for the economy—and plainly it is—it only makes sense to find a way to manage it more effectively.

Of all the naysayers' concerns, the most serious have to do with assimilation: fears that today's newcomers cannot or will not become Americans. Certainly, a lot more should be done to encourage and assist immigrants to assimilate. But it does not help to pretend that they are not arriving or to fantasize that tough enforcement can undo the laws of supply and demand. On the contrary, such denial and the vast illegal world of second-class noncitizens it creates are among the biggest barriers to assimilation today. That is all the more reason for Americans to open their eyes and face up to the facts of the immigrant influx.

Patrick J. Buchanan  **NO**

La Reconquista

$\mathbf{A}$s the [immigrant] invasion rolls on, with California as the preferred destination, sociologist William Frey has documented an out-migration of African Americans and Anglo-Americans from the Golden State in search of cities and towns like the ones they grew up in. Other Californians are moving into gated communities. A country that cannot control its borders isn't really a country anymore, Ronald Reagan warned us some twenty years ago.

Concerns about a radical change in America's ethnic composition have been called un-American. But they are as American as Benjamin Franklin, who once asked, "Why should Pennsylvania, founded by the English, become a Colony of Aliens, who will shortly be so numerous as to Germanize us instead of our Anglifying them . . . ?" Franklin would never find out if his fears were justified. German immigration was halted during the Seven Years War.

Former president Theodore Roosevelt warned, "The one absolutely certain way of bringing this nation to ruin, of preventing all possibility of its continuing to be a nation at all, would be to permit it to become a tangle of squabbling nationalities."

Immigration is a necessary subject for national debate, for it is about who we are as a people. Like the Mississippi, with its endless flow of life-giving water, immigration has enriched America throughout history. But when the Mississippi floods its banks, the devastation can be enormous. Yet, by the commands of political correctness, immigration as an issue is off the table. Only "nativists" or "xenophobes" could question a policy by which the United States takes in more people of different colors, creeds, cultures, and civilizations than all other nations of the earth combined. The river is rising to levels unseen in our history. What will become of our country if the levees do not hold?

❧

In late 1999, this writer left Tucson and drove southeast to Douglas, the Arizona border town of eighteen thousand that had become the principal invasion corridor into the United States. In March alone, the U.S. Border Patrol had apprehended twenty-seven thousand Mexicans crossing illegally, half again as many illegal aliens crossing in one month as there are people in Douglas.

From Patrick J. Buchanan. *The Death of the West: How Dying Populations and Immigrant Invasions Imperil Our Country and Civilization* (Thomas Dunne Books, 2002). Copyright © 2002 by Patrick J. Buchanan. Reprinted by permission of St. Martin's Press, LLC. Notes omitted.

While there, I visited Theresa Murray, an eighty-two-year-old widow and a great-grandmother who lives in the Arizona desert she grew up in. Her ranch house was surrounded by a seven-foot chain-link fence that was topped with coils of razor wire. Every door and window had bars on it and was wired to an alarm. Mrs. Murray sleeps with a .32-caliber pistol on her bed table, because she has been burglarized thirty times. Her guard dogs are dead; they bled to death when someone tossed meat containing chopped glass over her fence. Theresa Murray is living out her life inside a maximum-security prison, in her own home, in her own country, because her government lacks the moral courage to do its duty and defend the borders of the United States of America.

If America is about anything, it is freedom. But as Theresa Murray says, "I've lost my freedom. I can't ever leave the house unless I have somebody watch it. We used to ride our horses clear across the border. We had Mexicans working on our property. It used to be fun to live here. Now, it's hell. It's plain old hell."

While Theresa Murray lives unfree, in hellish existence, American soldiers defend the borders of Korea, Kuwait, and Kosovo. But nothing is at risk on those borders, half a world away, to compare with what is at risk on our border with Mexico, over which pass the armies of the night as they trudge endlessly northward to the great cities of America. Invading armies go home, immigrant armies do not.

Who Killed the Reagan Coalition?

For a quarter of a century, from 1968 until 1992, the Republican party had a virtual lock on the presidency. The "New Majority," created by Richard Nixon and replicated by Ronald Reagan, gave the GOP five victories in six presidential elections. The key to victory was to append to the Republican base two Democratic blocs: Northern Catholic ethnics and Southern white Protestants. Mr. Nixon lured these voters away from the New Deal coalition with appeals to patriotism, populism, and social conservatism. Success gave the GOP decisive margins in the industrial states and a "Solid South" that had been the base camp of the Democratic party since Appomattox. This Nixon-Reagan coalition proved almost unbeatable. McGovern, Mondale, and Dukakis could carry 90 percent of the black vote, but with Republicans taking 60 percent of the white vote, which was over 90 percent of the total, the GOP inevitably came out on top.

This was the Southern Strategy. While the media called it immoral, Democrats had bedded down with segregationists for a century without similar censure. FDR and Adlai Stevenson had put segregationists on their tickets. Outside of Missouri, a border state with Southern sympathies, the only ones Adlai captured in 1956 were Dixiecrat states later carried by George Wallace.

Neither Nixon nor Reagan ever supported segregation. As vice president, Nixon was a stronger backer of civil rights than Senators John F. Kennedy or Lyndon Johnson. His role in winning passage of the Civil Rights Act of 1957 was lauded in a personal letter from Dr. Martin Luther King, who hailed Vice President Nixon's "assiduous labor and dauntless courage in seeking to make Civil Rights a reality."

For a quarter century, Democrats were unable to pick the GOP lock on the presidency, because they could not shake loose the Republican grip on the white vote. With the exception of Lyndon Johnson's landslide of 1964, no Democrat since Truman in 1948 had won the white vote. What broke the GOP lock on the presidency was the Immigration Act of 1965.

During the anti-Soviet riots in East Berlin in 1953, Bertolt Brecht, the Communist playwright, quipped, "Would it not be easier . . . for the government to dissolve the people and elect another?" In the last thirty years, America has begun to import a new electorate, as Republicans cheerfully backed an immigration policy tilted to the Third World that enlarged the Democratic base and loosened the grip that Nixon and Reagan had given them on the presidency of the United States.

In 1996, the GOP was rewarded. Six of the 7 states with the largest numbers of immigrants—California, New York, Illinois, New Jersey, Massachusetts, Florida, and Texas—went for Clinton. In 2000, 5 went for Gore, and Florida was a dead heat. Of the 15 states with the most foreign-born, Bush lost 10. But of the 10 states with the smallest shares of foreign-born—Montana, Mississippi, Wyoming, West Virginia, South Dakota, South Carolina, Alabama, Tennessee, and Arkansas—Bush swept all 10.

Among the states with the most immigrants, only Texas has been reliably Republican, but now it is going the way of California. In the 1990s, Texas took in 3.2 million new residents as the Hispanic share of Texas's population shot from 25 percent to 33 percent. Hispanics are now the major ethnic group in four of Texas's five biggest cities: Houston, Dallas, San Antonio, and El Paso. "Non-Hispanic Whites May Soon Be a Minority in Texas" said a recent headline in the *New York Times.* With the Anglo population down from 60 percent in 1990 to 53 percent, the day when whites are a minority in Texas for the first time since before the Alamo is coming soon. "Projections show that by 2005," says the *Dallas Morning News,* "fewer than half of Texans will be white."

⊷❦⊷

America is going the way of California and Texas. "In 1960, the U.S. population was 88.6 percent white; in 1990, it was only 75.6 percent—a drop of 13 percentage points in thirty years. . . . [By 2020] the proportion of whites could fall as low as 61 percent." So writes Peter Brimelow of *Forbes.* By 2005, Euro-Americans, the largest and most loyal share of the electorate the GOP has, will be a minority, due to an immigration policy that is championed by Republicans. John Stuart Mill was not altogether wrong when he branded the Tories "the Stupid Party."

⊷❦⊷

Hispanics are the fastest-growing segment of America's population. They were 6.4 percent of the U.S. population in 1980, 9 percent by 1990, and in 2000 over 12 percent. "The Hispanic fertility rates are quite a bit higher than the white or black population. They are at the levels of the baby boom era of the 1950s," says Jeffrey Passel, a demographer at the Urban Institute. At 35.4 million, Hispanics now equal African Americans in numbers and are becoming as Democratic in voting preferences. Mr. Bush lost the African-American vote eleven to one, but he also lost Hispanics two to one.

In 1996, when Clinton carried Latino voters seventy to twenty-one, he carried first-time Latino voters ninety-one to six. Aware that immigrants could give Democrats their own lock on the White House, Clinton's men worked relentlessly to naturalize them. In the year up to September 30, 1996, the Immigration and Naturalization Service swore in 1,045,000 immigrants as new citizens so quickly that 80,000 with criminal records—6,300 for serious crimes—slipped by. [Table 1 shows] the numbers of new citizens in each of the last five years.

Table 1

1996	1,045,000
1997	598,000
1998	463,000
1999	872,000
2000	898,315

California took a third of these new citizens. As non-Latino white registration fell by one hundred thousand in California in the 1990s, one million Latinos registered. Now 16 percent of the California electorate, Hispanics gave Gore the state with hundreds of thousands of votes to spare. "Both parties show up at swearing-in ceremonies to try to register voters," says Democratic consultant William Carrick. "There is a Democratic table and a Republican table. Ours has a lot of business. Theirs is like the Maytag repairman." With fifty-five electoral votes, California, home state of Nixon and Reagan, has now become a killing field of the GOP.

✿

Voting on referenda in California has also broken down along ethnic lines. In 1994, Hispanics, rallying under Mexican flags, opposed Proposition 187 to end welfare to illegals. In the 1996 California Civil Rights Initiative, Hispanics voted for ethnic preferences. In 1998, Hispanics voted to keep bilingual education. Anglo-Americans voted the other way by landslides.

Ron Unz, father of the "English for the Children" referendum that ended state-funded bilingual education, believes the LA riot of 1992 may have been the Rubicon on the road to the balkanization of California.

> The plumes of smoke from burning buildings and the gruesome television footage almost completely shattered the sense of security of middle-class Southern Californians. Suddenly, the happy "multicultural California" so

beloved of local boosters had been unmasked as a harsh, dangerous, Third World dystopia . . . the large numbers of Latinos arrested (and summarily deported) for looting caused whites to cast a newly wary eye on gardeners and nannies who just weeks earlier had seemed so pleasant and reliable. If multicultural Los Angeles had exploded into sudden chaos, what security could whites expect as a minority in an increasingly nonwhite California?

❧

Except for refugees from Communist countries like Hungary and Cuba, immigrants gravitate to the party of government. The obvious reason: Immigrants get more out of government—in free schooling for their kids, housing subsidies, health care—than they pay in. Arriving poor, most do not soon amass capital gains, estates, or incomes that can be federally taxed. Why should immigrants support a Republican party that cuts taxes they don't pay over a Democratic party that will expand the programs on which they do depend?

After Ellis Island, the Democratic party has always been the first stop for immigrants. Only after they have begun to move into the middle class do the foreign-born start converting to Republicanism. This can take two generations. By naturalizing and registering half a million or a million foreign-born a year, the Democrats are locking up future presidential elections and throwing away the key. If the GOP does not do something about mass immigration, mass immigration will do something about the GOP—turn it into a permanent minority that is home to America's newest minority, Euro-Americans.

As the ethnic character of America changes, politics change. A rising tide of immigration naturally shifts politics and power to the Left, by increasing the demands on government. The rapidly expanding share of the U.S. electorate that is of African and Hispanic ancestry has already caused the GOP to go silent on affirmative action and mute its calls for cuts in social spending. In 1996, Republicans were going to abolish the U.S. Department of Education. Now, they are enlarging it. As Hispanic immigration soars, and Hispanic voters become the swing voters in the pivotal states, their agenda will become America's agenda. It is already happening. In 2000, an AFL-CIO that had opposed mass immigration reversed itself and came out for amnesty for illegal aliens, hoping to sign up millions of illegal workers as dues-paying union members. And the Bush White House—in its policy decisions and appointments—has become acutely attentive to the Hispanic vote, often at the expense of conservative principles.

America's Quebec?

Harvard economist George Borjas, who studied the issue, found no net economic benefit from mass migration from the Third World. The added costs of schooling, health care, welfare, social security, and prisons, plus the added pressure on land, water, and power resources, exceeded the taxes that immigrants contribute. The National Bureau of Economic Research puts the cost of immigration at $80.4 billion in 1995. Economist Donald Huddle of Rice University estimates that the net annual cost of immigration will reach $108 billion by

2006. What are the benefits, then, that justify the risks we are taking of the balkanization of America?

Census 2000 revealed what many sensed. For the first time since statehood, whites in California are a minority. White flight has begun. In the 1990s, California grew by three million people, but its Anglo population actually "dropped by nearly half a million . . . surprising many demographers." Los Angeles County lost 480,000 white folks. In the exodus, the Republican bastion of Orange County lost 6 percent of its white population. "We can't pretend we're a white middle class state anymore," said William Fulton, research fellow at USC's Southern California Studies Center. State librarian Kevin Starr views the Hispanization of California as natural and inevitable:

> The Anglo hegemony was only an intermittent phase in California's arc of identity, extending from the arrival of the Spanish . . . the Hispanic nature of California has been there all along, and it was temporarily swamped between the 1880s and the 1960s, but that was an aberration. This is a reassertion of the intrinsic demographic DNA of the longer pattern, which is a part of the California-Mexican continuum.

The future is predictable: With one hundred thousand Anglos leaving California each year, with the Asian population soaring 42 percent in a single decade, with 43 percent of all Californians under eighteen Hispanic, America's largest state is on its way to becoming a predominantly Third World state.

No one knows how this will play out, but California could become another Quebec, with demands for formal recognition of its separate and unique Hispanic culture and identity—or another Ulster. As Sinn Fein demanded and got special ties to Dublin, Mexican Americans may demand a special relationship with their mother country, dual citizenship, open borders, and voting representation in Mexico's legislature. President Fox endorses these ideas. With California holding 20 percent of the electoral votes needed for the U.S. presidency, and Hispanic votes decisive in California, what presidential candidate would close the door to such demands?

"I have proudly proclaimed that the Mexican nation extends beyond the territory enclosed by its borders and the Mexican migrants are an important— a very important—part of this," said President Zedillo. His successor agrees. Candidates for president of Mexico now raise money and campaign actively in the United States. Gov. Gray Davis is exploring plans to have Cinquo de Mayo, the fifth of May, the anniversary of Juarez's 1862 victory over a French army at Puebla, made a California holiday. "In the near future," says Davis, "people will look at California and Mexico as one magnificent region." Perhaps we can call it Aztlan.

✥

America is no longer the biracial society of 1960 that struggled to erase divisions and close gaps in a nation 90 percent white. Today we juggle the rancorous and rival claims of a multiracial, multiethnic, and multicultural country. Vice President Gore captured the new America in his famous howler, when he translated our national slogan, "E Pluribus Unum," backward, as "Out of one, many."

Today there are 28.4 million foreign-born in the United States. Half are from Latin America and the Caribbean, a fourth from Asia. The rest are from Africa, the Middle East, and Europe. One in every five New Yorkers and Floridians is foreign-born, as is one of every four Californians. With 8.4 million foreign-born, and not one new power plant built in a decade, small wonder California faces power shortages and power outages. With endless immigration, America is going to need an endless expansion of its power sources—hydroelectric power, fossil fuels (oil, coal, gas), and nuclear power. The only alternative is blackouts, brownouts, and endless lines at the pump.

In the 1990s, immigrants and their children were responsible for 100 percent of the population growth of California, New York, New Jersey, Illinois, and Massachusetts, and over half the population growth of Florida, Texas, Michigan, and Maryland. As the United States allots most of its immigrant visas to relatives of new arrivals, it is difficult for Europeans to come, while entire villages from El Salvador are now here.

The results of the Third World bias in immigration can be seen in our social statistics. The median age of Euro-Americans is 36; for Hispanics, it is 26. The median age of all foreign-born, 33, is far below that of the older American ethnic groups, such as English, 40, and Scots-Irish, 43. These social statistics raise a question: Is the U.S. government, by deporting scarcely 1 percent of an estimated eleven million illegal aliens each year, failing in its constitutional duty to protect the rights of American citizens? Consider:

- A third of the legal immigrants who come to the United States have not finished high school. Some 22 percent do not even have a ninth-grade education, compared to less than 5 percent of our native born.
- Over 36 percent of all immigrants, and 57 percent of those from Central America, do not earn twenty thousand dollars a year. Of the immigrants who have come since 1980, 60 percent still do not earn twenty thousand dollars a year.
- Of immigrant households in the United States, 29 percent are below the poverty line, twice the 14 percent of native born.
- Immigrant use of food stamps, Supplemental Social Security, and school lunch programs runs from 50 percent to 100 percent higher than use by native born.
- Mr. Clinton's Department of Labor estimated that 50 percent of the real-wage losses sustained by low-income Americans is due to immigration.
- By 1991, foreign nationals accounted for 24 percent of all arrests in Los Angeles and 36 percent of all arrests in Miami.
- In 1980, federal and state prisons housed nine thousand criminal aliens. By 1995, this had soared to fifty-nine thousand criminal aliens, a figure that does not include aliens who became citizens or the criminals sent over by Castro in the Mariel boat lift.
- Between 1988 and 1994, the number of illegal aliens in California's prisons more than tripled from fifty-five hundred to eighteen thousand.

None of the above statistics, however, holds for emigrants from Europe. And some of the statistics, on low education, for example, do not apply to emigrants from Asia.

Nevertheless, mass emigration from poor Third World countries is "good for business," especially businesses that employ large numbers at low wages. In the spring of 2001, the Business Industry Political Action Committee, BIPAC, issued "marching orders for grass-roots mobilization." The *Wall Street Journal* said that the 400 blue-chip companies and 150 trade associations "will call for continued normalization of trade with China . . . and easing immigration restrictions to meet labor needs. . . ." But what is good for corporate America is not necessarily good for Middle America. When it comes to open borders, the corporate interest and the national interest do not coincide, they collide. Should America suffer a sustained recession, we will find out if the melting pot is still working.

But mass immigration raises more critical issues than jobs or wages, for immigration is ultimately about America herself.

What Is a Nation?

Most of the people who leave their homelands to come to America, whether from Mexico or Mauritania, are good people, decent people. They seek the same better life our ancestors sought when they came. They come to work; they obey our laws; they cherish our freedoms; they relish the opportunities the greatest nation on earth has to offer; most love America; many wish to become part of the American family. One may encounter these newcomers everywhere. But the record number of foreign-born coming from cultures with little in common with Americans raises a different question: What is a nation?

Some define a nation as one people of common ancestry, language, literature, history, heritage, heroes, traditions, customs, mores, and faith who have lived together over time on the same land under the same rulers. This is the blood-and-soil idea of a nation. Among those who pressed this definition were Secretary of State John Quincy Adams, who laid down these conditions on immigrants: "They must cast off the European skin, never to resume it. They must look forward to their posterity rather than backward to their ancestors." Theodore Roosevelt, who thundered against "hyphenated-Americanism," seemed to share Adams's view. Woodrow Wilson, speaking to newly naturalized Americans in 1915 in Philadelphia, echoed T.R.: "A man who thinks of himself as belonging to a particular national group in America has yet to become an American." This idea, of Americans as a separate and unique people, was first given expression by John Jay in *Federalist 2:*

> Providence has been pleased to give this one connected country to one united people—a people descended from the same ancestors, speaking the same language, professing the same religion, attached to the same principles of government, very similar in their manners and customs, and who, by their joint counsels, arms, and efforts, fighting side by side throughout

a long and bloody war, have nobly established their general liberty and independence.

But can anyone say today that we Americans are "one united people"?

We are not descended from the same ancestors. We no longer speak the same language. We do not profess the same religion. We are no longer simply Protestant, Catholic, and Jewish, as sociologist Will Herberg described us in his *Essay in American Religious Sociology* in 1955. We are now Protestant, Catholic, Jewish, Mormon, Muslim, Hindu, Buddhist, Taoist, Shintoist, Santeria, New Age, voodoo, agnostic, atheist, humanist, Rastafarian, and Wiccan. Even the mention of Jesus' name at the Inauguration by the preachers Mr. Bush selected to give the invocations evoked fury and cries of "insensitive," "divisive," and "exclusionary." A *New Republic* editorial lashed out at these "crushing Christological thuds" from the Inaugural stand. We no longer agree on whether God exists, when life begins, and what is moral and immoral. We are not "similar in our manners and customs." We never fought "side by side throughout a long and bloody war." The Greatest Generation did, but it is passing away. If the rest of us recall a "long and bloody war," it was Vietnam, and, no, we were not side by side.

We remain "attached to the same principles of government." But common principles of government are not enough to hold us together. The South was "attached to the same principles of government" as the North. But that did not stop Southerners from fighting four years of bloody war to be free of their Northern brethren.

In his Inaugural, President Bush rejected Jay's vision: "America has never been united by blood or birth or soil. We are bound by ideals that move us beyond our background, lift us above our interests, and teach us what it means to be a citizen." In his *The Disuniting of America*, Arthur Schlesinger subscribes to the Bush idea of a nation, united by shared belief in an American Creed to be found in our history and greatest documents: the Declaration of Independence, the Constitution, and the Gettysburg Address. Writes Schlesinger:

> The American Creed envisages a nation composed of individuals making their own choices and accountable to themselves, not a nation based on inviolable ethnic communities. For our values are not matters or whim and happenstance. History has given them to us. They are anchored in our national experience, in our great national documents, in our national heroes, in our folkways, our traditions, and standards. [Our values] work for us; and, for that reason, we live and die by them.

Bush Americans no longer agree on values, history, or heroes. What one-half of America sees as a glorious past the other views as shameful and wicked. Columbus, Washington, Jefferson, Jackson, Lincoln, and Lee—all of them heroes of the old America—are all under attack. Those most American of words, equality and freedom, today hold different meanings for different Americans. As for our "great national documents," the Supreme Court decisions that interpret our Constitution have not united us; for forty years they have divided us, bitterly, over prayer in school, integration, busing, flag burning, abortion, pornography, and the Ten Commandments.

Nor is a belief in democracy sufficient to hold us together. Half of the nation did not even bother to vote in the presidential election of 2000; three out of five do not vote in off-year elections. Millions cannot name their congress-man, senators, or the Supreme Court justices. They do not care.

Whether one holds to the blood-and-soil idea of a nation, or to the creedal idea, or both, neither nation is what it was in the 1940s, 1950s, or 1960s. We live in the same country, we are governed by the same leaders, but can we truly say we are still one nation and one people?

It is hard to say yes, harder to believe that over a million immigrants every year, from every country on earth, a third of them breaking in, will reforge the bonds of our disuniting nation. John Stuart Mill warned that "free institutions are next to impossible in a country made up of different national-ities. Among a people without fellow-feeling, especially if they read and speak different languages, the united public opinion necessary to the working of representative government cannot exist."

We are about to find out if Mill was right.

POSTSCRIPT

Should America Remain
a Nation of Immigrants?

Buchanan argues that the new immigration since 1968 from Mexico, other parts of Latin America, and Asia is destroying the core culture of the United States. He maintains that the new immigrants are responsible for America's rising crime rate, the increase in the number of households that are below the poverty level, and the increase in the use of food stamps, supplemental Social Security, and school lunch programs. Furthermore, maintains Buchanan, low-income Americans sustain real wage losses of 50 percent because of competition from legal and illegal immigration.

Buchanan also asserts that America is losing the cultural war. He holds that the Republican Party's white-based majority under Presidents Richard Nixon and Ronald Reagan has been undermined by an immigrant-based Democratic Party. He notes that the two biggest states—California and Texas—are beset with ethnic enclaves who do not speak English and whose political and cultural values are outside the American mainstream.

Although Buchanan expresses feelings that are felt by many Americans today, his analysis lacks historical perspective. Ever since Columbus encountered the first Native Americans, tensions between immigrants and native-born people have existed. During the four peak periods of immigration to the United States, the host group has felt overwhelmed by the newest groups entering the country. Buchanan quotes Benjamin Franklin's concern about the German immigrants turning Pennsylvania into a "Colony of Aliens, who will shortly be so numerous as to Germanize us instead of our Anglifying them." But Buchanan does not carry his observation to its logical conclusion. German immigration into the United States did not halt during the Seven Years War, as Buchanan contends. It continued during the nineteenth and early twentieth centuries, and Germans today constitute the largest white ethnic group in the country.

Buchanan also ignores the hostility accorded his own Irish-Catholic relatives by white, Protestant Americans in the 1850s, who considered the Irish crime-ridden, lazy, drunken ignoramuses living in ethnic enclaves who were inassimilable because of their "Papist" religious ceremonies. Irish males, it was said, often did not work but lived off the wages of their wives, who worked as maids. When menial jobs were performed mostly by Irish men, they were accused of lowering the wages of other working-class Americans. One may question whether the newest immigrants are different from Buchanan's own ancestors.

In an earlier article, "Too Many Immigrants," *Commentary* (April 200 Tamar Jacoby gives a spirited defense of the newest immigrants. She dism the argument for increased immigration restriction after the September 11 attacks on the World Trade Center and the Pentagon by distinguishing between a terrorist and an immigrant. She contends that the estimates about a future population explosion in the country might be exaggerated, especially if economic conditions improve in Third World countries when the global economy becomes more balanced.

Jacoby stresses the positive impact of the new immigrants, particularly those from India and other Asian countries who have contributed their skills to the computer industry in the Silicon Valley and other high-tech industrial parks across America. Jacoby also argues that even if poorer immigrants overuse America's health and welfare social services, many of them contribute portions of their pay to the Social Security trust fund, including illegal immigrants who might never receive a government retirement check. Jacoby does allow that although today's immigrants may be no poorer than those who came in the third wave at the turn of the twentieth century, today's unskilled immigrants are relatively further behind than the southern and eastern Europeans who came around 1900. This is the view of sociologist George J. Borjas in *Heaven's Door: Immigration and the American Economy* (Princeton University Press, 1999).

Most experts agree that changes need to be made in the U.S. immigration laws. Some groups, such as the Federation for American Immigration Reform (FAIR), would like to see a huge cut in the 730,000 legal immigrants, 100,000 refugees, and 200,000 illegal immigrants (Borjas's numbers) who came into America each year in the 1980s and 1990s. Borjas would add a point system to a numerical quota, which would take into account age, work experience, fluency in English, educational background, work experience, and the quality of one's job. Jacoby also favors an immigration policy that gives preference to immigrants with key job-related skills over those who use the loopholes in the law to reunite the members of their families. Unlike Buchanan, Jacoby maintains that the newest immigrants will assimilate as earlier groups did but only when their legal status as citizens is fully established.

In her most recent article published in this reader, Jacoby makes a number of suggestions for an immigration reform bill that Congress may or may not pass before the presidential election campaign season begins in early 2008. She believes that any comprehensive reform bill should be marketed with expanded quotas that paradoxically will improve the ability of the Immigration Naturalization Service (INS) to enforce the illegal entry laws.

Jacoby's suggestion for immigration reform will shock both liberals and opponents of immigration who fear economic competition for jobs for native American and cultural conservatives like Patrick Buchanan who consider the non-white Hispanic inadmissible. For example, she suggests that the numbers of legal immigrants be increased to 400,000 or more to keep the economy growing. Let the market decide the balance between the number of skilled and unskilled. These immigrants should be given "biometric" identity cards that are logged into a computer database system. This system would allow the INS to crack down on businesses that hire illegal immigrants while permitting agents to go after real terrorists. Finally, temporary immigrants should be given a choice when their visas expire to either return home or apply for permanent residency.

Whether Congress would consider Jacoby's suggestions remains to be seen. Even though Jacoby makes a strong case for economic job assimilation between immigrants and upward mobility of native-born workers, few Congresspersons would have the guts to suggest upping the number of yearly quotas of legal immigrants to 400,000 as Jacoby suggests. Historically it has always been much easier for politicians to track the immigrants as inadmissible because of their cultural differences and in some cases criminal behavior.

There is an enormous bibliography on the newest immigrants. A good starting point, which clearly explains the immigration laws and their impact on the development of American society, is Kenneth K. Lee, *Huddled Masses, Muddled Laws: Why Contemporary Immigration Policy Fails to Reflect Public Opinion* (Praeger, 1998). Another book that concisely summarizes both sides of the debate and contains a useful glossary of terms is Gerald Leinwand, *American Immigration: Should the Open Door Be Closed?* (Franklin Watts, 1995).

Because historians take a long-range view of immigration, they tend to weigh in on the pro side of the debate. See L. Edward Purcell, *Immigration: Social Issues in American History Series* (Oryx Press, 1995); Reed Ueda's *Postwar America: A Social History* (Bedford Books, 1995); and David M. Reimers, *Still the Golden Door: The Third World War Comes to America,* 2d ed. (Columbia University Press, 1997) and *Unwelcome Strangers: American Identity and the Turn against Immigration* (Columbia University Press, 1998).

Books continue to proliferate on immigration into the twenty-first century. Tamar Jacoby has edited a favorable collection in *Reinventing the Melting Pot: The New Immigrants and What It Means to Be American* (Basic, 2004). The ever controversial Samuel P. Huntington takes a more pessimistic Buchanan-like view in *Who Are We? The Cultural Core of American National Identity* (Simon & Schuster, 2004). Reviews of the book have been favorable in conservative journals *Commentary* (May 2004) and *Policy Review* (October/November 2004) but more critical in the sometimes liberal *The New Republic* and in Andrew Hacker's, "Patriot Games," *The New York Review of Books* (June 24, 2004). The same journal's issues on November 29, 2002 and December 2001 contain a lengthy two-part essay by Christopher Jenks in discussion of the book "Who Should Get In?"

Anne Boyer has listed a number of "Migration Related Resources" on the World Wide Web in the *OAH Magazine of History* special edition in *Migrations* (Fall 1999, pp. 47–48). Two examples will suffice here:

Teaching with Historic Places: Created by the National Park Service, *Teaching with Historic Places* lesson plans use historic locations across the United States to examine developments in American history. Approximately 60 lessons, complete with photos, maps, graphs, and readings, are either posted online or can be ordered free of charge through this Web site. Topics such as "Log Cabins in America: The Finnish Experience" and "Your City: Cigar Capital of the World" explore immigrants' lives in places outside the big East. See http://www.cr.nps.gov/nr/twhp/descrip.html.

Virtual Ellis Island Tour: Created by students and teachers at Queensbury Middle School in Queensbury, New York, this site works as a sample lesson for teachers as an educational tool for students. Using the Queensbury School's "Ellis Island Day" project as a guide, the site combines primary documents and photography to simulate an immigrant's experience upon arriving at Ellis Island. The site also contains suggestions for teachers planning similar activities as well as links to other sites on Ellis Island. See http://www.capital.net/~alta/index.html.

ISSUE 17

Is the Environmental Crisis "An Inconvenient Truth"?

YES: Jim Hansen, from "The Threat to the Planet," *The New York Review of Books* (July 13, 2006)

NO: Kevin Shapiro, from "Global Warming: Apocalypse Now?" *Commentary* (September 2006)

ISSUE SUMMARY

YES: NASA scientist Jim Hansen believes that the world will become a more desolate place to live in the foreseeable future unless we reduce or sequester the carbon emissions that are warming the atmosphere.

NO: Kevin Shapiro, a research fellow in neuroscience at Harvard University, believes the increase in CO_2 in the atmosphere is significant but not a cause for panic because what we "know" about global warming comes from computer-simulated models that have various biased built-in assumptions.

Historically, Americans have not been sympathetic to preserving the environment. For example, the first European settlers in the sixteenth and seventeenth centuries were awed by the abundance of land in the New World. They abandoned their Old World custom of practicing careful agricultural husbandry on their limited lands and instead solved their agricultural problems in North America by constantly moving to virgin land. The pioneers believed that the environment must be conquered, not protected or preserved.

The first real surge in the environmental movement occurred during the Progressive Era of the early twentieth century. Reformers were upset about the changes seen in America since the Civil War, such as an exploding population, massive immigration, political corruption, and the end of the frontier (as proclaimed by the 1890 census). The remedy for these problems, said the reformers, lay in strong governmental actions at the local, state, and national levels.

Environmentalists agreed that the government had to take the lead and stop the plundering of the remaining frontier before it was too late. But the movement split into two groups—conservationists and preservationists—a division that has continued in the movement to this day.

The Nixon administration pushed through the most important piece of environment regulation ever passed by the government: the National Environmental Policy Act of 1969, which established the Council for Environmental Quality (CEQ) for the purpose of coordinating all federal pollution control programs. This legislation empowered the Environmental Protection Agency (EPA) to set standards and implement CEQ policies on a case-by-case basis. The EPA thus became the centerpiece of the emerging federal environmental regulatory system.

In the late 1970s and early 1980s, a new urban-oriented environmentalism emerged. The two major concerns surrounded the safety of nuclear power and the sites where toxic wastes were dumped. For years, proponents of atomic power proclaimed that the technological benefits of nuclear power far outweighed the risksolm. Now the public began to have doubts.

More dangerous and more mysterious were the dangers from hazardous waste and pollutants stored improperly and often illegally across the country. The first widely known battle between local industry and the public occurred at Love Canal, near Niagara Falls, New York. In the 1950s, a working-class neighborhood was constructed around a canal that was being used as a dump site for waste by Hooker Chemical, a local company. Although the local government denied it, cancers and birth defects in the community reached epic proportions. On August 2, 1978, the New York State health commissioner declared Love Canal a great and imminent peril to the health of the general public. President Jimmy Carter declared the Hooker Chemical dump site a national emergency, and by the following spring, 237 families had been relocated. Controversies such as Love Canal made the public aware that toxic waste dumps and the accompanying fallout were nationwide problems. Congress passed several laws in the 1980s to deal with this issue. The Superfund Act of 1980 created a $1.6 billion fund to clean up toxic wastes, and the Nuclear Waste Policy Act of 1982 directed a study of nine potential sites where the radioactive materials left over from the creation of nuclear energy could be permanently stored.

In spite of the lax enforcement of the laws under the Reagan administration, the public became alarmed again in 1988 when Representative Mike Synar (D-Oklahoma) chaired a congressional subcommittee on the environment that uncovered contamination of 4,611 sites at 761 military bases, a number of which threatened the health of the nearby communities. Many of these sites still need to be cleaned up.

Is the environmental crisis real? In the following selectionsm Professor Jim Hansen, a scientist from the National Aeronautics Space Administration (NASA), believes that the world will become a more desolate place to live in the foreseeable future unless we reduce or sequester the carbon emissions that are warming the atmosphere. But Kevin Shapiro, a research fellow in neuroscience at Harvard University, believes the increase in carbon dioxide in the atmosphere is significant but not a cause for panic because what we know about global warming comes from computer-simulation models that have various built-in biased assumptions.

YES

Jim Hansen

The Threat to the Planet

1.

Animals are on the run. Plants are migrating too. The Earth's creatures, save for one species, do not have thermostats in their living rooms that they can adjust for an optimum environment. Animals and plants are adapted to specific climate zones, and they can survive only when they are in those zones. Indeed, scientists often define climate zones by the vegetation and animal life that they support. Gardeners and bird watchers are well aware of this, and their handbooks contain maps of the zones in which a tree or flower can survive and the range of each bird species.

Those maps will have to be redrawn. Most people, mainly aware of larger day-to-day fluctuations in the weather, barely notice that climate, the average weather, is changing. In the 1980s I started to use colored dice that I hoped would help people understand global warming at an early stage. Of the six sides of the dice only two sides were red, or hot, representing the probability of having an unusually warm season during the years between 1951 and 1980. By the first decade of the twenty-first century, four sides were red. Just such an increase in the frequency of unusually warm seasons, in fact, has occurred. But most people—who have other things on their minds and can use thermostats—have taken little notice.

Animals have no choice, since their survival is at stake. Recently after appearing on television to discuss climate change, I received an e-mail from a man in northeast Arkansas: "I enjoyed your report on *Sixty Minutes* and commend your strength. I would like to tell you of an observation I have made. It is the armadillo. I had not seen one of these animals my entire life, until the last ten years. I drive the same forty-mile trip on the same road every day and have slowly watched these critters advance further north every year and they are not stopping. Every year they move several miles."

Armadillos appear to be pretty tough. Their mobility suggests that they have a good chance to keep up with the movement of their climate zone, and to be one of the surviving species. Of course, as they reach the city limits of St. Louis and Chicago, they may not be welcome. And their ingenuity may be taxed as they seek ways to ford rivers and multiple-lane highways.

Problems are greater for other species, as Tim Flannery, a well-known Australian mammalogist and conservationist, makes clear in *The Weather Makers*.

Ecosystems are based on interdependencies—between, for example, flower and pollinator, hunter and hunted, grazers and plant life—so the less mobile species have an impact on the survival of others. Of course climate fluctuated in the past, yet species adapted and flourished. But now the rate of climate change driven by human activity is reaching a level that dwarfs natural rates of change. And barriers created by human beings, such as urban sprawl and homogeneous agricultural fields, block many migration routes. If climate change is too great, natural barriers, such as coastlines, spell doom for some species.

Studies of more than one thousand species of plants, animals, and insects, including butterfly ranges charted by members of the public, found an average migration rate toward the North and South Poles of about four miles per decade in the second half of the twentieth century. That is not fast enough. During the past thirty years the lines marking the regions in which a given average temperature prevails ("isotherms") have been moving poleward at a rate of about thirty-five miles per decade. That is the size of a county in Iowa. Each decade the range of a given species is moving one row of counties northward.

As long as the total movement of isotherms toward the poles is much smaller than the size of the habitat, or the ranges in which the animals live, the effect on species is limited. But now the movement is inexorably toward the poles and totals more than a hundred miles over the past several decades. If emissions of greenhouse gases continue to increase at the current rate—"business as usual"—then the rate of isotherm movement will double in this century to at least seventy miles per decade. If we continue on this path, a large fraction of the species on Earth, as many as 50 percent or more, may become extinct.

The species most at risk are those in polar climates and the biologically diverse slopes of alpine regions. Polar animals, in effect, will be pushed off the planet. Alpine species will be pushed toward higher altitudes, and toward smaller, rockier areas with thinner air; thus, in effect, they will also be pushed off the planet. A few such species, such as polar bears, no doubt will be "rescued" by human beings, but survival in zoos or managed animal reserves will be small consolation to bears or nature lovers.

In the Earth's history, during periods when average global temperatures increased by as much as ten degrees Fahrenheit, there have been several "mass extinctions," when between 50 and 90 percent of the species on Earth disappeared forever. In each case, life survived and new species developed over hundreds of thousands of years. The most recent of these mass extinctions defines the boundary, 55 million years ago, between the Paleocene and Eocene epochs. The evolutionary turmoil associated with that climate change gave rise to a host of modern mammals, from rodents to primates, which appear in fossil records for the first time in the early Eocene.

If human beings follow a business-as-usual course, continuing to exploit fossil fuel resources without reducing carbon emissions or capturing and sequestering them before they warm the atmosphere, the eventual effects on climate and life may be comparable to those at the time of mass extinctions. Life will survive, but it will do so on a transformed planet. For all foreseeable human generations, it will be a far more desolate world than the one in which civilization developed and flourished during the past several thousand years.

2.

The greatest threat of climate change for human beings, I believe, lies in the potential destabilization of the massive ice sheets in Greenland and Antarctica. As with the extinction of species, the disintegration of ice sheets is irreversible for practical purposes. Our children, grandchildren, and many more generations will bear the consequences of choices that we make in the next few years.

The level of the sea throughout the globe is a reflection primarily of changes in the volume of ice sheets and thus of changes of global temperature. When the planet cools, ice sheets grow on continents and the sea level falls. Conversely, when the Earth warms, ice melts and the sea level rises. In *Field Notes from a Catastrophe*, Elizabeth Kolbert reports on the work of researchers trying to understand the acceleration of melting, and in his new book and film *An Inconvenient Truth*, Al Gore graphically illustrates possible effects of a rising sea level on Florida and other locations.

Ice sheets waxed and waned as the Earth cooled and warmed over the past 500,000 years. During the coldest ice ages, the Earth's average temperature was about ten degrees Fahrenheit colder than today. So much water was locked in the largest ice sheet, more than a mile thick and covering most of Canada and northern parts of the United States, that the sea level was 400 feet lower than today. The warmest interglacial periods were about two degrees Fahrenheit warmer than today and the sea level was as much as sixteen feet higher.

Future rise in the sea level will depend, dramatically, on the increase in greenhouse gases, which will largely determine the amount of global warming. As described in the books under review, sunlight enters the atmosphere and warms the Earth, and then is sent back into space as heat radiation. Greenhouse gases trap this heat in the atmosphere and thereby warm the Earth's surface as we are warmed when blankets are piled on our bed. Carbon dioxide (CO_2), produced mainly by burning fossil fuels (coal, oil, and gas), is the most important greenhouse gas made by human beings. Methane (CH_4), which is "natural gas" that escapes to the atmosphere from coal mines, oil wells, rice paddies, landfills, and animal feedlots, is also an important greenhouse gas. Other significant warming agents are ground-level ozone and black soot, which arise mainly from incomplete combustion of fossil fuels and biofuels.

In order to arrive at an effective policy we can project two different scenarios concerning climate change. In the business-as-usual scenario, annual emissions of CO_2 continue to increase at the current rate for at least fifty years, as do non-CO_2 warming agents including methane, ozone, and black soot. In the alternative scenario, CO_2 emissions level off this decade, slowly decline for a few decades, and by mid-century decrease rapidly, aided by new technologies.

The business-as-usual scenario yields an increase of about five degrees Fahrenheit of global warming during this century, while the alternative scenario yields an increase of less than two degrees Fahrenheit during the same period. Warming can be predicted accurately based on knowledge of how Earth responded to similar levels of greenhouse gases in the past. (By drilling into glaciers to analyze air bubbles trapped under layers of snow, scientists can measure the levels of each gas in the atmosphere hundreds of thousands of years ago. By comparing the concentrations of different isotopes of oxygen in these air bubbles, they can measure the average temperature of past centuries.) Climate models by themselves yield similar answers. However, the evidence from the Earth's history provides a more precise and sensitive measure, and we know that the real world accurately included the effects of all feedback processes, such as changes of clouds and water vapor, that have an effect on temperature.

How much will sea level rise with five degrees of global warming? Here too, our best information comes from the Earth's history. The last time that the Earth was five degrees warmer was three million years ago, when sea level was about eighty feet higher.

Eighty feet! In that case, the United States would lose most East Coast cities: Boston, New York, Philadelphia, Washington, and Miami; indeed, practically the entire state of Florida would be under water. Fifty million people in the US live below that sea level. Other places would fare worse. China would have 250 million displaced persons. Bangladesh would produce 120 million refugees, practically the entire nation. India would lose the land of 150 million people.

A rise in sea level, necessarily, begins slowly. Massive ice sheets must be softened and weakened before rapid disintegration and melting occurs and the sea level rises. It may require as much as a few centuries to produce most of the long-term response. But the inertia of ice sheets is not our ally against the effects of global warming. The Earth's history reveals cases in which sea level, once ice sheets began to collapse, rose one meter (1.1 yards) every twenty years for centuries. That would be a calamity for hundreds of cities around the world, most of them far larger than New Orleans. Devastation from a rising sea occurs as the result of local storms which can be expected to cause repeated retreats from transitory shorelines and rebuilding away from them.

Satellite images and other data have revealed the initial response of ice sheets to global warming. The area on Greenland in which summer melting of ice took place increased more than 50 percent during the last twenty-five years. Meltwater descends through crevasses to the ice sheet base, where it provides lubrication that increases the movement of the ice sheet and the discharge of giant icebergs into the ocean. The volume of icebergs from Greenland has doubled in the last ten years. Seismic stations reveal a shocking increase in "icequakes" on Greenland, caused by a portion of an ice sheet lurching forward and grinding to a halt. The annual number of these icequakes registering 4.6 or greater on the Richter scale doubled from 7 in 1993 to 14 in the late 1990s; it doubled again by 2005. A satellite that measures minute changes in Earth's gravitational field found the mass of Greenland to have decreased by 50 cubic miles of ice in 2005. West Antarctica's mass decreased by a similar amount.

The effect of this loss of ice on the global sea level is small, so far, but it is accelerating. The likelihood of the sudden collapse of ice sheets increases as global warming continues. For example, wet ice is darker, absorbing more sunlight, which increases the melting rate of the ice. Also, the warming ocean melts the offshore accumulations of ice—"ice shelves"—that form a barrier between the ice sheets and the ocean. As the ice shelves melt, more icebergs are discharged from the ice sheets into the ocean. And as the ice sheet discharges more icebergs into the ocean and loses mass, its surface sinks to a lower level where the temperature is warmer, causing it to melt faster.

The business-as-usual scenario, with five degrees Fahrenheit global warming and ten degrees Fahrenheit at the ice sheets, certainly would cause the disintegration of ice sheets. The only question is when the collapse of these sheets would begin. The business-as-usual scenario, which could lead to an eventual sea level rise of eighty feet, with twenty feet or more per century, could produce global chaos, leaving fewer resources with which to mitigate the change in climate. The alternative scenario, with global warming under two degrees Fahrenheit, still produces a significant rise in the sea level, but its slower rate, probably less than a few feet per century, would allow time to develop strategies that would adapt to, and mitigate, the rise in the sea level.

3.

Both the Department of Energy and some fossil fuel companies insist that continued growth of fossil fuel use and of CO_2 emissions are facts that cannot be altered to any great extent. Their prophecies become self-fulfilling, with the help of government subsidies and intensive efforts by special interest groups to prevent the public from becoming well-informed.

In reality, an alternative scenario is possible and makes sense for other reasons, especially in the US, which has become an importer of energy, hemorrhaging wealth to foreign nations in order to pay for it. In response to oil shortages and price rises in the 1970s, the US slowed its growth in energy use mainly by requiring an increase from thirteen to twenty-four miles per gallon in the standard of auto efficiency. Economic growth was decoupled from growth in the use of fossil fuels and the gains in efficiency were felt worldwide. Global growth of CO_2 emissions slowed from more than 4 percent each year to between 1 and 2 percent growth each year.

This slower growth rate in fossil fuel use was maintained despite lower energy prices. The US is still only half as efficient in its use of energy as Western Europe, i.e., the US emits twice as much CO_2 to produce a unit of GNP, partly because Europe encourages efficiency by fossil fuel taxes. China and India, using older technologies, are less energy-efficient than the US and have a higher rate of CO_2 emissions.

Available technologies would allow great improvement of energy efficiency, even in Europe. Economists agree that the potential could be achieved most effectively by a tax on carbon emissions, although strong political leadership would be needed to persuasively explain the case for such a tax to the public. The tax could be revenue-neutral, i.e., it could also provide for tax credits or tax decreases for the public generally, leaving government revenue unchanged; and it should be introduced gradually. The consumer who makes a special effort to save energy could gain, benefiting from the tax credit or decrease while buying less fuel; the well-to-do consumer who insisted on having three Hummers would pay for his own excesses.

Achieving a decline in CO_2 emissions faces two major obstacles: the huge number of vehicles that are inefficient in their use of fuel and the continuing CO_2 emissions from power plants. Auto makers oppose efficiency standards and prominently advertise their heaviest and most powerful vehicles, which yield the greatest short-term profits. Coal companies want new coal-fired power plants to be built soon, thus assuring long-term profits.

The California legislature has passed a regulation requiring a 30 percent reduction in automobile greenhouse gas emissions by 2016. If adopted nationwide, this regulation would save more than $150 billion annually in oil imports. In thirty-five years it would save seven times the amount of oil estimated by the US Geological Services to exist in the Arctic National Wildlife Refuge. By fighting it in court, automakers and the Bush administration have stymied the California law, which many other states stand ready to adopt. Further reductions of emissions would be possible by means of technologies now being developed. For example, new hybrid cars with larger batteries and the ability to plug into wall outlets will soon be available; and cars whose bodies are made of a lightweight carbon composite would get better mileage.

If power plants are to achieve the goals of the alternative scenario, construction of new coal-fired power plants should be delayed until the technology needed to capture and sequester their CO_2 emissions is available. In the interim, new electricity requirements should be met by the use of renewable energies such as wind power as well as by nuclear power and other sources that do not produce CO_2. Much could be done to limit emissions by improving the standards of fuel efficiency in buildings, lighting, and appliances. Such improvements are entirely possible, but strong leadership would be required to bring them about. The most effective action, as I have indicated, would be a slowly increasing carbon tax, which could be revenue-neutral or would cover a portion of the costs of mitigating climate change.

The alternative scenario I have been referring to has been designed to be consistent with the Kyoto Protocol, i.e., with a world in which emissions from developed countries would decrease slowly early in this century and the developing countries would get help to adopt "clean" energy technologies that would limit the growth of their emissions. Delays in that approach—especially US refusal both to participate in Kyoto and to improve vehicle and power plant efficiencies—and the rapid growth in the use of dirty technologies have resulted in an increase of 2 percent per year in global CO_2 emissions during the past ten years. If such growth continues for another decade, emissions in 2015 will be 35 percent greater than they were in 2000, making it impractical to achieve results close to the alternative scenario.

The situation is critical, because of the clear difference between the two scenarios I have projected. Further global warming can be kept within limits (under two degrees Fahrenheit) only by means of simultaneous slowdown of CO_2 emissions and absolute reduction of the principal non-CO_2 agents of global warming, particularly emissions of methane gas. Such methane emissions are not only the second-largest human contribution to climate change but also the main cause of an increase in ozone—the third-largest human-produced greenhouse gas—in the troposphere, the lowest part of the Earth's atmosphere. Practical methods can be used to reduce human sources of methane emission, for example, at coal mines, landfills, and waste management facilities. However, the question is whether these reductions will be overwhelmed by the release of frozen methane hydrates—the ice-like crystals in which large deposits of methane are trapped—if permafrost melts.

If both the slowdown in CO_2 emissions and reductions in non-CO_2 emissions called for by the alternative scenario are achieved, release of "frozen methane" should be moderate, judging from prior interglacial periods that were warmer than today by one or two degrees Fahrenheit. But if CO_2 emissions are not limited and further warming reaches three or four degrees Fahrenheit, all bets are off. Indeed, there is evidence that greater warming could release substantial amounts of methane in the Arctic. Much of the ten-degree Fahrenheit global warming that caused mass extinctions, such as the one at the Paleocene-Eocene boundary, appears to have been caused by release of "frozen methane." Those releases of methane may have taken place over centuries or millennia, but release of even a significant fraction of the methane during this century could accelerate global warming, preventing achievement of the alternative scenario and possibly causing ice sheet disintegration and further long-term methane release that are out of our control.

Any responsible assessment of environmental impact must conclude that further global warming exceeding two degrees Fahrenheit will be dangerous. Yet because of the global warming already bound to take place as a result of the continuing long-term effects of greenhouse gases and the energy systems now in use, the two-degree Fahrenheit limit will be exceeded unless a change in direction can begin during the current decade. Unless this fact is widely communicated, and decision-makers are responsive, it will soon be impossible to avoid climate change with far-ranging undesirable consequences. We have reached a critical tipping point.

4.

The public can act as our planet's keeper, as has been shown in the past. The first human-made atmospheric crisis emerged in 1974, when the chemists Sherry Rowland and Mario Molina reported that chlorofluorocarbons (CFCs) might destroy the stratospheric ozone layer that protects animal and plant life from the sun's harmful ultraviolet rays. How narrowly we escaped disaster was not realized until years later.

CFC appeared to be a marvelous inert chemical, one so useful as an aerosol propellant, fire suppressor, and refrigerant fluid that CFC production increased 10 percent per year for decades. If this business-as-usual growth of CFCs had continued just one more decade, the stratospheric ozone layer would have been severely depleted over the entire planet and CFCs themselves would have caused a larger greenhouse effect than CO_2.

Instead, the press and television reported Rowland and Molina's warning widely. The public, responding to the warnings of environmental groups, boycotted frivolous use of CFCs as propellants for hair spray and deodorant, and chose non-CFC products instead. The annual growth of CFC usage plummeted immediately from 10 percent to zero. Thus no new facilities to produce CFCs were built. The principal CFC manufacturer, after first questioning the scientific evidence, developed alternative chemicals. When the use of CFCs for refrigeration began to increase and a voluntary phaseout of CFCs for that purpose proved ineffective, the US and European governments took the lead in negotiating the Montreal Protocol to control the production of CFCs. Developing countries were allowed to increase the use of CFCs for a decade and they were given financial assistance to construct alternative chemical plants. The result is that the use of CFCs is now decreasing, the ozone layer was damaged but not destroyed, and it will soon be recovering.

Why are the same scientists and political forces that succeeded in controlling the threat to the ozone layer now failing miserably to deal with the global warming crisis? Though we depend on fossil fuels far more than we ever did on CFCs, there is plenty of blame to go around. Scientists present the facts about climate change clinically, failing to stress that business-as-usual will transform the planet. The press and television, despite an overwhelming scientific consensus concerning global warming, give equal time to fringe "contrarians" supported by the fossil fuel industry. Special interest groups mount effective disinformation campaigns to sow doubt about the reality of global warming. The government appears to be strongly influenced by special interests, or otherwise confused and distracted, and it has failed to provide leadership. The public is understandably confused or uninterested.

I used to spread the blame uniformly until, when I was about to appear on public television, the producer informed me that the program "must" also include a "contrarian" who would take issue with claims of global warming. Presenting such a view, he told me, was a common practice in commercial television as well as radio and newspapers. Supporters of public TV or advertisers, with their own special interests, require "balance" as a price for their continued financial support. Gore's book reveals that while more than half of the recent newspaper articles on climate change have given equal weight to such contrarian views, virtually none of the scientific articles in peer-reviewed journals have questioned the consensus that emissions from human activities cause global warming. As a result, even when the scientific evidence is clear, technical nit-picking by contrarians leaves the public with the false impression that there is still great scientific uncertainty about the reality and causes of climate change.

The executive and legislative branches of the US government seek excuses to justify their inaction. The President, despite conclusive reports from the Intergovernmental Panel on Climate Change and the National Academy of Sciences, welcomes contrary advice from Michael Crichton, a science fiction writer. Senator James Inhofe, chairman of the Committee on Environment and Public Works, describes global warming as "the greatest hoax ever perpetrated on the American people" and has used aggressive tactics, including a lawsuit to suppress a federally funded report on climate change, to threaten and intimidate scientists.

Policies favoring the short-term profits of energy companies and other special interests are cast by many politicians as being in the best economic interests of the country. They take no account of the mounting costs of environmental damage and of the future costs of maintaining the supply of fossil fuels. Leaders with a long-term vision would place greater value on developing more efficient energy technology and sources of clean energy. Rather than subsidizing fossil fuels, the government should provide incentives for fossil-fuel companies to develop other kinds of energy.

Who will pay for the tragic effects of a warming climate? Not the political leaders and business executives I have mentioned. If we pass the crucial point and tragedies caused by climate change begin to unfold, history will judge harshly the scientists, reporters, special interests, and politicians who failed to protect the planet. But our children will pay the consequences.

The US has heavy legal and moral responsibilities for what is now happening. Of all the CO_2 emissions produced from fossil fuels so far, we are responsible for almost 30 percent, an amount much larger than that of the next-closest countries, China and Russia, each less than 8 percent. Yet our responsibility and liability may run higher than those numbers suggest. The US cannot validly claim to be ignorant of the consequences. When nations must abandon large parts of their land because of rising seas, what will our liability be? And will our children, as adults in the world, carry a burden of guilt, as Germans carried after World War II, however unfair inherited blame may be?

The responsibility of the US goes beyond its disproportionate share of the world's emissions. By refusing to participate in the Kyoto Protocol, we delayed its implementation and weakened its effectiveness, thus undermining the attempt of the international community to slow down the emissions of developed countries in a way consistent with the alternative scenario. If the US had accepted the Kyoto Protocol, it would have been possible to reduce the growing emissions of China and India through the Protocol's Clean Development Mechanism, by which the developed countries could offset their own continuing emissions by investing in projects to reduce emissions in the developing countries. This would have eased the way to later full participation by China and India, as occurred with the Montreal Protocol. The US was right to object to quotas in the Kyoto Protocol that were unfair to the US; but an appropriate response would have been to negotiate revised quotas, since US political and technology leadership are essential for dealing with climate change.

It is not too late. The US hesitated to enter other conflicts in which the future was at stake. But enter we did, earning gratitude in the end, not condemnation. Such an outcome is still feasible in the case of global warming, but just barely.

As explained above, we have at most ten years—not ten years to decide upon action, but ten years to alter fundamentally the trajectory of global greenhouse emissions. Our previous decade of inaction has made the task more difficult, since emissions in the developing world are accelerating. To achieve the alternative scenario will require prompt gains in energy efficiencies so that the supply of conventional fossil fuels can be sustained until advanced technologies can be developed. If instead we follow an energy-intensive path of squeezing liquid fuels from tar sands, shale oil, and heavy oil, and do so without capturing and sequestering CO_2 emissions, climate disasters will become unavoidable.

5.

When I recently met Larry King, he said, "Nobody cares about fifty years from now." Maybe so. But climate change is already evident. And if we stay on the business-as-usual course, disastrous effects are no further from us than we are from the Elvis era. Is it possible for a single book on global warming to convince the public, as Rachel Carson's *Silent Spring* did for the dangers of DDT? Bill McKibben's excellent book *The End of Nature* is usually acknowledged as having been the most effective so far, but perhaps what is needed is a range of books dealing with different aspects of the global warming story.

Elizabeth Kolbert's *Field Notes*, based on a series of articles she wrote for *The New Yorker*, is illuminating and sobering, a good book to start with. The reader is introduced to some of the world's leading climate researchers who explain the dangers in reasonably nontechnical language but without sacrificing scientific accuracy. The book includes fascinating accounts of how climate changes affected the planet in the past, and how such changes are occurring in different parts of the world right now. If *Field Notes* leaves the reader yearning for more experience in the field, I suggest *Thin Ice* by Mark Bowen, which captures the heroic work of Lonnie Thompson in extracting unique information on climate change from some of the most forbidding and spectacular places on the planet.[1]

Tim Flannery's *The Weather Makers* puts needed emphasis on the effects of human-made climate change on other life on the planet. Flannery is a remarkable scientist, having discovered and described dozens of mammals in New Guinea, yet he writes for a general audience with passion and clarity. He considers changes in climate that correspond to what I have defined as the business-as-usual and alternative scenarios. Flannery estimates that when we take account of other stresses on species imposed by human beings, the alternative scenario will lead to the eventual extinction of 20 percent of today's species, while continuing with business-as-usual will cause 60 percent to become extinct. Some colleagues will object that he extrapolates from meager data, but estimates are needed and Flannery is as qualified as anyone to make them. Fossil records of mass extinctions support Flannery's shocking estimate of the potential for climate change to extinguish life.

Flannery concludes, as I have, that we have only a short time to address global warming before it runs out of control. However, his call for people to reduce their CO_2 emissions, while appropriate, oversimplifies and diverts attention from the essential requirement: government leadership. Without such leadership and comprehensive economic policies, conservation of energy by individuals merely reduces demands for fuel, thus lowering prices and ultimately promoting the wasteful use of energy. I was glad to see that in a recent article in these pages, he wrote that an effective fossil energy policy should include a tax on carbon emissions.[2]

A good energy policy, economists agree, is not difficult to define. Fuel taxes should encourage conservation, but with rebates to taxpayers so that the government revenue from the tax does not increase. The taxpayer can use his rebate to fill his gas-guzzler if he likes, but most people will eventually reduce their use of fuel in order to save money, and will spend the rebate on something else. With slow and continual increases of fuel cost, energy consumption will decline. The economy will not be harmed. Indeed, it will be improved since the trade deficit will be reduced; so will the need to protect US access to energy abroad by means of diplomatic and military action. US manufacturers would be forced to emphasize energy efficiency in order to make their products competitive internationally. Our automakers need not go bankrupt.

Would this approach result in fewer ultraheavy SUVs on the road? Probably. Would it slow the trend toward bigger houses with higher ceilings? Possibly. But experts say that because technology has sufficient potential to become more efficient, our quality of life need not decline. In order for this to happen, the price of energy should reflect its true cost to society.

Do we have politicians with the courage to explain to the public what is needed? Or may it be that such people are not electable, in view of the obstacles presented by television, campaign financing, and the opposition of energy companies and other special interests? That brings me to Al Gore's book and movie of the same name: *An Inconvenient Truth*. Both are unconventional, based on a "slide show" that Gore has given more than one thousand times. They are filled with pictures—stunning illustrations, maps, graphs, brief explanations, and stories about people who have important parts in the global warming story or in Al Gore's life. The movie seems to me powerful and the book complements it, adding useful explanations. It is hard to predict how this unusual presentation will be received by the public; but Gore has put together a coherent account of a complex topic that Americans desperately need to understand. The story is scientifically accurate and yet should be understandable to the public, a public that is less and less drawn to science.

The reader might assume that I have long been close to Gore, since I testified before his Senate committee in 1989 and participated in scientific "roundtable" discussions in his Senate office. In fact, Gore was displeased when I declined to provide him with images of increasing drought generated by a computer model of climate change. (I didn't trust the model's estimates of precipitation.) After Clinton and Gore were elected, I declined a suggestion from the White House to write a rebuttal to a *New York Times* Op-Ed article that played down global warming and criticized the Vice President. I did not hear from Gore for more than a decade, until January of this year, when he asked me to critically assess his slide show. When we met, he said that he "wanted to apologize," but, without letting him explain what he was apologizing for, I said, "Your insight was better than mine."

Indeed, Gore was prescient. For decades he has maintained that the Earth was teetering in the balance, even when doing so subjected him to ridicule from other politicians and cost him votes. By telling the story of climate change with striking clarity in both his book and movie, Al Gore may have done for global warming what *Silent Spring* did for pesticides. He will be attacked, but the public will have the information needed to distinguish our long-term well-being from short-term special interests.

An Inconvenient Truth is about Gore himself as well as global warming. It shows the man that I met in the 1980s at scientific roundtable discussions, passionate and knowledgeable, true to the message he has delivered for years. It makes one wonder whether the American public has not been deceived by the distorted images of him that have been presented by the press and television. Perhaps the country came close to having the leadership it needed to deal with a grave threat to the planet, but did not realize it.

Notes

1. Henry Holt, 2005. See the review by Bill McKibben, "The Coming Meltdown," *The New York Review*, January 12, 2006.

2. See "The Ominous New Pact," *The New York Review*, February 23, 2006.

Kevin Shapiro  **NO**

Global Warming: Apocalypse Now?

In 1906 the Swedish chemist Svante Arrhenius published a popular book speculating on the origins of the earth and of life upon it. (An English translation, *Worlds in the Making,* appeared in 1908.) In a nutshell, Arrhenius proposed that the solar system was born of a collision between cool stars, with the sun and the planets forming from the resulting nebular debris. The planets, he thought, were then seeded by living spores that had been propelled through the cosmos by electromagnetic radiation.

Unfortunately for Arrhenius, few of these ideas ever achieved wide currency, and most of them were considered far-fetched even at the turn of the last century. One, however, has lately experienced something of a revival: the notion that the earth's climate is maintained within bounds that are favorable to life by the concentration of carbon dioxide (CO_2) in the atmosphere. As early as 1896, Arrhenius had proposed that surface temperatures rise in proportion to atmospheric CO_2, which absorbs radiated heat that would otherwise escape into space. Noting that CO_2 can be generated by the burning of coal, Arrhenius predicted that the growth of industry might eventually result in a warmer planet (in modern terms, this would be called "anthropogenic forcing")—a salutary outcome from a Scandinavian point of view, since a more temperate climate would likely be a boon to agriculture in the North.

This "greenhouse effect" is the cornerstone of the contemporary notion of global warming.[1] A hundred years after Arrhenius wrote, the concentration of CO_2 in the atmosphere has already nearly doubled, and the earth's surface is on average about 0.6°C warmer—enough to convince many scientists and laypeople that Arrhenius was right at least about this. In 2001, the official estimate of the Intergovernmental Panel on Climate Change was that we should expect a warming of about 3°C, give or take a few degrees, in the decades ahead.

But today's prophets of climate change are not quite so sanguine as Arrhenius about the prospect of anthropogenic forcing. This is because, according to some models, even a relatively small rise in global mean temperature would result in dramatic changes in local climate patterns. While climate modelers generally agree that farmers in subarctic latitudes will benefit from warmer summers and milder winters, their forecast for the rest of the planet approximates the apocalypse: famine, drought, hurricanes, floods, mass extinctions—the list goes on. Most of these calamities, said to be of such a scale that they could threaten the viability of human civilization, are predicted to result from changes in weather patterns that would follow from rising temperatures in the oceans and the lower atmosphere.

❧

The earth's climate is an extraordinarily complex system, and most climatologists would probably concur that local perturbations cannot be foretold with precision. But given the magnitude of the prospective problem, many pundits and policymakers—with the backing of the scientific establishment—have become less interested in improving our understanding of climate change than in pressing for an immediate solution. By this they mean somehow reducing (or at least stabilizing) the concentration of CO_2 in the atmosphere.

This is a difficult proposition, to say the least. About 70 percent of electricity in the United States is generated by the combustion of fossil fuels, mostly coal; our transportation network, which accounts for about a quarter of our greenhouse-gas emissions, is almost entirely dependent on petroleum. The picture in the rest of the world is not much better, as economic pressures dictate the construction of new coal-fired power plants not only in China and India but also in Germany and Eastern Europe. Despite all the fanfare surrounding Russia's ratification of the Kyoto Protocol in November 2004, bringing the treaty into force, most experts agree that, because of relatively modest emissions targets, allowances for international trading of carbon credits, and the exemption of major polluters like China, it will have no discernible impact on global CO_2 emissions.

Nevertheless, as the intellectual class has increasingly become convinced of the reality of man-made climate change—recent "converts" range ideologically from Gregg Easterbrook of the liberal *New Republic* to Ron Bailey of the libertarian *Reason*—environmentalists have correspondingly stepped up their efforts to build public support for some sort of action. The media now regularly proclaim the impending reality of climate change and encourage alarm. ABC News, offering not so much as a bow toward a scientific approach, recently asked viewers to submit stories about "global warming" in their own communities. Even the July 2006 issue of *Condé Nast Traveler*, not generally known for coverage of science and technology issues, includes tips for travelers who feel guilty about the damaging emissions generated by their airplane flights.

Among the more serious efforts to sway the debate are two new books, Tim Flannery's *The Weather Makers: How Man Is Changing the Climate and What It Means for Life on Earth*[2] and Elizabeth Kolbert's *Field Notes from a Catastrophe*,[3] along with Al Gore's much ballyhooed film, *An Inconvenient Truth*. Each of these presents a more or less comprehensive view of the scientific case for global warming, and describes in vivid detail some of the changes already attributed to rising temperatures: melting permafrost in Alaska, the crack-up of the Larsen B ice shelf in Antarctica, thinning sea ice in the Arctic, fiercer and more numerous hurricanes in the Atlantic. And each suggests that the threat of global warming is supported by an overwhelming scientific consensus that, in their view, leaves absolutely no room for dissent.

━◦◉◦━

The basic elements of the consensus are relatively easy to comprehend. Indeed, the three most important have already been mentioned. One is that surface thermometers have registered a global mean increase in temperature of about 0.6°C over the last century, give or take 0.15°C. This means that global temperatures are now higher than they have been in at least a thousand years, and perhaps since before the last major ice age. Likewise, atmospheric CO_2 has increased from preindustrial levels of around 250 parts per million by volume (ppmv) to around 378 ppmv, a level probably not seen since the Pliocene era, around 3.5 million years ago, when atmospheric CO_2 was higher for reasons that are basically unknown. There is little doubt, however, that at least some of the current increase is attributable to human activity.

So much for the data. The rest of what we "know" about global warming comes from intricate computer simulations, called general circulation models (or GCM's), which make use of these data and innumerable other observations about the earth's atmosphere in order to predict the effects of continuing increases in CO_2. Almost all the models forecast more warming, with the amount depending on various assumptions built into them. Although it is not clear from these results exactly why we should be alarmed—more on this later— Kolbert, Flannery, and Gore do their best to make sure that we *are* alarmed, enough to be willing to take drastic action. Each of them takes a slightly different rhetorical tack, but the ultimate message is always the same: we are on the verge of a catastrophe.

Kolbert's book, which grew out of a series of articles written for the *New Yorker* in 2005, adopts a journalistic style; she reports from the "front lines," as it were, embedding her essential points in well-crafted vignettes and conversations with scientists. She treks to Alaska, where an expert in permafrost tells her that temperatures have already become dangerously high. In Greenland, she observes cracks and crevasses in the ice sheet, which seem to suggest that the island's glaciers are melting. Experts on mosquitos, frogs, and butterflies attest to ecological changes that similarly portend a warming earth. Some people, it seems, have already bitten the bullet: Kolbert describes how the Dutch are abandoning their 500-year-old battle against the seas, dismantling their dikes and designing floating houses.

Despite its grim tidings, *Field Notes* is almost a pleasure to read, thanks to Kolbert's casually elegant prose and attention to detail. Indeed, the anecdotal approach makes for a story both more interesting and less convincing than Kolbert might have hoped. By allowing scientists to present the case for global warming in their own words, Kolbert perhaps inadvertently gives the reader a glimpse into the doubts that still exist even among the most ardent believers in the problem—and into those believers' very human biases.

As compared with *Field Notes,* Tim Flannery's *The Weather Makers* is more flamboyant, more decisive, and far more belligerent. Flannery, an Australian zoologist and something of a scientific celebrity, does little to hide his contempt for those who fail to take the problem of climate change as seriously as he does.

The Weather Makers starts off on an encouraging note, with an acknowledgment that climate change is difficult to evaluate impartially because the scientific issues are bound up in competing political and economic interests. Unfortunately, this pretense of evenhandedness collapses by the first chapter, which introduces the Gaia hypothesis—roughly, the idea that the earth's oceans, soil, atmosphere, and living creatures function together as a kind of superorganism, resisting changes that would alter the global climate. It is our failure to adopt a Gaian view, Flannery suggests, that has led us into the current global-warming predicament. (James Lovelock, the British scientist who proposed the Gaia hypothesis in the late 1960's, has predicted that global warming will lead to a mass extinction of the human population—a sort of Gaian "final solution" to the problem of anthropogenic pollution.)

In Flannery's view, the "consensus" based on climate change models is too conservative. He thinks that climate change has already taken off in full force, and the outlook for the future is dire indeed. Where Kolbert is circumspect about warming trends at the poles, Flannery suggests that the entire polar ecosystem is on the brink of collapse, and that coral reefs bleached by overheated oceans may never recover. Droughts in the American West, Australia, and Africa are all attributed to global warming, as are Europe's recent heat waves and floods. And this is just the beginning: Flannery predicts a rapid rise in global temperatures that will wipe out innumerable animal and plant species, not to mention agriculture in much of the world.

Is there anything we can do to mitigate the coming disaster? *The Weather Makers* devotes considerable attention to exploring possible solutions. These include geosequestration (pumping CO_2 back into the earth's crust) and alternative energy sources like hydrogen, nuclear, wind, and solar power. Not surprisingly, Flannery comes down on the side of wind and solar power, suggesting that these would be the most economical and democratic choices. Why democratic? Because, he imagines, each community and household can control its own electricity generation with wind farms and solar panels, while alternatives like nuclear power will merely perpetuate corporate control of the power grid.

Flannery reserves his greatest ire for big business, and for the conservative politicians he sees as subservient to it. In the end, he seems to think that if we fail to break free of our captivity to "big oil" and "big coal," the imperative to regulate the climate will leave us with no choice but to submit to some sort of world government.

Somewhere in-between Kolbert's measured warning and Flannery's hysterical fearmongering lies *An Inconvenient Truth*. Narrated in its entirety by Al Gore, the film is part documentary, part hagiography: ominous warnings about the threat of climate change are interleaved with flashbacks to Gore's childhood and other formative moments in the former Vice President's career.

The movie covers much of the same ground as *Field Notes* and *The Weather Makers,* but with less concern for factual accuracy. Gore all but explicitly blames global warming for the disastrous effects of Hurricane Katrina; even Flannery only goes so far as to offer Katrina as an example of the kind of disaster that *might* become more prevalent in a warming world, and climatologists themselves are divided over whether global warming implies an increase in tropical-storm activity. In another segment, an animated polar bear is shown swimming for his life in an ice-free Arctic sea. Presumably the filmmakers resorted to animation because, in fact, most polar-bear populations are not under such imminent threat.

Gore's overall strategy is to present the worst of worst-case scenarios as if they were inevitable, barring a miraculous reduction in atmospheric CO_2. He suggests, for example, that Greenland's ice cap is in danger of melting, which in turn would cause the jet stream to shut down—a bit like the scenario dramatized in the 2004 disaster film *The Day After Tomorrow*. Needless to say, most earth and atmospheric scientists consider the likelihood of such an event to be vanishingly low. Animated maps show sea levels rising to inundate Miami, New York, and Shanghai, which is more than even the most extreme predictions would seem to allow.

One might note that *An Inconvenient Truth* contains more than its share of ironies and curious lacunae. Gore suggests that viewers can help cut back on their own carbon emissions by taking mass transit. And yet, during much of the movie, Gore is shown either riding in a car or traveling on a plane—by himself. He berates Americans for our reliance on fossil fuels, but, chatting amiably with Chinese engineers, seems peculiarly unconcerned by Chinese plans to build hundreds of new coal-fired power plants. Indeed, he compares vehicle-emission standards in the United States unfavorably with China's. Touting "renewable" fuels like those derived from biomass (which at present offer no carbon savings compared with traditional fuels), he does not mention nuclear power or other practical carbon-reducing alternatives to coal, oil, and gas.

In the end, *An Inconvenient Truth* brings nothing new to the global-warming debate, except perhaps its insistence that the "debate" is over. Its effectiveness as a film—the *New York Times* has called it "surprisingly engaging"—hinges, one suspects, on the degree to which the viewer is likely *a priori* to have a favorable view of Al Gore. Those who basically like him, or hope to see him run again for the presidency, have described his performance as earnest and energetic, and have found his appeal persuasive; Franklin Foer, the editor of the *New Republic,* was so impressed that he pronounced the film likely to become a "seminal political document." To others, he comes across as a self-absorbed, condescending know-it-all.

Politics aside, however, does Gore have a point? Is it really true that the threat of climate change impels us to take action?

❧⟨◉⟩❧

The data themselves—that is to say, actual observations of the earth's climate—are hardly grounds for much excitement. For example, the fact that global temperatures and CO_2 levels are correlated in the climatological record is not in itself cause for panic. Consider the "smoking gun" for many global-warming alarmists—the Vostok ice core, an 11,775-foot-long sliver of Antarctic ice that has allowed scientists to extrapolate atmospheric CO_2 and temperature anomalies over roughly the past 420,000 years, showing that temperature and CO_2 have risen and fallen roughly in tandem over this time frame.

But the key word here is "roughly." The Vostok data make it clear that at the onset of the last glaciation, temperatures began to decline thousands of years before a corresponding decline in atmospheric CO_2. This observation cannot be replicated by current climate models, which require a *previous* fall in CO_2 for glaciation to occur. Moreover, an analysis published in *Science* in 2003 suggests that the end of one glacial period, called Termination III, preceded a rise in CO_2 by 600 to 1,000 years. One explanation for this apparent paradox might be that global warming, whatever its initial trigger, liberates CO_2 from oceans and permafrost; this additional CO_2 might then contribute in turn to the natural greenhouse effect.

Should we worry that adding even more CO_2 to the atmosphere by burning fossil fuels could contribute to a runaway warming effect? Probably not. In simple physical terms, each extra unit of CO_2 added to the atmosphere contributes less to the greenhouse effect than the previous unit, just as extra layers of paint applied to a pane of glass contribute less and less to its opacity. For this reason, we have already experienced 75 percent of the warming that should be attributable to a simple doubling of atmospheric CO_2 since the late 19th century, a benchmark we have not yet reached but one that is frequently cited as dangerous by those who fear global warming. Moreover, it seems unlikely that we can do very much about it.

Most models, of course, predict much *more* warming to come. This has to do with the way they account for the effects of clouds and water vapor, which are assumed to amplify greatly the response to man-made greenhouse gases. The problem with this assumption is that it is probably wrong.

Many scientists who study clouds—including MIT's Richard Lindzen, a prominent skeptic of climate-change alarmism—argue that the data show the opposite to be true: namely, that clouds act to limit, rather than aggravate, warming trends. In any case, the GCM's have failed miserably to simulate observed changes in cloud cover. Flannery, to his credit, is cognizant of this criticism, and acknowledges that the role of clouds is poorly understood. By way of a response, he draws attention to a computer simulation showing a high degree of correspondence between observed and predicted cloud cover for one model on a single day—July 1, 1998. Overall, however, GCM simulations of clouds are a source of significant error.

Indeed, the models are subject to so much uncertainty that it is hard to understand why anyone would bother to get worked up about them. Generally speaking, the GCM's simulate two kinds of effects on climate: natural forcing, which includes the impact of volcanic eruptions and solar radiation, and anthropogenic forcing, which includes greenhouse gases and so-called aerosols, or particulate pollution. But the behavior of most of these factors is unknown.

The major models assume, for example, that aerosols act to cancel warming; this effect is said to "explain" the apparent decline in global temperatures from the 1940's to the 1970's, when the popular imagination was briefly obsessed with the possibility of global cooling. Some scientists, however, are now claiming that the opposite is true, and that aerosols actually exacerbate warming.

Whatever the case, the impact of aerosols is so poorly understood that the term essentially refers to a parameter that can be adjusted to make the models' predictions correspond to actual observations. Making inferences from the models about the "true" state of the earth's climate is therefore an exercise in circular reasoning. To be sure, the business of fine-tuning GCM's provides a livelihood for many climatologists, and may one day yield valuable insights into the workings of the earth's climate. But the output of these models is hardly a harbinger of the end of civilization.

❧

If the empirical basis for alarmism about global warming is so flimsy, it is reasonable to ask what can account for the disproportionately pessimistic response of many segments of society.

Part of the problem is that global warming has ceased to be a scientific question—by which I do not mean that the interesting scientific issues have actually been settled, but that many of those concerned about global warming are no longer really interested in the science. As Richard Lindzen has reminded us, the Kyoto Protocol provides an excellent illustration. Although there is widespread scientific agreement that the protocol will do next to nothing to affect climate change, politicians worldwide continue to insist that it is vital to our efforts to combat the problem of global warming, and scientists largely refrain from contradicting them.

Some have suggested that the underlying reason for this is economic. After all, public alarm is a powerful generator of science funding, a fact that is not lost on theorists and practitioners. In 2003, the National Research Council, the public-policy arm of the National Academy of Sciences, criticized a draft of the U.S. National Climate Change Plan for placing too much emphasis on improving our knowledge about the climate and too little on studying the likely impacts of global warming—the latter topic being sure to produce apprehension, and hence grants for more research. By the same token, the Kyoto process seems to lumber on in part because of the very large number of diplomats and bureaucrats whose prestige and livelihoods depend on maintaining the perception that their jobs are indispensable.

Money aside, it may be that many scientists have a knack for overinterpreting the importance of their own work. It is of course exciting to think that one's research concerns an unprecedented phenomenon with far-reaching political implications. But not only can this lead to public misperception, it can encourage a politicization of the scientific literature itself. Scientists skeptical of the importance of anthropogenic warming have testified that it is difficult to publish their work in prestigious journals; when they do publish, their articles are almost always accompanied by rebuttals.

In fact, the scientific "consensus" on climate change—at least, as it is summarized by Gore, Flannery, and the like—includes a very large number of disparate observations, only a small number of which are pertinent to understanding the actual determinants of contemporary climate change. The fact, for example, that certain species have become scarce or extinct is frequently presented as a cause for alarm about the climate. But such ecological shifts are often the result of idiosyncratic local conditions, and in any case are largely irrelevant to the broader issue of global warming.

❧

In recent years the issue of climate change has also been used as a tool to embarrass the political Right, and especially the Bush administration—which, after Bill Clinton declined to submit the Kyoto Protocol to the Senate for ratification, withdrew the U.S. signature from the pact. Although efforts to portray conservatives as insensitive to environmental issues are not new, what *is* new is the scope of the alleged problem, which requires not merely a targeted solution (like the phasing-out of chlorofluorocarbons in response to ozone depletion) but a radical change in our mode of energy generation and specifically a wholesale shift away from fossil fuels.

The really curious element here is that many of those who seem to have become convinced of the reality of climate change appear rather unwilling to take meaningful steps toward cleaner sources of energy. Like Flannery, they simply assert that a carbon-free economy will somehow be much more efficient and productive than one powered by fossil fuels—because, of course, we will be rid of evil and greedy energy companies, which many alarmists suspect are at the root of the problem.

Practically speaking, however, they have little to offer. Very few Democratic politicians have advocated the construction of new nuclear-power plants, a key element of the Bush administration's energy plan and probably our best bet to avoid an increased reliance on coal. Although Senator Edward M. Kennedy (among other Democrats) signed a bill that would require the U.S. to derive 20 percent of its energy from renewable sources by 2020, he has strenuously opposed a wind farm planned off the coast of Cape Cod, visible from his Hyannisport family estate.

The overall effect of these inconsistent policy goals—limiting fossil-fuel consumption without activating any viable substitutes—will be to drive up the price of energy, a move that will probably not much affect the affluent but will be quite problematic for the rest of us. Al Gore will be able to continue to crisscross the country by jet, while feeling virtuous about having encouraged the shift worker to reduce his energy consumption by using public transportation. And if the problem of global warming does not eventuate, so much the better. Alarmists will be able to reassure themselves that they have forestalled a catastrophe, even if this comes at considerable expense to the economy as a whole.

There are many good reasons to wean ourselves from a dependence on fossil fuels, not least to cease enriching unsavory regimes in places like Saudi Arabia, Iran, and Venezuela. But in combating climate change, we should not ignore the damage done by the proponents of global-warming themselves in diverting money and energy away from more obvious and well-substantiated problems. Unfortunately, many people seem to be more concerned with the supposed menace of global warming, about which we can realistically do very little, than with problems like infectious disease, about which we can do quite a bit. Speaking of inconvenient truths, this is a real one.

Notes

1. Technically speaking, the greenhouse effect refers to the warming attributable to all greenhouse gases, including not only CO_2 but also water vapor, methane, and others. The contribution to the greenhouse effect of CO_2 produced by combustion is properly called the Callendar effect, after the British scientist, Guy Stewart Callendar, who proposed it in 1938.
2. Atlantic Monthly Press, 384 pp., $24.00.
3. Bloomsbury USA, 192 pp., $22.95.

POSTSCRIPT

Is the Environmental Crisis "An Inconvenient Truth"?

Professor Jim E. Hansen leads the NASA Institute for space studies in New York City, which is a division of the Goddard Space Flight Center in Greenbelt, Maryland. Trained in astrophysics at the University of Iowa, Hansen has written dozens of scholarly and popular scientific articles over the past 30 years, many of which have appeared in the intellectual journal, *The New York Review of Books.* Contentious in personality, Hansen has had his argument with both the Clinton and Bush administrations. He has accused the latter in trying to shut him up because he claims the current administration suppresses and tones down reports that support the theory of "global warming," a phrase he coined in an article in 1998.

Hansen believes that meltdowns that are occurring in Greenland are a reflection of the warming of the earth's atmosphere. He believes the amount of carbon dioxide (CO_2) emissions and non-CO_2 emissions can be curbed by practical methods at coal mines, landfills, and waste management facilities. In the 1980s, says Hansen, the public responded by eliminating the use of hairspray and deodorant that emitted chlorofluorocarbons (CFCs). These CFCs had the potential to destroy the stratosphere ozone layer that protects animal and plant life from the sun's harmful ultraviolet rays. If the ozone layer was protected in public and governmental action in the 1980s, why hasn't this occurred today?

Hansen feels that the mainstream has hampered the scientific consensus that global warming is a serious problem. When scientists appear on television or radio, they are always paired with an opposition member, usually a non-scientist. Consequently, the public believes that global warming is not a fact. In addition, the Bush administration is hostile to scientists who support global warming because it could have major effects on the way energy companies and the current American economy operates.

Kevin Shapiro, a research fellow in neuroscience and a student at Harvard Medical School, takes issue with the advocates of global warming on several grounds. He doesn't see any scientific consensus on the issue of global warming. While he admits that the earth's temperature has become 3°C warmer in the past decade, he does not see this as a cause for panic. He questions whether the scientific models that have charted climate changes over the past thousand years are historically accurate—much less have the ability to predict the future. He believes that nature produces more changes in the atmosphere than pollution-producing CO_2 from the world's factories.

Finally, Shapiro takes pot shots at the liberal scientist and politicians. Contrary to Hansen, who believes mainstream media won't give global warming scientists a fair shake on television and radio without a rebuttal from the other side, Shapiro says scientists who oppose global warming are rarely able to write for a prestigious scientific journal. When they do, they are countered by an opposing article. He also attacks limousine liberals Al Gore and Ted Kennedy: Gore for crisscrossing across the country in a jet plane while preaching to workers to ride public transportation, and Kennedy for rejecting windmills powering a farm that is visible from his Hyannis Port family compound.

The debate over global warming has become heated and personal. At the center of the debate is Al Gore. The former vice president has exhibited an interest in environmental issues for two decades. His book *Earth in the Balance* (Houghton Mifflin, 1992) became the focus of attention when vice president Dan Quayle attacked it on one of the 1992 presidential campaign debates. Hamstrung by a Republican-controlled Congress under President Clinton, Gore nevertheless continued to study the importance of global warming during his vice-presidency, and after his narrow loss in the 2000 presidential race. His book *An Inconvenient Truth* (Rodale, 2006), a vivid pictorial and textual analysis, became a best-seller, and his lecture turned into a documentary with the same name that won an Oscar at the 2007 Academy Awards.

The scholarly debate can be followed on the Internet, national newspapers such as *The New York Times,* reports from liberal and conservative interest groups, and think tanks as well as liberal and conservative intellectual's magazines such as *New Republic, The Nation, The American Prospect, Commentary, The National Review,* and the *Weekly Standard.*

The (liberal) *New York Review of Books* has published a review of essays over the last decade reviewing the latest reports and books on global warming. See Daniel Kelves "Endangered Environment" (February 20, 1997); Bill McKibbin, "Acquaintance of Earth" (May 25, 2000), "Some Like It Hot" (July 5, 2005), "The Coming Meltdown" (January 12, 2006), "How Close to Catastrophe" (November 10, 2006); Tim Flannery, "Endgame" (August 11, 2005); Peter Canby, "The Specter Haunting Alaska" (November 17, 2005); and Al Gore, introduction to the 1994 reprint of Rachel Carson's classic *Silent Spring* (Houghton Mifflin, 1962).

Critics of global warming have been able to shift their attacks challenging abstract scientific data to the personna and presentation of Al Gore's *An Inconvenient Truth.* The American Enterprise Institute (AEI), a Washington D.C. conservative think tank, offered $10,000 to refute the former vice president's book and movie. Who won the award is not clear, but Steven F. Hayward, a resident scholar at the AEI, has written a number of reports on the AEI online, "The Fate of Earth in the Balance," Eco-Solutions, "Gore on the Rocks," and "Scenes from the Climate Inquisition," which are available on the AEI Web site as an Adobe Acrobat PDF. Haywood has also narrated *An Inconvenient Truth . . . or a Convenient Fiction?* This 50-minute movie was shot in the offices of the Heritage Foundation, another Washington D.C. conservative think tank, and disputes point-by-point Gore's depiction of global warming as the ultimate disaster. The producer of the movie was the Pacific Research Foundation, a free-market think tank based in San Francisco, which funded an earlier attack in 1994 edited by

John A. Baden on Gore's first book, *Environmental Gore: A Constructive Response to Earth in the Balance* (Pacific Research Institute, 1994). Although many of Gore's critics are right-wing "talk radio" hosts and journalists who make personal attacks against the former vice president, there is some other serious research from conservatives besides Haywood challenging global warming theories. One example is the 40-page report on "Issue in the Current State of Climate Science," *Century for Science and Public Policy* (March 2006), which uses similar approaches as Gore's *Inconvenient Truth,* but where charts ad diagrams reach different conclusions.

Politics continues to play a major role in the issue with both sides "warming" up for the presidential election of 2008. When he warned Congress of a "planetary emergency" in March 2007, Gore received both cheers and jeers. The Bush administration has been hostile and indifferent to the issue. The president refused to sign the Kyoto Accords, and there have been accusations by Hansen and others of being forced to tone down the conclusions of the scientific studies. But even the president mentioned "Climate Change" in his 2007 State of the Union message and suggested that we develop alternative vehicles.

But there are some hopeful signs for global warming enthusiasts. Ten businesses and four environmental groups agreed in January 2007 to work together on a Cap and Trade climate system plan in order to curb and lower emissions of greenhouse gases. In April 2007, the Supreme Court ruled that a reluctant EPA did have the authority under the Clean Air Act to control the carbon dioxide being emitted from tailpipes of cars and trucks. But according to some analysts, these emissions represent slightly less than one-quarter of the country's total bent trapping gasses. Scientific and popular journals continue to publicize the issue. The United Nation's Intergovernmental Panel on Climate Change issued its fourth report since 1995, which declares that the increase on the human population was using so much energy. See Bill McKibbi's assessment of this report in "Warning on Warning," *The New York Review of Books* (March 15, 2005). *Time Magazine* (April 9, 2007) published a special double issue on "The Global Warming Survival Guide: 51 Things You Can Do to Make a Difference." Gregg Easternbook, a recent convert on the issue of "Global Warming: Who Loses and Who Wins," *Atlantic Monthly* (April 2007), believes that "Climate change in the next century and beyond could be enormously disruptive, spreading disease and sparking wars. It could also be a windfall for some people, business, and nations." While some warm-weather countries and U.S. southern states might become uninhabitable, new paradise could be found in Moscow, Siberia, Buffalo (New York), and the North Pole. Finally, National Public Radio's Diane Rehm Show on March 21, 2007, featured a panel discussion of Easternbook, David Sandalow of The Brookings Institution, Andrew Revkin from *The New York Times,* and James Connaughton, who chairs the White House Council on Environmental Quality. Informed and with disagreements kept under emotional control, this panel decision can be accessed from the National Public Radio station at http://www.npr.org/stations.

The best historical overviews of the controversy are Hal K. Rothmans' *Saving the Planet: The American Response to the Environment in the Twentieth Century*

(Ivan Dee, 2000) and *The Greeting of a Nation? Environmentalism in the United States since 1945* (Harcourt Brace, 1998). Two excellent articles in the issue are Stewart L. Udall, "How the West Was Won," *American Heritage* (February/March 2000) and John Stele Gordon, "The American Environment," *American Heritage* (October 1993). Professor Otis L. Graham, Jr. has edited a collection of essays on *Environmental Politics and Policy, 1960s–1990s* (Pennsylvania Sate University Press, 2000), in which Graham divides the controversy between eco-optimists and eco-pessimists. Graham places himself among the latter and sees few solutions to stop the eventual destruction of the planet.

Contributors to This Volume

EDITOR

LARRY MADARAS is a professor of history and political science at Howard Community College in Columbia, Maryland. He received a B.A. from the College of the Holy Cross in 1959 and an M.A. and a Ph.D. from New York University in 1961 and 1964, respectively. He has also taught at Spring Hill College, the University of South Alabama, and the University of Maryland at College Park. He has been a Fulbright Fellow and has held two fellowships from the National Endowment for the Humanities. He is the author of dozens of journal articles and book reviews.

AUTHORS

GLENN C. ALTSCHULER is Thomas and Dorothy Litwin Professor of American Studies and dean of the School of Continuing Education and Summer Sessions at Cornell University. He is the author of several books on American history and popular culture, including *Changing Channels: America in TV Guide*.

CONRAD BLACK is a well-known publisher and author of the recent biography of *Franklin Delano Roosevelt: Champion of Freedom* (Public Affairs Press, 2003).

PATRICK J. BUCHANAN is a syndicated columnist and a founding member of three public affairs shows, "The McLaughlin Group," "The Capital Gang," and "Crossfire." He has served as senior adviser to three American presidents, ran twice for the Republican nomination for president (1992 and 1996), and was the Reform Party's presidential candidate in 2000. He is the author of *A Republic, Not an Empire: Reclaiming America's Destiny* (Regnery, 1999).

JOSEPH A. CALIFANO, JR., President Lyndon Johnson's special assistant for domestic affairs, currently runs the Center on Addiction and Substance Abuse at Columbia University. He is the author of *The Triumph and Tragedy of Lyndon Johnson: The White House Years* (Simon & Schuster, 1991).

CLAYBORNE CARSON is a professor of history at Stanford University in Stanford, California. He is also editor and director of the Martin Luther King, Jr., Papers Project at the university's Martin Luther King., Jr., Center for Nonviolent Social Change, which published in 2000 the fourth volume of a 14-volume edition of King's speeches, sermons, and writings. His publications include *A Knock at Midnight: Inspiration from the Great Sermons of Reverend Martin Luther King, Jr.*, coedited with Peter Holloran (Warner Books, 2000) and *Guide to American History* (Viking Penguin, 1999).

DANIEL DEUDNEY is an assistant professor in the department of political science at the Johns Hopkins University in Baltimore, Maryland. He is the author of *Pax Automica: Planetary Geopolitics and Republicanism* (Princeton University Press, 1993).

THOMAS BYRNE EDSALL is a widely respected political journalist who has written numerous books and articles for *The New Republic, The Atlantic, The Washington Post,* and *The New York Times*.

SARA M. EVANS is Distinguished McKnight University Professor of History at the University of Minnesota, where she has taught women's history since 1976. She is the author of several books, including *Personal Politics: The Roots of Women's Liberation in the Civil Rights Movement and the New Left* (1979) and *Born for Liberty: A History of Women in America*, 2nd ed. (1997). Born in a Methodist parsonage in South Carolina, she was a student activist in the civil rights and antiwar movements in North Carolina and has been an active feminist since 1967.

ADAM FAIRCLOUGH is a professor at the University of Leeds, where he holds the chair of modern American history. He has written extensively on the civil rights movement and is the author of *Teaching Equality: Black Schools in the Age of Jim Crow* (University of Georgia Press, 2001) and *Race and Democracy: The Civil Rights Struggle in Louisiana, 1915–1972* (University of Georgia Press, 1999).

RICHARD M. FRIED is a professor of history at the University of Illinois at Chicago and the author of *The Russians Are Coming! The Russians Are Coming! Pageantry and Patriotism in Cold-War America* (Oxford University Press, 1998).

JOHN LEWIS GADDIS is the Robert A. Lovett Professor of History at Yale University in New Haven, Connecticut. He has also been Distinguished Professor of History at Ohio University, where he founded the Contemporary History Institute, and he has held visiting appointments at the United States Naval War College, the University of Helsinki, Princeton University, and Oxford University. He is the author of many books, including *We Now Know: Rethinking Cold War History* (Oxford University Press, 1997).

JIM HANSEN is director of the NASA Goddard Institute for Space Studies and adjunct professor of Earth and Environmental Sciences at Columbia University's Earth Institute. His opinions are expressed here, he writes, "as personal views under the protection of the First Amendment of the United States Constitution."

TSUYOSHI HASEGAWA is professor of history and director of the Center for Cold War Studies at the University of California Santa Barbara.

JOHN EARL HAYNES is a twentieth-century political historian with the Library of Congress. He is coauthor, with Harvey Klehr and K. M. Anderson, of *The Soviet World of American Communism* (Yale University Press, 1998) and, with Harvey Klehr and Fridrikh I. Firsov, of *The Secret World of American Communism* (Yale University Press, 1996).

JOAN HOFF-WILSON is a professor of history at Indiana University in Bloomington, Indiana, and coeditor of the *Journal of Women's History*. She is a specialist in twentieth-century American foreign policy and politics and in the legal status of American women. She has received numerous awards, including the Stuart L. Bernath Prize for the best book on American diplomacy. She has published several books, including *Herbert Hoover: The Forgotten Progressive* (Little, Brown, 1975) and *Without Precedent: The Life and Career of Eleanor Roosevelt* (Indiana University Press, 1984), coedited with Marjorie Lightman.

G. JOHN IKENBERRY, currently a Wilson Center Fellow, is a professor of political science at the University of Pennsylvania and a nonresident senior fellow at the Brookings Institution. He is the author of *After Victory: Institutions, Strategic Restraint and the Rebuilding of Order after Major Wars* (Princeton University Press, 2000) and *American Foreign Policy: Theoretical Essays*, 3rd ed. (Addison-Wesley Longman, 1998).

TAMAR JACOBY a senior fellow at the Manhattan Institute and writes extensively on race, ethnicity, and other subjects. Her articles and book reviews have appeared in a variety of periodicals, including *The New York Times*, *The Wall Street Journal*, *The New Republic*, *Commentary*, and *Foreign Affairs*. Before joining the institute, she was a senior writer and justice editor for *Newsweek*. Her publications include *Someone Else's House: America's Unfinished Struggle for Integration* (Basic Books, 1998).

D. CLAYTON JAMES holds the John Biggs Chair of Military History at Virginia Military Institute in Lexington, Virginia. He is the author of the best-selling and prize-winning three-volume work *The Years of MacArthur* (Houghton Mifflin, 1970–1985), as well as numerous other works of military history.

HARVEY KLEHR is the Andrew W. Mellon Professor of Politics and History at Emory University. He is coauthor, with Kyrill M. Anderson and John Earl Haynes, of *The Soviet World of American Communism* (Yale University Press, 1998) and, with John Earl Haynes and Fridrikh I. Firsov, of *The Secret World of American Communism* (Yale University Press, 1996).

MICHAEL L. KURTZ is dean of the Graduate School at Southeastern Louisiana University in Hammond, Louisiana, where he has also served as professor of history. He is editor of *Louisiana since the Longs: Nineteen-Sixty to Century's End* (Center for Louisiana Studies, 1998).

ROBERT JAMES MADDOX is professor emeritus of history at Penn State University and is the author of two dozen books and articles on recent American history with a specialty on Cold War diplomacy.

H. R. McMASTER graduated from the U.S. Military Academy at West Point in 1984. Since then, he has held numerous command and staff positions in the military, and during the Persian Gulf War, he commanded Eagle Troop, 2d Armored Cavalry Regiment in combat. He is the author of *A Distant Thunder* (HarperCollins, 1997).

CHARLES MURRAY is a Bradley Fellow at the American Enterprise Institute in Washington, D.C., a privately funded public policy research organization. His publications include *The Underclass Revisited* (American Enterprise Institute for Public Policy Research, 1999) and *Does Prison Work?* (Institute of Economic Affairs, 1997).

J. RONALD OAKLEY was a professor of history at Davidson County Community College in Greensboro, North Carolina.

ARNOLD A. OFFNER is Cornelia F. Hugel Professor of History and head of the history department at Lafayette College. He is the author of *American Appeasement: United States Foreign Policy and Germany, 1933–1938* (1969) and *Origins of the Second World War: American Foreign Policy and World Politics, 1917–1941* (1975) and with Theodore A. Wilson co-edited *Victory in Europe, 1945: The Allied Triumph over Germany and the Origins of the Cold War* (1999). He has recently completed a book-length study of President Harry S. Truman and the origins of the Cold War.

PRESIDENT'S COMMISSION ON THE ASSASSINATION OF PRESIDENT JOHN F. KENNEDY was appointed by President Lyndon Johnson on November 29, 1963, to investigate the assassination of President Kennedy. Johnson directed the commission (commonly known as the Warren commission) to evaluate matters relating to the assassination and the subsequent killing of the alleged assassin and to report its findings and conclusions to him.

BRUCE J. SCHULMAN is professor of history and director of American Studies at Boston University. A frequent contributor to publications such as *The New York Times* and *The Los Angeles Times*, Schulman lives in Brookline, Massachusetts.

KEVIN SHAPIRO is a research fellow in neuroscience, is a student at Harvard Medical School, and writes science articles for *Commentary* magazine.

JOHN S. SPANIER is a professor of political science at the University of Florida. In addition, he has lectured extensively at other universities, including the United States Military Academy at West Point and the Naval War College, where he was a visiting professor of strategy in 1983 to 1984. He is the author or coauthor of a number of publications, including *Games Nations Play*, 4th ed. (CQ Press, 1993) and *American Foreign Policy since WWII*, coauthored with Steven W. Hook (CQ Press, 2000).

RONALD STEEL is a former foreign service officer and a political journalist who has written numerous books and articles including a biography of the famed journalist Walter Lippman.

BRIAN VANDEMARK teaches history at the United States Naval Academy at Annapolis, Maryland. He served as research assistant on Clark Clifford's autobiography, *Counsel to the President: A Memoir* (Random House, 1991), and as a collaborator on former secretary of defense Robert S. McNamara's Vietnam memoir *In Retrospect: The Tragedy and Lessons of Vietnam* (Times Books, 1995).

ROBERT WEISBROT is professor of history at Colby College in Maine and is the author of *Freedom Bound*, an important history of the civil rights revolution.

ANNE SHARP WELLS is an assistant editor with *The Journal of Military History*. She is the author of *Historical Dictionary of World War II: The War against Japan* (Scarecrow Press, 1999) and coauthor, with D. Clayton James, of *America and the Great War, 1914–1920* (Harlan Davidson, 1998).

SEAN WILENTZ, Dayton-Stockton Professor of History and director of the Program in American Studies at Princeton University, is the author of numerous books on American history and politics. He lives in Princeton, New Jersey.

J. DAVID WOODARD is a professor of history of political science at the University of South Carolina and is the author of a number of books and articles about the modern conservative movement.

Index